Living Liturgy

Living Liturgy

Spirituality, Celebration, and Catechesis for Sundays and Solemnities

Year B • 2000

Joyce Ann Zimmerman, C.PP.S.
Thomas A. Greisen
Kathleen Harmon, S.N.D. de N.
Thomas L. Leclerc, M.S.

A Liturgical Press Book

THE LITURGICAL PRESS
Collegeville, Minnesota

Design by Ann Blattner. Art by Helen Siegl.

The readings from the *Lectionary for Mass,* volume 1, copyright © 1970, 1997, 1998 Confraternity of Christian Doctrine, Inc., Washington, D.C. All rights reserved. No part of this work may be reproduced or transmitted in any form or by any means, electronic or mechanical, including photocopying, recording, or by any information storage and retrieval system, without permission in writing from the copyright owner.

The English translation of the Psalm Responses, some Alleluia and Gospel verses, and the Lenten Gospel Acclamations, some Summaries, the Titles and Conclusion of the Readings, and the Introduction to the Lectionary for Mass from the *Lectionary for Mass* © 1969, 1981, 1997, International Committee on English in the Liturgy, Inc. (ICEL); the Alternative Opening Prayers and the English translation of the Opening Prayers from *The Roman Missal* © 1973, ICEL; excerpts from the English translation of the *Book of Blessings* © 1987, ICEL. All rights reserved.

The poetic English translations of the sequences of the Roman Missal are taken from the *Roman Missal* approved by the National Conference of Catholic Bishops of the United States © 1964 by the National Catholic Welfare Conference, Inc. All rights reserved.

© 1999 by The Order of St. Benedict, Inc., Collegeville, Minnesota. All rights reserved. No part of this book may be reproduced in any form or by any means, electronic or mechanical, including photocopying, recording, taping, or any retrieval system, without the written permission of The Liturgical Press, Collegeville, MN 56321. Printed in the United States of America.

1	2	3	4	5	6	7	8

Library of Congress Cataloging-in-Publication Data

Living liturgy : spirituality, celebration, and catechesis for Sundays
   and solemnities : year B, 2000 / Joyce Ann Zimmerman ... [et al.].
         p.   cm.
   Includes bibliographical references.
   ISBN 0-8146-2567-3 (alk. paper)
     1. Church year.   2. Bible—Liturgical use.   3. Catholic Church—
Liturgy.   I. Zimmerman, Joyce Ann, 1945–   .
BV30.L56   1999
264'.02—dc21   99-28091
                                                                                                      CIP

Abbreviations

BofB	*Book of Blessings*. International Commission on English in the Liturgy. Collegeville: The Liturgical Press, 1989.
EACW	*Environment and Art in Catholic Worship*. In *The Liturgy Documents: A Parish Resource*. 3rd edition. Chicago: Liturgy Training Publications, 1991.
GIRM	*General Instruction of the Roman Missal*. In *The Liturgy Documents*.
L	*Lectionary*
SC	*Sacrosanctum Concilium*. The Constitution on the Sacred Liturgy. Vatican II. In *The Liturgy Documents*.
BB	*Breaking Bread*. Portland, OR: Oregon Catholic Press, 1998.
CBW3	*Canadian Book of Worship III*. Ottawa, Ontario: Canadian Conference of Catholic Bishops, 1994.
CH	*The Collegeville Hymnal*. Collegeville: The Liturgical Press, 1990.
G	*Gather*. Chicago: GIA Publications, Inc., 1988.
G2	*Gather*. 2nd edition. Chicago: GIA Publications, Inc., 1994.
LMGM	*Lead Me, Guide Me*. Chicago: GIA Publications, Inc., 1987.
LP	*Lectionary Psalms—Michel Guimont*. Chicago: GIA Publications, Inc., 1998.
PC	*Psalms for the Cantor*. Schiller Park, IL: World Library Publications, 1985.
RS	*Ritual Song*. Chicago: GIA Publications, Inc., 1996.
W3	*Worship*. 3rd edition. Chicago: GIA Publications, Inc., 1986.
WC	*We Celebrate*. Schiller Park, IL: World Library Publications, 1997.
GIA	GIA Publications, Inc.
OCP	Oregon Catholic Press
WLP	World Library Publications

Contributors

Joyce Ann Zimmerman, C.PP.S., is the director of the Institute for Liturgical Ministry in Dayton, Ohio; founding editor and columnist for *Liturgical Ministry*; and is a past advisor to the U.S. Bishops' Committee on the Liturgy. She is also an adjunct professor of liturgy, liturgical consultant, and frequent facilitator of workshops and days of recollection on liturgy. She has published numerous scholarly and pastoral liturgical works. She holds civil and pontifical doctorates of theology.

Thomas A. Greisen is a priest of the Archdiocese of Omaha, Nebraska, who is the director of spiritual development for lay ministry for the archdiocese, a spiritual director, and an associate pastor. He has been the director of spiritual formation for college seminarians and a professor of spirituality. He holds graduate degrees in theology and spirituality.

Kathleen Harmon, S.N.D. de N., is the music director for programs of the Institute for Liturgical Ministry in Dayton, Ohio, and the author of the *Music Notes* column for *Liturgical Ministry*. An educator and musician, she facilitates liturgical music workshops and cantor-formation programs, teaches private voice lessons, and is a past parish music director. She holds a graduate degree in music and is completing doctoral studies in liturgy.

Thomas L. Leclerc, M.S., is a priest of the Missionaries of La Salette (Hartford Province). He has been director of theology for his congregation, an associate pastor in parishes in Georgia and Connecticut, and has been involved with adult education in the Archdioceses of Atlanta and Boston. He is a professor of theology at St. Anselm College in Manchester, New Hampshire, and holds a doctorate of theology in Hebrew Bible/Old Testament.

Contents

Using this Resource   ix

Season of Advent   1

Season of Christmas   23

Ordinary Time I   47

Season of Lent   81

Easter Triduum   115

Season of Easter   125

Ordinary Time II   159

Appendix A   277

Appendix B   287

Using this Resource

Living Liturgy: Spirituality, Celebration, and Catechesis for Sundays and Solemnities is about seeing the Paschal Mystery as central to liturgy and how we can live it in our everyday lives. By Paschal Mystery we mean, first, the entire mystery of Jesus Christ—that is, his life, passion, death, resurrection, ascension, sending of the Spirit, and promised second coming. Second, we also mean *our* participation in this Mystery because we are Christ's body, the Church. Liturgy both enacts in the here and now Christ's Mystery as well as sends us forth to live it.

CELEBRATING AND LIVING THE PASCHAL MYSTERY

Living Liturgy is a resource that offers practical, simple means for reflecting on, celebrating, and living liturgy. Ideally, this resource is used *during the week before* we actually gather for Mass. Because so much is at stake, *all* are called to take seriously the readying of ourselves for our Sunday celebrations. Sometimes we hear people say something like "I'm going to Mass now." This kind of language may capture the simple action of transporting ourselves from home to a worship space, but *going* to Mass hardly captures the depth of reality that we celebrate in this central ritual action. By readying ourselves during the previous week, we come to liturgy aware of its power in our lives and ready to offer God praise and thanksgiving.

READYING OURSELVES

Often when preparing for Sunday liturgy, we think more in terms of parish staff responsibility and the visible ministers. But we might fruitfully speak of a "ministry of the assembly" that is no less than the surrender of each worshiper to God's action within us, transforming us into ever more perfect images of the risen Christ. We join with others who are baptized and in that gathering make visible the body of Christ. As body of Christ we are challenged to that "full, conscious, and active participation" (SC, no. 14) that concretizes our surrender to God's Mystery present and active in our worship and lives. Together we are challenged by God's prophetic Word and nourished by God's gift of heavenly food.

MINISTRY OF THE ASSEMBLY

Those who serve the community in specific ministries—presider, deacon, music ministers, hospitality ministers, altar ministers (including acolytes, sacristans, environmental artists, those who clean the space and linens, janitors, etc.), lectors, Eucharistic ministers—have a particular trust to carry out for a given liturgy. These ministers must not only ready themselves along with the whole assembly, but also prepare themselves in special ways for doing their ministries well. This necessarily includes spiritual preparation, suggestions for which are a key component of *Living Liturgy*.

SPECIFIC MINISTRIES

UNIQUE FEATURES

Many excellent resources for preparing Sunday Eucharistic liturgies are already available. *Living Liturgy* is not meant to replace them nor compete with them, but is intended to complement them. Certain unique features mark this resource.

1. PROMOTES LIVING THE PASCHAL MYSTERY

1. *Living Liturgy* helps us to reflect on and live the Paschal Mystery. This suggests that our worship is more than what takes place in the hour or so we spend together in praise and thanksgiving. Celebrating liturgy on Sunday ought to make a difference in the way we live. It ought to make a difference in how we relate to God, others, self. For liturgy to make this difference in our lives, we need to carefully ready ourselves—each and every one of us—so that our surrender to God's action might be more complete and fruitful. The Scripture readings for each Sunday or solemnity are included in this resource for the convenience of the user. Praying God's Word, pondering the mystery of God's salvific deeds, and reflecting on questions that take us deeper into the lived Mystery are all ways to help us celebrate well so that we might live well God's Mystery.

2. WORD-DRIVEN

2. *Living Liturgy* is Word-driven. The *General Instruction of the Roman Missal* makes quite clear (in no. 8) that the Liturgy of the Word is neither an appendage nor a preamble to the Liturgy of the Eucharist. They form one single act of worship. Therefore, our starting point is the Word itself, especially the Gospels for there we learn about Jesus' identity and mission and are challenged to take this up as our own way of living. We reflect and pray over God's Word, hoping that it might become a word on our own lips and burning in our hearts. The word is proclaimed as a prophetic reminder of God's mighty deeds of salvation on our behalf. It is because of those mighty deeds—climaxing in the Paschal Mystery—that we are called to share in this sacred meal.

3. INTEGRATES SPIRITUALITY, CELEBRATION, AND CATECHESIS

3. *Living Liturgy* integrates spirituality and celebration, catechesis and pastoral practice, the ministry of the assembly and the specific, visible ministries. No single aspect of readying ourselves for liturgy can stand alone. Each aspect of preparation—spirituality, celebration, and catechesis—is linked to another so that celebrating and living go hand-in-hand.

4. INTEGRATES PASTORAL PRACTICE AND THEOLOGY

4. *Living Liturgy* was written by a pastorally-experienced team with expertise in liturgy, Scripture, spiritual direction, and liturgical music. Hopefully this integrating, team approach emulates the reality of our Christian communities: that we learn from each other of the fullness of God's Mystery and by learning together we enrich each other.

5. INCLUDES SOLEMNITIES

5. *Living Liturgy* includes material for each of the solemnities in addition to the Sundays. The solemnities are inspiring festivals—few in number on the 1969 revised General Roman Calendar—that are intimately connected to our annual unfolding of the Paschal Mystery. Although most of them are not holy days of obligation, they nonetheless are privileged liturgical celebrations that we ought not let pass by unnoticed. Even though most of the members of our liturgical assemblies may not be able to celebrate Mass on these special days, the material here can still be used in private prayer and reflection to help break open another facet of the Paschal Mystery.

6. SIMPLE AND CONSISTENT FORMAT

6. *Living Liturgy* is a resource whose format is simple and consistent. The paragraphs are short and to-the-point to aid using only snatches at a time for reflection. In this way the content is, hopefully, a catalyst for assembly members to enter more deeply into the Paschal Mystery, both at Mass and at home. This resource is divided into three major headings: spirituality, celebration, and catechesis. The various individual sections appear on the pages in the same place to assure familiarity with the format (with a few exceptions because of the structure of those celebrations).

SPIRITUALITY

To foster spirituality, the reflections on the Gospel and living the Paschal Mystery highlight one main point, chosen from many possible ones. A main point enabled a more focused and practical reflection that generated the various questions and suggestions for living a liturgical spirituality. This main point also guided the choice of opening prayer included in this resource (frequently it is the alternative opening prayer given in the Sacramentary that best captures the import of the Gospel).

CELEBRATION

Some parts of the Mass more directly flow from God's Word, particularly the Gospel. Therefore, we chose to include in the section headed "celebration" those elements of the ritual shaped by the readings and liturgical season: option of sprinkling rite or form of the penitential rite; commentary on the responsorial psalm; and model general intercessions. The introductory remarks and *Lord, have mercy* invocations as well as the general intercessions are models that can be used as starting points for adapting them for particular liturgies.

CATECHESIS

The material included under catechesis is meant to lead to a better understanding of the elements of liturgy. These catechetical points flow from aspects of the readings appointed for a particular Sunday or from the liturgical season; seasonal notes are often included here.

GENERAL INTERCESSIONS

The format of the model general intercessions deserves separate comment. At liturgy, the general intercessions are an exercise of our share in the priesthood of Christ (for this reason, in the early Church the unbaptized were always dismissed before the profession of faith and these prayers) during which we pray for *all of humanity* (GIRM, no. 45). They are called "general" intercessions precisely because they are intended to reach out to a much wider group than the assembled community and its needs. At devotional prayer (and special celebrations of the Eucharist; see GIRM, no. 46) more specific intentions might be appropriately offered up. The four categories (Church, world, those in need, local community) are specified in the *General Instruction of the Roman Missal* (no. 46). Within these categories, a wide range of intercessions is possible. We have combined the possibility of both silence (indicated by the ellipses, a time for personal prayer) and response (GIRM, no. 47). The language of the intentions is drawn from the readings (especially the Gospel) and helps us to draw our reflection on God's Word toward a practical, lived expression of God's Word. Suggested music for the general intercessions is included as a way to underscore their structure as litany (which are always preferably sung; choir parts are included in Appendix B).

OTHERS WHO MIGHT BENEFIT BY USING THIS RESOURCE AND SUGGESTIONS FOR USE

Living Liturgy might be beneficial for a wide spectrum of members of a liturgical community, each having a personal copy so they might refer to it frequently during prayer and reflection throughout the week. **Parents** and **teachers** could profit well by simplifying its content and sharing it with younger members of the liturgical community. **Members of faith-sharing groups** and **R.C.I.A. catechumens, candidates, and sponsors** could use it as the focus of weekly prayer and reflection together. These groups might begin with the *Lord, have mercy* litany and/or opening prayer for the Sunday (given in the text for convenience), share the readings (also given in the text) and reflection material, take time to apply it to themselves in order to see concrete applications in their specific situations for living the Paschal Mystery, and conclude with praying the general intercessions (and, in this devotional context, adding specific ones of their own that reflect immediate needs and concerns). A similar process might be adopted by various **liturgy planning committees** or **other pastoral groups**, shortening the length of reflection time in lieu of the other work that would need to be accomplished.

LIVING LITURGY!

The Mystery of God's salvific action is wide and deep. We are, indeed, privileged to share in the unfolding of these great events. None of us—nor our lives—is so insignificant that who we are and how we live does not affect all others in this great journey toward realizing our fulfillment in everlasting praise of the Divine Majesty in heaven. We can spend time doing no more important thing than intensifying a spirituality based in praying and reflecting on God's Word, celebrating the Paschal Mystery, and catechizing ourselves and others in God's ways. When we do so, we are living liturgy!

Season of Advent

First Sunday of Advent

FAITH-SHARING
- Advent season is often overwhelmed by busy Christmas preparations. What might you do in your life to remain watchful and alert for the many comings of Christ?
- How important is the second coming of Christ to you? For what do you long?
- Isaiah and Paul describe two different "worlds" of Christian living. Which describes where you are? How might each shape your Advent prayer?
- How has Christ already come to you? How do you meet others' longing for Christ's presence?

PRESIDERS
In what ways are you a "gatekeeper" for your people? What helps you to remain watchful and alert for the many comings of Christ?

DEACONS
"May he not come suddenly and find you sleeping." What helps you to remain awake in faith? When are you more likely to "sleep" in faith?

HOSPITALITY MINISTERS
How might your greeting "infect" people with the joyful expectation of Advent?

MUSIC MINISTERS
The Church begins each new liturgical year watching for Christ. How do you help those involved in music ministry in your parish "keep watching"?

ALTAR MINISTERS*
Much of your ministry entails getting the space ready for the assembly and for the liturgy. How might these preparations help you to make yourself ready internally for the coming of Christ?

LECTORS
How might your preparation for reading God's word be a kind of "watchful" waiting for God's coming?

EUCHARISTIC MINISTERS
"Lord . . . let us see your face and we shall be saved." How might you help others to see the face of Christ?

---

* "Altar ministers" includes acolytes, sacristans, environment artists, those who clean the sacred space, take care of altar linens, janitors, etc.

Spirituality

Reflecting on the Gospel

"A watched pot never boils." So the adage goes. Everything about this time of year seems to turn December (and Advent) into a "watched pot." Society is propelling us toward Christmas with alarming speed. We get a regular countdown of the number of shopping days until Christmas. Snarled traffic, Salvation Army bell ringers, Christmas music everywhere are some of the constant reminders of the holidays ahead. In the midst of all this, do we miss what we're watching for?

This Sunday's Gospel includes the image of "gatekeeper," one who keeps watch. Indeed, Jesus admonishes us to "Be watchful! Be alert!" He is addressing all of us. *We* are the gatekeepers. The first and second readings spell out more concretely what being a gatekeeper means.

In the first reading Isaiah describes what is happening in his time: the people have chosen their own ways, the way of sinning. But without God they are lost, pulled in many directions with nothing satisfying them. And so they lament God's absence and cry out that God would "rend the heavens and come down." Isaiah's world is one in which our own human frailty and weakness are very evident. Without God we, too, "have all withered like leaves." Like Israel, we await "awesome deeds we could not hope for."

Paul gives us a glimpse of this very situation, a world in which Jesus has come to bestow on us the "grace of God" which has "enriched [us] in every way . . . so that [we] are not lacking in any spiritual gift." Paul declares that "God is faithful" and in Christ Jesus we share in a new nearness to God, that of "fellowship with his Son." Paul describes a world in which fullness of life abounds—that for which we are waiting has come and in Christ the awesome deeds of God are already evident.

To be gatekeeper means we look at Isaiah's world with all its longing, a world where God is hidden because of sinfulness; but at the same time we see Paul's world where the fullness of God's nearness has already been realized. We must be alert that our watching does not miss what we wait for. We await the fullness of Christ's coming in a world still darkened by sinfulness. In spite of our watching, this is the mystery we can so easily miss: in the midst of our own sinfulness, God comes!

Living the Paschal Mystery

"Paschal Mystery" means the whole mystery of Jesus Christ: his life, passion, death, resurrection, ascension, sending of the Spirit, and second coming in glory. Furthermore, through our baptism *we* participate in this same Mystery. So the Paschal Mystery describes the thrust of our daily Christian living—baptized into Christ's death so that we might live a new life (see Rom 6:3-11).

The Paschal Mystery stands at the very center of our waiting, for Advent captures this dying/rising dynamic of the Paschal Mystery (Isaiah's world of sinfulness/Paul's world of fullness in Christ-who-comes). Advent is a season of joyful expectation and celebration of Christ's comings: in glory at the end of time, in flesh on that first Christmas, in sacramental mystery in everyday life. Our God is coming! Be watchful! Be alert!

GOSPEL [Mark 13:33-37; L2B]

Jesus said to his disciples: "Be watchful! Be alert! You do not know when the time will come. It is like a man traveling abroad. He leaves home and places his servants in charge, each with his own work, and orders the gatekeeper to be on the watch. Watch, therefore; you do not know when the lord of the house is coming, whether in the evening, or at midnight, or at cockcrow, or in the morning. May he not come suddenly and find you sleeping. What I say to you, I say to all: 'Watch!'"

Working with the Word

Key words and phrases from the Gospel: be watchful, be alert, gatekeeper

Connecting to last Sunday, the Solemnity of Our Lord Jesus Christ the King: The Christ whom we enthroned in glory last week is the Christ we await this Sunday, the Christ who will return in the Second Coming.

Connecting to the culture: All the ways society tries to meet its longings (e.g., consumerism, pleasure, acquisitions) mask over the deeper human longing for what truly satisfies—life in God. We are constantly faced with a choice: to seek what *we* think might satisfy our deepest longings, or to beg God to "rend the heavens and come down" (first reading).

Exegetical points: There is a Christological shift from the first reading to the Gospel: in the first reading, Isaiah looks for God to come down; in the Gospel, Mark refers to *Christ's* coming.

The reading from Isaiah takes the form of a communal lament. In the plaintive tone of the passage we hear the community's anguish over their experience of the absence of God ("you have hidden your face from us"). The mourning and confession of sin that characterize a lament are intended to move God to save those who cry out for deliverance. As the first reading of Advent, this section poignantly speaks of life without God ("like withered leaves . . . carried away by the wind") and gives heartfelt voice to our longing for God to come and save us ("rend the heavens and come down"). The liturgical setting of this reading (the first Sunday of Advent) invites us to interpret it Christologically, that is, what faithful Israel expected of God, Christians now expect of Christ: as Emmanuel, Jesus will come in glory with salvation for his people. The "watching" that Jesus counsels keeps the community alert to the coming day of deliverance.

To the point: On this first Sunday of the liturgical year, a key image from the Gospel is that of gatekeeper: one who stands at the gate between two worlds. The one world—described by Isaiah—speaks of human longing for God. The other world—described by Paul in the second reading—gives thanks for God's responding to our longing for the coming of Christ. What began with Christ's life, death, and resurrection is yet to be fulfilled when he comes in glory.

Celebration

Model Penitential Rite
Presider: We begin Advent today, a time to celebrate God's nearness. Let us reflect on God's goodness to us and open our hearts to give thanks and praise . . . [pause]

    Lord Jesus, you admonish us to "Be watchful! Be alert!": Lord . . .
    Christ Jesus, you will come again in glory: Christ . . .
    Lord Jesus, you are already present to us in sacraments and grace: Lord . . .

Responsorial Psalm
"Lord, make us turn to you; let us see your face and we shall be saved."
The entire Liturgy of the Word this Sunday is a dialogue between us and God. We call out to God "rend the heavens and come down" (first reading); "rouse your power and come to save us" (psalm). We cry out "you have hidden your face from us" (first reading) and then beg "let us see your face" (psalm). On our side of this dialogue we hold God responsible for both our sinful situation and our redemption: "Why do you let us wander . . . [why do you] harden our hearts?" (first reading). But in the Gospel Jesus turns the table on us: "Watch!" he commands. We must participate in bringing about our redemption.

The second reading points out that this redemption has already been given to us in Christ. In Christ the God whose face seems hidden has in fact turned completely toward us. Our task is to watch so that we may see, and this is our prayer as we sing this Sunday's psalm.

Model General Intercessions
Presider: In Christ our God is always present to us and this nearness of God gives us hope that our prayers will be answered.

Response:

[musical notation: Lord, hear our prayer.]

Cantor:

[musical notation: we pray to the Lord,]

That the Church may be found watchful and alert when Christ comes in his glory . . . [pause]

That all people of the world may recognize that their deepest longing is for God . . . [pause]

That those who choose their own way over God's way may have ears to hear and eyes to see God's awesome deeds of salvation . . . [pause]

That our Advent preparation for Christ's coming may be marked by joyful expectation and grateful hearts . . . [pause]

Presider: O God, you come to us in many ways, always announcing the wonders of your gift of salvation: hear these our prayers that we might be better prepared for your coming. We ask this through Christ our Lord. **Amen.**

OPENING PRAYER
Let us pray

Pause for silent prayer

All-powerful God,
increase our strength of will for doing good
that Christ may find an eager welcome at his coming
and call us to his side in the kingdom of heaven,
where he lives and reigns with you and the Holy Spirit,
one God, for ever and ever. **Amen.**

RESPONSORIAL PSALM
[Ps 80:2-3, 15-16, 18-19]

℟. (4) Lord, make us turn to you; let us see your face and we shall be saved.

O shepherd of Israel, hearken,
    from your throne upon the cherubim, shine forth.
Rouse your power,
    and come to save us.

℟. Lord, make us turn to you; let us see your face and we shall be saved.

Once again, O LORD of hosts,
    look down from heaven, and see;
take care of this vine,
    and protect what your right hand has planted,
    the son of man whom you yourself made strong.

℟. Lord, make us turn to you; let us see your face and we shall be saved.

May your help be with the man of your right hand,
    with the son of man whom you yourself made strong.
Then we will no more withdraw from you;
    give us new life, and we will call upon your name.

℟. Lord, make us turn to you; let us see your face and we shall be saved.

FIRST READING
[Isa 63:16b-17, 19b; 64:2-7]

You, LORD, are our father,
    our redeemer you are named forever.
Why do you let us wander, O Lord, from your ways,
    and harden our hearts so that we fear you not?
Return for the sake of your servants,
    the tribes of your heritage.
Oh, that you would rend the heavens and come down,

with the mountains quaking before
    you,
while you wrought awesome deeds we
    could not hope for,
    such as they had not heard of from of
        old.
No ear has ever heard, no eye ever seen,
    any God but you
    doing such deeds for those who wait
        for him.
Would that you might meet us doing
    right,
    that we were mindful of you in our
        ways!
Behold, you are angry, and we are
    sinful;
    all of us have become like unclean
        people,
    all our good deeds are like polluted
        rags;
we have all withered like leaves,
    and our guilt carries us away like the
        wind.
There is none who calls upon your
    name,
    who rouses himself to cling to you;
for you have hidden your face from us
    and have delivered us up to our guilt.
Yet, O LORD, you are our father;
    we are the clay and you the potter:
    we are all the work of your hands.

SECOND READING
[1 Cor 1:3-9]

Brothers and sisters:
Grace to you and peace from God our
    Father
    and the Lord Jesus Christ.

I give thanks to my God always on your
    account
    for the grace of God bestowed on you
        in Christ Jesus,
    that in him you were enriched in
        every way,
    with all discourse and all knowledge,
    as the testimony to Christ was
        confirmed among you,
    so that you are not lacking in any
        spiritual gift
    as you wait for the revelation of our
        Lord Jesus Christ.
He will keep you firm to the end,
    irreproachable on the day of our Lord
        Jesus Christ.
God is faithful,
    and by him you were called to
        fellowship with his Son, Jesus
        Christ our Lord.

Catechesis

Cantors

As you prepare to sing this psalm, pray about where in your life you need to turn to God, where you need to see God's face more clearly. A family issue? A relationship at work? A struggle with yourself?

Choir

At the conclusion of choir rehearsal this week, pray a litany begging for the grace to watch for the coming of God. Use the refrain of the responsorial psalm as a sung response. Petitions could include "in our families . . . ," "in war-torn countries . . . ," "in our relationships . . . ," "among the poor . . . ," etc. You might want also to add petitions spontaneously. After each petition pause briefly to allow for silent prayer before singing the response.

Music Directors

It is important to select seasonally appropriate service music for Advent. Because Advent is a season of expectation, the service music should not be as exuberant as what you will sing during the Christmas season. Yet Advent is joyful, so the music need not have the somberness of what you use during Lent. Whatever you select, use it for the entire Advent season so that the music, along with the liturgical prayers, colors, and environment, will help the assembly enter into the spirit of the season.

Richard Proulx' *Missa Emmanuel* [RS; SATB arrangement GIA #G- 3489] is a setting of the Mass based on "O Come, O Come, Emmanuel." It is meant to be sung unaccompanied. If using the entire setting throughout all of Advent might become tedious, consider using just the Lamb of God.

Liturgy Committee

How might you help your liturgical community to enter better into Advent as a season focusing on the many comings of Christ? Do your preparations (including for the environment of the sacred space) help reflect the richness and breadth of this liturgical season? What are your priorities during Advent?

Although Advent is not primarily a *penitential* season (like Lent is), Isaiah does give us motivation for doing penance during Advent: "Would that you might meet us doing right." Christ will come at the end of time to judge the living and the dead. Our Advent penance is undertaken so that we might be prepared for Christ's second coming and its accompanying judgment.

The appropriate color for Advent is *royal* purple which picks up on the motif of the second coming of Christ with which we begin the season. This is a different color from the violet, penitential color we use during Lent.

The Advent wreath is a much-beloved Advent custom, kept both in our homes and churches. No. 1512 of the *Book of Blessings* states that when it is used in church it should not distract us from the actions of the liturgy. Placing the Advent wreath at the main entrance where all may see it might be a good pastoral alternative. The *Book of Blessings* (chapter 47) stipulates that the blessing of the Advent wreath during Mass takes place after the general intercessions (not as a replacement for the introductory rites). On subsequent Sundays the candles are lighted without blessing or ceremony (BofB, no. 1513).

NOVEMBER 28, 1999

Second Sunday of Advent

FAITH-SHARING
- Does Christ's second coming mean anything for the way you live your Christian commitment?
- What concrete ways are you like John the Baptist, the messenger of Christ's coming? Who are the "John the Baptists" in your faith life?
- How do you already see God's glory manifested in your life?
- What are your expectations for Christ's coming?

PRESIDERS
Generally you are in the role of John the Baptist—announcer of Christ's coming to others. Who announces to you? Who are your "John the Baptists"?

DEACONS
Identify the many ways in which your ordained ministry announces God's salvation to others. What might you do in your life to be a better messenger?

HOSPITALITY MINISTERS
How is your greeting of others (both in your life and in church before liturgy) really a way for you to be Christ's messenger?

MUSIC MINISTERS
How do your behaviors help those you lead in music ministry hasten the day of Christ's coming?

ALTAR MINISTERS
What sort of persons ought you be . . . waiting for and hastening the coming of the day of God? Practically, how are you "waiting for"? How are you "hastening" the coming of God?

LECTORS
Your ministry is one of announcing the word of God to the community. How does your life also announce God to others, and how might this help you proclaim the word better?

EUCHARISTIC MINISTERS
You minister the body of Christ to others. How is this ministry both a heralding of Christ's presence and a preparing for his second coming?

Spirituality

Reflecting on the Gospel

Some people like them. Some people don't. Those previews usually included at the beginning of VCR movies. The people who like them like to know what is coming available. They can plan ahead for their future movie-watching. The people who don't like them want to get on right away to the main feature: skip all the preview stuff and get to the important thing. The three readings for this, the Second Sunday of Advent, are something like previews and main feature. Only the main feature isn't what we might expect.

Both the first reading from Isaiah and the Gospel speak of preparing the way of the Lord. Isaiah and John the Baptist are messengers announcing "previews." Naturally, at this time of year, we would leap to think that the "main feature" is about Christmas, Christ's first coming at birth. Yet, the reading from the second letter of Peter gives us a very different picture. Here the "movie" is about the second coming, a motif that dominated the Liturgy of the Word last Sunday.

In John's time Jesus had come; the Old Testament expectation of the Messiah had been realized. For us today, too, salvation has *already dawned*. At the same time we are also waiting for the fullness of revelation. The *full light* of day is yet to come. We live in a "now" of salvation but we know that there is even more to come. Like John we must be voices crying out to prepare the way of the Lord. We already enjoy the glory of Christ's life, death, and resurrection. Yet there is a future glory that still awaits us. What might this glory be?

Living the Paschal Mystery

"Eschatology" is a term that refers to the end times and the future glory that awaits those who are faithful to God's gift of salvation. It includes Christ's second coming—accompanied by the end of this world as we know it, by the final judgment, and the general resurrection—and the gathering of all things to the Creator to share forever in the divine glory.

The first coming of Christ (what we celebrate at Christmas) already ushered in these eschatological times. The kingdom of God is inaugurated and is already upon us. But this "already" of God's reign is still "not yet." Its fullness will only be realized at the second coming.

This play between the "already" and the "not yet" of God's reign is the Mystery we grapple with during these first two Sundays of Advent. Salvation is already upon us. What we are doing *now* is critical, as critical as what John the Baptist was doing to announce Jesus' first coming. The way we live our lives makes a difference, not only for our own salvation but also because—since we have been baptized in the Holy Spirit and already share in God's divine life—we are to *announce* God's reign to others. The role of John the Baptist is transferred to us: what John was to Christ's first coming we are to be to Christ's second coming. The most poignant announcement of and preparation for Christ's second coming is living our lives in such a way that we are "without spot or blemish before him, at peace."

DECEMBER 5, 1999

GOSPEL [Mark 1:1-8; L5B]

The beginning of the gospel of Jesus Christ the Son of God.
 As it is written in Isaiah the prophet:
  Behold, I am sending my messenger ahead of you;
   he will prepare your way.
  A voice of one crying out in the desert:
   "Prepare the way of the Lord,
   make straight his paths."
 John the Baptist appeared in the desert proclaiming a baptism of repentance for the forgiveness of sins. People of the whole Judean countryside and all the inhabitants of Jerusalem were going out to him and were being baptized by him in the Jordan River as they acknowledged their sins. John was clothed in camel's hair, with a leather belt around his waist. He fed on locusts and wild honey. And this is what he proclaimed: "One mightier than I is coming after me. I am not worthy to stoop and loosen the thongs of his sandals. I have baptized you with water; he will baptize you with the Holy Spirit."

Working with the Word

Key words and phrases from the Gospel: my messenger, prepare the way, John the Baptist, coming after me, baptize you with the Holy Spirit

Connecting to the second reading: While the community of Second Peter (c. 120–140 C.E.) believed God's gift of salvation had come in Christ, they also knew that salvation was not fully realized. They were looking to Christ's second coming for this fulfillment and saw the delay as an opportunity both for personal repentance and to prepare the way for that second coming.

Connecting to the culture: Both in our contemporary culture and in our liturgical communities, our tendency is to focus on Christ's first coming (Christmas). And this Sunday's readings tell us that what we are waiting for is *more* than that: "new heavens and a new earth" that will be realized in Christ's second coming.

Exegetical points: After the title, Mark's Gospel begins with a composite quote from two different prophets. The first line is from Malachi 3:1—though modified from the Hebrew and Greek versions which have God "sending my messenger ahead of *me*." In Mark, the messenger comes in advance of *you*, i.e., the Lord. Later in Malachi (3:23), the messenger is identified as Elijah, whom Jews expected to return from heaven just before the Messiah comes. The second prophecy which Mark quotes is taken from this Sunday's first reading from Isaiah. It is the job-description for Malachi's messenger: to prepare the way of the Lord. Taking the two prophetic texts together, the "you" whom Malachi's messenger precedes is identified as the Lord: the messenger's job is to prepare the way of the Lord.

Mark then goes on to identify the messenger as John the Baptist. John's odd clothing (camel's hair garment and leather belt) explicitly recalls Elijah in 2 Kgs 1:8. Mark's point, then, is that the long-expected Elijah, whose coming will precede that of the Messiah, has appeared in the person of John the Baptist. John's frank admission that "One mightier than I is coming" sets the scene for the appearance of Jesus.

To the point: The beginning of the good news is Christ's first coming. But that was just the beginning. Our Advent longings and expectations move us beyond Bethlehem to engage our world in justice and truth, thus preparing for a "new heavens and a new earth."

Celebration

Model Penitential Rite

Presider: In today's Gospel John is the messenger who cries out to prepare the way of the Lord. Let us prepare for the Lord's coming in this Eucharist . . . [pause]

    Lord Jesus, you are the Messiah mightier than John: Lord . . .
    Christ Jesus, you baptize us with the Holy Spirit: Christ . . .
    Lord Jesus, you call us to share in the glory of your kingdom: Lord . . .

Responsorial Psalm

"Lord, let us see your kindness, and grant us your salvation."

Again on this Second Sunday of Advent, the readings present us with a dialogue. In the first reading and Gospel a "voice cries out . . . prepare the way of the LORD." In the responsorial psalm we answer, "I will hear what God proclaims." What is it that God proclaims? Make straight what is crooked, smooth out what is rough (first reading). Repent of sin, and look for the One who is to come (Gospel).

How do we hear what God proclaims? The readings tell us that it is through God's messengers, Isaiah and John the Baptist. But the psalm tells us that it is justice which "prepare[s] the way of [God's] steps." In other words, we hear God's call by listening to the Word and we respond by living according to that Word. Peter tells us this when he asks, "what sort of persons ought you to be" while we are "waiting for and hastening the coming of the day of God" (second reading). As we sing this psalm the "kindness" and "salvation" we are praying to see is in our own lives.

Model General Intercessions

Presider: Since Christ will come in glory to gather all things to the Creator, let us make our needs known so that our world might be ready for the day of the Lord.

Response:

[Musical notation: Lord, hear our prayer.]

Cantor:

[Musical notation: we pray to the Lord,]

That the members of the Church might prepare for Christ's coming by living without spot or blemish . . . [pause]

That the peoples of the world might make straight the paths of their lives, always keeping focused on God . . . [pause]

That all who have strayed from the path of righteousness and peace may listen to messengers who call them back to God's way . . . [pause]

That we might prepare ourselves by worthy lives to share in God's coming reign of glory . . . [pause]

Presider: God of glory, you sent your Son to live among us and draw us into your kingdom of justice and peace: hear these our prayers that we might be ready for the fullness of your glory. We pray through Jesus Christ our Lord. **Amen.**

OPENING PRAYER

Let us pray

Pause for silent prayer

God of power and mercy,
open our hearts in welcome.
Remove the things that hinder us from
    receiving Christ with joy,
so that we may share his wisdom
and become one with him when he
    comes in glory,
for he lives and reigns with you and the
    Holy Spirit,
one God, for ever and ever. **Amen.**

RESPONSORIAL PSALM
[Ps 85:9-10, 11-12, 13-14]

R/. (8) Lord, let us see your kindness,
and grant us your salvation.

I will hear what God proclaims;
    the LORD—for he proclaims peace to
    his people.
Near indeed is his salvation to those
    who fear him,
    glory dwelling in our land.

R/. Lord, let us see your kindness, and
grant us your salvation.

Kindness and truth shall meet;
    justice and peace shall kiss.
Truth shall spring out of the earth,
    and justice shall look down from
    heaven.

R/. Lord, let us see your kindness, and
grant us your salvation.

The LORD himself will give his benefits;
    our land shall yield its increase.
Justice shall walk before him,
    and prepare the way of his steps.

R/. Lord, let us see your kindness, and
grant us your salvation.

FIRST READING [Isa 40:1-5, 9-11]

Comfort, give comfort to my people,
    says your God.
Speak tenderly to Jerusalem, and
    proclaim to her
    that her service is at an end,
    her guilt is expiated;
indeed, she has received from the hand
    of the LORD
    double for all her sins.
        A voice cries out:
In the desert prepare the way of the LORD!
    Make straight in the wasteland a
        highway for our God!
Every valley shall be filled in,
    every mountain and hill shall be
        made low;

the rugged land shall be made a plain,
  the rough country, a broad valley.
Then the glory of the LORD shall be
    revealed,
  and all people shall see it together;
  for the mouth of the LORD has spoken.

Go up onto a high mountain,
  Zion, herald of glad tidings;
cry out at the top of your voice,
  Jerusalem, herald of good news!
Fear not to cry out
  and say to the cities of Judah:
  Here is your God!
Here comes with power
  the Lord GOD,
  who rules by his strong arm;
here is his reward with him,
  his recompense before him.
Like a shepherd he feeds his flock;
  in his arms he gathers the lambs,
carrying them in his bosom,
  and leading the ewes with care.

SECOND READING [2 Pet 3:8-14]

Do not ignore this one fact, beloved,
  that with the Lord one day is like a
    thousand years
  and a thousand years like one day.
The Lord does not delay his promise, as
    some regard "delay,"
  but he is patient with you,
  not wishing that any should perish
  but that all should come to repentance.
But the day of the Lord will come like a
    thief,
  and then the heavens will pass away
    with a mighty roar
  and the elements will be dissolved by
    fire,
  and the earth and everything done on
    it will be found out.

Since everything is to be dissolved in
    this way,
  what sort of persons ought you to be,
  conducting yourselves in holiness and
    devotion,
  waiting for and hastening the coming
    of the day of God,
  because of which the heavens will be
    dissolved in flames
  and the elements melted by fire.
But according to his promise
  we await new heavens and a new
    earth
  in which righteousness dwells.
Therefore, beloved, since you await
    these things,
  be eager to be found without spot or
    blemish before him, at peace.

Catechesis

Cantors

As you prepare to sing this psalm, spend some time reflecting on what helps you hear God speaking in your life, and what impedes your hearing. What habits or attitudes need to be maintained, and which need to be "smoothed" out?

Choir

This Sunday's second reading asks, "What sort of persons ought you to be" as you wait for the final coming of Christ? How you act helps bring closer the day of Christ's coming. You might reflect on questions like these this week: How do you treat one another in the choir? How do you treat the other liturgical ministers? What is your attitude toward the assembly?

Music Directors

"Comfort, Comfort, O My People" [BB, RS, WC, W3] is based on this Sunday's first reading from Isaiah. The hymn was written for the solemnity of the Nativity of John the Baptist and first published in 1671. Despite the tender words, the hymn is meant to be sung at a moderate, dance-like pace. It would work well for the presentation of gifts, or as a choral prelude.

"Wake You Power" [BB] by Huub Oosterhuis and Tom Lowenthal is an energetic song which especially fits Advent year B readings because of their imagery of God's power coming to save us. The song is responsorial in style. The offbeat, back-and-forth entrances of choir and cantor in the verses give the piece an anticipated energy that coincides with the "already/not yet" feel of Advent. The SATB setting is available in the collection *Wake Your Power* [OCP #9784]. It would be suitable as the entrance song for all four Sundays of Advent.

Another energetic responsorial-style entrance song suitable for this Sunday is Michael Joncas' "A Voice Cries Out" [BB, RS]. The choir parts are available in *Choral Praise Comprehensive Edition* [SATB for refrain only; OCP #10317] and *Choral Praise* [SATB for refrain and verses; OCP #8723 and 9093].

Liturgy Committee

How might you help yourselves (and the members of the liturgical community whom you serve) better understand that the God-like way you live now is directly related to the future coming of Christ in the fullness of his glory (see the second reading)? Are your Christmas preparations only concerned with Christ's first coming? How might your patient waiting *now* hasten Christ's coming?

The second reading for this Sunday repeats the motivation for doing penance during Advent: to prepare for the final judgment at Christ's second coming.

We note that Advent is not a four-*week* season but a four-*Sunday* season. This highlights for us the importance of the four Sundays of Advent and their readings. We've already seen how the first two Sundays help us reflect on the second coming, which colors all of these first two weeks.

DECEMBER 5, 1999

THE IMMACULATE CONCEPTION OF THE BLESSED

FAITH-SHARING
- Where can you see yourself as an ancestor of Adam and Eve's fears and self-willfulness? How, like Mary, could you become more trusting of God?
- Do you have experiences of God gracing you without merit (i.e., before you "earn" or "deserve" it)?
- How might you make this solemnity more than a legal obligation?

PRESIDERS
Are the holydays of obligation simply days of more "work" for you as an ordained priest, or are they opportunities for celebrating salvation?

DEACONS
In what ways could your ministry embody Gabriel's message for others: "Do not be afraid . . . you have found favor with God . . . nothing will be impossible for God"?

HOSPITALITY MINISTERS
Gabriel's greeting to Mary assured her, "Do not be afraid . . . you have found favor with God." How might your hospitality help people to experience this for themselves? assure people of God's favor?

MUSIC MINISTERS
How can you help those you direct to see their music ministry as a way of living out the holiness for which they have been chosen in Christ?

ALTAR MINISTERS
Mary is *the* handmaid, *the* servant of the Lord. What does Mary teach you about being servant?

LECTORS
"May it be done to me according to your word." As you pray over the readings, what needs to be "done" to you? by you?

EUCHARISTIC MINISTERS
In Christ, God has blessed you "with every spiritual blessing in the heavens." How has your ministry revealed this to you? If you could remember this, how would it affect your daily living?

Spirituality

Reflecting on the Gospel
Pius IX defined the Immaculate Conception of Mary as a dogma of the Church in 1854. Confusion reigns concerning the meaning of the Immaculate Conception. This solemnity is about *Mary's* conception in the womb of St. Ann; *she* was free from sin from the very first moment of her life.

Although the Gospel relates the story of Jesus' conception (it is the same Gospel selected for the solemnity of the Annunciation of the Lord), it does give us hints that scripturally substantiate the dogma concerning Mary's conception: (1) "Hail, full of grace! The Lord is with you"—surely the body that was to harbor the human life of the Son of God would be pure and spotless from all time; (2) "the child to be born will be called holy"—surely Mary, too, was holy; (3) "May it be done to me according to your word"—this response of Mary echoes God's creative word, "Let there be . . ."; Mary is the first of all creation, the new Eve, free from all stain of sin.

The first reading from Genesis also brings us back to the beginning of creation. God promised the serpent that "I will put enmity between you and the woman, and between your offspring and hers"; that most perfect offspring is Christ, the light through whom the darkness of evil is dispelled. Eve "became the mother of all the living," but Mary is the new Eve who cooperates with God's plan of salvation and reverses the harm caused by Adam and Eve's sin. Adam and Eve were afraid because they were naked. Mary calms all fears and models for us an utter trust in God's will—"May it be done to me."

The second reading is a reassuring one that helps us understand that Mary's holiness is not beyond the reach of any one of us. Like Mary we, too, have been "blessed . . . in Christ with every spiritual blessing in the heavens." God showed Mary special favor but we, too, are offered "adoption" because of God's great love for each of us. In Christ "we were also chosen." This great mystery of Mary's holiness that we celebrate is a clue to our own call to holiness, stripping ourselves of all our fears in order to better surrender to and trust in God.

This festival is a holy day of obligation in the United States. It would be a shame if people from the U.S. celebrate Eucharist as if it were simply mandated with no deeper meaning. It would be a shame if people from other countries where Mass is not obligatory would treat this day like any other day. The solemnities are included on the liturgical calendar because they open up for us in special ways the mystery of God's salvation offered to us. How can we not respond with joy and enthusiasm? Make this day a special one for celebrating redemption, a special day of thanksgiving for Mary our mother!

Living the Paschal Mystery
As we meditate on Mary's life with the celebration of Mary's Immaculate Conception, we are drawn into a deeper living of the Paschal Mystery: like Mary, we are challenged to surrender ourselves without reserve to God's plan of salvation. The Adam and Eve in us—with all of our fears and self-willfulness—must die so that "every spiritual blessing in the heavens" will come to life in us!

VIRGIN MARY

DECEMBER 8, 1999

GOSPEL [Luke 1:26-28; L689]

The angel Gabriel was sent from God to a town of Galilee called Nazareth, to a virgin betrothed to a man named Joseph, of the house of David, and the virgin's name was Mary. And coming to her, he said, "Hail, full of grace! The Lord is with you." But she was greatly troubled at what was said and pondered what sort of greeting this might be. Then the angel said to her, "Do not be afraid, Mary, for you have found favor with God. Behold, you will conceive in your womb and bear a son, and you shall name him Jesus. He will be great and will be called Son of the Most High, and the Lord God will give him the throne of David his father, and he will rule over the house of Jacob forever, and of his kingdom there will be no end." But Mary said to the angel, "How can this be, since I have no relations with a man?" And the angel said to her in reply, "The Holy Spirit will come upon you, and the power of the Most High will overshadow you. Therefore the child to be born will be called holy, the Son of God. And behold, Elizabeth, your relative, has also conceived a son in her old age, and this is the sixth month for her who was called barren; for nothing will be impossible for God." Mary said, "Behold, I am the handmaid of the Lord. May it be done to me according to your word." Then the angel departed from her.

Working with the Word

Key words and phrases from the Gospel: Hail, full of grace! The Lord is with you.

Connecting to the other readings: The first reading reminds us that from the days of creation God works for our salvation. The second reading reminds us that God accomplishes all things (i.e., our salvation) according to the divine will. These texts underscore Mary's *pure* body as the temple of Christ, prepared for from all time as part of God's salvific plan.

Connecting to our culture: By this time in December the Christmas music is on the radio, colored lights are blinking in yards and the stores, so many shopping days until Christmas are being noted. In the midst of this frenzy the liturgical year celebrates the quiet expectancy of Advent and, with this solemnity, the wondrous conception of Mary. Such a contrast!

Exegetical points: The concluding verses of the passage from Genesis are sometimes called "The First Gospel." The divine announcement of eternal enmity between the offspring of the serpent and the woman does more than provide an etiology for human aversion to snakes—part of the original purpose for telling the story. Two interpretive trends moved this natural story in a theological direction. The human heel striking at the serpent's head seems to suggest human domination and victory over the serpent. Once the serpent began to be interpreted as the devil (cf. Wis 2:24; John 8:44; Rev 12:9; 20:2), it became a story of the human necessity to resist evil. Under the influence of Paul's Adam-Christ typology (1 Cor 15) in which the first Adam's disobedience brought sin while the obedience of the second Adam (Christ) brought salvation, Eve became a type for Mary. Thus, the offspring of the Eve (= Mary) would refer to Jesus who would strike at the very head of evil. So, even as the first sin enters the world in the Garden of Eden, it is met with a divine assurance that evil will not prevail and that a savior will come. The theological impulse that drives this kind of imaginative interpretation is the conviction that God's plan for human salvation is carefully laid out, that each step in the unfolding of that plan is taken with foresight and in accordance with God's loving and saving intentions for humanity. This is a fitting context in which to consider the Immaculate Conception: God's wondrous salvific foresight.

To the point: What the solemnity asserts about Mary, Scripture asserts about all of us: we were chosen "before the foundation of the world, to be holy and without blemish before him" (second reading).

Celebration

Model Penitential Rite

Presider: God preserved Mary pure and spotless from the moment of her conception. Let us reflect on our own sinfulness and ask God to make us spotless . . . [pause]

> Son of Mary, you call all of us to holiness: Lord . . .
> Son of God, you were born of Mary so that we might gain salvation: Christ . . .
> Son of Mary, nothing is impossible with God: Lord . . .

Responsorial Psalm

"Sing to the Lord a new song, for he has done marvelous deeds."
The responsorial psalm for the solemnity of the Immaculate Conception of the Blessed Virgin Mary is the same one that will be used for the Mass during the day on Christmas (Psalm 98) except that the refrain is different. On this solemnity the refrain reflects Mary's own words in her *Magnificat,* "The Almighty has done great things for me" (Luke 1:49). The loss of grace described in the reading from Genesis is completely reversed in the person of Mary, who is "full of grace" (Gospel). But God's marvelous deeds do not end with her. We, too, have been chosen in Christ for great things (second reading). And so we sing this psalm of praise *with* Mary, knowing that in our own lives salvation has been promised and is already begun.

Model General Intercessions

Presider: God is the God of salvation who calls all of us to the same holiness and purity that Mary enjoyed. Let us offer up our prayers that we might one day reach the fullness of life.

Response:

Lord, hear our prayer.

Cantor:

we pray to the Lord,

That the people of God may come to be holy and without blemish before God . . . [pause]

That the people of the world may witness to the spiritual blessings that God offers . . . [pause]

That all mothers have the strength to rear their children according to God's plan . . . [pause]

That we honor Mary our mother by imitating her fidelity to God . . . [pause]

Presider: O God, you preserved Mary free from all sin so that she might be a perfect vessel to nurture your Son: hear these our prayers that we might come to everlasting life. We ask this through Christ our Lord. **Amen.**

OPENING PRAYER
Let us pray

Pause for silent prayer

Father,
you prepared the Virgin Mary
to be the worthy mother of your Son.
You let her share beforehand
in the salvation Christ would bring by his death,
and kept her sinless from the first moment of her conception.
Help us by her prayers to live in your presence without sin.
We ask this through our Lord Jesus Christ, your Son,
who lives and reigns with you and the Holy Spirit,
one God, for ever and ever. **Amen.**

RESPONSORIAL PSALM
[Ps 98:1, 2-3, 3-4]

℟. (1a) Sing to the Lord a new song, for he has done marvelous deeds.

Sing to the LORD a new song,
 for he has done wondrous deeds;
his right hand has won victory for him,
 his holy arm.

℟. Sing to the Lord a new song, for he has done marvelous deeds.

The LORD has made his salvation known:
 in the sight of the nations he has revealed his justice.
He has remembered his kindness and his faithfulness
 toward the house of Israel.

℟. Sing to the Lord a new song, for he has done marvelous deeds.

All the ends of the earth have seen
 the salvation by our God.
Sing joyfully to the LORD, all you lands;
 break into song; sing praise.

℟. Sing to the Lord a new song, for he has done marvelous deeds.

FIRST READING
[Gen 3:9-15, 20]

After the man, Adam, had eaten of the tree,
 the LORD God called to the man and asked him, "Where are you?"
He answered, "I heard you in the garden;
 but I was afraid, because I was naked,
 so I hid myself."
Then he asked, "Who told you that you were naked?

You have eaten, then,
 from the tree of which I had
  forbidden you to eat!"
The man replied, "The woman whom
 you put here with me—
 she gave me fruit from the tree, and
  so I ate it."
The LORD God then asked the woman,
 "Why did you do such a thing?"
The woman answered, "The serpent
 tricked me into it, so I ate it."

Then the LORD God said to the serpent:
 "Because you have done this, you
  shall be banned
   from all the animals
   and from all the wild creatures;
 on your belly shall you crawl,
  and dirt shall you eat
  all the days of your life.
 I will put enmity between you and the
  woman,
  and between your offspring and
   hers;
 he will strike at your head,
  while you strike at his heel."
The man called his wife Eve,
 because she became the mother of all
  the living.

SECOND READING
[Eph 1:3-6, 11-12]

Brothers and sisters:
Blessed be the God and Father of our
 Lord Jesus Christ,
 who has blessed us in Christ
  with every spiritual blessing in the
   heavens,
 as he chose us in him, before the
  foundation of the world,
 to be holy and without blemish before
  him.
In love he destined us for adoption to
 himself through Jesus Christ,
 in accord with the favor of his will,
 for the praise of the glory of his grace
 that he granted us in the beloved.

In him we were also chosen,
 destined in accord with the purpose
  of the One
 who accomplishes all things according
  to the intention of his will,
 so that we might exist for the praise of
  his glory,
 we who first hoped in Christ.

Catechesis

Cantors
In singing the responsorial psalm for this solemnity, you sing not only about the "marvelous deeds" God has accomplished in Mary, but also about the same works God has wrought in every human being. As you prepare to sing this psalm, you might spend some time looking for God's saving interventions in human life—in your own life—and give God praise.

Choir
Like Mary, all have been chosen in Christ to be holy (second reading). What does it mean to be holy? How do you support one another in the choir, in your families, in your parish to be faithful to this holiness?

Music Directors
This solemnity is not so much about Mary as it is about God's great deeds to which Mary so completely responded. It would be well to select hymns which enable the assembly to sing God's praises *with* Mary. The *Magnificat* would be an excellent hymn either during Communion (here using a cantor- or choir-led responsorial setting would perhaps be best) or as a hymn of praise for the whole assembly to sing after Communion (here perhaps a strophic version). If the assembly does sing a hymn of praise after Communion, it would be good not to sing a recessional hymn. You might use a joyful organ postlude to send the community on its way.

Liturgy Committee
Often Mass attendance on solemnities is sparse even when they are holy days of obligation. What can you do as a committee to help people understand that solemnities are really "Sundays" as far as celebrating the events of our salvation is concerned?

The solemnity of the Immaculate Conception of the Blessed Virgin Mary, the patronal feast of the United States, brings the ritual requirements and special features of all solemnities: (1) first Evening Prayer is celebrated; (2) there is a proper Mass with three readings as on Sundays; (3) the Gloria (even during Advent) and Creed are used; (4) often the first reading is from the New Testament; and (5) often the second reading carries the meaning or theological import of the festival.

Although this festival occurs during Advent and the sacred space is rather reserved in joyful expectation of Christmas, it is very appropriate to enhance the environment so the space is quite festive. Fresh flowers and good use of joyful color might be chosen.

DECEMBER 8, 1999

Third Sunday of Advent

FAITH-SHARING
- How would you describe your identity and mission, vis-à-vis the coming of Christ?
- How do you testify to the light in your everyday living? What lights up your life?
- How have you experienced being "sent" by God?

PRESIDERS
When have you recently experienced being "sent from God"? When do you testify to the light well? When have you fallen into the temptation of becoming "center stage" rather than pointing to Christ the Light? When have you fallen into self-grandeur rather than pointing to Christ the Light?

DEACONS
Isaiah's passage paints the Advent mission of the Church. As you pray over this text, what might you do to incarnate Christ for others?

HOSPITALITY MINISTERS
". . . there is one among you whom you do not recognize." How might you greet others to show that you recognize the Christ in them?

MUSIC MINISTERS
Your role as leader of music in liturgy is like that of John the Baptist—to lead without calling attention to yourself. What do you need to do to keep the focus on Christ?

ALTAR MINISTERS
"My soul proclaims the greatness of the Lord." How is this true about you?

LECTORS
Your proclamation of the readings is one way of testifying to the Light. Do your neighbors recognize you as one testifying to the Light by how you live?

EUCHARISTIC MINISTERS
"He has filled the hungry with good things." This is certainly true during the Communion procession. How do you fill the hungry with good things outside the liturgy?

Spirituality

Reflecting on the Gospel
When we think about it, much of our lives is directed toward future events. Right now we are looking forward to Christmas. Maybe we look forward to getting our driver's license or going to college. Or we look forward to our next birthday (especially if it's a "big" one!) or to a raise in pay or promotion or a different, better job. We eagerly look forward to marriage or the birth of a child or grandchild. We look forward, perhaps, to the leisure of retirement. We all have many longings, and how easy it is, sometimes, to settle for intermediate goals. In this Sunday's Gospel John the Baptist could have fulfilled the longing for the Messiah of those who approached him. He could have said, "Sure, it's me!" This might have been especially attractive to him, considering the concept of Messiah in John's time was to be the one who would restore Israel to its status of wealth and power during the time of David. Who wouldn't choose wealth and power?

But John didn't! Instead, he fulfilled his mission as the one *sent by God* who would "*testify* to the light." John's identity and mission are clearly set forth in this Gospel. Who is he? Not the Christ, but he is one sent by God. Not only does he reject overtures to make him the Messiah, but he goes on to say that one is "among you whom you do not recognize . . . whose sandal strap I am not worthy to untie." It is because the priests and Levites and Pharisees (and us!) do not recognize Christ among them that they look to John.

What does John do? He testifies to the light, cries out, makes straight the way of the Lord. What do those do who are not sent by God but are sent by humans? They question! They search! They have unfulfilled longings! They mistakenly settle for someone less than the one for whom they truly long. And, so, a question needs to be put to us: Are we sent by God who give testimony to the light, or are we sent by others to question? How we answer that question depends upon whether we recognize the Christ who is among us. Do we?

Living the Paschal Mystery
Why, then, do we baptize? This question, put forth by the Gospel, captures in a few words our own identity and mission. Our baptism plunges us into Christ's saving Mystery. Our baptism transforms us into the body of Christ, an identity we all share in common. As such, we share in John's mission to announce the presence of Christ among us and we share in Christ's mission to announce what God has already accomplished (see the second reading): "a year of favor from the LORD" (first reading). Baptism sharpens our salvific longings so that we, hopefully, don't settle for intermediate goals or place our belief in someone other than Christ. The work of John the Baptist continues in us, the Church. John, then, is a precursor for the Church. And this is what the Church does: testifies, cries out, makes straight the way to the Lord.

This Third Sunday of Advent is a turning point in this season of longing—we now look to the Christ among us, the Christ who was born in Bethlehem long ago and who is present to us now in the Church. For this we "rejoice always."

DECEMBER 12, 1999

GOSPEL [John 1:6-8, 19-28; L8B]

A man named John was sent from God. He came for testimony, to testify to the light, so that all might believe through him. He was not the light, but came to testify to the light.

And this is the testimony of John. When the Jews from Jerusalem sent priests and Levites to him to ask him, "Who are you?" he admitted and did not deny it, but admitted, "I am not the Christ." So they asked him, "What are you then? Are you Elijah?" And he said, "I am not." "Are you the Prophet?" He answered, "No." So they said to him, "Who are you, so we can give an answer to those who sent us? What do you have to say for yourself?" He said: "I am *the voice of one crying out in the desert, make straight the way of the Lord*, as Isaiah the prophet said." Some Pharisees were also sent. They asked him, "Why then do you baptize if you are not the Christ or Elijah or the Prophet?" John answered them, "I baptize with water; but there is one among you whom you do not recognize, the one who is coming after me, whose sandal strap I am not worthy to untie." This happened in Bethany across the Jordan, where John was baptizing.

Working with the Word

Key words and phrases from the Gospel: sent, testify to the light, crying out, make straight the way

Connecting to the first reading: Who is the "I" and "me" of the first reading? We tend to hear this passage ("bring glad tidings to the poor . . .") only from the perspective of Luke's Gospel (Luke 4:18-19) where the passage is applied to Jesus. Does not the Lectionary suggest that this reading is applied to John (the Gospel is about John's identity and mission) and, as disciples, to us (we are functioning as John for our times)?

Connecting to our culture: The irony is that on this, the Third Sunday of Advent, Christ is not on the scene! So the task of "keeping Christ in Christmas" (messages and billboards abound by now) is far too narrow. The mission of John challenges us to testify to and incarnate Christ in the world. How do we testify to Christ in the world? By our Christian living (see the "job description" in the first reading).

Exegetical points: In this Sunday's Gospel, there are three individuals or groups who are "sent" (Greek verb: *apostellō*). The first is John the Baptist (v. 6) who is sent by God "to testify to the light." His bold testimony stands in contrast to the others who are sent: both the priests and Levites who are sent by the Jews from Jerusalem (v. 19) and the Pharisees (v. 24) come to question John. These are paradigmatic responses to God's sending Jesus as the light of the world: one will either testify to it or, by questioning, find oneself in opposition to the light.

The priests and Levites ask John whether he is the "Prophet." This is a reference to Deut 18:15 where God promises to send a prophet like Moses. Various biblical passages anticipate the coming of such a figure (e.g., 1 Macc 4:41-50; 14:41), and Acts 3:22 identifies Jesus as this "prophet like Moses." In Qumran, this figure is discussed in passages that describe the eschatological defeat of enemies. Those who question John the Baptist pair this prophet-like-Moses with Elijah, a pair we find explicitly in accounts of the transfiguration. In the community of John the Evangelist, some were exalting the role of John the Baptist. This passage seems to undercut such attempts.

To the point: John is identified as someone who is sent to testify to the light, to cry out, to make straight the way. These metaphors are further explained in the selection from Isaiah as bringing glad tidings, etc. The Advent mission of the Church is the mission of John.

Celebration

Model Penitential Rite

Presider: John the Baptist was sent by God to give testimony to the light that shines among us. Let us reflect on how that light shines today in our own lives . . . [pause]

> Lord Jesus, you are the light that has come into the world: Lord . . .
> Christ Jesus, you are the Messiah who has come to save us: Christ . . .
> Lord Jesus, you are the one for whom we long: Lord . . .

Responsorial Psalm

"My soul rejoices in my God."

This Sunday's responsorial psalm draws from the *Magnificat* (Luke 1:46-55). On the one hand, it is relatively rare that a text other than one of the psalms is used for the responsorial psalm. (In the three years of the Sunday cycle of readings, only four other Sundays have texts other than psalms, and this Sunday's selection is the only one from the New Testament). On the other hand, there are many texts throughout the Bible that are psalms, though they are not found in the book of Psalms. The point is this: the designation of a text as a "psalm" does not depend on its placement in that particular book. Psalms are poetic prayers, songs, or hymns that express everything from praise and thanks to lamentations and confessions of sin.

The *Magnificat* is a beautiful psalm of praise to God for having chosen Mary for a special role in the salvific events. It thus serves both as a fitting response to this Sunday's first reading and as a bridge to the Gospel reading, as both readings describe individuals (the prophet and John the Baptist) who have been chosen for a particular mission.

Model General Intercessions

Presider: John humbled himself before the One who is greater. We humble ourselves before God as we cry out to God with our needs.

Response:

[musical notation: Lord, hear our prayer.]

Cantor:

[musical notation: we pray to the Lord,]

That the Church might faithfully make straight all paths toward God . . . [pause]

That all people might embrace the faith to see the Light that dwells among us . . . [pause]

That those who long for someone less than the Messiah might cry out to God for enlightenment . . . [pause]

That we here gathered might draw nearer to God at this time of preparation for Christmas . . . [pause]

Presider: Ever faithful God, you sent your Son as the light of the world to dwell among us: hear these our prayers that we might always long only for you. We pray through Jesus Christ our Lord. **Amen.**

ALTERNATIVE OPENING PRAYER

Let us pray

Pause for silent prayer

Father of our Lord Jesus Christ,
ever faithful to your promises
and ever close to your Church:
the earth rejoices in hope of the Savior's coming
and looks forward with longing to his return at the end of time.
Prepare our hearts and remove the sadness
that hinders us from feeling the joy and hope
which his presence will bestow,
for he is Lord for ever and ever. **Amen.**

RESPONSORIAL PSALM

[Luke 1:46-48, 49-50, 53-54]

℟. (Isaiah 61:10b) My soul rejoices in my God.

My soul proclaims the greatness of the Lord;
 my spirit rejoices in God my Savior,
for he has looked upon his lowly servant.
 From this day all generations will call me blessed:

℟. My soul rejoices in my God.

The Almighty has done great things for me,
 and holy is his Name.
He has mercy on those who fear him
 in every generation.

℟. My soul rejoices in my God.

He has filled the hungry with good things,
 and the rich he has sent away empty.
He has come to the help of his servant Israel
 for he has remembered his promise of mercy.

℟. My soul rejoices in my God.

FIRST READING
[Isa 61:1-2a, 10-11]

The spirit of the Lord GOD is upon me,
  because the LORD has anointed me;
he has sent me to bring glad tidings to
    the poor,
  to heal the brokenhearted,
to proclaim liberty to the captives
  and release to the prisoners,
to announce a year of favor from the
    LORD
  and a day of vindication by our God.

I rejoice heartily in the LORD,
  in my God is the joy of my soul;
for he has clothed me with a robe of
    salvation
  and wrapped me in a mantle of
    justice,
like a bridegroom adorned with a
    diadem,
  like a bride bedecked with her jewels.
As the earth brings forth its plants,
  and a garden makes its growth spring
    up,
so will the Lord GOD make justice and
    praise
  spring up before all the nations.

SECOND READING
[1 Thess 5:16-24]

Brothers and sisters:
Rejoice always. Pray without ceasing.
In all circumstances give thanks,
  for this is the will of God for you in
    Christ Jesus.
Do not quench the Spirit.
Do not despise prophetic utterances.
Test everything; retain what is good.
Refrain from every kind of evil.

May the God of peace make you
  perfectly holy
  and may you entirely, spirit, soul, and
    body,
  be preserved blameless for the
    coming of our Lord Jesus Christ.
The one who calls you is faithful,
  and he will also accomplish it.

Catechesis

Cantors
Mary's *Magnificat* proclaims the goodness and mercy of God. As you sing it this Sunday, you make the same proclamation: you, too, have seen that goodness. When? Where? How?

Choir
Through your ministry as a choir you are called to see and announce the presence of Christ in and to one another, in and to the assembly. How can you make the extra demands placed upon the choir as Christmas approaches an opportunity to fulfill this mission?

Music Directors
The readings of the past two weeks of Advent have kept your eyes looking toward the second coming of Christ. This Sunday begins to turn your focus toward the Christ coming at Christmas. Advent hymns which express this focus include "Awake! Awake, and Greet the New Morn" [CBW3, RS, W3]. This could be used for entrance or as a hymn of praise after Communion. Have the choir only sing v. 3, sopranos and altos singing the first two phrases softly, tenors and basses singing the last two more strongly. "O Come, Divine Messiah" [BB, CH, CBW3, RS, W3, WC] could be sung at the presentation of the gifts, as a song after Communion, or as a recessional. "He Will Come" [CH] uses a gentle Welsh folk melody for a Willard Jabusch text that is exceptional in its imagery, e.g., "years of groping, years of hoping, all fulfilled when He will come," and "down among us He has chosen here to taste our cup of life." Text and melody are well integrated, the beauty of one adding to the beauty of the other. (This one's a hidden treasure that needs wider publication.)

Liturgy Committee
At this time, everyone is caught up in preparations for Christmas. This is not a bad thing, unless your longings change focus. How might you both enjoy the Christmas preparations at the same time that you remain focused on longing for a greater presence of Christ in your life?

This Sunday has traditionally been called *"gaudete"* (Latin for "rejoice") Sunday, taken from the introductory verse ("introit," given in the Sacramentary): "Rejoice in the Lord always; again I say, rejoice! The Lord is near" (Phil 4:4-5; see also the second reading). The presider wore rose vestments (still permitted, but not required) as a sign of rejoicing, "the Lord is near." The rose was also a reminder that Advent penance was half over. Since the penance of Advent is understood in a different light now, it is better not to emphasize this "almost over" aspect of Advent penance.

DECEMBER 12, 1999

Fourth Sunday of Advent

FAITH-SHARING
- How is God's plan for salvation being worked out in your life?
- What enables you to say *yes* like Mary said yes?
- What does God's presence within you bring about in your life?
- It's always easier to *do* than to *be*. What changes must you make in your life so that you can truly *be* God's presence for others?
- How will you *be* during the last week before Christmas?

PRESIDERS
Especially at this time of year, the demands of ministry push you toward *doing* rather than *being*. How might you bring better balance to these two?

DEACONS
How does your service promote an awareness of God's dwelling within those whom you serve? Within you?

HOSPITALITY MINISTERS
"The Lord is with you." As you reflect on this greeting, how is this true for you? How might you promote this awareness in those you greet?

MUSIC MINISTERS
How does awareness of God's presence within you and within the assembly influence the way in which you lead the music of worship?

ALTAR MINISTERS
You will have much service to offer during the last week before Christmas. How can you do it in such a way that you are truly ministering God's presence for others?

LECTORS
How does your proclamation of the Word enable the Word to be enfleshed in the here-and-now for the members of your liturgical community?

EUCHARISTIC MINISTERS
How is your greeting each communicant with "Body of Christ" or "Blood of Christ" another way of saying "The Lord is with you"?

Spirituality

Reflecting on the Gospel

Finally, with this Fourth Sunday of Advent, the readings *explicitly* direct our attention to the coming feast. The annunciation account in the Gospel also draws our attention to the concrete role Mary played in the events of salvation. Of all the Sundays in the year, this one might truly be called a "Marian" Sunday! Further, connecting the annunciation account with the first reading opens up a promise-fulfillment typology; that is, what God promised in the Hebrew Scriptures came to fulfillment in Christ.

In the first reading, though David's intentions to build a temple for God seem honorable—they are, after all, initially approved by Nathan the Prophet—they are not carried out when God countervenes the prophet's word and denies David the right to build a temple. God retains his role as God: God will build a house (dynasty) for David, will "adopt" David's son as God's own son (see Ps 2:7 for the notion of divine adoption of the king by God), and will give him an everlasting kingdom and throne—all promises that the New Testament sees fulfilled in Jesus.

If we pair this first reading with the Gospel, there is a contrast—perhaps unintended—between the over-reaching David and the more cooperative Mary. Chosen as David had been, Mary does not lose sight of the fact that the initiative must lie with God. The plans, the purpose, and the accomplishment of salvation will be God's doing. By her faithful cooperation, Mary herself is shaped by God into a living Temple fit to bear the Divine Presence. These events show us in astounding ways that nothing is impossible with God.

Both readings draw our attention not to the house, but to *what is housed*: God's presence. The prophet Nathan answered David with "Go, do . . . for the Lord is with you." Gabriel greets Mary with "The Lord is with you." In response, David wanted to build a space to house the Divine Presence; Mary opened up the space of her very own being to house the Divine Presence. Mary's *yes* that was the surrender of her whole being—"may it be done to me"—was enabled by God's presence already within her. Our challenge is to recognize and respond to God's presence already within us. This is what true preparation for Christmas is all about.

Living the Paschal Mystery

On the last two Sundays the Gospel has referred to preparing the way of the Lord. Just as for Mary in this Sunday's Gospel, this makes concrete demands on *our* lives. Yet, it is not what *we* do that brings Divine Presence to us, it is what *God* accomplishes in us. And what God does for us always far surpasses anything we do for God. The incredible mystery of Christmas—we now enter into our final week of joyful preparation—is about God's presence to us in so many unthinkable ways. We are challenged to take up these readings' many reminders of God's presence—God has been with us wherever we went, destroyed our enemies, enabled us to dwell in peace, established a kingdom for us that will last forever, adopted us as sons and daughters, filled us with grace, overshadowed us with the Holy Spirit—and to respond as Mary did: "May it be done to me according to your word."

DECEMBER 19, 1999

GOSPEL [Luke 1:26-38; L11B]

The angel Gabriel was sent from God to a town of Galilee called Nazareth, to a virgin betrothed to a man named Joseph, of the house of David, and the virgin's name was Mary. And coming to her, he said, "Hail, full of grace! The Lord is with you." But she was greatly troubled at what was said and pondered what sort of greeting this might be. Then the angel said to her, "Do not be afraid, Mary, for you have found favor with God.

"Behold, you will conceive in your womb and bear a son, and you shall name him Jesus. He will be great and will be called Son of the Most High, and the Lord God will give him the throne of David his father, and he will rule over the house of Jacob forever, and of his kingdom there will be no end." But Mary said to the angel, "How can this be, since I have no relations with a man?" And the angel said to her in reply, "The Holy Spirit will come upon you, and the power of the Most High will overshadow you. Therefore the child to be born will be called holy, the Son of God. And behold, Elizabeth, your relative, has also conceived a son in her old age, and this is the sixth month for her who was called barren; for nothing will be impossible for God." Mary said, "Behold, I am the handmaid of the Lord. May it be done to me according to your word." Then the angel departed from her.

Working with the Word

Key words and phrases from the Gospel: full of grace, the Lord is with you, nothing will be impossible for God, may it be done to me

Connecting to the first reading: In the first reading, the initiative is with David who wants to build a house *for* God. In contrast, in the Gospel the initiative is with God who announces what will be done *for* humanity. Mary models the proper response to God's initiative.

Connecting to our culture: We always seem to need to be on the initiative. "Responders" tend to be understood as passive and weak. Culturally, our instinct is like David's: we desire to do something for God. In the first reading, God's response to David is that God will do more for David (build an everlasting dynasty) than David could ever do for God (build a temple).

Exegetical points: The pairing of this Sunday's first reading from 2 Samuel and the Gospel of the annunciation from Luke is traditionally understood along typological lines: the Ark that houses the Divine Presence foreshadows Mary as *Theotokos*—the one who bears the Divine Presence in her womb.

The world-view behind 2 Samuel is rich. In that ancient world, kingship and temple-building go together. Myths in which combat among the gods gives rise to new creation show the victorious god being acclaimed as king who then builds himself a temple. This pattern is also found in the Song of the Sea in Exodus 15 in which YHWH the Divine Warrior is acclaimed as king and builds his sanctuary (vv. 17-18). In the earthly realm, David, the divinely appointed king who has finally defeated all his enemies, desires to build a temple for the Lord. Some see on David's part a pretentious move to establish a kingship on the model of his pagan neighbors, or at the very least, to become God's patron rather than recognize himself as the one whose patron is God. God undercuts such possibilities both by denying David the right to build a temple and by making David realize that his throne is established solely by divine grace.

To the point: This Sunday's readings draw us to reflect on God's many and varied actions: (1) what God did for David; (2) what God did for humanity through Mary; (3) what God is doing for us during these Advent and Christmas seasons; and (4) what God will do for us during the new millennium.

Celebration

Model Penitential Rite

Presider: Our mighty God came to Mary and dwelt within her. Let us reflect on the God who dwells within each of us and let our hearts overflow with praise . . . [pause]

> Lord Jesus, you were conceived by the power of the Holy Spirit: Lord . . .
> Christ Jesus, you made Mary's womb your Temple: Christ . . .
> Lord Jesus, you are the holy one, the Son of God: Lord . . .

Responsorial Psalm

"Forever I will sing the goodness of the Lord."

The section of Psalm 89 used for this Sunday's responsorial psalm is the psalmic version of the first reading, the story of God's promise to build David a house—a dynasty—which will last forever. The one who sits on the throne of this dynasty will call God "father," and all blessings will come through him to the people Israel.

We are not given the rest of Psalm 89, however. In vv. 32-35 God promises to remain faithful even if David's sons are not. God swears to punish any who forsake the law, but "my kindness I will not take from him. . . . I will not violate my covenant." Yet in vv. 39-52 God does just this—withholds divine protection and permits the destruction of the kingdom. By the time of Christ there has been no king on the throne of David for over five centuries. What has happened to God's promise of fidelity?

The answer is given in the Gospel. God sends an angel to announce the birth of One who will inherit David's throne. Here will be the Son of David who can most fully cry out, "You are my Father." Here will be the restoration of the dynasty and all its blessings for the people. Truly God is faithful, and truly can we sing of God's goodness forever.

Model General Intercessions

Presider: God faithfully dwells among us, and so we bring our prayers to the Divine Majesty with confidence.

Response:

Lord, hear our prayer.

Cantor:

we pray to the Lord,

That the Church may always be "full of grace" . . . [pause]

That those who rule people today may draw their power from God . . . [pause]

That those who experience the absence of God because of lack of faith or despair may come to experience that God is always faithful . . . [pause]

That we may prepare for Christmas by saying to God daily "may it be done to me according to your word" . . . [pause]

Presider: Mighty God, you sent your Spirit to overshadow Mary and your Son dwelt within her: come and do not delay, hear our prayers and dwell among us. We ask this through that same Son, Jesus Christ our Lord. **Amen.**

ALTERNATIVE OPENING PRAYER

Let us pray
  [as Advent draws to a close for the
  faith that opens our lives to the Spirit
  of God]

Pause for silent prayer

Father, all-powerful God,
your eternal Word took flesh on our earth
when the Virgin Mary placed her life
at the service of your plan.
Lift our minds in watchful hope
to hear the voice which announces his
  glory
and open our minds to receive the Spirit
who prepares us for his coming.
We ask this through Christ our Lord.
  Amen.

RESPONSORIAL PSALM
[Ps 89:2-3, 4-5, 27, 29]

℟. (2a) Forever I will sing the goodness of the Lord.

The promises of the Lord I will sing
  forever;
  through all generations my mouth
    shall proclaim your faithfulness.
For you have said, "My kindness is
  established forever";
  in heaven you have confirmed your
    faithfulness.

℟. Forever I will sing the goodness of the Lord.

"I have made a covenant with my
  chosen one,
  I have sworn to David my servant:
forever will I confirm your posterity
  and establish your throne for all
    generations."

℟. Forever I will sing the goodness of the Lord.

"He shall say of me, 'You are my father,
  my God, the Rock, my savior.'
Forever I will maintain my kindness
  toward him,
  and my covenant with him stands
    firm."

℟. Forever I will sing the goodness of the Lord.

FIRST READING
[2 Sam 7:1-5, 8b-12, 14a, 16]

When King David was settled in his
  palace,
  and the Lord had given him rest from
    his enemies on every side,
  he said to Nathan the prophet,

"Here I am living in a house of cedar,
  while the ark of God dwells in a tent!"
Nathan answered the king,
  "Go, do whatever you have in mind,
  for the LORD is with you."
But that night the LORD spoke to Nathan
  and said:
  "Go, tell my servant David, 'Thus
    says the LORD:
  Should you build me a house to dwell
    in?'

It was I who took you from the pasture
  and from the care of the flock
  to be commander of my people Israel.
I have been with you wherever you
    went,
  and I have destroyed all your enemies
    before you.
And I will make you famous like the
  great ones of the earth.
I will fix a place for my people Israel;
  I will plant them so that they may
    dwell in their place
  without further disturbance.
Neither shall the wicked continue to
  afflict them as they did of old,
  since the time I first appointed judges
    over my people Israel.
I will give you rest from all your
  enemies.
The LORD also reveals to you
  that he will establish a house for you.
And when your time comes and you
  rest with your ancestors,
  I will raise up your heir after you,
    sprung from your loins,
  and I will make his kingdom firm.
I will be a father to him,
  and he shall be a son to me.
Your house and your kingdom shall
  endure forever before me;
  your throne shall stand firm forever."

SECOND READING
[Rom 16:25-27]

Brothers and sisters:
To him who can strengthen you,
  according to my gospel and the
    proclamation of Jesus Christ,
  according to the revelation of the
    mystery kept secret for long ages
  but now manifested through the
    prophetic writings and,
  according to the command of the
    eternal God,
  made known to all nations to bring
    about the obedience of faith,
  to the only wise God, through Jesus
    Christ
  be glory forever and ever. Amen.

Catechesis

Cantors
The goodness about which you sing in this psalm is God's promise to remain faithful to you, a promise fulfilled in the coming of Christ. Take some time this week to thank God for Christ and for the fulfillment which Christ has brought to humankind.

Choir
God desires to be present among and within you. Because of your baptism you, like Mary, "house" God. How during this final week of Advent can you deepen your "yes" to being this dwelling?

Music Directors
Hymns about Mary and her role in the birth of Christ are appropriate on this Sunday. "The Angel Gabriel from Heaven Came" [CBW3, W3] uses a delightful Basque carol to tell the story of the annunciation and would work well either at the presentation of the gifts or as a choral prelude. John Bell's "No Wind at the Window" [RS] would also be suitable at either of these two places in the liturgy. If the choir sings it, you might add some emphasis to the final phrase by omitting the sharp in the final chord until the last verse. Put a *fermata* on the last syllable of "conviction" in the final line, follow it by a *caesura*, then use *tenutos* on the concluding "Tell God I say yes."

In line with the imagery of house or dwelling place in this Sunday's readings, a beautiful choral prelude would be Owen Ascott's "O Holy Mary" [BB] with its refrain "O holy Dwelling Place of God. O holy Temple of the Word . . ." Choir parts are available [OCP, *Choral Praise* #9093 and 8723; *Choral Praise Comprehensive Edition* #10317; octavo #8724, which includes solo instrument part].

Liturgy Committee
This week will include a flurry of Christmas preparation, both in your homes and parishes. How might you keep your focus on Divine Presence during this whole time? How might your preparations be done in such a way as to witness to the Divine Presence already dwelling within you?

This time of Advent might be called the Church's liturgical "Marian season." Some kind of devotional Marian prayer (e.g., a holy hour) would be very appropriate. The *Magnificat* could be a "centerpiece" for the prayer.

The phrase "The Lord is with you" that is used in both the first reading and Gospel for this Sunday only occurs two other times in English translations of the Scriptures: in Judges 6:12 (where it is the angel's greeting to Gideon) and in 2 Chronicles 15:2 (where Azariah assures King Asa of God's abiding presence so long as he opens himself to God). The similar phrase, "The Lord be with you," only occurs in the English Scriptures five times (Ruth 2:4; 1 Sam 17:37; 20:13; 1 Chron 22:11, 16). Sometimes presiders like to use the two phrases interchangeably, but in fact they are different. The first phrase—with indicative verb *is*—states the *fact* of God's presence; the second phrase—with optative mood verb *be*—expresses a *wish* and, in its liturgical use, is an indication of action that is yet to unfold in the liturgy. That yet-to-be-accomplished action is God's transforming us by grace. For this reason, presiders are cautioned about changing the liturgical text by interchanging the phrases.

DECEMBER 19, 1999

Season of Christmas

THE NATIVITY OF THE LORD

FAITH-SHARING
- How has the Christ in others brought light and life to you?
- How do you bring light and life to others?
- What family activities do you share together that capture the religious spirit of Christmas?
- How can your activities during the Christmas season be extended through the year so that God's peace reigns?

PRESIDERS
Your presiding at the Christmas Masses is your gift of God's presence to the people. How might remembering this affect how you welcome those Catholics who come to liturgy so infrequently?

DEACONS
At this time of the year when giving is foremost, how might you understand your service as your gift to the community?

HOSPITALITY MINISTERS
A good many worshipers you greet on Christmas only come to church this one day of the year. How might your greeting make them feel welcome in God's presence? How might you put them at ease? How might you help them pray/worship better?

MUSIC MINISTERS
Many last-minute demands will be placed upon you this week. In the midst of it, be sure to take time to prepare *yourself* through personal prayer for your ministry.

ALTAR MINISTERS
How might the reverence and awe with which you serve at the church help others to know the Word is made flesh?

LECTORS
How does your proclamation of the Word help enflesh the Word in the world today?

EUCHARISTIC MINISTERS
How might you better recognize the Word made flesh as the body of Christ (in the Eucharist, in the people)?

Spirituality

Reflecting on the Gospel

"Merry Christmas!" How many times will this greeting be given and received over the next week? Why is Christmas merry? For many reasons, but among them: our being together with family and friends; reminiscing; the generous gift-giving to our loved ones and to those whom we don't know but are less fortunate than ourselves; the familiar, traditional music, lights, decorations, good food; time off from work and other chores that allow for a different (even if not a more leisurely) pace of life. Each of us can add to the list of what makes Christmas merry in terms of family customs or out-of-the-ordinary occurrences (e.g., a time for engagement to be married) or other events that fulfill personal hopes and dreams. All this makes this season a wonderful one for most of us.

On the other hand, the harsh reality of our society is that Christmas is anything but merry for all too many citizens. For some, poverty keeps them from providing for their loved ones in the way they would like; for others, alienation and loneliness divide and separate rather than unite; for still others selfishness and greed and self-centeredness keep family or friends at bay and result in emptiness and isolation.

The four Gospels given for the Vigil and three Masses for Christmas help us bridge these two very discordant realities. At the Vigil Mass the Gospel from Matthew relates Joseph's bewilderment at learning Mary, his betrothed, is pregnant; Jewish law required harsh punishment. God visits him in a dream through an angel so that Joseph could take Mary into his home. The Gospel for the Mass at Midnight relates how Jesus, the Savior of the world, is born in material poverty but has angels of the Most High announce his birth to all the world with great joy. The Gospel for the Mass at Dawn sends the shepherds to Bethlehem to find everything as the angels said—the infant with his parents—and they go away "glorifying and praising God." And, finally, the Gospel for the Mass during the Day reveals to us the lofty divinity of this humble babe, testified to by John the Baptist, one who dwells among us so that *we* might, too, see his glory and give praise to God.

Christmas is a time for more than merriment. It is a time to be aware of how blessed we are by God's saving presence. Christ came into the world as an infant wrapped in swaddling clothes and lying in a manger so that we might sing joyfully that today a Savior has been born for us! It is a time *for us* to give glory and praise to our God. Glory to God in the highest! Peace!

Living the Paschal Mystery

For the selfish and self-centered, Christmas might be more a time of dying. For the generous and those who are other-centered, Christmas might be more a time of rising. Reaching out to others doesn't depend on social, economic, or religious status. It simply depends on our recognizing that Christ came into the world to dwell among us. Christ isn't choosey . . . he loves all, infinitely. This is what "Savior" means. This is what the angels sang "Glory!" about. This is why the shepherds were awe-stricken. The "good news of great joy that will be for all the people" is that a "Savior has been born."

For the Vigil Mass

GOSPEL [Matt 1:1-25; L13ABC]

The book of the genealogy of Jesus Christ, the son of David, the son of Abraham.

Abraham became the father of Isaac, Isaac the father of Jacob, Jacob the father of Judah and his brothers. Judah became the father of Perez and Zerah, whose mother was Tamar. Perez became the father of Hezron, Hezron the father of Ram, Ram the father of Amminadab. Amminadab became the father of Nahshon, Nahshon the father of Salmon, Salmon the father of Boaz, whose mother was Rahab. Boaz became the father of Obed, whose mother was Ruth. Obed became the father of Jesse, Jesse the father of David the king.

David became the father of Solomon, whose mother had been the wife of Uriah. Solomon became the father of Rehoboam, Rehoboam the father of Abijah, Abijah the father of Asaph. Asaph became the father of Jehoshaphat, Jehoshaphat the father of Joram, Joram the father of Uzziah. Uzziah became the father of Jotham, Jotham the father of Ahaz, Ahaz the father of Hezekiah. Hezekiah became the father of Manasseh, Manasseh the father of Amos, Amos the father of Josiah. Josiah became the father of Jechoniah and his brothers at the time of the Babylonian exile.

After the Babylonian exile, Jechoniah became the father of Shealtiel, Shealtiel the father of Zerubbabel, Zerubbabel the father of Abiud. Abiud became the father of Eliakim, Eliakim the father of Azor, Azor the father of Zadok. Zadok became the father of Achim, Achim the father of Eliud, Eliud the father of Eleazar. Eleazar became the father of Matthan, Matthan the father of Jacob, Jacob the father of Joseph, the husband of Mary. Of her was born Jesus who is called the Christ.

Thus the total number of generations from Abraham to David is fourteen generations; from David to the Babylonian exile, fourteen generations; from the Babylonian exile to the Christ, fourteen generations.

Now this is how the birth of Jesus Christ came about. When his mother Mary was betrothed to Joseph, but before they lived together, she was found with child through the Holy Spirit. Joseph her husband, since he was a righteous man, yet unwilling to expose her to shame, decided to divorce her quietly. Such was his intention when, behold, the angel of the Lord appeared to him in a dream and said, "Joseph, son of David, do not be afraid to take Mary your wife into your home. For it is through the Holy Spirit that this child has been conceived in her. She will bear a son and you are to name him Jesus, because he will save his people from their sins." All this took place to fulfill what the Lord had said through the prophet: *Behold, the virgin shall conceive and bear a son, and they shall name him Emmanuel,* which means "God is with us." When Joseph awoke, he did as the angel of the Lord had commanded him and took his wife into his home. He had no relations with her until she bore a son, and he named him Jesus.

For the Mass at Midnight

GOSPEL [Luke 2:1-14; L14ABC]

In those days a decree went out from Caesar Augustus that the whole world should be enrolled. This was the first enrollment, when Quirinius was governor of Syria. So all went to be enrolled, each to his own town. And Joseph too went up from Galilee from the town of Nazareth to Judea, to the city of David that is called Bethlehem, because he was of the house and family of David, to be enrolled with Mary, his betrothed, who was with child. While they were there, the time came for her to have her child, and she gave birth to her firstborn son. She wrapped him in swaddling clothes and laid him in a manger, because there was no room for them in the inn.

Now there were shepherds in that region living in the fields and keeping the night watch over their flock. The angel of the Lord appeared to them and the glory of the Lord shone around them, and they were struck with great fear. The angel said to them, "Do not be afraid; for behold, I proclaim to you good news of great joy that will be for all the people. For today in the city of David a savior has been born for you who is Christ and Lord. And this will be a sign for you: you will find an infant wrapped in swaddling clothes and lying in a manger." And suddenly there was a multitude of the heavenly host with the angel, praising God and saying: "Glory to God in the highest and on earth peace to those on whom his favor rests."

For the Mass at Dawn

GOSPEL [Luke 2:15-20; L15ABC]

When the angels went away from them to heaven, the shepherds said to one another, "Let us go, then, to Bethlehem to see this thing that has taken place, which the Lord has made known to us." So they went in haste and found Mary and Joseph, and the infant lying in the manger. When they saw this, they made known the message that had been told them about this child. All who heard it were amazed by what had been told them by the shepherds. And Mary kept all these things, reflecting on them in her heart. Then the shepherds returned, glorifying and praising God for all they had heard and seen, just as it had been told to them.

For the Mass during the Day

GOSPEL [John 1:1-18; L16ABC]

In the beginning was the Word, and the Word was with God, and the Word was God. He was in the beginning with God. All things came to be through him, and without him nothing came to be. What came to be through him was life, and this life was the light of the human race; the light shines in the darkness, and the darkness has not overcome it.

A man named John was sent from God. He came for testimony, to testify to the light, so that all might believe through him. He was not the light, but came to testify to the light. The true light, which enlightens everyone, was coming into the world.

He was in the world, and the world came to be through him, but the world did not know him. He came to what was his own, but his own people did not accept him.

But to those who did accept him he gave power to become children of God, to those who believe in his name, who were born not by natural generation nor by human choice nor by a man's decision but of God.

And the Word became flesh and made his dwelling among us, and we saw his glory, the glory as of the Father's only Son, full of grace and truth.

John testified to him and cried out, saying, "This was he of whom I said, 'The one who is coming after me ranks ahead of me because he existed before me.'" From his fullness we have all received, grace in place of grace, because while the law was given through Moses, grace and truth came through Jesus Christ. No one has ever seen God. The only Son, God, who is at the Father's side, has revealed him.

Spirituality, cont.

Working with the Word

At the Vigil Mass—*Key words and phrases from the Gospel:* Joseph, son of David; name him Jesus; fulfill . . . said through the prophet; name him Emmanuel

To the point: We note that the Gospel for the Vigil Mass is an annunciation *to Joseph*. What is announced? More than the *fact* of Christ's birth is the meaning of the birth; i.e., that he saves us from our sin and is God with us. This is the fulfillment of God's age-old prophecy of salvation and presence.

Mass at Midnight—*Key words and phrases from the Gospel:* house and family of David, savior has been born for you, shepherds, swaddling clothes, lying in a manger

To the point: We see in this Gospel a contrast between the lofty origins and the lowly birth of Jesus. Descended from the royal house of David, he is born in a manger. Acclaimed by choirs of angels, he is visited by shepherds in the dark. Contrary to expectation, it is in the night, in poverty, on the fringes of the city, that "a savior has been born *for you*."

Mass at Dawn—*Key words and phrases from the Gospel:* angels went away, shepherds, go . . . to Bethlehem, saw, made known the message

To the point: The shepherds had been told, they came and saw, and they made known the message. We are here, we've been told the story, the Savior has been made known to us. All that remains is for us to go and make known the message.

Mass during the Day—*Key words and phrases from the Gospel:* What came to be through him was life, become children of God, the Word became flesh

To the point: In addition to the human interest around Christmas—infant wrapped in swaddling clothes, infant in a manger, angels, shepherds—this Gospel reveals a fuller meaning of Christ's birth. All that God had wanted for creation and salvation is accomplished in Jesus Christ. This is what it means to say that God's Word becomes flesh. Further, what it means *for us* is that God in Christ gave to us "power to become children of God" and "grace in place of grace."

DECEMBER 25, 1999

Celebration

From Mass during the Day

ALTERNATIVE OPENING PRAYER

Let us pray
   [in the joy of Christmas because the Son of God lives among us]

Pause for silent prayer

God of love, Father of all,
the darkness that covered the earth
has given way to the bright dawn of
   your Word made flesh.
Make us a people of this light.
Make us faithful to your Word,
that we may bring your life to the
   waiting world.
Grant this through Christ our Lord.
   Amen.

For the Vigil Mass

RESPONSORIAL PSALM
[Ps 89:4-5, 16-17, 27, 29]

℟. (2a) Forever I will sing the goodness of the Lord.

I have made a covenant with my chosen one,
   I have sworn to David my servant:
forever will I confirm your posterity
   and establish your throne for all generations.

℟. Forever I will sing the goodness of the Lord.

Blessed the people who know the joyful shout;
   in the light of your countenance, O LORD, they walk.
At your name they rejoice all the day,
   and through your justice they are exalted.

℟. Forever I will sing the goodness of the Lord.

He shall say of me, "You are my father, my God, the rock, my savior."
Forever I will maintain my kindness toward him,
   and my covenant with him stands firm.

℟. Forever I will sing the goodness of the Lord.

Model Penitential Rite

Presider: Today we join the angels and lift our hearts with joy to praise our God who is among us. Let us prepare ourselves to hear the Word of salvation and receive the gift of life . . . [pause]

   Lord Jesus, you are the Word become flesh: Lord . . .
   Christ Jesus, you are Emmanuel—God with us: Christ . . .
   Lord Jesus, you are the Savior of the world: Lord . . .

Responsorial Psalm

The audience to whom the good news of the birth of the Savior is announced grows with each Gospel for the Masses of Christmas. This progression in the proclamation is also evident in the responsorial psalms. The verses from Psalm 89 (a royal psalm about both the establishment of David's kingdom and its subsequent destruction) chosen for the Vigil Mass indicate that the promises of God to David are being fulfilled in this child born of Mary. The responsorial psalms for the next three Masses are in sequence (Pss 96–98), part of a collection of psalms proclaiming God's kingship.

The Gospel at midnight is about Jesus' birth in the night, announced by angels to the shepherds. Psalm 96 declares that this Savior has been given the kingship belonging to David and "he shall rule the world with justice." In the Gospel at dawn, what angels had announced at midnight, the shepherds now proclaim. Having sought and found the newborn Savior, they begin broadcasting what they have seen. Psalm 97 declares "The LORD is king . . . [let] all peoples see his glory." The first reading from the Mass during the Day praises those who announce the good news of God's kingship ("how beautiful . . . are the feet of [those] who bring glad tidings . . . God is King!"). The plan of God which has existed from the beginning has become flesh (Gospel) and "of his fullness we have all received." Psalm 98 cries out, "All the ends of the earth have seen the saving power of God."

Model General Intercessions

Presider: On this wondrous day when we celebrate the nearness of our God, let us make our prayers known with confidence in God's care for us.

Response: Lord, hear our prayer.

Cantor: we pray to the Lord,

That the Church may welcome in peace and joy Christ's abiding presence among us . . . [pause]

That the people of the world may welcome the Light of the world who pours life into their hearts . . . [pause]

That those without joy or family or friends this Christmas may experience the nearness of God and find peace . . . [pause]

That we here gathered may share the glory of God's only Son who is full of grace and truth . . . [pause]

Presider: O wondrous God, you give us joy in this celebration of the birth of your Son: hear these our prayers that we may sing with the angels your glory and praise always. We pray through that same Son, Jesus Christ our Lord. **Amen.**

For the Mass at Midnight

RESPONSORIAL PSALM
[Ps 96:1-2, 2-3, 11-12, 13]

℟. (Luke 2:11) Today is born our Savior, Christ the Lord.

Sing to the Lord a new song;
   sing to the Lord, all you lands.
Sing to the Lord; bless his name.

℟. Today is born our Savior, Christ the Lord.

Announce his salvation, day after day.
   Tell his glory among the nations;
among all peoples, his wondrous deeds.

℟. Today is born our Savior, Christ the Lord.

Let the heavens be glad and the earth rejoice;
   let the sea and what fills it resound;
   let the plains be joyful and all that is in them!
Then shall all the trees of the forest exult.

℟. Today is born our Savior, Christ the Lord.

They shall exult before the Lord, for he comes;
   for he comes to rule the earth.
He shall rule the world with justice
   and the peoples with his constancy.

℟. Today is born our Savior, Christ the Lord.

For the Mass at Dawn

RESPONSORIAL PSALM
[Ps 97:1, 6, 11-12]

℟. A light will shine on us this day: the Lord is born for us.

The Lord is king; let the earth rejoice;
   let the many islands be glad.
The heavens proclaim his justice,
   and all peoples see his glory.

℟. A light will shine on us this day: the Lord is born for us.

Light dawns for the just;
   and gladness, for the upright of heart.
Be glad in the Lord, you just,
   and give thanks to his holy name.

℟. A light will shine on us this day: the Lord is born for us.

For the Mass during the Day

RESPONSORIAL PSALM
[Ps 98:1, 2-3, 3-4, 5-6]

℟. (3c) All the ends of the earth have seen the saving power of God.

Sing to the Lord a new song,
   for he has done wondrous deeds;
his right hand has won victory for him,
   his holy arm.

℟. All the ends of the earth have seen the saving power of God.

The Lord has made his salvation known:
   in the sight of the nations he has revealed his justice.
He has remembered his kindness and his faithfulness
   toward the house of Israel.

℟. All the ends of the earth have seen the saving power of God.

All the ends of the earth have seen
   the salvation by our God.
Sing joyfully to the Lord, all you lands;
   break into song; sing praise.

℟. All the ends of the earth have seen the saving power of God.

Sing praise to the Lord with the harp,
   with the harp and melodious song.
With trumpets and the sound of the horn
   sing joyfully before the King, the Lord.

℟. All the ends of the earth have seen the saving power of God.

For the Vigil Mass

FIRST READING [Isa 62:1-5]

For Zion's sake I will not be silent,
   for Jerusalem's sake I will not be quiet,
until her vindication shines forth like the dawn
   and her victory like a burning torch.
Nations shall behold your vindication,
   and all the kings your glory;
you shall be called by a new name
   pronounced by the mouth of the Lord.
You shall be a glorious crown in the hand of the Lord,
   a royal diadem held by your God.
No more shall people call you "Forsaken,"
   or your land "Desolate,"
but you shall be called "My Delight,"
   and your land "Espoused."
For the Lord delights in you
   and makes your land his spouse.
As a young man marries a virgin,
   your Builder shall marry you;
and as a bridegroom rejoices in his bride
   so shall your God rejoice in you.

For the Mass at Midnight

FIRST READING [Isa 9:1-6]

The people who walked in darkness
   have seen a great light;
upon those who dwelt in the land of gloom
   a light has shone.
You have brought them abundant joy
   and great rejoicing,
as they rejoice before you as at the harvest,
   as people make merry when dividing spoils.
For the yoke that burdened them,
   the pole on their shoulder,
and the rod of their taskmaster
   you have smashed, as on the day of Midian.
For every boot that tramped in battle,
   every cloak rolled in blood,
   will be burned as fuel for flames.
For a child is born to us, a son is given us;
   upon his shoulder dominion rests.
They name him Wonder-Counselor, God-Hero,
   Father-Forever, Prince of Peace.
His dominion is vast
   and forever peaceful,
from David's throne, and over his kingdom,
   which he confirms and sustains
by judgment and justice,
   both now and forever.
The zeal of the Lord of hosts will do this!

For the Mass at Dawn

FIRST READING [Isa 62:11-12]

See, the Lord proclaims
   to the ends of the earth:
say to daughter Zion,
   your savior comes!
Here is his reward with him,
   his recompense before him.
They shall be called the holy people,
   the redeemed of the Lord,
and you shall be called "Frequented,"
   a city that is not forsaken.

Catechesis

Cantors
Keeping in mind the progression within the responsorial psalms used for the four Masses for Christmas will add depth to your understanding of the one you are to sing. You are shouting with all the world that the Savior has come.

Choir
One of the challenging things for choirs on Christmas is postponing the family celebration of the feast until *after* the liturgy. It is difficult to sing and pray well when you are too full or too exhausted. In a sense, Advent doesn't end for the choir on Christmas Eve. But the very waiting to fully celebrate will bring the resurrection of a deeper participation in your liturgical ministry.

Music Directors
Christmas hymns abound, and the assembly loves to sing them; make sure each hymn chosen fits its function in the liturgy. The entrance and recessional hymns need a tempo and style that "process." The hymns during the presentation of gifts and Communion need to be more meditative or reflective. For example, carols such as "Silent Night" and "What Child Is This?" are not suitable for entrance or recessional, but are better suited for the presentation of gifts or Communion. Examples of good entrance or recessional carols are "Joy to the World" and "Good Christian Friends, Rejoice."

Liturgy Committee
How might you—through your preparations and enhancement of the sacred space—help the members of your liturgical community connect the joy of this feast with salvation?

While it is permitted for pastoral reasons to choose readings from the Vigil or any of the three Christmas Masses to be celebrated at any time, the rubric indicates that complete sets of readings are used, not mixed and matched (e.g., first reading and responsorial psalm from one Mass, second reading from another, and a Gospel from yet another is not permitted). Further, in parishes where multiple Christmas Masses are celebrated, if possible preference should be given to use all four Masses since they lead us through a fuller reflection on the feast (note the gradual unfolding indicated under "To the point"). At the Vigil Mass, since this is often celebrated with many children present, it would be pastorally wise to use the short form of the Gospel.

It is popular to do all kinds of "nonliturgical" things at the Christmas Eve children's Mass (e.g., replacing the Liturgy of the Word with a Christmas pageant, having Santa Claus, birthday cakes, including wrapped presents in the presentation of gifts). However, this tends to distract from the real meaning of the feast, a celebration of Christ coming to dwell among you as your Savior. Care must be taken to lead your children to this deeper understanding of the Mystery.

Christmas is one of the easiest feasts to "decorate" and is one of the easiest to overdo things. Your sacred space must be lush, indeed, but not distract from the central focus of altar-table, ambo, and presider's chair. The creche ought not be dominant, and is best placed, perhaps, in a shrine area or at the entrance to the sacred space. Flashing or chasing lights—popular as they might be for the home—are distracting in church.

For the Mass during the Day
FIRST READING [Isa 52:7-10]

How beautiful upon the mountains
   are the feet of him who brings glad
      tidings,
announcing peace, bearing good news,
   announcing salvation, and saying to
      Zion,
"Your God is King!"

Hark! Your sentinels raise a cry,
   together they shout for joy,
for they see directly, before their eyes,
   the LORD restoring Zion.
Break out together in song,
   O ruins of Jerusalem!
For the LORD comforts his people,
   he redeems Jerusalem.
The LORD has bared his holy arm
   in the sight of all the nations;
all the ends of the earth will behold
   the salvation of our God.

For the Vigil Mass
SECOND READING [Acts 13:16-17, 22-25]

See Appendix A, p. 277.

For the Mass at Midnight
SECOND READING [Titus 2:11-14]

See Appendix A, p. 277.

For the Mass at Dawn
SECOND READING [Titus 3:4-7]

See Appendix A, p. 277.

For the Mass during the Day
SECOND READING [Heb 1:1-6]

See Appendix A, p. 277.

DECEMBER 25, 1999

The Holy Family of Jesus, Mary, and Joseph

FAITH-SHARING
- What are some concrete ways the Holy Family might be a model for your family life?
- What can you do to strengthen and support families in your liturgical community, especially those having difficulties?
- Christmas reveals that the Divine Word becomes flesh and is found in simplicity and poverty (a poor manger in little Bethlehem). Where/how has the Divine become flesh in the simplicity and poverty of your family life? What is your simplicity and poverty?

PRESIDERS
How can you model a holiness that gives hope to the families you encounter in your ministry?

DEACONS
How might your service strengthen and support families in your liturgical community?

HOSPITALITY MINISTERS
How might your greeting the assembly members as they come to worship (or in your everyday encounters) convey that all are members of God's family?

MUSIC MINISTERS
This Sunday's readings present you with some of the greatest "mentors" in your faith. How are you, as musical leader in your parish, a "mentor" of faith?

ALTAR MINISTERS
In what ways is your helping at the church serving God's family and strengthening it?

LECTORS
How might reading and pondering the Word of God on a regular basis help strengthen your family relationships?

EUCHARISTIC MINISTERS
How might the reverence with which you minister the Body or Blood of Christ model the reverence with which family members treat each other?

Spirituality

Reflecting on the Gospel

Man, woman, 1.7 children. Such is society's concept of the "nuclear" family. But these statistics hardly bear out the reality of our society where there has been a wholesale attack on the nuclear family. All too many of our children grow up with a depleted sense of family life. This Sunday's feast can appear initially as irrelevant, while in fact it offers a sense of hope.

The feast can appear irrelevant because so many families today might find it particularly difficult to identify with the Holy Family. This "ideal" family, after all, has two saints for parents and one child, the Son of God! How can any family today measure up to the holiness of this ideal family? Can we imagine Joseph and Mary going through some of the painful experiences that many families today face (e.g., divorce, drugs, alcohol, stealing, sex, peer pressure)? It's unthinkable! They are hardly "normal," so how can they be a model for families today?

Recent Gospels and this Sunday offer us some hope. Jesus was certainly an unusual child! He was conceived miraculously, born among spectacular happenings, and received in the Temple amid curious prophecies. How might Joseph and Mary have really *felt* about all this? How much did they really understand? Was their path with this child a smooth one? Already this Sunday's Gospel hints that they struggled as much as we do: "The child's father and mother were amazed at what was said about him." They had to learn, too, how to rear this most unusual child! And things weren't always so easy for Joseph and Mary; consider the anxiety and pain they felt until they found Jesus in the temple. Even Jesus' own attitude as an adult toward family is somewhat ambivalent as he subordinates natural blood relations to a new family made up of those "who hear the word of God and act on it" (Luke 8:21). For Christians, "family"—for all its centrality—is defined not primarily by blood ties or marriage, but by shared commitment to Jesus. And herein lies our hope.

For whatever difficulties face families today—and they are myriad!—we are never alone in our struggle. Jesus is always present to teach us how to be holy. The holiness of families is not dependent on the "correct" number of children or certain "correct" ways of relating. The holiness of families is dependent on each member surrendering self to the other for the sake of the other, as Jesus did for us. This means giving ourselves to another without counting the cost. This means keeping Jesus, the light of the world, at the center of our family living. This means being God's holy family first.

Living the Paschal Mystery

Following closely on Christmas, Simeon recognizes Jesus as "a light . . . to the Gentiles, and glory for your people Israel." The challenge to families today is also to recognize that Light and follow the Light, no matter the cost. Our younger generation, however, cannot follow the Light if they haven't been shown the Light. We are called every day to die to ourselves so that Christ's light might shine in our world. This is no small challenge. The adage says that "actions speak louder than words." If adults don't *live* in Jesus' light, then there is no model for children to choose living in the Light, either.

GOSPEL [Luke 2:22-40; L17B]

When the days were completed for their purification according to the law of Moses, they took him up to Jerusalem to present him to the Lord, just as it is written in the law of the Lord, *Every male that opens the womb shall be consecrated to the Lord,* and to offer the sacrifice of *a pair of turtledoves or two young pigeons,* in accordance with the dictate in the law of the Lord. Now there was a man in Jerusalem whose name was Simeon. This man was righteous and devout, awaiting the consolation of Israel, and the Holy Spirit was upon him. It had been revealed to him by the Holy Spirit that he should not see death before he had seen the Christ of the Lord. He came in the Spirit into the temple; and when the parents brought in the child Jesus to perform the custom of the law in regard to him, he took him into his arms and blessed God, saying: "Now, Master, you may let your servant go in peace, according to your word, for my eyes have seen your salvation, which you prepared in sight of all the peoples, a light for revelation to the Gentiles, and glory for your people Israel." The child's father and mother were amazed at what was said about him; and Simeon blessed them and said to Mary his mother, "Behold, this child is destined for the fall and rise of many in Israel, and to be a sign that will be contradicted—and you yourself a sword will pierce—so that the thoughts of many hearts may be revealed." There was also a prophetess, Anna, the daughter of Phanuel, of the tribe of Asher. She was advanced in years, having lived seven years with her husband after her marriage, and then as a widow until she was eighty-four. She never left the temple, but worshiped night and day with fasting and prayer. And coming forward at that very time, she gave thanks to God and spoke about the child to all who were awaiting the redemption of Jerusalem.

When they had fulfilled all the prescriptions of the law of the Lord, they returned to Galilee, to their own town of Nazareth. The child grew and became strong, filled with wisdom; and the favor of God was upon him.

Working with the Word

Key words and phrases from the Gospel: according to the law (5x), light for revelation to the Gentiles, glory of your people Israel

Connecting to the first and second readings: Israel's pattern of righteousness is traced to obedient Abraham and Sarah: "Abram put his faith in the LORD, who credited it to him as an act of righteousness." Abraham's descendants, faithful Israel symbolized by Simeon and Anna, recognize in Christ the fulfillment of God's promise of salvation.

Connecting to the biblical culture: By going to the temple Joseph, Mary, and Jesus act not as a "nuclear family" but as part of the family of Israel. In the first century, "family" was an extended family tied to the whole nation Israel. Further, the broader biblical background that provides the context for the first reading and most of Israel's history is the extended family (for a hint of this, see Luke 2:44). Archaeology tells us that single-family homes were most often found adjoining one another—sharing a common courtyard and even common walls—forming a family compound that housed a multifamily household. "Nuclear families" found their identity in the extended family.

Exegetical points: The Gospel tells us five times that everything Mary and Joseph did in this episode was "according to the law." As they fulfill all that the law requires, they and the child are greeted by two prophets, Simeon and Anna. On the one hand, these pious and devout elders represent faithful Israel greeting the Messiah. The presence of these two prophetic figures testifies to Jesus' status as superior to that of John the Baptist who received one prophecy from his father Zechariah. On the other hand, the encounter between these prophets and the Holy Family fulfilling the law indicates that the "Law and the Prophets" are coming to completion in Jesus. It is entirely fitting that this should take place in the Temple: the presence of God in Israel and for the world is now to be found in the One whom Simeon hails as "salvation," a "light for revelation to the Gentiles," and "glory for your people Israel."

To the point: We don't have to look to the "ideal" Holy Family or outside our own families to find holiness. The family is the first and primary community in which the love of God is experienced in a tangible way. Holiness is love willing to sacrifice (Abraham) and suffer (Mary) for the sake of one another. By Christ's sacrificial love for us, we are God's family.

Celebration

Model Penitential Rite

Presider: By our baptism we are made members of God's holy family. Let us reflect on our willingness to surrender to a deep relationship with God . . . [pause]

> Lord Jesus, you are the Savior of all people: Lord . . .
> Christ Jesus, you are a revealing Light for those in darkness: Christ . . .
> Lord Jesus, you are the strength and wisdom of your people: Lord . . .

Responsorial Psalm

"The Lord remembers his covenant forever."

The responsorial psalm for the feast of the Holy Family is taken from Psalm 105. Psalms 105 and 106 were probably composed together for use at a festival celebrating Israel's identity as God's people. The first recounts God's wondrous deeds from the time of the patriarchs, through the Exodus, to the period of settlement in the promised land. The second tells of Israel's sins and infidelities through this same history and ends with the petition, "Save us, O LORD." In these readings for Holy Family, we celebrate those who have been faithful throughout history: Abraham and Sarah, Mary and Joseph, Anna and Simeon. The readings tell us that the foundation of such fidelity is always God's reliability. Because God "remembers his covenant forever" (psalm), these righteous ones could cling to God's promise even when the wait was long and the present seemed to belie their confidence.

The first occurrence of "Hallelujah" (praise the LORD) comes at the end of Psalm 104, and is taken up in Psalms 105 and 106. Psalm 105 ends with "Hallelujah" and Psalm 106 both begins and ends with this shout. Though it is not included in the verses from Psalm 105 chosen for this Sunday, surely we can be singing it in our hearts as we celebrate God's fidelity and the faithfulness of those who have gone before us.

Model General Intercessions

Presider: Because we are members of God's family, we are confident that God cares for us by hearing our prayers.

Response: Lord, hear our prayer.

Cantor: we pray to the Lord,

That the Church may be righteous and devout, worshiping night and day with prayer and song . . . [pause]

That families may grow in their relationships with each other, become stronger, and find the favor of God upon them . . . [pause]

That troubled and deeply grieved families may find consolation in Christ, the light of the world . . . [pause]

That all of us may grow in holiness by faithfully living as God's children . . . [pause]

Presider: Loving God, you call us to live as your family through the power of the Holy Spirit and the sacrifice of your Son: hear these our prayers that we might grow in holiness and live more perfectly as your children. We ask this through that same Son, Jesus Christ our Lord. **Amen.**

OPENING PRAYER

Let us pray
 [for peace in our families]

Pause for silent prayer

Father,
help us to live as the holy family,
united in respect and love.
Bring us to the joy and peace of your
 eternal home.
Grant this through our Lord Jesus
 Christ, your Son,
who lives and reigns with you and the
 Holy Spirit,
one God, for ever and ever. **Amen.**

RESPONSORIAL PSALM
[Ps 105:1-2, 3-4, 6-7, 8-9]

℟. (7a, 8a) The Lord remembers his covenant forever.

Give thanks to the LORD, invoke his name;
 make known among the nations his
  deeds.
Sing to him, sing his praise,
 proclaim all his wondrous deeds.

℟. The Lord remembers his covenant forever.

Glory in his holy name;
 rejoice, O hearts that seek the LORD!
Look to the LORD in his strength;
 constantly seek his face.

℟. The Lord remembers his covenant forever.

You descendants of Abraham, his
 servants,
 sons of Jacob, his chosen ones!
He, the LORD, is our God;
 throughout the earth his judgments
  prevail.

℟. The Lord remembers his covenant forever.

He remembers forever his covenant
 which he made binding for a
  thousand generations
which he entered into with Abraham
 and by his oath to Isaac.

℟. The Lord remembers his covenant forever.

FIRST READING [Gen 15:1-6; 21:1-3]

The word of the LORD came to Abram in
 a vision, saying:
 "Fear not, Abram!
  I am your shield;
  I will make your reward very great."
But Abram said,
 "O Lord GOD, what good will your
  gifts be,

if I keep on being childless
and have as my heir the steward of
my house, Eliezer?"
Abram continued,
"See, you have given me no offspring,
and so one of my servants will be my
heir."
Then the word of the LORD came to him:
"No, that one shall not be your heir;
your own issue shall be your heir."
The LORD took Abram outside and said,
"Look up at the sky and count the
stars, if you can.
Just so," he added, "shall your
descendants be."
Abram put his faith in the LORD,
who credited it to him as an act of
righteousness.

The LORD took note of Sarah as he had
said he would;
he did for her as he had promised.
Sarah became pregnant and bore
Abraham a son in his old age,
at the set time that God had stated.
Abraham gave the name Isaac to this
son of his
whom Sarah bore him.

SECOND READING [Heb 11:8, 11-12, 17-19]

Brothers and sisters:
By faith Abraham obeyed when he was
called to go out to a place
that he was to receive as an inheritance;
he went out, not knowing where he
was to go.
By faith he received power to generate,
even though he was past the normal
age
—and Sarah herself was sterile—
for he thought that the one who had
made the promise was trustworthy.
So it was that there came forth from one
man,
himself as good as dead,
descendants as numerous as the stars
in the sky
and as countless as the sands on the
seashore.

By faith Abraham, when put to the test,
offered up Isaac,
and he who had received the
promises was ready to offer his
only son,
of whom it was said,
"Through Isaac descendants shall
bear your name."
He reasoned that God was able to raise
even from the dead,
and he received Isaac back as a symbol.

Catechesis

Cantors
Abraham and Sarah, Mary and Joseph, Anna and Simeon were able to remain faithful because they kept their focus on God's constancy. How can you imitate their attitude? Be aware that singing this Sunday's psalm is a way of participating in their outlook, even if you find yourself struggling with faith.

Choir
This Sunday you celebrate not just blood-related families but the entire "family" of God: all those persons who remain faithful to their covenant relationship with God and one another, no matter what the cost. End rehearsal this week with a prayer of thanksgiving for specific members of your parish, your city, and the worldwide Church who are (have been) your mentors in the faith.

Music Directors
Often carols which sing about the infant Jesus or about Jesus, Mary, and Joseph as a family are used on this Sunday. The readings of year B suggest, however, that you consider texts which speak about God's ancient promise fulfilled at last in Christ, and the heritage handed down through the centuries from those who maintained faith in that promise.

Two such hymns suited for presentation of the gifts would be "Lo, How a Rose E'er Blooming" and "Of the Father's Love Begotten." Bernadette Gasslein's "In the Darkness Shines the Splendor" [CBW3], which plays on the significance of Christ in "ev'ry human story," would be excellent for Communion. Especially relevant as a hymn of praise after Communion would be the Canticle of Simeon, which goes by different names in different hymnbooks ("Lord, Bid Your Servant Go in Peace"; "Lord God, You Now Have Set Your Servant Free"; "Now Let Your Servant God"; "Canticle of Simeon").

Liturgy Committee
Christmas is one of only two festivals during the entire liturgical year that has an octave (Easter is the other). This means that Christmas and the seven days following are all of the same solemnity. Christmas is so important in the liturgical life of the Church that it is celebrated for eight days. What might you do to sustain this eight-day celebration in your parish? In your lives?

This Sunday's feast is an "idea feast"; that is, it is a historical development (it became popular in the nineteenth century) resulting from devotional life or theologizing about salvific events. Although there is Gospel precedent for a "Holy Family," there is no Gospel incident that suggests this feast. The "idea," however, is entirely consistent with and derives from the Christmas mystery being celebrated.

The alternate readings given for year B were chosen for reflection so that there would be a better rotation of readings over the three-year Lectionary cycle. These alternate readings are a feature of the revised Lectionary. The longer form of the Gospel reading should be used (unless pastoral reasons dictate otherwise; e.g., a Mass with children) because it places Joseph and Mary's keeping the Law within the larger context of the prophecies about this child.

DECEMBER 26, 1999

Solemnity of the Blessed Virgin Mary,

FAITH-SHARING
- How can you turn New Year's resolutions (which you quickly forget) into a serious renewal of your commitment to live as children of God and heirs of heaven?
- As you end one year, what do you need to let go? As you begin this new year (and millennium), what do you need to nurture?
- When have you experienced freedom from slavery and joy for being God's heir?
- How might you interiorize Aaron's blessing so you can share it with others?

PRESIDERS
People address you as "Father." How does the meaning of this festival in honor of Mary as mother shed light on your ordained ministry? How/when is your ministry part of the "proof" that your people are no longer slaves, but children (and heirs) of God?

DEACONS
How might remembering that God dwells within you shape your ministry during this new year?

HOSPITALITY MINISTERS
How can your welcome and greeting of "Happy New Year!" be a genuine prayer of blessing for all those you meet?

MUSIC MINISTERS
When your musical leadership leads the assembly to deepen their identity as daughters and sons of God, it is a continuation of God's blessing over them. This is an awesome participation in the work of God, but it is a power given you because of your divine adoption. How do you use this power?

ALTAR MINISTERS
"Then the shepherds returned, glorifying and praising God for all they had heard and seen." What have you heard and seen this past year that moves you to glorify and praise God?

LECTORS
Mary "kept all these things, reflecting on them in her heart." How might your imitating Mary enrich your living and proclaiming the readings?

EUCHARISTIC MINISTERS
How might you become more profoundly a part of God's blessing and mercy for others in this New Year?

Spirituality

Reflecting on the Gospel

Happy New Year! Happy New Millennium! How unique it is for us some five billion humans on the earth today to be alive to witness the beginning of a new millennium! It's difficult to grasp the cultural, societal, industrial, agricultural, technological, and religious changes that have taken place over the last one thousand years. It is equally difficult to image how our world will look to those who are alive to celebrate the fourth millennium. As stupendous as these past changes and future possibilities are, as Christians we celebrate an even deeper mystery. We celebrate the third millennium of Christ's birth. How fitting that on this, the first day of the third millennium, we celebrate the solemnity of the Blessed Virgin Mary, the Mother of God.

The readings for this day are as expansive as the new millennium we celebrate. The first reading from the book of Numbers takes us back over three thousand years and finds Aaron commanded to bless the people whom God has freed from the slavery of Egypt. The Gospel takes us back two thousand years to that first Christmas. Jesus, "conceived in the womb" of Mary, is given the name "Jesus," which means "savior." God's saving deeds—which actually began with creation—come to a new fulfillment in Christ. Now salvation brings a freedom from the slavery of sin. The second reading from the letter to the Galatians, although historically situated in the same century as the Gospel, really propels us forward, into the future. Jesus is born of a woman, and so we receive adoption. But more. Because we are God's children, we are also God's *heirs* which means that some day—who knows how many more millennia?—all will share in the fullness of divine life.

We celebrate today a Marian festival, under the title of Blessed Virgin Mary, Mother of *God*. On this, the octave day of Christmas, we see a further unfolding of the Christmas festival. Because God loves us so much, the Son was born of our flesh and lived among us. In this, humanity is raised up to share in divinity. Because of this, we join the shepherds in "glorifying and praising God." Because of this, we are blessed, too: "The LORD bless you and keep you! The LORD let his face shine upon you, and be gracious to you! The LORD look upon you kindly and give you peace!"

Living the Paschal Mystery

Adoption carries with it responsibilities. Salvation is a gift of God, but we must cooperate with God's grace (first given through baptism). Mary is a model *par excellence* of this cooperation. Mary assented, conceived, gave birth, and now we are adopted as children of God. No wonder we honor Mary during this season of celebrating God's mighty deeds of salvation! Mary "kept all these things, reflecting on them in her heart." What God was asking of her wasn't easy. This child born of her was no ordinary child. All the events of conception and birth confirm the special identity and mission of her Son. Mary reflected, pondered, worked out in her daily *yes* to God the meaning of all this. And where did she faithfully go? Even to Calvary. So must we, so that we may share someday in the glory that Mary already experiences.

MOTHER OF GOD

JANUARY 1, 2000

GOSPEL [Luke 2:16-21; L18ABC]

The shepherds went in haste to Bethlehem and found Mary and Joseph, and the infant lying in the manger. When they saw this, they made known the message that had been told them about this child. All who heard it were amazed by what had been told them by the shepherds. And Mary kept all these things, reflecting on them in her heart. Then the shepherds returned, glorifying and praising God for all they had heard and seen, just as it had been told to them. When eight days were completed for his circumcision, he was named Jesus, the name given him by the angel before he was conceived in the womb.

Working with the Word

Key words and phrases from the second reading and Gospel: born of a woman, adoption, heir, conceived in the womb

Connecting to Christmas Day: The Christmas celebration—spread over an octave—is framed by the divinity and humanity of Christ. At the Christmas Mass during the Day, with the Prologue of John as the Gospel, we reflected on the mystery of the incarnation from the divine point-of-view. On this Sunday we reflect on the mystery from the human point-of-view: Jesus is born of a woman.

Connecting to our culture: A devotional approach to Christmas sometimes focuses on the tender images of Mary as mother and intercessor for us. Her role also—more deeply—tells us that humanity can bear and reveal divinity because the Word became *flesh* through Mary.

Exegetical points: Paul's Letter to the Galatians spells out for believers the significance of the incarnation: we have been "adopted" as children of God. The language of adoption is used in the Hebrew Scriptures to describe God's relationship to Israel (Jer 3:19) and, more prominently, to the Davidic king (Ps 2:7; 2 Sam 7:14). The biblical stories that deal with adoption indicate that adopted children are fully heirs along with the biological children of the adoptive parents. This seems to be Paul's point. While Christians are not children of God in the same way that Jesus is the Son of God, we are, nevertheless, truly heirs of his divine heritage and have the same rights to call God "Abba."

Contrary to the commonly held view that "Abba" is an intimate form of address equivalent to our words "daddy" or "papa" (initially made popular by J. Jeremias, who later recanted his findings as naive), "Abba" is, in fact, the Aramaic form of the word for "father." Some scholars believe that the use of this term by early Christians in Galatia and Rome (and perhaps elsewhere) may reflect a genuine tradition that remembers Jesus using this term in his own prayer.

To the point: Jesus, fully human, is also fully divine; therefore, Mary is the Mother of God. Since Jesus is born of a woman, we have received adoption as children of God. Because Jesus shares our humanity, we share his divinity. The consequence of this event is that we have been raised to the royal status of heirs, children of God.

Celebration

Model Penitential Rite

Presider: Jesus was born of Mary so that we might be children of God. Let us praise and thank God for this great privilege . . . [pause]

> Lord Jesus, you are Son of Mary: Lord . . .
> Christ Jesus, you are Son of God: Christ . . .
> Lord Jesus, your Spirit dwells in our hearts so that we are children of God: Lord . . .

Responsorial Psalm

"May God bless us in his mercy."

Because the Lectionary omits v. 7 of the responsorial psalm used for this solemnity ("The earth has yielded its fruits; God, our God, has blessed us"), it is not evident that this psalm of praise is also a psalm of petition for a fruitful harvest. Israel believed that a bountiful harvest would be tangible proof of God's greatness. Such abundance would lead all nations to praise and reverence God.

The readings suggest that God has indeed blessed the earth with plenitude, for the flesh of Mary has yielded the fruit of Christ. Through this fruit all peoples have received a blessing beyond compare: adoption as God's own daughters and sons. Out of human flesh comes the harvesting of divinity. "May the nations be glad and exult."

Model General Intercessions

Presider: As adopted children of God, we can be confident that God will hear our prayers and grant us what we need. And so we pray.

Response:

(musical notation: "Lord, hear our prayer.")

Cantor:

(musical notation: "we pray to the Lord,")

That all members of the Church live in ways that witness to the grace that is theirs by adoption . . . [pause]

That people everywhere may reflect on the wonderful things God has done and come to a deeper faith . . . [pause]

That those who have no mother or are alienated from their mothers may find comfort in Mary . . . [pause]

That we may respond faithfully to the blessings of kindness and peace God bestows on us during this new year and new millennium . . . [pause]

Presider: God, our Abba, hear these the prayers of your children and respond to our needs so that one day we might, as heirs, share in your everlasting life. We ask this through your Son Jesus Christ our Lord. **Amen.**

ALTERNATIVE OPENING PRAYER

Let us pray

Pause for silent prayer

Father,
source of light in every age,
the virgin conceived and bore your Son
who is called Wonderful God, Prince of Peace.
May her prayer, the gift of a mother's love,
be your people's joy through all ages.
May her response, born of a humble heart,
draw your Spirit to rest on your people.
Grant this through Christ our Lord.
Amen.

RESPONSORIAL PSALM

[Ps 67:2-3, 5, 6, 8]

℟. (2a) May God bless us in his mercy.

May God have pity on us and bless us;
  may he let his face shine upon us.
So may your way be known upon earth;
  among all nations, your salvation.

℟. May God bless us in his mercy.

May the nations be glad and exult
  because you rule the peoples in equity;
  the nations on the earth you guide.

℟. May God bless us in his mercy.

May the peoples praise you, O God;
  may all the peoples praise you!
May God bless us,
  and may all the ends of the earth fear him!

℟. May God bless us in his mercy.

FIRST READING
[Num 6:22-27]

The LORD said to Moses:
"Speak to Aaron and his sons and tell them:
This is how you shall bless the Israelites.
Say to them:
The LORD bless you and keep you!
The LORD let his face shine upon you, and be gracious to you!
The LORD look upon you kindly and give you peace!
So shall they invoke my name upon the Israelites,
and I will bless them."

SECOND READING
[Gal 4:4-7]

Brothers and sisters:
When the fullness of time had come,
God sent his Son,
born of a woman, born under the law,
to ransom those under the law,
so that we might receive adoption as sons.
As proof that you are sons,
God sent the Spirit of his Son into our hearts,
crying out, "Abba, Father!"
So you are no longer a slave but a son,
and if a son then also an heir, through God.

Catechesis

Cantors

Let your singing of this psalm combine praise and petition: thanksgiving for what God has given you in Christ, and prayer that you recognize your identity as daughter or son of God.

Choir

Often you might think of your singing as your gift to God, but actually the reverse is true. You are able to stand and sing at the Table of the Lord because you are God's adopted children. Mary understood this—that even her ability to say yes to her role in the Incarnation was a gift of God. Let your singing this solemnity be a thanksgiving to God for what has been given to you.

Music Directors

This solemnity of Mary offers you a good opportunity to examine the hymns you sing about her. Which ones portray her as a naive young girl, or only as a heavenly mother whose sweetness answers any need? In reality, Mary was a strong woman who met the challenges of discipleship with great courage. Hymns such as "Mary, Woman of the Promise" [BB, CBW3] have this to say about your relationship with her: "Mary, model of compassion; Wounded by your offspring's pain, When our hearts are torn by sorrow, Teach us how to love again." Other examples of hymns which express Mary's strength are "I Sing a Maid" [CBW3, G, G2, RS] and "Mary, Mother of Good Counsel" [CBW3]. All of these would be appropriate either as prelude or at the presentation of gifts. A fine choice for a hymn of praise after Communion would be the *Magnificat*. Singing this would, furthermore, make an excellent sequence to having sung the Canticle of Simeon on the feast of the Holy Family.

Liturgy Committee

Don't try to address all the motifs for this solemnity. The readings lead you in the direction of celebrating Mary as Mother of God and observing the octave of Christmas. This is really still a Christmas celebration (the last day of the octave). How might you sustain this eight-day celebration of God's salvation throughout the new year?

This solemnity is perhaps one of the most difficult days of the entire liturgical year to prepare. In fact, this year seven different motifs converge on this one day. First, and foremost, it is the solemnity of the Blessed Virgin Mary, Mother of God; it is a Marian feast. Second, and next most important, it is the octave day of Christmas (this is what shapes the choice of readings) and, hence, is connected to the great festival you've been celebrating for the last eight days. Consonant with the octave, it is also the day of Jesus' circumcision (third motif) and the day he receives the name given him by Gabriel at conception (fourth motif). Fifth, it is New Year's Day and, unique to this year, New Millennium Day (sixth motif). Finally, it is traditionally a world day of prayer for peace (seventh motif). Although all of these motifs are worthy of your attention, the liturgy really should focus on the solemnity of Mary and the octave of Christmas.

Because this solemnity falls on a Saturday this year, it is not a holy day of obligation in the United States. However, it would be well to encourage members of your parish to celebrate liturgically this wonderful festival.

JANUARY 1, 2000

The Epiphany of the Lord

FAITH-SHARING
- Who or what are the stars in your life that lead you to God?
- When are you like Herod and plot against the reign of God? When are you like the chief priests and scribes and are indifferent toward the reign of God?
- What gifts can you offer to the Messiah-King as your way of offering homage?

PRESIDERS
With how much abandon do you follow the Messiah's star in your ordained ministry?

DEACONS
How does your ministry of service lead others to do homage before God?

HOSPITALITY MINISTERS
How might you greet others so that the universality of salvation is evident? How can you instill confidence in others that they are redeemed?

MUSIC MINISTERS
How might you use your music-making as an act of homage to God? Do you ever find yourself using it as a way to gain homage for yourself?

ALTAR MINISTERS
In what way is your service an act of homage to the Messiah-King?

LECTORS
In what way do the Scriptures offer light to your darkness (see the first reading from Isaiah)? How do you share the light of Christ with others?

EUCHARISTIC MINISTERS
For a variety of reasons, some may not be welcome to the Eucharistic table. What are other ways that you might invite them to the universality of Christ's salvation? How might you be a "star" that directs others to Christ?

Spirituality

Reflecting on the Gospel

For most of us, the Christmas trees and lights and music are gone, we are back to work or school on Monday, and (in general) we have a sense that Christmas is over. It's "back to business as usual." Yet, with this Sunday's feast of the Epiphany of the Lord, we have one more staging of the Christmas mystery. The Gospel leads us to ask, for whom does Christ come?

The Gospel shows an interesting paradox. Those whom we would expect to be open to the birth of the Messiah (e.g., Herod, chief priests, scribes) are not open to his manifestation. Strangers from the East (the Magi) come looking for the "newborn king of the Jews." Magi were a class of wise men who were (among other things) astrologers and interpreters of dreams. They were hardly mainstream Jews who would be looking for the Messiah. Yet it is these foreigners who recognize Jesus and pay him homage.

Symbolism abounds in this Gospel. The Magi come from the East, the direction of the rising sun and of light and the direction of Christ's second coming. Notice that the Gospel neither numbers nor names the Magi. Tradition (since the third century theologian Origen) has set their number at three, probably because of the mention of the three gifts (see the first reading). Since the ninth century names have been given—Caspar, Melchior, and Balthasar. Further, Caspar has been depicted as a black man, symbolizing that the Messiah was to be manifested to all peoples, regardless of race, religion, or nationality. From the sixth century the Magi have been designated as kings (see the responsorial psalm).

Why did such an outstanding story find its way in Matthew's Gospel? (No other Gospel records this incident.) Matthew's Gospel is one structured around five discourses on the coming of God's kingdom. At the outset of the Gospel, set within the narration of Christ's birth, Matthew underscores the universality of God's reign and, by extension, the universality of salvation (the second reading). But even more. Sometimes Matthew's Gospel is considered an early "handbook for preachers" with a liturgical intent. "Do him homage" is a phrase that occurs three times in this feast's Gospel. In fact, it seems as though the writer of Matthew's Gospel brings these wise men from afar precisely to *do homage*. The gift-offering is but another sign of their recognition of Jesus as someone worthy of obeisance. Even though they were astrologers and star-watching would be of great interest to them, would "star-following" across countries be equally natural? Probably not! They saw a great phenomena, and left all to follow. Would we be so willing to follow God's signs?

Living the Paschal Mystery

Salvation is meant for all, if we are but willing to follow God's signs of the gift. This feast, in the Western Church, is one celebrating the universality of salvation. The wise men call us to abandon our own directions and desires, our own country and kinsfolk to find the Messiah. The wise men were led to the manger in Bethlehem. We are led to the cross and resurrection as we find them in our daily living.

JANUARY 2, 2000

GOSPEL [Matt 2:1-12; L20ABC]

When Jesus was born in Bethlehem of Judea, in the days of King Herod, behold, magi from the east arrived in Jerusalem, saying, "Where is the newborn king of the Jews? We saw his star at its rising and have come to do him homage." When King Herod heard this, he was greatly troubled, and all Jerusalem with him. Assembling all the chief priests and the scribes of the people, he inquired of them where the Christ was to be born. They said to him, "In Bethlehem of Judea, for thus it has been written through the prophet: *And you, Bethlehem, land of Judah, are by no means least among the rulers of Judah; since from you shall come a ruler, who is to shepherd my people Israel.*" Then Herod called the magi secretly and ascertained from them the time of the star's appearance. He sent them to Bethlehem and said, "Go and search diligently for the child. When you have found him, bring me word, that I too may go and do him homage." After their audience with the king they set out. And behold, the star that they had seen at its rising preceded them, until it came and stopped over the place where the child was. They were overjoyed at seeing the star, and on entering the house they saw the child with Mary his mother. They prostrated themselves and did him homage. Then they opened their treasures and offered him gifts of gold, frankincense, and myrrh. And having been warned in a dream not to return to Herod, they departed for their country by another way.

Working with the Word

Key words and phrases from the Gospel: Magi from the East, king of the Jews, star, do him homage, go and search diligently

Connecting to the Christmas season: In the Christmas Mass at Midnight, we heard in the Gospel, "a savior has been born *for you*." In the Gospel for the feast of the Holy Family we heard Simeon bless God with the words "a light for revelation to the Gentiles, and glory to your people Israel." In Isaiah the prophet speaks about God's glory that will shine over the people who are covered in darkness (first reading). In the Gospel for this Sunday it is the light of a star that brings the magi to the presence of the Messiah.

Connecting to the early Church: The early Church identified with the main characters in this Sunday's Gospel. They pondered what gifts *they* could offer to Christ. One tradition saw gold as the virtuous life, incense as prayer rising to God, and myrrh as sacrifice and suffering. Another tradition saw gold as representing the kingship of Christ, incense his divinity, and the myrrh as his suffering.

Exegetical points: Matthew's Gospel is addressed to a mixed community of Jewish and Gentile converts. Chapter 1 is addressed to Matthew's Jewish constituents; it highlights Jesus' Davidic ancestry and gives a prominent role to St. Joseph, whom Matthew casts in the image of Joseph the patriarch who has dreams and saves his family by bringing them to Egypt (Gen 37ff). This Sunday's passage, from chapter 2, features Gentiles who are represented by the "Magi" (a term restored in place of the more precise but less evocative term "astrologers"). They receive "revelation" or guidance from a sign in nature. The Magi, who come from afar, i.e., outside the land of Judah, come to worship and offer gifts to the "king of the Jews," a title which reappears only at the crucifixion of Jesus (Matt 27:11, 29, 37). At the crucifixion it will again be Gentiles (the centurion and those who were keeping watch over Jesus [Matt 27:54]) who acknowledge Jesus as "the Son of God." Thus, at the beginning and end of Matthew's Gospel, Gentiles—outsiders—are presented as those who recognize the true identity of Jesus and who worship him.

To the point: Epiphany as the manifestation of Christ evokes from us a response of worship. Worship extends beyond what we do in our liturgical actions as a community; it embraces our entire human life as a living sacrifice of praise.

Celebration

Model Penitential Rite

Presider: The wise men in today's Gospel leave all to follow the star to Bethlehem so they can do homage to the newborn Messiah-king. Let us open our hearts to do homage to God during this celebration . . . [pause]

> Lord Jesus, you are the Messiah-king: Lord . . .
> Christ Jesus, you are the light of the world and the glory of God: Christ . . .
> Lord Jesus, you receive our homage and gifts: Lord . . .

Responsorial Psalm

"Lord, every nation on earth will adore you."

Psalm 72 was both a royal psalm used at coronation ceremonies and a messianic text which looked forward to the fullness of God's reign over all nations. In Israel's theology of kingship, the king was to be the arm of God's righteousness among the people. His role was to protect the well-being of the kingdom by seeing to it that the poor and needy were given justice. The full meaning of the Hebrew word *shalom*, used in v. 7, was more than peace—it meant a situation where everyone had what she or he needed to live. The health of the nation, then, was measured by the condition of every member, most particularly the poor, and responsibility for that condition rested with the king.

The early Church saw Christ as the fulfillment of this kingly role. It was he who "rescue[d] the poor" and had "pity for the lowly," who brought the flowering of "justice" and "profound peace." Moreover, the second reading and the Gospel reveal that his kingdom was not limited to Israel but was to encompass all the earth. In Christ the kingdom of *shalom* has come for all people.

Model General Intercessions

Presider: We pay homage to God when we show our dependence on God's goodness and give our needs over to God's care. And so we pray.

Response:

[musical notation: Lord, hear our prayer.]

Cantor:

[musical notation: we pray to the Lord,]

May the Church always go and search diligently for the manifestations of Christ's unexpected presence . . . [pause]

May all people of the world see the glory of God and be open to God's offer of salvation . . . [pause]

May those who do not recognize the signs of God's presence in themselves and in the world see and become radiant . . . [pause]

May we here gathered follow Christ faithfully throughout this new year . . . [pause]

Presider: O God, you are great and wonderful are your works: hear these our prayers that we may see your presence in the people and world about us. We ask this through Christ our Lord. **Amen.**

OPENING PRAYER

Let us pray
  [that we will be guided by the light of faith]

Pause for silent prayer

Father,
you revealed your Son to the nations
  by the guidance of a star.
Lead us to your glory in heaven
  by the light of faith.
We ask this through our Lord Jesus
  Christ, your Son,
who lives and reigns with you and the
  Holy Spirit,
one God, for ever and ever. **Amen.**

RESPONSORIAL PSALM

[Ps 72:1-2, 7-8, 10-11, 12-13]

℟. (cf. 11) Lord, every nation on earth will adore you.

O God, with your judgment endow the king,
  and with your justice, the king's son;
he shall govern your people with justice
  and your afflicted ones with judgment.

℟. Lord, every nation on earth will adore you.

Justice shall flower in his days,
  and profound peace, till the moon be no more.
May he rule from sea to sea,
  and from the River to the ends of the earth.

℟. Lord, every nation on earth will adore you.

The kings of Tarshish and the Isles shall offer gifts;
  the kings of Arabia and Seba shall bring tribute.
All kings shall pay him homage,
  all nations shall serve him.

℟. Lord, every nation on earth will adore you.

For he shall rescue the poor when he cries out,
  and the afflicted when he has no one to help him.
He shall have pity for the lowly and the poor;
  the lives of the poor he shall save.

℟. Lord, every nation on earth will adore you.

FIRST READING
[Isa 60:1-6]

Rise up in splendor, Jerusalem! Your
    light has come,
        the glory of the Lord shines upon you.
See, darkness covers the earth,
    and thick clouds cover the peoples;
but upon you the LORD shines,
    and over you appears his glory.
Nations shall walk by your light,
    and kings by your shining radiance.
Raise your eyes and look about;
    they all gather and come to you:
your sons come from afar,
    and your daughters in the arms of
        their nurses.

Then you shall be radiant at what you
        see,
    your heart shall throb and overflow,
for the riches of the sea shall be emptied
        out before you,
    the wealth of nations shall be brought
        to you.
Caravans of camels shall fill you,
    dromedaries from Midian and Ephah;
all from Sheba shall come
    bearing gold and frankincense,
    and proclaiming the praises of the
        LORD.

SECOND READING
[Eph 3:2-3a, 5-6]

Brothers and sisters:
You have heard of the stewardship of
    God's grace
        that was given to me for your benefit,
        namely, that the mystery was made
            known to me by revelation.
It was not made known to people in
        other generations
    as it has now been revealed
    to his holy apostles and prophets by
        the Spirit:
    that the Gentiles are coheirs, members
        of the same body,
    and copartners in the promise in
        Christ Jesus through the gospel.

Catechesis

Cantors
The refrain to the psalm is not only a statement but also an invitation that every nation adore God. Your voice needs to carry the sound of homage as you sing it. How can you deepen this attitude within yourself?

Choir
Your ministry is more than just making music; it is an act of worship, of homage. The extent to which your singing is homage of God affects not only your own participation in the liturgy but the assembly's as well. You might want to pray this week for the gift of adoration.

Music Directors
Bernadette Farrell's Communion song "Bread of Life" [BB] with its Christmas verses is especially applicable for Epiphany because it speaks of Christ the "radiant light in our darkness" who is "salvation of all the world." The SATB arrangement is published in *Choral Praise* [OCP #10317 and 9093]. A second good choice for Communion would be Huub Oosterhuis' "In Deepest Night" [BB], which sings of Christ as the prince of peace for whom "once for all, his hour has come." The SATB arrangement, published by OCP [octavo #8715GC; *Choral Praise* #8723 and 9093] is something of a challenge but well worth the effort. The SATB arrangement might be better used as a choral prelude than at Communion.

Liturgy Committee
How might your ministry this year in preparing liturgies for your liturgical community bring others to recognize Christ as the light who brings salvation for all? How can your preparation help people understand that their participation in liturgy is a participation in the Mystery of Christ?

The feast of the Epiphany of the Lord originally comes from the Eastern Church. It was a feast that combined a broad range of rich events: Christ's baptism in the Jordan, the wedding feast at Cana, and the visit of the Magi. Eventually the Eastern and Western Churches shared each other's feast, and the celebration of the Epiphany in the West came to have the more narrow focus of the visit of the Magi and the manifestation of Christ to the Gentiles. In the Western Church today, the baptism of the Lord is celebrated on the Sunday after Epiphany (most years) and the Gospel of the wedding feast of Cana is proclaimed on the second Sunday in Ordinary Time, year C.

Since January 1 is on a Saturday this year and not a holy day of obligation, this Sunday's feast of the Epiphany may be the first time you see many of the people. Be careful, however, that you don't turn this Epiphany celebration into a new year celebration.

JANUARY 2, 2000

THE BAPTISM OF THE LORD

FAITH-SHARING
- List your understanding of the effects of baptism. Which ones are really important to you?
- How might you make your baptismal commitment something that motivates the way you live each day?
- What would it be like for you to hear God say about you: "This is my beloved [daughter, son] with whom I am well pleased"? How differently might you live when remembering this?

PRESIDERS
How might your entire ministry be an announcement to your people of their Christian dignity: "This is my beloved [daughter, son] with whom I am well pleased"?

DEACONS
In what concrete ways can you identify your ministry of service with that of Jesus?

HOSPITALITY MINISTERS
How might your greeting help others to know their dignity as daughters and sons of God?

MUSIC MINISTERS
How is your ministry of leading liturgical music a participation in the identity and mission of Jesus?

ALTAR MINISTERS
How might your reverent service help you deepen your participation in the identity and mission of Jesus?

LECTORS
How can you prepare for and proclaim God's word so that it "shall not return . . . void"?

EUCHARISTIC MINISTERS
How can you improve your ministering of Christ's Body and Blood so that the communicant understands her or his identity as the risen Christ for others?

Spirituality

Reflecting on the Gospel

The experience of baptism in parishes is quite varied. In some parishes when baptisms take place at the Sunday celebration of Eucharist, they are a prolongation of the Mass time and tend to be an annoyance. In other parishes, baptisms are a joyful celebration and a true welcoming of the new member into the Christian community. When numbers are very large, it may necessitate baptisms to occur in separate celebrations when most of the community cannot or do not participate, running the risk of seeing this as a private celebration. These contrasts raise perhaps the most significant question about baptism: is it a private deal, or something connected to the whole community? This Sunday's feast and its Gospel address this question.

John baptized with water for the repentance of sins. Jesus never sinned. Then why was he baptized by John? The answer is given in the voice from heaven: "You are my beloved Son; with you I am well pleased." Jesus' baptism is a statement about Jesus' own identity as "beloved Son." At the same time Jesus' baptism has to do with others. Why was the Father pleased with Jesus? Because he fulfilled his mission, did the Father's will. And that mission includes the "word . . . that goes forth from my mouth . . . achieving the end for which I sent it" (first reading) and the "Spirit, the water, and the blood" (second reading) that testify that Jesus is the beloved Son who was faithful to the Father's will.

The first thing that happens in Mark's Gospel (other than the story of John the Baptist in the desert) is Jesus' baptism and the inauguration of his mission. Jesus' public ministry proceeds from an authorization by the Father. We will see in the weeks ahead how Jesus' authority, derived from the Father, is developed by Mark in his Gospel. This is a continuing story of Jesus, but also a continuing story of how he touches each one of us individually, personally—but even more importantly, how Jesus binds us into a beloved community, his very own Body. This is why our baptisms, preferably, take place in the presence of as many of the community as possible.

Living the Paschal Mystery

This Sunday is a bridge between Christmas and Ordinary Time. It reminds us that the mystery of the Incarnation is so much more than the birth of an infant. God's Word-made-flesh is the One who bridges divinity and humanity. Jesus' baptism revealed who he is: beloved Son. When we come up out of our own baptismal waters, we share in that divine election and are also sons and daughters of God. We are baptized with the Holy Spirit; through the Spirit we receive our own identity (God's life, grace) and mission (to believe and work to build the kingdom).

If we share in Jesus' identity, we also share in his mission. This means that salvation is no easy road. Like Jesus, we must make God's reign present, we must cast out demons and heal the sick, we must preach boldly, we must do the Father's will. Like Jesus, we must take up our cross. Only when we so die to ourselves can we be assured also of sharing in the life of his resurrection. This is how the Paschal Mystery plays itself out in real ways in our everyday lives.

JANUARY 9, 2000

GOSPEL [Mark 1:7-11; L21B]

This is what he proclaimed: "One mightier than I is coming after me. I am not worthy to stoop and loosen the thongs of his sandals. I have baptized you with water; he will baptize you with the Holy Spirit."

It happened in those days that Jesus came from Nazareth of Galilee and was baptized in the Jordan by John. On coming up out of the water he saw the heavens being torn open and the Spirit, like a dove, descending upon him. And a voice came from the heavens, "You are my beloved Son; with you I am well pleased."

Working with the Word

Key words and phrases from the Gospel: he will baptize you with the Holy Spirit, coming up out of the water, You are my beloved Son, with you I am well pleased

Connecting to the first two readings and the Eastern Church: The first two readings include the image of water, which certainly connects them to baptism. However, the use of water in the baptismal theology of the Eastern Church is different from its predominant use in the Western Church (where the paradigm reference for baptismal theology is Romans 6, in which we are plunged into water so that we might die with Christ and rise with him). In the Eastern Church, the paradigm Gospel story is that of Nicodemus (John 3)—centered around new life through the waters of a new birth; a parallel notion of water is alluded to in the first two readings given as an option for year B in the Lectionary.

Connecting to the biblical culture: In the biblical culture baptizing was a common occurrence. Some communities (the Essenes, for example) required it as an initiation rite. What is unique in this Sunday's account of Jesus' baptism is that a "voice came from the heavens" and revealed Jesus' identity ("beloved Son") and mission (to please God, do God's will).

Exegetical points: John's message, that a mightier one is coming after him who will baptize with the Holy Spirit, is immediately confirmed when Jesus is baptized and he hears the heavenly voice and the Holy Spirit descends on Jesus as he emerges from the water. The combined symbolism of water and spirit in Jesus' baptism evokes the story of creation in which the spirit hovers over the waters (Gen 1:2). The appearance of Jesus signals a new beginning for the created order.

The quote, "You are my beloved Son, with you I am well pleased," paraphrases a combination of Old Testament passages. Most obvious is Isaiah 42:1, the call of the Servant of the Lord; but it also echoes Psalm 2:7, the divine adoption of the Davidic king. The "beloved" aspect echoes Genesis 22:2 in which Abraham is told to sacrifice Isaac, his "beloved son." Thus, "servant," "king," "beloved" are all aspects of the identity of Jesus.

To the point: Those who share in Jesus' baptism also share in his identity and mission. Our own baptisms, then, rather than preponderantly focusing on washing away original sin, are concerned more with our taking up Jesus' identity and mission.

Celebration

Rite of Blessing and Sprinkling Holy Water

Presider: Dear friends, this water will be used to remind us of our baptism. Let us ask God to bless it, and to keep us faithful to the Spirit he has given us.

[*Continue with form B of the blessing of water*]

Responsorial Psalm

"You will draw water joyfully from the springs of salvation."

This Sunday's responsorial "psalm" is not a psalm in the strict sense for it is not one from the book of Psalms. It is one of the biblical canticles, those poetic texts which share many literary characteristics with the psalms. What makes this song from Isaiah so appropriate for the feast of the Baptism of the Lord is its obvious reference to water (which connects all three readings), but also its repeated use of the Hebrew word *yeshu'a* (seven times, including the refrain). *Yeshu'a* means savior or salvation. Its English form is the name "Jesus." The one who at his baptism is identified as God's "beloved Son" is *Yeshu'a*. The water the first reading invites us to come and drink from without payment is *Yeshu'a*. Let us without hesitation obey the call of this canticle to "acclaim [this] name," to "proclaim how exalted" it is.

Model General Intercessions

Presider: Through our baptism we are privileged to be called daughters and sons of God. We know that God will not refuse us what we ask. And so we pray.

Response:

[musical notation: Lord, hear our prayer.]

Cantor:

[musical notation: we pray to the Lord,]

That all the baptized may witness faithfully to the life and mission of Jesus . . . [pause]

That all people of the world may renew with their God an everlasting covenant that brings life . . . [pause]

That those who have great difficulty accepting Jesus might have the grace to keep God's commandments and thereby be led to God's life . . . [pause]

That our community may grow in our appreciation of sharing in Jesus' life and mission . . . [pause]

Presider: Father in heaven, you spoke words long ago about Jesus and you speak those words to us today: hear these our prayers that we might one day be united with you and your Son Jesus, with the Holy Spirit, one God, for ever and ever. **Amen.**

OPENING PRAYER

Let us pray
   [that we will be faithful to our baptism]
Pause for silent prayer

Almighty, eternal God,
when the Spirit descended upon Jesus
at his baptism in the Jordan,
you revealed him as your own beloved Son.
Keep us, your children born of water and
   the Spirit,
faithful to our calling.
We ask this through our Lord Jesus Christ,
   your Son,
who lives and reigns with you and the
   Holy Spirit,
one God, for ever and ever. **Amen.**

RESPONSORIAL PSALM
[Isa 12:2-3, 4bcd, 5-6]

R. (3) You will draw water joyfully from the springs of salvation.

God indeed is my savior;
   I am confident and unafraid.
My strength and my courage is the LORD,
   and he has been my savior.
With joy you will draw water
   at the fountain of salvation.

R. You will draw water joyfully from the springs of salvation.

Give thanks to the LORD, acclaim his name;
   among the nations make known his
      deeds,
   proclaim how exalted is his name.

R. You will draw water joyfully from the springs of salvation.

Sing praise to the LORD for his glorious
   achievement;
   let this be known throughout all the earth.
Shout with exultation, O city of Zion,
   for great in your midst
   is the Holy One of Israel!

R. You will draw water joyfully from the springs of salvation.

FIRST READING [Isa 55:1-11]

Thus says the LORD:
All you who are thirsty,
   come to the water!
You who have no money,
   come, receive grain and eat;
come, without paying and without cost,
   drink wine and milk!
Why spend your money for what is not
   bread,
   your wages for what fails to satisfy?
Heed me, and you shall eat well,
   you shall delight in rich fare.
Come to me heedfully,
   listen, that you may have life.
I will renew with you the everlasting
   covenant,
   the benefits assured to David.
As I made him a witness to the peoples,
   a leader and commander of nations,

so shall you summon a nation you knew not,
   and nations that knew you not shall run
      to you,
because of the LORD, your God,
   the Holy One of Israel, who has
      glorified you.

Seek the LORD while he may be found,
   call him while he is near.
Let the scoundrel forsake his way,
   and the wicked man his thoughts;
let him turn to the LORD for mercy;
   to our God, who is generous in forgiving.
For my thoughts are not your thoughts,
   nor are your ways my ways, says the
      LORD.
As high as the heavens are above the earth
   so high are my ways above your ways
      and my thoughts above your thoughts.

For just as from the heavens
   the rain and snow come down
and do not return there
   till they have watered the earth,
      making it fertile and fruitful,
giving seed to the one who sows
   and bread to the one who eats,
so shall my word be
   that goes forth from my mouth;
my word shall not return to me void,
   but shall do my will,
      achieving the end for which I sent it.

SECOND READING [1 John 5:1-9]

Beloved:
Everyone who believes that Jesus is the
   Christ is begotten by God,
   and everyone who loves the Father
      loves also the one begotten by him.
In this way we know that we love the
   children of God
   when we love God and obey his
      commandments.
For the love of God is this,
   that we keep his commandments.
And his commandments are not
   burdensome,
   for whoever is begotten by God
      conquers the world.
And the victory that conquers the world is
   our faith.
Who indeed is the victor over the world
   but the one who believes that Jesus is
      the Son of God?
This is the one who came through water
   and blood, Jesus Christ,
   not by water alone, but by water and
      blood.
The Spirit is the one who testifies,
   and the Spirit is truth.
So there are three that testify,
   the Spirit, the water, and the blood,
   and the three are of one accord.
If we accept human testimony,
   the testimony of God is surely greater.
Now the testimony of God is this,
   that he has testified on behalf of his Son.

Catechesis

Cantors

Perhaps the most significant thing you can learn about the canticle you sing this Sunday is the realization that the "salvation" from which you will "draw water joyfully" is the very person of Jesus himself. How does this affect your understanding of salvation?

Choir

You may be heaving a sigh of relief that the extra musical challenges and added rehearsals of the Christmas season are over. But beware, with this first Sunday in Ordinary Time, the real work—accepting as ours the identity and mission of Jesus—is just beginning. How does this challenge you as a choir?

Music Directors

The sprinkling rite used this Sunday does not celebrate Easter nor does it have the penitential significance of cleansing from sin, but is focused instead on discipleship. An example of a suitable text to sing during the rite is "Music for the Sprinkling Rite" [CBW3] which states, "Water and Spirit give birth to a life of greater worth" and "we share this holy pow'rs!" A second suitable choice might be "Send Us Flowing Water" [WC] with its repetition of "we shall all receive . . . we shall all believe." The syncopated Gospel style and overlapping choir entrances of this piece communicate a sense of energy fitting for a new start into Ordinary Time.

For other music during the liturgy, you might consider texts which call you to the challenge of Ordinary Time (re-committing ourselves to the identity and mission of Jesus); for example, "This Is the Spirit's Entry Now" [CH, W3] which reflects on the call to join Christ in his mission and journey to the cross (suitable for the presentation of gifts), "Baptized in Living Water" [WC] which speaks of our initiation into Christ and his mission (hymn of praise after Communion), and "Baptized in Water" [G, G2, RS, W3] which is short and energetic (an excellent recessional hymn sending the assembly back into the living of Ordinary Time).

Liturgy Committee

Does the way you celebrate baptisms in your liturgical community bring out how baptism enables you to share in Jesus' identity and mission?

The baptism of Jesus serves a similar function in both the liturgical calendar and in the Gospel of Mark. This Sunday is unique in that it is the last day of the Advent-Christmas-Epiphany festal cycle and also begins Ordinary Time. In Mark's Gospel, the baptism ends the prologue and introduces Jesus' public ministry. For readers, unlike the original disciples, the rest of Mark's Gospel unfolds with the knowledge conveyed in Jesus' baptism: that the story we are about to hear is the story of the Son of God. For Christians, baptism makes us participants in that life-giving story.

Since proper readings are given for year B, we have chosen to focus on these in order to assure a broader range of readings over the three-year cycle of the Lectionary.

The feast of the Baptism of the Lord is really the First Sunday in Ordinary Time. As such, the Monday after begins the weekdays in Ordinary Time. It is best to remove the Christmas things, even if the poinsettias are still fine! We have moved into a different liturgical season.

JANUARY 9, 2000

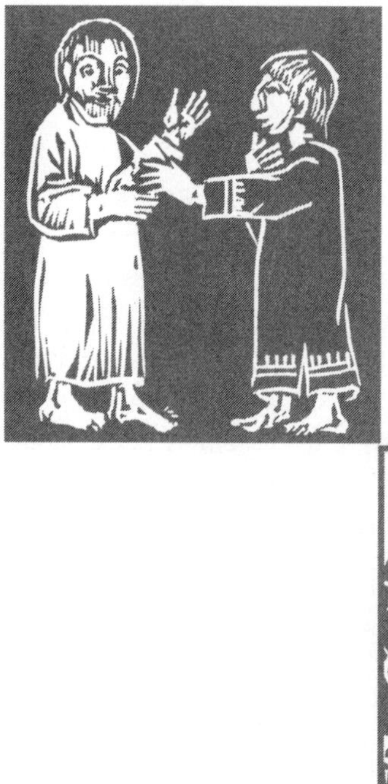

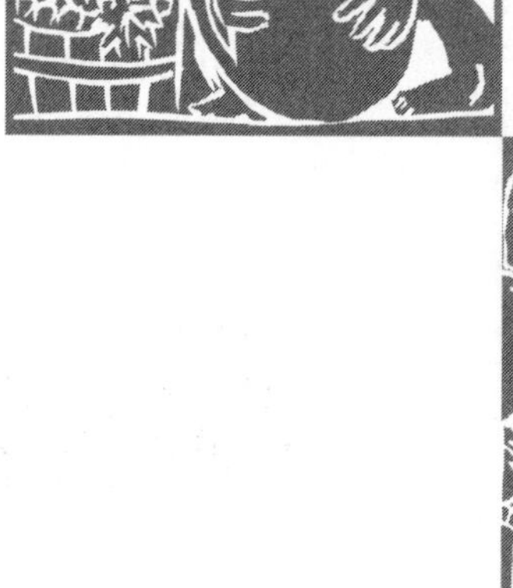

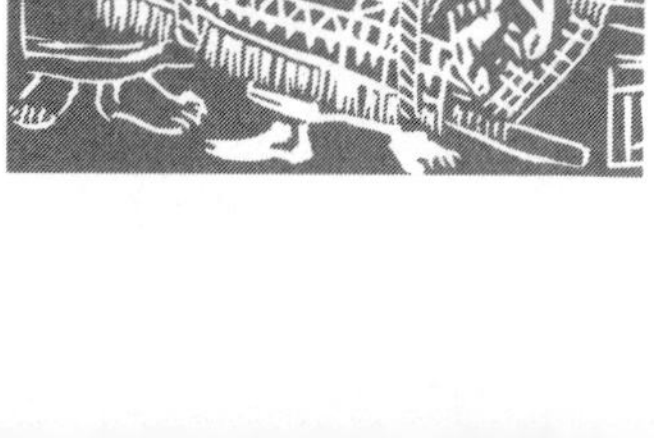

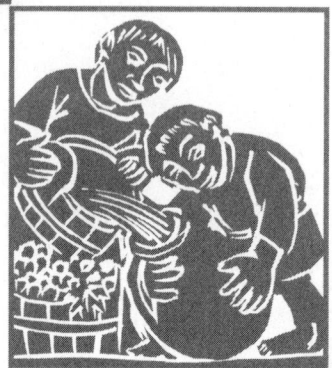

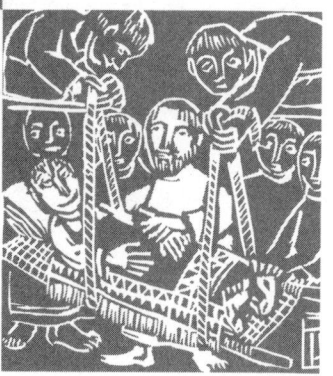

Ordinary Time I

Second Sunday in Ordinary Time

FAITH-SHARING
- Where have you seen Jesus during the past week?
- How have you shown Jesus to others?
- For what are you looking?
- What are you leaving in order to get it?
- Where do you want to stay?

PRESIDERS
When is John the Baptist announcing to you "Behold, the Lamb of God"? Reflect on how your ministry is the place of "seeing" and "staying" with Jesus.

DEACONS
How might you express in your ministry of service this week that you are choosing to "stay" with Jesus?

HOSPITALITY MINISTERS
Jesus invites those in the Gospel to "come, and you will see." Each person whom you greet is coming to see Jesus. How might that influence the way you greet them? How might your greeting assist them to see Jesus?

MUSIC MINISTERS
What are you looking for in choosing to be in music ministry? ego and personal gratification or Jesus and service? or . . . ?

ALTAR MINISTERS
Jesus asked the disciples who were following him, "What are you looking for?" "Looking for" is a kind of attentiveness. How might you practice being attentive to the little things that enable the liturgy to unfold with grace and beauty?

LECTORS
From the Church's earliest beginnings, a profound way of "staying" with Jesus was by meditating on the Scriptures. As you prayerfully prepare the Sunday readings, recognize how you are "staying" with Jesus. Allow this preparation to help you proclaim the readings as one who has "seen" the Lamb of God.

EUCHARISTIC MINISTERS
Mother Teresa would gaze on Jesus in the Eucharist so she would recognize him in the poor. How does your "seeing" Christ in the Eucharist help you to "see" Christ in others: family, friends, peers, those who come to you for Communion on Sunday?

Spirituality

Reflecting on the Gospel

Ordinary Time begins with a spotlight on Jesus, whom we are called to follow. Throughout the many Sundays of Ordinary Time we will continually learn what discipleship means: to walk with Jesus toward Jerusalem and his dying and rising.

Before we can follow, we need to recognize the call—not an easy task! In the first reading for this Sunday we hear God call Samuel, and in the Gospel we hear Jesus call disciples. Samuel at first misunderstands God's call, because he "was not familiar with the Lord." Neither did the disciples know Jesus; John the Baptist points him out to them saying, "Behold, the Lamb of God."

Jesus' answer, "Come, and you will see," to the disciples' question, "Where are you staying?" makes clear to us that faithful discipleship is learned through *experience*. Jesus doesn't just answer the disciples' question directly; rather, he issues an invitation to come and stay with him and find out for themselves. So it is with us. We can't expect all the answers to what it means to follow Jesus. The Church knows this. This is why we have such a long period of Ordinary Time: a long time to figure out what discipleship—following Jesus—means. But we must be willing to come, to see, and to stay. COME. SEE. STAY. The elements of discipleship are (1) the call from God (come); (2) a personal experience and relationship with God (see); and (3) fidelity to the call over a lifetime (stay). We must be willing to *encounter* Jesus in the ordinary circumstances of our daily living.

Living the Paschal Mystery

The long journey of discipleship during Ordinary Time is our invitation to live as Jesus did, to enter into the rhythm of life as he did—dying and rising. As baptized Christians our basic call is to *live* the Paschal Mystery. By "Paschal Mystery" we refer both to Christ's own dying and rising as well as to our own daily dying and rising with Christ. This is what it means to be a disciple. To answer our baptismal call is to embrace this Mystery and in this way we "stay" with Jesus and experience the Mystery for ourselves.

Really, two challenges present themselves here. First, to hear the call and follow in Jesus' footsteps of dying and rising. Second, to see this dying and rising in all the ordinary, "un-divine" circumstances of life. For example, money may be tight for the family. This means that everyone must "die" to their wants and make do with less. But it can also mean that the family must take time to talk together, work things out, perhaps spend more time together which can lead to the "rising" of a new life of stronger relationships in the family. Hearing the call is seeing through the little deaths we meet every day to the opportunities for new life that are always offered if we take the time to see.

JANUARY 16, 2000

GOSPEL [John 1:35-42; L65B]

John was standing with two of his disciples, and as he watched Jesus walk by, he said, "Behold, the Lamb of God." The two disciples heard what he said and followed Jesus. Jesus turned and saw them following him and said to them, "What are you looking for?" They said to him, "Rabbi"—which translated means Teacher—, "where are you staying?" He said to them, "Come, and you will see." So they went and saw where Jesus was staying, and they stayed with him that day. It was about four in the afternoon. Andrew, the brother of Simon Peter, was one of the two who heard John and followed Jesus. He first found his own brother Simon and told him, "We have found the Messiah"—which is translated Christ—. Then he brought him to Jesus. Jesus looked at him and said, "You are Simon the son of John; you will be called Cephas"—which is translated Peter.

Working with the Word

Key words and phrases from the Gospel: Behold, the Lamb of God; come; see; stay

Connecting to the liturgical year: This is the first time we gather for a Sunday in Ordinary Time. What characterizes Ordinary Time is a sequential reading from one of the synoptic Gospels (year B: Mark) that takes us with Jesus to Calvary and Easter.

Connecting to cultures: In the ancient world a person derived his or her identity and importance from whomever he or she was a disciple of. In our culture, we derive our identity from independence. We see here the contrast between relationship (discipleship) and self-reliance.

Exegetical points: Verbs of seeing occur three times in this Sunday's short passage and more than one hundred times in John's Gospel. The first and last words of Jesus deal with sight: "Come and see" (1:39) and "Blessed are those who have not seen and have believed" (20:29; chapter 21 is widely accepted as an appendix). Throughout the Gospel, seeing is a first step on the way to believing. In this passage, Jesus invites Andrew and his companion to "come and see"; he is inviting them to begin a journey that will lead to believing in him. John then remarks, "They went . . . and saw . . . and stayed."

John uses "staying" or "remaining" forty times in the Gospel to refer to the enduring quality of relationship between the Father and the Son, as well as between the Son and those who follow the Son. Jesus' response, "Come and see," is, here, an invitation to experience him and, on the basis of that experience, "stay" as his disciples.

To the point: "What are you looking for?" Hopefully, we come to liturgy because we've heard the call to discipleship in some way. We're looking to God for something. What is it that we want from God? How does staying with Jesus answer "what we are looking for"?

Celebration

Model Penitential Rite

Presider: As we prepare to celebrate the mystery of Christ's love, let us reflect on how God has called us to be disciples and how we have responded . . . [*pause*]

> Lamb of God, you call us to follow you as faithful disciples: Lord . . .
> Messiah, we encounter you in word and sacrament: Christ . . .
> Teacher, you are present to us in the ordinary circumstances of our lives: Lord . . .

Responsorial Psalm

"Here am I, Lord; I come to do your will."

This psalm, like the first reading and Gospel it bridges, speaks of an encounter with divine presence. We wait, listen attentively, and then respond actively. In all three cases—Samuel, the disciples of John, the psalmist—it is God who is present first. God calls Samuel in the night. Jesus walks by John and his disciples. God stoops toward the psalmist and hears her or his cry.

God then empowers. Samuel's words are never "without effect." Andrew brings his brother to Jesus, and Simon was "empowered by God's word" to become "rock" for the Church. The psalmist sings a new song and justice is announced to the people.

This psalm invites us to sing of our willingness to become aware of the personal presence of God in our lives, to listen attentively to whatever God is saying, and to respond to God's call with a sense of confident empowerment.

Model General Intercessions

Presider: Confident that our gracious God hears our every cry, we present our needs:

Response: Lord, hear our prayer.

Cantor: we pray to the Lord,

That all members of the Church may be faithful disciples of Jesus . . . [pause]

That all those seeking salvation may find and stay with the Messiah, the Anointed One . . . [pause]

That those who cannot hear or who refuse to hear God's call may be open to God's persistent and loving presence . . . [pause]

That we here gathered may be ministers of God's call for others . . . [pause]

Presider: O God, you call us as your disciples to spread the good news of your salvation: hear our cry for the grace of response. We pray through Jesus Christ our Lord. **Amen.**

ALTERNATIVE OPENING PRAYER

Let us pray

Pause for silent prayer

Almighty and ever-present Father,
your watchful care reaches from end to end
and orders all things in such power
that even the tensions and the tragedies of sin
cannot frustrate your loving plans. Help us to embrace your will,
give us the strength to follow your call,
so that your truth may live in our hearts
and reflect peace to those who believe in your love.
We ask this in the name of Jesus the Lord. **Amen.**

RESPONSORIAL PSALM

[Ps 40:2, 4, 7-8, 8-9, 10]

℟. (8a and 9a) Here am I, Lord; I come to do your will.

I have waited, waited for the LORD,
    and he stooped toward me and heard my cry.
And he put a new song into my mouth,
    a hymn to our God.

℟. Here am I, Lord; I come to do your will.

Sacrifice or offering you wished not,
    but ears open to obedience you gave me.
Holocausts or sin-offerings you sought not;
    then said I, "Behold I come."

℟. Here I am, Lord; I come to do your will.

"In the written scroll it is prescribed for me,
    to do your will, O my God, is my delight,
and your law is within my heart!"

℟. Here am I, Lord; I come to do your will.

I announced your justice in the vast assembly;
    I did not restrain my lips, as you, O LORD, know.

℟. Here am I, Lord; I come to do your will.

FIRST READING [1 Sam 3:3b-10, 19]

Samuel was sleeping in the temple of the LORD
    where the ark of God was.
The LORD called to Samuel, who answered, "Here I am."

Samuel ran to Eli and said, "Here I am.
   You called me."
"I did not call you," Eli said. "Go back
   to sleep."
So he went back to sleep.
Again the LORD called Samuel, who rose
   and went to Eli.
"Here I am," he said. "You called me."
But Eli answered, "I did not call you, my
   son. Go back to sleep."
At that time Samuel was not familiar
   with the LORD,
   because the LORD had not revealed
      anything to him as yet.
The LORD called Samuel again, for the
   third time.
Getting up and going to Eli, he said,
   "Here I am. You called me."
Then Eli understood that the LORD was
   calling the youth.
So he said to Samuel, "Go to sleep, and
   if you are called, reply,
   Speak, LORD, for your servant is
      listening."
When Samuel went to sleep in his place,
   the LORD came and revealed his
      presence,
   calling out as before, "Samuel,
      Samuel!"
Samuel answered, "Speak, for your
   servant is listening."
Samuel grew up, and the LORD was with
   him,
   not permitting any word of his to be
      without effect.

SECOND READING [1 Cor 6:13c-15a, 17-20]

Brothers and sisters:
The body is not for immorality, but for
   the Lord,
   and the Lord is for the body;
   God raised the Lord and will also
      raise us by his power.
Do you not know that your bodies are
   members of Christ?
But whoever is joined to the Lord
   becomes one Spirit with him.
Avoid immorality.
Every other sin a person commits is
   outside the body,
   but the immoral person sins against
      his own body.
Do you not know that your body
   is a temple of the Holy Spirit within
      you,
   whom you have from God, and that
      you are not your own?
For you have been purchased at a price.
Therefore glorify God in your body.

Catechesis

Cantors

When you lead the assembly in this Sunday's responsorial psalm, your song needs to come from a heart that has practiced listening and responding to God's call. Using the melody of the psalm refrain, begin each day this week with the prayer, "Here am I, Lord, I come to do your will." Then ask for the grace to become aware of some specific way God is calling you each day, and for the confidence to respond.

Choir

At the conclusion of choir rehearsal this week, lead the choir in a litany begging for grace to hear and respond to God's call in daily life. Use the refrain of the responsorial psalm as a sung response. Petitions could include "for the Church . . . ," "for the world . . . ," "for our families . . . ," "for our parish . . . ," "for those struggling to respond to God's call . . . ." After each petition pause briefly to allow for silent prayer before singing the response. Invite the choir to add similar petitions.

Music Directors

As Ordinary Time begins, it is important to return to a setting of service music in keeping with this non-festal season. Select a setting which is less complex or embellished than what you have been singing during the Christmas season. Examples: Richard Proulx' "Community Mass," the "St. Louis Jesuits' Mass," Jan Vermulst's "People's Mass," Owen Alstott's "Heritage Mass," and Stephen Somerville's "Good Shepherd Mass." In order to help the assembly enter into the spirit of Ordinary Time, use the same setting for this and the next seven Sundays in Ordinary Time. For Mass settings which do not include a Glory to God, you might use Carroll T. Andrews' through-composed version from his "A New Mass for Congregations," James Chepponis' responsorial "Melodic Gloria," or John Lee's antiphonal arrangement from his "Congregational Mass."

One popular song which this Sunday's readings bring immediately to mind is Dan Schutte's "Here I Am, Lord." This piece is intended to be done in responsorial fashion, with choir or cantor singing the verses (God's call) and the assembly the refrain (their answer). The meditative style makes it better suited for the presentation of gifts than for the entrance hymn or recessional. Its text also is better placed at the presentation of gifts where it can aptly express the assembly's response to the proclamation just heard rather than at Communion.

Liturgy Committee

At the beginning of this new liturgical season, it would be well to evaluate the overall planning. Is there anything you can do in your preparation of liturgies to help people enter into the journey of Jesus toward Calvary and Easter? A question the committee might ask is, "Is there any way we can help people see this and the next seven Sundays as a journey, with each week's Gospel connected one to another?"

Last Sunday's feast of the Baptism of the Lord takes the place of the first Sunday in Ordinary Time; hence, the weekdays last week were of the first week in Ordinary Time. Baptism is the "foundation" for Ordinary Time: Jesus' baptism was the source for his ministry, and so it is for Christians.

JANUARY 16, 2000

Third Sunday in Ordinary Time

FAITH-SHARING
- What is "good" about the good news?
- What are signs around you that the kingdom of God is truly at hand?
- What are signs around you that people still thwart the establishment of God's reign?
- Are you willing to embrace the cross in order to do your part to bring about more fully God's reign?

PRESIDERS
Be aware this week of how you hear God's call to die and rise in the ordinary circumstances of your ministry.

DEACONS
How might you recognize in those you serve an opportunity for bringing about more fully God's reign?

HOSPITALITY MINISTERS
How might your greeting people this week with a warm smile and/or handshake be a mediation of God's presence that truly helps to bring about God's reign?

MUSIC MINISTERS
How does the music you choose/sing invite people to deeper discipleship? to taking up the cross?

ALTAR MINISTERS
Jonah served the people of Nineveh even by announcing the unpleasant message of impending doom. How might your accepting in a spirit of charity any unpleasant tasks that might face you this week help bring about the presence of God and God's reign?

LECTORS
Jonah preached in such a way that the Ninevites listened and changed their lives. How might you live this week to announce that the reign of God is at hand? How might you proclaim the readings so that the assembly realizes that *now* is the time of fulfillment, now the kingdom of God is at hand?

EUCHARISTIC MINISTERS
The good news of God's reign being present is that all people are called to be cherished members of the body of Christ. How might the goodness you see in another bring about God's reign and build up the body?

Spirituality

Reflecting on the Gospel

All of us have encountered at some time or another a threat, and, probably, most of us didn't react very well. If we felt we were the stronger party, we might have called the other's bluff. If we felt we were the weaker party, we might have done as the other wished, but with resentment and anger. The use of threats may result in a desired action, but such a negative approach ultimately harms relationships. On the other hand, all of us react favorably to an invitation which leaves us truly free to accept or decline. Because it respects our freedom, the positive approach of invitation strengthens our relationship with the one inviting.

The Jesus we encounter in this Sunday's Gospel does not come with threats, but with an invitation: "Come after me." He does not threaten us with going to hell if we don't follow him. Rather, he simply calls. Why should we respond? Because, as Jesus announces in the first part of the Gospel, "This is the time of fulfillment. The kingdom of God is at hand." We respond because Jesus shows us throughout his public ministry what it means to have the kingdom of God at hand: the sick are healed, the dead are raised, the poor are given hope, the lost are found, the lowly are raised up.

To be called to be a disciple of Jesus means that we, too, must announce that the kingdom of God is at hand. We are called to announce the good news, the Gospel. The challenge is not only to hear and respond to the call, but also to realize that this call means living it every day in all the circumstances of our lives. By *our* lives others will know that this is a time of fulfillment. Like Jesus we, too, must preach and heal, nourish and forgive, respect and admonish, love and reconcile.

The good news we announce as disciples does have its cost. This Sunday's Gospel opens with the statement that John the Baptist has been arrested. The announcement not only foreshadows the fate of Jesus, but it also reveals one important aspect of discipleship: we will have to take up the cross. Ultimately, these weeks of Ordinary Time are about our journey to the cross.

Living the Paschal Mystery

Strange, this "good" news that leads us to a cross! What is so "good" about that? Our Christian faith tells us that when we hear and respond to Jesus' call to follow, to come to the cross, we do not walk alone. Jesus has announced the time of fulfillment, that the kingdom of God is at hand. He calls *us* to participate in announcing the good news of the kingdom. And so *we* walk with Jesus. We walk with him to the cross; we also walk with him into resurrection—and *that* is the *good* news!

JANUARY 23, 2000

GOSPEL [Mark 1:14-20; L68B]

After John had been arrested, Jesus came to Galilee proclaiming the gospel of God: "This is the time of fulfillment. The kingdom of God is at hand. Repent, and believe in the gospel."

As he passed by the Sea of Galilee, he saw Simon and his brother Andrew casting their nets into the sea; they were fishermen. Jesus said to them, "Come after me, and I will make you fishers of men." Then they abandoned their nets and followed him. He walked along a little farther and saw James, the son of Zebedee, and his brother John. They too were in a boat mending their nets. Then he called them. So they left their father Zebedee in the boat along with the hired men and followed him.

Working with the Word

Key words and phrases from the Gospel: Gospel, time of fulfillment, kingdom of God is at hand

Connecting to last Sunday's Gospel: Last Sunday the Gospel from John opened with a call; this Sunday the Gospel closes with a call. Sandwiched in between is Jesus' proclamation of the good news, here given in synopsis form: "This is the time of fulfillment. The kingdom of God is at hand. Repent, and believe in the Gospel."

Connecting to our culture: For a culture that is "full," what does God (the Gospel) offer? The challenge is to inspire people with the Gospel message so that they are motivated to *live* the good news. We might be more aware of all those people who are *already* putting their belief in God into actions, for example, members of the St. Vincent de Paul Society, volunteers with Habitat for Humanity, parishioners who prepare lunches for grieving families after funerals, Eucharistic ministers who take time with the sick, etc.

Exegetical points: As we begin reading from Mark's Gospel in Ordinary Time, it will be helpful to keep three features in mind. (1) The entire Gospel centers on the question, "Who is Jesus?" In Mark's theology, Jesus' identity can only be fully revealed and understood on the cross: his passion and death—the concern of fully half the Gospel—are the key that unlocks the secret of his true identity. A related theme woven throughout Mark's Gospel is the disciples' failure to understand Jesus and his mission. (2) At every step of the way, Jesus encounters resistance and, as the controversy grows, his death becomes inevitable. The mention of John the Baptist's arrest in the Gospel's opening line already foreshadows Jesus' similar fate. (3) Throughout Mark's Gospel, the call to discipleship and the requirements of fidelity to Jesus are everywhere evident. Implied is the truth that to follow Jesus is to do as he did and to expect a similar fate.

To the point: The subject of Jesus' Gospel ("good news") is "The kingdom of God is at hand," i.e., God's presence and rule over people are being established as Jesus (1) expels the powers of evil, (2) heals the sick, and (3) forgives sins.

Celebration

Model Penitential Rite

Presider: As we prepare to celebrate Jesus' dying and rising in these sacred mysteries, let us reflect on God's call to announce the kingdom of God and ask ourselves how we have responded to that call . . . [pause]

> Lord Jesus, you announce that the kingdom of God is at hand: Lord . . .
> Christ Jesus, you call followers to announce your good news: Christ . . .
> Lord Jesus, you invite us to journey with you to the cross and resurrection: Lord . . .

Responsorial Psalm

"Teach me your ways, O Lord."

In the first reading the Ninevites listen to Jonah's call to repentance and immediately reform their lives. In the Gospel the disciples hear Jesus' announcement of the kingdom of God and abandon all to follow him. In Psalm 25 we pray for this same readiness to hear and to learn the ways of God. We acknowledge that the kingdom of God is at hand and ask for the grace to live our lives accordingly. Psalm 25, then, is a blueprint for the journey of Ordinary Time which we have just begun, when God teaches and we learn the ways of discipleship.

Model General Intercessions

Presider: Jesus announces the good news, the time of fulfillment, and so we are encouraged to present our needs to God, knowing that our prayers are answered.

Response:

Lord, hear our prayer.

Cantor:

we pray to the Lord,

May the Church follow Jesus in announcing the good news of his death and resurrection . . . [pause]

May world leaders witness truthfully to the good news of God's reign . . . [pause]

May those who refuse to hear God's good news be turned toward goodness and truth . . . [pause]

May we here gathered proclaim by our charity and unity with all Christians that the kingdom of God is at hand . . . [pause]

Presider: O God, you unfailingly hear the prayers of those who follow your call: hear these our prayers and grant us the courage to follow in your Son's footsteps in announcing the good news. We pray in the name of that Son, Jesus Christ our Lord. **Amen.**

ALTERNATIVE OPENING PRAYER

Let us pray
   [pleading that our vision may
   overcome our weakness]

Pause for silent prayer

Almighty Father,
the love you offer
always exceeds the furthest expression
   of our human longing,
for you are greater than the human
   heart.
Direct each thought, each effort of our
   life,
so that the limits of our faults and
   weaknesses
may not obscure the vision of your glory
or keep us from the peace you have
   promised.
We ask this through Christ our Lord.
Amen.

RESPONSORIAL PSALM
[Ps 25:4-5, 6-7, 8-9]

℟. (4a) Teach me your ways, O Lord.

Your ways, O Lord, make known to me;
   teach me your paths,
guide me in your truth and teach me,
   for you are God my savior.

℟. Teach me your ways, O Lord.

Remember that your compassion, O
   Lord,
   and your love are from of old.
In your kindness remember me,
   because of your goodness, O Lord.

℟. Teach me your ways, O Lord.

Good and upright is the Lord;
   thus he shows sinners the way.
He guides the humble to justice
   and teaches the humble his way.

℟. Teach me your ways, O Lord.

FIRST READING
[Jonah 3:1-5, 10]

The word of the LORD came to Jonah, saying:
 "Set out for the great city of Nineveh, and announce to it the message that I will tell you."
So Jonah made ready and went to Nineveh,
 according to the LORD's bidding.
Now Nineveh was an enormously large city;
 it took three days to go through it.
Jonah began his journey through the city,
 and had gone but a single day's walk announcing,
 "Forty days more and Nineveh shall be destroyed,"
 when the people of Nineveh believed God;
 they proclaimed a fast
 and all of them, great and small, put on sackcloth.

When God saw by their actions how they turned from their evil way,
 he repented of the evil that he had threatened to do to them;
 he did not carry it out.

SECOND READING
[1 Cor 7:29-31]

I tell you, brothers and sisters, the time is running out.
From now on, let those having wives act as not having them,
 those weeping as not weeping,
 those rejoicing as not rejoicing,
 those buying as not owning,
 those using the world as not using it fully.
For the world in its present form is passing away.

Catechesis

Cantors

Reflect this week on where in your life God is calling you to greater discipleship. Pray the responsorial psalm each day so that when you cantor it on Sunday your song comes from a deepened desire to follow the way God leads.

Choir

Singing with a choir is more than just a musical commitment—it is a ministry in response to God's call. In terms of this Sunday's readings, are there any rehearsal habits you might assess in order to minister better? For example, Do you arrive on time? Do you stay focused on the musical task at hand? Do you socialize with everyone in the choir? Do you use your voice to support the group sound, rather than to compete? Do you keep prayer the focus of your singing rather than performance?

Music Directors

There are numerous settings of Psalm 25 available. Many of these, however, use the refrain text intended for the season of Advent ("To you, O Lord, I lift my soul"). Using this refrain with this Sunday's readings will weaken the nuance of Psalm 25. The refrain given in the Lectionary, "Teach me your ways, O Lord," more clearly connects the first reading and the Gospel in terms of God's call to hear and respond. Robert Kreutz has a fine setting, with melodic verses, in *Psalms for the Cantor,* v. VII [WLP]. Another good setting is that of Richard Proulx in *Worship,* 3rd ed. [GIA]. Here the verses can be sung to either a contemporary psalm tone, or a Gelineau tone.

Because John L. Bell's "The Summons" [RS, G2] repeats the question of this Sunday's Gospel (Will you come . . . ? Will you leave . . . ? Will you love . . . ?), it would work well during the procession with the gifts as a summation of the Gospel's call. Have the choir or cantor sing the verses and the assembly respond on the energetic refrain.

Liturgy Committee

Sometimes liturgy committees are tempted to prepare liturgies in such a way that they remove the real sting of what following Jesus entails: coming to the cross. There is only one question you need ask when preparing liturgies: How does this help you enter more fully into living the Paschal Mystery? How might you answer this question in your life this week?

These thirty-four weeks of non-festal time are named "Sundays in Ordinary Time" first, because they derive not from a feastday as such (they used to be called Sundays "after Pentecost") but from the Mystery of Jesus Christ and, second, because they are numbered or "counted time" (from the Latin word *ordinarius* and its cognates which mean "according to order," "regular"). Although the Latin is translated in the *editio typica* by "ordinary," you must not think these Sundays are prosaic or unimportant. In fact, they make up the longest liturgical season of the year, the Church's teaching time.

It is always appropriate to use green plants to enhance the liturgical environment, but be careful that their use doesn't convey that the assembly is walking into a greenhouse! *Live* plants are suitable; artificial plants, although practical, don't convey the same meaning.

JANUARY 23, 2000

Fourth Sunday in Ordinary Time

FAITH-SHARING
- When are you astonished and amazed at Jesus' teaching?
- How has your amazement had an impact on your discipleship?
- Where do you need to grow toward greater integrity of word and deed?

PRESIDERS
A typical day can include a flood of words and deeds. In what ways are your words and deeds compatible? When are they not? Are you able to identify an area where you need to grow toward integrity?

DEACONS
What set Jesus apart from the scribes is that he taught with authority. That is, Jesus' teaching "authored" life! In the past week, which of your acts "authored" life? Are you able to recognize and celebrate the entrance of the kingdom of God in these moments?

HOSPITALITY MINISTERS
How might you greet those you meet this week as "the Holy One of God," thus becoming more aware that Jesus dwells in all the baptized who are members of his Body?

MUSIC MINISTERS
This would be a good week to meditate on the words of a twelfth-century bishop: "See that what you sing with your mouth you believe with your heart, and that what you believe with your heart you obey in your works."

ALTAR MINISTERS
Psalm 95 reminds us that you prepare to "bow down in worship" and "kneel before the Lord" by resisting a hard heart. Prepare for your service around the worship table by sensitizing your heart to the daily needs of those around you.

LECTORS
Jesus had integrity because his words and deeds corresponded. How do your deeds correspond with the words you proclaim at liturgy?

EUCHARISTIC MINISTERS
The unclean spirit called Jesus "the Holy One of God!" When you minister Communion, you minister the Holy One of God. How might you see the holy in those you meet this week so that you can better minister the Body of Christ?

Spirituality

Reflecting on the Gospel

"Do as I say and not as I do" is an adage that most of us have probably heard invoked at one time or another. It is always much easier to say what is right and good than it is to do it. Often our youth have a legitimate complaint against us when they are asked to live in ways that they don't see us model.

This is something of the situation between the scribes and Jesus depicted in this Sunday's Gospel. The scribes were the "learned" members of the Jewish community and knew well the Hebrew Scriptures. They were the ones who knew the Law and how to fulfill its letter. But in spite of their knowledge, the scribes mentioned in this Gospel were not recognized as having authority because their manner of living did not flow from their knowledge of Scripture. In other words, they knew God's word as an intellectual exercise, but they had not received it into their hearts; it had no affect on their actions.

Jesus, on the other hand, is recognized as one having authority because he acts according to his word. Even the unclean spirit recognizes this integrity of Jesus' word and deed when it proclaims that he is "the Holy One of God!" Jesus' authority, however, is not a "power over," but a truth that calls forth *life*. His is an authority that derives from modeling how a true servant of God lives.

The people in the synagogue who witnessed these events were amazed and astonished at Jesus' authority: "even the unclean spirits . . . obey him." As disciples of Jesus, we are called to the same integrity of word and deed. Herein lies our challenge. The authority that comes from an integrity of word and deed is a whole new way to teach: model the good news by living it.

Living the Paschal Mystery

The good news is that, because of baptism, we are the body of Christ and, therefore, we possess the *same* authority as Jesus to confront and overcome the power of evil. We all face evil. This is part of original sin, the human condition. Nonetheless, we have been given *the* gift essential to triumph over the power of evil: we come weekly to the Eucharistic table and reaffirm that we are Christ's body. We come to reaffirm our response to God's call to be disciples.

Authentic discipleship implies working toward integrity: words and deeds coinciding in such a way that our lives manifest the same integrity as Jesus' life. Goodness overcomes evil when we demonstrate such integrity. We are easily amazed and astonished at the eloquent words of others. Sometimes we ourselves might even talk fancy words about God. These words are truly eloquent and fruitful, however, only when our everyday actions witness to their truth.

JANUARY 30, 2000

GOSPEL [Mark 1:21-28; L71B]

Then they came to Capernaum, and on the sabbath Jesus entered the synagogue and taught. The people were astonished at his teaching, for he taught them as one having authority and not as the scribes. In their synagogue was a man with an unclean spirit; he cried out, "What have you to do with us, Jesus of Nazareth? Have you come to destroy us? I know who you are—the Holy One of God!" Jesus rebuked him and said, "Quiet! Come out of him!" The unclean spirit convulsed him and with a loud cry came out of him. All were amazed and asked one another, "What is this? A new teaching with authority. He commands even the unclean spirits and they obey him." His fame spread everywhere throughout the whole region of Galilee.

Working with the Word

Key words and phrases from the Gospel: astonished, amazed, teaching, authority, Holy One of God

Connecting to the first reading: Moses was a prophet who spoke God's word with authority; now Jesus is the one God raises up to speak with authority—not just as a prophet, but as the Holy One of God.

Connecting to the culture: This Gospel opens with the words "Then they came to Capernaum." This was Jesus' "hometown" as an adult, as Nazareth had been in his youth. In Nazareth he had no authority; in Capernaum he has an authority that amazes his onlookers.

Exegetical points: This Sunday's Gospel begins a series of four Sundays which feature healing stories. Each one gives evidence of Jesus' claim in last Sunday's Gospel that the kingdom is at hand. Although this Sunday's passage mentions "teaching" four times, the actual content of his message is not included. Instead, the focus is on what Jesus *did*. This suggests the essential connection between the words and deeds of Jesus (the same link that is made in the Hebrew for "word," *dabar*): the "amazing" authority of Jesus' teaching in the synagogue is confirmed when he expels the demon from the afflicted man.

The setting in the synagogue, the home turf of the official religious establishment, already hints at the larger conflict Jesus will have with the scribes and religious leaders whose authority Jesus exposes—on their own "home court"!—as bankrupt.

It is significant that Jesus' first healing or mighty deed is the expelling of a demon. This reveals both the real nature of the conflict underlying the Gospel (divine vs. demonic, good vs. evil), and the scope of Jesus' authority—even demons obey him! The establishment of the kingdom of God means that the kingdom of evil is cast out and overthrown (cf. Mark 3:27).

To the point: Last Sunday Jesus preached "the kingdom of God is at hand." The proof of his claim is revealed this Sunday in his confrontation with evil which is displaced. The basis of Jesus' authority is that his words ("the kingdom of God is at hand") and his deeds (expels the demon) are one.

Celebration

Model Penitential Rite

Presider: As we prepare to hear God's word and be nourished at God's table, let us open ourselves to the authority of the divine presence . . . [pause]

>Holy One of God, you speak with authority: Lord . . .
>Holy One of God, you cast out the power of evil: Christ . . .
>Holy One of God, your fame is spread throughout the world: Lord . . .

Responsorial Psalm

"If today you hear his voice, harden not your hearts."

Whose voice are we hearing? In the first reading Moses and the prophets speak the words of God and do so in the recognizable voice of a fellow human being, a "kinsman." In the Gospel reading, Jesus does the same—speaks the word of God in a human voice. But he does so with an authority far beyond anything the people have heard before. The words he speaks are a direct and victorious confrontation with the forces of evil which can possess the human heart. Truly this is good news!

This Sunday's psalm raises the question each of us faces in our struggle with faithful discipleship: will we surrender to this authority? The reality is that, despite how good the news, many elements in our hearts resist. The psalmist pleads with us to remain faithful in our listening to God, knowing full well how real is the possibility that we may choose otherwise.

Model General Intercessions

Presider: God hears our prayer and has the authority to grant our needs, and so we pray.

Response:

[musical notation: Lord, hear our prayer.]

Cantor:

[musical notation: we pray to the Lord,]

That all those with leadership roles in the Church speak with the authority that comes from an integrity of word and deed . . . [pause]

That world leaders govern with honesty and truth . . . [pause]

That those burdened by evil encounter the Holy One of God . . . [pause]

That we allow our amazement and astonishment at the integrity of God's word to lead us to true discipleship . . . [pause]

Presider: God most holy, you are ever faithful in word and deed: receive these our prayers that we might have what we need to be better disciples of your Son. We pray through Jesus Christ our Lord. **Amen.**

ALTERNATIVE OPENING PRAYER
Let us pray

Pause for silent prayer

Father in heaven,
from the days of Abraham and Moses
until this gathering of your Church in prayer,
you have formed a people in the image of your Son.
Bless this people with the gift of your kingdom.
May we serve you with our every desire
and show love for one another even as you have loved us.
Grant this through Christ our Lord.
Amen.

RESPONSORIAL PSALM
[Ps 95:1-2, 6-7, 7-9]

℞. (8) If today you hear his voice, harden not your hearts.

Come, let us sing joyfully to the LORD;
  let us acclaim the rock of our salvation.
Let us come into his presence with thanksgiving;
  let us joyfully sing psalms to him.

℞. If today you hear his voice, harden not your hearts.

Come, let us bow down in worship;
  let us kneel before the LORD who made us.
For he is our God,
  and we are the people he shepherds,
  the flock he guides.

℞. If today you hear his voice, harden not your hearts.

Oh, that today you would hear his voice:
  "Harden not your hearts as at Meribah,
  as in the day of Massah in the desert,
where your fathers tempted me;
  they tested me though they had seen my works."

℞. If today you hear his voice, harden not your hearts.

FIRST READING
[Deut 18:15-20]

Moses spoke to all the people, saying:
"A prophet like me will the LORD,
   your God, raise up for you
   from among your own kin;
   to him you shall listen.
This is exactly what you requested of
   the LORD, your God, at Horeb
   on the day of the assembly, when you
   said,
   'Let us not again hear the voice of the
   LORD, our God,
   nor see this great fire any more, lest
   we die.'
And the LORD said to me, 'This was well
   said.
I will raise up for them a prophet like
   you from among their kin,
   and will put my words into his
   mouth;
   he shall tell them all that I command
   him.'
Whoever will not listen to my words
   which he speaks in my name,
   I myself will make him answer for it.
But if a prophet presumes to speak in
   my name
   an oracle that I have not commanded
   him to speak,
   or speaks in the name of other gods,
   he shall die."

SECOND READING
[1 Cor 7:32-35]

Brothers and sisters:
I should like you to be free of anxieties.
An unmarried man is anxious about the
   things of the Lord,
   how he may please the Lord.
But a married man is anxious about the
   things of the world,
   how he may please his wife, and he is
   divided.
An unmarried woman or a virgin is
   anxious about the things of the Lord,
   so that she may be holy in both body
   and spirit.
A married woman, on the other hand,
   is anxious about the things of the
   world,
   how she may please her husband.
I am telling you this for your own
   benefit,
   not to impose a restraint upon you,
   but for the sake of propriety
   and adherence to the Lord without
   distraction.

*C*atechesis

Cantors

In order for your leading of the psalm to be genuine, it needs to come from a heart which knows that it struggles to hear and be faithful to the voice of God. Spend time this week examining where in your life you struggle with those "voices" which compete with Christian discipleship. Is it the voice of consumerism? Of social pressure? Of timidity in face of a situation which needs to be confronted? Reflect on why these voices are attractive, and ask for the grace to hear and respond to the deeper voice of Christ speaking in your heart.

Choir

The ministry of liturgical music invites you to use your voice with authority in worship. This week choose to use your voice in daily living with this same authority. For example, instead of gossiping, say a word of praise; instead of arguing or bickering, say a word of appeasement; instead of silence, speak a word of honest confrontation.

Music Directors

One purpose of the entrance hymn is to accompany the procession which begins the liturgy. But it is not just the ministers who process. On a symbolic level, it is the entire assembly who journeys from the "doorway" of the liturgy to its heart, the ritual enactment of the Paschal Mystery. The hymn accompanying this journey, then, needs to support this movement. Its text needs to express praise, worship, sacramental celebration, gathering, or be directly related to the Gospel of the day or to the liturgical season. And its meter needs to be rhythmically strong as befits a processional hymn.

One hymn which would function well for this Sunday's entrance is Bryn Rees' "The Kingdom of God" [RS, W3, WC]. Its text speaks of Christ's authoritative power over sin, and also of the "challenge and choice" disciples face because of the "crisis of judgment" the announcement of the kingdom lays before us. Although its time signature is 3/4, the hymn is actually in 1. Lead it by giving strong weight to the first note of each measure. On one of the inner verses you might play only the first chord of each measure, following it with two quarter rests, to emphasize the challenge which both hymn and readings bring before you.

A second well-suited hymn would be Jeff Cothran's "Glorious in Majesty" [G, G2, RS, W3]. Its text speaks of the glory of Christ victorious over the powers of darkness as well as of the invitation to come to him and live in his word. Its meter is 4/4. To increase the sense of momentum, you might repeat the bass note of the accompaniment in a slightly detached quarter rhythm in the pedal or left hand.

Liturgy Committee

The liturgy committee has a weighty responsibility to do seasonal planning and prepare liturgies. You must continually learn more about the liturgy so you can fulfill your ministry in even better ways. How might a resolution to read on a regular basis a solid article on some aspect of liturgy increase your "authority"?

Sometimes liturgies are flooded with words, words, words. You must be careful that the words of the ritual are carefully balanced with the ritual actions. Be careful about extraneous commentaries and remarks that tend to draw people out of the ritual and focus attention elsewhere.

JANUARY 30, 2000

Fifth Sunday in Ordinary Time

FAITH-SHARING
- What needs healing in your life?
- Are there things you need to do or stop doing before you can receive healing?
- Jesus models a rhythm of healing (deeds), prayer (intimacy with God), and preaching (words). How balanced is your life in this regard?
- What acts of service are you involved in that bring about the reign of God to your family? your parish? your neighborhood?

PRESIDERS
Ponder what needs healing in you—physical, spiritual, Job-like drudgery? How is Jesus healing this? How can the awareness of your infirmity assist you in preaching this Sunday's Gospel?

DEACONS
After being healed by Jesus, Peter's mother-in-law "began to wait on them." Who does Jesus want you to wait on? Is there someone you are intentionally or subconsciously neglecting?

HOSPITALITY MINISTERS
Psalm 147 reminds you that before God you remain uniquely attended to: God "calls each by name." How might your greeting and assistance during the liturgy affirm each one's uniqueness and goodness?

MUSIC MINISTERS
The ministry of music can be a never-ending cycle of planning and preparation. Do you include prayer as part of your planning and preparation?

ALTAR MINISTERS
How might taking some time for personal prayer in preparation for your ministry transpose it from "getting a job done" to service that helps make present God's kingdom?

LECTORS
Jesus' ministry flows from his prayerful relationship to his Father. How does your prayer life influence your proclamation of the Scriptures? What grace of healing do you need to seek in order to announce God's good news?

EUCHARISTIC MINISTERS
Those who are ill or possessed came to Jesus. That same procession of humanity continues today. Prepare for Sunday by "feeding" people this week through offering time and care with the intent to heal.

Spirituality

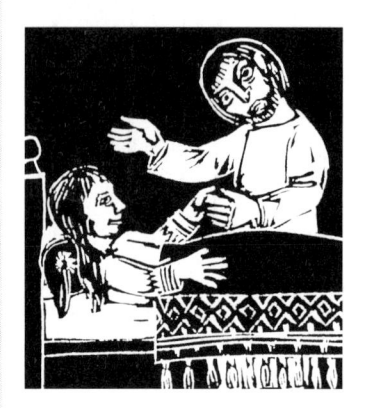

Reflecting on the Gospel

Illness, pain, suffering, weakness, forces of evil. Each of us has a sense that these realities—in spite of modern advances—are really beyond our control and we seek divine intervention. We seek miracles when things are beyond us. That is why the subject of healing is a very popular one. This Sunday's Gospel may bring to mind all our good desires to overcome the evils of life.

In the Gospel selection, not surprisingly, "they brought to [Jesus] all who were ill or possessed by demons." In fact, "the whole town was gathered at the door" of Simon and Andrew's house. We can imagine that they were gathered there with heightened expectation, and with a great sense of hope and awe and wonder. Nor were they disappointed, for Jesus "cured many." There had already been encouragement to bring the sick and possessed to Jesus: he had cured the man at the synagogue who was possessed (last Sunday's Gospel) and he had healed Simon's mother-in-law. He can do these things! He has already shown us his authority!

But our Gospel doesn't end with this good news, good as it is. After the evening of healings, Jesus rises "very early before dawn" and goes off to pray. When found by Simon and the others who pursued him, Jesus proceeded to nearby villages to preach. These three movements help us to put the healings into perspective: (1) the healings are a sign of Jesus' authority and of the good things to come when we respond to that authority; (2) Jesus' ministry flows from his prayerful relationship to his Father; and (3) Jesus has come to preach that the kingdom of God is at hand.

Since we are all in need of healing in some form or another, we can easily place ourselves in this Gospel. The first reading from Job reminds us that "evil" doesn't have to be disease or possession or systemic evil, but can include the drudgery and burdens of daily life. Jesus heals us from diminished living, too. And, just as Simon's mother-in-law immediately arose from her bed and "waited on them" so, too, when we encounter the reconciling, healing touch of Jesus are we called to respond with that service which helps to make God's kingdom present to others.

Living the Paschal Mystery

In all these healings (and we will be hearing more in the Sundays to come), we receive glimpses of the greater mystery being revealed by Jesus, the movement from death to life. The evil that affects all of our lives in one way or another is a reminder that the kingdom of God is "not yet" fully established. The healings and good news of Jesus' preaching are reminders that the kingdom is "already" gradually being revealed in the words and deeds of Jesus, whose mission it is to inaugurate God's kingdom.

By means of encounters with individuals in the healings, Jesus establishes a relationship with others so that he might preach the good news that God's kingdom is at hand. The healings performed by Jesus inaugurate the kingdom of God. *We are living during the time of fulfillment!*

GOSPEL [Mark 1:29-39; L74B]

On leaving the synagogue Jesus entered the house of Simon and Andrew with James and John. Simon's mother-in-law lay sick with a fever. They immediately told him about her. He approached, grasped her hand, and helped her up. Then the fever left her and she waited on them.

When it was evening, after sunset, they brought to him all who were ill or possessed by demons. The whole town was gathered at the door. He cured many who were sick with various diseases, and he drove out many demons, not permitting them to speak because they knew him.

Rising very early before dawn, he left and went off to a deserted place, where he prayed. Simon and those who were with him pursued him and on finding him said, "Everyone is looking for you." He told them, "Let us go on to the nearby villages that I may preach there also. For this purpose have I come." So he went into their synagogues, preaching and driving out demons throughout the whole of Galilee.

Working with the Word

Key words and phrases from the Gospel: for this purpose have I come, preaching, driving out demons, healing

Connecting to the first reading: Job speaks for the people who come to Jesus for healing. Job's words give expression to the cries of the anonymous crowd who had gathered at Simon's door in the Gospel.

Connecting to biblical culture: In some traditions in the Hebrew Scriptures, sickness, poverty, etc. were assumed to be punishment for sin. For Jesus, these conditions reflect the power of evil in the world and provide an opportunity to reflect God's greater power: the good news.

Exegetical points: Jesus clearly states the purpose of his mission: "Let us go . . . that I may preach . . . For this purpose have I come." Again, the content of his preaching is not explicitly expressed. Instead, the focus is on the healings and exorcisms Jesus performs. In his ministry, the words and deeds of Jesus are inseparable, the words giving meaning to his deeds, his deeds confirming his words. In this way, too, the announcement of God's kingdom is actualized as evil is driven out and the sick are healed. Taken together, the readings from last Sunday and this Sunday show Jesus driving a demon out of a man and healing a woman, at work in the synagogue and at home with his disciples, with strangers and with companions. The mission of Jesus is addressed to all sorts of people, in all kinds of environments, and all varieties of ills—a truly expansive and inclusive ministry.

This passage also contains the first of repeated commands in Mark's Gospel to various characters not to disclose the identity of Jesus. Mark's point seems to be that any statement about Jesus that does not include acknowledgment of his suffering and death is incomplete and will surely lead to misunderstanding. Only the cross will reveal Jesus' full identity—and the nature of true discipleship.

To the point: The purpose for which Jesus came is to announce and inaugurate God's kingdom, a reign of wholeness, healing, restoration, and life. As Simon's mother-in-law demonstrates, the response to healing and restoration is service, discipleship.

Celebration

Model Penitential Rite

Presider: In today's Gospel we find Jesus going off to a deserted place to pray. We ourselves have come to this place to be in communion with God. Let us open our hearts and surrender ourselves to divine presence . . . [pause]

> Lord Jesus, you teach us to withdraw to pray: Lord . . .
> Christ Jesus, you heal those who come to you: Christ . . .
> Lord Jesus, you preach the good news of the kingdom of God at hand: Lord . . .

Responsorial Psalm

"Praise the Lord, who heals the brokenhearted."

The pervasive pain of life which Job decries is answered by the good news that God does heal all human brokenness. The kingdom of evil will be destroyed by the kingdom of God which the words and deeds of Jesus have inaugurated. Through these verses of Psalm 147, we respond with hope-filled confidence in the good news which has been announced.

Model General Intercessions

Presider: Our God heals us of all ills and overcomes any evil so that we may know the purpose for which Jesus has come. Therefore, let us speak our prayers of need with confidence.

Response:

Lord, hear our prayer.

Cantor:

we pray to the Lord,

That the Church may remember the purpose for which Jesus has come, and be faithful in preaching the good news of the time of fulfillment . . . [pause]

That Christians of the world may remember the purpose for which Jesus has come, and overcome the forces of evil among them . . . [pause]

That those in need of healing may remember the purpose for which Jesus has come, and be open to his approach . . . [pause]

That our community here gathered may remember the purpose for which Jesus has come, and reach out in service to others . . . [pause]

Presider: O healing God, you include all in your kingdom: hear our prayers of need that we might better serve you in one another. We pray through Jesus Christ our Lord. **Amen.**

ALTERNATIVE OPENING PRAYER

Let us pray

Pause for silent prayer

In faith and love we ask you, Father,
to watch over your family gathered
   here.
In your mercy and loving kindness
no thought of ours is left unguarded,
no tear unheeded, no joy unnoticed.
Through the prayer of Jesus
may the blessings promised to the poor
   in spirit
lead us to the treasures of your heavenly
   kingdom.
We ask this in the name of Jesus the
   Lord. **Amen.**

RESPONSORIAL PSALM
[Ps 147:1-2, 3-4, 5-6]

℟. (cf. 3a) Praise the Lord, who heals the brokenhearted.
   or:
℟. Alleluia.

Praise the LORD, for he is good;
   sing praise to our God, for he is
      gracious;
   it is fitting to praise him.
The LORD rebuilds Jerusalem;
   the dispersed of Israel he gathers.

℟. Praise the Lord, who heals the brokenhearted.
   or:
℟. Alleluia.

He heals the brokenhearted
   and binds up their wounds.
He tells the number of the stars;
   he calls each by name.

℟. Praise the Lord, who heals the brokenhearted.
   or:
℟. Alleluia.

Great is our Lord and mighty in power;
   to his wisdom there is no limit.
The LORD sustains the lowly;
   the wicked he casts to the ground.

℟. Praise the Lord, who heals the brokenhearted.
   or:
℟. Alleluia.

FIRST READING
[Job 7:1-4, 6-7]

Job spoke, saying:
Is not man's life on earth a drudgery?
  Are not his days those of hirelings?
He is a slave who longs for the shade,
  a hireling who waits for his wages.
So I have been assigned months of
    misery,
  and troubled nights have been
    allotted to me.
If in bed I say, "When shall I arise?"
  then the night drags on;
  I am filled with restlessness until the
    dawn.
My days are swifter than a weaver's
    shuttle;
  they come to an end without hope.
Remember that my life is like the wind;
  I shall not see happiness again.

SECOND READING
[1 Cor 9:16-19, 22-23]

Brothers and sisters:
If I preach the gospel, this is no reason
    for me to boast,
  for an obligation has been imposed on
    me,
  and woe to me if I do not preach it!
If I do so willingly, I have a recompense,
  but if unwillingly, then I have been
    entrusted with a stewardship.
What then is my recompense?
That, when I preach,
  I offer the gospel free of charge
  so as not to make full use of my right
    in the gospel.
Although I am free in regard to all,
  I have made myself a slave to all
  so as to win over as many as possible.
To the weak I became weak, to win over
    the weak.
I have become all things to all, to save at
    least some.
All this I do for the sake of the gospel,
  so that I too may have a share in it.

Catechesis

Cantors
You need to sing this psalm with a combination of tender-heartedness for those who are suffering and confidence in the God who brings healing. How this week can you bring the good news of hope to someone who is suffering?

Choir
Your music ministry announces the good news of the kingdom of God in many ways: through the community you build with one another, through the willing service you offer the parish, through the prayerfulness with which you lead the assembly's singing. In your prayer at the end of rehearsal this week, thank God for these graces and pray for continued fidelity.

Music Directors
Fred Pratt Green's text "When Jesus Came Preaching" [RS, W3] fits the import of this Sunday's Gospel well, connecting Jesus' mission with our own as his disciples. This hymn could be used either as entrance or recessional. Or you might use it in both places, singing it as the entrance hymn, then playing an instrumental improvisation on its tune as the recessional.

Howard S. Olson's text "Good News" [LMGM, RS] uses an Ethiopian tune with refrain. The verses tell the story of Jesus' preaching, his conflict with the elders, his death on the cross. The refrain relates the good news to the healing of broken hearts. This hymn would fit the presentation of gifts, or it could be sung by the choir alone as a prelude. Keep the verses light to maintain the ballad-like quality of the tune.

Liturgy Committee
The strength of God is especially needed at times of illness. How often does your parish offer a communal celebration of the sacrament of the sick for your ill parishioners? Do you connect taking Communion to the ill and homebound with Jesus' healing ministry?

Mark's Gospel tends to cluster material; the Gospel pericopes (selections) from the fifth through the eighth Sundays in Ordinary Time in year B all include healing stories. These are not mere repetitions, but each Sunday these healing stories move you deeper into Mark's overall agenda: to announce the inauguration of God's kingdom. Look each week for what is new in the readings that furthers your understanding of the establishment of God's reign.

A note on liturgical color: All of these Sundays in Ordinary Time use the color green, which is the color of the growing season and is to remind you of life. The liturgical color green signifies your growing in the life of Christ.

FEBRUARY 6, 2000

Sixth Sunday in Ordinary Time

FAITH-SHARING
- How are you unclean?
- Who are the unclean around you?
- Do you risk to touch them?
- Are you an agent for restoration?
- What is it that should banish one from the community?
- What must be accomplished in order to overcome all things that alienate?

PRESIDERS
In the midst of many demands, how might you set aside truly sufficient time to go "outside in deserted places" so that you can keep the reign of God in perspective?

DEACONS
Do you choose those whom you wish to serve, or are you willing to reach out to the truly marginalized?

HOSPITALITY MINISTERS
What are the ways in which your ministry is truly one of inclusion?

MUSIC MINISTERS
One of the restorations the leper in this Sunday's Gospel experiences is that of his being able to return to the worship of the community. How does your music ministry invite people to greater participation in worship?

ALTAR MINISTERS
"Moved with pity, [Jesus] stretched out his hand, [and] touched him . . ." Pity or compassion was the attitude that motivated Jesus' action. How might your service be different when it is motivated by compassion and sensitivity to what needs to be done?

LECTORS
The healed leper proclaimed the event of his healing freely, making the story public. What healing or good news might you share with another as a means of proclaiming the reign of God is at hand?

EUCHARISTIC MINISTERS
Jesus *wills* your healing. And this healing brings those marginalized back into communion with others. Recognize the marginalized in your family, workplace, neighborhood. What kind of touch is necessary to bridge them with the larger community?

Spirituality

Reflecting on the Gospel

Even today, when leprosy isn't a common disease in most of the world, it still elicits repulsion in us. In Scripture, leprosy referred to any number of skin diseases, but no matter which, the result was the same: exclusion from the community. In a purely physical sense, this was bad enough for it meant isolation and alienation. Jewish law, however, added a further demoralizing expulsion. Because one afflicted with leprosy was ritually unclean or impure, he or she was forbidden participation in community worship. The leper, therefore, was not only cut off from family and friends, but also cut off from worship—giving the impression of being cut off from God!

Imagine the sense of alienation and isolation that drives this leper to kneel before Jesus (a posture of submission) and *beg* to be made clean. Jesus responds to this outpouring of emotion with deep feelings of his own ("Moved with pity") and then does the unimaginable: he reaches out and *touches* the leper. This *touch* must have required great compassion on the part of Jesus, so much so that it took precedence over the law and Jesus' own risk of ritual impurity. The leper is healed and then admonished to show himself to the priest, in fulfillment of the law, in order to regain ritual purity and be restored to the worship of the community.

The final verses of the Gospel put this healing episode into an even broader context than the good fortune of the leper who is cleansed and restored to community and worship. In spite of Jesus' "stern warning" to tell no one, the man can't contain the good news but instead proclaims what has happened to him: he was unclean, and now he is clean; he was alienated, and now he is restored; he was an isolated individual, and now he is once again a member of the community. The conviction of his preaching must have had its effect, because Jesus could not "enter a town openly" and "people kept coming to him from everywhere."

The leper is healed of isolation, alienation, and ritual impurity. This summarizes for us what it is that Jesus truly does will; that is, an inauguration of the reign of God such that *everyone* is included. Membership in the community and ritual purity have to do with right relationships with God and each other. God pushes no one away from membership in the kingdom but instead God acts upon us so that we are included. *That* is good news.

Living the Paschal Mystery

Each of us at certain times in our lives experiences isolation and alienation from loved ones and God like that of the leper in this Gospel. Through Jesus' touch the Paschal Mystery is revealed to us. Death is transformed into life, the ultimate isolation of the cross becomes the ultimate restoration of the resurrection. We participate in this Paschal Mystery both by opening ourselves to the restoring touch of Jesus and by offering his restoring touch to the most alienated among us.

Our own surrender (humble submission) to God's will by reaching out to the alienated and isolated ones around us brings about God's kingdom. Like the leper, we can't keep still, but must preach.

FEBRUARY 13, 2000

GOSPEL [Mark 1:40-45; L77B]

A leper came to Jesus and kneeling down begged him and said, "If you wish, you can make me clean." Moved with pity, he stretched out his hand, touched him, and said to him, "I do will it. Be made clean." The leprosy left him immediately, and he was made clean. Then, warning him sternly, he dismissed him at once.

He said to him, "See that you tell no one anything, but go, show yourself to the priest and offer for your cleansing what Moses prescribed; that will be proof for them."

The man went away and began to publicize the whole matter. He spread the report abroad so that it was impossible for Jesus to enter a town openly. He remained outside in deserted places, and people kept coming to him from everywhere.

Working with the Word

Key words and phrases from the Gospel: [unclean], clean, moved with pity, I do will it, touched

Connecting to the first reading: The selection from Leviticus outlines the physical results of leprosy: rent garments, bare head, beard muffled, crying out "unclean," dwelling apart. In the Gospel Jesus goes contrary to the law in order to heal the isolation and alienation. When Jesus says "I do will it," he is expressing more than a desire to heal. He is also stating the purpose for which he has come: the inauguration of the reign of God.

Connecting to the biblical culture: Leprosy in the Bible was a descriptive term that referred to a broad range of skin diseases and afflictions, not to what we now call Hansen's disease. Diagnosis with leprosy made one "unclean," which in this case was a ritual, not a moral, condition. Uncleanness was a physical condition that could come about naturally (e.g., seminal or menstrual discharge, childbirth, certain diseases), or it could be the result of deliberate acts (e.g., sexual transgression, idolatrous practices, homicide). Uncleanness could be passed on to others through contact or proximate contact; it could be washed away by bathing or laundering, and other rites.

Exegetical points: The effects of the diagnosis of leprosy with its declaration of unclean were devastating. In addition to the personal experience of *physical* impairment and the accompanying *psychological* diminishment, there were *social* and *religious* consequences as well. A leprous/unclean person was cut off socially and forced to live apart from the community (to prevent spreading impurity), and was prohibited from participating in religious rites (to avoid polluting sacred space with one's uncleanness). When Jesus heals the leper, then, he addresses far more than the man's physical condition. Jesus' healing touch restores the man's physical wholeness, and with it his psychological sense of well-being; but he also makes it possible for the man to rejoin the community and to resume a life of worship and praise.

To the point: "I do will it." The response last week to Jesus' healing was restoration to service (Simon's mother-in-law); this week it is restoration to worship (go and offer the sacrifice prescribed).

Celebration

Model Penitential Rite

Presider: God calls forth each of us from our diverse places in order to fashion us into a community. Let us surrender ourselves to God's compassionate touch . . . [pause]

> Lord Jesus, you touch us when we are isolated and alienated: Lord . . .
> Christ Jesus, you will that we all be restored to your community of love: Christ . . .
> Lord Jesus, you send us to spread the good news of your reign: Lord . . .

Responsorial Psalm

"I turn to you, Lord, in time of trouble, and you fill me with the joy of salvation." In this Sunday's Gospel the leper begs, "If you will to do so, you can cure me." Jesus' immediate answer is, "I do will it." He touches the leper, heals him, and restores him to community. Jesus could heal the man because the man, humble about himself, approaches to ask for help. The responsorial psalm repeats the gesture of this leper. In singing it we kneel before God, honest about our sinfulness, and rise joyfully in the knowledge of our salvation.

Model General Intercessions

Presider: Let us confidently place our needs before our God who heals and restores.

Response:

Lord, hear our prayer.

Cantor:

we pray to the Lord,

That members of the Church, the community of Christ, may be moved to pity and include all who are isolated and alienated . . . [pause]

That world leaders do will that all people be treated with dignity and equality . . . [pause]

That those who are isolated and alienated may experience a healing touch and be restored to family and community . . . [pause]

That this assembly may have the courage to preach and live the good news of inclusion of everyone in God's kingdom . . . [pause]

Presider: O God of healing, you hear our every cry for cleansing and restoration: hear our prayers today that all people might enjoy the company of the community of your saints. We pray through Jesus Christ our Lord. **Amen.**

ALTERNATIVE OPENING PRAYER
Let us pray

Pause for silent prayer

Father in heaven,
the loving plan of your wisdom took flesh in Jesus Christ,
and changed mankind's history
by his command of perfect love.
May our fulfillment of his command reflect your wisdom
and bring your salvation to the ends of the earth.
We ask this through Christ our Lord.
Amen.

RESPONSORIAL PSALM
[Ps 32:1-2, 5, 11]

℟. (7) I turn to you, Lord, in time of trouble, and you fill me with the joy of salvation.

Blessed is he whose fault is taken away,
 whose sin is covered.
Blessed the man to whom the LORD imputes not guilt,
 in whose spirit there is no guile.

℟. I turn to you, Lord, in time of trouble, and you fill me with the joy of salvation.

Then I acknowledged my sin to you,
 my guilt I covered not.
I said, "I confess my faults to the LORD,"
 and you took away the guilt of my sin.

℟. I turn to you, Lord, in time of trouble, and you fill me with the joy of salvation.

Be glad in the LORD and rejoice, you just;
 exult, all you upright of heart.

℟. I turn to you, Lord, in time of trouble, and you fill me with the joy of salvation.

FIRST READING
[Lev 13:1-2, 44-46]

The LORD said to Moses and Aaron,
"If someone has on his skin a scab or
  pustule or blotch
 which appears to be the sore of
  leprosy,
 he shall be brought to Aaron, the
  priest,
 or to one of the priests among his
  descendants.
If the man is leprous and unclean,
 the priest shall declare him unclean
 by reason of the sore on his head.

"The one who bears the sore of leprosy
 shall keep his garments rent and his
  head bare,
 and shall muffle his beard;
 he shall cry out, 'Unclean, unclean!'
As long as the sore is on him he shall
  declare himself unclean,
 since he is in fact unclean.
He shall dwell apart, making his abode
 outside the camp."

SECOND READING
[1 Cor 10:31–11:1]

Brothers and sisters,
whether you eat or drink, or whatever
  you do,
 do everything for the glory of God.
Avoid giving offense, whether to the
  Jews or Greeks or
 the church of God,
 just as I try to please everyone in
  every way,
 not seeking my own benefit but that
  of the many,
 that they may be saved.
Be imitators of me, as I am of Christ.

Catechesis

Cantors
In preparing to sing this psalm, reflect on a time in your life when you experienced the joy of being reconnected to the other person(s) in some broken relationship. Where was the grace of God evident? Know that in singing this psalm you proclaim, as the leper did, what you have come to believe about the saving power of God.

Choir
Every group inevitably experiences tensions among the members. How do you handle this as a choir? Do you have any "in group/out group" dynamics which need to be examined?

Music Directors
Brian Wren's "I Come with Joy" [CBW3, RS, W3, WC] speaks of the "joy" of being "forgiven, loved, and free" and of the Eucharistic community in which "strangers are friends." The text intimates the relationship between salvation and community as the "I" of verses 1 and 2 becomes the "us" of verses 3 to 5. Set to the familiar American tune LAND OF REST, this hymn could be used either for the entrance hymn or for a hymn of thanksgiving after Communion.

One of the most misunderstood musical elements in the Eucharistic rite concerns the option of a song after Communion. Popularly called the "Communion meditation," it is most often sung by either the choir alone or a soloist. The *General Instruction of the Roman Missal* (no. 56j), however, directs that after Communion "a hymn, psalm, or other song of praise may be sung by the entire congregation." This directive raises a whole new understanding of the purpose of a song after Communion. First, it is to be a hymn of praise rather than a meditation. Second, it is to be sung by the entire assembly. In other words, this hymn serves a *liturgical* rather than a *devotional* function. Through it the assembly expresses together their gratitude at having been fed at the table of the Lord.

Liturgy Committee
The Gospel announces the inauguration of God's kingdom—a reign of healing and inclusion. How might your efforts in this regard direct the assembly to the profundity and richness of what you do at Eucharist?

From early on, the Church responded to apostates (those who had alienated themselves from the community by denying the faith, especially during times of persecution) with charity. The Order of Penitents arose as a way to gracefully restore members. Some of its practices parallel the Levitical requirements for lepers: rend their garments, remain isolated from the community. It was a joyous occasion on Holy Thursday when the penitents were restored to community membership so they could participate in the Lord's Supper that evening. The sacrament of penance has tended to focus on individual guilt rather than on community restoration. Everyone needs to see again the relationship of the sacrament of penance to baptism and Eucharist.

FEBRUARY 13, 2000

Seventh Sunday in Ordinary Time

FAITH-SHARING
- How has forgiveness enriched your life? In giving it? Receiving it?
- How have you been paralyzed by your withholding of forgiveness?
- How are forgiveness and reconciliation continuing manifestations of the presence of God's kingdom in your midst?
- What needs forgiving?
- How is forgiveness a necessary attitude for the true disciple of Jesus?

PRESIDERS
Besides the sacrament of penance, what are other ways that you announce the good news of forgiveness to people? How could your own experience of being forgiven shape your homily for this Sunday?

DEACONS
Four men carried the paralytic to Jesus. "Jesus saw *their* faith" and forgave the man's sins. Whom do you need to carry—in prayer, in life—to Jesus for healing and forgiveness? Is *your* faith sufficient to bring about God's healing and forgiving word?

MUSIC MINISTERS
How do you respond when your musical expectations are not met? Can you be forgiving, merciful, understanding of the human condition?

HOSPITALITY MINISTERS
How is forgiveness related to an attitude of true hospitality?

ALTAR MINISTERS
In this Sunday's Gospel, the people are filled with awe: "We have never seen anything like this." How might the awe of your being forgiving have an impact on your service at the altar-table?

LECTORS
How might the practice of forgiving those around you (home, work, leisure) lead you to better proclaim God's good news of salvation?

EUCHARISTIC MINISTERS
How does forgiveness help you understand more deeply the meaning of the "body of Christ"?

Spirituality

Reflecting on the Gospel

This Sunday's Gospel serves well Mark's overall agenda of revealing who Jesus is. He is the one who, by word and deed, announces the good news of the kingdom. In him, words and deeds together communicate, simultaneously say that God is doing something new! And in this Gospel story, what's the new that is springing forth? Forgiveness of sins.

The scene is this: Jesus returns "home" to Capernaum; news spreads; a crowd gathers; Jesus preaches to them. Four men bring to Jesus a paralytic lying on a mat. The crowd is large; ingenious and persistent, the men lower the paralytic through the roof into Jesus' presence. Upon seeing the paralytic, Jesus responds in a most unusual way. Rather than reaching out to him, taking him by the hand, and lifting him up off the mat (all gestures which we would expect from Jesus because we have seen him do these in previous Sundays' Gospels), Jesus *says* to the paralytic "your sins are forgiven."

To this, the scribes who are sitting there respond with anger. As the first reading from Isaiah indicates, the scribes knew full well that it is only God who can forgive sins. For Jesus to claim this authority for himself is blasphemy (claiming to be God). Jesus goes on to validate his *words* of forgiveness by *healing* the man's paralysis. Truly, his words and his deeds are integrated and proclaim loudly that Jesus is exactly who he will later show himself to be on the cross, the Son of God.

The paralytic's response is recorded ("went away in the sight of everyone"), as is the crowd's ("astounded and glorified God"). What is our response? Why do we gather Sunday after Sunday to hear these words and to commune at the table of the Lord? Do we *truly* hear the good news proclaimed: that we are forgiven, healed, and united with one another in a way possible only because of the power of God?

Living the Paschal Mystery

Forgiveness comes from God, but it does require something from us. The four men in this Gospel story *acted* to bring the paralytic to Jesus. They *overcame* obstacles to reach him, motivated by the expectation that Jesus would do what he had done for so many others. They had faith in Jesus' power and they acted on this faith.

This kind of faith demands dying. We must die to hanging onto our infirmities, to excuses for why we are powerless to act, to paralysis in face of obstacles to healing and forgiveness. When we embrace this kind of dying, we place ourselves in the presence of Jesus, and there discover the resurrection.

The healings of Jesus don't merely expel demons or cure infirmities; they touch the deepest part of our woundedness. Forgiveness of sins communicates a depth of healing between us and God, within ourselves, between ourselves and one another that we cannot achieve by our own power. Such forgiveness brings a healing and freedom—we can walk now!

FEBRUARY 20, 2000

GOSPEL [Mark 2:1-12; L80B]

When Jesus returned to Capernaum after some days, it became known that he was at home. Many gathered together so that there was no longer room for them, not even around the door, and he preached the word to them. They came bringing to him a paralytic carried by four men. Unable to get near Jesus because of the crowd, they opened up the roof above him. After they had broken through, they let down the mat on which the paralytic was lying. When Jesus saw their faith, he said to the paralytic, "Child, your sins are forgiven." Now some of the scribes were sitting there asking themselves, "Why does this man speak that way? He is blaspheming. Who but God alone can forgive sins?" Jesus immediately knew in his mind what they were thinking to themselves, so he said, "Why are you thinking such things in your hearts? Which is easier, to say to the paralytic, 'Your sins are forgiven,' or to say, 'Rise, pick up your mat and walk'? But that you may know that the Son of Man has authority to forgive sins on earth"—he said to the paralytic, "I say to you, rise, pick up your mat, and go home." He rose, picked up his mat at once, and went away in the sight of everyone. They were all astounded and glorified God, saying, "We have never seen anything like this."

Working with the Word

Key words and phrases from the Gospel: your sins are forgiven, authority to forgive sins, in the sight of everyone, astounded and glorified God

Connecting to the Gospels of the last two Sundays: Aspects of Jesus' authority are being expanded: he heals, he casts out demons, he forgives sins. In each case, the response of discipleship is also expanded: healing ➔ service, worship; casting out demons ➔ wholeness; forgiveness ➔ witness in the sight of everyone.

Connecting to our culture: In the Hebrew Scriptures one notion of sin was "missing the mark," skewing relationships with God, self, others. For a long time in the Church, we have only considered sin in terms of omission and commission. In contemporary culture we try to place sin in a broader perspective, but in so doing have we lost any sense of sin? And with that, any sense of needing forgiveness?

Exegetical points: This passage both brings to a conclusion a series of the five healings we have been reading about since the Fourth Sunday in Ordinary Time, and introduces the first of five controversies that we hear about next.

This is the first occurrence of the title "Son of Man," which is Jesus' preferred way of referring to himself. In the Hebrew Scriptures, the title has two primary referents: (1) it is a generic reference to ordinary human beings; and (2) in some apocalyptic literature, it designates a God-appointed figure arising in the end times. Mark usually uses it in reference either to Jesus' future suffering/death and coming in glory, or to his authority, e.g., over the Sabbath or to forgive sins.

It is ironic that the authority of Jesus, which the crowd found so astonishing and refreshing on the fourth Sunday is greeted here by the scribes with accusations of blasphemy. This initial controversy features two elements that recur in the trial of Jesus: the prominent role of the scribes as accusers, and the charge of blasphemy (Mark 14:53-65). Even this early in the Gospel, Mark is laying the groundwork for the passion and death of Jesus.

To the point: The continuing unfolding of God's reign is manifested in Jesus' authority to forgive sins. What is the "new thing" of this Gospel? That Jesus forgives sins. Further, if *we* are disciples and witnesses to the good news, what does it mean for us to be a forgiving community?

Celebration

Model Penitential Rite
Presider: Jesus reveals to us that the kingdom of God is about forgiveness and healing. Let us reflect on our need for forgiveness and God's healing word . . . [pause]

    Lord Jesus, you preach the good news of healing: Lord . . .
    Christ Jesus, you forgive our weakness and sins: Christ . . .
    Lord Jesus, your deeds witness to the authority of your words: Lord . . .

Responsorial Psalm
"Lord, heal my soul, for I have sinned against you."
The reading from Isaiah tells us that God does something new: wipes out our offenses. In the Gospel reading Jesus enacts this truth about God by forgiving the sins of the paralytic. The paralytic, healed in spirit and in body, walks into the midst of the people who marvel at what they see. This Sunday's psalm reminds us that it is this mercy of God which sustains us. But it also invites us to reflect on the meaning of our discipleship. Do we, like Jesus, reach out to those in need of healing?

Model General Intercessions
Presider: God has the authority to heal and forgive, and to answer our prayers. And so we pray with confidence.

Response: Lord, hear our prayer.

Cantor: we pray to the Lord,

May all the people of God have the courage to utter the words, "you are forgiven" . . . [pause]

May the leaders of nations use their authority to bring about forgiveness and reconciliation . . . [pause]

May those who cannot forgive, forgive . . . [pause] . . . and may those who need forgiveness find forgiveness . . . [pause]

May our Christian community be quick to forgive each other and heal all injuries . . . [pause]

Presider: O God, you have the authority to heal and forgive: hear these our prayers that we might witness to the coming of your kingdom by our forgiving one another. We pray through Jesus Christ. **Amen**

OPENING PRAYER
Let us pray

Pause for silent prayer

Father,
keep before us the wisdom and love
you have revealed in your Son.
Help us to be like him
in word and deed,
for he lives and reigns with you and the
    Holy Spirit,
one God, for ever and ever. **Amen.**

RESPONSORIAL PSALM
[Ps 41:2-3, 4-5, 13-14]

℟. (5b) Lord, heal my soul, for I have sinned against you.

Blessed is the one who has regard for
    the lowly and the poor;
    in the day of misfortune the Lord will
        deliver him.
The Lord will keep and preserve him;
    and make him blessed on earth,
    and not give him over to the will of
        his enemies.

℟. Lord, heal my soul, for I have sinned against you.

The Lord will help him on his sickbed,
    he will take away all his ailment
        when he is ill.
Once I said, "O Lord, have pity on me;
    heal me, though I have sinned against
        you."

℟. Lord, heal my soul, for I have sinned against you.

But because of my integrity you sustain
    me
    and let me stand before you forever.
Blessed be the Lord, the God of Israel,
    from all eternity. Amen. Amen.

℟. Lord, heal my soul, for I have sinned against you.

FIRST READING
[Isa 43:18-19, 21-22, 24b-25]

Thus says the LORD:
Remember not the events of the past,
    the things of long ago consider not;
see, I am doing something new!
    Now it springs forth, do you not
        perceive it?
In the desert I make a way,
    in the wasteland, rivers.
The people I formed for myself,
    that they might announce my praise.
Yet you did not call upon me, O Jacob,
    for you grew weary of me, O Israel.
You burdened me with your sins,
    and wearied me with your crimes.
It is I, I, who wipe out,
    for my own sake, your offenses;
    your sins I remember no more.

SECOND READING
[2 Cor 1:18-22]

Brothers and sisters:
As God is faithful,
    our word to you is not "yes" and
        "no."
For the Son of God, Jesus Christ,
    who was proclaimed to you by us,
        Silvanus and Timothy and me,
    was not "yes" and "no," but "yes" has
        been in him.
For however many are the promises of
    God, their Yes is in him;
    therefore, the Amen from us also goes
        through him to God for glory.
But the one who gives us security with
    you in Christ
    and who anointed us is God;
    he has also put his seal upon us
    and given the Spirit in our hearts as a
        first installment.

Catechesis

Cantors

In this psalm you sing about what Jesus enacts in the Gospel—that God, fully aware of our sinfulness, forgives and heals. Use the psalm refrain this week to guide your prayer. Be humble and honest about your own sinfulness. Ask for God's mercy. Then praise God for continued forgiveness.

Choir

Use the hymn "There's a Wideness in God's Mercy" for prayer at the end of rehearsal this week. Before singing it, spend a moment in silent prayer acknowledging your personal sinfulness, thanking God for forgiveness, and asking for the grace to forgive others.

Music Directors

"There's a Wideness in God's Mercy" [BB, CBW3, RS, W3, WC] speaks of the breadth of God's forgiving love and invites you to gather where "there is welcome for the sinner." You might sing it for the presentation of gifts, using a broad tempo to communicate the stretching embrace of God's mercy. Or you might sing it for the entrance, using a slightly quicker tempo to support the procession. (If, however, your presider and ministers rush this procession instead of pacing it appropriately to fit the requirement of an entrance into liturgy, save this hymn for the presentation of gifts. Rushing its tempo would destroy the power of its text.)

Liturgy Committee

Catechesis on the use of silence during liturgies would be helpful. These are not just "empty" or rest times, but they allow you to hear and respond better to the good news of God's words and sacramental deeds. How might silence improve the quality of the community's prayer? Of their living?

Sometimes you can best hear God's good news and a word of forgiveness in the pauses for silence between words, not in a multiplicity of words themselves. It might be well to take time to review what the *General Instruction on the Roman Missal* has to say about silences during the Eucharistic liturgy (see GIRM, nos. 23, 32, 56j, 88, 121).

At times the very structure of a particular element in the ritual requires a pause for silence. (1) In the introductory rites, those assembled should be given time to recollect themselves and surrender themselves to God's action. The community needs to consider those times when they can't hear God and ask for forgiveness. (2) After the invitation to pray the opening prayer or the prayer after Communion ("Let us pray . . .") there should be a pause for the assembly to call to mind their intention and pray. What follows is really a "collect" (to use the older term) that concludes all these prayers. (3) After the announcement of an intention at the general intercessions (recall that the structure of the general intercessions proposed here is an *announcement* of intentions, not prayers directed to God), there should be a pause to allow time for the assembly's personal prayer. This is followed after all the intentions by the presider's concluding "collect" prayer.

FEBRUARY 20, 2000

Eighth Sunday in Ordinary Time

FAITH-SHARING
- How do you grow in intimacy with God, self, others?
- What are some habits of relationship—trusting your spouse, child, co-worker—that you need to change, perhaps find a whole new way of relating?
- Is your relationship with Jesus simply an old garment, or is there a transforming, fresh newness to your intimacy? What is it?
- Are you willing to be a new skin?
- What does the balance of old and new religious practices look like in your life?

PRESIDERS
How might reflecting on Jesus' intimate union with you help you balance the old and the new in your life?

DEACONS
In what ways is your diaconal service an "incarnation" of God's espousal love for the people?

HOSPITALITY MINISTERS
The psalm response states that "The Lord is kind and merciful." How might you welcome people into God's "kindness" and "mercy"?

MUSIC MINISTERS
New ways, old ways—contemporary music, or traditional? When is which music the better choice? Take some time this week to talk with others about how music of any kind is meant to support the liturgical prayer of the assembly.

ALTAR MINISTERS
Serving because it is "job" is considerably different from serving those you love. How does Jesus' love for you affect the way you serve . . . in church? in daily family life?

LECTORS
That which is "new" and "good" news is the great intimacy God shows you in Jesus. How can you proclaim the readings this Sunday so that your proclamation announces the "new" and "good" of your faith?

EUCHARISTIC MINISTERS
God's espousal love for you in Jesus transforms you. In what ways have you been changed/transformed by being a disciple? By being a Eucharistic minister? Where is the new wine of Jesus bursting forth in your life?

Spirituality

Reflecting on the Gospel

The opening lines of this Gospel set up another conflict situation for Jesus, this time between him and people who criticize his disciples for not fasting. Jesus' reply to the people, however, reveals that this Gospel is not really about fasting practices. Rather, fasting is a context for the revelation of yet another piece of the good news and of the mystery of Jesus' identity.

In response to the people, Jesus delivers two seemingly diverse "homilets." First, he gives a reason why his disciples do not fast: "the bridegroom is with them." This teaching implants some compelling clues about Jesus' identity and mission. Jesus applies to himself the metaphor of bridegroom, an image that his hearers knew the Scriptures used for God (see the first reading from the prophet Hosea). In using it Jesus implies that he is the bridegroom and that his presence is why the kingdom is at hand. Furthermore, his claim has messianic implications. In Jesus the mission of inaugurating the kingdom has begun. Jesus alludes to how this mission will work itself out when he refers to the time "when the bridegroom will be taken away." "Bridegroom" is an intimate image pointing to the close relationship we can have with Jesus and, hence, also pointing to our involvement in bringing about God's reign.

The second "homilet" concerns tension between the old and the new. Jesus uses two everyday occurrences familiar to his hearers—mending old clothes and storing new wine. Before sewing new cloth onto an old garment, we must shrink the new in order to protect the old. In order to save the new wine, we must discard the old wineskins. The text curtly concludes here, giving no further explanation of what the images of old and new mean. We are drawn, then, to interpret the second "homilet" in light of the first.

Fasting belonged to the old dispensation of religious practices. Jesus' hint about fasting "on that day" suggests that fasting is important and that there are appropriate times for it. Nevertheless, with the coming of Jesus, the bridegroom, a new dispensation has been inaugurated, one in which illnesses are healed, demons are thrown out, and sins are forgiven. What is called for now is not a fast, but an embracing of this new reign of God. Something new is here, and it comes in terms of an intimacy between God and humankind that is far beyond the reckoning of any human imagining.

Living the Paschal Mystery

The intimacy with Jesus that is the fruit of our baptism—we are the body of Christ—requires a whole new way of conceiving of God and being in relationship with others. The "old" revelation of God as bridegroom is deepened and re-"newed" in the revelation of Jesus: our bridegroom is now God-flesh-and-bones-before-us. The intimacy of God's espousal relationship moves from transcendence to incarnational immanence. Such nearness to God has an impact on how we relate with each other: ". . . whatever you did for one of these least brothers [or sisters] of mine, you did for me" (Matt 25:40).

FEBRUARY 27, 2000

GOSPEL [Mark 2:18-22; L83B]

The disciples of John and of the Pharisees were accustomed to fast. People came to him and objected, "Why do the disciples of John and the disciples of the Pharisees fast, but your disciples do not fast?" Jesus answered them, "Can the wedding guests fast while the bridegroom is with them? As long as they have the bridegroom with them they cannot fast. But the days will come when the bridegroom is taken away from them, and then they will fast on that day. No one sews a piece of unshrunken cloth on an old cloak. If he does, its fullness pulls away, the new from the old, and the tear gets worse. Likewise, no one pours new wine into old wineskins. Otherwise, the wine will burst the skins, and both the wine and the skins are ruined. Rather, new wine is poured into fresh wineskins."

Working with the Word

Key words and phrases from the Gospel: bridegroom, new, old

Connecting to the first reading: In spite of the fact that there is much written about fasting in the Hebrew Scriptures, the first reading from Hosea does not focus on fasting and so provides the clue that this Gospel isn't really about fasting but about the presence of the bridegroom. Now Jesus implies that he is the bridegroom, giving us a further hint about his identity.

Connecting to the culture: Contemporaries of Jesus would have known that in their Scriptures God was the bridegroom. What is new here, and unexpected, is Jesus' claim to be the bridegroom. By using this imagery, Mark suggests that the new kind of discipleship isn't only teacher/student or master/disciple, but is also a discipleship of intimacy and mutuality.

Exegetical points: The Lectionary skips Mark 2:13-17 in which Jesus calls Levi, the tax collector, and then has dinner in his house. Some scribes and Pharisees object that Jesus eats with tax collectors and sinners, to which Jesus makes his famous reply, "Those who are well do not need a physician, but the sick do. I did not come to call the righteous but sinners." This controversy over eating with sinners leads directly into this Sunday's controversy about fasting.

The two images Jesus uses move in opposite directions. The image of the patch on a garment focuses on what is done to save the old. The image of new wine skin for the new wine puts the focus on keeping what is new. Mark concludes with a ringing endorsement of the new: "new wine is poured into fresh wineskins." Matthew, in his appeal to both Jews and Christians, wants to preserve both. Luke, with his historical interests, concludes "the old is good." This is a wonderful example of how the Gospel is adapted to the pastoral needs of each local community.

To the point: Mark continues to unfold a richer understanding of discipleship, namely, we have an espousal relationship with God in Jesus that transforms us! Its manifestations include righteousness, justice, love, mercy, fidelity (see the first reading). This is what is new in the Gospel.

Celebration

Model Penitential Rite

Presider: The bridegroom of today's Gospel calls us to a special intimacy with him and each other. We pause to recognize the divine presence and open ourselves to whatever newness God is offering . . . [pause]

> Lord Jesus, you are the bridegroom present among us: Lord . . .
> Christ Jesus, you call us to intimate relationship with you and each other: Christ . . .
> Lord Jesus, you remind us to respect the old as we embrace the new: Lord . . .

Responsorial Psalm

"The Lord is kind and merciful."

The first reading from Hosea assures us that God longs to be one with us so deeply that God can express it only in spousal terms. God's relationship with us is both personal and permanent. Through it we come to learn who God is. The psalm includes what this knowing is about: God's kindness and mercy, compassion and forgiveness. The good news which Jesus announces in the Gospel is that this God who desires such intimacy with us is here in him. Old ways of relating do not count, for a new way is here.

Model General Intercessions

Presider: Since our God desires intimacy with us, we are confident that our needs are heard. And so we pray.

Response:

(musical notation: Lord, hear our prayer.)

Cantor:

(musical notation: we pray to the Lord,)

That the Church may more fully open herself to the love offered by her bridegroom, Christ . . . [pause]

That all peoples of the world may work toward a community of love, mercy, and peace . . . [pause]

That those who suffer deep anguish over the old and the new may find balance in Jesus our bridegroom . . . [pause]

That we here gathered may find a fresh newness to our relationships . . . [pause]

Presider: O loving God, you call all people to be your very own and hold them to yourself with mercy and fidelity: hear these our prayers that we may more fittingly be your loving people. We pray through Jesus Christ our Lord. **Amen.**

ALTERNATIVE OPENING PRAYER

Let us pray
  [that the peace of Christ may find welcome in the world]

Pause for silent prayer

Father in heaven,
form in us the likeness of your Son
and deepen his life within us.
Send us as witnesses of gospel joy
into a world of fragile peace and broken promises.
Touch the hearts of all men with your love
that they in turn may love one another.
We ask this through Christ our Lord.
Amen.

RESPONSORIAL PSALM
[Ps 103:1-2, 3-4, 8, 10, 12-13]

℟. (8a) The Lord is kind and merciful.

Bless the LORD, O my soul;
  and all my being, bless his holy name.
Bless the LORD, O my soul,
  and forget not all his benefits.

℟. The Lord is kind and merciful.

He pardons all your iniquities,
  heals all your ills.
He redeems your life from destruction,
  crowns you with kindness and compassion.

℟. The Lord is kind and merciful.

Merciful and gracious is the LORD,
  slow to anger and abounding in kindness.
Not according to our sins does he deal with us,
  nor does he requite us according to our crimes.

℟. The Lord is kind and merciful.

As far as the east is from the west,
  so far has he put our transgressions from us.
As a father has compassion on his children,
  so the LORD has compassion on those who fear him.

℟. The Lord is kind and merciful.

FIRST READING
[Hos 2:16b, 17b, 21-22]

Thus says the LORD:
I will lead her into the desert
   and speak to her heart.
She shall respond there as in the days of
   her youth,
   when she came up from the land of
     Egypt.
I will espouse you to me forever:
   I will espouse you in right and in
     justice,
   in love and in mercy;
I will espouse you in fidelity,
   and you shall know the Lord.

SECOND READING
[2 Cor 3:1b-6]

Brothers and sisters:
Do we need, as some do,
   letters of recommendation to you or
     from you?
You are our letter, written on our hearts,
   known and read by all,
   shown to be a letter of Christ
     ministered by us,
   written not in ink but by the Spirit of
     the living God,
   not on tablets of stone but on tablets
     that are hearts of flesh.

Such confidence we have through Christ
   toward God.
Not that of ourselves we are qualified
   to take credit for anything as coming
     from us;
   rather, our qualification comes from
     God,
   who has indeed qualified us as
     ministers of a new covenant,
   not of letter but of spirit;
   for the letter brings death, but the
     Spirit gives life.

Catechesis

Cantors
This Sunday you will sing about the kindness and mercy of God. As you prepare, reflect on where in your life you have experienced this mercy. Pray for all people that they may come to know this God who is so compassionate.

Choir
Your regular interaction with one another as a choir is an opportunity to keep growing in relationships. What new ways of relating are you developing? Where do you need to examine your ways of relating?

Music Directors
Each procession in the Eucharistic liturgy has a different purpose. When choosing music, let what you select fit each purpose.

The entrance procession is meant to help the assembly "move" into the liturgy. To support this movement, choose music with a strong processional feel such as "God Is Here! As We His People" [RS, W3, WC] or the responsorial style "Out of Darkness" [BB, G2].

The procession with the gifts is meant to be practical, to get the bread and wine to the altar. Choose music with a gentler rhythm and mood. When possible, select a text which correlates with the Gospel so that the hymn can help the assembly assimilate the Word as well as move ritually from Word to Eucharist.

The Communion procession celebrates our coming to the table of the Lord and our oneness in the Body of Christ. Choose music which expresses joy, uplift, fullness in Christ, for example, "I Received the Living God" [RS, W3, WC] or any of the settings of "Take and Eat."

Because the recessional hymn is not really part of the rite, it can be omitted. It might be good sometimes to use a choir or instrumental piece to accompany the assembly's departure.

Liturgy Committee
Controversies about the "old" liturgy and the "new" liturgy are probably going to be around for a long time yet. Rather than something that frightens or daunts you, it might help to understand this as a natural part of your growing into new life. How do the old and new balance in your parish? Family? Personal life?

Fridays have traditionally been a day of fasting as a way to commemorate the cross. For centuries that fasting was specified by abstinence—no meat. Pope Paul VI relaxed the abstinence requirement, but Fridays are still recommended as days of fasting and penance. You might want to revisit your observance of Friday, especially relating your religious practices to your participation in the Bridegroom's messianic banquet at the Sunday Eucharist. The Friday fast is related to Sunday as Good Friday is to Easter. The one-hour Communion fast has a similar purpose: to empty yourselves and prepare yourselves for being fed on such lavish food.

FEBRUARY 27, 2000

Ninth Sunday in Ordinary Time

FAITH-SHARING
- From what are *you* being delivered?
- How are you disciples/instruments of deliverance for others?
- How is deliverance a mystery that ushers you into the greatest mystery of all, the Paschal Mystery?
- What level of law do you observe? literal? its deepest meaning?

PRESIDERS
Multiple liturgies (sometimes even miles apart) with numerous parish activities on a weekend can leave you scattered and wearied. In the midst of this reality, how does God's deliverance come to you? How do you preserve any semblance of Sunday rest and holiness for yourself?

DEACONS
Your service enfleshes God's deliverance for the people. To whom have you brought deliverance this week? How does this have an impact on your Sunday observance?

HOSPITALITY MINISTERS
How can your hospitality prepare those who gather for the "holiness" and "rest" of Sunday?

MUSIC MINISTERS
Sunday is often your biggest workday. You can observe its rest even while doing your ministry by remembering that your music-making is part of the celebration of God's saving actions. How might you rest in God's deliverance even while you work?

ALTAR MINISTERS
In the midst of all the weekend activities, how do you keep Sunday holy? How does your service around the altar communicate the holiness of the day?

LECTORS
What are some of God's mighty deeds of deliverance in your life? How can remembering these affect your proclamation of the good news—in daily life, in the liturgy?

EUCHARISTIC MINISTERS
Jesus gave his Body and Blood so that you could be delivered from all kinds of bondage. Are you willing to give of yourself to assist those around you? Do you place limits on your self-giving? Are you able to see how these choices affect your Eucharistic ministry?

Spirituality

Reflecting on the Gospel

Just as the controversy in last Sunday's Gospel didn't ultimately concern the question of fasting, neither is the controversy in this Sunday's Gospel about Sabbath law and practices but is really about who Jesus is and his mission.

The first reading from Deuteronomy gives us a clue about the reason for Sabbath (and Sunday) observance. The beginning of the reading refers to the command (from the Decalogue or Ten Commandments) to keep this day holy. Then the ancient writer goes on to say that weekly rest is commanded because Israel was "once a slave in Egypt" and it was God's "strong hand and outstretched arm" that delivered them from slavery to freedom in the Promised Land. The motive for the holiness and rest of this day, then, derives from the action of a strong and caring God who delivered Israel from oppression. To keep this day of the week holy by resting is to acknowledge God's mighty acts of salvation. This cuts to the very core of who Israel understands itself to be: the people whom God has chosen and delivered. No wonder, then, the Pharisees are so outraged at Jesus' disciples' picking grain on the Sabbath. Fidelity to Sabbath observance was central to Israel's expression of its identity as the people saved by God.

The controversy is heightened and made even more explicit in the second part of the Gospel where Jesus pushes the manner of keeping the Law even further. There is no problem with saving a life on the Sabbath, a tradition long attested to in the rabbinic literature. But Jesus calls forward a man whose withered hand is clearly not a life-threatening malady. Angry and grieved at the Pharisees' "hardness of heart," Jesus delivers the man from his infirmity. With this act, Jesus raises the issue of observance of Law vs. the meaning of the Law, and the controversy between himself and the leading Jews moves to open hostility . . . they begin to plot how to put him to death. It's the hard heart that watches and schemes; the grieving heart longs to bring deliverance—and this longing for deliverance and action to bring it about manifest the profoundest understanding of Sabbath rest.

Living the Paschal Mystery

This Sunday's Gospel is one of the most practical and challenging of all the year because it hits us exactly where most of us need to spend some time reflecting and, probably, make some changes in our lives. Why do we keep Sunday as the Lord's day, and why is it a day of rest?

Is not our Sunday rest also a deliverance (as Sabbath is an observance of the Hebrew's deliverance)? From what are *we* delivered? What are God's great deeds of deliverance in our lives? Jesus is the one who surrendered himself to the cross, was raised, and gave his Body and Blood for our salvation. Our weekly celebration of Eucharist and observance of rest on Sunday make present and call us continually to enter into the Paschal Mystery, the mystery of *our* deliverance. Just as God delivered Israel, so Jesus is the one who delivers us and saves us. How well we keep our Sunday celebration and rest is one of the most important ways we surrender ourselves in discipleship.

GOSPEL [Mark 2:23–3:6; L86B]

As Jesus was passing through a field of grain on the sabbath, his disciples began to make a path while picking the heads of grain. At this the Pharisees said to him, "Look, why are they doing what is unlawful on the sabbath?" He said to them, "Have you never read what David did when he was in need and he and his companions were hungry? How he went into the house of God when Abiathar was high priest and ate the bread of offering that only the priests could lawfully eat, and shared it with his companions?" Then he said to them, "The sabbath was made for man, not man for the sabbath. That is why the Son of Man is lord even of the sabbath."

Again he entered the synagogue. There was a man there who had a withered hand. They watched him closely to see if he would cure him on the sabbath so that they might accuse him. He said to the man with the withered hand, "Come up here before us." Then he said to them, "Is it lawful to do good on the sabbath rather than to do evil, to save life rather than to destroy it?" But they remained silent. Looking around at them with anger and grieved at their hardness of heart, he said to the man, "Stretch out your hand." He stretched it out and his hand was restored. The Pharisees went out and immediately took counsel with the Herodians against him to put him to death.

Working with the Word

Key words and phrases from the Gospel: Sabbath, Is it lawful?, hardness of heart, put him to death

Connecting to the first reading: The motive for Sabbath observance is God's deliverance of Israel from bondage. The Jewish understanding of Sabbath is absolutely *central* to their religious expression because it is tied into the Exodus event. Jesus *enacts* the meaning of Sabbath by his deliverance of the man with the withered hand.

Connecting to the culture: We must move our understanding of Sunday observance beyond just attending Mass to keeping a day commemorating God's saving deeds *for us*.

Exegetical points: Jesus' apparent disregard for the Sabbath is a major factor that leads to his death, which is explicitly mentioned for the first time at the conclusion of this Gospel: the Pharisees "took counsel with the Herodians against him to put him to death."

When Jesus delivers the man with the withered hand from his infirmity, he is enacting the deepest meaning of the Sabbath as "deliverance." To use last Sunday's image of the wine and wineskins: the law enshrining Sabbath *observance* is the wineskin; the *meaning* of the Sabbath is the wine. While the Pharisees are concerned about the wineskins, Jesus is concerned about the wine. The new wine is the inauguration of God's kingdom which is one of healing and deliverance.

The issue of the Sabbath highlights the great differences that separate Jesus and some of the religious establishment. As the religious authorities cling to the legal requirements rather than the meaning of the Sabbath law, they must leave the man in bondage to infirmity. More insidiously, they would rather use the law to entrap Jesus than to redeem the needy man!

To the point: Healing the man who, strictly speaking, has no life-threatening malady commemorates the Sabbath more than observing the letter of the law and doing nothing. Jesus acts out of the deeper meaning behind Sabbath rest—remembering God's deliverance of Israel from bondage.

Celebration

Model Penitential Rite

Presider: Each Sunday we come together as a community to praise and thank God for the saving deeds done on our behalf. Let us open ourselves to this great mystery of salvation . . . [pause]

> Lord Jesus, you are grieved at our hardness of heart: Lord . . .
> Christ Jesus, you heal us of all that keeps us in bondage: Christ . . .
> Son of Man, you are the Son of Man and lord even of the Sabbath: Lord . . .

Responsorial Psalm

"Sing with joy to God our help."

Psalm 81 was probably a liturgical psalm used every autumn as part of the Feast of Booths *(Sukkoth)* when the Israelites marked the gathering of the harvest by remembering their sojourn in the desert and renewing their covenant with God. The ritual began with a blowing of the trumpet at the new moon, and implied a renewal of commitment to the requirements of the Law. This Sunday's reading from Deuteronomy tells us that the purpose of the Sabbath law of rest was to remember the saving acts by which God had freed the people from slavery. Fully aware of this, Jesus honors the Sabbath when he frees the man with the withered hand from his infirmity (Gospel). When we sing this Sunday's psalm we remember how God has delivered *us* and, like the Israelites, recommit ourselves to faithful response.

Model General Intercessions

Presider: As Jesus compassionately healed the man with the withered hand, so are we confident that he heals us of all infirmities and answers our needs. And so we pray.

Response:

Lord, hear our prayer.

Cantor:

we pray to the Lord,

That the body of Christ may truly know who is the Lord of the Sabbath and respond by keeping the Lord's day as a day of celebration and rest . . . [pause]

That judges and juries may always take to heart the true meaning of laws and render decisions for the good of all . . . [pause]

That those burdened with infirmities of all kinds may be delivered by the merciful hand of God . . . [pause]

That our community may find rest and comfort in the restoring mystery of Jesus . . . [pause]

Presider: O God, you delivered Israel from bondage to a land flowing with milk and honey: hear these our prayers that we might be restored to rest in you. We pray through Jesus Christ our Lord. **Amen.**

OPENING PRAYER

Let us pray

Pause for silent prayer

Father,
your love never fails.
Hear our call.
Keep us from danger
and provide for all our needs.
Grant this through our Lord Jesus
    Christ, your Son,
who lives and reigns with you and the
    Holy Spirit,
one God, for ever and ever. **Amen.**

RESPONSORIAL PSALM

[Ps 81:3-4, 5-6, 6-8, 10-11]

℟. (2a) Sing with joy to God our help.

Take up a melody, and sound the
    timbrel,
    the pleasant harp and the lyre.
Blow the trumpet at the new moon,
    at the full moon, on our solemn feast.

℟. Sing with joy to God our help.

For it is a statute in Israel,
    an ordinance of the God of Jacob,
who made it a decree for Joseph
    when he came forth from the land of
    Egypt.

℟. Sing with joy to God our help.

An unfamiliar speech I hear:
    "I relieved his shoulder of the burden;
    his hands were freed from the basket.
In distress you called, and I rescued
    you."

℟. Sing with joy to God our help.

"There shall be no strange god among
    you
    nor shall you worship any alien god.
I, the LORD, am your God
    who led you forth from the land of
    Egypt."

℟. Sing with joy to God our help.

FIRST READING
[Deut 5:12-15]

Thus says the LORD:
    "Take care to keep holy the sabbath day
        as the LORD, your God, commanded you.
Six days you may labor and do all your work;
    but the seventh day is the sabbath of the LORD, your God.
No work may be done then, whether by you, or your son or daughter,
    or your male or female slave,
    or your ox or ass or any of your beasts,
    or the alien who lives with you.
Your male and female slave should rest as you do.
For remember that you too were once a slave in Egypt,
    and the LORD, your God, brought you from there
    with his strong hand and outstretched arm.
That is why the LORD, your God, has commanded you
    to observe the sabbath day."

SECOND READING
[2 Cor 4:6-11]

Brothers and sisters:
God who said, *Let light shine out of darkness,*
    has shone in our hearts to bring to light
    the knowledge of the glory of God on the face of Jesus Christ.
But we hold this treasure in earthen vessels,
    that the surpassing power may be of God and not from us.
We are afflicted in every way, but not constrained;
    perplexed, but not driven to despair;
    persecuted, but not abandoned;
    struck down, but not destroyed;
    always carrying about in the body the dying of Jesus,
    so that the life of Jesus may also be manifested in our body.
For we who live are constantly being given up to death
    for the sake of Jesus,
    so that the life of Jesus may be manifested in our mortal flesh.

Catechesis

Cantors
Since Psalm 81 is a covenant renewal song, spend some time this week reflecting on your own baptismal covenant with Christ. What promise has Christ made to you? What response does he ask of you in return? How can you sing joyfully about this relationship this Sunday?

Choir
Sunday is truly a day of celebration when you bring to the liturgy the fruit of your rehearsal work during the week. Ask God to bless your rehearsal so that its fruits may lead people to greater fidelity to the covenant.

Music Directors
A hymn especially appropriate to this Sunday's Gospel is "I Danced in the Morning" [G, G2, RS, W3; in BB as "Lord of the Dance"]. The story-telling of this text requires that all its verses be sung, and this makes it too long (for most situations) for the entrance processional. It has been used effectively as a hymn of praise after Communion. The assembly might stand to sing it, and the organist vary the accompaniment to fit each verse.

Rudolph Currie has a wonderful setting of this Sunday's psalm refrain [RS, W3] in which he sets the melody against a running eighth-note obbligato in the accompaniment. The dance-like result fits the joy of the text. Be sure to follow his indication to solo-out the tenor line where it becomes the melody.

Liturgy Committee
A temptation for those who work often with liturgy is to watch and critique the liturgy rather than surrender and enter into it. That posture (of watching and critiquing) is dangerous, since it is close to the posture of the Pharisees: "They watched him closely . . . so that they might accuse him." It is the grieving heart of Jesus to bring deliverance that demonstrates the real meaning of "keeping holy the Sabbath." How do you balance being responsible for the liturgy with entering personally into its celebration?

This Sunday's Gospel is a good example of what can sometimes happen if the short form of the Gospel is proclaimed. Here, the short form truncates the power of the message and where it's going: who the Sabbath is made for is not the point of the passage (unless the short form is proclaimed), but rather God's deliverance and restoration which result in the controversy that ultimately leads to Jesus' death.

MARCH 5, 2000

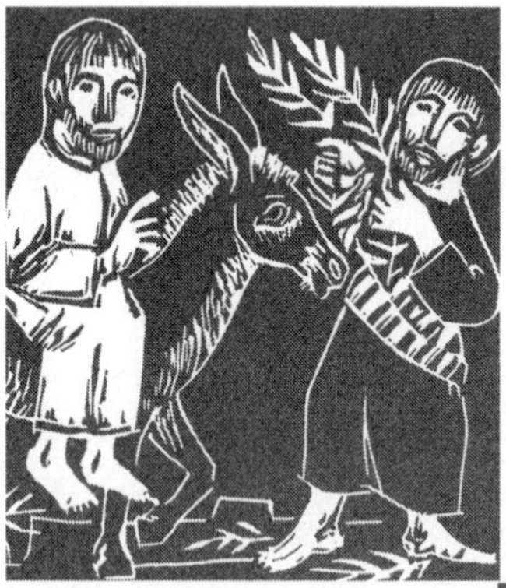

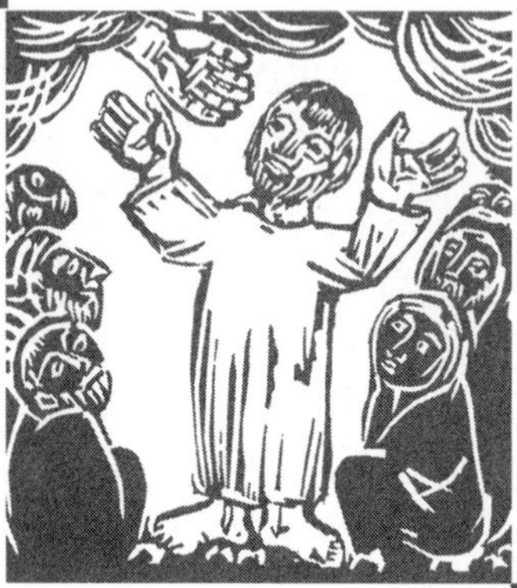

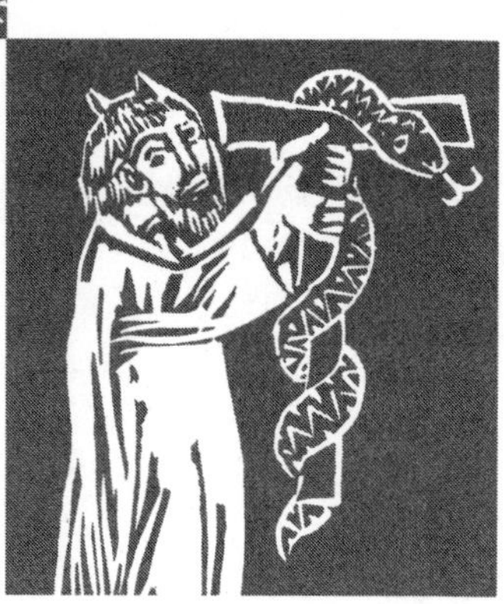

Season of Lent

First Sunday of Lent

FAITH-SHARING
- What drives you out into the desert, to face the sin within you and find the mercy of God?
- Who are the angels that minister to you while you remain in the desert?
- What is the turmoil in yourself that reminds you of the controversy baptismal living always stirs up?
- "Repent, and believe in the gospel." From what do you need to repent? What helps you to believe and live the Gospel more deeply?
- What will be your Lenten penance?

PRESIDERS
In what circumstances has your ordained ministry led you to the desert to face your own sinfulness?

DEACONS
What shape must your service to the community take during Lent so that the people's journey to the cross and resurrection is a sure one?

HOSPITALITY MINISTERS
Who needs hospitality due to the desert of his/her life? How might your greeting be like the angels who ministered to Jesus?

MUSIC MINISTERS
How can you prepare yourself so that your musical leadership during Lent reveals your willingness to enter with the Church into this period of conversion and renewal?

ALTAR MINISTERS
You usually help to get the liturgical space ready for the Lenten season. What needs "getting ready" in your life so you can live a good Lent?

LECTORS
How might the Word shape your Lenten living and penance?

EUCHARISTIC MINISTERS
While people are in the midst of the Lenten desert, how might you help them to know that "the kingdom of God is at hand"?

Spirituality

Reflecting on the Gospel
If someone were to ask us what is our favorite liturgical season, most of us would probably say Christmas or Easter. It would be a rare person who would vote Lent as their favorite liturgical season! In spite of our disaffection for Lent, it still seems to be a time of the year when even the religiously "lukewarm" feel compelled to do at least something. The widespread response to Lent is attested even by the fast-food chains, which offer specials on fish sandwiches during these six weeks. Lent is a time hardly to be ignored. It's sort of like medicine: we don't like it, but we take it because it's good for us.

It is highly unlikely that when the angels ministered to Jesus in the desert they fed him cheap fish sandwiches! This is hardly what Lent is all about. What it is about is facing evil and turning from it. The first Sunday of Lent begins with Mark's account of Jesus' first recorded words: "The kingdom of God is at hand. Repent and believe." Essentially, Lent is about conversion: repenting, and turning away from evil. Repentance, which is a total turning of oneself toward God, leads to believing, which is a way of living in God's kingdom.

In some respects it is easy to dismiss Jesus' struggle with Satan in the desert as nothing more than a nice scriptural story; if we had angels ministering to us, probably Lent wouldn't be so wearisome! But not even angels can diminish the sense of crisis in the reading. The line "after John had been arrested" is one that can arrest our own too-easy dismissal of this account. Jesus' ministry unfolds in the midst of turmoil. With our hindsight, we know that Jesus didn't escape the fate of John: he also was killed by his enemies. This Gospel is totally within the range of our own human experience. When Jesus preached repentance, he knew from his own experience the struggle he was asking of us. It's no easy season, this Lent.

Living the Paschal Mystery
Historically, Lent is a season of final, intense preparation for baptism by the elect. The whole Church joins in a conversion process with those to be baptized or make their profession of faith. Lent is conversion and journey; its goal is a renewed sense of our identity as daughters and sons of God.

The first reading from Genesis for this Sunday speaks of the covenant God made with Noah: that waters will never again destroy "all mortal beings." At the same time, it was those destroying waters that brought life to Noah and his family, the righteous ones. The second reading from the First Letter of Peter explicitly relates baptism to saving waters. By our baptism we make a new covenant with God ("appeal to God for a clear conscience") that initiates in us a new relationship to God through Jesus Christ, the resurrected One who "is at the right hand of God."

Lent is a time for us to assess our baptismal, covenantal relationship with God. It is our time to face evil and choose to live in righteousness. By so doing, we—with Christ—proclaim by our lives that the "kingdom of God is at hand." Living the Paschal Mystery calls us to die to the sin within us so that we can rise to the life given us in baptism.

MARCH 12, 2000

GOSPEL [Mark 1:12-15; L23B]

The Spirit drove Jesus out into the desert, and he remained in the desert for forty days, tempted by Satan. He was among wild beasts, and the angels ministered to him.

After John had been arrested, Jesus came to Galilee proclaiming the gospel of God: "This is the time of fulfillment. The kingdom of God is at hand. Repent, and believe in the gospel."

Working with the Word

Key words and phrases from the Gospel: Spirit drove; tempted; kingdom of God is at hand; repent, and believe in the Gospel

Connecting to Mark's Gospel: This story of Jesus being tempted in the desert comes immediately on the heels of his baptism. He comes up out of the water and is *driven* into the desert by the Spirit. Jesus' baptism not only inaugurates his public ministry, but instigates a confrontation with evil. The same Spirit who confirms his identity at his baptism is the one who drives him into the desert.

Connecting to Ash Wednesday and early Christian culture: The Gospel assigned for Ash Wednesday (Matt 6:1-6, 16-18) is a telling one with which to begin Lent. It mentions three practices that the early Church always connected with doing penance: almsgiving (practicing charity), prayer, and fasting, each of which addresses a key relationship: to others (almsgiving), to God (prayer), and to ourselves (fasting). We are reminded that Lent is a time to look at our whole selves and all our relationships.

Exegetical points: Mark's account of the temptations of Jesus in the wilderness is the shortest of the three Synoptics. The context for this brief passage is important—both for the Gospel and the liturgical season. The temptations follow immediately upon the baptism of Jesus. Liturgically, Lent is oriented to the paschal celebration of baptism and the sacraments of initiation at the Easter Vigil. In the Gospel, the context tells us that baptism leads to confrontation with evil.

The Greek verb we translate "tempt" can mean either "to tempt" in the sense of "seduce to sin" or it can mean "to put to the test," which is the sense whenever this verb occurs in Mark. The test is between the power of evil and the power of the "beloved Son." Once in the wilderness, Jesus encounters both "wild beasts" (minions of evil?) and angels. The testing in the wilderness is more than a personal struggle of Jesus; in Jesus, the kingdom of God engages the kingdom of evil to its ultimate defeat. Jesus' frontal assault on evil—note the action of the Spirit who drives Jesus into the wilderness—begins with his very first mighty deed, which is to cast out an unclean spirit in a possessed man (Mark 1:28ff).

To the point: The irony is that Jesus' baptism thrusts him *into* the conflict with evil. The first and primary conflict is between the Son of God and Satan. This same conflict is one we must also face because, through baptism, we share in Jesus' life and ministry.

Celebration

Model Penitential Rite

Presider: Sisters and brothers in Christ, we have begun Lent, that solemn time of the year for us to name the sin within ourselves, to repent, and to believe in Jesus' Gospel. Let us reflect on the mercy and forgiveness of God, the reality of evil in our lives and world, and ask God to strengthen us on our Lenten journey . . . [pause]

Confiteor: I confess . . .

Responsorial Psalm

"Your ways, O Lord, are love and truth to those who keep your covenant."
In the first reading God promises not death but life. Never again will God "destroy all mortal beings." What God offers instead is forgiveness of sin and guidance along the path of righteousness (psalm). Leading the way is Christ, who chose to suffer for our sins that "he might lead [us] to God" (second reading). For our part, we ask God in the responsorial psalm to remember the compassion and kindness which motivated the covenant with all creation after the flood (first reading). We seek forgiveness of sin and gentle instruction toward what is right. Just as the flood prefigured baptism (second reading) so, then, does this psalm encapsulate all of Lent. In singing it we choose to enter again our Lenten journey of conversion.

Model General Intercessions

Presider: Just as the angels ministered to Jesus in the desert, so will our God hear our prayers. And so we make known our needs.

Response:

Lord, hear our prayer.

Cantor:

we pray to the Lord,

May all members of the Church take seriously their baptismal commitment to "repent, and believe in the gospel" . . . [pause]

May the people of the world respond faithfully to their relationship with their God . . . [pause]

May those who are isolated and have no one to minister to them know the care and mercy of God . . . [pause]

May all of us here gathered walk with those about to be baptized or profess their faith, encouraging them and strengthening ourselves in our baptismal commitment . . . [pause]

Presider: Merciful God, you sent angels to care for your Son in the desert and you care for us by your love and forgiveness: grant these our prayers that our Lent may bring us nearer to you. We ask this through our Lord Jesus Christ. **Amen.**

ALTERNATIVE OPENING PRAYER

Let us pray
 [at the beginning of Lent for the spirit of repentance]

Pause for silent prayer

Lord our God,
you formed man from the clay of the earth
and breathed into him the spirit of life,
but he turned from your face and sinned.
In this time of repentance
we call out for your mercy.
Bring us back to you
and to the life your Son won for us
by his death on the cross,
for he lives and reigns for ever and ever.
Amen.

RESPONSORIAL PSALM
[Ps 25:4-5, 6-7, 8-9]

℟. (cf. 10) Your ways, O Lord, are love and truth to those who keep your covenant.

Your ways, O Lord, make known to me;
 teach me your paths,
guide me in your truth and teach me,
 for you are God my savior.

℟. Your ways, O Lord, are love and truth to those who keep your covenant.

Remember that your compassion, O Lord,
 and your love are from of old.
In your kindness remember me,
 because of your goodness, O Lord.

℟. Your ways, O Lord, are love and truth to those who keep your covenant.

Good and upright is the Lord,
 thus he shows sinners the way.
He guides the humble to justice,
 and he teaches the humble his way.

℟. Your ways, O Lord, are love and truth to those who keep your covenant.

FIRST READING
[Gen 9:8-15]

God said to Noah and to his sons with him:
"See, I am now establishing my covenant with you
 and your descendants after you
 and with every living creature that was with you:
 all the birds, and the various tame and wild animals
 that were with you and came out of the ark.
I will establish my covenant with you,

that never again shall all bodily
   creatures be destroyed
by the waters of a flood;
there shall not be another flood to
   devastate the earth."
God added:
"This is the sign that I am giving for all
   ages to come,
of the covenant between me and you
   and every living creature with you:
I set my bow in the clouds to serve as
   a sign
of the covenant between me and the
   earth.
When I bring clouds over the earth,
   and the bow appears in the clouds,
I will recall the covenant I have made
   between me and you and all living
   beings,
so that the waters shall never again
   become a flood
to destroy all mortal beings."

SECOND READING
[1 Pet 3:18-22]

Beloved:
Christ suffered for sins once,
   the righteous for the sake of the
      unrighteous,
   that he might lead you to God.
Put to death in the flesh,
   he was brought to life in the Spirit.
In it he also went to preach to the spirits
   in prison,
   who had once been disobedient
   while God patiently waited in the
      days of Noah
   during the building of the ark,
   in which a few persons, eight in all,
   were saved through water.
This prefigured baptism, which saves
   you now.
It is not a removal of dirt from the body
   but an appeal to God for a clear
      conscience,
   through the resurrection of Jesus
      Christ,
   who has gone into heaven
   and is at the right hand of God,
   with angels, authorities, and powers
      subject to him.

Catechesis

Cantors
In leading this psalm, you are modeling for the assembly two aspects of the Lenten call to conversion: honesty about sinfulness and certainty about the divine compassion which confronts it. Spend some time this week praying about these. You will be walking the way of love and truth about which you are singing.

Choir
How can you as a choir live out the Lenten call to conversion and renewal of covenant? Perhaps this is a season to examine your ways of relating to one another, to the assembly, to the liturgy. What attitudes or behaviors need conversion? Where do forgiveness and healing need to be sought?

Music Directors
With the beginning of Lent a change is needed in the service music you have been singing. What you choose will be relative to what you have available and to what you use during the other seasons of the liturgical year. Its style should fit the mood and purpose of Lent. Ideally, it will be a setting which the parish identifies with Lent because its use is reserved for this season. Some examples of acclamation settings which would be especially appropriate are David Hurd's "New Plainsong Mass," Robert Batastini's setting of the Lectionary chants, Vermulst's "People's Mass," and the "St. Louis Jesuits' Mass."

One of the significant things about the use of Psalm 25 on this Sunday is that it is the first psalm to speak of the covenant, a motif that plays an important role in the readings of this day. In order for the role of the psalm to be clear, then, the setting you sing needs to use the refrain given in the Lectionary. Settings which use this refrain are available in LP, PC v. II, and W3.

Liturgy Committee
Lectionary overview: In all three years of the Lectionary cycle, the first two Sundays of Lent always have been assigned the Gospels of Jesus' temptation in the desert and the transfiguration. Then the third to fifth Sundays form unique units in each of the three years, and the sixth Sunday is always a passion account from one of the three Synoptic Gospels. How might you prepare these Sundays so that Lent unfolds as a journey toward the cross and resurrection?

Because so many members of your liturgical community may not be able to receive ashes on Ash Wednesday, it is pastorally tempting to distribute them at the Sunday liturgies. This practice should be avoided because it distracts from the import of this Sunday as initiating our baptismal, covenantal journey.

Be careful about imposing symbolism on Lent; e.g., creating "deserts" in our sacred spaces or putting sand in the holy water fonts. Allow the Lenten Lectionary and the liturgy itself to suggest symbols that help us enter into the depth of the season. The order of the day should convey reserve, simplicity, emptiness, space, silence, slower movements, good use of violet purple (as opposed to the eschatological, royal purple of Advent)—all this touched by subtle suggestions of the coming celebration of new life.

MARCH 12, 2000

Second Sunday of Lent

FAITH-SHARING
- ". . . give[s] us everything else along with him." Who has loved you in such a way that you have a glimpse of God's excessive love for you?
- How do you experience the downs and ups—the Paschal Mystery dying and rising—of desert and transfiguration in your own life?
- This Gospel is filled with hope and glory. How does this encourage you during your Lenten journey?
- What needs to die in you so that you might experience joy and glory?

PRESIDERS
Notice God's lavishness—did not spare an only Son, did not hold back. Where do you hold back in ministry? How might you become more extravagant in your sacrificial giving?

DEACONS
How might your service to the community reflect the sacrificial love of God for you?

HOSPITALITY MINISTERS
How might your greeting encourage those who are faltering in their Lenten resolves?

MUSIC MINISTERS
What is the death being asked of you as music minister? Where do you see the resurrection?

ALTAR MINISTERS
"It is good that we are here." How might you serve so that the assembly senses the good of being with God?

LECTORS
Recall your personal glimpses of glory. How might this recollection help you communicate the hope within this Sunday's readings?

EUCHARISTIC MINISTERS
How are you a part of sustaining people in the midst of downs and ups, deserts and transfigurations?

Spirituality

Reflecting on the Gospel
We've all had the experience of being utterly speechless, whether out of amazement or surprise or fear. We can well identify with Peter, who "hardly knew what to say." Like Peter, we would probably also blurt out something that wouldn't quite fit the occasion, wouldn't quite make sense. After all, in face of theophany—God's self-revelation—who would know how to respond?

This Gospel of the transfiguration has a Lenten light cast on it in Mark's Gospel. The story comes after Jesus' first prediction of his passion. Peter rebuked him for these dire predictions (Mark 8:33). In this Gospel we again see Peter responding in an inappropriate way. No wonder! Who would want to embrace the cross? Or, even more scandalous, what kind of God gives an only Son over to death? Peter is as clueless about the answer as we are. Because, by human standards, we have no response to such extraordinary love.

The Gospel does give us a hint about a response to being delivered over to suffering and death. Jesus commands his disciples to tell no one of the transfiguration until "the Son of Man had risen from the dead." Here is the key. Here is what we know: death leads to glory, to life!

Living the Paschal Mystery
Last Sunday we began Lent "down" in the desert. This week we are taken "up" to the mountain top. This down and up journey characterizes well the Paschal Mystery and characterizes our lives. It's as though the Church knows in her wisdom that we humans need glimpses of glory if we are to journey faithfully along the road to conversion. Without these glimpses of glory—these hopeful reassurances—we might lose courage along the way.

Jesus' dying and rising is another image we might use for the down and up journey before us. The hard part of our Lenten journey is the dying to self. We like to hold on to our own selfishness and self-centeredness. We don't like to admit that we are less than perfect. It is easy to find fault with others. Going down into the desert calls us to surrender ourselves to God, to be obedient even as Abraham was, to be willing to sacrifice everything, even our own future. Only when we embrace such a total surrender can we even begin to fathom the glory of the mountain top. As Paul's Letter to the Romans assures us, won't the God who did not spare the only Son "give us everything else along with him"?

In the down and up, the dying and rising, of these first two Sundays of Lent we have a microcosm of the relationship of Lent to Easter. Lent is our time in the desert, to face our temptations and open ourselves to the Spirit who is always present to us to guide us and comfort us. If we journey well and purposefully, when we come to the glory of Easter morning we will see that the journey has brought us a joy that far outweighs any personal sacrifices we might have made along the way. But the best thing of all is that as we embrace conversion, we ourselves begin to take on the glow of the transfigured Christ. That is our gift to each other this Lent that encourages all of us along the way.

MARCH 19, 2000

GOSPEL [Mark 9:2-10; L26B]

Jesus took Peter, James, and John and led them up a high mountain apart by themselves. And he was transfigured before them, and his clothes became dazzling white, such as no fuller on earth could bleach them. Then Elijah appeared to them along with Moses, and they were conversing with Jesus. Then Peter said to Jesus in reply, "Rabbi, it is good that we are here! Let us make three tents: one for you, one for Moses, and one for Elijah." He hardly knew what to say, they were so terrified. Then a cloud came, casting a shadow over them; from the cloud came a voice, "This is my beloved Son. Listen to him." Suddenly, looking around, they no longer saw anyone but Jesus alone with them.

As they were coming down from the mountain, he charged them not to relate what they had seen to anyone, except when the Son of Man had risen from the dead. So they kept the matter to themselves, questioning what rising from the dead meant.

Working with the Word

Key words and phrases from the Gospel: transfigured, cloud, my beloved Son, what rising from the dead meant

Connecting to the preface (P13): The context for the Sunday and this Gospel is Jesus' impending death; the transfiguration tries to prepare the disciples for the scandal of the cross and the new life that follows. Peter, James, and John now catch a glimpse of Jesus' identity.

Connecting to our culture: There is a deep bond between parent and child that still plays itself out, even in our culture with fragmented families. Parents sacrifice much for their children—"children are the future"—and instinctively recognize both their vulnerability and their potential. The readings today help us reflect on this deep parental bond.

Exegetical points: As Jesus is revealed in the transfiguration as the "beloved Son," the Lectionary invites us to hear echoes from this Sunday's first reading from Genesis in which God refers to Abraham's son as "the son whom you love." Later in the story, the translation becomes more explicit: "you did not withhold from me your own beloved son." Christian exegetes have been quick to see many such connections to Christ's own sacrifice in the story of the binding of Isaac. In addition to both stories centering on an only beloved son, both scenes—the binding of Isaac and the transfiguration—take place on a mountain. In one story, the beloved son is spared from death; in the other, we know that the beloved son will not be spared, a point taken up by Paul in the second reading. In the portion of the first story omitted from the Lectionary, Abraham lays on Isaac's shoulders the wood for the sacrifice, evoking images of Jesus carrying the wood on which he would be sacrificed. The offering God requires of Abraham—a holocaust—is a total offering to God. The ram in the thicket has been imaginatively seen as the paschal lamb with a crown of thorns, again finding Christological significance in the Genesis reading. But quite apart from this artful reading of details, the theological significance of the narrative should not be lost. The stunning obedience of Abraham leads to the renewal of an even more stunning promise from God—countless descendants, land, blessing. The sacrifice of Christ, too, results in stunning blessings—his own glorification and the salvation of all.

To the point: A father's great love for his son (Abraham ➔ Isaac and God ➔ Jesus) is at the heart of this Sunday's readings. God's great love won't permit the sacrifice of Isaac. But God's greater love won't spare the only Son *for us*. That same love will vindicate Jesus in the glory of the resurrection, which we glimpse this Sunday in the transfiguration.

Celebration

Model Penitential Rite

Presider: In the Gospel for today we hear about Jesus being transfigured before Peter, James, and John. From a cloud a voice says, "This is my beloved Son. Listen to him." Let us open our hearts to the times we have not listened to God's Word . . . [pause]

Confiteor: I confess . . .

Responsorial Psalm

"I will walk before the Lord, in the land of the living."
Psalm 116 is a psalm of thanksgiving for having been delivered from death. Such thanksgiving is contingent upon having actually faced death. For Abraham, this was the near loss of his son Isaac whose death he believed God desired as a sign of fidelity (first reading). For the disciples who witnessed Christ's transfiguration, the connection between death and deliverance remained yet a mystery (Gospel). For us the connection has been clearly revealed in Christ, who died for us and now intercedes for us at the right hand of God (second reading). Our singing of this psalm is an expression of what we have come to know through faith: that death willingly undertaken out of servanthood (Abraham) or Sonship (Christ) is the door to life.

Model General Intercessions

Presider: A God who loves us so much as to be willing to sacrifice an only Son is surely a God who will listen to our needs and respond to them. So we are encouraged to pray.

Response:

[musical notation: Lord, hear our prayer.]

Cantor:

[musical notation: we pray to the Lord,]

That all members of the Church might have glimpses of the glory awaiting those who are faithful to the demands of the Gospel . . . [pause]

That the world may know the peace that comes from people surrendering to conversion . . . [pause]

That those who have suffered the loss of a child may be comforted by God's great love . . . [pause]

That all of us here gathered may listen to the beloved Son and grasp more clearly what rising from the dead means . . . [pause]

Presider: Loving Father, you loved us so much as to give your only Son up to the cross for our salvation: hear these our prayers that we might complete our Lenten journey as a transformed people ready to sing your Easter praises. We ask this through Christ our Lord. **Amen.**

OPENING PRAYER
Let us pray

Pause for silent prayer

God our Father,
help us to hear your Son.
Enlighten us with your word,
that we may find the way to your glory.

We ask this through our Lord Jesus
 Christ, your Son,
who lives and reigns with you and the
 Holy Spirit,
one God, for ever and ever. **Amen.**

RESPONSORIAL PSALM
[Ps 116:10, 15, 16-17, 18-19]

℟. (116:9) I will walk before the Lord, in the land of the living.

I believed, even when I said,
 "I am greatly afflicted."
Precious in the eyes of the Lord
 is the death of his faithful ones.

℟. I will walk before the Lord, in the land of the living.

O Lord, I am your servant;
 I am your servant, the son of your
  handmaid;
 you have loosed my bonds.
To you will I offer sacrifice of
  thanksgiving,
 and I will call upon the name of the
  Lord.

℟. I will walk before the Lord, in the land of the living.

My vows to the Lord I will pay
 in the presence of all his people,
in the courts of the house of the Lord,
 in your midst, O Jerusalem.

℟. I will walk before the Lord, in the land of the living.

FIRST READING
[Gen 22:1-2, 9a, 10-13, 15-18]

God put Abraham to the test.
He called to him, "Abraham!"
"Here I am!" he replied.
Then God said:
 "Take your son Isaac, your only one,
  whom you love,
 and go to the land of Moriah.
There you shall offer him up as a
 holocaust
 on a height that I will point out to
  you."

When they came to the place of which
 God had told him,

Abraham built an altar there and
  arranged the wood on it.
Then he reached out and took the knife
  to slaughter his son.
But the LORD's messenger called to him
  from heaven,
  "Abraham, Abraham!"
"Here I am!" he answered.
"Do not lay your hand on the boy," said
  the messenger.
"Do not do the least thing to him.
I know now how devoted you are to
  God,
  since you did not withhold from me
    your own beloved son."
As Abraham looked about,
  he spied a ram caught by its horns in
    the thicket.
So he went and took the ram
  and offered it up as a holocaust in
    place of his son.

Again the LORD's messenger called to
  Abraham from heaven and said:
  "I swear by myself, declares the LORD,
  that because you acted as you did
  in not withholding from me your
    beloved son,
  I will bless you abundantly
  and make your descendants as
    countless
  as the stars of the sky and the sands of
    the seashore;
  your descendants shall take
    possession
  of the gates of their enemies,
  and in your descendants all the
    nations of the earth shall find
    blessing—
  all this because you obeyed my
    command."

SECOND READING
[Rom 8:31b-34]

Brothers and sisters:
If God is for us, who can be against us?
He who did not spare his own Son
  but handed him over for us all,
  how will he not also give us
    everything else along with him?

Who will bring a charge against God's
  chosen ones?
  It is God who acquits us, who will
    condemn?
Christ Jesus it is who died—or, rather,
  was raised—
  who also is at the right hand of God,
  who indeed intercedes for us.

Catechesis

Cantors
To "walk before the Lord, in the land of the living" does not mean that you shall never face death. The Gospel, in fact, tells you just the opposite. How can you sing this psalm with both the courage and confidence it requires?

Choir
The disciples in this Sunday's Gospel did not know what "rising from the dead" meant. Neither will you unless you are willing, like Christ, to die. In what ways are you being invited to die? Where in your lives is the resurrection/transfiguration trying to break out?

Music Directors
An excellent hymn for the presentation of the gifts would be "God Spoke to Our Father Abraham" [W3]. The text relates Abraham's sacrifice of Isaac to God's offering of his Son on the cross. The lamb offered in Isaac's stead becomes the Lamb acclaimed by John the Baptist whose "death destroys the sin of the world."

"'Tis Good, Lord, to Be Here" [CH, RS, W3, WC] would be a good text to sing as a hymn of praise after Communion, for it fits not only the transfiguration story but the season of Lent. Part of the "being here" is the transformation of the community which takes place through the Eucharistic action and Communion. But, as with the disciples in the Gospel, you cannot remain on the mountain. You must return to the demands of daily living. Thanks, however, to the transfiguration and to the Eucharistic banquet, you know what the future promises and you know who it is who walks with you.

Liturgy Committee
These first two Sundays of Lent capture well in Gospel stories the dying and rising mystery of Christ. How might you help the members of your liturgical community to connect these two Sundays and to experience better the reality of the Paschal Mystery in their own daily dying and rising?

On the mountain top Peter, James, and John got a glimpse of the fullness of Christ's glory. Fullness can best be appreciated by a prior experience of emptiness. Such is the intent behind the Lenten fast. You empty yourselves so that you hunger only for God and are filled by him. (This is similarly true for the Communion fast but since it has been reduced to fasting just one hour before Communion, it is hardly enough to really give you a *physical* hunger for God.) Your Lenten fasting practices are more earnest and austere than those during the rest of the year and are an opportunity for you to sincerely *hunger* for God and reflect on the grace of your own self-emptying.

MARCH 19, 2000

St. Joseph, Husband of the Blessed Virgin

Spirituality

Reflecting on the Gospel

Violence seems to surround us these days, no matter where we live. Anger, harshness, and bitterness seem to be part of our everyday lives. Newspapers, tabloids, and TV inundate us with stories of infidelity, injustice, and deceit. Sometimes this even invades our own lives, families, communities. This solemnity of Joseph, husband of Mary, is a pleasant respite in the midst of all this and shows us that there is an alternative way to live with each other.

The Lectionary provides two choices for a Gospel; we have chosen to reflect on the selection from Matthew. The opening lines are two carefully crafted sentences, the conclusion of Matthew's long genealogy of Jesus, that clearly evade any hint of referring to Joseph as the father of Jesus. He is called "the husband of Mary." At the same time this Gospel presents Joseph as having an *active* role in the incarnation events.

Joseph acts as a strong and determined, yet gentle and compassionate man in this Gospel. Already betrothed to Joseph, Mary's pregnancy puts Joseph in a dilemma. Adultery is punished by stoning in the Mosaic Law. Instead, Joseph the righteous man (the one who is obedient to the law) "decided to divorce her"; Joseph the compassionate man was "unwilling to expose her to shame" and planned on carrying out the Law "quietly." Further, Joseph must have been a man of great faith and very intimate with his God, for he acted upon a dream, "did as the angel of the Lord had commanded him," and "took his wife into his home." It must have taken great strength of character for Joseph to see through the letter of the Law and fulfill what became for him God's will.

After Jesus was born, it was Joseph, then, who fulfilled with both strength of character and compassionate obedience the role of the traditional Jewish father. What did Jesus learn from Joseph? Joseph would have taught him Jewish Law. He would have taught him Jewish prayer. He would have taught him how to keep Sabbath. He would have taught him Scripture. He would have accompanied him to the synagogue. He would have taken him to Jerusalem for the pilgrimage feasts (hence, the finding in the Temple story when Jesus was twelve). From living with Joseph, Jesus would have been taught *through example* about righteousness, compassion, and listening to the voice of God.

Living the Paschal Mystery

Jesus taught his disciples to pray "thy will be done" in the Our Father; no doubt, he learned this from both the teaching and example of Joseph. Jesus began learning obedience at a very early age. When he faced the most serious demand for obedience in his life in Gethsemane the night before he died, he had a lifetime of saying *yes* to draw upon for strength. Joseph can be for us a model for living the Paschal Mystery since his obedience to God's will—"Do not be afraid to take Mary your wife into your home"—necessitated a dying to self. Joseph, a "righteous man," took into his home a wife "found with child" "before they lived together." The shame brought into Joseph's house was transformed into glory: this day we honor him as one now living eternal life.

FAITH-SHARING
- How might you come to the kind of trusting faith that Joseph had?
- How is your exercise of righteousness and compassion a participation in God's plan of salvation?
- Joseph models for you righteousness, compassion, listening to the voice of God, obedience, great strength of character. In what ways are you like Joseph? Where do you need to grow?

PRESIDERS
How do you find and work out the balance between righteousness and compassion in your own ordained ministry?

DEACONS
God's promises made to David are fulfilled in Christ *through Joseph*. Where/how are God's promises of compassion and salvation for his people fulfilled *through you? Through whom* have you received God's promises?

HOSPITALITY MINISTERS
Joseph was obedient to God and endured the shame of accepting the pregnant Mary into his home. What does Joseph teach you about hospitality?

MUSIC MINISTERS
What can Joseph teach you about persistent day in, day out fidelity to your ministry when no progress seems to be occurring with the choir, the cantors, the assembly?

ALTAR MINISTERS
Joseph is a great model of a quiet servant who is active and an integral participant in God's saving work. What can you learn from Joseph with respect to your ministry?

LECTORS
Joseph heard the angel of the Lord speak in a dream and acted on it. How might you ponder God's Word so that you act on it?

EUCHARISTIC MINISTERS
Joseph had great strength of faith to see through the letter of the Law and fulfill God's will. How do you sustain people so they fulfill God's will? What "food" do they need to endure suffering, loneliness, boredom, lack of faith, etc.? What sustenance do *you* need?

MARY

MARCH 20, 2000

GOSPEL [Matt 1:16, 18-21, 24a; L543]

Jacob was the father of Joseph, the husband of Mary. Of her was born Jesus who is called the Christ.

Now this is how the birth of Jesus Christ came about. When his mother Mary was betrothed to Joseph, but before they lived together, she was found with child through the Holy Spirit. Joseph her husband, since he was a righteous man, yet unwilling to expose her to shame, decided to divorce her quietly. Such was his intention when, behold, the angel of the Lord appeared to him in a dream and said, "Joseph, son of David, do not be afraid to take Mary your wife into your home. For it is through the Holy Spirit that this child has been conceived in her. She will bear a son and you are to name him Jesus, because he will save his people from their sins." When Joseph awoke, he did as the angel of the Lord had commanded him and took his wife into his home.

Working with the Word

Key words and phrases from the Gospel: righteous man, unwilling to expose her to shame, did as the angel . . . commanded him, took his wife into his home

Connecting the three readings: The lineage of Jesus is referred to in each of the three readings. Especially is the second reading key: Paul, in contrasting faith and the Law, cites the faith of Abraham rather than Moses the law-giver, reminding us that righteousness goes beyond keeping the Law; it means having faith.

Connecting to biblical culture: A betrothed couple was considered legally married. Ending a betrothal, consequently, required a bill of divorce. Jewish law would have considered Mary's pregnancy as evidence of adultery, a sin punishable by stoning to death.

Exegetical points: Jewish marriages proceeded in two stages. The first was engagement or betrothal. This was a formal and legally binding commitment between the man and woman. To break off the engagement required a decree of divorce. During this first stage, the woman remained at her family's home. After some months, she moved into her husband's home (the second stage). It is during this first stage that this Sunday's Gospel takes place. Mary is betrothed but she does not yet live with Joseph. When Joseph discovers that she is pregnant, he evidently presumes that Mary has been unfaithful. Technically, her infidelity could be punished under the Law by stoning to death (Deut 22:21-23). The translation of verse 19 implies that *since* Joseph is a righteous man, he was expected to pursue the legal option; *yet* he is unwilling to follow that route. Compassionately, he decides not to submit her to the demands of the law. It is interesting to note that Joseph chose the route of compassion and mercy even before the angel appears to him. The angel's message is not intended to move Joseph to greater righteousness or mercy, but to inform his ignorance of the truth of Mary's situation. Joseph's acceptance of a dream-message shows both a faithful and obedient man.

To the point: Joseph is an *active player* in the unfolding plan of salvation. He is a righteous man, had faith, did as the Lord commanded, and had compassion. Through Joseph, who is the connection to the royal house, God's promises made to David are fulfilled in Christ.

Celebration

Model Penitential Rite

Presider: Joseph was a just and compassionate husband to Mary and a father to Jesus. Let us reflect on our own righteousness and compassion . . . [pause]

> Lord Jesus, you were taught righteousness and compassion by your foster father Joseph: Lord . . .
> Son of David, you came to save your people from their sins: Christ . . .
> Lord Jesus, you are son of David, Son of God: Lord . . .

Responsorial Psalm

"The son of David will live forever."
In Psalm 89 the "son of David" who will "live forever" is, literally, David's offspring to whom God has promised both divine sonship and everlasting dynasty (first reading). But the Gospel names Joseph "son of David," a man born centuries later and surely not a king. How is it that this title is given to Joseph?

Over time, as Israel watched the destruction of the kingdom due to the infidelity of David's descendants, the title took on a note of expectancy: people longed for the House of David to be revived by a just and righteous descendant. The story of Abraham tells us that fidelity to God also meant "hoping against hope" when what had been promised was long in coming (second reading). As we sing the responsorial psalm for this solemnity of St. Joseph, then, we celebrate the fidelity, righteousness, and hope which this true son of David models for us.

Model General Intercessions

Presider: St. Joseph is the husband of Mary, the foster father of Jesus, and the patron of the universal Church. His compassion draws him to intercede before God for us. And so we are encouraged to pray for our needs and know that they will be answered.

Response:

[Musical notation: Lord, hear our prayer.]

Cantor:

[Musical notation: we pray to the Lord,]

That all members of the Church may live out of righteousness and compassion . . . [pause]

That nations may be obedient to God's will and cooperate in the divine plan of salvation . . . [pause]

That children lacking positive role models in their lives may be in touch with someone who can guide them wisely . . . [pause]

That our community may have strong faith and enlivening dreams . . . [pause]

Presider: O God, you gave Mary and Jesus the strong and compassionate Joseph to watch over them and guide them: be with us and grant our prayers that we might enjoy eternal life. We ask this through Christ our Lord. **Amen.**

OPENING PRAYER
Let us pray

Pause for silent prayer

Father,
you entrusted our Savior to the care of St. Joseph.
By the help of his prayers
may your Church continue to serve its Lord, Jesus Christ,
who lives and reigns with you and the Holy Spirit,
one God, for ever and ever. **Amen.**

RESPONSORIAL PSALM
[Ps 89:2-3, 4-5, 27, 29]

℟. (37) The son of David will live forever.

The promises of the LORD I will sing forever,
    through all generations my mouth will proclaim your faithfulness,
for you have said, "My kindness is established forever";
    in heaven you have confirmed your faithfulness.

℟. The son of David will live forever.

"I have made a covenant with my chosen one;
    I have sworn to David my servant:
forever will I confirm your posterity
    and establish your throne for all generations."

℟. The son of David will live forever.

"He shall say of me, 'You are my father, my God, the Rock my savior!'
Forever I will maintain my kindness toward him,
    my covenant with him stands firm."

℟. The son of David will live forever.

FIRST READING
[2 Sam 7:4-5a, 12-14a, 16]

The Lord spoke to Nathan and said:
  "Go, tell my servant David,
    'When your time comes and you rest
      with your ancestors,
  I will raise up your heir after you,
    sprung from your loins,
  and I will make his kingdom firm.
It is he who shall build a house for my
  name.
And I will make his royal throne firm
  forever.
I will be a father to him,
  and he shall be a son to me.
Your house and your kingdom shall
  endure forever before me;
  your throne shall stand firm forever.'"

SECOND READING
[Rom 4:13, 16-18, 22]

Brothers and sisters:
It was not through the law
  that the promise was made to
    Abraham and his descendants
  that he would inherit the world,
  but through the righteousness that
    comes from faith.
For this reason, it depends on faith,
  so that it may be a gift,
  and the promise may be guaranteed
    to all his descendants,
  not to those who only adhere to the law
  but to those who follow the faith of
    Abraham,
  who is the father of all of us, as it is
    written,
  I have made you father of many nations.
He is our father in the sight of God,
  in whom he believed, who gives life
    to the dead
  and calls into being what does not
    exist.
He believed, hoping against hope,
  that he would become "the father of
    many nations,"
  according to what was said, "Thus
    shall your descendants be."
That is why "it was credited to him as
  righteousness."

Catechesis

Cantors

As you prepare to sing the psalm for this solemnity of St. Joseph, reflect on who in your life have been models of fidelity, righteousness, and hope. How might you thank God for the blessing they have been for you?

Choir

Who are the persons who have been most important in teaching you the ways of God—love of the Eucharist, faithfulness to the commandments, openness to Scripture, participation in the Church? You might want to end rehearsal this week with prayer for them.

Music Directors

"Come Now, and Praise the Humble Servant" [W3] uses the imagery of "David's house and line." It would work as the entrance hymn if sung at a moderately fast tempo with the dotted half-note as the basic beat. "Joseph, Be Our Guide and Pattern" is given different treatment in CBW3 and W3. The Canadian book uses a tune with dramatic leaps (REGENT SQUARE) which gives the text—and Joseph—strength and energy (perhaps because Joseph is their national patron?). W3 uses the tune ORIEL which, because the melody moves almost entirely by steps, makes the text—and Joseph—seem passive. Sing it to the more energetic tune and use it for the entrance. A third fine hymn for Joseph is Thomas Troeger's poetically moving "The Hands that First Help Mary's Child." Phrases such as "When Joseph marveled at the size of that small breathing frame" give this text an immediacy that makes the incarnation come alive. The final verse is challenging with its reference to the crucifixion and your call to follow there.

Liturgy Committee

It is a challenge to encourage your parishioners to celebrate solemnities. Even if they cannot be present at Eucharist, you may want to encourage people (perhaps through a bulletin note) to pray the Evening Prayer from the Liturgy of the Hours for the solemnity or use some devotional prayer to St. Joseph.

This solemnity is transferred this year to Monday, March 20 because nothing may replace a Sunday of Lent. As with all solemnities, the Eucharistic celebration has three readings, a Gloria (even though it is Lent), and Creed.

Two choices for a Gospel are given in the Lectionary. We chose to focus on the selection from Matthew and reserve the selection from Luke for next year, year C, which is the year Luke's Gospel is read.

Although it is Lent, it is appropriate to use fresh flowers and have a festive atmosphere in the sacred space (without overdoing it).

MARCH 20, 2000

The Annunciation of the Lord

FAITH-SHARING
- What are the ways you, like Mary, bear Christ within yourself? Identify some of the "swords" and the "fruit."
- The name Jesus means "savior." As Christ-bearers, how do you also mediate salvation for others?
- Where are you being invited to surrender to God's will? What are the obstacles to your *yes*?

PRESIDERS
The angel Gabriel visited Mary, a young and probably poor girl, in an obscure little village in Galilee; and no one knew that it occurred. What are the small and insignificant moments in your ministry when you encounter God?

DEACONS
When immersed in the Paschal Mystery, we encounter "swords" and "fruit." What helps you with "swords"? How might you remember better the "fruit"?

HOSPITALITY MINISTERS
Through baptism you are "Christ-bearers" (Emmanuel). How have you encountered Christ through others? How have you witnessed Christ to others?

MUSIC MINISTERS
Do you let yourself "listen to/hear" all of the liturgy, or are you attentive only to the musical elements which involve you?

ALTAR MINISTERS
"Sacrifice and offering you did not desire, but a body you prepared for me." How might you look beyond merely preparing the church building to preparing your "body," your life?

LECTORS
Gabriel announced to Mary God's invitation to participate in the saving plan. In what way is your proclamation to the assembly like Gabriel's announcement? How have you responded to the word *you* announce?

EUCHARISTIC MINISTERS
Mary said, "May it be done to me according to your word." If you were to be like Mary, what is the "it" for you?

Spirituality

Reflecting on the Gospel

Gabriel was one busy angel during the unfolding of the incarnation events! All the TV angels and plastic statues and saccharine pictures of angels so popular today cannot even begin to stir up the piety and wonder and grace that Gabriel inaugurated in his two annunciation visits.

The story from Luke's Gospel of the announcement of the birth of Jesus to Mary has numerous parallels with the announcement of the birth of John to Zechariah. In both cases it is Gabriel who brings good tidings. Both were troubled at the angel's appearance. Both are told "Do not be afraid." Both question the news of conception on "biological" grounds: Zechariah says he and Elizabeth are too old; Mary says she is too young (has yet to have sexual relations). Both women do end up pregnant. For all these similarities, however, the responses of Zechariah and Mary are still subtly but significantly different and offer a tremendous lesson for us.

Zechariah responded to the announcement of wondrous events with a question, "How shall I *know* this?" His request is really for a sign and shows a profound doubt of the possibility of fulfillment of Gabriel's announcement. Zechariah is given a most evident sign: Zechariah will be speechless until Gabriel's word is fulfilled. Mary, too, responded to the announcement of wondrous events with a question, "How can this *be*?" Her request is really for further action and already shows a profound surrender to what Gabriel announces. The angel's response to Mary is one of explanation and reassurance; Mary is given a sign in Elizabeth's pregnancy—a sign for which she did not ask. Mary's "May it be done to me according to your word" is the verbalization of her surrender. As was said by Isaiah (first reading), the conception by a virgin *is* the sign in itself.

Both of these responses culminated in the great songs of praise we know as Gospel canticles: Zechariah utters the *Benedictus* (Luke 1:68-79) when his tongue is loosed at John's circumcision and naming; Mary utters the *Magnificat* in response to Elizabeth's greeting (Luke 1:46-55). Each of these songs is a salvation hymn. Each time we sing them we are invited to respond to God's announcement to us of divine wonders in our own lives. Do we doubt and ask for signs, like Zechariah? Or do we ponder in faith what God speaks to us and believe, responding like both Mary and her Son with "Behold, I come to do your will" (second reading). By the union of their wills with God *we* have been consecrated. *We* are the highly favored ones of God because "nothing will be impossible with God."

Living the Paschal Mystery

In our baptism we are immersed in the Paschal Mystery: God invites us, like Mary, to participate in the divine plan—"The Holy Spirit will come upon you, and the power of the Most High will overshadow you." Like Mary, we spend our entire lives living out our baptism by surrendering to God's will—"May it be done to me according to your word." Like Mary, we bear the cost of the Paschal Mystery: our hearts are pierced by swords of family strife, illness, grief, etc. Yet, like Mary, we bear the fruit of this great Mystery: we are privileged to bear Christ within us.

GOSPEL [Luke 1:26-38; L545]

The angel Gabriel was sent from God to a town of Galilee called Nazareth, to a virgin betrothed to a man named Joseph, of the house of David, and the virgin's name was Mary. And coming to her, he said, "Hail, full of grace! The Lord is with you." But she was greatly troubled at what was said and pondered what sort of greeting this might be. Then the angel said to her, "Do not be afraid, Mary, for you have found favor with God. Behold, you will conceive in your womb and bear a son, and you shall name him Jesus. He will be great and will be called Son of the Most High, and the Lord God will give him the throne of David his father, and he will rule over the house of Jacob forever, and of his kingdom there will be no end." But Mary said to the angel, "How can this be, since I have no relations with a man?" And the angel said to her in reply, "The Holy Spirit will come upon you, and the power of the Most High will overshadow you. Therefore the child to be born will be called holy, the Son of God. And behold, Elizabeth, your relative, has also conceived a son in her old age, and this is the sixth month for her who was called barren; for nothing will be impossible for God." Mary said, "Behold, I am the handmaid of the Lord. May it be done to me according to your word." Then the angel departed from her.

Working with the Word

Key words and phrases from the Gospel: Hail, full of grace!; name him Jesus; Son of the Most High; give him the throne of David his father; rule; his kingdom; holy, the Son of God

Connecting to the second reading: The selection from Hebrews moves us away from miraculous conception and birth and focuses on Jesus who came to be sacrificed: "Behold, I come to do your will" was not only said by Jesus but also captures Mary's *yes*.

Connecting to the culture: During the century before Jesus' birth, there was great messianic expectation. There were varied elements to this expectation. One motif was awaiting David's heir to re-establish the tribes of Israel politically. In the early Church, Jesus was understood as God's anointed king, chosen from David's lineage. However, as we know, his kingship is different from the original messianic expectation.

Exegetical points: As the title of the solemnity suggests, this is a festival of the Lord. The various titles and descriptions of Jesus are, therefore, noteworthy: he will be called "Son of the Most High," and "holy, the Son of God"; he will inherit the "throne of David his father," "he will rule over the house of Jacob," and "of his kingdom there will be no end." All these statements are rich with Old Testament references. The "Most High" is a title used by Abraham for God (Gen 14:22); the use of "the house of Jacob" and the "house of David" place this passage firmly within the ancient and sacred traditions of Israel. Further, the "sonship" of Jesus, especially in light of the frequent references to David, could suggest the divine adoption of the Davidic heir, i.e., the ancient tradition that saw the King of Judah as God's own adopted son (see Pss 2:7; 110:2-3; cf. also Ps 89:27). This royal aspect is reinforced by the references to his eternal "rule" and his "kingdom." Even on this rich referential level, the message to Mary is astounding: the long moribund kingship of David which apparently ended with Zerubbabel in the sixth century B.C.E. is about to be revived! But for readers of the Gospel, something even greater is about to unfold. Luke signals this with the unparalleled virgin birth. The uniqueness of the conception and birth befit, not primarily the privilege of Mary, but the status of Jesus as the Son of God Most High.

To the point: Christ and Mary are our models for how salvation is accomplished by fidelity to God's will. For this reason Christ came into the world: "Behold, I come to do your will." Like Mary, we, too, must conform our wills to God's.

Celebration

Model Penitential Rite

Presider: Mary's response to Gabriel was "Behold, I am the handmaid of the Lord." Let us reflect on our own *yes* to God and ask that it be firm and unshakable . . . [pause]

Son of Mary, you were conceived by the power of the Holy Spirit: Lord . . .
Son of God, your kingdom has no end: Christ . . .
Son of the Most High, you offer your body for our salvation: Lord . . .

Responsorial Psalm

"Here am I, Lord; I come to do your will."
In the first reading, even though God commands him to do so, Ahaz will not ask God for a sign. Christ (second reading) and Mary (Gospel), on the other hand, respond to God's request without hesitation. The metaphor the responsorial psalm gives for such willingness is "ears open to obedience." The etiology of this image was the Semitic custom of piercing the ear of a slave as a sign of the obedience that the slave was expected to render. Exod 21:6 and Deut 15:17 give a further nuance to this practice, for in both references the slave whose ear is pierced has refused his freedom even though it has been granted him by Jewish law.

The obedience of which the psalm speaks, then, is freely undertaken, not coerced, and it is lifelong. Its source is an openness truly to hear the will of God written "within [the] heart," and its fruit is a joyful proclamation of that will among the people. Its model is Christ, whose self-offering enables us to sing with him, "Here am I, Lord; I come to do your will."

Model General Intercessions

Presider: All power belongs to God, even to have a virgin conceive by the Holy Spirit. Let us bring our prayers to this saving God.

Response:

[Musical notation: Lord, hear our prayer.]

Cantor:

[Musical notation: we pray to the Lord,]

That the Church, like Mary, always find favor with God . . . [pause]

That the nations, like Mary, do God's will . . . [pause]

That the poor, like Mary, have no fear . . . [pause]

That we, like Mary, surrender ourselves to God in faith . . . [pause]

Presider: O saving God, you reach out to humanity with the most wondrous of deeds: hear these our prayers that we may bear your Son's name with grace and fidelity. We ask this through that same Son, Jesus Christ our Lord. **Amen.**

OPENING PRAYER
Let us pray

Pause for silent prayer

God our Father,
your Word became man and was born of
  the Virgin Mary.
May we become more like Jesus Christ,
whom we acknowledge as our
  Redeemer, God and man.
We ask this through our Lord Jesus
  Christ, your Son,
who lives and reigns with you and the
  Holy Spirit,
one God, for ever and ever. **Amen.**

RESPONSORIAL PSALM
[Ps 40:7-8, 8-9, 10, 11]

℟. (8a and 9a) Here am I, Lord; I come to do your will.

Sacrifice or offering you wished not,
  but ears open to obedience you gave
    me.
Holocausts and sin-offerings you sought
  not;
  then said I, "Behold, I come";

℟. Here am I, Lord; I come to do your will.

"In the written scroll it is prescribed for
  me.
To do your will, O God, is my delight,
  and your law is within my heart!"

℟. Here am I, Lord; I come to do your will.

I announced your justice in the vast
  assembly;
  I did not restrain my lips, as you, O
    LORD, know.

℟. Here am I, Lord; I come to do your will.

Your justice I kept not hid within my
  heart;
  your faithfulness and your salvation I
    have spoken of;
I have made no secret of your kindness
  and your truth
  in the vast assembly.

℟. Here am I, Lord; I come to do your will.

FIRST READING
[Isa 7:10-14; 8:10]

The LORD spoke to Ahaz, saying:
  Ask for a sign from the LORD, your God;
  let it be deep as the netherworld, or high as the sky!
But Ahaz answered,
  "I will not ask! I will not tempt the LORD!"
Then Isaiah said:
  Listen, O house of David!
Is it not enough for you to weary people,
  must you also weary my God?
Therefore the Lord himself will give you this sign:
  the virgin shall conceive, and bear a son,
  and shall name him Emmanuel,
  which means "God is with us!"

SECOND READING
[Heb 10:4-10]

Brothers and sisters:
It is impossible that the blood of bulls and goats
  takes away sins.
For this reason, when Christ came into the world, he said:
  "Sacrifice and offering you did not desire,
    but a body you prepared for me;
  in holocausts and sin offerings you took no delight.
  Then I said, 'As is written of me in the scroll,
  behold, I come to do your will, O God.'"

First Christ says, "Sacrifices and offerings,
  holocausts and sin offerings,
  you neither desired nor delighted in."
These are offered according to the law.
Then he says, "Behold, I come to do your will."
He takes away the first to establish the second.
By this "will," we have been consecrated
  through the offering of the body of Jesus Christ once for all.

Catechesis

Cantors

Your role as cantor is an embodiment of the listening and responding which characterize real obedience. The assembly listens as you sing the verses of the psalm, and responds with the refrain. Through this interaction you are, together, responding to the word of God proclaimed in the readings and to the call for obedience which these readings are making upon your lives. Cantoring, then, is far more than singing the words of a psalm; it is an act of discipleship! How might you make this more evident in your cantoring? in your Christian living?

Choir

Singing is as much an act of listening as it is a making of sound. Your ears need to be as open as your mouth. One way to practice this "obedience" is to discipline yourself to listen to the other sections of the choir when they are rehearsing a phrase or passage, rather than "tuning out" or becoming distracted. The resultant choral sound will be all the richer for you will understand its individual elements more clearly.

Music Directors

Because this solemnity is more about Christ who is the source and model of obedience than about Mary, the music ought not focus on Marian hymns. The music would better focus on Christ as the source and goal of our *yes* to discipleship. Especially fitting for either the presentation of the gifts or Communion would be "Yes, Lord" [LMGM] with its "My soul says yes . . . Yes to your will . . ." Also suitable for the presentation of the gifts would be "With Jesus for Hero" (CH, W3]. "O Christ the Great Foundation" [CH, W3] would be a good hymn of praise after Communion.

Liturgy Committee

How do you prepare your liturgies so that you can elicit from your assemblies the faithful *yes* that you hear Mary speak in this solemnity's Gospel?

The Annunciation of the Lord is a dominical feast (feast of the Lord) on the 1969 General Roman Calendar, not a Marian feast. This Gospel is also proclaimed on the Fourth Sunday of Advent, where Marian overtones are more clearly evident. Throughout the history of this feast (dating from the sixth century in the Eastern Church and the seventh century in the Western Church) it has been variously a dominical or Marian feast. This reminds us that Mary cannot ever be far from our thoughts when we consider the great deeds of salvation.

This solemnity comes during Lent, so we want to have a "tempered" celebration at the same time that we strive to celebrate joyfully this festival of salvation.

MARCH 25, 2000

Third Sunday of Lent

FAITH-SHARING

- How can you grow in your grasp that you are temples of God, and your bodies, too, will be raised up? How might this give you hope to persevere in your Lenten penance?
- Describe your covenantal relationship with God. What concrete shapes does this take in your everyday living?
- How does your keeping of God's law witness to your relationship with God?
- If Jesus were to visit you as his temple, what would need cleansing?

PRESIDERS

"Zeal for your house will consume me." How is your zeal? What consumes you?

DEACONS

The "sign" Jesus offers his questioners is his very life and death. What does your daily living "signify"? Christ crucified? self-interest?

HOSPITALITY MINISTERS

In what way was Jesus performing an act of hospitality in the temple that you might also model?

MUSIC MINISTERS

Yours is a ministry, so to speak, "within the temple." Do you strive to serve God and God's people, rather than personal ends?

ALTAR MINISTERS

How is your service related to "cleansing the Temple"? What needs to be cleansed in you, who are God's temple?

LECTORS

"When he was raised from the dead . . . they came to believe the Scripture." What leads you to believe the Scripture you proclaim?

EUCHARISTIC MINISTERS

How might you better recognize that those to whom you give Communion are temples of God, the living body of Christ?

Spirituality

Reflecting on the Gospel

Walk in most Roman Catholic churches today and what do we find at the entrance? Usually, racks full of pamphlets, Catholic papers, and books for sale. On some Sundays there might be tables set up for bake sales or raffle tickets. There's a box to place gifts for the poor, lost and found, and sometimes sign-up sheets for this or that. If Jesus walked in our churches today, would he have the same reaction as at the Temple?

This Sunday's Gospel takes place at Passover. Many visitors had come to Jerusalem to make their offering at the Temple. Moneychangers and sacrificial animals for sale, offering boxes, and other forms of commerce were a normal part of the Temple area, just as the similar purchasing that might take place in any Catholic parish church today. So what's the big deal? Why use a whip? Why overthrow tables? Was Jesus just having a bad day?

The first reading gives us a clue to an accurate response to these questions and an explanation for Jesus' actions. The reading is from the book of Exodus and tells of the Law given to Moses. It is key to understand, here, the relationship between law and covenant. The law was more than just a list of commandments for the people to keep, and surely more than some kind of checklist for good conduct. The law was the measure of the covenantal relationship between God and Israel. God was the One who brought them out of Egyptian slavery; God was the One who bestowed "mercy . . . on the children of those who love me." Merely keeping commandments in themselves was not an expression of Israel's love for God; keeping the commandments *because of what God had done for them,* because of the unique relationship that existed between them was what made Israel holy and God's people.

The merchants and moneychangers were keeping the law; this kind of commerce was natural to the Temple area. That wasn't the point. The point is, "my Father's house" was a marketplace for some; that is, the commerce was no longer directed toward temple worship and expressing one's love and covenantal relationship to God. Instead, the commerce was directed to the merchants' and bankers' own self interests. In face of this unfaithful behavior, Exodus says that God is "a jealous God, inflicting punishment . . . for wickedness."

Are our churches places of self interest and our own endeavors, or places where we express our own covenantal relationship with God, a covenant sealed by "Christ crucified" (second reading) and "raised from the dead"?

Living the Paschal Mystery

Through baptism our bodies are made temples of God. Our Lenten penitential practices (prayer, fasting, and almsgiving) are our concrete ways to enter into the dying and rising Mystery of Christ. Like Christ, we become living signs of God's love and fidelity. The witness of our lives is a living sign of our covenantal relationship with God, a relationship of love and mercy. How are we doing as a sign this Lent?

GOSPEL [John 2:13-25; L29B]

Since the Passover of the Jews was near, Jesus went up to Jerusalem. He found in the temple area those who sold oxen, sheep, and doves, as well as the money changers seated there. He made a whip out of cords and drove them all out of the temple area, with the sheep and oxen, and spilled the coins of the money changers and overturned their tables, and to those who sold doves he said, "Take these out of here, and stop making my Father's house a marketplace." His disciples recalled the words of Scripture, *Zeal for your house will consume me.* At this the Jews answered and said to him, "What sign can you show us for doing this?" Jesus answered and said to them, "Destroy this temple and in three days I will raise it up." The Jews said, "This temple has been under construction for forty-six years, and you will raise it up in three days?" But he was speaking about the temple of his body. Therefore, when he was raised from the dead, his disciples remembered that he had said this, and they came to believe the Scripture and the word Jesus had spoken.

While he was in Jerusalem for the feast of Passover, many began to believe in his name when they saw the signs he was doing. But Jesus would not trust himself to them because he knew them all, and did not need anyone to testify about human nature. He himself understood it well.

Working with the Word

Key words and phrases from the Gospel: Passover . . . was near, went up to Jerusalem, Temple, temple of his body, raised from the dead

Connecting to the next two Sundays: These three Sundays form a unit preparing us for the passion. One of the charges at Jesus' trial (destroy this temple . . .) is from this incident.

Connecting to our culture: The Gospel hints that our body is a temple as Jesus' body was a temple. How does society view the human body? Do we view our bodies as temples or idols?

Exegetical points: In a major departure from the order of the Synoptic Gospels, John places the cleansing of the Temple at the beginning of the Gospel rather than in Jesus' final week before his death. In this, John is continuing a pattern in which Jesus progressively replaces the feasts, customs, and institutions of Judaism. The grace and truth that come in Jesus surpass the law that comes through Moses (John 1:17); the water used in rites of purification is replaced by a messianic abundance of choice wine (John 2:1-11; cf. Isa 25:6); and now in this Sunday's passage, the Temple in Jerusalem is replaced by the temple of Jesus' own body. The replacement pattern becomes even more explicit in John 4:21-24 when Jesus assures the Samaritan woman that the days of Temple worship are coming to an end.

Even in these opening chapters of John, the passion is already in view. In addition to situating this event in the context of the feast of Passover, John 2:19 (on the destruction of the Temple) alludes to the tradition in the synoptic Gospels where the destruction of the Temple appears as a taunt against Jesus during his crucifixion (Matt 27:40; Mark 15:29). John goes on to alert his readers that the destruction of the Temple really refers to the destruction of Jesus' body in death. John then indicates that the full meaning of Jesus' saying would become clear only after the resurrection (v. 22). Passover, destruction of the Temple, resurrection are all signposts on the way to Christ's glorification on the cross.

As a reading during Lent, the cleansing of the Temple offers a paschal image: the elect preparing for their baptism can see in this passage a symbol of their interior purification which Jesus brings about in them.

To the point: Jesus' dying and rising is the pattern of our baptismal living of dying and rising. We are called to die to our self-interests so that our covenant relationship with God is the focus or direction of our lives.

Celebration

Model Penitential Rite

Presider: As Church, we are Christ's body made visible in the world today. How faithful have we been to the life given us by God? How well have we responded to God's love and mercy? . . . [pause]

Confiteor: I confess . . .

Responsorial Psalm

"Lord, you have the words of everlasting life."

The whole of Psalm 19 from which the responsorial psalm for this Sunday is taken has three sections. The first (vv. 2-7) sings about the sun "joyfully [running] its course" from one end of the heavens to the other. "Nothing," says the psalm, "escapes its heat." The second (vv. 8-11) sings the praises of God's Law, from which all good comes. The third (vv. 12-15) is an acknowledgment of sin, both unconscious and willful, with a plea that God keep the psalmist faithful.

Just as the sun gives light to the earth, so does the Law give light to humankind. Both leave no corner in shadow. Both are gifts of God. Yet, how easily humans fail to live in the light! In the temple Jesus, who understands "human nature" well, confronts this darkness with directness and force (Gospel). He is "the power . . . and the wisdom of God" (second reading) who brings the light of God's judgment to bear upon human behavior. He is the personification of the covenant and the Law and it is of him we sing when we pray this responsorial psalm.

Model General Intercessions

Presider: God understands human nature very well, and still God loves us faithfully. We place our needs into the hands of this loving and kind God.

Response:

Lord, hear our prayer.

Cantor:

we pray to the Lord,

May the Church ever grow in being the living temple of God, witnessing to others God's love and mercy . . . [pause]

May the people of all nations heed the commandments of God written into their hearts and bring the world to peace and reconciliation . . . [pause]

May those who twist laws for their own gain come during this Lent to conversion and repentance . . . [pause]

May all of us be consumed with zeal for God and express it by faithful prayer, fasting, and charity . . . [pause]

Presider: Loving and kind God, you offer us a covenant of new life in which we are your temple: hear these our prayers and help us to persevere in our Lenten penance. We ask this through Christ our Lord. **Amen.**

OPENING PRAYER

Let us pray

Pause for silent prayer

Father,
you have taught us to overcome our sins
  by prayer, fasting and works of mercy.
When we are discouraged by our
    weakness,
give us confidence in your love.
We ask this through our Lord Jesus
    Christ, your Son,
who lives and reigns with you and the
    Holy Spirit,
one God, for ever and ever. **Amen.**

RESPONSORIAL PSALM [Ps 19:8, 9, 10, 11]

℟. (John 6:68c) Lord, you have the words of everlasting life.

The law of the LORD is perfect,
    refreshing the soul;
the decree of the LORD is trustworthy,
    giving wisdom to the simple.

℟. Lord, you have the words of everlasting life.

The precepts of the LORD are right,
    rejoicing the heart;
the command of the LORD is clear,
    enlightening the eye.

℟. Lord, you have the words of everlasting life.

The fear of the LORD is pure,
    enduring forever;
the ordinances of the LORD are true,
    all of them just.

℟. Lord, you have the words of everlasting life.

They are more precious than gold,
    than a heap of purest gold;
sweeter also than syrup
    or honey from the comb.

℟. Lord, you have the words of everlasting life.

FIRST READING [Exod 20:1-17]

In those days, God delivered all these
    commandments:
  "I, the LORD, am your God,
  who brought you out of the land of
      Egypt, that place of slavery.
You shall not have other gods besides me.
You shall not carve idols for yourselves
  in the shape of anything in the sky
      above
  or on the earth below or in the waters
      beneath the earth;
  you shall not bow down before them
      or worship them.
For I, the LORD, your God, am a jealous
    God,

inflicting punishment for their
    fathers' wickedness
  on the children of those who hate me,
    down to the third and fourth
      generation;
  but bestowing mercy down to the
    thousandth generation
  on the children of those who love me
    and keep my commandments.
"You shall not take the name of the
  LORD, your God, in vain.
For the LORD will not leave unpunished
  the one who takes his name in vain.
"Remember to keep holy the sabbath day.
Six days you may labor and do all your
    work,
  but the seventh day is the sabbath of
    the LORD, your God.
No work may be done then either by
  you, or your son or daughter,
  or your male or female slave, or your
    beast,
  or by the alien who lives with you.
In six days the LORD made the heavens
    and the earth,
  the sea and all that is in them;
  but on the seventh day he rested.
That is why the LORD has blessed the
  sabbath day and made it holy.
"Honor your father and your mother,
  that you may have a long life in the
    land
  which the LORD, your God, is giving
    you.
You shall not kill.
You shall not commit adultery.
You shall not steal.
You shall not bear false witness against
  your neighbor.
You shall not covet your neighbor's
  house.
You shall not covet your neighbor's wife,
  nor his male or female slave, nor his
    ox or ass,
  nor anything else that belongs to him."

SECOND READING [1 Cor 1:22-25]

Brothers and sisters:
Jews demand signs and Greeks look for
    wisdom,
  but we proclaim Christ crucified,
    a stumbling block to Jews and
      foolishness to Gentiles,
  but to those who are called, Jews and
    Greeks alike,
  Christ the power of God and the
    wisdom of God.
For the foolishness of God is wiser than
    human wisdom,
  and the weakness of God is stronger
    than human strength.

Catechesis

Cantors

Read and reflect on the entirety of Psalm 19 as you prepare to sing the portion of it assigned for this Sunday's responsorial psalm. The comparison of the law to the light of the sun, and the honesty with which the psalmist prays to remain faithful to the law reveal that the law is not a list of things to do or not do, but the guide to a living and loving relationship. It is out of this relationship that you wish to sing.

Choir

What judgment would Christ have to bring upon your behaviors as a choir? When rehearsing in the church space, do you remember that it is a sacred place? In your relating to one another, do you remember that each of you is a temple of God?

Music Directors

The sixth-century Latin hymn "O Sun of Justice" [RS, W3] would make a fitting entrance hymn for this Sunday. The text calls on Christ to "dispel the darkness of our hearts," and calls the assembly to use this "time acceptable" for conversion and renewal. CBW3 uses a different translation of the text with the especially beautiful additional verse, "As spring awakes the frozen earth, So Easter blooms from Lent's restraints. Rejoice, for Christ will conquer death And bring his grace to make us saints." RS and W3 use the traditional chant melody for the hymn. CBW3 uses the hymn tune WAREHAM.

Liturgy Committee

In your ministry of planning, preparing, and evaluating liturgies, do you act more like the merchants and moneychangers or like Jesus? For example, is "getting it right" more important than leading the assembly toward a deeper worship experience? Or are you so "anything goes as long as it works and the people go away happy" that the focus shifts from praying in God's house to something else?

For parishes with catechumens and candidates in the RCIA, this third Sunday of Lent begins the scrutinies. At that Mass the readings from year A are recommended, even during year B (and at this Mass, then, use the preface for the third Sunday [P14]). Admittedly, this always raises a pastoral problem: preferably, two different sets of readings would be used (from year A at the Mass where the scrutinies are celebrated, and year B for the other Masses) but this, then, would require the preparation of two different homilies and, possibly, two sets of hymn selections.

It is best to use the long form of the first reading, for if the short form is chosen then the notion of covenant (clarifying its Lenten context) is largely missed.

MARCH 26, 2000

Fourth Sunday of Lent

FAITH-SHARING
- When has God spoken to you "early and often"? How have you responded?
- Does your daily living witness a preference for darkness or light? How might you come closer to the Light during this Lent?
- What might help you to come more surely to the light?
- "God so loved the world . . ." When/how have you experienced this love of God for you?

PRESIDERS
How do you witness to others that you are coming to the light?

DEACONS
How might your loving service invite and encourage others to seek the light rather than darkness?

HOSPITALITY MINISTERS
How might the warmth of your greeting bring light to those who seem to be in darkness?

MUSIC MINISTERS
What light does Jesus' death and resurrection shed upon your ministry of leading the assembly in liturgical song?

ALTAR MINISTERS
Ironically, your unselfish ministry puts you in the position of being "lifted up" for all to see. How might you serve so that others are drawn to the light?

LECTORS
In what ways can you *live* the light so that you can proclaim God's word as light-giving?

EUCHARISTIC MINISTERS
How do you share your own life and light with others when you minister the Body or Blood of Christ? How is this especially true if you bring Communion to the sick or homebound?

Spirituality

Reflecting on the Gospel

A radio station created quite a stir in its listening area when it brought out an ad campaign that featured a woman on a billboard with two prominent, half-naked breasts. In response to the outrage, the station manager said, "We got what we wanted; people are talking about the station." Isn't it interesting how we can have offensive billboards and commercials at the same time that we have religious ones such as those announcing John 3:16 (a line from this Sunday's Gospel)? Do religious billboards and banners create a stir like that radio station did? And *if* the John 3:16 billboards created an equal stir, what would the response be? Just talk, or do these billboards do what this Sunday's Gospel does: call us to conversion and belief?

The Liturgy of the Word this Sunday contrasts condemnation and salvation, and employs such images as captivity and return, weeping and joy, dead and raised up, lifted up (on the cross) and eternal life, darkness and light. The contrasts are as stark and revealing as that between billboards with breasts or Scripture. How fickle we human beings can be! How saved we human beings are!

"God so loved the world" that we have been given every means possible to believe and be saved. "And this is the verdict": some still choose darkness over light, in spite of being given the incredible gift of Truth, God's own Son who was raised up on a cross for us. What does God ask in return for such great gifts as a Son's sacrifice and our eternal life? God asks for the total sacrifice of our own lives. Perhaps such a high cost explains why we prefer darkness and billboards with breasts—they don't cost us anything!

Living the Paschal Mystery

A line in the first reading is as heart-rending and plaintive as is the responsorial psalm: "Early and often did the Lord . . . send . . . messengers to them, for he had compassion . . . But they mocked the messengers of God." Can it be any clearer to us that our God desires our salvation? And offers us every means possible to enter into eternal life?

Lent is a kind of "messenger" given by a compassionate God and Church for us to assess our relationship with God, self, and others. The Liturgy of the Word casts our Lenten penance as a contrast between dying and rising. We would naturally think of penance as a dying to self, and it is that. But it's not only that. The positive aspect of penance is that the dying always leads to life, resurrection. We are barely half way through Lent and we are already invited to go through Lent with the *risen* Christ. Even in our journey of repentance and conversion we are already shown that we will be given far more than we could ever give: all we need do is come to the light and life eternal is ours.

Of course, the real challenge is that the words of Scripture must leap from the page through proclamation into our hearts and sear so deeply that we *live* God's word. In other words, we must move from paying lip service to Scripture and belief *toward* concrete, everyday actions that witness to our choice to come to the light: prayer, fasting, charitable works. The Paschal Mystery isn't a concept; it is a life to be lived!

APRIL 2, 2000

GOSPEL [John 3:14-21; L32B]

Jesus said to Nicodemus: "Just as Moses lifted up the serpent in the desert, so must the Son of Man be lifted up, so that everyone who believes in him may have eternal life."

For God so loved the world that he gave his only Son, so that everyone who believes in him might not perish but might have eternal life. For God did not send his Son into the world to condemn the world, but that the world might be saved through him. Whoever believes in him will not be condemned, but whoever does not believe has already been condemned, because he has not believed in the name of the only Son of God. And this is the verdict, that the light came into the world, but people preferred darkness to light, because their works were evil. For everyone who does wicked things hates the light and does not come toward the light, so that his works might not be exposed. But whoever lives the truth comes to the light, so that his works may be clearly seen as done in God.

Working with the Word

Key words and phrases from the Gospel: lifted up, gave his only Son, have eternal life, saved, not be condemned, darkness to light

Connecting to the first three Sundays of Lent: Last Sunday's Gospel moved us toward Jerusalem by the charge against Jesus ("destroy this temple . . ."); this Sunday's Gospel also moves us toward Jerusalem by being "lifted up," a reference not only to death on a cross but—more importantly—to being lifted up in glory. We have the same dying-rising dynamic between these two Sundays as we had between the first two Sundays of Lent.

Connecting to our culture: We often see billboards and banners (especially at sports events where there is national exposure) advertising John 3:16 ("For God so loved the world that he gave his only Son, so that everyone who believes in him might not perish but might have eternal life"). The verse is rightly called "the Gospel in miniature" because it is really a summary of the whole Paschal Mystery. We've got the quote right; do we follow through on our living it?

Exegetical points: John's love of "double meaning" is evident in the first verse of this Sunday's Gospel. The most obvious meaning of the expression "lifted up" is the physical act of placing something on high—in this context, Moses placing the bronze serpent on a pole (Numbers 21), and Jesus being placed high on the cross. Just as the Hebrews who had been bitten by poisonous snakes found healing by looking upon the bronze serpent, all who look upon the crucified Jesus with faith will find salvation. In both instances, the instrument that brings death—serpent and cross—also brings life. The meaning of Jesus' life-giving death is stated explicitly in v. 16, "the Gospel in miniature."

But the expression "lifted up" also means "to be exalted." While for Mark the cross means suffering and ignominy, for John the cross fulfills "the hour" of Christ's glorification. The cross is Jesus' throne of glory, the moment when he is exalted as King of the Jews and Savior of the world. For this reason, the Church has long preferred the Passion according to John on Good Friday, for more than the story of Jesus' death, John's Gospel is the story of Jesus' exaltation and human salvation.

To the point: What needs to be done has been done: Christ has suffered, died, and is risen. God desires our salvation, not our condemnation; but God does not compel us to accept the gift of salvation. By our lives we choose either to walk in darkness or light.

Celebration

Model Penitential Rite

Presider: Today's Gospel offers us a clear choice: choose darkness, the realm of evil and sin, or come to the light where we can hear the promise of eternal life. Let us consider our living during the past week and whether we choose darkness or light . . . [pause]

Confiteor: I confess . . .

Responsorial Psalm

"Let my tongue be silenced, if I ever forget you!"
This Sunday's responsorial psalm is difficult to relate to unless we understand it in the context of Israel's exile in Babylon. The exile was devastating and they had brought it upon themselves through their unfaithfulness to the covenant (first reading). Psalm 137 echoes the bitterness of the exile and is a reflection upon the utter barrenness of that experience. It is also a plea never again to forget what it means to be God's people. The second reading tells us that we, too, have been restored to life "even when we were dead in our transgressions." The only Son of God has come not to condemn but to save us (Gospel). Yet, just as with the Israelites, we must choose. The responsorial psalm invites us to remember who we are so that we will walk in the light.

Model General Intercessions

Presider: "God so loved the world that he sent his only Son." We can make our needs known to such a God with great confidence that they will be answered.

Response:

[musical notation: Lord, hear our prayer.]

Cantor:

[musical notation: we pray to the Lord,]

For the Church to believe so firmly as to inspire and encourage candidates and catechumens during their final preparation for baptism . . . [pause]

For the people of the world to be saved through response to the presence of God's kingdom . . . [pause]

For those who have chosen darkness to repent and believe and come to the light . . . [pause]

For our community to perform works that are clearly seen as done in God . . . [pause]

Presider: Early and often, O God, you have called us to be your faithful people: hear these our prayers that we might turn toward you in repentance and peace and so come to enjoy eternal life. We ask this through Christ our Lord. **Amen.**

OPENING PRAYER
Let us pray
Pause for silent prayer

Father of peace,
we are joyful in your Word,
your Son Jesus Christ,
who reconciles us to you.
Let us hasten toward Easter
with the eagerness of faith and love.

We ask this through our Lord Jesus
  Christ, your Son,
who lives and reigns with you and the
  Holy Spirit,
one God, for ever and ever. **Amen.**

RESPONSORIAL PSALM [Ps 137:1-2, 3, 4-5, 6]

℟. (6ab) Let my tongue be silenced, if I ever forget you!

By the streams of Babylon
  we sat and wept when we
    remembered Zion.
On the aspens of that land
  we hung up our harps.

℟. Let my tongue be silenced, if I ever forget you!

For there our captors asked of us
  the lyrics of our songs,
and our despoilers urged us to be joyous:
  "Sing for us the songs of Zion!"

℟. Let my tongue be silenced, if I ever forget you!

How could we sing a song of the LORD
  in a foreign land?
If I forget you, Jerusalem,
  may my right hand be forgotten!

℟. Let my tongue be silenced, if I ever forget you!

May my tongue cleave to my palate
  if I remember you not,
if I place not Jerusalem
  ahead of my joy.

℟. Let my tongue be silenced, if I ever forget you!

FIRST READING [2 Chr 36:14-16, 19-23]

In those days, all the princes of Judah,
  the priests, and the people
  added infidelity to infidelity,
  practicing all the abominations of the
    nations
  and polluting the LORD's temple
  which he had consecrated in Jerusalem.

Early and often did the LORD, the God of
  their fathers,
  send his messengers to them,
  for he had compassion on his people
    and his dwelling place.
But they mocked the messengers of God,
  despised his warnings, and scoffed at
    his prophets,

until the anger of the LORD against his
    people was so inflamed
that there was no remedy.
Their enemies burnt the house of God,
    tore down the walls of Jerusalem,
    set all its palaces afire,
    and destroyed all its precious objects.
Those who escaped the sword were
    carried captive to Babylon,
    where they became servants of the
        king of the Chaldeans and his sons
    until the kingdom of the Persians
        came to power.
All this was to fulfill the word of the
    LORD spoken by Jeremiah:
"Until the land has retrieved its lost
    sabbaths,
during all the time it lies waste it shall
    have rest
while seventy years are fulfilled."
In the first year of Cyrus, king of Persia,
    in order to fulfill the word of the LORD
        spoken by Jeremiah,
    the LORD inspired King Cyrus of Persia
        to issue this proclamation throughout
            his kingdom,
        both by word of mouth and in writing:
"Thus says Cyrus, king of Persia:
All the kingdoms of the earth
    the LORD, the God of heaven, has
        given to me,
and he has also charged me to build
    him a house
in Jerusalem, which is in Judah.
Whoever, therefore, among you belongs
    to any part of his people,
let him go up, and may his God be
    with him!"

SECOND READING [Eph 2:4-10]

Brothers and sisters:
God, who is rich in mercy,
    because of the great love he had for us,
    even when we were dead in our
        transgressions,
    brought us to life with Christ—by
        grace you have been saved—,
    raised us up with him,
    and seated us with him in the heavens
        in Christ Jesus,
    that in the ages to come
he might show the immeasurable
        riches of his grace
    in his kindness to us in Christ Jesus.
For by grace you have been saved
    through faith,
    and this is not from you; it is the gift
        of God;
    it is not from works, so no one may
        boast.
For we are his handiwork, created in
    Christ Jesus for the good works
    that God has prepared in advance,
    that we should live in them.

Catechesis

Cantors

The Liturgy of the Word for this Sunday presents you with two constants in your experience: human sinfulness and God's salvation. To sing this psalm well, you need to be honest about your own sinfulness, the times and ways that you have been in exile from God and from the community, and conscious of the real ways that God has forgiven you and restored you to fullness of life.

Choir

A good hymn to use this week for prayer before or after rehearsal would be "What Wondrous Love Is This." You might first pray it together by reciting the verses, then spend some time in silent prayer, then conclude by singing it softly.

Music Directors

"By the Babylonian Rivers" [RS, W3] is a paraphrase of Psalm 137 set to a Latvian folk tune, the original text of which compared orphans in a conquered land to the captives in Babylon. The final verse connects cross and resurrection, "Let the Cross be benediction For those bound in tyranny; By the power of resurrection Loose them from captivity." The hymn would function well for the entrance procession.

Psalm 137 occurs as the responsorial psalm only this once in the three-year cycle. Its intensely plaintive text calls for an equally plaintive setting. RS and W3 use a Gelineau tone effectively set for either organ or woodwinds. The refrain by Frank Schoen is chromatically intense, and may be difficult for the assembly to get on first hearing, but is worth the effort. WC has a through-composed setting by Mike Hay which requires a competent cantor who can handle a high tessitura and a melodic line independent of the accompaniment. Both of these settings are immensely expressive of the psalm text. One regrets how seldom assemblies get to sing them.

Liturgy Committee

Penance as something to be endured rather than something joyfully embraced is an outgrowth of medieval and later spirituality that concentrated heavily on the sinfulness of humanity. The earlier understanding of penance had a much more positive context. Penance was considered a *sacramental*; that is, it was a tangible reality (prayer, fasting, and almsgiving) that helped people grasp a spiritual reality (conversion and new relationship with God). Early Christians fasted much more often than Christians today tend to do because, rather than merely burdensome, penance was directed to participating in the Paschal Mystery. How might you help yourself and others acquire a more positive meaning to penance?

A Lectionary note: this is the only Sunday in the entire three-year cycle that a selection from Chronicles (a historical book) is read.

This Fourth Sunday of Lent was called *laetare* (rejoice, be joyful) Sunday, from the introductory verse (introit), and rose vestments were worn (they are still permitted). It marked the halfway point and encouraged people in their penitential practices. Since there is now a more positive context for penance (especially with the readings of this Sunday that remind one of the "rising" aspect of the Paschal Mystery), it is preferable not to separate this Sunday from the other Sundays of Lent.

APRIL 2, 2000

Fifth Sunday of Lent

FAITH-SHARING
- What have you learned from your suffering? What kind of obedience might *you* learn from suffering?
- What shape does the grain of wheat dying take in your everyday living?
- What, concretely, does it mean to follow Jesus by being servant?
- When have you glimpsed the glory of the cross in your own life?

PRESIDERS
How do you model in your ministry the servanthood that comes from dying to self?

DEACONS
What is the difference in your ministry to the community between being "servant" or "employee"?

HOSPITALITY MINISTERS
In what ways is hospitable ministry really being servant for others?

MUSIC MINISTERS
How can you help those you lead to see that the most genuine fruit their music ministry bears comes from dying to self rather than from any other signs of seeming success?

ALTAR MINISTERS
How might your service at church lead others to be drawn to Jesus?

LECTORS
What steps in preparation for your ministry do you take to ensure that God's word will be written upon people's hearts?

EUCHARISTIC MINISTERS
How might you minister and live Eucharist so that both the suffering of the cross and the glory of the resurrection are manifested?

Spirituality

Reflecting on the Gospel

Dead Man Walking was a box-office hit movie several years ago. Reruns, video rentals, articles, and conversations about it still come up every now and then. The story is a disturbing one to catch the fancy of the public. Does it merely witness to our growing callousness to violence, fed by so much of it in the media? Is our sense of entertainment so warped that we see imposed death as fascinating and capturing our attention? Or is something else at work? In this particular case, the movie and spinoffs continue to draw public attention to the issues of "an eye for an eye" restitution, our penal system, and capital punishment. At what price does redemption come? This Sunday's Gospel addresses this question.

The Gospel begins with people wanting to "see Jesus." Were they drawn because of his miracles? because of his confrontations with authorities? because of his teachings? mixed motives? Andrew and Philip tell Jesus people want to see him, but the Gospel never tells us whether they did see Jesus or not. Rather, Jesus responds with a meditative monologue (to "see" Jesus is to "see" the passion) that sets us up for the coming events of a Last Supper with his disciples, the trial, passion, death, and resurrection (immediate in John's Gospel, coming yet in a couple weeks for our unfolding of the liturgical year). "The hour has come." Jesus is a dead man walking.

Living the Paschal Mystery

Death is something that we try to avoid, prolonging the inevitable as much as possible. By contrast, Jesus embraces his death. He is the grain of wheat that dies. Those of us who want to participate in his Paschal Mystery must also lose our life and serve.

Was the prospect of suffering and dying easy for Jesus? Apparently not: "I am troubled now." He is not swerved from the purpose for which he came (to reconcile us to his Father). As the second reading tells us, "he learned obedience from what he suffered." The key image in John's Gospel is that of Jesus being "lifted up from the earth." On the one hand, this means his being physically lifted up on the cross. It also means lifted up in exaltation for, in John, the cross *is* exaltation; cross and exaltation can never be separated.

By our baptism we have the new covenantal relationship with God written upon our hearts (see the first reading). Baptism is the sign of our being drawn to Jesus so that we, too, might be lifted up and glorified with him. Like Jesus, we must learn obedience through suffering, that is, by dying to self which often takes the form of following Jesus in service of others. These are no mere words. They demand of us a life very much different from that which the media teaches us about happiness. Dying to self means that we live counter-culturally: not for ourselves and our own gain but for the happiness and salvation of others.

If we take living the Paschal Mystery seriously, we are "dead man [people] walking." The door opening onto life is death to self. Our own glorification is the fruit of obedience learned through service. Who among us is willing to be a "dead man walking"? We must follow Jesus to the cross. And glory.

APRIL 9, 2000

GOSPEL [John 12:20-33; L35B]

Some Greeks who had come to worship at the Passover Feast came to Philip, who was from Bethsaida in Galilee, and asked him, "Sir, we would like to see Jesus." Philip went and told Andrew; then Andrew and Philip went and told Jesus. Jesus answered them, "The hour has come for the Son of Man to be glorified. Amen, amen, I say to you, unless a grain of wheat falls to the ground and dies, it remains just a grain of wheat; but if it dies, it produces much fruit. Whoever loves his life loses it, and whoever hates his life in this world will preserve it for eternal life. Whoever serves me must follow me, and where I am, there also will my servant be. The Father will honor whoever serves me.

"I am troubled now. Yet what should I say? 'Father, save me from this hour'? But it was for this purpose that I came to this hour. Father, glorify your name." Then a voice came from heaven, "I have glorified it and will glorify it again." The crowd there heard it and said it was thunder; but others said, "An angel has spoken to him." Jesus answered and said, "This voice did not come for my sake but for yours. Now is the time of judgment on this world; now the ruler of this world will be driven out. And when I am lifted up from the earth, I will draw everyone to myself." He said this indicating the kind of death he would die.

Working with the Word

Key words and phrases from the Gospel: see Jesus, hour has come, grain of wheat . . . dies, for this purpose I came, lifted up, draw everyone to myself

Connecting to last Sunday: The condemnation spoken of in last Sunday's Gospel is not of persons (God desires *all* to be saved) but of *evil*. The "judgment on this world" is so that "the ruler of this world [Satan] will be driven out."

Connecting to our culture: We tend to have a one-dimensional view of the cross as an instrument of suffering. In this Gospel John is pointing to more: the cross is a means for Jesus to be glorified. In John the cross is a throne upon which Jesus is exalted. [The crosses in the Eastern Church are always ornate and usually without a body; if Christ is on the cross, it is the glorified, priestly, victorious, risen One.]

Exegetical points: This last numbered Sunday of Lent finds some Greeks asking to see Jesus. From this seemingly simple request, the Gospel seems to take a strange detour as Jesus launches into a discourse about the hour of his glorification. "Hour" and "glorification" are two prominent themes in the Fourth Gospel. In this Sunday's brief passage, Jesus refers to "the/this hour" three times, while the noun "glory" and the verb "glorify" each occur twice. In John's Gospel, when the "hour" is not referring to a particular time of day, it refers to a significant period in the life of Jesus, namely, his passion, death, resurrection, and ascension. These are not so much four discrete episodes as they are one event—the single "hour" of his glorification. As Jesus explains, "the hour . . . for the Son of Man to be glorified" means that it is time for the grain of wheat to fall, die, and thus produce much fruit. Indeed, "it was for this purpose that I came to this hour." Thus, last week's suggestion that the life-giving death and resurrection of Jesus is the hour of his glory is now confirmed and made explicit. This Sunday's passage concludes by recalling last week's Gospel, "when I am lifted up from the earth, I will draw everyone to myself." With this end in view, it is now clear why the Gospel begins as it does. The request of the Greeks to "see" Jesus can be met in its deepest Johannine sense only when his glory is revealed, for "seeing" Jesus means having faith in him as the glorified Son of God.

To the point: Like those in this Gospel, we want to see Jesus. Jesus reveals himself in a most unexpected way, lifted up on the cross. The unexpected is that this cross is not a scandal but a throne of glory.

Celebration

Model Penitential Rite

Presider: If we wish to be glorified with Christ, we must follow him to the cross and become the servant of all. To prepare ourselves to celebrate this liturgy, let us think over our past few weeks of Lent and judge how well we have been a servant of others . . . [pause]

Confiteor: I confess . . .

Responsorial Psalm

"Create a clean heart in me, O God."

Psalm 51 is so familiar to us that we may miss its significance. Almost always a psalmist confronted with suffering claims innocence of any evildoing which would have merited the suffering (see Psalm 26, for example). Precisely what makes Psalm 51 unusual is that the psalmist does not do this. Instead he or she readily acknowledges guilt ("wipe out my offense . . . wash me from my guilt") and asks not for forgiveness, but for transformation ("Create a clean heart in me, O God").

The Liturgy of the Word for this Sunday presents an ongoing dialogue between God and human beings. God continually offers us a new heart and a new covenant (first reading). With Psalm 51 we continually acknowledge our need for forgiveness and transformation. The second reading proclaims that the transformation has been completed in Christ. And the Gospel tells us that—for him and for us—the way is through death.

Model General Intercessions

Presider: Let us pray to God that we may follow Christ and die to ourselves so that we may share in his glory.

Response:

[Musical notation: "Lord, hear our prayer."]

Cantor:

[Musical notation: "we pray to the Lord,"]

That the Church may always have members who are like grains of wheat that fall to the ground and die and then bear much fruit . . . [pause]

That all people of the world may serve God, responding to the new covenant written in their hearts . . . [pause]

That those who love too much themselves and their own life in the world may come to repentance and conversion during this Lent . . . [pause]

That all of us may willingly come to the cross so that God may glorify us as Jesus was glorified . . . [pause]

Presider: Merciful God, you supported and encouraged your own Son with the promise of glory: hear these our prayers that our Lenten penance may bring us to conversion so one day we will be united with you in glory. We ask this through your Son, Jesus Christ our Lord. **Amen.**

OPENING PRAYER

Let us pray
 [for the courage to follow Christ]

Pause for silent prayer

Father,
help us to be like Christ your Son,
who loved the world and died for our
 salvation.
Inspire us by his love,
guide us by his example,
who lives and reigns with you and the
 Holy Spirit,
one God, for ever and ever. **Amen.**

RESPONSORIAL PSALM
[Ps 51:3-4, 12-13, 14-15]

℟. (12a) Create a clean heart in me, O God.

Have mercy on me, O God, in your
 goodness;
 in the greatness of your compassion
 wipe out my offense.
Thoroughly wash me from my guilt
 and of my sin cleanse me.

℟. Create a clean heart in me, O God.

A clean heart create for me, O God,
 and a steadfast spirit renew within
 me.
Cast me not out from your presence,
 and your Holy Spirit take not from
 me.

℟. Create a clean heart in me, O God.

Give me back the joy of your salvation,
 and a willing spirit sustain in me.
I will teach transgressors your ways,
 and sinners shall return to you.

℟. Create a clean heart in me, O God.

FIRST READING
[Jer 31:31-34]

The days are coming, says the LORD,
　when I will make a new covenant
　　with the house of Israel
　　and the house of Judah.
It will not be like the covenant I made
　with their fathers
　　the day I took them by the hand
　　to lead them forth from the land of
　　　Egypt;
　for they broke my covenant,
　　and I had to show myself their master,
　　　says the LORD.
But this is the covenant that I will make
　with the house of Israel after those
　　days, says the LORD.
I will place my law within them and
　write it upon their hearts;
　　I will be their God, and they shall be
　　　my people.
No longer will they have need to teach
　their friends and relatives
　　how to know the LORD.
All, from least to greatest, shall know
　me, says the LORD,
　　for I will forgive their evildoing and
　　　remember their sin no more.

SECOND READING
[Heb 5:7-9]

In the days when Christ Jesus was in the
　flesh,
　he offered prayers and supplications
　　with loud cries and tears
　to the one who was able to save him
　　from death,
　and he was heard because of his
　　reverence.
Son though he was, he learned
　obedience from what he suffered;
　and when he was made perfect,
　he became the source of eternal
　　salvation for all who obey him.

Catechesis

Cantors

Just as last Sunday's responsorial psalm required honesty from you about sinfulness and redemption, so does Psalm 51. The transformation of heart prayed for is as personal and deep as the sinfulness that has been acknowledged. Arriving at such honesty is painful, but it is also a moment of resurrection, for it opens the door for God's loving entry. Then Psalm 51 becomes a song of joy.

Choir

The people gathering for worship are seeking to see Jesus. Do you show him to them? Does the assembly see through your manner of acting, praying, singing at liturgy that you are willing to die to self so that Christ may live in you?

Music Directors

Thomas Troeger and Carol Doran's "Before the Fruit Is Ripened by the Sun" [CH, W3] was written expressly for this Sunday in the Lectionary. The step-wise rise and fall of each melodic phrase captures the cycle of death and resurrection expressed in the poetry of the text, "Before the fruit is ripened by the sun . . . A seed is dropped and buried in the soil . . . Before we gain the grace that came through loss . . . We face with Christ the seed's renewing death." The pace and mood of the hymn would make it appropriate during the presentation of the gifts.

Liturgy Committee

How might you help others see liturgy as a "school" for learning obedience from suffering and servanthood from following Jesus?

　An ongoing discussion among liturgical design artists, liturgists, and parish liturgical personnel is whether the processional cross should have a corpus or not. The answer really depends upon the theology of the cross that is at the basis of the decision. The Western Church—especially influenced by Renaissance art—has tended to include a corpus of a suffering Christ. As already noted, the Eastern Church tends to follow Johannine theology and omits the corpus or has one of Jesus the resurrected One or Jesus the high priest. Neither is wrong, but it does raise questions about a theology of redemption that needs to be revisited from time to time.

APRIL 9, 2000

Palm Sunday of the Lord's Passion

Faith-Sharing

- What are the circumstances in your lives that bring you to flip-flop from "Hosanna!" to "Crucify him!"?
- What are the circumstances in your lives that bring you to declare "Truly this is the Son of God!"?
- What steps do you need to take in your everyday life (e.g., change in schedule) in order to enter deeply into the Mystery you celebrate this week?
- What is your response when the cross of Jesus visits one of your loved ones—abandon like the disciples? assist like Simon the Cyrenian? mock like passers-by? suffer with like the women at the foot of the cross?

Presiders

Holy Week is a demanding one for clergy. How can you shift the "demand" from concern about time, schedules, etc. to concern about the Mystery?

Deacons

When faced with the cross in your life, what helps you to remain hopeful, trusting in resurrection?

Hospitality Ministers

How might you combine the joy of the procession with palms with the triumph of the cross in your greeting of the assembly?

Music Ministers

How can you use music to help the assembly see that you celebrate not just the historical death of one man, but the participation of all the cosmos in that Mystery?

Altar Ministers

The services this week are unusual and more complex than you are used to. How can you help yourself be as attentive as you need as well as be able to pray and enter the celebration of the Mystery?

Lectors

How might you live this week the words you proclaim so they carry the depth of the Mystery being celebrated?

Eucharistic Ministers

How might your ministering Communion model the joy and the compassion of the Savior?

Spirituality

Reflecting on the Gospel

We all like a good parade. And we don't like it to rain on our parade. Millions line the streets of New York to participate as spectators in Macy's Thanksgiving parade and millions more watch it on TV. Even those who are not football fans still enjoy the various bowl parades around New Year's Day. Many of us participate personally in local parades that often take place on, for example, Memorial Day or Veterans Day. There is something about a parade that catches us up in the moment and carries us beyond ourselves into something bigger, something shared by many.

This is something of the atmosphere surrounding the entry of Jesus into Jerusalem. Never mind that the crowd still misunderstood the identity and mission of the Messiah. Never mind that they were still looking to participate in the restoration of the Davidic kingdom, which would surely be a sign of God's favor and redemption. Never mind that they joyfully gave themselves over to something (earthly kingdom) that was actually much less than was being offered (God's kingdom). Despite all their misunderstanding, they were still drawn in by the event of Jesus' entry into Jerusalem.

A few days after this joyful occasion—one seemingly unmarked by obstacles or opponents—the mood would be very different. Probably some of the same people who shouted "Hosanna!" on Sunday were the same ones who shouted "Crucify him!" on Friday. This "king" was mocked and crowned with pain. His own words of truth were twisted to condemn him. His closest disciples abandoned him. Only the women stood helplessly by as he hung on the cross. And one more—a centurion, a nonbeliever—stood there and proclaimed the truth that has resounded for two millennia: "Truly this man was the Son of God!"

Living the Paschal Mystery

The incredible contrast in moods between the two Gospels proclaimed in this Sunday's liturgy capture well the broad dynamic of the Paschal Mystery. The triumph with which we begin this Sunday is the triumph we celebrate next Sunday: the glory of the Lord shining forth for all to see and share. Sandwiched in between is the scandal and ignominy of the cross. What seemed to end in utter failure is resurrected in complete glory.

We all want the parade. But we don't want the rain. We want a glorious share in Christ's triumphant victory over sin and death. But we don't want the cross. We want resurrection. But not the dying.

It can't be. Christ showed us by his own way of living and by his ministry that the only way to share in his glory is to die to self by becoming servants and disciples following him to the cross. The only way to enjoy the passionate glory of risen life is to suffer the risk of dying. All of this is something that takes place more than just this once a year. It is the everyday of our ordinary human living, when we choose to respond to another instead of ignoring him or her, having patience rather than snapping, talking things through rather than staying angry. The Paschal Mystery unfolds in the little things in life that we turn into big ways to say *yes* to the Christ in others.

GOSPEL [at the procession with palms: Mark 11:1-10; L37B]

When Jesus and his disciples drew near to Jerusalem, to Bethphage and Bethany at the Mount of Olives, he sent two of his disciples and said to them, "Go into the village opposite you, and immediately on entering it, you will find a colt tethered on which no one has ever sat. Untie it and bring it here. If anyone should say to you, 'Why are you doing this?' reply, 'The Master has need of it and will send it back here at once.'" So they went off and found a colt tethered at a gate outside on the street, and they untied it. Some of the bystanders said to them, "What are you doing, untying the colt?" They answered them just as Jesus had told them to, and they permitted them to do it. So they brought the colt to Jesus and put their cloaks over it. And he sat on it. Many people spread their cloaks on the road, and others spread leafy branches that they had cut from the fields. Those preceding him as well as those following kept crying out: "Hosanna! Blessed is he who comes in the name of the Lord! Blessed is the kingdom of our father David that is to come! Hosanna in the highest!"

GOSPEL [Mark 14:1–15:47; L38B]

See Appendix A, p. 277.

Working with the Word: At the Procession with the Palms

Key words and phrases from the Gospel: Blessed is he who comes in the name of the Lord, hosanna in the highest

Connecting to the first five Sundays of Lent: With the joyous procession with palms and the music acclaiming Jesus as Messiah and King, the mood of the last five weeks dramatically shifts. We enter into this most solemn week of the year, and heighten the contrasting relationship between dying and rising, servanthood and glory, a kingdom of this world and the Kingdom of God.

Connecting to the culture: Processions are a journey from one place to another (and sometimes back to the originating point). The procession with palms invites us to process symbolically with Jesus into Jerusalem, the city of David and his city. What does this procession mean for us? Are we going to abandon Jesus—like the many, including his disciples, of long ago—or are we going to follow him faithfully to the cross?

To the point: Jesus' entry into Jerusalem is perceived by the crowd as a triumphal one. They were ready to acclaim him as a king in the line of David. They were less than ready for the turn of events that followed.

Working with the Word: At Mass

Key words and phrases from the Gospel: put him to death, poured [perfumed oil] on his head, truly this man was the Son of God

Connecting to the first reading: This third Song of the Servant from Isaiah is a first-person description of the suffering. It is the prayer of one who willingly and with full consciousness and acceptance undertakes the suffering as part of his mission.

Connecting to the second reading: Obedience is the key to the typology between Adam and Christ. This hymn recorded in the letter to the Philippians does not stop with obedience even "to the point of death," but moves us to the exaltation ("every tongue confess that Jesus Christ is Lord, to the glory of God the Father").

Connecting to the biblical culture: Crucifixion was a horribly agonizing death reserved only for the most heinous criminals. Death by crucifixion (and not, perhaps, by beheading like John the Baptist) speaks of the depth to which Jesus had shaken the Jewish establishment.

To the point: By being lifted up on the cross at what seems to be the conclusion of his mission, Jesus is recognized for who he is: the king of the Jews who is the Son of God.

Celebration

Responsorial Psalm

"My God, my God, why have you abandoned me?"

Psalm 22 uses three thematic progressions which explain its connection in Christian tradition to the passion. The first progression is one of abandonment, first by God ("My God, my God, why have you abandoned me?"), then by fellow human beings ("all who see me scoff at me"), until, finally, the psalmist is surrounded only by ravening animals (vv. 12-17). The second progression, though diametrically opposite the first, emerges simultaneously. The distant God of verses 2-3 becomes in verse 11 the intimate God known from birth ("From my mother's womb you are my God"). The third progression (vv. 23-32) is a prayer of thanksgiving into which an ever-widening circle is invited: immediate family, the offspring of Jacob, all nations, future generations, all the ends of the earth, the afflicted, the poor, even the dead. The praise is eschatological and cosmic. The effect of such a thrust is to transform our response to the proclamation of the passion. The psalm reminds us that this proclamation is not a retelling of the pain of one individual but the anamnesis (remembering) of the transformation of all humanity, even of all creation.

Model General Intercessions

Presider: On this day that begins in seeming triumph, let us recall in humility that we are dependent upon our God for all our needs. And so we pray.

Response:

Lord, hear our prayer.

Cantor:

we pray to the Lord,

May the Church enter into this Holy Week alive to a passion for love and mercy . . . [pause]

May the people of the world turn from ungodly ways and accept the kingdom of God ransomed by Jesus . . . [pause]

May the sick, the suffering, and the dying be consoled by looking to the cross of Jesus . . . [pause]

May we here gathered greet the Lord this week with joyful hearts and grateful spirit . . . [pause]

Presider: Triumphant and redeeming God, you sacrificed your only Son so that we might rise to new life: hear these our prayers that we might be strengthened in our resolve to enter into these sacred mysteries with openness and surrender. We ask this through Jesus Christ our Lord. **Amen.**

ALTERNATIVE OPENING PRAYER

Let us pray

Pause for silent prayer

Almighty Father of our Lord Jesus Christ,
you sent your Son
to be born of a woman and to die on a cross,
so that through the obedience of one man,
estrangement might be dissolved for all men.
Guide our minds by his truth
and strengthen our lives by the example of his death,
that we may live in union with you
in the kingdom of your promise.
Grant this through Christ our Lord.
Amen.

RESPONSORIAL PSALM
[Ps 22:8-9, 17-18, 19-20, 23-24]

℟. (2a) My God, my God, why have you abandoned me?

All who see me scoff at me;
    they mock me with parted lips, they wag their heads:
"He relied on the LORD; let him deliver him,
    let him rescue him, if he loves him."

℟. My God, my God, why have you abandoned me?

Indeed, many dogs surround me,
    a pack of evildoers closes in upon me;
they have pierced my hands and my feet;
    I can count all my bones.

℟. My God, my God, why have you abandoned me?

They divide my garments among them,
    and for my vesture they cast lots.
But you, O LORD, be not far from me;
    O my help, hasten to aid me.

℟. My God, my God, why have you abandoned me?

I will proclaim your name to my brethren;
    in the midst of the assembly I will praise you:
"You who fear the LORD, praise him;
    all you descendants of Jacob, give glory to him;
revere him, all you descendants of Israel!"

℟. My God, my God, why have you abandoned me?

FIRST READING
[Isa 50:4-7]

The Lord God has given me
   a well-trained tongue,
that I might know how to speak to the
   weary
   a word that will rouse them.
Morning after morning
   he opens my ear that I may hear;
and I have not rebelled,
   have not turned back.
I gave my back to those who beat me,
   my cheeks to those who plucked my
     beard;
my face I did not shield
   from buffets and spitting.

The Lord God is my help,
   therefore I am not disgraced;
I have set my face like flint,
   knowing that I shall not be put to
     shame.

SECOND READING
[Phil 2:6-11]

Christ Jesus, though he was in the form
   of God,
   did not regard equality with God
     something to be grasped.
Rather, he emptied himself,
   taking the form of a slave,
   coming in human likeness;
   and found human in appearance,
   he humbled himself,
   becoming obedient to the point of
     death,
     even death on a cross.
Because of this, God greatly exalted him
   and bestowed on him the name
   which is above every name,
   that at the name of Jesus
   every knee should bend,
   of those in heaven and on earth and
     under the earth,
   and every tongue confess that
   Jesus Christ is Lord,
   to the glory of God the Father.

Catechesis

Cantors

Perhaps more than any other responsorial psalm during the year, Psalm 22 invites you to identify with Christ most deeply. The few verses from this psalm which are used this Sunday give only the merest glimpse of the psalm's depth and of its connection with the meaning of what you celebrate this week. Because of your baptism you participate with him in his death and resurrection. You need to spend time with him in prayer this week so that you can sing with him in both his suffering and his praise.

Choir

More rehearsal time and liturgical participation will be required of you this week than any other time during the year. The temptation will be to get caught up in the activity and miss its deeper purpose. Perhaps the best prayer before or after rehearsals this week would be simply silent time.

Music Directors

To highlight the movement within the responsorial psalm from abandonment to praise, you might have the cantor sing the first three strophes a cappella, and add accompaniment on the last verse. At liturgies where there is no choir you might support the assembly on the refrain with simple, open chords.

Liturgy Committee

The rubrical notes in the Lectionary allow for a procession by the whole assembly from another place only at the principal Mass. It would be good pastoral practice to use the solemn entrance at all other Masses in the parish. The procession or solemn entrance takes the place of the introductory rites. How might you live this week so that the meaning of the procession is carried into Good Friday?

The title for this Sunday, "Palm Sunday of the Lord's Passion," already alerts us to the two foci for this day: the triumphal entry of Jesus into Jerusalem amidst jubilation and the waving of palm branches, and the proclamation of the Passion. A procession with palms is attested to as early as the fifth century in Jerusalem, and from about the eighth century in the Western Church (although the title for this Sunday was used before that). Pagan Greeks and Romans regarded some tree branches as having the power to ward off evil spirits; it is not surprising that Christian people took their palm or olive (or other branches) home from Palm Sunday services and used them in their homes also as protective talismans. Eventually the prayer for the blessing of palms included the notion of protection. Today the prayer of blessing does not include protection, although some people still use the palms in their homes in such a way.

The various missalettes that are published still include in the printed Passion account a people's part. This has two undesirable effects: it encourages the people to *follow along* the proclamation rather than actively *listen* to it and it changes the notion of proclamation as a unique communication *between* proclaimer and the rest of the assembly. The Passion accounts are best proclaimed (or sung) by one person or three persons taking the various parts.

Since the readings for this Sunday (and throughout the Triduum) are so rich, the homilies would best serve the community if they were very short and focused.

APRIL 16, 2000

Easter Triduum

Holy Thursday

FAITH-SHARING
- To whom are you "master" and "teacher"? How do you play this out in your everyday living?
- Whose "feet" are you called to wash? Who washes your "feet"?
- In what ways does the Eucharist sustain you throughout your week? How does it help you to serve others?

PRESIDERS
What helps you to stoop to serve the "lowly" as well as the "great"?

DEACONS
How do you loose the bonds (responsorial psalm) of those in need? How does Eucharist sustain you in this?

HOSPITALITY MINISTERS
"He loved them to the end." How might your greeting this night and in your life help people to experience this love?

MUSIC MINISTERS
How is your music-making a gift of self-surrendering love? What are the various demands of your service?

ALTAR MINISTERS
How is "foot washing" a good metaphor for your ministry?

LECTORS
Paul relates to the Corinthians what he "received from the Lord . . . I also handed on to you." How do you hand on to others what you receive from ministering God's Word?

EUCHARISTIC MINISTERS
How might you convey the meaning of Jesus' washing the disciples' feet when you minister Christ's Body and Blood?

EASTER TRIDUUM

The Easter Triduum begins with the Evening Mass of the Lord's Supper on Holy Thursday and concludes with Evening Prayer on Easter Sunday. The most solemn three days of the entire liturgical year, they bring to a climax our liturgical celebration of the Paschal Mystery. Let us keep these days holy by surrendering in quiet prayer to the Mystery of salvation.

OPENING PRAYER

Let us pray

Pause for silent prayer

God our Father,
we are gathered here to share in the supper
which your only Son left to his Church to reveal his love.
He gave it to us when he was about to die
and commanded us to celebrate it as the new and
    eternal sacrifice.
We pray that in this eucharist
we may find the fullness of love and life.
Grant this through our Lord Jesus Christ, your Son,
who lives and reigns with you and the Holy Spirit,
one God, for ever and ever. **Amen.**

Readings: Exod 12:1-8, 11-14; Ps 116:12-13, 15-16bc, 17-18; 1 Cor 11:23-26; John 13:1-15

Reflecting on the Gospel

It was the lowliest boy slave's job to wash the feet of guests. This assignment of the "least" among the slaves suggests that washing feet is not a very pleasant task. Feet are very personal, in spite of often being bare. They tend to be ticklish. Sometimes they are dirty. Sometimes they smell. Feet support our weight. They balance us. They connect us to the earth. They ground us.

On this holy night, when we celebrate Jesus' giving us his very own Body and Blood for our nourishment, the Gospel tells of washing feet. Jesus, the "master" and "teacher," assumes the posture of the lowliest of slaves and does what no master or teacher would do: he stoops to wash the feet of his disciples. This Gospel, on this night, introduces a startling context for the Eucharistic mystery: there is an intimate connection between serving others and being nourished at the Messianic Banquet, between dying to self and rising to new life, between doing what no others would stoop to do and "com[ing] from God and . . . returning to God."

On this holy night, when we celebrate Jesus' giving us his very own Body and Blood for our nourishment (second reading), we are reminded that freedom from slavery (first reading) is given to us only when we surrender ourselves to God and others (stoop and wash feet). This surrender is the answer to the psalmist's question, "How shall I make a return to the Lord for all the good he has done for me?" This dying is such a small price to pay for being reckoned "precious in the eyes of the LORD"!

Living the Paschal Mystery

"He loved them to the end." With these words St. John's Gospel opens us to the deepest mystery of the Paschal Triduum. Jesus gave us his all—the most tremendous gift of his Body and Blood, and the self-surrendering gift of his very own life. Facing suffering, Jesus loved us. Facing death, Jesus loved us. Facing mockery, Jesus loved us. Herein is the meaning of St. John's words: "I have given you a model to follow, so that as I have done for you, you should also do." Of such is our life!

The Holy Thursday Mass of the Lord's Supper might look just like a festive Sunday Mass except for two elements: the washing of feet and the solemn Eucharistic procession followed by adoration. These two ritual elements balance each other: losing ourselves to serve others (washing feet) is counterbalanced by our kneeling in awe before the love and life outpoured in the Eucharistic Mystery (procession and adoration). Dying and rising. Of such is our life!

APRIL 20, 2000

GOSPEL [John 13:1-15; L39ABC]

Before the feast of Passover, Jesus knew that his hour had come to pass from this world to the Father. He loved his own in the world and he loved them to the end. The devil had already induced Judas, son of Simon the Iscariot, to hand him over. So, during supper, fully aware that the Father had put everything into his power and that he had come from God and was returning to God, he rose from supper and took off his outer garments. He took a towel and tied it around his waist. Then he poured water into a basin and began to wash the disciples' feet and dry them with the towel around his waist. He came to Simon Peter, who said to him, "Master, are you going to wash my feet?" Jesus answered and said to him, "What I am doing, you do not understand now, but you will understand later." Peter said to him, "You will never wash my feet." Jesus answered him, "Unless I wash you, you will have no inheritance with me." Simon Peter said to him, "Master, then not only my feet, but my hands and head as well." Jesus said to him, "Whoever has bathed has no need except to have his feet washed, for he is clean all over; so you are clean, but not all." For he knew who would betray him; for this reason, he said, "Not all of you are clean." So when he had washed their feet and put his garments back on and reclined at table again, he said to them, "Do you realize what I have done for you? You call me 'teacher' and 'master,' and rightly so, for indeed I am. If I, therefore, the master and teacher, have washed your feet, you ought to wash one another's feet. I have given you a model to follow, so that as I have done for you, you should also do."

RESPONSORIAL PSALM
[Ps 116:12-13, 15-16bc, 17-18]

R̊. (cf. 1 Corinthians 10:16) Our blessing-cup is a communion with the Blood of Christ.

How shall I make a return to the Lord
  for all the good he has done for me?
The cup of salvation I will take up,
  and I will call upon the name of the Lord.

R̊. Our blessing-cup is a communion with the Blood of Christ.

Precious in the eyes of the Lord
  is the death of his faithful ones.
I am your servant, the son of your handmaid;
  you have loosed my bonds.

R̊. Our blessing-cup is a communion with the Blood of Christ.

To you will I offer sacrifice of thanksgiving,
  and I will call upon the name of the Lord.
My vows to the Lord I will pay
  in the presence of all his people.

R̊. Our blessing-cup is a communion with the Blood of Christ.

FIRST READING [Exod 12:1-8, 11-14]

The Lord said to Moses and Aaron in the land of Egypt,
  "This month shall stand at the head of your calendar;
    you shall reckon it the first month of the year.
  Tell the whole community of Israel:
    On the tenth of this month every one of your families
    must procure for itself a lamb, one apiece for each
      household.
  If a family is too small for a whole lamb,
    it shall join the nearest household in procuring one
    and shall share in the lamb
    in proportion to the number of persons who partake of it.
  The lamb must be a year-old male and without blemish.
  You may take it from either the sheep or the goats.
  You shall keep it until the fourteenth day of this month,
    and then, with the whole assembly of Israel present,
    it shall be slaughtered during the evening twilight.
  They shall take some of its blood
    and apply it to the two doorposts and the lintel
    of every house in which they partake of the lamb.
  That same night they shall eat its roasted flesh
    with unleavened bread and bitter herbs.

"This is how you are to eat it:
  with your loins girt, sandals on your feet and your staff in
    hand,
  you shall eat like those who are in flight.
It is the Passover of the Lord.
For on this same night I will go through Egypt,
  striking down every firstborn of the land, both man and beast,
  and executing judgment on all the gods of Egypt—I, the Lord!
But the blood will mark the houses where you are.
Seeing the blood, I will pass over you;
  thus, when I strike the land of Egypt,
  no destructive blow will come upon you.

"This day shall be a memorial feast for you,
  which all your generations shall celebrate
  with pilgrimage to the Lord, as a perpetual institution."

SECOND READING [1 Cor 11:23-26]

Brothers and sisters:
I received from the Lord what I also handed on to you,
  that the Lord Jesus, on the night he was handed over,
  took bread, and, after he had given thanks,
  broke it and said, "This is my body that is for you.
  Do this in remembrance of me."
In the same way also the cup, after supper, saying,
  "This cup is the new covenant in my blood.
  Do this, as often as you drink it, in remembrance of me."
For as often as you eat this bread and drink the cup,
  you proclaim the death of the Lord until he comes.

GOOD FRIDAY

FAITH-SHARING

- Whose kingdom do you follow, God's or Caesar's? What behaviors/actions/attitudes support your response?
- What truth do you proclaim by the very living of your life? What truth do others see in you?
- Where, still, are your areas of unbelief? How might you bring unbelief to belief?
- How do you already share in Jesus' glorification?
- What is the "good" of Good Friday for you?

PRESIDERS

In what ways do you *choose* the destiny that your ordination bears? Wherein is the belief? the glory?

DEACONS

Yours is a ministry of service to the community. How does your service carry out the intentions of Good Friday's solemn general intercessions?

HOSPITALITY MINISTERS

How might your greeting on Good Friday and in your everyday living attest to the glory of the cross?

MUSIC MINISTERS

To help convey their solemnity, ideally the Passion and solemn general intercessions need to be sung. Why?

ALTAR MINISTERS

The sacred space for the Good Friday celebration is completely unadorned. How does your service "adorn" the environment with the deepest meaning of the Good Friday liturgy? How are you "passionate" about your ministry?

LECTORS

Isaiah proclaims in the first reading "Yet it was our infirmities that he bore, our sufferings that he endured." How might you give over your infirmities and sufferings to Jesus so that you can proclaim the Word with greater power?

EUCHARISTIC MINISTERS

The Eucharist that is shared on Good Friday is "presanctified," that is, consecrated on Holy Thursday. In what way are *you* presanctified?

OPENING PRAYER

Lord,
by shedding his blood for us,
your Son, Jesus Christ,
established the paschal mystery.
In your goodness, make us holy
and watch over us always.
We ask this through Christ our Lord. **Amen.**

Readings: Isa 52:13–53:12; Ps 31:2, 6, 12-13, 15-16, 17, 25; Heb 4:14-16; 5:7-9; John 18:1–19:42

Reflecting on the Gospel

Today, the day of all days that draws forth from everyone—unenthusiastic and fervent alike—reverent silence, earnest devotion, awed dolor . . . today, the day of all days when we feel the scourging whips and pierce of the thorns, when we cringe at the mockery and cowardice and obstinance, when we hear "Crucify him!" and when we walk with Jesus who carries his own instrument of death, when we stand at the foot of the cross with the women and the beloved disciple . . . today, this day, is a day of triumph and glory!

John presents Jesus as the one who is in charge of his own destiny and *chooses* that destiny. At the beginning of the Passion account, it is Jesus who goes to the soldiers and guards and asks them—not once, but twice!—"Whom are you looking for?" Twice, to their reply "Jesus the Nazarene," Jesus answers "I AM" (see John 17:6: "I revealed [the Father's] name to those whom you gave me out of the world" and Exod 3:14: "I AM sent me [Moses] to you [Pharaoh]"). At the end of the Passion account, Jesus, "aware that everything was now finished," says "I thirst" (he chooses to drink the cup of salvation given him) and "It is finished." He then "bow[s] his head" and "hand[s] over the spirit."

In between the beginning and end of John's Passion account is the charged exchange between Pilate and Jesus over kingship and truth. Here Jesus reiterates what John has had on Jesus' lips from the very beginning of his Gospel: that Jesus is one with God (see John 1:1-2), that some would believe in him ("his own") and others would reject him (John 1:10-12), that Jesus reveals the Father's glory because he is "full of grace and truth" (John 1:14). The hour of Jesus' crucifixion is a time for revelation of truth, not ignominy; is a time for Jesus' glorification, not defeat; is a time for Jesus to *choose* to die for our salvation, not be a victim at the hands of disbelievers. The great mystery of Good Friday is that Jesus' death returns him to glory with the Father and brings us believers a share in that glory.

Living the Paschal Mystery

Our solemn proclamation of John's Passion this day is counterbalanced by the solemn general intercessions. The victory of Jesus' death celebrated on Good Friday is brought into the here and now by the challenge of the prayer intentions to bring about peace and tranquility, responsiveness to God's love, seeking the truth with sincerity, faithfulness to God's covenant, following all that is right, healing the sick, comforting the dying, giving safety to travelers, freeing those deprived of liberty, and ridding the world of falsehood, hunger, and disease. In this way are we reminded that the work of salvation is ongoing, is that in which we cooperate with Jesus through our efforts to help others. Only by taking up the cross of others' needs can we, too, rise to glory in Christ.

APRIL 21, 2000

GOSPEL [John 18:1–19:42; L40ABC]

Jesus went out with his disciples across the Kidron valley to where there was a garden, into which he and his disciples entered. Judas his betrayer also knew the place, because Jesus had often met there with his disciples. So Judas got a band of soldiers and guards from the chief priests and the Pharisees and went there with lanterns, torches, and weapons. Jesus, knowing everything that was going to happen to him, went out and said to them, "Whom are you looking for?" They answered him, "Jesus the Nazarene." He said to them, "I AM." Judas his betrayer was also with them. When he said to them, "I AM," they turned away and fell to the ground. So he again asked them, "Whom are you looking for?" They said, "Jesus the Nazarene." Jesus answered, "I told you that I AM. So if you are looking for me, let these men go." This was to fulfill what he had said, "I have not lost any of those you gave me." Then Simon Peter, who had a sword, drew it, struck the high priest's slave, and cut off his right ear. The slave's name was Malchus. Jesus said to Peter, "Put your sword into its scabbard. Shall I not drink the cup that the Father gave me?"

So the band of soldiers, the tribune, and the Jewish guards seized Jesus, bound him, and brought him to Annas first. He was the father-in-law of Caiaphas, who was high priest that year. It was Caiaphas who had counseled the Jews that it was better that one man should die rather than the people.

Simon Peter and another disciple followed Jesus. Now the other disciple was known to the high priest, and he entered the courtyard of the high priest with Jesus. But Peter stood at the gate outside. So the other disciple, the acquaintance of the high priest, went out and spoke to the gatekeeper and brought Peter in. Then the maid who was the gatekeeper said to Peter, "You are not one of this man's disciples, are you?" He said, "I am not." Now the slaves and the guards were standing around a charcoal fire that they had made, because it was cold, and were warming themselves. Peter was also standing there keeping warm.

The high priest questioned Jesus about his disciples and about his doctrine. Jesus answered him, "I have spoken publicly to the world. I have always taught in a synagogue or in the temple area where all the Jews gather, and in secret I have said nothing. Why ask me? Ask those who heard me what I said to them. They know what I said." When he had said this, one of the temple guards standing there struck Jesus and said, "Is this the way you answer the high priest?" Jesus answered him, "If I have spoken wrongly, testify to the wrong; but if I have spoken rightly, why do you strike me?" Then Annas sent him bound to Caiaphas the high priest.

Now Simon Peter was standing there keeping warm. And they said to him, "You are not one of his disciples, are you?" He denied it and said, "I am not." One of the slaves of the high priest, a relative of the one whose ear Peter had cut off, said, "Didn't I see you in the garden with him?" Again Peter denied it. And immediately the cock crowed.

Then they brought Jesus from Caiaphas to the praetorium. It was morning. And they themselves did not enter the praetorium, in order not to be defiled so that they could eat the Passover. So Pilate came out to them and said, "What charge do you bring against this man?" They answered and said to him, "If he were not a criminal, we would not have handed him over to you." At this, Pilate said to them, "Take him yourselves, and judge him according to your law." The Jews answered him, "We do not have the right to execute anyone," in order that the word of Jesus might be fulfilled that he said indicating the kind of death he would die. So Pilate went back into the praetorium and summoned Jesus and said to him, "Are you the King of the Jews?" Jesus answered, "Do you say this on your own or have others told you about me?" Pilate answered, "I am not a Jew, am I? Your own nation and the chief priests handed you over to me. What have you done?" Jesus answered, "My kingdom does not belong to this world. If my kingdom did belong to this world, my attendants would be fighting to keep me from being handed over to the Jews. But as it is, my kingdom is not here." So Pilate said to him, "Then you are a king?" Jesus answered, "You say I am a king. For this I was born and for this I came into the world, to testify to the truth. Everyone who belongs to the truth listens to my voice." Pilate said to him, "What is truth?"

When he had said this, he again went out to the Jews and said to them, "I find no guilt in him. But you have a custom that I release one prisoner to you at Passover. Do you want me to release to you the King of the Jews?" They cried out again, "Not this one but Barabbas!" Now Barabbas was a revolutionary.

Then Pilate took Jesus and had him scourged. And the soldiers wove a crown out of thorns and placed it on his head, and clothed him in a purple cloak, and they came to him and said, "Hail, King of the Jews!" And they struck him repeatedly. Once more Pilate went out and said to them, "Look, I am bringing him out to you, so that you may know that I find no guilt in him." So Jesus came out, wearing the crown of thorns and the purple cloak. And he said to them, "Behold, the man!" When the chief priests and the guards saw him they cried out, "Crucify him, crucify him!" Pilate said to them, "Take him yourselves and crucify him. I find no guilt in him." The Jews answered, "We have a law, and according to that law he ought to die, because he made himself the Son of God." Now when Pilate heard this statement, he became even more afraid, and went back into the praetorium and said to Jesus, "Where are you from?" Jesus did not answer him. So Pilate said to him, "Do you not speak to me? Do you not know that I have power to release you and I have power to crucify you?" Jesus answered him, "You would have no power over me if it had not been given to you from above. For this reason the one who handed me over to you has the greater sin." Consequently, Pilate tried to release him; but the Jews cried out, "If you release him, you are not a Friend of Caesar. Everyone who makes himself a king opposes Caesar."

Continued in Appendix A, p. 279.

Easter Vigil

FAITH-SHARING
- How timely and timeless is *this* night for you? How is this special for you?
- How is Christ the light of your life? How do you let Christ's light shine through you?
- What are the stories of salvation God has written in, with, for your life?
- How do you experience your baptismal entry into Jesus' death in your life? your baptismal entry into resurrection?
- How is every Eucharist a celebration of resurrection for you?

PRESIDERS
How is your presiding this night different from all others?

DEACONS
In your proclaiming the light of Christ and the Exultet, how are you challenging yourself to live differently?

HOSPITALITY MINISTERS
What shape does your vigil-watching greeting take? your resurrection greeting?

MUSIC MINISTERS
There is much music to sing this night. How might you encourage people to enter into the mystery of salvation through their singing?

ALTAR MINISTERS
You must be attentive to the movement of the four parts of the service: the Service of Light, the Liturgy of the Word, the Liturgy of Baptism, and the Liturgy of the Eucharist. How might your ministry help others enter into the flow of the Vigil?

LECTORS
The Word is especially important at the Easter Vigil, for you proclaim God's mighty deeds of salvation. How are these deeds borne out in your life?

EUCHARISTIC MINISTERS
How does your giving and receiving the Body of Christ proclaim the resurrection?

OPENING PRAYER
Let us pray

Pause for silent prayer

Lord God,
you have brightened this night
with the radiance of the risen Christ.
Quicken the spirit of sonship in your Church;
renew us in mind and body
to give you whole-hearted service.

Grant this through our Lord Jesus Christ, your Son,
who lives and reigns with you and the Holy Spirit,
one God, for ever and ever. **Amen.**

Readings: Gen 1:1–2:2; Ps 104:1-2, 5-6, 10, 12, 13-14, 24, 35; Gen 22:1-18; Ps 16:5, 8, 9-10, 11; Exod 14:15–15:1; Exod 15:1-2, 3-4, 5-6, 17-18; Isa 54:5-14; Ps 30:2, 4, 5-6, 11-12, 13; Isa 55:1-11; Isa 12:2-3, 4, 5-6; Bar 3:9-15, 32–4:4; Ps 19:8, 9, 10, 11; Ezek 36:16-17a, 18-28; Ps 42:3, 5; 43:3, 4; Rom 6:3-11; Ps 118:1-2, 16-17, 22-23; Mark 16:1-7

Reflecting on the Liturgy and Scriptures

"This." We use the word all the time. Grammatically, it's a demonstrative pronoun that points out a particular person, place, or thing that is immediately present. During the Service of Light at the Easter Vigil "this" is a prevalent word: "on this holy night," "this is the passover of the Lord," "let this place resound with joy," "this holy light," "this is our passover feast," "this is the night when first you saved our fathers," "this is the night when the pillar of fire destroyed the darkness of sin," "this is the night when Christians everywhere . . . are restored to grace and grow together in holiness," "this is the night when Jesus Christ broke the chains of death and rose triumphant from the grave," "of this night Scripture says: 'The night will be as clear as day: it will become my light, my joy,'" "this holy night," "this night," "accept this Easter candle."

The timeliness and timelessness of "this" collapses into our vigil-watching: God's creating good creatures and very good humanity; God's entering into covenantal relationship with believing humanity; God's setting the chosen and holy people free; God's sending prophets to announce enduring love, mercy, abundance of life, Law, splendor, cleansing, and a new heart and a new spirit; God's calling us to new life through being baptized into Jesus' death and resurrection; and, finally, God's raising Jesus from the dead. The time of "this" is *now!*

Living the Paschal Mystery

How does our vigil-watching help us enter more deeply into the Mystery of this night? It is precisely out of the very retelling of God's mighty deeds of salvation that we celebrate baptisms or renew our baptismal commitment with God and come to the Eucharistic table to be fed. Let us not shorten our vigil-watching to bare minimum! Let us recite faithfully and attentively God's mighty deeds of salvation. Let us keep watch through this night until darkness gives way to the splendor of light. If anything, we could add to our retelling: the fall and expulsion from the Garden of Eden (Genesis 3), Noah's faithfulness (Genesis 7–9), Joseph's sojourn into Egypt (Genesis 37–47), the first Passover (Exod 12:1-24), Jonah (Jonah 1:1–4:11), God's answer to Job (Job 38:2-28), the assumption of Elijah (2 Kgs 2:1-22), the promise of a new covenant (Jer 31:31-34), the valley of the dry bones (Ezek 37:1-14), or the canticle of the three children (Dan 3:1-90). What a story we tell!

APRIL 22, 2000

GOSPEL [Mark 16:1-7; L41B]

When the sabbath was over, Mary Magdalene, Mary, the mother of James, and Salome bought spices so that they might go and anoint him. Very early when the sun had risen, on the first day of the week, they came to the tomb. They were saying to one another, "Who will roll back the stone for us from the entrance to the tomb?" When they looked up, they saw that the stone had been rolled back; it was very large. On entering the tomb they saw a young man sitting on the right side, clothed in a white robe, and they were utterly amazed. He said to them, "Do not be amazed! You seek Jesus of Nazareth, the crucified. He has been raised; he is not here. Behold the place where they laid him. But go and tell his disciples and Peter, 'He is going before you to Galilee; there you will see him, as he told you.'"

RESPONSORIAL PSALM
[Ps 104:1-2, 5-6, 10, 12, 13-14, 24, 35]

R℣. (30) Lord, send out your Spirit, and renew the face of the earth.

Bless the LORD, O my soul!
    O LORD, my God, you are great indeed!
You are clothed with majesty and glory,
    robed in light as with a cloak.

R℣. Lord, send out your Spirit, and renew the face of the earth.

You fixed the earth upon its foundation,
    not to be moved forever;
with the ocean, as with a garment, you covered it;
    above the mountains the waters stood.

R℣. Lord, send out your Spirit, and renew the face of the earth.

You send forth springs into the watercourses
    that wind among the mountains.
Beside them the birds of heaven dwell;
    from among the branches they send forth their song.

R℣. Lord, send out your Spirit, and renew the face of the earth.

You water the mountains from your palace;
    the earth is replete with the fruit of your works.
You raise grass for the cattle,
    and vegetation for man's use,
producing bread from the earth.

R℣. Lord, send out your Spirit, and renew the face of the earth.

How manifold are your works, O LORD!
    In wisdom you have wrought them all—
    the earth is full of your creatures.
Bless the LORD, O my soul!

R℣. Lord, send out your Spirit, and renew the face of the earth.

FIRST READING [Gen 1:1–2:2]

In the beginning, when God created the heavens and the earth,
    the earth was a formless wasteland, and darkness covered the abyss,
    while a mighty wind swept over the waters.

Then God said,
    "Let there be light," and there was light.
God saw how good the light was.
God then separated the light from the darkness.
God called the light "day," and the darkness he called "night."
Thus evening came, and morning followed—the first day.

Then God said,
    "Let there be a dome in the middle of the waters,
    to separate one body of water from the other."
And so it happened:
    God made the dome,
    and it separated the water above the dome from the water below it.
God called the dome "the sky."
Evening came, and morning followed—the second day.

Then God said,
    "Let the water under the sky be gathered into a single basin,
    so that the dry land may appear."
And so it happened:
    the water under the sky was gathered into its basin,
    and the dry land appeared.
God called the dry land "the earth,"
    and the basin of the water he called "the sea."
God saw how good it was.
Then God said,
    "Let the earth bring forth vegetation:
    every kind of plant that bears seed
    and every kind of fruit tree on earth
    that bears fruit with its seed in it."
And so it happened:
    the earth brought forth every kind of plant that bears seed
    and every kind of fruit tree on earth
    that bears fruit with its seed in it.
God saw how good it was.
Evening came, and morning followed—the third day.

Then God said:
    "Let there be lights in the dome of the sky,
    to separate day from night.
Let them mark the fixed times, the days and the years,
    and serve as luminaries in the dome of the sky,
    to shed light upon the earth."
And so it happened:
    God made the two great lights,
    the greater one to govern the day,
    and the lesser one to govern the night;
    and he made the stars.

Continued in Appendix A, p. 281.

Easter Sunday

FAITH-SHARING
- How does this festival challenge your seeing and believing? What draws you to see and believe?
- How do you live the splendor and glory of Christ's resurrection in your daily life? Do people see this splendor and glory reflected in you?
- What draws you spontaneously to utter alleluia?
- How are you an Easter person?

PRESIDERS
The Triduum liturgies are challenging, demanding, and exhausting. How do you feel about them? How is this reflected in your ministry?

DEACONS
In the first reading from Acts Peter speaks about how Jesus "went about doing good." In what ways and at what times does this describe your life?

HOSPITALITY MINISTERS
How might your greeting help the assembly "seek what is above" (second reading)?

MUSIC MINISTERS
How might the Easter Sequence embellish the Gospel procession, helping the assembly receive the Easter Gospel with greater faith?

ALTAR MINISTERS
How might the care with which you serve the sacred space proclaim that you desire to "appear with [Christ] in glory" (second reading)?

LECTORS
How does your proclamation of God's word help you to be "witnesses chosen by God in advance" (first reading) to make the resurrected Christ visible in the world today?

EUCHARISTIC MINISTERS
How does your ministering the Body and Blood of Christ proclaim Easter glory? How does it draw forth from you seeing and believing?

ALTERNATIVE OPENING PRAYER
Let us pray

Pause for silent prayer

God our Father, creator of all,
today is the day of Easter joy.
This is the morning on which the Lord appeared to men
who had begun to lose hope
and opened their eyes to what the scriptures foretold:
that first he must die, and then he would rise
and ascend into his Father's glorious presence.
May the risen Lord
breathe on our minds and open our eyes
that we may know him in the breaking of bread,
and follow him in his risen life.

Grant this through Christ our Lord. **Amen.**

Readings: Acts 10:34a, 37-43; Ps 118:1-2, 16-17, 22-23; Col 3:1-4; John 20:1-9)

Reflecting on the Gospel

ALLELUIA! A word more sonorous than instructive, more musical than declarative, more acclamatory than explanatory. It is an exclamation that captures the depths of joy and wonderment and exaltation of this festival and all that it means for us. For six weeks we have fasted from this word; now we cannot stop singing it out. To try to explain the word is to miss all that it evokes and excites in us. We do know that it somehow captures for us in this one remarkable word all the praise that we wish to sing forth at this time of new life.

The Gospel for the Mass of Easter Day is something like our alleluia. It is filled with joy and wonder while at the same time its "loose ends" leave us guessing. Mary Magdalene arrives at the tomb first "early in the morning, while it was still dark," and sees the stone rolled back; but rather than going into the tomb she runs to Peter and John to tell them "We don't know where they put him." Peter and John run to the tomb (this is a day for running . . . our excitement can't be contained, slowed down, checked), but John arrives first and rather than going in he waits for Peter. Peter goes into the tomb, and discovers the burial clothes not in a heap, left hurriedly by those who might steal a body, but discovers the "cloth that had covered his head, not with the burial cloths but rolled up in a separate place," as if someone had carefully and deliberately arranged the cloths. Then John goes into the tomb, and "he saw and believed."

"While it was still dark" Mary and the disciples begin to catch a glimpse of the brightness, shining light, splendor, and radiance of the resurrection. And they believed. Our alleluias give utterance to the brightness of the splendor that is ours by our share in Christ's death and resurrection. No wonder all we can do is sing ALLELUIA! ALLELUIA! ALLELUIA!

Living the Paschal Mystery

"Saw" and "believed." Two words that are at the heart of John's Gospel. The high point of this Gospel—and, indeed, the high point of this whole paschal festival—is to see and believe. Finally, the glory that is given Jesus by the Father is revealed in all its splendor and power. He is risen! Alleluia! In coming to the messianic table, we already share in the splendor of Christ's glory. How can we do anything less than see and believe? How can we utter anything less than ALLELUIA! ALLELUIA! ALLELUIA!

APRIL 23, 2000

GOSPEL [John 20:1-9; L42ABC]

On the first day of the week, Mary of Magdala came to the tomb early in the morning, while it was still dark, and saw the stone removed from the tomb. So she ran and went to Simon Peter and to the other disciple whom Jesus loved, and told them, "They have taken the Lord from the tomb, and we don't know where they put him." So Peter and the other disciple went out and came to the tomb. They both ran, but the other disciple ran faster than Peter and arrived at the tomb first; he bent down and saw the burial cloths there, but did not go in. When Simon Peter arrived after him, he went into the tomb and saw the burial cloths there, and the cloth that had covered his head, not with the burial cloths but rolled up in a separate place. Then the other disciple also went in, the one who had arrived at the tomb first, and he saw and believed. For they did not yet understand the Scripture that he had to rise from the dead.

RESPONSORIAL PSALM
[Ps 118:1-2, 16-17, 22-23]

℟. (24) This is the day the Lord has made; let us rejoice and be glad.
    or:
℟. Alleluia.

Give thanks to the LORD, for he is good,
    for his mercy endures forever.
Let the house of Israel say,
    "His mercy endures forever."

℟. This is the day the Lord has made; let us rejoice and be glad.
    or:
℟. Alleluia.

"The right hand of the LORD has struck with power;
    the right hand of the LORD is exalted.
I shall not die, but live,
    and declare the works of the LORD."

℟. This is the day the Lord has made; let us rejoice and be glad.
    or:
℟. Alleluia.

The stone which the builders rejected
    has become the cornerstone.
By the LORD has this been done;
    it is wonderful in our eyes.

℟. This is the day the Lord has made; let us rejoice and be glad.
    or:
℟. Alleluia.

FIRST READING
[Acts 10:34a, 37-43]

Peter proceeded to speak and said:
    "You know what has happened all over Judea,
    beginning in Galilee after the baptism
    that John preached,
    how God anointed Jesus of Nazareth
    with the Holy Spirit and power.
He went about doing good
    and healing all those oppressed by the devil,
    for God was with him.
We are witnesses of all that he did
    both in the country of the Jews and in Jerusalem.
They put him to death by hanging him on a tree.
This man God raised on the third day and granted that he be visible,
    not to all the people, but to us,
    the witnesses chosen by God in advance,
    who ate and drank with him after he rose from the dead.
He commissioned us to preach to the people
    and testify that he is the one appointed by God
    as judge of the living and the dead.
To him all the prophets bear witness,
    that everyone who believes in him
    will receive forgiveness of sins through his name."

SECOND READING
[Col 3:1-4]

Brothers and sisters:
If then you were raised with Christ, seek what is above,
    where Christ is seated at the right hand of God.
Think of what is above, not of what is on earth.
For you have died, and your life is hidden with Christ in God.
When Christ your life appears,
    then you too will appear with him in glory.

SEQUENCE

See Appendix A, p. 285.

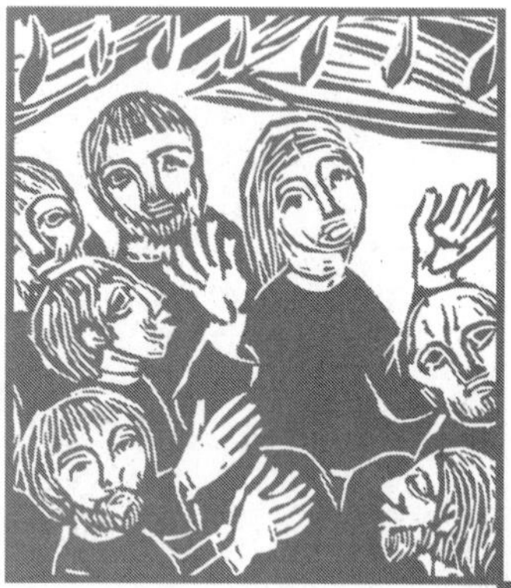
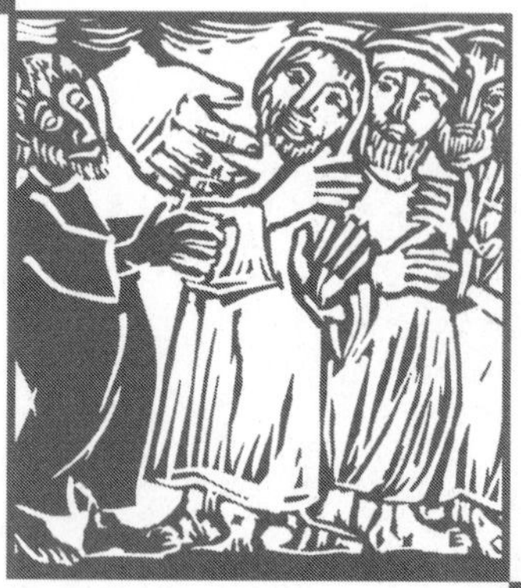
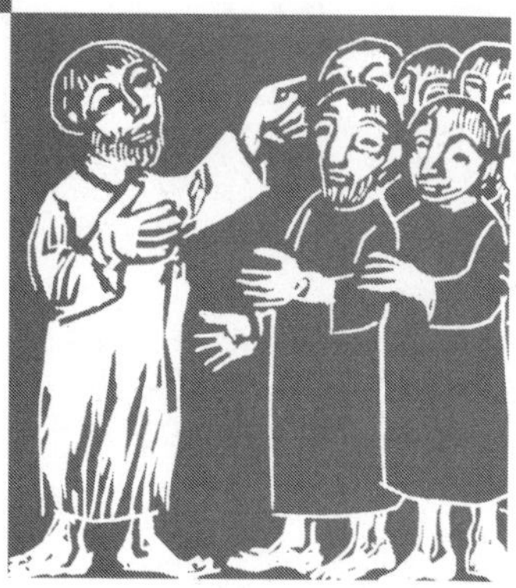

Season of Easter

Second Sunday of Easter

FAITH-SHARING

- In what ways can you identify with the disciples being "locked in" or "locked up"? How has the resurrection touched those "locked" places in your life?
- When have you experienced "not seeing"? believing?
- How might Easter help you enter more deeply into a "new order" of life? How can you carry this beyond the Easter season into your whole year?

PRESIDERS

What are some events in your ordained living that bring you to utter "My Lord and my God!"?

DEACONS

How might your service to the community help "unlock" closed doors in peoples' lives? Help unlock closed doors in your life?

HOSPITALITY MINISTERS

How might your presence and welcoming of people as they gather for liturgy help to keep Easter an ongoing experience in peoples' lives?

MUSIC MINISTERS

How is the music you sing during this season a liturgical celebration of your having entered with Christ into a new way of being?

ALTAR MINISTERS

How does the resurrection come alive in your service? in your everyday living?

LECTORS

Proclamation is not done merely with the voice; just as important is the proclamation through living. How might you live the new resurrection order (peace, forgiveness, love, fidelity to the commandments, etc.) so that your proclamation of the Word calls others to Easter living?

EUCHARISTIC MINISTERS

At Communion you distribute the risen Lord. How might you distribute the Easter experience through your daily living?

Spirituality

Reflecting on the Gospel

This Second Sunday of Easter is called the "octave day." For eight days now we have celebrated with great solemnity Jesus' resurrection. Just as with Christmas, we have the intuition that this celebration is too extraordinary to celebrate on only one day . . . we need a longer period of time to voice our joy, to sing our alleluias.

Further, we have the intuition that the incredible thing that happened to Jesus—being raised to new life—is not only an extraordinary event, but it is also something that has repercussions beyond what happened to Jesus. The Gospels give us examples of resuscitation: Jesus brought Lazarus and the daughter of Jairus back to life. But their being raised up was a return to the life that they formerly had. As tremendous as that is—who of us, having lost dear ones to accidents or illnesses, wouldn't want to bring them back?—something even greater happened to Jesus. While Lazarus and Jairus' daughter would die again, Jesus will live for ever! Jesus' resurrection is to a whole new life, one where he returned to abide in glory with the Father.

This Sunday's Gospel relates two scenes: one on Easter night and the other a week later. In both cases, the disciples were in a room with locked doors. Locked in. Locked up. The Gospel relates being locked: the disciples were locked in fear, Thomas was locked in doubt ("Unless I see . . ."), and we are locked in sin. Before the resurrection, we are paralyzed by our own inability to break out of whatever fetters us.

The new order of the resurrection opens up the possibility of overcoming fear with peace ("Peace be with you"), doubt with believing ("blessed are those who have not seen and have believed"), and sin with forgiveness ("Whose sins you forgive are forgiven them"). The new order opens up the possibility of having new "life in his name." Our hearts and lips continue to sing alleluia beyond these eight days of celebrating resurrection because the life that is promised is a life already given.

Living the Paschal Mystery

Sometimes in the hustle and bustle of everyday living we can lose sight of where we are in the liturgical year. Even this wonderful Easter festival can grow dim after we've eaten the last of the Easter eggs and the chocolate bunnies. The challenge of the Easter season is to proclaim that Jesus is alive even long after Easter Sunday because the resurrection really has ushered in a whole new order of living. The fifty-day celebration of resurrection calls forth from us great joy and jubilation. It also challenges us to become aware of God's living presence in our lives in new ways. It challenges our faith to move beyond belief in a long-ago historical event to a faith enlivened by an experience of that living presence today. It challenges us to hope in our own resurrection such that God's living presence in us becomes a source of consolation and hope and forgiveness and peace and love for all those we meet in our everyday living. It challenges us to increase our charity so that others may be less burdened and more able to experience for themselves God's living presence. Most of all, Easter challenges us to live as Jesus did: surrender ourselves to the Father's will and by so doing we ourselves are surprised by the new life to which the Father raises us, even now. Alleluia!

126

APRIL 30, 2000

GOSPEL [John 20:19-31; L44B]

On the evening of that first day of the week, when the doors were locked, where the disciples were, for fear of the Jews, Jesus came and stood in their midst and said to them, "Peace be with you." When he had said this, he showed them his hands and his side. The disciples rejoiced when they saw the Lord. Jesus said to them again, "Peace be with you. As the Father has sent me, so I send you." And when he had said this, he breathed on them and said to them, "Receive the Holy Spirit. Whose sins you forgive are forgiven them, and whose sins you retain are retained."

Thomas, called Didymus, one of the Twelve, was not with them when Jesus came. So the other disciples said to him, "We have seen the Lord." But he said to them, "Unless I see the mark of the nails in his hands and put my finger into the nailmarks and put my hand into his side, I will not believe."

Now a week later his disciples were again inside and Thomas was with them. Jesus came, although the doors were locked, and stood in their midst and said, "Peace be with you." Then he said to Thomas, "Put your finger here and see my hands, and bring your hand and put it into my side, and do not be unbelieving, but believe." Thomas answered and said to him, "My Lord and my God!" Jesus said to him, "Have you come to believe because you have seen me? Blessed are those who have not seen and have believed."

Now Jesus did many other signs in the presence of his disciples that are not written in this book. But these are written that you may come to believe that Jesus is the Christ, the Son of God, and that through this belief you may have life in his name.

Working with the Word

Key words and phrases from the Gospel: peace be with you, are forgiven, we have seen the Lord

Connecting to last Sunday's and next Sunday's Gospels: The Lectionary gives us appearance accounts of the risen Lord on each of the first three Sundays of Easter. The wisdom of the Church captured in the Lectionary is to provide us the time to savor the reality of Christ's resurrection, so that not having seen, we nonetheless believe.

Connecting to the biblical and our culture: One of the main differences between the Pharisees and the Sadducees concerned the issue of belief in an afterlife. The one clear Old Testament reference to afterlife is found in Dan 12:1-3, in which afterlife is given not to everyone but to the very good and the very evil. After Jesus' resurrection, we Christians believe in the afterlife (and resurrection) for everyone; its fruits are already in the here and now (peace, forgiveness, love, etc.).

Exegetical points: Even though the end of this Sunday's Gospel focuses on Thomas and the importance of believing in the fact of the resurrection (see also the second reading's emphasis on believing, faith, and testimony), John and the first two readings also describe the effects of the resurrection in the lives of believers. From the Gospel perspective, the effects are "peace" and, especially, the forgiveness of sins. What Jesus experiences as the new life of resurrection believers experience as the peace of his risen presence and freedom from sin. Similarly, the reading from Acts describes how those who believe in Jesus and his resurrection live their daily lives in a community of shared goods and mutual support. The second reading likewise describes how believers put their faith into action—by loving God and keeping the commandments.

Two earlier passages from John's Gospel help us understand this Sunday's episode. Jesus tells his disciples, "it is better for you that I go. For if I do not go, the Advocate will not come to you. But if I go, I will send him to you" (16:7). Earlier on Easter morning, the risen Jesus said to Mary Magdalene, "Stop holding on to me, for I have not yet ascended to the Father" (20:17). Now, on Easter night, Jesus appears to the disciples and gives them the Spirit. In the theology of St. John, Easter, Ascension, and Pentecost are one event that happens on Easter day.

To the point: The power and source of all these visible manifestations of a new order of life—peace, forgiveness, and love which are expressed in community life and fidelity to God's commandments—is the resurrection of Jesus.

Celebration

Rite of Blessing and Sprinkling Holy Water

Presider: Dear friends, Easter is a time to share in the joy of being baptized or received into the Church. This water will be used to remind us of baptism and draw us more deeply into our life with the risen Christ. Let us ask God to bless it.

[Continue with form C of the blessing of water]

Responsorial Psalm

"Give thanks to the Lord for he is good, his love is everlasting."

Psalm 118, which concludes the "Hallel Songs" (Ps 113–118), was originally a processional song in praise of God's saving the people from destruction by an enemy. This ceremony began with a call to worship: all Israel, all priests, all who feared the Lord were invited to praise God for unending mercy (vv. 1-4). It continued with a procession through Jerusalem during which a soloist sang verses about facing death with confidence in God and a choir responded with verses about God's powerful intervention to save. The rejected stone which became the cornerstone (vv. 22-23) may have referred to Israel itself, a small nation considered easy to conquer by more powerful neighbors. Or it may have referred to the stone of the Temple itself, symbol of God, the rock of salvation.

It is easy to see why the New Testament would apply the image of the rejected stone to Christ (Matt 21:42; Acts 4:11; 1 Pet 2:7), and why the Lectionary would select parts of this psalm for use during the Easter season. We celebrate our victory in Christ over the enemy sin and death. In singing this psalm we call one another and all who believe to give praise for what God has done.

Model General Intercessions

Presider: The pledge of the resurrection is that the Father raises us to new life. Let us make our needs known, confident that the God of life hears our every prayer.

Response:

Lord, hear our prayer.

Cantor:

we pray to the Lord,

That the Church may witness that Jesus is "Lord and God" in all that it says and does . . . [pause]

That leaders of all nations may strive for the peace offered by the resurrected Jesus . . . [pause]

That those locked in fear or doubt or sin may be opened to peace, belief, and forgiveness . . . [pause]

That we here gathered may be of one heart and one mind . . . [pause]

Presider: O God of surprises, you raised your Son to new life on that first Easter Sunday: hear these our prayers that we may one day enjoy the fullness of life that the resurrection promises. We pray through the risen Christ, Jesus our Lord. **Amen.**

ALTERNATIVE OPENING PRAYER

Let us pray
 [as Christians thirsting for the risen life]

Pause for silent prayer

Heavenly Father and God of mercy,
we no longer look for Jesus among the dead,
for he is alive and has become the Lord of life.
From the waters of death you raise us with him
and renew your gift of life within us.
Increase in our minds and hearts
the risen life we share with Christ
and help us to grow as your people
toward the fullness of eternal life with you.
We ask this through Christ our Lord.
Amen.

RESPONSORIAL PSALM
[Ps 118:2-4, 13-15, 22-24]

℟. (1) Give thanks to the Lord for he is good, his love is everlasting.
 or:
℟. Alleluia.

Let the house of Israel say,
 "His mercy endures forever."
Let the house of Aaron say,
 "His mercy endures forever."
Let those who fear the Lord say,
 "His mercy endures forever."

℟. Give thanks to the Lord for he is good, his love is everlasting.
 or:
℟. Alleluia.

I was hard pressed and was falling,
 but the Lord helped me.
My strength and my courage is the Lord,
 and he has been my savior.
The joyful shout of victory
 in the tents of the just.

℟. Give thanks to the Lord for he is good, his love is everlasting.
 or:
℟. Alleluia.

The stone which the builders rejected
 has become the cornerstone.
By the Lord has this been done;
 it is wonderful in our eyes.
This is the day the Lord has made;
 let us be glad and rejoice in it.

℟. Give thanks to the Lord for he is good, his love is everlasting.
 or:
℟. Alleluia.

FIRST READING
[Acts 4:32-35]

The community of believers was of one heart and mind,
    and no one claimed that any of his possessions was his own,
    but they had everything in common.
With great power the apostles bore witness
    to the resurrection of the Lord Jesus,
    and great favor was accorded them all.
There was no needy person among them,
    for those who owned property or houses would sell them,
    bring the proceeds of the sale,
    and put them at the feet of the apostles,
    and they were distributed to each according to need.

SECOND READING
[1 John 5:1-6]

Beloved:
Everyone who believes that Jesus is the Christ is begotten by God,
    and everyone who loves the Father loves also the one begotten by him.
In this way we know that we love the children of God
    when we love God and obey his commandments.
For the love of God is this,
    that we keep his commandments.
And his commandments are not burdensome,
    for whoever is begotten by God conquers the world.
And the victory that conquers the world is our faith.
Who indeed is the victor over the world
    but the one who believes that Jesus is the Son of God?

This is the one who came through water and blood, Jesus Christ,
    not by water alone, but by water and blood.
The Spirit is the one that testifies,
    and the Spirit is truth.

Catechesis

Cantors

In singing this responsorial psalm you are leading the assembly in a song of praise to God for the victory over death granted you in Christ. In keeping with the structure of the psalm and with the festivity of the season, you might lead the first strophe as a litany with assembly or choir responding on the "His mercy endures forever," sing the second strophe as a solo, and have the choir sing the final strophe.

Choir

It would not be surprising if you found it hard to sustain the Easter celebration for seven weeks. It might help to keep in mind that Easter joy is not a passing feeling, but an abiding awareness that you and the other members of the body of Christ have been transformed; having died, you are now risen. Let this realization be what animates your liturgical singing these weeks.

Music Directors

Easter is the season to use your most festive, energetic, musically embellished set of acclamations. The acclamations are the primary musical element in the liturgy because they are parts of the liturgical text sung by the assembly at key moments of assent. Singing them is one of the ways the assembly enacts its priestly participation in the unfolding of the liturgy.

Furthermore, developing and using seasonal sets of acclamations helps the assembly participate in the liturgical dynamic of the whole year. The interplay between festal seasons and Ordinary Time is one of the ways the liturgy helps us to see and enter into the relationship between dying and rising which is the Paschal Mystery. The time it takes to develop seasonal acclamation sets for your parish or liturgical community is worth the effort. It must begin with reflection on the purpose of the acclamations as liturgical enactment.

Liturgy Committee

The resurrection is both a historical fact accomplished and an eschatological reality promised. Therefore, the focus can't simply be on empty tombs or images of the resurrected Christ, but the focus must be on your experience of resurrection today: peace, forgiveness, care of those in need, unity in community. How can you promote these fruits as evidence in your liturgical community that, though not seeing, you still believe?

This Sunday is the octave of Easter; note that the weekdays of the past week are celebrated as solemnities and have proper readings in the Sunday Lectionary (see L261-266). Further, since Easter is a fifty-day celebration, as much as possible the environment should be kept as fresh as on Easter Sunday itself. Another way to underscore the unity of these fifty days is to celebrate the Rite of Blessing and Sprinkling Holy Water on all eight Sundays of Easter (beginning with Easter Sunday and ending with Pentecost).

Before the revised liturgical calendar, this Sunday was called "Whit Sunday" because this was the day in the early Church when the neophytes (the newly baptized) put off their white baptismal robes and wore regular clothes. Now they "fully belonged" to the community.

APRIL 30, 2000

Third Sunday of Easter

FAITH-SHARING

- As with the disciples, the risen Christ asks you: What troubles you? What questions arise in your hearts? How has Christ's resurrection offered you peace?
- When and how have you recognized the risen Christ in the breaking of bread?
- When have you been incredulous with joy? amazed? Have these times ever been more than good feelings but also signs of the risen Christ?
- To what does your life witness? What is one thing you might do to witness better your belief in the risen Christ?

PRESIDERS

Besides *ex opere operato,* how do you make the risen Christ present in your ministry of forgiving sins? How might you help yourself connect the long hours you spend ministering the Sacrament of Penance with the presence of the risen Christ?

DEACONS

How might your service be a sign of forgiveness to those to whom you reach out?

HOSPITALITY MINISTERS

How can you help your community invite *all* to your table of fellowship?

MUSIC MINISTERS

As a liturgical season, Easter is about more than just the singing of resurrection hymns. What is that "more," and how can your ministry help the assembly enter into it?

ALTAR MINISTERS

How might your "hidden" ministry be a witness to the risen Christ?

LECTORS

How might you live the resurrected Christ so that your proclamation of the Word witnesses to his presence to all nations? in your neighborhood?

EUCHARISTIC MINISTERS

How might remembering the Body of Christ you minister in Communion help you to witness better to the presence of the risen Christ to those you meet in your daily life?

Spirituality

Reflecting on the Gospel

The occult fascinates us. It also scares us. In this Sunday's Gospel Jesus assures the disciples that he is not a ghost: "Touch me and see, because a ghost does not have flesh and bones as you can see I have." In the Gospel it is Easter Sunday evening. Jesus is trying to convince the disciples that he is real and alive. Last Sunday he invited Thomas to touch his wounds; this Sunday Jesus asks for a piece of fish and eats it in front of them. For sure, ghosts don't eat! This risen Jesus is not a ghost! But what or who is he? Simple flesh and bones like us, as he was before the resurrection? Hardly, for locked doors (last Sunday) don't keep Jesus from standing "in their midst." He's not a ghost, that's for sure. But what or who is he?

First of all, Jesus is the One made known to the disciples (and to us) "in the breaking of bread." The two disciples who journeyed to Emmaus (the story in Luke's Gospel that this Sunday's selection follows and picks up) recognized Jesus in table fellowship. It is through the hospitality of simple table fellowship that eyes can be opened for the disciples to see and believe.

Second, the risen Jesus can now be seen as the one who fulfills the Jewish expectations about the Messiah. Luke describes how the resurrection of Jesus enlightens the disciples to the understanding of the Scriptures. According to Jesus, all that happened to him (his suffering, death, and resurrection) is explained this way: "[it is] written . . . in the law of Moses and in the prophets and psalms." The long-prepared saving plans of God reach their culmination in the Mystery of Jesus.

But this is not all we are shown about the risen Jesus. Ultimately, the risen Jesus is known in those who are called to be his witnesses. These witnesses preach repentance and forgiveness "in his name" to "all the nations." The reality of the resurrection is known in the new order this event brings forth: repentance and forgiveness. This resurrection is real. This Jesus is alive. This is no ghost!

Living the Paschal Mystery

"Then he opened their minds to understand the Scriptures." This is similar to the line that is used earlier in Luke's Gospel to describe what happened to the two disciples on their way to Emmaus (see Luke 24:32). What does "opened their minds" mean? Surely, more than an intellectual exercise in understanding. The end of this Sunday's Gospel makes clear what this line means and, indeed, what even the resurrection means: we are to be *witnesses of all these things*. There is a very practical, concrete reality to the resurrection that involves us in those very events. The resurrection is about much more than Jesus' being raised from the dead. The new order that it establishes means that each of us is to preach repentance and forgiveness of sins. To "preach" means, first, that we proclaim by our living. This means that if we are to witness to or preach forgiveness, we ourselves must be forgiving people. If we are to witness to or preach repentance, we must be repenting people. The resurrection, then, makes a difference in our lives. It challenges us to do what is utterly basic to the Gospels: repent and forgive. Ghosts don't do these things. Real, alive-in-Christ people do!

MAY 7, 2000

GOSPEL [Luke 24:35-48; L47B]

The two disciples recounted what had taken place on the way, and how Jesus was made known to them in the breaking of bread.

While they were still speaking about this, he stood in their midst and said to them, "Peace be with you." But they were startled and terrified and thought that they were seeing a ghost. Then he said to them, "Why are you troubled? And why do questions arise in your hearts? Look at my hands and my feet, that it is I myself. Touch me and see, because a ghost does not have flesh and bones as you can see I have." And as he said this, he showed them his hands and his feet. While they were still incredulous for joy and were amazed, he asked them, "Have you anything here to eat?" They gave him a piece of baked fish; he took it and ate it in front of them.

He said to them, "These are my words that I spoke to you while I was still with you, that everything written about me in the law of Moses and in the prophets and psalms must be fulfilled." Then he opened their minds to understand the Scriptures. And he said to them, "Thus it is written that the Christ would suffer and rise from the dead on the third day and that repentance, for the forgiveness of sins, would be preached in his name to all the nations, beginning from Jerusalem. You are witnesses of these things."

Working with the Word

Key words and phrases from the Gospel: look, touch, see, understand, witnesses

Connecting to the first three Sundays of Easter: These Gospels seem similar because they each relate accounts of Jesus' post-resurrection appearances, but in reality they open us to an ever-widening circle of witnesses to the meaning of the resurrection: on the First Sunday of Easter, Mary of Magdala, Peter, and John encounter the empty tomb ("for they did not yet understand the Scripture that he had to rise from the dead"); on the Second Sunday of Easter, the disciples encounter the person of the risen Christ ("We have seen the Lord"); and on this Third Sunday of Easter, the disciples encounter the risen Messiah who is the fulfillment of Sacred Scripture to which we give witness to all nations ("Thus it is written that the Christ . . . would be preached").

Connecting to our culture: The meaning of Easter resurrection cannot be captured simply by events two millennia ago nor in events that will happen at Christ's second coming. The meaning of Easter resurrection also encompasses *our witnessing* now to repentance and the forgiveness of sins.

Exegetical points: Peter's preaching (first reading) appropriately begins and ends with Scripture references: the entire history of Israel and their election is signaled by reference to the God of Abraham, Isaac, and Jacob; the fulfillment of prophecy is suggested by the designation of Jesus as God's "servant" and the "Righteous One"; and Peter concludes by asserting that the suffering and death of Jesus came about in "fulfillment" of what had been "announced beforehand" through "the prophets." Peter also indicates that the effects and the consequences of the fulfillment of Scripture in the death-resurrection of Jesus are repentance, conversion, and forgiveness of sins (on this, see also the second reading). It is significant that in the readings of Easter thus far, resurrection is understood both as an event and in terms of its manifest effects in the lives of believers. More than a matter of credal statements, resurrection is the charter for a new way of living.

To the point: We are not just to be "incredulous for joy" and "amazed" at Jesus' resurrection, but we are to go and be witnesses.

Celebration

Rite of Blessing and Sprinkling Holy Water
Presider: Dear friends, for the third week in a row we hear in the Gospel about Jesus' appearing to his disciples, convincing them and us that the resurrection is real. Today he commands his disciples to be witnesses to what has happened. We bless this water as a reminder of our baptism; by being plunged into Jesus' death and resurrection we are to be witnesses to the new life he offers.

[Continue with form C of the blessing of water]

Responsorial Psalm
"Lord, let your face shine on us."
Psalm 4 from which this Sunday's responsorial psalm is taken is a song of confidence in which the psalmist's sense of distress is outweighed by his or her absolute trust in God who will save. The plea that God hear the cry for help (first strophe) is followed by a statement of certitude that God will respond (second strophe). On the one hand, the psalm is sung by Christ whom God has saved from death. But it is also sung by us who have been saved *through* Christ's death. In the body of the risen Christ God turns on us a face of such radiance that we are freed from fear, from misunderstanding, from disbelief (Gospel). Even more, we are saved from sin, past (first reading) and future (second reading). What deeper security and peace can God grant us?

Model General Intercessions
Presider: One way we witness to Jesus' resurrected life is by the confidence we have in our prayers being answered when we make our needs known to the Father. And so we pray.

Response:

[Musical notation: Lord, hear our prayer.]

Cantor:

[Musical notation: we pray to the Lord,]

That the Church may faithfully see and touch the risen Christ in others . . . [pause]

That the leaders of the world may be quick to forgive and slow to condemn . . . [pause]

That those who feel that their sins cannot be forgiven may encounter the risen Christ and experience his forgiveness . . . [pause]

That we here gathered may be hospitable in welcoming all to our tables, seeing Christ in those with whom we share table fellowship . . . [pause]

Presider: Wondrous God, you raised your Son to new life and call us now to witness to his resurrection: hear these our prayers that we might preach by the goodness of our lives the good news to all nations. We ask this through Christ our Lord. **Amen.**

ALTERNATIVE OPENING PRAYER
Let us pray

Pause for silent prayer

Father in heaven, author of all truth,
a people once in darkness has listened to your Word
and followed your Son as he rose from the tomb.
Hear the prayer of this newborn people
and strengthen your Church to answer your call.
May we rise and come forth into the light of day
to stand in your presence until eternity dawns.
We ask this through Christ our Lord.
Amen.

RESPONSORIAL PSALM
[Ps 4:2, 4, 7-8, 9]

℟. (7a) Lord, let your face shine on us.
or:
℟. Alleluia.

When I call, answer me, O my just God,
 you who relieve me when I am in distress;
 have pity on me, and hear my prayer!

℟. Lord, let your face shine on us.
or:
℟. Alleluia.

Know that the LORD does wonders for his faithful one;
 the LORD will hear me when I call upon him.

℟. Lord, let your face shine on us.
or:
℟. Alleluia.

O LORD, let the light of your countenance shine upon us!
 You put gladness into my heart.

℟. Lord, let your face shine on us.
or:
℟. Alleluia.

As soon as I lie down, I fall peacefully asleep,
 for you alone, O LORD,
 bring security to my dwelling.

℟. Lord, let your face shine on us.
or:
℟. Alleluia.

FIRST READING
[Acts 3:13-15, 17-19]

Peter said to the people:
"The God of Abraham,
 the God of Isaac, and the God of Jacob,
 the God of our fathers, has glorified his servant Jesus,
 whom you handed over and denied in Pilate's presence
 when he had decided to release him.
You denied the Holy and Righteous One
 and asked that a murderer be released to you.
The author of life you put to death,
 but God raised him from the dead; of this we are witnesses.
Now I know, brothers,
 that you acted out of ignorance, just as your leaders did;
 but God has thus brought to fulfillment
 what he had announced beforehand through the mouth of all the prophets,
 that his Christ would suffer.
Repent, therefore, and be converted, that your sins may be wiped away."

SECOND READING
[1 John 2:1-5a]

My children, I am writing this to you so that you may not commit sin.
But if anyone does sin, we have an Advocate with the Father,
 Jesus Christ the righteous one.
He is expiation for our sins,
 and not for our sins only but for those of the whole world.
The way we may be sure that we know him is to keep
 his commandments.
Those who say, "I know him," but do not keep his commandments
 are liars, and the truth is not in them.
But whoever keeps his word,
 the love of God is truly perfected in him.

Catechesis

Cantors
It is your experience of the resurrection which gives you the confidence to sing this Sunday's psalm. Part of that experience is knowing that in Christ you have been and will be forgiven your sins. Pray this week that your singing be filled with this steadfast assurance.

Choir
The readings for this Sunday remind us that one of the key testimonies to the resurrection is the forgiveness of sins. How can you be witnesses of this as a choir among yourselves? for the assembly? for the parish?

Music Directors
The reference in this Sunday's Gospel to the experience of recognizing Christ in the breaking of bread makes using hymns with this reference appropriate, especially for Communion. Even more appropriate, however, would be hymns which call us to witness to the resurrection and to the forgiveness of sins. "Christ the Lord Is Risen Again" (CH) is a fifteenth-century text set to a medieval French tune associated with the Christmas season. The text speaks of the resurrected Christ bidding us "tell abroad How the lost may be restored, How the penitent restored . . ." The gentle melody fits either the presentation of the gifts or Communion. David Hurd's "Morning of Splendor" [W3] prays that the meaning of the resurrection break forth in our hearts, minds, souls, voices, and lives. Its unusual melodic contour, however, suggests that unless you have a musically adept assembly, you let the choir alone sing it during the presentation of the gifts.

Liturgy Committee
The first reading for the eight Sundays of Easter is always taken from the Acts of the Apostles which record how the Easter faith was received and lived in the early Christian communities. What might you do in your liturgical community to strengthen the people's Easter faith? to keep it alive throughout the year?

Especially Easter Sunday and its octave were privileged times in the early Church for mystagogy, those marvelous sermons that explained the meaning of the initiation sacraments. However, all of the Easter season might be considered "mystagogical," for during this time we are plumbing the meaning of Christ's death and resurrection. It is appropriate to celebrate baptisms on any of these eight Sundays; this is particularly important to keep in mind if the RCIA has a large number of catechumens and candidates so that the Easter Vigil baptisms take a disproportionately large amount of time. Those who are baptized on a Sunday of Easter rather than at the Vigil aren't being "cheated," but themselves are "witnesses" to the Easter mystery being prolonged over the seven weeks of Easter.

MAY 7, 2000

Fourth Sunday of Easter

FAITH-SHARING
- When have you heard the voice of Jesus as your Good Shepherd? How might you improve your hearing his voice? Improve your following it?
- In what ways have you lived as Jesus the Good Shepherd—for whom and how have you laid down your life in self-sacrifice?
- "See what love the Father has bestowed on us . . ." When have you experienced this love? How is this love being made known to others through you?

PRESIDERS
When is your ministry that of the Good Shepherd? that of the hired man? What is God asking you to "lay down" for the benefit of your sheep?

DEACONS
If you were examined for your good deeds, as Peter in the first reading, what would be the verdict?

HOSPITALITY MINISTERS
"Beloved, we are God's children now." How might you witness this through your ministry of hospitality?

MUSIC MINISTERS
Your ministry requires a lot of shepherding. Whenever you are tired or discouraged, remember that there is One who shepherds you with great love.

ALTAR MINISTERS
In your simple and "hidden" service, have you ever felt like the rejected stone? How is your service really a cornerstone?

LECTORS
How might your everyday dying and rising in Christ help you to proclaim the word with more conviction?

EUCHARISTIC MINISTERS
How does your ministering Communion help others "see [Jesus] as he is" (second reading)?

Spirituality

Reflecting on the Gospel

Jesus is risen! But where does that leave us? Last Sunday the Gospel challenged us to preach and witness. But where does that leave us? Abandoned? Sheep without a shepherd? This Sunday's Gospel tells us otherwise. We have a shepherd. And he is good.

The Greek word for "good" in this Gospel means having merit in accordance with a purpose. Jesus is the "good" shepherd because he accomplished what he came to do: bring us salvation. This Gospel gives us two important insights that carry us further into the Mystery of resurrection.

First, Jesus tells us that "I know mine and mine know me." Here "know" doesn't refer to a cold, distant intellectual exercise so much as it describes "being known" in the context of an intimate relationship. Notice, John uses the same word to describe the communion and unity between the Father and Jesus: "Just as the Father knows me and I know the Father." Jesus' relationship with us, therefore, is much more than a shepherd "owning" the sheep. Rather, our relationship with Jesus is so intimate that we are to "be called children of God" (second reading). In other words, the manner in which Jesus our Good Shepherd "knows" us brings about a new, resurrected identity—an intimacy and communion with each other that makes us all "one flock" and makes us "God's children *now*."

Second, Jesus is the *good* shepherd precisely because he laid down his life for his sheep. By choosing to lay down his life, we see and learn that his voice will never abandon us—not even at death! In that, we "know" the incredible love and care that Jesus has for us. In that, we experience the power of the resurrection.

The resurrection is not a historical event that confirms Jesus "made it," is now returned to the Father, and we are left to fend for ourselves. This Sunday's Gospel of the Good Shepherd is an incredibly reassuring one in which we hear in the metaphor of the good shepherd Jesus' pledge to continue to care for us and love us just as he loves the Father and the Father loves him. His call to us to preach and witness to the resurrection is a call from One who is blameless in his own fidelity to his purpose: to lay down his life, take it up again, and have abiding concern for his followers. Would we need anything more to prompt us to continue to exclaim our Alleluias?

Living the Paschal Mystery

This Sunday is Mother's Day. Motherhood could be a kind of metaphor for living the Paschal Mystery. When mothers live this Gospel, when they themselves are "good shepherds" towards their children, they bring the resurrection experience to life in the here and now. Like a good shepherd, a mother spends her life for her children, knows them with tenderness and understanding, has concern for them, loves them. In this way, then, the Mystery of resurrection isn't really far beyond our grasp. Resurrection is in the opening of ourselves to the loving intimacy Jesus offers by opening ourselves to the love that mothers (and fathers), spouses, children, friends offer us. In this we glimpse and live the new life of the resurrection.

MAY 14, 2000

GOSPEL [John 10:11-18; L50B]

Jesus said: "I am the good shepherd. A good shepherd lays down his life for the sheep. A hired man, who is not a shepherd and whose sheep are not his own, sees a wolf coming and leaves the sheep and runs away, and the wolf catches and scatters them. This is because he works for pay and has no concern for the sheep. I am the good shepherd, and I know mine and mine know me, just as the Father knows me and I know the Father; and I will lay down my life for the sheep. I have other sheep that do not belong to this fold. These also I must lead, and they will hear my voice, and there will be one flock, one shepherd. This is why the Father loves me, because I lay down my life in order to take it up again. No one takes it from me, but I lay it down on my own. I have power to lay it down, and power to take it up again. This command I have received from my Father."

Working with the Word

Key words and phrases from the Gospel: lays down life, they will hear my voice, one flock, one shepherd

Connecting to the Lectionary for the eight Sundays of Easter: The first three Sundays of Easter concentrate on the fact of Jesus' resurrection—empty tomb, finger in the nail marks, no ghost. This Sunday begins to tell us what resurrection means—that this Jesus, as the one who lays down his life, is the very Good Shepherd of God the Father whose shepherding will bring about "one flock, one shepherd." The next four Sundays, as we will see, say something about how we disciples experience and live the resurrection.

Connecting to our culture: Almost none of us has any practical experience of sheep and shepherding. Nevertheless, we all have real experience of what Jesus did for us: laid down his life and knew his own.

Exegetical points: The effects of the resurrection continue to be dramatized and unfolded. The Gospel description of Jesus as the "good shepherd" does two things. First, it sets up a contrast between Jesus and the self-serving and corrupt "shepherds" of Israel's past—wicked kings and leaders whose lack of concern for their people resulted in internal decay and external ruin. Indeed, the corruption of Israel's kings so disgusted God that Ezekiel prophesied how God would personally come to be their shepherd (Ezek 37:11-16). The second point follows from this: in Jesus, God's desire to shepherd the people personally is fulfilled. What Ezekiel expected to be exercised by God is now accomplished in Jesus. Jesus does this at the cost of laying down his own life for the sheep.

To the point: Jesus' good shepherding is manifested in his dying and rising: he "lays down his life for his sheep" (dying) and has power to take it up again (rising).

Celebration

Rite of Blessing and Sprinkling Holy Water

Presider: Dear friends, the Good Shepherd knows us and leads us to new life. We bless this water and use it to remind us of our baptism, the sacrament that unites us with the risen Christ so we can hear his voice.

[*Continue with form C of the blessing of water*]

Responsorial Psalm

"The stone rejected by the builders has become the cornerstone."

The psalm notes for the second Sunday of Easter state that Psalm 118 (used also this Sunday) was originally a processional song used by the Jewish community to celebrate victory over an enemy. But the psalm may have been formulated even earlier as an individual's song of thanksgiving. It would easily have evolved into a communal thanksgiving because for the Israelites the individual relationship with God could never be separated from the communal. The source of personal relationship with God was the communal covenant. Any individual experience of God's salvific intervention was always understood in terms of, and intensified by, this communal relationship.

Often we Christians relate to the image of the Good Shepherd only on an individual basis. After all, the text of Psalm 23 is in the first person singular. Yet this Sunday's Gospel, coupled with Psalm 118, tells us that our shepherd relationship with Jesus is communal, that individual salvation is part of communal redemption, that the intimacy we have been granted by Christ ("I know mine and mine know me") is intended for all people ("I have other sheep . . . these also I must lead"). In singing this psalm, we acknowledge that the resurrection offered in Christ is meant for all and that our surrender to its effects in our lives is the "cornerstone" of salvation for the world.

Model General Intercessions

Presider: The Father knows the Son and knows those of us who are one with the Son. We are confident of God's love and that our prayers will be heard.

Response:

Lord, hear our prayer.

Cantor:

we pray to the Lord,

That the Church may always hear the voice of the Good Shepherd, heed that voice, and follow him to life everlasting . . . [pause]

That leaders of all nations may lead with goodness and righteousness . . . [pause]

That those who have lost the way or strayed from the path of goodness may heed God's voice that calls them back . . . [pause]

That we here gathered may rejoice in the unity we share in the risen Lord and never let our Alleluia! cease . . . [pause]

Presider: Good and gracious God, you care for your children with the love of a parent: hear these our prayers and grant that we might one day share in the glory of your risen Son. We pray through Christ our Lord. **Amen.**

ALTERNATIVE OPENING PRAYER

Let us pray

Pause for silent prayer

God and Father of our Lord Jesus Christ,
 though your people walk in the valley of darkness,
no evil should they fear;
for they follow in faith the call of the shepherd
 whom you have sent for their hope and strength.
Attune our minds to the sound of his voice,
lead our steps in the path he has shown,
that we may know the strength of his outstretched arm
and enjoy the light of your presence for ever.
We ask this in the name of Jesus the Lord. **Amen.**

RESPONSORIAL PSALM

[Ps 118:1, 8-9, 21-23, 26, 28, 29]

℟. (22) The stone rejected by the builders has become the cornerstone.
 or:
℟. Alleluia.

Give thanks to the Lord, for he is good,
 for his mercy endures forever.
It is better to take refuge in the Lord
 than to trust in man.
It is better to take refuge in the Lord
 than to trust in princes.

℟. The stone rejected by the builders has become the cornerstone.
 or:
℟. Alleluia.

I will give thanks to you, for you have answered me
 and have been my savior.
The stone which the builders rejected
 has become the cornerstone.
By the Lord has this been done;
 it is wonderful in our eyes.

℟. The stone rejected by the builders has become the cornerstone.
 or:
℟. Alleluia.

Blessed is he who comes in the name of the Lord;
 we bless you from the house of the Lord.
I will give thanks to you, for you have answered me
 and have been my savior.
Give thanks to the Lord, for he is good;
 for his kindness endures forever.

℟. The stone rejected by the builders has become the cornerstone.
or:
℟. Alleluia.

FIRST READING
[Acts 4:8-12]

Peter, filled with the Holy Spirit, said:
"Leaders of the people and elders:
If we are being examined today
about a good deed done to a cripple,
namely, by what means he was saved,
then all of you and all the people of Israel should know
that it was in the name of Jesus Christ the Nazarene
whom you crucified, whom God raised from the dead;
in his name this man stands before you healed.
He is *the stone rejected by you, the builders, which has become the cornerstone.*
There is no salvation through anyone else,
nor is there any other name under heaven
given to the human race by which we are to be saved."

SECOND READING
[1 John 3:1-2]

Beloved:
See what love the Father has bestowed on us
that we may be called the children of God.
Yet so we are.
The reason the world does not know us is that it did not know him.
Beloved, we are God's children now;
what we shall be has not yet been revealed.
We do know that when it is revealed we shall be like him,
for we shall see him as he is.

Catechesis

Cantors

In singing this psalm, you give thanks to God for resurrection—in your life and in the lives of all people. Spend some time this week reflecting on how your personal experience of resurrection flows from and builds up the communal experience of the whole Church.

Choir

Just as the resurrection is not a private, individual experience, neither is your liturgical celebration of it. The most important aspect of your ministry as a choir is the witness you give to the communal nature of the Church. You are an icon of the "one flock" under the "one Shepherd."

Music Directors

The Gospel from last Sunday ended with the command that you witness the resurrection to all the world. This Sunday's Gospel promises the presence of the Good Shepherd who will never abandon you. The Easter season Lectionary is inviting you to see the connection between resurrection, the abiding presence of Christ, and mission. The hymn text which most strongly captures this connection is Ralph Wright's "Sing of One Who Walks beside Us" [CBW3] which speaks of the nearness of the risen Christ in the midst of the continuing struggle with darkness, doubt, and fear. Set to the tune HOLY MANNA, it would serve well at either the presentation of the gifts or as a song after Communion. Another good choice would be "Jesus, Shepherd of Our Souls" [W3] in which Fred Kaan connects Jesus' shepherding with mission ("May we with a shepherd's heart Love the people round us . . ."). Its gentle tune would be appropriate for the presentation of the gifts.

Liturgy Committee

This period of a fifty-day celebration of Easter is sometimes referred to as the "Great Sunday" because these fifty days are considered a unity. Look for patterns in the Lectionary that help you draw the fifty days into a unity. What might you do in your parish or in your families to help preserve the unity of these days?

Mother's Day is the busiest day of the year for long distance phone calls. Of course, everyone wants to honor mothers on this day! Be careful, however, that the liturgy of the Fourth Sunday of Easter remains just that . . . an *Easter* celebration.

One way, perhaps, to pay respect to this day would be to have a grandmother, mother, and daughter be the gift bearers. Be careful about bringing up "symbols" of motherhood; remember, the gifts of bread and wine represent ourselves and our lives surrendered to God. For parishes in the United States, the *Book of Blessings* gives an "Order for the Blessing of Mothers on Mother's Day" (chapter 55). Intercessions are provided that may be adapted and added to the general intercessions for this Sunday; a special prayer over the people before the concluding blessing of Mass is also given. For parishes in Canada, *A Book of Blessings* provides that intercessions may be added to those of the day (p. 233) and a blessing may be given to mothers after the homily (p. 51).

MAY 14, 2000

Fifth Sunday of Easter

FAITH-SHARING
- How do you "remain" in Christ? Who helps you to remain in Christ?
- How do you get cut off from Christ?
- Contrast the fruit of your life when you remain in Christ to what happens in your life when you are cut off.
- What needs to be pruned in you in order for you to "bear more fruit"?

PRESIDERS
When do you feel you have spoken out the most "boldly in the name of Christ"? What fosters that in you?

DEACONS
"Let us love not in word and speech but in deed and truth." How is your diaconal ministry a love "in deed and truth"?

HOSPITALITY MINISTERS
"By this is my Father glorified . . ." How might your hospitality bring glory to God? How might your hospitality enable others to witness to God's glory?

MUSIC MINISTERS
There is more to the image of the vine and the branches than just singing a hymn about it. Does your ministry of music rise organically from a love of Christ and of the liturgy?

ALTAR MINISTERS
What is the fruit of your altar ministry? What difference does it make in your daily, Christian living?

LECTORS
"[Saul] spoke out boldly in the name of the Lord." What does bold proclaiming look like during the Liturgy of the Word? in your everyday living?

EUCHARISTIC MINISTERS
". . . a branch cannot bear fruit on its own unless it remains on the vine." How might you minister God's nourishment to God's people outside of the liturgy?

Spirituality

Reflecting on the Gospel

We have an incredible drive for intimacy. "Love" is the catchword for today's society, especially touted by the entertainment media. This Sunday's Gospel addresses our need for *genuine* intimacy. St. John uses a metaphor—the vine and branches—to tell us exactly how intimate Christ is with us; and this is the kind of intimacy that we desperately seek.

Christ is the vine; we are the branches. In Jesus' dying and rising we witness and experience his great love for us, his giving of his life to us. So long as we *remain* vitally connected to Christ our vine, love and life are ours. However, the word "remain" implies that we have a choice. In fact, the Gospel outlines a very clear choice: remain attached to the vine and bear fruit, or be "thrown out" and "burned."

How do we remain in Christ, then? The First Letter of John (second reading) gives us a clear answer: "let us love not in word or speech but in deed and truth." We remain in Christ not when we *talk a good talk* but whenever we choose to love in deed. These loving deeds are the fruit of our remaining in Christ. And this fruit honors God—"By this is my Father glorified." That means that the worship we offer the Father flows from the deeds of our everyday living; worship and life are intimately connected.

John tries to capture the intimacy God offers us in Christ by using the metaphor of vine and branches. Our life flows from Christ's life; we are nourished and sustained by the Father. This Sunday's Gospel begins to open up for us the fact that sharing in the resurrection carries with it the choice to be a disciple. But whatever demands (dying) discipleship makes on us, they pale in face of the tremendous intimacy that is offered. For faithful Christians, our greatest desires for intimacy are fulfilled in Christ. No wonder we still sing Alleluia!

Living the Paschal Mystery

Remaining in Christ has its practical demands. To be sure, we are not without the nourishment and care that will sustain us—Christ is our vine; the Father is our vine grower. Nonetheless, to remain in Christ means that we must *live* as Jesus did: "not in word or speech but in deed and truth." In other words, being the branch grafted onto Christ's life is real, to the extent that we believe and love.

How are we grafted onto this Christ-vine? Essentially, this is what the initiation sacraments (baptism, confirmation, Eucharist) are all about: becoming the branch that is grafted onto the vine and receiving its life and love from the vine. This is another reason why the Easter season is a privileged time for celebrating these sacraments in the Church. These readings encourage us by stating explicitly the kind of loving, intimate relationship that can be ours in Christ. They also challenge us in that living in Christ must make a difference in how we live—we baptized Christians live everyday life within the Mystery of Christ's dying and rising. The Easter season helps us grasp this more clearly. This is another reason why we still sing Alleluia!

MAY 21, 2000

GOSPEL [John 15:1-8; L53B]

Jesus said to his disciples: "I am the true vine, and my Father is the vine grower. He takes away every branch in me that does not bear fruit, and every one that does he prunes so that it bears more fruit. You are already pruned because of the word that I spoke to you. Remain in me, as I remain in you. Just as a branch cannot bear fruit on its own unless it remains on the vine, so neither can you unless you remain in me. I am the vine, you are the branches. Whoever remains in me and I in him will bear much fruit, because without me you can do nothing. Anyone who does not remain in me will be thrown out like a branch and wither; people will gather them and throw them into a fire and they will be burned. If you remain in me and my words remain in you, ask for whatever you want and it will be done for you. By this is my Father glorified, that you bear much fruit and become my disciples."

Working with the Word

Key words and phrases from the Gospel: I am the true vine, Father is the vine grower, you are the branches, remain in me

Connecting to the Third Sunday of Easter: The Gospel for the Third Sunday of Easter challenged us to be witnesses to the resurrection; this Gospel and readings spell out what witness means: remain in Christ (Gospel), speak out boldly (first reading), love in deed and truth and keep the commandments (second reading).

Connecting to our culture: "Hatch," "match," and "dispatch"—is this not the way all too many Christians view their connection to Christ? Resurrection life in believers is something which must be *maintained*. "Conversion," "baptism," "new life" are not one-shot deals. Conversion or baptism may be identified as a particular event, but the ongoing reality of life in Christ must be sustained. A vine is either attached to the branch and sustained each day or it is "thrown out" to "wither" and "be burned." So it is with our Christian discipleship.

Exegetical points: The key to the Gospel for this Sunday is the verb "remain" which occurs eight times. The metaphor of the vine and the branches is organic: its vitality depends on the life that flows from the vine into the branches. The flow of life is evident when the branches "bear fruit" (five times). It is not enough for the branch to have been connected to the vine at one time, or for the connection to be weak, dangling, or broken. The branch can be vital only by "remaining" on the vine. This, finally, is the meaning of the metaphor of "vine and branches": it expresses the organic and vital aspect of the relationship between the Master and his disciples, a relationship that is life-giving and productive.

Notice again the dynamism of John's theology: believing is not a mental activity but is expressed in concrete ways; for example, by loving one another. Or, in terms from the Gospel, believing is evident in bearing fruit. There is only one way to fulfill the commandment to love, or to bear fruit—it is by the power Jesus gives us in his Spirit. Stated negatively, "Without me you can do nothing."

To the point: "Remaining" in Christ is bi-directional. On the one hand, "remaining" demands of us more than intellectual assent; it calls us to keep the commandments. On the other hand, we are not left alone in this endeavor; the Father is the vine grower who continues to give the Son as the vine that nourishes and sustains us.

Celebration

Rite of Blessing and Sprinkling Holy Water

Presider: Dear friends, we are called to share in the life and love of the risen Christ. We bless this water as a reminder that we are baptized into him; let us celebrate with joy the new life given to us.

[*Continue with form C of the blessing of water*]

Responsorial Psalm

"I will praise you, Lord, in the assembly of your people."

Only recently we prayed parts of Psalm 22 as the responsorial psalm on Palm Sunday of the Lord's Passion. On this, the Fifth Sunday of Easter, we pray it again, using more verses from its second half where the intense suffering and the sense of abandonment of the first part has been transformed into salvation and praise of God. In this Sunday's Gospel Jesus invites us to "remain" in him, as branches which rise organically from a vine. What does it mean to remain in him? We must "[speak] out boldly" (first reading). We must "keep [God's] commandments" (second reading). And the psalm says that we must be faithful through death. We will only be able to sing God's praises before the people if we have embraced the dying which must precede resurrection. Already the call to discipleship which the resurrection entails is upon us. May we remain! May we sing praise before the world!

Model General Intercessions

Presider: Jesus called us to confidence in God and promised that whatever we ask, it shall be done for us. Let us pray in the risen Savior's name.

Response:

Lord, hear our prayer.

Cantor:

we pray to the Lord,

Remaining in Christ, may the Church ever deepen her belief and love in the risen Lord . . . [pause]

Remaining in God, may all nations keep God's commandments and do what pleases the Almighty . . . [pause]

May all those cut off from God return to God as the source of their life and nourishment . . . [pause]

Remaining in the Spirit, may all of us glorify God by the fruits of our living . . . [pause]

Presider: O God who is the vine grower, you sustain us with your steadfast care: hear these our prayers that we may remain in the risen Christ and he in us. We ask this through that same Jesus Christ our Lord. **Amen.**

OPENING PRAYER

Let us pray

Pause for silent prayer

God our Father,
look upon us with love.
You redeem us and make us your
    children in Christ.
Give us true freedom
and bring us to the inheritance you
    promised.
We ask this through our Lord Jesus
    Christ, your Son,
who lives and reigns with you and the
    Holy Spirit,
one God, for ever and ever. **Amen.**

RESPONSORIAL PSALM
[Ps 22:26-27, 28, 30, 31-32]

℟. (26a) I will praise you, Lord, in the
    assembly of your people.
    or:
℟. Alleluia.

I will fulfill my vows before those who
    fear the LORD.
    The lowly shall eat their fill;
they who seek the LORD shall praise him:
    "May your hearts live forever!"

℟. I will praise you, Lord, in the
    assembly of your people.
    or:
℟. Alleluia.

All the ends of the earth
    shall remember and turn to the LORD;
all the families of the nations
    shall bow down before him.

℟. I will praise you, Lord, in the
    assembly of your people.
    or:
℟. Alleluia.

To him alone shall bow down
    all who sleep in the earth;
before him shall bend
    all who go down into the dust.

℟. I will praise you, Lord, in the
    assembly of your people.
    or:
℟. Alleluia.

And to him my soul shall live;
    my descendants shall serve him.
Let the coming generation be told of the
    LORD
    that they may proclaim to a people
        yet to be born
    the justice he has shown.

℟. I will praise you, Lord, in the
    assembly of your people.
    or:
℟. Alleluia.

FIRST READING
[Acts 9:26-31]

When Saul arrived in Jerusalem he tried to join the disciples,
 but they were all afraid of him,
 not believing that he was a disciple.
Then Barnabas took charge of him and brought him to the apostles,
 and he reported to them how he had seen the Lord,
 and that he had spoken to him,
 and how in Damascus he had spoken out boldly in the name of Jesus.
He moved about freely with them in Jerusalem,
 and spoke out boldly in the name of the Lord.
He also spoke and debated with the Hellenists,
 but they tried to kill him.
And when the brothers learned of this, they took him down to Caesarea
 and sent him on his way to Tarsus.
The church throughout all Judea, Galilee, and Samaria was at peace.
It was being built up and walked in the fear of the Lord,
 and with the consolation of the Holy Spirit it grew in numbers.

SECOND READING
[1 John 3:18-24]

Children, let us love not in word or speech
 but in deed and truth.
Now this is how we shall know that we belong to the truth
 and reassure our hearts before him
 in whatever our hearts condemn,
 for God is greater than our hearts and knows everything.
Beloved, if our hearts do not condemn us,
 we have confidence in God
 and receive from him whatever we ask,
 because we keep his commandments and do what pleases him.
And his commandment is this:
 we should believe in the name of his Son, Jesus Christ,
 and love one another just as he commanded us.
Those who keep his commandments remain in him, and he in them,
 and the way we know that he remains in us
 is from the Spirit he gave us.

Catechesis

Cantors

You sing today not only about resurrection but about your willingness to remain with the discipleship which resurrection entails. Are you willing?

Choir

Why would you not want to "remain" with Christ when resurrection has come? Christ knew—and so do you—that the struggle is not over. Striving to live "in deed and truth" by "[loving] one another" (second reading) is not easy. You have to stick to it. How are you called to live this specifically as a choir?

Music Directors

Two songs directly connected to this Sunday's readings are "We Have Been Told" [BB, G, G2, RS] and "Now We Remain" [BB, G, G2, RS]. Both are generally sung during Communion, but would also fit during the presentation of the gifts. A third song to consider is the African piece "Jesus Has Conquered Death" [LMGM], which calls us to follow the risen Lord. Its lively call-response style would lend itself well to either entrance or recessional. Sing it either a cappella or use drums.

Liturgy Committee

This is a particularly challenging time of the year liturgically: your attention is focused on the unity of the Easter fifty days; at the same time, practically, spring is the customary season for first Communions, graduations, and weddings. You must always monitor your liturgies, that the Easter season is not eclipsed by these other pastoral celebrations. Is there any catechesis that you need to do in your parish in this regard? How might you go about that?

Throughout the fifty days of Easter the paschal candle is lit as a reminder of the presence of the risen Christ who lives and is present in the Church. It is as large and prominent as the resurrection is large and prominent in the life and belief of Christians. When the Easter candle is prominent outside of the Easter season—especially at baptisms and funerals and also at evening prayer—it is in order to remind the assembly how intimately connected their life is with Christ's. All candles used at liturgy really are smaller copies of the Easter candle. Lit candles are reminders that Christ is the light of the world that dispels the darkness of sin and calls everyone to risen life.

MAY 21, 2000

Sixth Sunday of Easter

FAITH-SHARING

- What does it mean to be Christ's friend? Which commandments do you have difficulty keeping? How might your relying on Christ's friendship help you?
- How is it evident in your life that you have been chosen by God to bear fruit?
- Where is God asking you to lay down your life for another?

PRESIDERS

Who do you have a hard time calling "friend"? How does your experience of God's love for you help you to call the person friend?

DEACONS

How is "laying down your life" a metaphor for diaconal service?

HOSPITALITY MINISTERS

"God shows no partiality." How might you better imitate God's hospitality at the parish? in daily life?

MUSIC MINISTERS

The fruit you have been called to bear is not your music-making itself but the love you reveal through it. This is a self-effacing love which leads people to look not at you, but at the risen Christ.

ALTAR MINISTERS

". . . everyone who loves is begotten of God." In what way is your service "begotten of God"?

LECTORS

Your proclamation of God's Word helps the community "know what [the] master is doing." How does your living the Word help you proclaim it better?

EUCHARISTIC MINISTERS

In what ways does your ministering the Body or Blood of Christ bring you joy? How can you share that joy with others as the fruit of God's friendship with you?

Spirituality

Reflecting on the Gospel

"Love is a many splendored thing." So the old movie song goes. In common parlance the many splendors of love tend to be seen as a "feeling good" love that makes few demands on the beloved. This kind of love is usually portrayed as something fairly easy to come by: we "fall" in love. In contrast, more recently we hear about "tough love," a kind of love that seems at face value to be rather harsh but that is really given with the good of the beloved in mind. Although there may be touches of both of these kinds of love in what Jesus says in this Sunday's Gospel, he really takes the notion of Christian love to a much different place.

In this Gospel, what is love? Two points come clear. First, surely Christian loving is not something we do on our own; we are able to love because of Christ (onto whom we are grafted; see last Sunday's Gospel) and the life that he gives. The key is that *we have been chosen*. In other words, Christian loving is something way beyond the many splendored thing we sing about; this love is the fulfillment of our search for intimacy and belonging that is initiated by and completed in Christ.

Second, the love of Christ is a fruitful love because the lover does the unthinkable: lays down his life. Our preference is to skip to the joy that Jesus speaks about in this Sunday's Gospel; Jesus invites us to remain in his love so that our "joy might be complete." And what is this complete joy? Jesus' joy in us is complete when it calls forth from us as total a self-surrender as was Jesus'. This is what real life is about; this is what real love is about. We must *give* without counting the cost.

Clearly our fifty-day celebration of Easter is not something apart from the cares and demands of our everyday living. Jesus' Gospel message is always practical, something that squares up with the messiness of our everyday lives. Resurrection life is filled with love and joy and friends when it is grounded in the stark reality of self-surrender. Jesus gave 100 percent; so must we. And then is our joy complete. This is why we still sing the many-splendored Alleluia!

Living the Paschal Mystery

The love that exists between the Father and Jesus, and between Jesus and his disciples, is to exist also among the disciples themselves: "love one another as I love you." The dynamism of resurrected life is that it is not content with a "me and Jesus" relationship. It is essentially directed towards others, drawing in even those who are radically unlike us—as the first reading vividly demonstrates. Such selfless love cannot originate in human capabilities but originates in God: "This is love: not that we have loved God, but that he has loved us" (second reading). The active aspect of love (as opposed to feelings, sentiment, or emotionalism) is underscored by the disciples' close association with the command of Jesus. The selfless aspect of this obedient love is also stated clearly: to lay down one's life for one's friends. Ultimately, the life of the resurrection is reached only through dying to self. This was Jesus' path. So is it ours as his disciples.

MAY 28, 2000

GOSPEL [John 15:9-17; L56B]

Jesus said to his disciples: "As the Father loves me, so I also love you. Remain in my love. If you keep my commandments, you will remain in my love, just as I have kept my Father's commandments and remain in his love.

"I have told you this so that my joy may be in you and your joy might be complete. This is my commandment: love one another as I love you. No one has greater love than this, to lay down one's life for one's friends. You are my friends if you do what I command you. I no longer call you slaves, because a slave does not know what his master is doing. I have called you friends, because I have told you everything I have heard from my Father. It was not you who chose me, but I who chose you and appointed you to go and bear fruit that will remain, so that whatever you ask the Father in my name he may give you. This I command you: love one another."

Working with the Word

Key words and phrases from the Gospel: remain in my love, you are my friends, this I command you

Connecting to last Sunday's Gospel: This passage follows immediately upon last Sunday's Gospel of the vine and the branches. Notice once again the emphasis on "remaining" (four times). This time, however, the way the disciples remain united to Jesus is through love (nine times). Lest there be any mistake about the nature of love, Jesus equates remaining in his love with keeping his commandments. The organic closeness of the vine (from last Sunday) is now shifted to the metaphor of the intimacy of friendship.

Connecting to Jewish culture: Jews and Gentiles were two mutually exclusive peoples. Yet Christ's love overcomes such divisions by drawing all peoples into the joy of friendship with him. In Christ, God shows no partiality in extending this friendship (first reading). No one is excluded.

Exegetical points: Last Sunday's rather impersonal metaphor of the vine and branches is personalized in explicit terms of intimacy. The more personal term, however, is not "love," as we might expect. In the Old Testament, "love" is a standard expression for covenant loyalty and the obedience expected of the vassal towards the overlord. In this Gospel, the connection between commandment and love points in the direction of covenant obedience. The more intimate and personal term is "friend." As if to underscore the personal aspect of the relationship between Jesus and the disciples, Jesus explicitly rejects the term "slave" and underscores the fact that "I have called you friends." There are specific qualities to this friendship. Friends do not keep secrets: "I have told you everything I have heard from my father." Friends share the same values—what is important to one is important to the other: "keep my commandments." Friends sacrifice for one another: they "lay down one's life for one's friend."

To the point: The reality of love is that God gives it first ("It was not you who chose me, but I who chose you") and it has its cost ("love one another as I love you . . . lay down [your] life").

Celebration

Rite of Blessing and Sprinkling Holy Water

Presider: Dear friends, Jesus laid down his life for us and was raised to new glory. We bless this water and use it to remind us that we, too, are to lay down our lives by loving one another.

[*Continue with form C of the blessing of water*]

Responsorial Psalm

"The Lord has revealed to the nations his saving power."
Psalm 98 from which this Sunday's responsorial psalm is taken connects God's actions throughout history with God's final eschatological intervention. Verses 1 to 3 celebrate that God "has done wondrous deeds," "has won victory," "has remembered kindness." Verse 9 (not used this Sunday) proclaims "he comes . . . He will rule the world with justice . . ." The psalm symbolizes the completion of God's eschatological plan by its use of the number seven (a number symbolizing completion, fulfillment): it names God seven times, describes seven divine actions, lists seven divine attributes, and uses seven verbs of praise. The concluding strophe is an exuberant acclamation from the faithful who invite all of creation to join in.

In the liturgical year, we first used Psalm 98 in the Christmas Mass during the day. Its use on this Sixth Sunday of Easter tells us that God's plan for the salvation of the world begun with the birth of Jesus is now being completed. The gift of the Spirit poured out on Cornelius' family (first reading) is a foreshadowing of the explosion of the Spirit we will celebrate on Pentecost. It is for the completion of this plan that we have been chosen and sent (Gospel).

Model General Intercessions

Presider: Jesus told his disciples that whatever we ask the Father in his name, the Father will give us. And so we are bold to pray.

Response:

Lord, hear our prayer.

Cantor:

we pray to the Lord,

That the Church's Easter life may be expressed in love and joy . . . [pause]

That leaders of nations may truly love their people so that justice and peace for all may be their fruit . . . [pause]

That those excluded from communities because of race, nationality, gender, or economic status may be invited into a community of friends . . . [pause]

That all of us may keep God's commandments faithfully and remain in love . . . [pause]

Presider: Loving Father, you sent your Son to live among us and now he calls us friends: hear these the prayers of the people you chose and lead us to everlasting life. We ask this through Jesus Christ our Lord. **Amen.**

OPENING PRAYER
Let us pray

Pause for silent prayer

Ever-living God,
help us to celebrate our joy
in the resurrection of the Lord
and to express in our lives
the love we celebrate.

Grant this through our Lord Jesus
  Christ, your Son,
who lives and reigns with you and the
  Holy Spirit,
one God, for ever and ever. **Amen.**

RESPONSORIAL PSALM
[Ps 98:1, 2-3, 3-4]

℟. (cf. 2b) The Lord has revealed to the nations his saving power.
  or:
℟. Alleluia.

Sing to the LORD a new song,
  for he has done wondrous deeds;
his right hand has won victory for him,
  his holy arm.

℟. The Lord has revealed to the nations his saving power.
  or:
℟. Alleluia.

The LORD has made his salvation
    known:
  in the sight of the nations he has
    revealed his justice.
He has remembered his kindness and
    his faithfulness
  toward the house of Israel.

℟. The Lord has revealed to the nations his saving power.
  or:
℟. Alleluia.

All the ends of the earth have seen
  the salvation by our God.
Sing joyfully to the LORD, all you lands;
  break into song; sing praise.

℟. The Lord has revealed to the nations his saving power.
  or:
℟. Alleluia.

FIRST READING
[Acts 10:25-26, 34-35, 44-48]

When Peter entered, Cornelius met him
 and, falling at his feet, paid him
 homage.
Peter, however, raised him up, saying,
 "Get up. I myself am also a human
 being."
Then Peter proceeded to speak and said,
 "In truth, I see that God shows no
 partiality.
Rather, in every nation whoever fears
 him and acts uprightly
 is acceptable to him."
While Peter was still speaking these
 things,
 the Holy Spirit fell upon all who were
 listening to the word.
The circumcised believers who had
 accompanied Peter
 were astounded that the gift of the
 Holy Spirit
 should have been poured out on the
 Gentiles also,
 for they could hear them speaking in
 tongues and glorifying God.
Then Peter responded,
 "Can anyone withhold the water for
 baptizing these people,
 who have received the Holy Spirit
 even as we have?"
He ordered them to be baptized in the
 name of Jesus Christ.

SECOND READING
[1 John 4:7-10]

Beloved, let us love one another,
 because love is of God;
 everyone who loves is begotten by
 God and knows God.
Whoever is without love does not know
 God, for God is love.
In this way the love of God was
 revealed to us:
 God sent his only Son into the world
 so that we might have life through
 him.
In this is love:
 not that we have loved God, but that
 he loved us
 and sent his Son as expiation for our
 sins.

Catechesis

Cantors
The responsorial psalm for this Sunday is an acclamation of joy that God's saving power has been revealed to all peoples. How does your manner of living—at home, at work, on the street—continue this revelation?

Choir
Jesus' gift to you was the surrender of his life. Now he asks the same gift of you (Gospel). Can you do it? How is your fidelity to the ministry of the choir a kind of surrender? How in that surrender do you experience intimacy with Jesus?

Music Directors
The song "We Have Been Told" [BB, G, G2, RS] directly fits the text of this Sunday's Gospel and could be used for either the presentation of the gifts or Communion. Also appropriate would be "I Have Loved You" [BB, G, G2, RS]. A strong text which refers to your being not servants but friends and images your mission as disciples to tell the world's "grim, demonic chorus: 'Christ is risen! Get you gone!'" is found in Brian Wren's "Christ Is Risen! Shout Hosanna!" [G2]. The given tune is not strong enough, however, to carry the intensity of the text. Substitute another in 87 87D meter, such as ABBOT'S LEIGH, BEACH SPRING, or HYRFRYDOL.

Liturgy Committee
From earliest Easter practice there was to be no fasting or kneeling during Easter season; it is a time of joy in the resurrected life of Christ. How is this practice and posture observed in your parish community? Is there catechesis that might be given in order to deepen the people's grasp of the meaning of the Easter season: the Bridegroom is present among us.

In Canada and some dioceses in the United States Ascension Thursday is transferred to the Seventh Sunday of Easter. The rubric note in the U.S. Lectionary for the Sixth Sunday of Easter notes that the second reading and Gospel for the Seventh Sunday may be proclaimed on the Sixth Sunday when Ascension replaces the Seventh Sunday. This underscores the importance of the Gospel for the Seventh Sunday, taken from the priestly prayer of Christ in John's Gospel.

MAY 28, 2000

The Ascension of the Lord

FAITH-SHARING

- How might you better connect your baptismal commitment and Jesus' commissioning his disciples to proclaim the Gospel in your everyday living?
- What gifts have you been given so that you might preach the Gospel effectively?
- How might people see in your very living a confirmation of the Gospel being preached?
- Christ's ascension into heaven is a pledge of eternal glory. How are you faithful to Jesus' commandments so that you might attain this glory?

PRESIDERS

Is your preaching the Gospel the fulfillment of a job or your expression of the gifts given to you? How is this evident?

DEACONS

"The Lord worked with them and confirmed the word through accompanying signs." What signs have accompanied your ministry?

HOSPITALITY MINISTERS

How might your hospitality in church and in your everyday living invite people to look around them for the presence of Christ?

MUSIC MINISTERS

How and when is music a proclamation of the good news?

ALTAR MINISTERS

How might your "hidden" service assure the presence of Christ in your community?

LECTORS

Do you only proclaim God's word in church, or is it evident in your life? When? How?

EUCHARISTIC MINISTERS

How might you minister Communion so that each communicant believes herself or himself to be participating in the risen Christ's glory?

Spirituality

Reflecting on the Gospel

"Up, up, and away!" This may well be our sentiment on this festival if we disconnect the ascension from the resurrection and Pentecost. If so, it would be an occasion for great sadness, for the one who is like us in all things except sin would be absent. Even the readings—at a surface level—suggest "up, up, and away": "was taken up into heaven" (Gospel), "he was lifted up" (first reading), "he ascended on high" (second reading). But a deeper reading takes us in a very different direction: Jesus remains *present here,* among us. So why would we want to be "standing there looking at the sky"? In the account of the ascension in the first reading, the word "looking" occurs three times. In all three cases, the disciples' looking is directed at Jesus. Here is the key. Keep our sights on Jesus. The readings play this out in two ways.

First, concerning Jesus: he ascended into glory and "took his seat at the right hand of God." This God-man, who identified with us humans to the point of taking on our flesh at the incarnation, now has returned to his rightful place of glory. Just as the incarnation raises the dignity of humanity to a new relationship with the divinity, so does the ascension. By Jesus' ascending into heaven, humanity itself is raised up to this place of glory. Thus, Jesus' ascension is an elevation of our own human dignity to a share in God's life and glory. Jesus' ascension is a pledge that he has not abandoned humanity but instead is present to us in a new, glorified way that involves us *inextricably* in the work of salvation. We look to the glorified, ascended Christ so we can be "worthy of the call [we] have received" (second reading).

Second, then, concerning us: the ascension account in the Gospel for this solemnity is sandwiched between Jesus' commission to the disciples ("Go into the whole world and proclaim the Gospel to every creature") and their actual going forth after the ascension ("they went forth and preached everywhere"). After Jesus' ascension *his* mission (that of *one person*) is now taken up by *all his disciples.* We, then, are not simply onlookers, but we become the instruments by which salvation is announced and the kingdom continues to be inaugurated throughout the whole world. We look to the glorified, ascended Christ as we "wait for 'the promise of the Father . . . [to] be baptized with the Holy Spirit.'"

It would be daunting to us to think that we alone continue Jesus' mission after his ascension. But not so. The Gospel assures us that "the Lord work[s] with [us]." What dignity is ours! We are given the gifts to walk in the footsteps of Jesus on this earth, assured that we, too, will one day ascend to share in his glory. Need we any more motivation than that, "called to the one hope of [our] call" (second reading)?

Living the Paschal Mystery

Entering into the dying and rising Mystery of Christ means taking up his mission to preach the good news of the coming of God's kingdom. We know we are faithful to that mission when the Lord "confirm[s] [our] word through accompanying signs." What are the signs around us that confirm our taking up Jesus' mission?

JUNE 1, 2000

GOSPEL [Mark 16:15-20; L58B]

Jesus said to his disciples: "Go into the whole world and proclaim the gospel to every creature. Whoever believes and is baptized will be saved; whoever does not believe will be condemned. These signs will accompany those who believe: in my name they will drive out demons, they will speak new languages. They will pick up serpents with their hands, and if they drink any deadly thing, it will not harm them. They will lay hands on the sick, and they will recover."

So then the Lord Jesus, after he spoke to them, was taken up into heaven and took his seat at the right hand of God. But they went forth and preached everywhere, while the Lord worked with them and confirmed the word through accompanying signs.

Working with the Word

Key words and phrases from the Gospel: go into the whole world, saved, condemned, the Lord was taken up, confirmed the word through accompanying signs

Connecting to Easter and Pentecost: To isolate the ascension from Easter and Pentecost is to minimize it. With Easter, ascension, and Pentecost we are talking about one Mystery: Christ raised up (Easter) into glory with the Father (ascension) ushers forth his new presence in the world—Jesus' disciples bearing the Spirit (Pentecost).

Connecting to our culture: Our culture (because of the history of the development of the liturgical calendar) has over-historicized these events. The restoration of the fifty days in the 1969 General Roman Calendar invites us to see once again these events as one Mystery.

Exegetical points: This Gospel passage is often called "The Longer Ending" and is universally acknowledged as a non-Marcan text added to smooth the otherwise abrupt ending in the original Mark. It was known to, and quoted by, the Fathers of the second century and has been considered (and declared by Trent to be) a canonical text. In content, it is similar to material found in Luke and John. As it stands, the report of the ascension is almost incidental. Of greater importance is the commission to the disciples to proclaim the Gospel and the concluding assertion that (1) the disciples went and preached the Gospel; (2) that the Lord—despite his ascension to the right hand of God—worked with them; and (3) their preached word was confirmed by their mighty deeds. While not an original Marcan text, it certainly is consistent with Mark's view that the words and deeds of Jesus (and now the disciples) have an inner integrity. As wondrous as the deeds might be (driving out demons, snake-handling, immunity from deadly drinks, healing the sick), the emphasis is clearly on the word proclaimed. Just as Jesus had begun his ministry by proclaiming the Gospel (Mark 1:14), the work of the disciples begins in the same way: "Go . . . and proclaim the gospel." Jesus had preached, "Repent and believe in the gospel" (Mark 1:15); the Gospel as announced by the disciples will also invite belief; the effects of both belief and unbelief are also spelled out.

To the point: While the solemnity of the Ascension celebrates an event that happened to Jesus, its significance is that the mission of Jesus is transferred to the disciples. Ascension commissions the disciples to take up the work of Jesus as their own. At stake is nothing less than salvation and condemnation.

Celebration

Rite of Blessing and Sprinkling Holy Water
Presider: Dear friends, the Lord Jesus ascended into heaven and commissioned us to "proclaim the gospel to every creature." We bless this water now as a reminder of our own baptism and our commitment to live and preach the good news of salvation.

[Continue with form C of the blessing of water]

Responsorial Psalm
"God mounts his throne to shouts of joy: a blare of trumpets for the Lord."
Psalm 47, most of which is used for the responsorial psalm for this solemnity, describes a liturgical procession in which the Ark of the Covenant—which for the Israelites was a sign of the presence of God—was carried into the Temple. The trumpet blasts and the shouting were not metaphoric but real. What the Israelites were ritualizing was God's kingship over them as the chosen people and over all the earth. It is easy to see why the Lectionary assigns this psalm to the celebration of the ascension of Christ into heaven. The risen Christ, who holds all power, all judgment, all victory, ascends to the throne of God. His kingship is established. It is for us to spread the word, to carry out the commission given us in all three readings, to cry out, "All you peoples, clap your hands . . . the Lord, the awesome, is the great king over all the earth" (psalm).

Model General Intercessions
Presider: Our Savior, the Lord Jesus Christ, ascended into heaven and intercedes for us at the right hand of God. With confidence in such an advocate, we make our needs known to God.

Response:

Lord, hear our prayer.

Cantor:

we pray to the Lord,

That the Church be filled with the gifts of the Spirit and faithfully carry out the mission to proclaim the Gospel to every creature . . . [pause]

That the world may recognize the signs of God's grace working in all God-fearing people . . . [pause]

That those weak in faith be strengthened by the power of the risen Christ who intercedes for us with God . . . [pause]

That all of us gathered here may look for the risen Christ in those around us . . . [pause]

Presider: God of power and glory, you raised your Son to new life and gave him a place at your right hand: hear these our prayers that we might receive new life and one day be with you in glory. We pray through the risen Christ our Lord. **Amen.**

ALTERNATIVE OPENING PRAYER
Let us pray

Pause for silent prayer

Father in heaven,
our minds were prepared for the coming
 of your kingdom
when you took Christ beyond our sight
so that we might seek him in his glory.

May we follow where he has led
and find our hope in his glory,
for he is Lord for ever. **Amen.**

RESPONSORIAL PSALM
[Ps 47:2-3, 6-7, 8-9]

℟. (6) God mounts his throne to shouts of joy: a blare of trumpets for the Lord.
 or:
℟. Alleluia.

All you peoples, clap your hands,
 shout to God with cries of gladness,
for the LORD, the Most High, the awesome,
 is the great king over all the earth.

℟. God mounts his throne to shouts of joy: a blare of trumpets for the Lord.
 or:
℟. Alleluia.

God mounts his throne amid shouts of joy;
 the LORD, amid trumpet blasts.
Sing praise to God, sing praise;
 sing praise to our king, sing praise.

℟. God mounts his throne to shouts of joy: a blare of trumpets for the Lord.
 or:
℟. Alleluia.

For king of all the earth is God;
 sing hymns of praise.
God reigns over the nations,
 God sits upon his holy throne.

℟. God mounts his throne to shouts of joy: a blare of trumpets for the Lord.
 or:
℟. Alleluia.

FIRST READING
[Acts 1:1-11]

In the first book, Theophilus,
 I dealt with all that Jesus did and taught
 until the day he was taken up,
 after giving instructions through the Holy Spirit
 to the apostles whom he had chosen.
He presented himself alive to them
 by many proofs after he had suffered,

appearing to them during forty days
and speaking about the kingdom of
God.
While meeting with them,
he enjoined them not to depart from
Jerusalem,
but to wait for "the promise of the
Father
about which you have heard me
speak;
for John baptized with water,
but in a few days you will be baptized
with the Holy Spirit."

When they had gathered together they
asked him,
"Lord, are you at this time going to
restore
the kingdom to Israel?"
He answered them, "It is not for you to
know the times or seasons
that the Father has established by his
own authority.
But you will receive power when the
Holy Spirit comes upon you,
and you will be my witnesses in
Jerusalem,
throughout Judea and Samaria,
and to the ends of the earth."
When he had said this, as they were
looking on,
he was lifted up, and a cloud took
him from their sight.
While they were looking intently at the
sky as he was going,
suddenly two men dressed in white
garments stood beside them.
They said, "Men of Galilee,
why are you standing there looking at
the sky?
This Jesus who has been taken up from
you into heaven
will return in the same way as you
have seen him going into heaven."

SECOND READING
[Eph 4:1-13]

See Appendix A, p. 285.

Catechesis

Cantors
The first strophe of this responsorial psalm captures the commission which all three of this solemnity's readings leave with you: to be witnesses of the risen Christ to all nations. Your song not only celebrates a fulfillment (Christ does reign) but also issues an invitation (that all peoples recognize his victory).

Choir
The Israelites shouted and sang when the Ark was carried into the Temple. The whole world knew of their joy over God and kingship. How do you invite others into the kingdom?

Music Directors
How can the music you sing on this solemnity connect resurrection, ascension, and the mission which will be fully given to you at Pentecost? How is this so, not just through the texts you sing (ascension hymns are earmarked in every hymnal), but even more through the surrender to the Paschal Mystery in your lives which your singing is meant to celebrate and support? This is the "sign" which confirms your mission (Gospel).

Liturgy Committee
Helium-filled balloons and unbridled joy on this day hardly capture the serious nature of the commission Jesus gave to his disciples (and us) before his ascension. You have two catechetical challenges before you with respect to this solemnity: (1) make sure this festival is perceived as one part of the *whole* Mystery of Christ's life, suffering, death, resurrection, ascension, Pentecost, and second coming; (2) make sure the parishioners don't think that Jesus has *absented* himself, but is still very much present and working out salvation with us. How will you go about this catechesis?

In the Johannine tradition Easter, ascension, and Pentecost all take place on one day underscoring the unity of the Mystery. In the Luke/Acts tradition these are three distinct events occurring over fifty days. It is out of this latter tradition that we have this solemnity of the Ascension of the Lord on the fortieth day after Easter. There are a number of ways that you might ritually sustain the unity of the fifty days: use of the rite of blessing and sprinkling holy water throughout the season, using the homily to continually connect the Sundays to one another, repetition of hymns and service music, maintaining the environment with fresh greens and flowers.

The paschal candle is no longer extinguished after the Gospel on the solemnity of the Ascension. The suppressing of this ritual act in the revised liturgy emphasizes that Christ really hasn't *absented* himself, but is still present in the Christian community as the glorified, risen One.

Eucharistic Prayer I is not used that frequently on Sundays in parishes. There is a special form of the "In union with the whole Church . . ." for Ascension that may prove pastorally effective on this day.

JUNE 1, 2000

Seventh Sunday of Easter

FAITH-SHARING
- What is the evil around you (and in your life) that you need to pray to God to keep you from?
- How in your life do you experience Jesus protecting and guarding you? How does this challenge the way you live your life?
- After living, praying, reflecting on these Sundays of Easter, how would you see Easter and Pentecost as related, as two facets of the one Paschal Mystery?

PRESIDERS
How does your ministry confirm your parishioners in their baptismal consecration?

DEACONS
In what ways does your ministry of service to the community help them experience the complete joy of sharing in Christ?

HOSPITALITY MINISTERS
How does your joyful greeting and hospitality confirm those you meet every day of their belonging to Christ?

MUSIC MINISTERS
As a music minister, do you see yourself as "consecrated" for mission?

ALTAR MINISTERS
When you do service *in Jesus' name*, what difference does that make in your performance? in your daily living?

LECTORS
How must you live so that you can proclaim the Scriptures with truth?

EUCHARISTIC MINISTERS
How does your ministry of the Body and Blood of Christ nourish the consecration of the communicants and send them into the world to be the presence of Christ?

Spirituality

Reflecting on the Gospel
This priestly prayer of Christ that concludes John's Supper Discourse hovers over us as the Spirit hovers over us at Pentecost. Its function in the Gospel mirrors its function in the liturgical calendar: it is a summation of what has preceded and it prepares for what follows. As a summation, Jesus reports in prayer to his Father all that he has done on behalf of his disciples: he has drawn them into the same unity that Jesus enjoys with the Father; he has protected and guarded them; he has given them God's word. As a preparation for what follows, Jesus prays that God will "keep them from the evil one" and "consecrate them in truth." These blessings already received form the foundation of the missionary activity about to begin.

The Easter Lectionary is a marvelous construction that prepares us for our mission to continue preaching the good news of Jesus. These eight Sundays form a wonderful unit. The first three Sundays are all appearance accounts and gradually unfold for us the meaning of resurrection. The fifth through the seventh Sundays are a gradual unfolding of the meaning of discipleship and they begin to prepare us for our return to Ordinary Time when the meaning of discipleship is made even more explicit. The hinge Sunday is the fourth, Good Shepherd Sunday, where we reflect on Jesus as the Good Shepherd who lays down his life. With Pentecost, we are empowered in the Spirit to be good shepherds who must also lay down our lives. We might schematize this as follows.

Easter ————————> Good Shepherd ————————> Pentecost
↓ He is risen!   ↓ care, guard, protect   ↓ discipleship

The Gospels for these Sundays follow the Johannine tradition where resurrection, ascension, and Pentecost all happen on one day while the liturgical calendar follows the Luke/Acts tradition of discrete events spread over fifty days. In the Gospel sequence, before Jesus returns to the Father he consecrates (sets apart, makes holy) his disciples in preparation for their being sent to continue his mission. We must move on. We assume the shepherding ministry of Christ in the world. During this last week of Easter we sing our Alleluia! with much greater insight: our joy is complete because we do not belong to this world, either. We have been consecrated in truth. We belong to Christ. Alleluia!

Living the Paschal Mystery
Just as the early community took charge after Jesus' ascension (e.g., the first reading), so do we take charge in our own time. Jesus didn't promise us an easy time; he did pray to "keep [us] from the evil one." Already by the time of the writing of John's Gospel, the early Christian community had begun to experience conflict and persecution. They knew the cost of Jesus' consecrating them in truth. Our own times are also filled with conflict and persecution. The second reading helps us remain faithful: "God remains in us, and his love is brought to perfection in us." The Paschal Mystery includes our own struggle with faithfulness to God's will for salvation; at the same time it includes our own resurrection to new life. Alleluia!

GOSPEL [John 17:11b-19; L60B]

Lifting up his eyes to heaven, Jesus prayed, saying: "Holy Father, keep them in your name that you have given me, so that they may be one just as we are one. When I was with them I protected them in your name that you gave me, and I guarded them, and none of them was lost except the son of destruction, in order that the Scripture might be fulfilled. But now I am coming to you. I speak this in the world so that they may share my joy completely. I gave them your word, and the world hated them, because they do not belong to the world any more than I belong to the world. I do not ask that you take them out of the world but that you keep them from the evil one. They do not belong to the world any more than I belong to the world. Consecrate them in the truth. Your word is truth. As you sent me into the world, so I sent them into the world. And I consecrate myself for them, so that they also may be consecrated in truth."

Working with the Word

Key words and phrases from the Gospel: but now I am coming to you, consecrate, sent

Connecting to the Fourth Sunday of Easter: The good shepherd imagery in the Gospel of the Fourth Sunday of Easter is echoed and demonstrated this Sunday in that Jesus is *the* One who protects and guards us through his priestly prayer (Gospel).

Connecting to biblical culture: By the Gospel's oblique reference to Judas ("the son of destruction" who "was lost"), the Gospel is explicitly tied to the first reading from Acts. Matthias' election was important in the early Church since it completed the circle of the Twelve, who parallel the twelve tribes of Israel. The Twelve were an important sign that God's reign of restoration had now begun in Christ.

Exegetical points: The Gospel for this Sunday is taken from John's account of Jesus' Supper Discourse and Prayer, which runs from chapter 14 through chapter 17. These four chapters are entirely the words of Jesus and contain no narrative material at all. Here Jesus speaks at length about the Advocate and his coming, about the relationship between Jesus and his disciples (vine and branches, friends), and about their relationship to the world. The verses of this Sunday's Gospel stop just before the final six verses of the entire Lord's Supper Discourse. The function of this passage is to end the discourse and prepare for what happens next—the arrest and trial of Jesus, his crucifixion and resurrection.

To the point: As Jesus prepares to return to the Father ("But now I am coming to you."), he consecrates the disciples (and us) so they can be his continuing presence in the world. This is what will come to full power in the liturgy next Sunday on Pentecost.

Celebration

Rite of Blessing and Sprinkling Holy Water
Presider: Dear friends, at our initiation into the Church we were consecrated by being anointed with chrism and we were set apart as disciples to proclaim Christ's Gospel. Let us bless this water, reminding us that we have been consecrated in truth.

[Continue with form C of the blessing of water]

Responsorial Psalm
"The Lord has set his throne in heaven."
The second reading for this Sunday assures us, "God is love, and whoever remains in love remains in God." The internal verse of the responsorial psalm spells out what divine love is: kindness which surpasses the height of heaven, and forgiveness which is wider than the universe. Other verses from Psalm 103 (see vv. 13-18) tell of God's compassion toward human fragility. In the Gospel Jesus prays, "Father, keep them." He can send us "into the world" which "hates" us because he knows what love protects and guides us. This is the love which John asks that we let come to "perfection in us" (second reading). The disciples do this when with the grace of God, they choose to move beyond the loss of Judas to a new beginning (first reading). When we sing this psalm we proclaim with them that we are not afraid to take on the mission we have been given. For we know the love which will sustain us.

Model General Intercessions
Presider: Having been consecrated in truth, we are confident that the Father hears these our prayers.

Response:

[Music: Lord, hear our prayer.]

Cantor:

[Music: we pray to the Lord,]

That the Church may protect and guard all those who bear Jesus' name . . . [pause]

That the leaders of the world may protect and guard all those entrusted to their care . . . [pause]

That those who are vulnerable and alienated may find protection and belonging in a loving community . . . [pause]

That we may protect and guard the truth that has been given us . . . [pause]

Presider: Holy Father, you are one with your Son and so you protect us and guard us from all harm: hear these our prayers that we may always be one with you and your Son Jesus Christ, in the unity of the Holy Spirit, one God for ever and ever. **Amen.**

OPENING PRAYER
Let us pray

Pause for silent prayer

Father,
help us keep in mind that Christ our Savior
lives with you in glory
and promised to remain with us until the end of time.

We ask this through our Lord Jesus Christ, your Son,
who lives and reigns with you and the Holy Spirit,
one God, for ever and ever. **Amen.**

RESPONSORIAL PSALM
[Ps 103:1-2, 11-12, 19-20]

℟. (19a) The Lord has set his throne in heaven.
or:
℟. Alleluia.

Bless the LORD, O my soul;
 and all my being, bless his holy name.
Bless the LORD, O my soul,
 and forget not all his benefits.

℟. The Lord has set his throne in heaven.
or:
℟. Alleluia.

For as the heavens are high above the earth,
 so surpassing is his kindness toward those who fear him.
As far as the east is from the west,
 so far has he put our transgressions from us.

℟. The Lord has set his throne in heaven.
or:
℟. Alleluia.

The LORD has established his throne in heaven,
 and his kingdom rules over all.
Bless the LORD, all you his angels,
 you mighty in strength, who do his bidding.

℟. The Lord has set his throne in heaven.
or:
℟. Alleluia.

FIRST READING [Acts 1:15-17, 20a, 20c-26]
Peter stood up in the midst of the brothers
 —there was a group of about one hundred and twenty persons
 in the one place—.
He said, "My brothers,
 the Scripture had to be fulfilled

which the Holy Spirit spoke beforehand
through the mouth of David, concerning Judas,
who was the guide for those who arrested Jesus.
He was numbered among us
and was allotted a share in this ministry.
"For it is written in the Book of Psalms:
May another take his office.
"Therefore, it is necessary that one of the men
who accompanied us the whole time
the Lord Jesus came and went among us,
beginning from the baptism of John
until the day on which he was taken up from us,
become with us a witness to his resurrection."
So they proposed two, Judas called Barsabbas,
who was also known as Justus, and Matthias.
Then they prayed,
"You, Lord, who know the hearts of all,
show which one of these two you have chosen
to take the place in this apostolic ministry
from which Judas turned away to go to his own place."
Then they gave lots to them, and the lot fell upon Matthias,
and he was counted with the eleven apostles.

SECOND READING [1 John 4:11-16]

Beloved, if God so loved us,
we also must love one another.
No one has ever seen God.
Yet, if we love one another, God remains in us,
and his love is brought to perfection in us.

This is how we know that we remain in him and he in us,
that he has given us of his Spirit.
Moreover, we have seen and testify
that the Father sent his Son as savior of the world.
Whoever acknowledges that Jesus is the Son of God,
God remains in him and he in God.
We have come to know and to believe in the love God has for us.

God is love, and whoever remains in love
remains in God and God in him.

Catechesis

Cantors
The connection between this Sunday's responsorial psalm and the readings of the day is not readily evident until one reads the whole of Psalm 103. The psalm contrasts human fragility and transience with the strength and permanence of God's love. What does this have to do with Jesus' sending us "into the world"? About what are you singing when you lead this responsorial psalm?

Choir
How are you "consecrated" for mission? How is your ministry as a choir a participation in the mission of Jesus? What does your singing at liturgy have to do with proclaiming the Gospel?

Music Directors
Music during liturgy is more than just the singing of acclamations and hymns. It is an active way of entering into the Mystery being celebrated, your participation in the death and resurrection of Christ. This means that the music chosen, and the manner in which it is done, must both reveal the Mystery and enable participation in it. This is a tall order, but it is one way you carry out the mission given you by Jesus.

Liturgy Committee
Mystagogy is a time for explaining the rites and power of initiation to those who have just entered the Church or professed their faith. The word "mystagogy" itself comes from two Greek words meaning "initiated" and "to conduct or lead." Mystagogy, then, means to be led into the meaning of initiation. Especially important in the fourth-and-fifth-century initiation processes, mystagogy was a time both to savor the powerful impact of the initiation rites on the individual as well as to reflect more deeply on its meaning for everyday living. The mystagogical catecheses given to the neophytes (the newly baptized) were frequently also attended by the whole community as a way to freshen each member's commitment to Christ. Given in the form of homilies, the preaching was always Christological (centered on the Mystery of Christ) and synthesized the truth of the Mystery with the neophytes' actual experience of the rites.

These "disciple" Sundays (Fifth, Sixth, and Seventh Sundays of Easter as well as Pentecost) encapsulate initiation: being grafted onto Christ, friendship in Christ, our unity with God and each other, consecrated in truth, and being missioned. How might this mystagogy be carried beyond the Easter season with a catechesis that draws the assembly more deeply into living the Paschal Mystery?

This Sunday occurs at the beginning of June and, consequently, reminds us of the temptation to see the summer months as a "vacation" from either being present at liturgy or an excuse for not preparing liturgy well. What needs to be done in order to assure the quality and fruitfulness of liturgy throughout the summer vacation months?

JUNE 4, 2000

Pentecost

FAITH-SHARING
- Jesus has given and gives his Spirit to you. In what ways do you receive that Spirit each day?
- What are the fruits of the Spirit that others can see manifest in your life?
- When do you most clearly experience the peace that Jesus gives?
- How would you describe the new life that you live in Christ? Has this Easter season made a difference in you?

PRESIDERS
In what ways do you call forth the gifts of the Spirit that are manifest in your parish?

DEACONS
The Spirit enabled the disciples locked in the upper room to proclaim Jesus' good news boldly. What helps you proclaim boldly?

HOSPITALITY MINISTERS
Three of the fruits of the Spirit that are mentioned in this Sunday's second reading are joy, kindness, and gentleness. How are these manifest in your ministry of hospitality?

MUSIC MINISTERS
How can you help those you lead to see their musical gifts as blessings of the Spirit given for service?

ALTAR MINISTERS
Generosity and faithfulness are listed in the second reading as fruits of the Spirit. How are these manifest in your ministry of service?

LECTORS
How might the gifts of patience and self-control help you in your ministry?

EUCHARISTIC MINISTERS
How might the gifts of love and peace be foundational for your ministering Communion, especially to the sick or homebound?

Spirituality

Reflecting on the Gospel

"Strong driving wind" and "tongues as of fire"—these are powerful images that express a powerful experience! The Scriptures lead us to believe that prior to Pentecost the disciples of Jesus huddled together behind locked doors—hardly behavior befitting those who had "seen the Lord." Yet, after Pentecost the disciples' behavior changed dramatically: they burst the confines of lock and preached boldly and witnessed heroically. The creative and prophetic presence of the God of Israel paved the way for the glorious presence of God's only Son, Christ Jesus; the Lord's resurrection and return to the right hand of God paved the way for an even more startling presence, the power of the Spirit in each of us to profess that Jesus is Lord.

Without Pentecost, our hearts and lives would be like that of the disciples in this Sunday's Gospel: "doors were locked . . . for fear." Without Pentecost, we would also forfeit the most intimate of God's presences: Christ's risen life within each of us. And here is the key. Pentecost ushers in a *new creation*. Jesus *breathed* on the gathered disciples, similar to how God breathed life into Adam (Gen 2:7) at creation. Our receiving the Spirit means that we are (becoming) a new creation.

The second reading from Galatians clearly contrasts the old and new orders of creation. Sinful humanity behaves wretchedly: "immorality, impurity, lust, idolatry," etc. Spirit-filled humanity who is the new creation behaves splendidly: "love, joy, peace, patience, kindness," etc. The contrast is stark and clear. The way to get to the new creation is also quite clear: "those who belong to Christ Jesus have crucified their flesh . . . [and] live in the Spirit." The new relationship we now enjoy in Christ is one of unique intimacy: God *dwells within us*. And by sharing in the very Life of the risen Christ through the Spirit, we also share in Jesus' ministry of healing and forgiving, of doing the Father's will and thus bringing to fruition the reign of God.

Living the Paschal Mystery

Pentecost has popularly been called the "birthday of the Church." We greatly reduce the mystery of God's presence if we understand this phrase to refer to the beginning of the institutional church. Pentecost is *our* birth into new life, new creation. It is our celebration of being God's redeemed people who now share in the mission of the divine Son through the Spirit. This is the great Mystery we celebrate—our Mystery, too! This is one of the reasons why the Easter season is a privileged time for celebrating baptisms, for in our baptism we first receive the Spirit and the new life that is ours as those who bear Christ's name and mission ("As the Father has sent me, so I send you").

This Pentecost solemnity brings to a climax the fifty-day celebration of Easter. But we must be careful not to put away our Easter joy too quickly. Pentecost may be the end of the Easter season, but it is also a celebration of the beginning of our new life in Christ. Rather than our Alleluias being over, they are just beginning! They bear fruit in the practical ways in our life that we "renew the face of the earth" (responsorial psalm).

GOSPEL [John 20:19-23; L63B]

On the evening of that first day of the week, when the doors were locked, where the disciples were, for fear of the Jews, Jesus came and stood in their midst and said to them, "Peace be with you." When he had said this, he showed them his hands and his side. The disciples rejoiced when they saw the Lord. Jesus said to them again, "Peace be with you. As the Father has sent me, so I send you." And when he had said this, he breathed on them and said to them, "Receive the Holy Spirit. Whose sins you forgive are forgiven them, and whose sins you retain are retained."

Working with the Word

Key words and phrases from the Gospel: send, breathed on them, receive the Holy Spirit

Connecting to the Second Sunday of Easter: This Sunday's Gospel is the first half of the same Gospel that we read on the Second Sunday of Easter. The setting is the upper room on Easter Sunday evening. By omitting the scenes of Thomas' belief/unbelief, the focus is now clearly on the giving of the Spirit and the forgiveness of sins.

Connecting to our culture: If someone would simply read to us the list of "the works of the flesh" from the second reading, it might seem like a recap of the daily newspaper or nightly TV news! It would seem as though things haven't changed much in the last two millennia! We are in need of Paul's warning and insight to "live by the Spirit" as much as the Galatians were.

Exegetical points: In Luke's scheme (in the first reading), Pentecost is fifty days after Easter and coincides with the Jewish feast of the same name. Jewish Pentecost was a pilgrimage feast which, like Passover, brought Jews from outlying areas and distant regions to Jerusalem. The contrasts between John's and Luke's versions of Pentecost are instructive. Luke's rendition of Pentecost is presented as a classic theophany—an appearance of God in wind and fire; it is manifest as a public event before all Israel ("Jews from every nation under heaven"); it is interpreted in classic Old Testament terms as one of "the mighty acts of God" which reveals God's power to save. All this is typical of Luke's penchant to "dramatize" his theology in carefully detailed, "historicized" events.

John's account is significantly different. First comes the commission ("I send you"). Then comes the power to undertake that commission ("Receive the Holy Spirit"). The giving of the Spirit has as its primary reference not a Jewish feast, but the resurrection of Jesus. It is the risen Jesus who confers directly the Spirit on those gathered. The giving of the Spirit is presented not as a theophany, but as a new creation—breath/spirit evoking Gen 1:2 (see also Wis 15:11). Newly created and commissioned, the disciples are sent to forgive (or retain) sins.

To the point: The disciples are empowered when they receive the Spirit by Jesus' breathing on them. As a result, discipleship is not a "job," but our being recreated in the Spirit, manifesting the fruits of the Spirit by living a whole new way of life.

Celebration

Rite of Blessing and Sprinkling Holy Water

Presider: Dear friends, the risen Christ breathed on his disciples and they received the Holy Spirit. We now bless this water and use it as a sign of our baptism, when we first received the Holy Spirit.

[Continue with form C of the blessing of water]

Responsorial Psalm

"Lord, send out your Spirit, and renew the face of the earth."

Psalm 104 is a poetic masterpiece praising God for the marvels of creation. Its form unfolds in a seven-part structure modeled after the creation account of Genesis chapter 1. Its connection with the liturgical celebration of Pentecost is easy to see. In Hebrew understanding, the cause of creation is God's breath or spirit *(ruach)*. Take breath away and creatures die; give them divine breath/spirit and they live (vv. 29-30). The Gospel reveals that Pentecost is the giving of a new creation through the Spirit/breath of Jesus. This new creation is a total transformation of ourselves into a new way of life (second reading). The psalm refrain is our prayer that God continue this new creation in us, and through us in all the earth.

Model General Intercessions

Presider: In peace and by the power of the Spirit let us present our needs to God.

Response:

Lord, hear our prayer.

Cantor:

we pray to the Lord,

Receiving the Spirit, may the Church carry the presence of the risen Christ to all corners of the earth . . . [pause]

Receiving the Spirit, may world leaders be prompted to bring peace and reconciliation to all . . . [pause]

Receiving the Spirit, may those who are locked in sin seek forgiveness . . . [pause]

Receiving the Spirit, may all of us gathered here manifest the fruits of the Spirit in all we do . . . [pause]

Presider: God of life, you send your Spirit among us to guide us in all we do: hear these our prayers that we may rejoice in the new life you give. We ask this through our Lord Jesus Christ, your Son, who lives and reigns with you in the unity of the Holy Spirit, one God, for ever and ever. **Amen.**

ALTERNATIVE OPENING PRAYER

Let us pray

Pause for silent prayer

Father of light,
from whom every good gift comes,
send your Spirit into our lives
with the power of a mighty wind,
and by the flame of your wisdom
open the horizons of our minds.
Loosen our tongues to sing your praise
in words beyond the power of speech,
for without your Spirit
man could never raise his voice in
 words of peace
or announce the truth that Jesus is Lord,
who lives and reigns with you and the
 Holy Spirit,
one God, for ever and ever. **Amen.**

RESPONSORIAL PSALM

[Ps 104:1, 24, 29-30, 31, 34]

℟. (cf. 30) Lord, send out your Spirit, and renew the face of the earth.
 or:
℟. Alleluia.

Bless the LORD, O my soul!
 O LORD, my God, you are great indeed!
How manifold are your works, O LORD!
 The earth is full of your creatures.

℟. Lord, send out your Spirit, and renew the face of the earth.
 or:
℟. Alleluia.

If you take away their breath, they perish
 and return to their dust.
When you send forth your spirit, they
 are created,
 and you renew the face of the earth.

℟. Lord, send out your Spirit, and renew the face of the earth.
 or:
℟. Alleluia.

May the glory of the LORD endure forever;
 may the LORD be glad in his works!
Pleasing to him be my theme;
 I will be glad in the LORD.

℟. Lord, send out your Spirit, and renew the face of the earth.
 or:
℟. Alleluia.

FIRST READING [Acts 2:1-11]

When the time for Pentecost was fulfilled,
 they were all in one place together.
And suddenly there came from the sky
 a noise like a strong driving wind,
 and it filled the entire house in which
  they were.
Then there appeared to them tongues as
 of fire,
 which parted and came to rest on
  each one of them.

And they were all filled with the Holy
    Spirit
        and began to speak in different
            tongues,
        as the Spirit enabled them to proclaim.
Now there were devout Jews from every
    nation under heaven
        staying in Jerusalem.
At this sound, they gathered in a large
    crowd,
    but they were confused
        because each one heard them
            speaking in his own language.
They were astounded, and in
    amazement they asked,
    "Are not all these people who are
        speaking Galileans?
Then how does each of us hear them in
    his native language?
We are Parthians, Medes, and Elamites,
    inhabitants of Mesopotamia, Judea
        and Cappadocia,
    Pontus and Asia, Phrygia and
        Pamphylia,
    Egypt and the districts of Libya near
        Cyrene,
    as well as travelers from Rome,
    both Jews and converts to Judaism,
        Cretans and Arabs,
    yet we hear them speaking in our
        own tongues
    of the mighty acts of God."

SECOND READING [Gal 5:16-25]

Brothers and sisters, live by the Spirit
    and you will certainly not gratify the
        desire of the flesh.
For the flesh has desires against the Spirit,
    and the Spirit against the flesh;
    these are opposed to each other,
    so that you may not do what you want.
But if you are guided by the Spirit, you
    are not under the law.
Now the works of the flesh are obvious:
    immorality, impurity, lust, idolatry,
    sorcery, hatreds, rivalry, jealousy,
    outbursts of fury, acts of selfishness,
    dissensions, factions, occasions of envy,
    drinking bouts, orgies, and the like.
I warn you, as I warned you before,
    that those who do such things will not
        inherit the kingdom of God.
In contrast, the fruit of the Spirit is love,
    joy, peace,
    patience, kindness, generosity,
    faithfulness, gentleness, self-control.
Against such there is no law.
Now those who belong to Christ Jesus
    have crucified their flesh
    with its passions and desires.
If we live in the Spirit, let us also follow
    the Spirit.

SEQUENCE
See Appendix A, p. 285.

Catechesis

Cantors
In the final strophe of this Sunday's psalm, you pray that God "be glad in his works." You are praying that the new creation be completed that was made possible by the death and resurrection of Jesus. It must begin with you and your surrender to the Spirit.

Choir
Singing is a release of the spirit through breath and sound. Through baptism all of you have been given the Spirit of Jesus. Think of what power you release when you lead the singing of the body of Christ at liturgy!

Music Directors
Pentecost celebrates our full insertion into the life, death, and mission of Jesus. Select hymns which convey the sense of the urgency and import of this mission. "We Know that Christ Is Raised" [CH, CBW3, W3, WC] combines a strong text with a strong tune. Verses such as "A new creation comes to life and grows As Christ's new body takes on flesh and blood. The universe restored and whole will sing: Alleluia!" captures well the meaning of Pentecost. The hymn would be excellent for the entrance procession. A second hymn with similarly strong text and tune is "The Church of Christ in Every Age" [BB, CH, RS, W3], which could be used for either entrance or the presentation of the gifts.

Liturgy Committee
The renewal of liturgy in parishes often feels like an up-hill journey. This Sunday of "strong driving wind" and "tongues as of fire" reminds you to pray to the Spirit for guidance in your efforts. May the Spirit's new life course through you and give you renewed courage and strength of purpose!

John 20:19-23 was chosen for the Gospel reflection because this one recounts the actual giving of the Spirit rather than the promise of the Spirit as in John 15:26-27; 16:12-15. For the second reading the passage from Galatians was chosen, which is the option for year B.

This Sunday is one of only two (Easter being the other) that has an obligatory sequence. Originally, these popular musical compositions were crafted in order to embellish and prolong the Gospel procession on high feast days. It would be well to begin the Gospel procession with the sequence and process with the Gospel book throughout the assembly in solemn fashion (with candles and incense). This way, hopefully, the sequence can be a joyful expression of this festival rather than a long, "dead" time.

The Monday after Pentecost returns us to weekdays of the tenth week in Ordinary Time. Therefore, the solemnities the Church celebrates on the next two Sundays are solemnities in Ordinary Time; these solemnities are connected to the Easter *Mystery*, but not to the Easter *season*.

JUNE 11, 2000

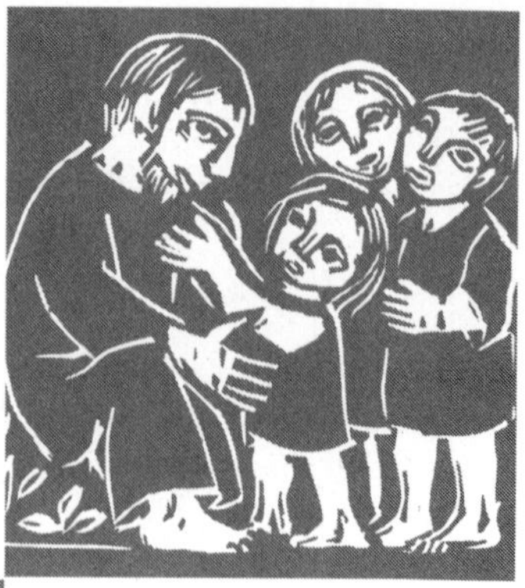

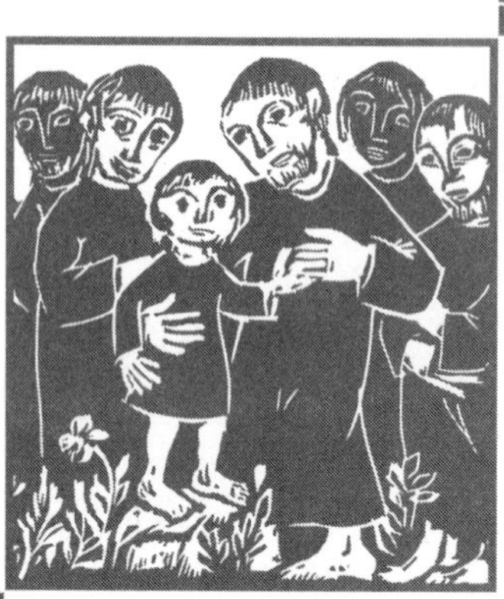

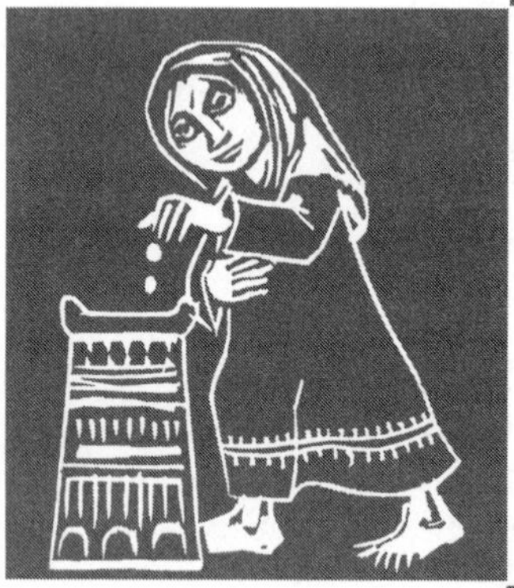

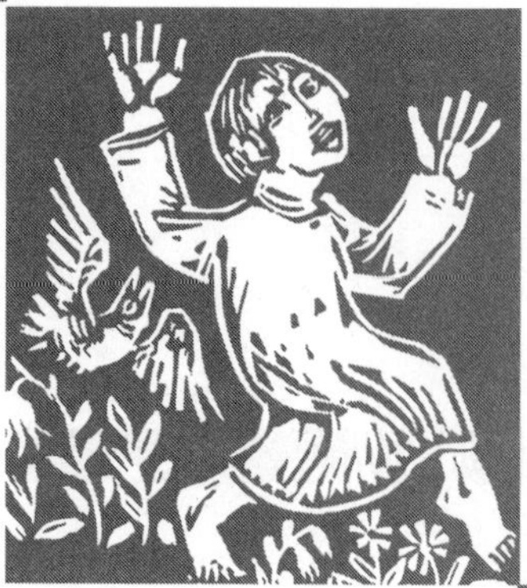

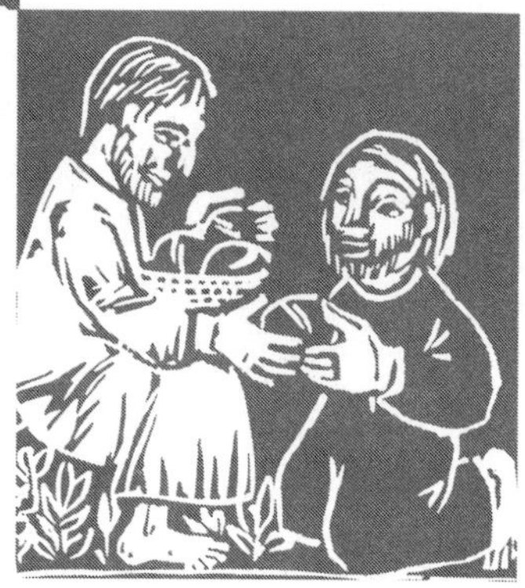

Ordinary Time II

The Solemnity of the Most Holy Trinity

FAITH-SHARING

- In what ways have you experienced God as Triune—Father, Son, Holy Spirit? In what ways is your prayer affected by your belief in God as Triune?
- How does doubt affect your ability to worship?
- What is it like for you to contemplate the awesome majesty of God?
- How might you make the sign of the cross with more awareness and fervor?

PRESIDERS

"This is why you must now know, and fix in your heart . . ." What do you need to "know" again and "fix in your heart" to preach this Trinity Sunday?

DEACONS

How might your service be a model that teaches others how a believer in God lives?

HOSPITALITY MINISTERS

How does your hospitality and greeting (at church and elsewhere) help others to prostrate themselves in worship before the Triune God?

MUSIC MINISTERS

In your prayer this week, visualize each individual whom you direct in music ministry and make the Sign of the Cross over them.

ALTAR MINISTERS

Through baptism you have received "a Spirit of adoption." How might remembering this help you to serve better?

LECTORS

"Moses said to the people . . ." What do *you* say to the people through your daily living?

EUCHARISTIC MINISTERS

What is Christ asking you to "suffer with him" so that you may "be glorified with him" (second reading)?

Spirituality

Reflecting on the Gospel

Legend has it that St. Patrick used the shamrock in his preaching to explain the Trinity: three leaves but one stem and one clover. Sometimes a triangle is used as a symbol for the Trinity. These two examples bring home to us the difficulty we have with the mystery of the Trinity. This solemnity is sometimes referred to as a "devotional" or "idea" feast. That is, it derives from our own theological reflection and is not so closely tied to the presenting of the mystery of salvation as the other solemnities. In fact, this is the only solemnity that in one way or another does not connect to the Paschal Mystery of Christ.

Nevertheless, this festival has been around for a long time. Evidence of special emphasis on belief in the Trinity dates to early Christian times and the controversies that arose about defining the nature of Christ and, subsequently, God. We have data attesting to a feast dedicated to the Triune God on the Sunday after Pentecost since before the turn of the first millennium. From the fourteenth century this celebration has been on the calendar of the universal Church.

After having celebrated the high point of the Mystery of redemption during the Triduum and Easter season, on the First Sunday after Pentecost the Church reflects on the source of that Mystery—the Triune God. The unity of the Trinity is somewhat compromised by ascribing to each of the persons a particular saving act; this has been evident in our religious formation as well as in our interpretation of the Scriptures themselves. Thus, to the first Person we ascribe creation, to the second Person salvation, and to the third Person sanctification (hints of this are in this Sunday's readings). Sometimes in theology this is referred to as the "economic" Trinity . . . the God who acts. Having just celebrated what God "does" for us at the Triduum and Easter, the Church now invites us to contemplate the "immanent" Trinity . . . the God who is.

The Gospel is telling. It is a post-resurrection account. Jesus "ordered" (the Greek means "directed" or "appointed") the disciples to a mountain in Galilee. The eleven (an oblique reference to the betrayal of Judas) "saw him" and prostrated themselves in worship. This is the only incident in the Gospels where we find the apostles or disciples actually worshiping Jesus. The resurrection has opened for the disciples clearly a new relationship to Jesus. This relationship has its own new demands: Jesus is beheld as who he is—God to be worshiped. The first reading is equally telling. Recalling creation, the making of a people, and the giving of commandments, Moses asks the people, "Did anything so great ever happen before?" and declares that "the LORD is God in the heavens above and the earth below, and that there is no other." Hearing this, our response is like the disciples': we prostrate ourselves in worship.

Living the Paschal Mystery

As "children of God" (second reading), we have a unique, organic relationship to God. Living the Mystery of this organic relationship includes "mak[ing] disciples of all nations" (Gospel) as well as prostrating ourselves in worship. In reality, these are two sides of the same coin! Like the Trinity, our life is both doing and being.

GOSPEL [Matt 28:16-20; L165B]

The eleven disciples went to Galilee, to the mountain to which Jesus had ordered them. When they all saw him, they worshiped, but they doubted. Then Jesus approached and said to them, "All power in heaven and on earth has been given to me. Go, therefore, and make disciples of all nations, baptizing them in the name of the Father, and of the Son, and of the Holy Spirit, teaching them to observe all that I have commanded you. And behold, I am with you always, until the end of the age."

Working with the Word

Key words and phrases from the Gospel: saw him, worshiped, doubted

Connecting to first and second readings: Here we find a summary of God's mighty deeds: creating, speaking to us, calling a nation, giving commandments, leading us by the Spirit, adopting us as "heirs with Christ."

Connecting to the Gospel and our culture: Worship and doubt are not necessarily mutually exclusive. Those who struggle with the doctrine of the Trinity will find comfort in Matthew's frank description of the disciples who, upon seeing the risen Christ, "worshiped, but they doubted." Doubt, lack of understanding, and confusion do not preclude worship, nor do they prevent Jesus from giving a commission. The power that God has given Christ lies behind his sending out the disciples with authority to baptize, make disciples of all nations, and teach. In this daunting task, Jesus himself will be with those who undertake his work.

Exegetical points: The readings for the solemnity of the Trinity are not concerned with theological ruminations about the nature of the Trinity. Rather, the focus is on what God does and the impact God has on the life of believers. In Deuteronomy, belief that "the LORD is God . . . and that there is no other" expresses itself in keeping the commandments; such fidelity will result in prosperity and long life in the promised land. God is known through the election of the people, the giving of the Law, and the promise of the land. In Paul's Letter to the Romans, God is again known through what is given, but the nature of the gifts is different. God gives believers the Spirit which makes them children of God by adoption. The result of this adoption is that we can call God our "Abba, Father" and that we are "joint heirs with Christ."

To the point: Once we prescind from the mighty deeds of God, we have nothing to say—we are silent and awed before the majesty of God.

Celebration

Model Penitential Rite

Presider: Last Sunday we completed our Easter season celebration. This Sunday we contemplate the wonder of our Triune God. Let us open ourselves to the Mystery of God's presence to us . . . [pause]

> Lord Jesus, you were given all power in heaven and on earth: Lord . . .
> Christ Jesus, you made us disciples to preach to the nations: Christ . . .
> Lord Jesus, you are with us always, until the end of ages: Lord . . .

Responsorial Psalm

"Blessed the people the Lord has chosen to be his own."
The readings for this Sunday celebrating the mystery of the Trinity reveal God's desire to relate to us with unthinkable intimacy. God takes Israel as "a nation for himself" (first reading). God adopts us as children (second reading). Jesus promises us his personal presence "until the end" (Gospel). Of all God's mighty deeds, perhaps this offer of intimacy is the greatest. "Did anything so great ever happen before?" (first reading). The responsorial psalm conveys the utmost trust we can have in such a God, whose word is true, whose works are reliable, and whose kindness is granted to all who hope. This God chooses us to participate in the very core of the divine nature: intimate personal relationship. Not only is the mystery of the Trinity beyond comprehension, so is the design of the Trinity's heart (see Ps 33:11). Truly, blessed are we who have been chosen.

Model General Intercessions

Presider: From creation God has done mighty deeds for us. We are confident that God hears our prayers and continues to provide for us.

Response:

Lord, hear our prayer.

Cantor:

we pray to the Lord,

May all people in the Church faithfully worship the Triune God with praise and thanksgiving until the end of the age . . . [pause]

May leaders of nations use their power to spend themselves at the service of justice and peace . . . [pause]

May those who doubt find the God of wonders who leads to faith . . . [pause]

May our community be faithful to our mission to make disciples . . . [pause]

Presider: O God, you reveal yourself in mystery and majesty: hear these our prayers that one day we might dwell with you always. We ask this through Christ our Lord who lives and reigns with you and the Holy Spirit, one Triune God for ever and ever. **Amen.**

ALTERNATIVE OPENING PRAYER

Let us pray
 [to our God who is Father, Son, and Holy Spirit]

Pause for silent prayer

God, we praise you:
Father all-powerful, Christ Lord and Savior, Spirit of love.
You reveal yourself in the depths of our being,
 drawing us to share in your life and your love.
One God, three Persons,
be near to the people formed in your image,
 close to the world your love brings to life.
We ask you this, Father, Son, and Holy Spirit,
 one God, true and living, for ever and ever. **Amen.**

RESPONSORIAL PSALM
[Ps 33:4-5, 6, 9, 18-19, 20, 22]

℟. (12b) Blessed the people the Lord has chosen to be his own.

Upright is the word of the LORD,
 and all his works are trustworthy.
He loves justice and right;
 of the kindness of the LORD the earth is full.

℟. Blessed the people the Lord has chosen to be his own.

By the word of the LORD the heavens were made;
 by the breath of his mouth all their host.
For he spoke, and it was made;
 he commanded, and it stood forth.

℟. Blessed the people the Lord has chosen to be his own.

See, the eyes of the LORD are upon those who fear him,
 upon those who hope for his kindness,
to deliver them from death
 and preserve them in spite of famine.

℟. Blessed the people the Lord has chosen to be his own.

Our soul waits for the LORD,
 who is our help and our shield.
May your kindness, O LORD, be upon us
 who have put our hope in you.

℟. Blessed the people the Lord has chosen to be his own.

FIRST READING
[Deut 4:32-34, 39-40]

Moses said to the people:
"Ask now of the days of old, before your time,
ever since God created man upon the earth;
ask from one end of the sky to the other:
Did anything so great ever happen before?
Was it ever heard of?
Did a people ever hear the voice of God
speaking from the midst of fire, as you did, and live?
Or did any god venture to go and take a nation for himself
from the midst of another nation,
by testings, by signs and wonders, by war,
with strong hand and outstretched arm, and by great terrors,
all of which the LORD, your God,
did for you in Egypt before your very eyes?
This is why you must now know,
and fix in your heart, that the LORD is God
in the heavens above and on earth below,
and that there is no other.
You must keep his statutes and commandments that I enjoin on you today,
that you and your children after you may prosper,
and that you may have long life on the land
which the LORD, your God, is giving you forever."

SECOND READING
[Rom 8:14-17]

Brothers and sisters:
Those who are led by the Spirit of God are sons of God.
For you did not receive a spirit of slavery to fall back into fear,
but you received a Spirit of adoption,
through whom we cry, "Abba, Father!"
The Spirit himself bears witness with our spirit
that we are children of God,
and if children, then heirs,
heirs of God and joint heirs with Christ,
if only we suffer with him
so that we may also be glorified with him.

*C*atechesis

Cantors

When you sing this Sunday's responsorial psalm refrain, let your prayer turn in two directions. Remind yourself that *you* have been chosen to be God's own. And keep in mind *all* God's people. Pray for yourself and for all human beings to grow in intimacy with God.

Choir

This Sunday celebrates the Trinity, God in three persons who seeks deep intimacy with mere human creatures. And it celebrates your mission to tell the world about this desire of God's heart (Gospel). You might end choir rehearsal this week with the sign of the cross, made slowly and reflectively. Pause for spontaneous prayers for all those who do not know God, or who doubt God's closeness and care. Conclude by making the sign of the cross again.

Music Directors

St. Patrick's text "I Bind unto Myself Today" [CH] speaks in strongly relational terms of your connection to the Trinity. The text is long, so it would work best at Communion. Another hymn suitable for Communion is "God the Father, Son and Spirit" [LMGM]. The tune is an African chant, with the refrain set up in call and response style. John Bell's "Today I Awake" [G2] combines a very poetic text (e.g., "The Spirit inspires all life which is changing From fearing to faith, from broken to blest") with a sweeping lyrical melody; it would fit either the presentation of the gifts or Communion. Finally, Brian Wren, another gifted contemporary hymn text writer, offers "How Wonderful the Three-in-One" [G2, RS, WC]. In successive verses he names the persons of the Trinity "Creation's Lover," the "Lover's own Beloved," and their "Equal Friend," and calls them "our hope's beginning, way and end." The lilting 3/4 tune would be suitable for either Communion or the presentation of the gifts.

Liturgy Committee

Jesus commissioned the eleven to baptize "in the name of the Father, and of the Son, and of the Holy Spirit." You use these words and sign yourselves thousands of times. Is it merely a habit, or do you reflect on their meaning? "In the name" means in the possession of or protection of. The sign of the cross can be understood to be a surrender to God, a giving of your whole selves to the Triune God. How might you make these words and accompanying gesture something other than habit?

This Sunday is Father's Day, but it would not be liturgically appropriate to center the homily (or other parts of the Mass) around this holiday. It would be appropriate, however, to mention that Trinity Sunday offers a challenge to Fathers to be protective of and caring for their children. For the United States, The *Book of Blessings* (chapter 56) provides sample intercessions that may be added to the general intercessions for the day and a prayer over the people that may be used before the blessing of the people during the concluding rite. For Canada, *A Book of Blessings* mentions (p. 233) that intercessions may be added to those of the day and a blessing (given on p. 52) may be given the fathers after the homily.

JUNE 18, 2000

The Nativity of St. John the Baptist

FAITH-SHARING
- In what way is your whole life centered around John the Baptist's mission of preparing the way of the Lord?
- Like John the Baptist, you are "not worthy to unfasten the sandals of [Christ's] feet" and yet, like John, you can pray Psalm 139 about yourselves: "I praise you for I am wonderfully made." Which of these two self-descriptions is easier for you to believe? to live? What could you do to have better balance of these two?

PRESIDERS
What needs to decrease in you so that Christ's light in you might increase?

DEACONS
Your life and mission are to point to Jesus as the Savior of the world. How does your service point others to Jesus? help them experience Jesus as Savior?

HOSPITALITY MINISTERS
How does your ministry of greeting people make Jesus' presence and identity known? Is there anything you need to change in your manner of greeting?

MUSIC MINISTERS
Music can all too easily become the "star" of the liturgy. How can you stay faithful to the discipline of "I must decrease so that he may increase"?

LECTORS
How is every proclamation of God's word really an announcing of Jesus, making Jesus present?

EUCHARISTIC MINISTERS
The birth of John is the dawn of your salvation. When/where have you noticed the dawning of God's work in your life?

Spirituality

Reflecting on the Gospel

John the Baptist is a figure full of contrasts. We picture him as a desert dweller, wearing animal skins, foraging for what meager sustenance he can find in the desert to eat, a simple and humble man. Yet he is privileged in so many ways: miraculous conception and birth, special name (John = God's gracious gift, God has shown favor), "strong in spirit," cousin and forerunner of the Messiah.

Even more contrasts come to light when we compare John to Jesus. John is the precursor, Jesus is the long-awaited Messiah. John is the baptizer, Jesus is the one baptized. John baptized with water for repentance, Jesus baptizes with the Holy Spirit and fire. One of the more symbolic contrasts is between light and darkness. John is born during the summer solstice, at the time in the northern hemisphere when daylight is the longest. Daylight diminishes and the darkness of night increases as we move toward the winter solstice when Jesus is born during the longest of nights (in John 3:30 we hear John say, "He must increase; I must decrease"). The Light of the world enters at the time of greatest darkness. That Light dispels darkness so that the Light might bring forth life. The first reading from Isaiah says, referring to Jesus, that God "will make you a light to the nations, that my salvation may reach to the ends of the earth."

In addition to contrasts, a number of parallels are evident between the birth of John and the birth of Jesus. Both Elizabeth and Mary give birth to boys. There is great rejoicing (at John's birth, among the "neighbors and relatives"; at Jesus' birth, among the angels). There is fear among those witnessing these births because of the uncommon circumstances surrounding them. Both boys are circumcised, incorporating them into the people of Israel. Both boys are given special names assigned at their conceptions by Gabriel. Scriptures mention that both grew up in a way so as to fulfill their mission (John, "strong in spirit"; Jesus, in "wisdom and age and favor before God and man").

It would be pretty hard to miss the connection between John and Jesus and salvific events. More than celebrating the birth of a key player for announcing Jesus' mission, this solemnity celebrates the wonders of God's whole plan of salvation that is happening now. The second reading from Acts reminds us that "this word of salvation has been sent." John was beheaded because he boldly announced the dawn of salvation. But John's announcement could not really be silenced and Christ's light could not be extinguished.

Living the Paschal Mystery

Darkness and light are two images that we could substitute for dying and rising. John stepped aside so the true Light of the world could be recognized and followed. We must bring the light of the Christ who dwells within us to all the dark recesses of our world. At the same time we, like John, must step aside so that not ourselves but Christ is proclaimed. We must surrender ourselves so that the Light might shine. John's life and mission was to point to Jesus as the Savior of the world. Our life and mission is to do the same.

JUNE 24, 2000

GOSPEL [Luke 1:57-66, 80; L587]

When the time arrived for Elizabeth to have her child she gave birth to a son. Her neighbors and relatives heard that the Lord had shown his great mercy toward her, and they rejoiced with her. When they came on the eighth day to circumcise the child, they were going to call him Zechariah after his father, but his mother said in reply, "No. He will be called John." But they answered her, "There is no one among your relatives who has this name." So they made signs, asking his father what he wished him to be called. He asked for a tablet and wrote, "John is his name," and all were amazed. Immediately his mouth was opened, his tongue freed, and he spoke blessing God. Then fear came upon all their neighbors, and all these matters were discussed throughout the hill country of Judea. All who heard these things took them to heart, saying, "What, then, will this child be?" For surely the hand of the Lord was with him.

The child grew and became strong in spirit, and he was in the desert until the day of his manifestation to Israel.

Working with the Word

Key words and phrases from the Gospel: birth to a son; rejoiced; name; fear; What, then, will this child be?; hand of the Lord was with him; grew and became strong in spirit; manifestation to Israel

Connecting to the liturgical year: The parallels between John's and Jesus' conceptions and births are carried out most strikingly in the liturgical calendar. John's nativity festival comes during the summer solstice, nine months after the fall equinox when he was conceived (Luke 1:9 tells us Zechariah was in "the sanctuary of the Lord to burn incense"; this occurred once a year on *yom kippur*, the great Day of Atonement, during the fall equinox). At Jesus' conception Mary is told her cousin Elizabeth is in her sixth month of pregnancy, thus placing Jesus' conception at the spring equinox and his birth at the winter solstice.

Connecting to biblical culture: Miraculous events surrounding the birth of a child signaled the special mission of the child; e.g., Moses, Isaac, Samson, Samuel, John the Baptist, and preeminently so with Jesus.

Exegetical points: The choice of the first reading from Isaiah as a companion to the Gospel story of John's conception is striking. For parallelism, any number of Old Testament stories about extraordinary births could have been recounted, e.g., the stories of aged and/or barren Sarah, Rachel, Hannah, and Samson's mother would each have been fitting for the story of John's own conception to sterile and aged Elizabeth. Instead, the Church gives us a text—Isaiah's Second Song of the Servant— which is usually applied to Jesus. The liturgical feast thus provides a new and entirely appropriate context for interpretation: the call from his mother's womb, his razor-sharp ministry of the word, the apparent futility of his ministry that ends in prison, his ultimate vindication, his role in bringing forth the light of salvation—all these details are suitably applied to John. Thus, interpreting John's birth and ministry in light of the prophecy of Isaiah reveals the long intentionality of God who goes to such great lengths in preparing for our salvation.

To the point: The imagery in this solemnity's Scripture readings is strikingly similar to imagery used at the nativity and passion of Jesus, suggesting the close relationship of John's mission as precursor to Jesus' mission as savior. While John's mission was to *prepare* for Jesus' way, by our baptism we *take up* the very mission of Jesus, manifesting in our lives his passion, death, and resurrection.

Celebration

Model Penitential Rite

Presider: John was born to announce that the Light of the world had arrived. Let us pause and recognize that Light in our own lives . . . [pause]

Lord Jesus, you fulfilled the ancient prophecies and the preaching of John: Lord . . .
Christ Jesus, you are the Light of the world announced by John: Christ . . .
Lord Jesus, you have shown your great mercy toward us: Lord . . .

Responsorial Psalm

"I praise you for I am wonderfully made."

The readings for this solemnity correlate two miraculous births, that of Jesus and that of John the Baptist. The selfhood and identity of both were fashioned by God in the womb. The mission of both was to bring salvation, John as precursor, Jesus as fulfillment. The responsorial psalm is taken from one of the most known and loved texts in the psalter, Psalm 139. The psalm as a whole speaks of God's omniscience, omnipresence, and omnipotence, especially as these attributes characterize God's intimacy with the human person. The final stanza of the psalm (vv. 19-24) calls upon God to use the divine omnipotence against the powers of evil, both in the world and in the psalmist's heart.

In the births of Jesus and John the wisdom and omnipotence of God are manifest. For in the "secret" of their personhoods the divine plan to save humankind from the forces of evil and death unfolds.

Model General Intercessions

Presider: God worked wondrous things in bringing about the birth of John the Baptist. That same God works wondrous things on our behalf. And so we pray.

Response:

[Musical notation: Lord, hear our prayer.]

Cantor:

[Musical notation: we pray to the Lord,]

For the Church to give witness to Christ always and everywhere . . . [pause]

For people of the world to rejoice at God's many blessings . . . [pause]

For those paralyzed by fear to grow strong in spirit . . . [pause]

For ourselves to know our own mission in life . . . [pause]

Presider: God of salvation, you act in history to fulfill your promises: hear these our prayers that we might be faithful to our commitments. We ask this through your Son Jesus Christ our Lord. **Amen.**

OPENING PRAYER

Let us pray

Pause for silent prayer

God our Father,
you raised up St. John the Baptist
to prepare a perfect people for Christ the Lord.
Give your Church joy in spirit
and guide those who believe in you
into the way of salvation and peace.
We ask this through our Lord Jesus Christ, your Son,
who lives and reigns with you and the Holy Spirit,
one God, for ever and ever. **Amen.**

RESPONSORIAL PSALM
[Ps 139:1-3, 13-14, 14-15]

℟. (14a) I praise you for I am wonderfully made.

O LORD you have probed me and you know me;
   you know when I sit and when I stand;
   you understand my thoughts from afar.
My journeys and my rest you scrutinize,
   with all my ways you are familiar.

℟. I praise you for I am wonderfully made.

Truly you have formed my inmost being;
   you knit me in my mother's womb.
I give you thanks that I am fearfully, wonderfully made;
   wonderful are your works.

℟. I praise you for I am wonderfully made.

My soul also you knew full well;
   nor was my frame unknown to you
when I was made in secret,
   when I was fashioned in the depths of the earth.

℟. I praise you for I am wonderfully made.

FIRST READING
[Isa 49:1-6]

Hear me, O coastlands
   listen, O distant peoples.
The LORD called me from birth,
   from my mother's womb he gave me my name.
He made of me a sharp-edged sword
   and concealed me in the shadow of his arm.

He made me a polished arrow,
  in his quiver he hid me.
You are my servant, he said to me,
  Israel, through whom I show my glory.

Though I thought I had toiled in vain,
  and for nothing, uselessly, spent my strength,
yet my reward is with the LORD,
  my recompense is with my God.
For now the LORD has spoken
  who formed me as his servant from the womb,
that Jacob may be brought back to him
  and Israel gathered to him;
and I am made glorious in the sight of the Lord,
  and my God is now my strength!
It is too little, he says, for you to be my servant,
  to raise up the tribes of Jacob,
  and restore the survivors of Israel;
I will make you a light to the nations,
  that my salvation may reach to the ends of the earth.

SECOND READING
[Acts 13:22-26]

In those days, Paul said:
  "God raised up David as their king;
    of him he testified,
  'I have found David, son of Jesse, a man after my own heart;
    he will carry out my every wish.'
From this man's descendants God,
    according to his promise,
  has brought to Israel a savior, Jesus.
John heralded his coming by
    proclaiming a baptism of repentance
    to all the people of Israel;
  and as John was completing his course, he would say,
  'What do you suppose that I am? I am not he.
Behold, one is coming after me;
  I am not worthy to unfasten the sandals of his feet.'

"My brothers, children of the family of Abraham,
  and those others among you who are God-fearing,
  to us this word of salvation has been sent."

Catechesis

Cantors
Cantoring the responsorial psalm is an act of self-revelation, for it reveals the extent to which you are listening to and following the word of God in your life. The psalm for this solemnity should engender self-confidence for it proclaims that the self which you reveal has been "wonderfully made" by God. How do you share the gifts with which God has blessed you with others?

Choir
Because singing in the choir is a group ministry, it offers a concrete way to practice John the Baptist's virtue of keeping the focus off of himself so that the vision could be of Jesus. But living this virtue means dying to self, which is never easy. When you find yourself competing to be the "star," you might take some time to re-focus on who the real Light is.

Music Directors
"The Great Forerunner of the Morn" [RS, W3], a hymn about the birth of John the Baptist, was written in the seventh century by the Venerable Bede. Set to the tune WINCHESTER NEW, it projects our minds forward to the John who will cry on Jordan's bank at the beginning of Advent. The hymn is intended for the entrance procession. A perfect choice for a hymn of praise after Communion would be the Canticle of Zechariah (known variously as the *Benedictus*, "Blessed Be the God of Israel," etc.), which proclaims the salvation promised by God and announced by John.

Liturgy Committee
What might you do as a liturgy committee to encourage people, even in some small way, to celebrate these solemnities—either at home or with the parish?

  (1) Only three nativity (birth) festivals appear on the 1969 General Roman Calendar, the nativities of Jesus (December 25), Mary (September 8), and John the Baptist. (2) Our present liturgical calendar has very few solemnities (the highest degree of festivity), all of them chosen because they are connected with the unfolding of the Paschal Mystery in the course of a calendar year. (3) When the solemnities are not holy days of obligation or do not fall on Sunday, they largely get missed. Parishioners must be helped to understand the importance of these celebrations for their deeper entry into the saving Mystery of Christ.

  The environment should reflect the great feast day being celebrated. This is difficult on a weekday when many people probably are not present. But you must be careful not to "do less" because the numbers are fewer.

JUNE 24, 2000

The Solemnity of the Most Holy Body and

Faith-Sharing

- How might you better relate receiving Christ's Body and Blood and your *being* and *becoming* Christ's Body and Blood?
- When do you give your "body and blood" for others? What are the fruits of this self-surrender?
- The second reading from Hebrews says that "the blood of Christ . . . cleanse[s] our consciences from dead works to worship the living God." What are the dead works of which you need to be cleansed? How might you make your worship more fervent?

Presiders

"Christ came as high priest . . . entered . . . into the sanctuary . . . with his own blood." What is the extent of your vocational commitment? In what way do you unite your own blood to that of Christ's, the High Priest? Where do you hold back?

Deacons

How might the "shedding of blood" be a good metaphor for your service? What does this demand of you? How does it change the way you live?

Hospitality Ministers

How might your ministry invite others to be faithful to the new covenant sealed in Christ's blood?

Music Ministers

Living Eucharistically means being willing to lay down one's life for others. How does your ministry of music call you to this?

Altar Ministers

How are you rewarded for the self-surrender of your service?

Lectors

The psalmist writes, "How shall I make a return to the Lord for all the good he has done for me?" How shall *you*? To what extent is your ministry a "return to the Lord"?

Eucharistic Ministers

When does your life spill over in the joy that belongs to those who are nourished by Christ's Body and Blood?

Spirituality

Reflecting on the Gospel

Body of Christ. Amen. Blood of Christ. Amen. Body of Christ. Amen. Blood of Christ. Amen. Each time we celebrate Mass this acclamation and response are told out over and over again between minister and communicant. Usually the Communion hymn masks this litany of acclamations. Body of Christ! Blood of Christ! The litany is an echo of Christ's tremendous gift of self to us as well as an echo of the self-surrender of our own Christian living.

The origins of this festival date to the twelfth century (the feast for the universal Church dates from the thirteenth century) and the great devotion to the Eucharist that was prevalent at that time. Seldom partaking in Communion, the people expressed their devotion by "seeing" the consecrated host; the elevations at Mass come from this time, as well as the ever-popular Eucharistic processions. Although popular devotion centered on the host (the Body of Christ, the name *Corpus Christi* in Latin for the feast), Mass formularies from these centuries show us that from the beginning it was to be a solemn celebration of the Body *and* Blood of Christ and this is indicated by the title for the solemnity today.

The readings for year B stress more strongly than years A or C the blood. The first reading from Exodus relates how Moses sprinkled the blood of the holocaust on the people to seal the covenant. A holocaust was a whole, burnt offering; the animal was completely destroyed as a symbol of the total gift of those making the sacrifice. This "total gift" becomes so real in Christ (see the second reading); his total gift lifts us up to new life. The shedding of blood and the total self-surrender that it symbolizes are why the martyrs were held in such esteem in the early Church, for—like Christ—they even sacrificed their life-blood.

The shedding of blood spreads over all of salvation history, rising to its climax in Christ. We celebrate with great joy his tremendous gift of self. Is it no wonder that our litany—Body of Christ. Blood of Christ—continues on unending? Let us thank and praise God!

Living the Paschal Mystery

The second reading and Gospel for this solemnity do not belabor, but presume, the identification between the bread and wine and the Body and Blood of Christ. Instead, all the readings direct our attention to the effects of Jesus' giving his Body and Blood: his Eucharistic self-giving establishes a new covenant, "obtains eternal redemption," secures "the promised eternal inheritance" (Hebrews), and is given for the sake of "many" (Gospel). In this way, the celebration of the Body and Blood of Christ is an eloquent summation of the Paschal Mystery celebrated at Easter. The shedding of blood is paschal because it always requires a death, and in the history of salvation it always brings us to life (covenant). Thus, the body broken and the blood shed, while commemorating death, also celebrates life; his sacrifice becomes a gift; his defeat becomes our victory; his weakness is our strength, his brokenness is our healing, his Eucharist is our blessing. Our living needs to be a self-giving that brings these tremendous gifts to all we meet in the ordinary circumstances of our lives. As *we* share in his Body and Blood, we surrender ourselves to be like Christ—a Passover lamb for our world today.

BLOOD OF CHRIST

JUNE 25, 2000

GOSPEL [Mark 14:12-16, 22-26; L168B]

On the first day of the Feast of Unleavened Bread, when they sacrificed the Passover lamb, Jesus' disciples said to him, "Where do you want us to go and prepare for you to eat the Passover?" He sent two of his disciples and said to them, "Go into the city and a man will meet you, carrying a jar of water. Follow him. Wherever he enters, say to the master of the house, 'The Teacher says, "Where is my guest room where I may eat the Passover with my disciples?"' Then he will show you a large upper room furnished and ready. Make the preparations for us there." The disciples then went off, entered the city, and found it just as he had told them; and they prepared the Passover.

While they were eating, he took bread, said the blessing, broke it, gave it to them, and said, "Take it; this is my body." Then he took a cup, gave thanks, and gave it to them, and they all drank from it. He said to them, "This is my blood of the covenant, which will be shed for many. Amen, I say to you, I shall not drink again the fruit of the vine until the day when I drink it new in the kingdom of God." Then, after singing a hymn, they went out to the Mount of Olives.

Working with the Word

Key words and phrases from the Gospel: sacrificed, disciples . . . prepared the Passover, blood of the covenant

Connecting to the first and second readings: The shedding of blood is central to the unfolding of God's plan of salvation, from Mount Sinai (first reading) to its completion in Christ (second reading).

Connecting to our culture: Transubstantiation is a teaching of the Church meant to explain and serve the deeper mystery of the Body and Blood of Christ. It is not only *that* Christ is present in the Eucharist, but *why* he is present—for our "promised inheritance"! To preach only transubstantiation is to stop short of the full depth of the mystery!

Exegetical points: The Lord's Supper commemorates something old even as it institutes something new. The "old" is evident in Mark's chronology, which stresses that the Supper is clearly the Passover meal which commemorates God's great act of deliverance of the Hebrews from Egyptian bondage. This annual feast is carefully anticipated and prepared, as the details of vv. 12-16 demonstrate. What Jesus is about to do, he does with foresight, deliberation, and intention. In Mark, "*the* blood of the covenant" becomes "*my* blood of the covenant." This is the new: the covenant between God and humanity is sealed and solemnized, not by the blood of bulls, but with the blood of Christ—the very point the second reading from Hebrews is at pains to make. Hebrews rightly identifies this as a "new covenant" (see also Jer 31:31). Hebrews does not abandon the notion of deliverance inherent in the celebration of Passover, but the deliverance of which it speaks leads to an "eternal inheritance."

To the point: Christ's shedding his blood as the Passover Lamb inaugurates what we have desired for centuries through the blood of goats and calves: "promised eternal inheritance." As we partake of his Body and Blood, we both receive this inheritance and long for its fulfillment.

Celebration

Model Penitential Rite

Presider: Jesus gave us his Body and Blood as a memorial of the new covenant to which we are called. Let us prepare ourselves to celebrate this new covenant in Christ's Body and Blood . . . [pause]

> Lord Jesus, you took, blessed, broke, and gave the bread of life to us: Lord . . .
>
> Christ Jesus, you obtained our eternal redemption by shedding your blood: Christ . . .
>
> Lord Jesus, you are the mediator of a new covenant: Lord . . .

Responsorial Psalm

"I will take the cup of salvation, and call on the name of the Lord."

Psalm 116 was sung by a person offering a sacrifice of thanksgiving because God had saved her or him from imminent death. The psalm begins with "I love the Lord because he has heard my voice in supplication," and goes on to spell out the threat of death and the saving mercy of God. The verses used for this celebration of the Body and Blood of Christ are taken from the latter half of the hymn where the psalmist is making the promised offering. The "cup of salvation" is a libation of wine to be poured out in gratitude. The next verse—"Precious in the eyes of the LORD is the death of his faithful ones"—seems a contradiction until we learn of two different interpretations for the word "precious." The word sometimes meant "dear" or "valued," as in God's appreciation for the death of a martyr. But at other times it meant "too dear," that the death of a faithful person was too costly for God to bear. Surely both interpretations would apply to the death of Christ. Our singing of this psalm proclaims that the cup of salvation we take up is his blood, poured out that we might live. Precious Christ's death because precious our life.

Model General Intercessions

Presider: The God who sends the Son to give us his Body and Blood for our nourishment, is surely the God who hears our prayers. Let us pray.

Response: Lord, hear our prayer.

Cantor: we pray to the Lord,

That the Church give praise and thanksgiving always for the gift of Christ's Body and Blood . . . [pause]

That people everywhere be willing to surrender themselves for the good of others . . . [pause]

That the selfish and self-seeking may be guided to a transformation of life that is giving to others . . . [pause]

That we here gathered for this Eucharist may be nourished for the journey to eternal life . . . [pause]

Presider: God of life, you gave your only Son to be our Food for life: hear these our prayers that we may always be one with you in your kingdom. We pray through Jesus Christ our Lord. **Amen.**

ALTERNATIVE OPENING PRAYER

Let us pray
   [for the willingness to make present in our world the love of Christ shown to us in the eucharist]

Pause for silent prayer

Lord Jesus Christ,
we worship you living among us
   in the sacrament of your body and blood.
May we offer to our Father in heaven
   a solemn pledge of undivided love.
May we offer our brothers and sisters
   a life poured out in loving service of that kingdom
where you live with the Father and the Holy Spirit,
one God, for ever and ever. **Amen.**

RESPONSORIAL PSALM
[Ps 116:12-13, 15-16, 17-18]

℟. (13) I will take the cup of salvation, and call on the name of the Lord.
   or:
℟. Alleluia.

How shall I make a return to the LORD
   for all the good he has done for me?
The cup of salvation I will take up,
   and I will call upon the name of the LORD.

℟. I will take the cup of salvation, and call on the name of the Lord.
   or:
℟. Alleluia.

Precious in the eyes of the LORD
   is the death of his faithful ones.
I am your servant, the son of your handmaid;
   you have loosed my bonds.

℟. I will take the cup of salvation, and call on the name of the Lord.
   or:
℟. Alleluia.

To you will I offer sacrifice of thanksgiving,
   and I will call upon the name of the LORD.
My vows to the LORD I will pay
   in the presence of all his people.

℟. I will take the cup of salvation, and call on the name of the Lord.
   or:
℟. Alleluia.

FIRST READING [Exod 24:3-8]

When Moses came to the people
   and related all the words and
      ordinances of the LORD,
   they all answered with one voice,
   "We will do everything that the LORD
      has told us."

Moses then wrote down all the words of the LORD and,
> rising early the next day,
> he erected at the foot of the mountain an altar
> and twelve pillars for the twelve tribes of Israel.
Then, having sent certain young men of the Israelites
> to offer holocausts and sacrifice young bulls
> as peace offerings to the LORD,
Moses took half of the blood and put it in large bowls;
> the other half he splashed on the altar.
Taking the book of the covenant, he read it aloud to the people,
> who answered, "All that the LORD has said, we will heed and do."
Then he took the blood and sprinkled it on the people, saying,
> "This is the blood of the covenant
> that the LORD has made with you
> in accordance with all these words of his."

SECOND READING [Heb 9:11-15]

Brothers and sisters:
When Christ came as high priest
> of the good things that have come to be,
> passing through the greater and more perfect tabernacle
> not made by hands, that is, not belonging to this creation,
> he entered once for all into the sanctuary,
> not with the blood of goats and calves
> but with his own blood, thus obtaining eternal redemption.
For if the blood of goats and bulls
> and the sprinkling of a heifer's ashes
> can sanctify those who are defiled
> so that their flesh is cleansed,
> how much more will the blood of Christ,
> who through the eternal Spirit offered himself unblemished to God,
> cleanse our consciences from dead works
> to worship the living God.
For this reason he is mediator of a new covenant:
> since a death has taken place for deliverance
> from transgressions under the first covenant,
> those who are called may receive the promised eternal inheritance.

SEQUENCE

See Appendix A, p. 286.

Catechesis

Cantors

Do not forget that the cup of salvation offered in the psalm is the life of Christ poured out that you, and all, might live. How can you make a return for this good that has been done? How can you live Eucharistically, that is, giving thanks in all that you do?

Choir

Just as Christ has given his body and his blood that you might live, so are you called to do for others. Your participation in the Eucharist is a pledge of this commitment. In light of this, reflect this week on what you sing about as you receive the Body and Blood of Christ. Is it just the words of the hymn, or is it something deeper?

Music Directors

This Sunday suggests a good opportunity to reflect on the music you use for the Communion rite. Do the texts express your participation in the dying and rising of Christ? Do they call you to *be* the Body and Blood of Christ for one another and in the world? Do they draw you into the Body of Christ rather than invite you into private devotion during Mass?

The directives in the *General Instruction of the Roman Missal* state that the function of the Communion song is "to express outwardly the communicants' union in spirit by means of the unity of their voices, to give evidence of a joy of heart, and to make the procession to receive Christ's body more fully an act of community" (no. 56i). The document also indicates that the song should begin when the presider takes Communion. After Communion there may be time for silent prayer, or a "hymn, psalm, or other song of praise may be sung by the entire congregation" (no. 56j).

Liturgy Committee

Because almost all the assembly goes to Communion each time Mass is celebrated, it might become routine and simply one more act among the others. What catechesis is needed in your parish to help everyone understand that being nourished by Christ's Body and Blood is a tremendous privilege and includes pledging yourselves to the same kind of self-surrendering sacrifice for others that Christ modeled?

The readings for this Mass certainly point to the importance of blood in both the Hebrew and Christian Scriptures. While it is true that Christ is whole and complete in either the Sacred Host or the Precious Blood, to receive from the cup (a privilege restored by the liturgical renewal after Vatican II) *completes* the symbol of Christ's giving both his Body and his Blood for salvation. Yet, many of the people who receive Communion still choose not to take from the cup when it is offered. What catechesis needs to be shared in order that people are encouraged to receive *both* the Body and Blood?

This solemnity has an *optional* sequence, a beautiful text attributed to St. Thomas Aquinas of the thirteenth century. If you choose to use the sequence, it would fittingly be connected to an extended Gospel procession that would help capture and express the joy of this solemnity.

JUNE 25, 2000

Saints Peter and Paul, Apostles

FAITH-SHARING

- When Jesus asks you, "Who do you say that I am?"—how do you answer? Do you *live* that answer?
- Paul wrote, "I have competed well; I have finished the race; I have kept the faith." For what do you compete? Where is your zeal? What still needs attending before the race is finished for you?
- Who is excluded—in your family? your parish? What is one thing you can do to begin including them?

PRESIDER
As an ordained minister, are you more like Peter (mission to conserve tradition) or Paul (mission to pursue new directions?) How might you bring better balance between these two great apostles' missions within your own ministry?

DEACON
Who are the marginalized ones excluded in your parish that deserve your outreach "so that through [you] the proclamation might be completed"?

HOSPITALITY MINISTERS
How might you help people to experience liturgy as the gathering of diverse people into the "one family of Christ"?

MUSIC MINISTERS
How does liturgical music ministry participate in the mission of the Church?

ALTAR MINISTERS
How are you "poured out like a libation" through your service? How does this build up the Church?

LECTORS
Peter and Paul proclaimed the good news with words, but more importantly with their lives—even to death. How are you living the good news?

EUCHARISTIC MINISTERS
In what ways are you a minister of *communion* outside the liturgy? How does your life build up the people into "one family of Christ"?

Spirituality

Reflecting on the Gospel

We have evidence of a feast commemorating Peter and Paul together on June 29 from about the middle of the third century. From earliest times the apostles were held in great esteem in the Church (see Eph 2:19-20; Rev 21:14). What is interesting is that the Lectionary readings and preface proper to the solemnity do something different from what might be expected, and that difference gives us some insight into how we could approach this solemnity.

We might expect this solemnity to focus on two great men in our tradition. And at first glance it seems as though Peter gets a larger share of the festival than does Paul—both the Gospel and first reading focus on Peter while only the second reading comments about Paul. We might expect, too, that this solemnity would focus on some of the exhortatory, theological, or pastoral writings at hand from these two great apostles (e.g., 1 Pet 2:1-10 and 1 Cor 15:50-58). It is the preface for this solemnity, however, that gives us an interpretive clue: "Peter raised up the Church from the faithful flock of Israel. Paul brought your call to the nations, and became the teacher of the world. Each in his chosen way gathered into unity the one family of Christ." The preface directs our interpretation away from merely viewing these two great apostles as holy individuals or as insightful teachers toward contemplating the inclusivity of the Church: what God has built through these great apostles is "one family of Christ."

In addition, the Lectionary readings chosen for this solemnity give us a graphic, real-life picture of what discipleship entails. The first and second readings—referring to imprisonment and martyrdom—relate for us the cost of an inclusive Church. We don't just *read about* the Jesus event; we encounter two great men who *lived* to the fullest their respective encounters with Christ. These two apostles represent for us the Church's mission to conserve tradition (Peter's relationship with the Jewish-Christian communities) and her mission to being open to new directions (Paul's activity among the Gentile-Christians). By its nature our Church is inclusive and these two apostles and their joint festival remind us of that.

Living the Paschal Mystery

Peter and Paul both paid for their zeal with their lives. But that didn't seem to dampen that zeal. They were both imbued with the Holy Spirit and consumed by their passion for spreading the good news. This solemnity challenges us to live our own lives with the same inclusiveness and with the same concreteness. Religion isn't something we simply *do* (as in weekly worship) and then forget about. The word "religion" means that we are "bound" to relationships. Peter and Paul show us how intimate our relationship to Christ can be. They show us how inclusive of others we must be. They show us conversion and trust and surrender. They show us that to the question "Who do *you* say that I am?" we must respond with our very lives. They show us that living the Paschal Mystery means that *through us* the proclamation of Jesus as Messiah "might be completed." Then, as with Peter and Paul, we too have the "crown of righteousness" awaiting us.

JUNE 29, 2000

GOSPEL [Matt 16:13-19; L591]

When Jesus went into the region of Caesarea Philippi he asked his disciples, "Who do people say that the Son of Man is?" They replied, "Some say John the Baptist, others Elijah, still others Jeremiah or one of the prophets." He said to them, "But who do you say that I am?" Simon Peter said in reply, "You are the Christ, the Son of the living God." Jesus said to him in reply, "Blessed are you, Simon son of Jonah. For flesh and blood has not revealed this to you, but my heavenly Father. And so I say to you, you are Peter, and upon this rock I will build my church, and the gates of the netherworld shall not prevail against it. I will give you the keys to the kingdom of heaven. Whatever you bind on earth shall be bound in heaven; and whatever you loose on earth shall be loosed in heaven."

Working with the Word

Key words and phrases from the readings: killed, arrest Peter, prayer by the church, poured out like a libation, who do you say I am?, I will build my church

Connecting to the liturgical calendar: Both Peter and Paul have secondary feasts on the 1969 General Roman Calendar: the Conversion of St. Paul on January 25 and the Chair of Peter on February 22 (both have the rank of feast). The focus of this solemnity, then, is more on "Church" than on either individual.

Connecting to our culture: This solemnity holds tensions together as a unity: Peter/Paul, Jew/Gentile. This sheds light on polarities in our own culture: conservative/liberal, institutional/charismatic, etc. This is "catholicity" at its best. Not to be so "catholic" compromises the mission.

Exegetical points: While Matthew has other passages that shine the light on Peter (e.g., Matt 14:22-28; 17:24-27), the liturgy chooses to emphasize his role as one who professes Jesus and who is called to leadership of service. While the other synoptic Gospels also record Peter's profession of faith, only Matthew has Jesus blessing Peter with the keys of the kingdom. This image of Peter holding the keys gives rise to the tradition of Peter as heaven's gatekeeper.

An ecumenical consensus concerning the interpretation of this passage seems to have emerged which recognizes Peter's historical uniqueness among the first generation of Christians, but not his hereditary primacy passed on to successors throughout history. (It should be pointed out that this last statement is an *exegetical*, not a *doctrinal*, observation.) Indeed, the authority which Jesus confers on Peter in this passage is also given, in the very same words, to the entire Church in Matt 18:18.

The meaning of "binding" and "loosing" defies precise definition. What is agreed is the text's general affirming of authority conferred on Peter. The "gates of the netherworld" seems to be an allusion to the gates of death in Isa 38:10.

To the point: The honor of the solemnity isn't primarily directed toward the individuals Peter and Paul as it is to Jesus' mission which extends to both Jew and Gentile. Peter and Paul endured all things—even martyrdom—so that Christ's kingdom may be for all peoples.

Celebration

Model Penitential Rite

Presider: God called Peter and Paul to be great apostles in the Church. Let us pause and listen for God's call in our own lives . . . [pause]

> Lord Jesus, you call pastors and preachers to build up your Church: Lord . . .
> Christ Jesus, you reveal yourself to all peoples through your disciples: Christ . . .
> Lord Jesus, you call each of us to reveal your good news in our daily living: Lord . . .

Responsorial Psalm

"The angel of the Lord will rescue those who fear him."
The use of verses from Psalm 34 for this solemnity is very fitting. The angel of the Lord rescues Peter from impending death (first reading). The Lord has saved Paul from "the lion's mouth" and from "every evil threat" (second reading). Christ promises protection to the Church, against whom "the gates of the netherworld shall not prevail" (Gospel).

Such divine protection does not release disciples from fear, however. The psalm uses the word "fear" in both of its connotations—awe before the power of God, and terror in face of danger. The first frees from the shackles of the second by giving the apostles the courage they need to continue their mission. In singing this psalm we join Peter and Paul in their courage as we, too, carry out the mission of proclaiming salvation.

Model General Intercessions

Presider: God called fearless leaders to protect the Church and spread the good news and is just as present to us today. Let us voice our needs to such a caring God.

Response:

[musical notation: "Lord, hear our prayer."]

Cantor:

[musical notation: "we pray to the Lord,"]

That the Church always witness to her marks of being one, holy, catholic, and apostolic . . . [pause]

That the leaders of the world foster inclusivity and righteousness . . . [pause]

That those who are excluded because of race, gender, religion, sexual orientation, age, disabilities, or economic status find a home in God . . . [pause]

That we labor tirelessly—even to death—to reveal the Messiah to all we meet . . . [pause]

Presider: O God, you offer salvation to all peoples: hear our prayer on this festival of Peter and Paul and may your will be done. We ask this through Jesus Christ, the Son of the living God. **Amen.**

OPENING PRAYER
Let us pray
Pause for silent prayer

God our Father,
today you give us the joy
of celebrating the feast of the apostles Peter and Paul.
Through them your Church first received the faith.
Keep us true to their teaching.
Grant this through our Lord Jesus Christ, your Son,
who lives and reigns with you and the Holy Spirit,
one God, for ever and ever. **Amen.**

RESPONSORIAL PSALM
[Ps 34:2-3, 4-5, 6-7, 8-9]

℟. (8) The angel of the Lord will rescue those who fear him.

I will bless the Lord at all times;
 his praise shall be ever in my mouth.
Let my soul glory in the Lord;
 the lowly will hear me and be glad.

℟. The angel of the Lord will rescue those who fear him.

Glorify the Lord with me,
 let us together extol his name.
I sought the Lord, and he answered me
 and delivered me from all my fears.

℟. The angel of the Lord will rescue those who fear him.

Look to him that you may be radiant with joy,
 and your faces may not blush with shame.
When the poor one called out, the Lord heard,
 and from all his distress he saved him.

℟. The angel of the Lord will rescue those who fear him.

The angel of the Lord encamps
 around those who fear him, and delivers them.
Taste and see how good the Lord is;
 blessed the man who takes refuge in him.

℟. The angel of the Lord will rescue those who fear him.

FIRST READING [Acts 12:1-11]

In those days, King Herod laid hands
 upon some members of the church to harm them.
He had James, the brother of John, killed by the sword,
 and when he saw that this was pleasing to the Jews
 he proceeded to arrest Peter also.
—It was the feast of Unleavened Bread.—
He had him taken into custody and put in prison
 under the guard of four squads of

four soldiers each.
He intended to bring him before the
  people after Passover.
Peter thus was being kept in prison,
  but prayer by the church was
    fervently being made
    to God on his behalf.

On the very night before Herod was to
  bring him to trial,
  Peter, secured by double chains,
  was sleeping between two soldiers,
  while outside the door guards kept
    watch on the prison.
Suddenly the angel of the Lord stood by
  him
  and a light shone in the cell.
He tapped Peter on the side and
  awakened him, saying,
  "Get up quickly."
The chains fell from his wrists.
The angel said to him, "Put on your belt
  and your sandals."
He did so.
Then he said to him, "Put on your cloak
  and follow me."
So he followed him out,
  not realizing that what was happening
    through the angel was real;
  he thought he was seeing a vision.
They passed the first guard, then the
  second,
  and came to the iron gate leading out
    to the city,
  which opened for them by itself.
They emerged and made their way
  down an alley,
  and suddenly the angel left him.

SECOND READING [2 Tim 4:6-8, 17-18]

I, Paul, am already being poured out
  like a libation,
  and the time of my departure is at
    hand.
I have competed well; I have finished
    the race;
  I have kept the faith.
From now on the crown of
  righteousness awaits me,
  which the Lord, the just judge,
  will award to me on that day, and not
    only to me,
  but to all who have longed for his
    appearance.
The Lord stood by me and gave me
  strength,
  so that through me the proclamation
    might be completed
  and all the Gentiles might hear it.
And I was rescued from the lion's
  mouth.
The Lord will rescue me from every evil
  threat
  and will bring me safe to his heavenly
    kingdom.
To him be glory forever and ever. Amen.

Catechesis

Cantors

The responsorial psalm is not only about Peter and Paul, it is also about you. It is a prayer of confidence in God which gives you the courage to do the mission into which you were baptized. In leading the psalm you are modeling your choice to remain faithful to this mission no matter what the personal cost. When has it cost you to be faithful to your baptismal mission? Why? How did you respond?

Choir

This solemnity celebrates the universality of the salvation brought to you by Christ. It also reminds you of the cost of discipleship. You might end rehearsal this week with prayer for those who have chosen to be involved in the missionary work of the Church, especially in places where this work brings threat to their lives.

Music Directors

Two types of hymns fit this solemnity: one which specifically honors Peter and Paul, and one which reminds you of your mission to the world. "Two Noble Saints" [RS, W3] is taken from an eleventh-century Latin text and would be appropriate for the entrance. Also suitable for the entrance is the more generalized hymn about apostles, "Let All on Earth Their Voices Raise" [CBW3, W3]. Examples of hymns which speak of your mission to proclaim the good news are "Go Make of All Disciples" [CH, RS, WC, W3] and "God's Blessing Sends Us Forth" [WC], both of which would work well as recessionals.

Liturgy Committee

How might you promote through your parish's liturgy the same zeal for living the Paschal Mystery that Peter and Paul had?

Very early evidence indicates that the early Church had great regard for all the twelve apostles. These men were eye witnesses of the Jesus event and upon them the Church was built. The Eastern Church originally celebrated a feast of all the apostles; individuals were venerated chiefly in the communities where their tombs were located. Eventually, feasts of individual apostles made their way onto the general Roman calendar, as is the case today.

JUNE 29, 2000

THE SOLEMNITY OF THE MOST SACRED HEART

FAITH-SHARING
- When has your heart been pierced; how has your response been like God's response?
- How has God shown unfathomable love in your life?
- When have you been the unfaithful one that God has still loved tenderly and completely?

PRESIDERS
In what ways does the overwhelming love of God flow through you to others during your ministry? How might you open yourself to this more deeply?

DEACONS
When is your service a service of love? When is it not? When it isn't, what is one thing you could do about that?

HOSPITALITY MINISTERS
How might you keep your Fridays as a day of the cross so that your hospitality on Sunday rings with the love of Christ crucified and pierced?

MUSIC MINISTERS
Many blessings flow from the heart of Christ. How is your ministry one of them?

ALTAR MINISTERS
When is your pity stirred so that you serve others more faithfully?

LECTORS
". . . in [Christ] we have boldness of speech and confidence . . ." How could you live more "in Christ" so that you have boldness of speech and confidence when you proclaim the Word?

EUCHARISTIC MINISTERS
In what way might you distribute Communion so that you witness to this as a sacrament of love?

Spirituality

Reflecting on the Gospel

Here it is: the dead and pierced body is an icon of the "breadth and length and height and depth" of the love of Christ for us! There is so much power here, and yet so many of our society's references to hearts (e.g., Valentine's Day) and love are so insipid and trite. This solemnity challenges us to take ourselves to much greater depths, so that we "may come to believe" (Gospel).

On this Solemnity of the Sacred Heart the first reading from Hosea speaks on a symbolic level to the compassion and love associated with the heart. The love of God for Israel is described in terms of a parent-child relationship: God calling child Israel, teaching him to walk, holding him in God's arms and lifting him to God's cheeks, leading him with love, fostering and feeding and healing him. Despite God's blazing anger against Israel for repeated infidelity and sin, God's compassion averts the punishing flames because God's heart is overwhelmed with pity. The Letter to the Ephesians describes how that compassionate love of God for Israel is now extended to the Gentiles. God's love finds full expression in Christ whose own love is beyond measure.

And herein is the great mystery: Christ's love is beyond measure—"I will not let the flames consume you" (first reading) but I will let them consume me ("They will look upon him whom they have pierced"). The "heart" becomes a symbol of the whole person of Christ who sacrificed all according to "the plan of the mystery hidden from ages past in God" (second reading). Such a heart! Such a love!

Living the Paschal Mystery

This is the third "idea" feast we celebrate (the other two being the solemnities of the Holy Trinity and of the Body and Blood of Christ) that comes quickly on the heels of our Easter celebration. Historically, in the development of the liturgical calendar, this particular time was purposely chosen. These celebrations enable us to prolong right into Ordinary Time the joy and depth of Mystery that we solemnized through the fifty days of Easter.

It is of no small significance that this solemnity occurs on a Friday and not on a Sunday as the other two. Since it is not a holy day of obligation nor a Sunday, many people will not be able to share in the Eucharist, the sacrament that conveys the depths of Christ's love to the fullest. Still, this solemnity could be a special time for us to connect this and every Friday to the sacrificial and complete love of Christ for us. If every Sunday is a "little Easter" on which we celebrate Christ's resurrection (which is why *Sunday* is the privileged day for celebrating Eucharist), then surely every Friday is a "little Good Friday." Surely once a week is not too often to unite ourselves with the self-sacrificing love of Christ! Surely once a week is not too often to take special time to remember the love that God has for us! Surely once a week is not too often to examine ourselves on our willingness to emulate the heart of Christ! The Sacred Heart is an icon of all God has done for us. And all we are called to do for each other as Christ's Body.

JUNE 30, 2000

GOSPEL [John 19:31-37; L171B]

Since it was preparation day, in order that the bodies might not remain on the cross on the sabbath, for the sabbath day of that week was a solemn one, the Jews asked Pilate that their legs be broken and they be taken down. So the soldiers came and broke the legs of the first and then of the other one who was crucified with Jesus. But when they came to Jesus and saw that he was already dead, they did not break his legs, but one soldier thrust his lance into his side, and immediately blood and water flowed out. An eyewitness has testified, and his testimony is true; he knows that he is speaking the truth, so that you also may come to believe. For this happened so that the Scripture passage might be fulfilled: *Not a bone of it will be broken.* And again another passage says: *They will look upon him whom they have pierced.*

Working with the Word

Key words and phrases from the Gospel: so that you . . . may come to believe, pierced

Connecting to the first reading: God shows in human words the anguish of love pierced: "My heart is overwhelmed."

Connecting to our culture: Many parents today anguish over the love they have poured out over their children who persist in seriously destructive behaviors (e.g., drugs, alcohol, sex, etc.). Often they ask, "What did we do wrong?" Sometimes feeling unwarranted guilt or failure, these parents may be comforted by the experience of God whose love was rejected (first reading from Hosea) but became victorious in Christ (see second reading).

Exegetical points: The symbolic importance of Jesus' heart being pierced is the testimony, as the evangelist sites, of an eyewitness (the Beloved Disciple of vv. 26-27) who testifies that "immediately blood and water flowed out." Interpretations vary. In John's own Gospel Jesus had earlier equated water with the Spirit when he said, "Scripture says, 'Rivers of living water will flow from within him.'" He said this in reference to the Spirit that those who came to believe in him were to receive (John 7:38-39). And as Jesus dies, the evangelist notes—with typical double entendre—"Bowing his head, he handed over the spirit." So on one level, the water flowing from within Jesus at the moment of his death symbolizes the Spirit. The blood testifies to the reality of his physical and sacrificial death. The early Church Fathers saw in the water and the blood references to the two sacraments most closely associated with the death of Jesus, baptism and Eucharist.

To the point: What God would not permit to happen to us ("I will not let the flames consume you"), God does permit to happen to the only Son ("They will look upon him whom they have pierced") so that we "may be filled with all the fullness of God" (second reading).

Celebration

Model Penitential Rite

Presider: God has shown the depths of love to us by sending the Son to be pierced by a sword on the cross. Let us open ourselves to this great mystery of love . . . [pause]

> Lord Jesus, your heart was pierced and blood and water flowed from your side: Lord . . .
> Christ Jesus, you call us to boldness of speech and confidence in you: Christ . . .
> Lord Jesus, your love surpasses all knowledge: Lord . . .

Responsorial Psalm

"You will draw water joyfully from the springs of salvation."

These verses from Isaiah 12 are part of a biblical canticle similar in style to a psalm. The text is also used for the responsorial psalm for the Feast of the Baptism of the Lord, year B. The mission Jesus undertook on that day is completed in the death on the cross told of in this solemnity's Gospel. What was said about the use of Isaiah 12 on that Sunday applies here as well. In these verses and refrain the Hebrew word *yeshuʿa* is used seven times. *Yeshuʿa* means "savior" or "salvation." Its English form is "Jesus." The springs of salvation are the blood and water flowing from the pierced side of the crucified Christ (Gospel). Drinking it, we are "filled with the fullness of God" (second reading). We experience most graphically the love of God overflowing with tenderness and compassion (first reading). Our responsorial "psalm" is a song of joy for such love we have been shown from the heart of God.

Model General Intercessions

Presider: Just as blood and water poured forth from the heart of Christ crucified, so will God bestow on us God's everlasting love by hearing our prayers.

Response:

Lord, hear our prayer.

Cantor:

we pray to the Lord,

That the Church may always make known the manifold wisdom and love of God . . . [pause]

That all peoples of the world may experience the depths of love that God has shown from the beginning . . . [pause]

That those who pierce God's heart by sin may see their evil ways and turn back to God . . . [pause]

That all of us here, embraced by the tenderness of God's love, may bring to others the fullness of God . . . [pause]

Presider: God of unfathomable love, your heart has been pierced by our errant ways: hear these our prayers that your eternal purpose may be fulfilled. We ask this through Christ our Lord. **Amen.**

ALTERNATIVE OPENING PRAYER

Let us pray
  [that the love of Christ's heart may touch the world with healing and peace]

Pause for silent prayer

Father,
we honor the heart of your Son
broken by man's cruelty,
yet symbol of love's triumph,
pledge of all that man is called to be.

Teach us to see Christ in the lives we touch,
to offer him living worship
by love-filled service to our brothers and sisters.
We ask this through Christ our Lord.
Amen.

RESPONSORIAL PSALM
[Isa 12:2-3, 4, 5-6]

℟. (3) You will draw water joyfully from the springs of salvation.

God indeed is my savior;
  I am confident and unafraid.
My strength and my courage is the LORD,
  and he has been my savior.
With joy you will draw water
  at the fountain of salvation.

℟. You will draw water joyfully from the springs of salvation.

Give thanks to the LORD, acclaim his name;
  among the nations make known his deeds,
  proclaim how exalted is his name.

℟. You will draw water joyfully from the springs of salvation.

Sing praise to the LORD for his glorious achievement;
  let this be known throughout all the earth.
Shout with exultation, O city of Zion,
  for great in your midst
  is the Holy One of Israel!

℟. You will draw water joyfully from the springs of salvation.

FIRST READING
[Hos 11:1, 3-4, 8c-9]

Thus says the LORD:
When Israel was a child I loved him,
  out of Egypt I called my son.
Yet it was I who taught Ephraim to walk,
  who took them in my arms;

I drew them with human cords,
   with bands of love;
I fostered them like one
   who raises an infant to his cheeks;
yet, though I stooped to feed my child,
   they did not know that I was their
      healer.

My heart is overwhelmed,
   my pity is stirred.
I will not give vent to my blazing anger,
   I will not destroy Ephraim again;
for I am God and not a man,
   the Holy One present among you;
   I will not let the flames consume you.

SECOND READING
[Eph 3:8-12, 14-19]

Brothers and sisters:
To me, the very least of all the holy ones,
   this grace was given,
      to preach to the Gentiles the
         inscrutable riches of Christ,
      and to bring to light for all what is the
         plan of the mystery
      hidden from ages past in God who
         created all things,
      so that the manifold wisdom of God
         might now be made known through
         the church
      to the principalities and authorities in
         the heavens.
This was according to the eternal
   purpose
      that he accomplished in Christ Jesus
         our Lord,
      in whom we have boldness of speech
      and confidence of access through faith
         in him.

For this reason I kneel before the Father,
   from whom every family in heaven
      and on earth is named,
      that he may grant you in accord with
         the riches of his glory
      to be strengthened with power
         through his Spirit in the inner self,
      and that Christ may dwell in your
         hearts through faith;
      that you, rooted and grounded in
         love,
      may have strength to comprehend
         with all the holy ones
      what is the breadth and length and
         height and depth,
      and to know the love of Christ which
         surpasses knowledge,
      so that you may be filled with all the
         fullness of God.

Catechesis

Cantors

As you prepare to sing Isaiah 12, spend some time reflecting on the cost of your salvation. Christ opened his heart to you, not just figuratively, but actually. Everyone dreams of such love and here it is, freely and truly given. Sing of it with joy.

Choir

Because this solemnity is assigned to a Friday, you will probably not be singing as a choir for the celebration of Mass. But perhaps you can incorporate some prayer into your weekly rehearsal which connects the meaning of the Sacred Heart to the return to Ordinary Time. The responsorial psalm invites you to draw joyfully from the springs of salvation. These springs are the blood and water flowing from the heart of Jesus. It is drinking from this which will refresh and restore you in the months ahead of learning more and more about discipleship.

Music Directors

In the hymn "Come, Thou Font of Every Blessing" [CH] the font is the blood of Christ with "streams of mercy never ceasing." The tune would work for the entrance procession, but the text seems more suited for the presentation of the gifts or Communion. "Come and Let Us Drink of that New River" [CH, RS, W3] is a seventh-century text written by John of Damascus for the Office of Easter in the Greek Church. His first verse is "Come and let us drink of that new river, Not from barren rock divinely poured, But the fount of life that springs forever From the sacred body of our Lord." The simple, chant-like tune flows with the text and would work well at any point in the liturgy. Also appropriate at any point in this liturgy would be "What Wondrous Love Is This" [BB, CH, G2, RS, W3, WC], which would connect this solemnity to the sacrifice of the cross and to your weekly Friday remembrance of it.

Liturgy Committee

What can you do to help your parishioners celebrate the meaning of this feast not only on this Friday but on every Friday?

St. Margaret Mary Alacoque is perhaps best known for promoting keeping the Fridays in honor of the Sacred Heart (seventeenth century), although this devotion flourished at least three centuries before that. Pius IX made this feast obligatory for the universal Church and Leo XIII in 1899 declared that the whole world should be consecrated to the Sacred Heart during the twentieth century. It was Pius XI who revised the liturgy and chose readings and composed prayers that are still in use today.

Because this solemnity is not a holy day of obligation, there may be a temptation to limit the festivity. It would be well to prepare the liturgy with great care, especially bringing out its connection with the Triduum and Easter season and its challenge of everyday Paschal Mystery living.

JUNE 30, 2000

Thirteenth Sunday in Ordinary Time

FAITH-SHARING
- What are the "deaths" that face you every day? How do you relate this to Jesus' promise of life?
- How can your faith have an impact on other people's lives?
- When do you live in faith?
- What does it mean for you as disciples to build a kingdom of life?

PRESIDERS
You face severe illness and death so frequently in your ministry. Do you remain affected by them? In what ways does your ministerial "reaching out" and "touching" Jesus keep you in hope and faith about new life?

DEACONS
Jairus brought Jesus to his dying daughter. Whom have you brought to Jesus this past week? Who needs to be brought to Jesus?

HOSPITALITY MINISTERS
Jesus tends to the high official (Jairus) and the simple person (the woman) with equal concern. How might you treat the various members of the Body of Christ with equal attention?

MUSIC MINISTERS
The year in/year out commitment which the ministry of music requires is part of your ongoing dying to self. Whenever the task begins to feel lifeless, how can you re-connect with the presence of Jesus which gives it purpose?

ALTAR MINISTERS
Jesus waited on the needs of the sick and dying. How can you share the healing of Jesus with someone who has his or her life "oozing out"? How might this encounter help you minister better?

LECTORS
Sickness and death breed fear and discouragement. How might you proclaim the good news (in daily life and on Sunday) so that people receive hope and courage in God's rescue of them?

EUCHARISTIC MINISTERS
The Communion procession is filled with suffering people who—just like the woman afflicted with hemorrhage—want to touch Jesus and be touched by him. How does this affect your belief in and reverence for the Body of Christ?

Spirituality

Reflecting on the Gospel

In this Sunday's Gospel life is oozing out of both the twelve-year-old girl and the woman with the hemorrhage. All of us can understand this painful, human situation for we have either watched a loved one slowly lose life or we ourselves have experienced the drain of a life-threatening illness. We can all identify, then, with the desperation of the father, Jairus, or the reaching out of the woman with the hemorrhage.

Jairus pleads with Jesus because his "daughter is at the point of death." The woman with the hemorrhage has watched her life flow out of her for twelve years (since blood is taken to be the seat of life in Jewish culture). Both are staring death in the face. Jairus asks Jesus to lay his hands on his daughter; the woman merely reaches out and touches his cloak. Both Jairus and the woman assume postures of humility when seeking Jesus' help ("fell at his feet," "came up behind him"). Both have faith, and both have their wish for healing granted.

In addition to these parallels in the two scenes, contrasts also abound. Jairus is "one of the synagogue officials," no doubt a prominent Jew; yet he humbles himself before Jesus for the sake of his daughter. The crowd presses around Jesus, yet he looks for a single person who has touched him. Jairus and the woman take Jesus quite seriously, yet the mourners ridicule him. Death has encroached, yet death is turned back.

All of these comparisons and contrasts surely lead us to reflect on the power of death over us and Jesus' power over it. The first reading from Wisdom boldly proclaims that "God did not make death." No, death is not part of God's plan for us. The coming of Jesus and the establishment of God's reign restore the integrity of God's plan for creation by turning back the effects of death. Satan has control of the world only until Someone stronger comes. Jesus not only has the authority to heal and cast out demons and forgive sins; he also has authority over death!

Living the Paschal Mystery

Death is part of our human lives. Yet, Jesus' inauguration of God's kingdom vanquishes death and restores life. Like Jairus and the woman with the hemorrhage, all we need do to overcome death is reach out and touch the nearness of Jesus.

Death, however, not only means the cessation of physical life but also all those everyday "dyings to self" that call us to surrender our wills to God's will. In the Christian mystery, death is the doorway to life. Just as Jairus and the woman forgot their own stations in life and overcame their fears in order to receive life from Jesus, so must we surrender our own wills in order to encounter Jesus and receive life. God's kingdom of life is not built by avoiding death, but by embracing it. Living the Paschal Mystery is none other than our daily dying to self—overcoming our fears and reaching out to Jesus in humility—in all the little, practical ways that fill our daily routines. Paschal Mystery dying is as simple as smiling at the children even when we're bone tired or taking an hour out of our day to visit the sick. When we surrender in humility to his goodness and power, Jesus offers us life.

GOSPEL [Mark 5:21-43; L98B]

When Jesus had crossed again in the boat to the other side, a large crowd gathered around him, and he stayed close to the sea. One of the synagogue officials, named Jairus, came forward. Seeing him he fell at his feet and pleaded earnestly with him, saying, "My daughter is at the point of death. Please, come lay your hands on her that she may get well and live." He went off with him, and a large crowd followed him and pressed upon him.

There was a woman afflicted with hemorrhages for twelve years. She had suffered greatly at the hands of many doctors and had spent all that she had. Yet she was not helped but only grew worse. She had heard about Jesus and came up behind him in the crowd and touched his cloak. She said, "If I but touch his clothes, I shall be cured." Immediately her flow of blood dried up. She felt in her body that she was healed of her affliction. Jesus, aware at once that power had gone out from him, turned around in the crowd and asked, "Who has touched my clothes?" But his disciples said to Jesus, "You see how the crowd is pressing upon you, and yet you ask, 'Who touched me?'" And he looked around to see who had done it. The woman, realizing what had happened to her, approached in fear and trembling. She fell down before Jesus and told him the whole truth. He said to her, "Daughter, your faith has saved you. Go in peace and be cured of your affliction."

While he was still speaking, people from the synagogue official's house arrived and said, "Your daughter has died; why trouble the teacher any longer?" Disregarding the message that was reported, Jesus said to the synagogue official, "Do not be afraid; just have faith." He did not allow anyone to accompany him inside except Peter, James, and John, the brother of James. When they arrived at the house of the synagogue official, he caught sight of a commotion, people weeping and wailing loudly. So he went in and said to them, "Why this commotion and weeping? The child is not dead but asleep." And they ridiculed him. Then he put them all out. He took along the child's father and mother and those who were with him and entered the room where the child was. He took the child by the hand and said to her, *"Talitha koum,"* which means, "Little girl, I say to you, arise!" The girl, a child of twelve, arose immediately and walked around. At that they were utterly astounded. He gave strict orders that no one should know this and said that she should be given something to eat.

Working with the Word

Key words and phrases from the Gospel: Who touched me?, your faith has saved you, do not be afraid, just have faith

Connecting to the first reading: The good news is that God "fashioned all things that they might have being" (Wisdom). Death reveals the power of evil at work in the world, but God's plan for us is full, abundant life.

Connecting to the culture: In a contemporary culture that likes to deny death, defy death, postpone death, keep death at a distance, the Paschal Mystery invites us to see death as a doorway to life (that which we truly want).

Exegetical points: With Lent and Easter duly celebrated, we resume the in-course reading of Mark in Ordinary Time. Because the solemnities of the past two weeks and the number of Sundays in the year have abrogated Sundays 10, 11, and 12 in Ordinary Time, the Lectionary this year skips Mark 3:13–5:20 and picks up with this Sunday's passage. These two healing stories are examples of a typical Marcan device: intercalating (or "sandwiching") one story in the middle of another. In this way, Mark invites the reader to interpret the two stories in light of each other. The Gospel starts out as a typical healing story, but goes on to reveal Jesus as Lord of life.

Both the woman and Jairus must overcome their fear in order to have Jesus accomplish his work. The woman's faith is exactly what Jairus needs, as Jesus tells him, "Do not be afraid; just have faith." The power of faith is obscured in the present translation where the Greek word "to save" is translated as "made well": Jairus says to Jesus, "lay your hands on her that she may *be saved*"; and Jesus says to the woman, "your faith has *saved* you." Both healings point to the deeper truth: faith leads to salvation.

To the point: Mark is presenting the expanding reach of the power of the kingdom: over evil, illness, sin, death. While this expanding power unfolds, however, we're caught in living in the "already but not yet" of its "unfulfillment." The way we live is in faith and free from fear.

Celebration

Model Penitential Rite

Presider: God offers us new life when we come with faith. Let us place ourselves in God's hands and ask to be touched by divine mercy and healing.

> Lord Jesus, you desire that we get well and live: Lord . . .
> Christ Jesus, you tell us not to be afraid, just have faith: Christ . . .
> Lord Jesus, you invite us to arise to new life: Lord . . .

Responsorial Psalm

"I will praise you, Lord, for you have rescued me."
Psalm 30 is used four times in the Sunday Lectionary (Easter Vigil 4, Third Sunday of Easter C, Tenth Sunday in Ordinary Time C, and Thirteenth Sunday in Ordinary Time B) and each time the readings deal with deliverance from death. The "pit" from which the psalmist is rescued is Sheol, the land of the dead (not the same as our concept of hell). Notice how much of the text is in past tense. The psalmist can rest confident in deliverance yet to come ("with the dawn, rejoicing") because of deliverance already given ("you changed my mourning into dancing").

The first reading tells us that God "did not make death." Rather, it is clear from the actions of Jesus in the Gospel that what God wishes for human beings is the restoration of life. When we sing this psalm, we proclaim our absolute trust in God's promise to rescue us from death.

Model General Intercessions

Presider: God hears us as surely as Jesus heard the plea for healing from Jairus and the woman with the hemorrhage. So we, too, fall humbly at Jesus' feet and pray.

Response:

(musical notation: Lord, hear our prayer.)

Cantor:

(musical notation: we pray to the Lord,)

That the Church be not afraid but just have faith to proclaim Jesus' death and resurrection . . . [pause]

That people of the world not ridicule those who live in faith . . . [pause]

That those whose life is ebbing out from illness or lack of faith be touched by Jesus' presence . . . [pause]

That our community reach out and touch others in need . . . [pause]

Presider: Good and gracious God, you touch those with your presence who open themselves to you in faith: hear these our prayers that we may have life everlasting. We pray through Jesus Christ our Lord. **Amen.**

ALTERNATIVE OPENING PRAYER
Let us pray

Pause for silent prayer

Father in heaven,
the light of Jesus
has scattered the darkness of hatred and sin.
Called to that light
we ask for your guidance.
Form our lives in your truth, our hearts in your love.
We ask this through Christ our Lord.
Amen.

RESPONSORIAL PSALM
[Ps 30:2, 4, 5-6, 11, 12, 13]

℟. (2a) I will praise you, Lord, for you have rescued me.

I will extol you, O Lord, for you drew me clear
    and did not let my enemies rejoice over me.
O Lord, you brought me up from the netherworld;
    you preserved me from among those going down into the pit.

℟. I will praise you, Lord, for you have rescued me.

Sing praise to the Lord, you his faithful ones,
    and give thanks to his holy name.
For his anger lasts but a moment;
    a lifetime, his good will.
At nightfall, weeping enters in,
    but with the dawn, rejoicing.

℟. I will praise you, Lord, for you have rescued me.

Hear, O Lord, and have pity on me;
    O Lord, be my helper.
You changed my mourning into dancing;
    O Lord, my God, forever will I give you thanks.

℟. I will praise you, Lord, for you have rescued me.

FIRST READING
[Wis 1:13-15; 2:23-24]

God did not make death,
   nor does he rejoice in the destruction
     of the living.
For he fashioned all things that they
   might have being;
   and the creatures of the world are
     wholesome,
and there is not a destructive drug
   among them
   nor any domain of the netherworld
     on earth,
for justice is undying.
For God formed man to be
   imperishable;
   the image of his own nature he made
     him.
But by the envy of the devil, death
   entered the world,
   and they who belong to his company
     experience it.

SECOND READING
[2 Cor 8:7, 9, 13-15]

Brothers and sisters:
As you excel in every respect, in faith,
   discourse,
   knowledge, all earnestness, and in the
     love we have for you,
   may you excel in this gracious act
     also.

For you know the gracious act of our
   Lord Jesus Christ,
   that though he was rich, for your sake
     he became poor,
   so that by his poverty you might
     become rich.
Not that others should have relief while
   you are burdened,
   but that as a matter of equality
   your abundance at the present time
     should supply their needs,
   so that their abundance may also
     supply your needs,
   that there may be equality.
As it is written:
   Whoever had much did not have more,
     and whoever had little did not have less.

Catechesis

Cantors
When you sing this psalm you embody the confidence of the entire Body of Christ that God does save you from death, even when the whole world is groaning under its threat. Pray this week for those who are facing death in any form—physical, mental, emotional. Pray that you be a vessel of hope.

Choir
This Sunday is the return to the Sundays in Ordinary Time. How do you, during these summer months, maintain your commitment to your ministry? Perhaps the best way is not to think of these weeks as "down time," but to see them as continued opportunities to deepen your understanding of discipleship and of liturgy.

Music Directors
As you return to the Sundays in Ordinary Time, it is once again important to select a set of service music which fits this season. It might be well to select two sets, one to use from now until the Twenty-third Sunday in Ordinary Time; then a different set beginning on the Twenty-fourth Sunday when the readings already begin to take on a different flavor, moving toward Jerusalem and the cross. Check the music suggestions for the Second Sunday in Ordinary Time for examples of service music especially suitable for this period.

Maintaining your faith in the person and power of Jesus even when you cannot see, hear, or touch him is well-expressed in the familiar hymn "We Walk by Faith," found in most hymnals [both CH and W3 offer a less well-known tune for the text]. DUNLAP'S CREEK [W3] is especially suitable for the entrance because of its strong meter and sweeping melody.

Liturgy Committee
As you live in the tension of the "already but not yet," how do you help the assembly grow in faith and deal with their fear in face of human suffering and death?

Since the Gospel for this Sunday speaks so eloquently of death and life, it might be well to connect it to the Easter season that has recently been completed.

Tuesday is the 4th of July, but it would not be liturgically appropriate to sing patriotic hymns at the Sunday Mass (nor on Tuesday). The reason for this norm is that the music at liturgy must always fit the requirements of the ritual. Furthermore, because the Church is universal and does not belong to any particular culture or country (see EACW, no. 101), it is generally inappropriate to display flags in the sanctuary (although this is permitted on special occasions such as holidays). Praying for one's country is a different matter, however; the second of the general intercessions intentions—for the world, nations, leaders, etc.—indicates that such prayer is always fitting (see GIRM, no. 46b). On Tuesday it would be appropriate to use the opening prayer For the Nation, (State,) or City.

JULY 2, 2000

Fourteenth Sunday in Ordinary Time

FAITH-SHARING
- Is faith a noun for you? a verb? What are the implications of the difference?
- What is necessary to do the work of God?
- Who are your prophets?
- What is the role of the prophet?
- Do you welcome your prophets today?

PRESIDERS
What is prophetic about your ministry? What is it like for you to be a prophet sometimes "without honor" in your own ministry? Who are the prophets that God has sent into your life, and how have you received them?

DEACONS
Faith includes "mighty deeds" on behalf of the kingdom. What is prophetic about your diaconal service? What are the "mighty deeds" you are doing on behalf of the kingdom?

HOSPITALITY MINISTERS
In the Gospel, familiarity blinded some people to the real presence and power of Jesus. As you greet and welcome people, to what does your familiarity blind you?

MUSIC MINISTERS
How does the manner in which you do music reveal the reality of Jesus to the gathered assembly?

ALTAR MINISTERS
The psalmist guides your worship: "Our eyes are fixed on the Lord, pleading for his mercy." How does your service in the sanctuary and elsewhere assist the assembly to fix their eyes on the Lord?

LECTORS
Liturgical familiarity with any ministry often results in less sensitivity and openness to the presence and action of God in Jesus. How might you resist such familiarity with your proclamation of the Scriptures?

EUCHARISTIC MINISTERS
The very routine of weekly Mass can lessen your sensitivity to the "mighty deed" of God which the Eucharist is. How might you resist such loss of sensitivity to the presence of Christ in the bread and wine? in the assembly?

Spirituality

Reflecting on the Gospel

How many of us, at one time or another, have caught ourselves thinking, "Gee, if only I had lived when Jesus lived, seen those miracles, heard his powerful preaching, I would be able to believe more deeply in him. It would be easier. He would be right there." This Sunday's Gospel tells us otherwise. Contemporaries of Jesus *did* see his mighty deeds, did hear him teach and preach, and yet they "took offense at him." Even Jesus "was amazed at their lack of faith." All the miracles, the most eloquent preaching, inspired words of prophets, all the signs in the world won't help us see Jesus for who he really is if we don't have faith.

Faith, by its very nature, isn't something that can be proven. Oh, yes, if we leave faith at the level of doctrine, we might appeal to authorities or try to write logical proofs. The questions asked by the crowd at the synagogue suggest that they were attempting to do this very thing: "Where did this man get all this? What kind of wisdom has been given him?" In other words, they wanted to know who Jesus' teacher was, who his authority was. If his teacher were someone they knew of and respected, they might believe him. (Remember, St. Paul used this tack when he said that he was a disciple of Gamaliel, a respected Pharisee.) As it is, all they can cite about Jesus are familiar details such as his occupation and his relatives. Their questions reveal that they still do not understand who Jesus is, still are not able to accept him as someone from God. They saw but they didn't believe. So they did the natural, human thing: they protected themselves by taking offense.

Jesus' response is word ("A prophet is not without honor except . . . in his own house") and deed ("he was not able to perform any mighty deed there") and strong emotion ("He was amazed at their lack of faith"). The clear rejection of Jesus by the synagogue crowd disabled Jesus from doing God's work in his native place.

It is too easy to dismiss the events of this Sunday's Gospel selection as past history. After all, we like to think, if we had been there and seen those mighty deeds, we would have believed. Really?

Living the Paschal Mystery

To recognize God's prophets among us for who they are, to do the work of God, we must have the faith that conditions us to a receptivity of God's saving presence. Much more than assent to doctrine, faith is a total yes-response to God's words and deeds. Actually, assent to doctrine is the easy part. Much more difficult is the *yes* to enter into the dying and rising Mystery of Christ, God's plan of salvation for us. Our own faith is tested when we are faced in the ordinary circumstances of our lives with the choice to say *yes* and surrender to dying to ourselves. This is easier said than done. For example, when our children need time and direction, are we willing to surrender, even when we are dog tired? Or when a friend needs help, are we willing to surrender, even when we already have crowded schedules? Only by surrendering to these everyday dyings to self can we rise to God's saving new life. Only then do we demonstrate that we really have faith in Jesus.

GOSPEL [Mark 6:1-6; L101B]

Jesus departed from there and came to his native place, accompanied by his disciples. When the sabbath came he began to teach in the synagogue, and many who heard him were astonished. They said, "Where did this man get all this? What kind of wisdom has been given him? What mighty deeds are wrought by his hands! Is he not the carpenter, the son of Mary, and the brother of James and Joses and Judas and Simon? And are not his sisters here with us?" And they took offense at him. Jesus said to them, "A prophet is not without honor except in his native place and among his own kin and in his own house." So he was not able to perform any mighty deed there, apart from curing a few sick people by laying his hands on them. He was amazed at their lack of faith.

Working with the Word

Key words and phrases from the Gospel: Is he not the carpenter?, a prophet, in his own house, lack of faith

Connecting to last Sunday's Gospel: Last Sunday Jairus and the woman with the hemorrhage were filled with faith and this led to their restoration. This Sunday, the lack of faith of the crowd in the synagogue resulted in Jesus being unable to work "any mighty deeds" in his native place.

Connecting to today's culture: An important question in this age of science and consumerism and rigid fundamentalism is, What is faith? According to our tradition, faith is not merely assenting to a body of teaching; it is also an assent to do God's mighty deeds on behalf of others, so the kingdom may be built up (see Jas 2:14-26).

Exegetical points: The astonishment of the hometown crowd recaps the past several Sundays: the "wisdom" of Jesus was evident in the Gospels for the Tenth and Eleventh Sundays in Ordinary Time (omitted this year); his "mighty deeds" were the subject of the Gospels for the Twelfth (also omitted this year) and Thirteenth Sundays. This Sunday, the crowd fails entirely to see Jesus for who he is. They cannot get beyond their familiar categories: "carpenter," "son of Mary," "brother" of their neighbors and friends. If those who should know him best cannot recognize his true identity, little wonder that the religious authorities also fail to understand him and his mission. Rejection by his hometown anticipates rejection by the people, the authorities, and the nation at large. This is the expected lot of the prophet, as the first reading from Ezekiel confirms.

"Astonishment" usually accompanies miracle stories (faith was central to the stories of Jairus' daughter and the woman with the hemorrhage), but the astonishment here leads to scandal and lack of faith with the sad result that he "was not able to perform any mighty deed there."

To the point: Ironically, presumed familiarity leads not to greater openness and receptivity to the presence and action of God in Jesus, but to scandal, rejection, and lack of faith—surely a sobering thought for the Church that claims to be the family of Jesus. The greatest obstacle to building the kingdom of God is the lack of faith.

Celebration

Model Penitential Rite

Presider: Our God raises up prophets among us to lead us to God's house. Let us reflect on our own receptivity to God's presence in others, and ask for the faith to be open to God's mighty deeds of salvation . . . [pause]

    Jesus the carpenter, you labor tirelessly to fashion us into God's holy people: Lord . . .
    Christ the anointed prophet, you teach us words of truth and life: Christ . . .
    Jesus the son of Mary, you nourish our faith: Lord . . .

Responsorial Psalm

"Our eyes are fixed on the Lord, pleading for his mercy."
Perhaps few of us are prophets like Ezekiel or Jesus and find ourselves thrown into intense opposition with hard-hearted persons who resist the message of God. But every one of us is called to the service of the Lord. And every one of us meets hardships, difficulties, opposition as we carry out this mission. This Sunday's psalm invites us to keep our eyes focused on the Lord, who calls us and who supports us in our response.

Model General Intercessions

Presider: God always shows us a willingness to work mighty deeds on our behalf, if only we surrender ourselves to receive God's goodness. And so we pray.

Response:

(musical notation: "Lord, hear our prayer.")

Cantor:

(musical notation: "we pray to the Lord,")

That the Church, the family of Jesus, not take offense at Jesus' mighty deeds but embrace his gift of salvation . . . [pause]

That the world, the family of God, grow in faith and receptivity to God's continued deeds on behalf of all humanity . . . [pause]

That the sick and those lacking faith may recognize Jesus for who he is: the son of God . . . [pause]

That we here gathered may honor the prophets among us . . . [pause]

Presider: Mighty God, you work your deeds of salvation among those who receive you in faith: help our lack of faith and hear these our prayers. We pray through Jesus Christ our Lord. **Amen.**

ALTERNATIVE OPENING PRAYER
Let us pray

Pause for silent prayer

Father,
in the rising of your Son
death gives birth to new life.
The sufferings he endured restored hope
    to a fallen world.
Let sin never ensnare us
with empty promises of passing joy.
Make us one with you always,
so that our joy may be holy,
and our love may give life.
We ask this through Christ our Lord.
    Amen.

RESPONSORIAL PSALM
[Ps 123: 1-2, 2, 3-4]

℟. (2cd) Our eyes are fixed on the Lord, pleading for his mercy.

To you I lift up my eyes
    who are enthroned in heaven—
as the eyes of servants
    are on the hands of their masters.

℟. Our eyes are fixed on the Lord, pleading for his mercy.

As the eyes of a maid
    are on the hands of her mistress,
so are our eyes on the Lord, our God,
    till he have pity on us.

℟. Our eyes are fixed on the Lord, pleading for his mercy.

Have pity on us, O Lord, have pity on us,
    for we are more than sated with contempt;
our souls are more than sated
    with the mockery of the arrogant,
    with the contempt of the proud.

℟. Our eyes are fixed on the Lord, pleading for his mercy.

FIRST READING
[Ezek 2:2-5]

As the LORD spoke to me, the spirit entered into me
 and set me on my feet,
 and I heard the one who was speaking say to me:
Son of man, I am sending you to the Israelites,
 rebels who have rebelled against me;
 they and their ancestors have revolted against me to this very day.
Hard of face and obstinate of heart
 are they to whom I am sending you.
But you shall say to them: Thus says the LORD God!
And whether they heed or resist—for they are a rebellious house—
 they shall know that a prophet has been among them.

SECOND READING
[2 Cor 12:7-10]

Brothers and sisters:
That I, Paul, might not become too elated,
 because of the abundance of the revelations,
 a thorn in the flesh was given to me, an angel of Satan,
 to beat me, to keep me from being too elated.
Three times I begged the Lord about this, that it might leave me,
 but he said to me, "My grace is sufficient for you,
 for power is made perfect in weakness."
I will rather boast most gladly of my weaknesses,
 in order that the power of Christ may dwell with me.
Therefore, I am content with weaknesses, insults,
 hardships, persecutions, and constraints,
 for the sake of Christ;
 for when I am weak, then I am strong.

Catechesis

Cantors
This Sunday's psalm points out that it is not success or failure as a prophet which is important, but fidelity to the mission. What is your mission as cantor? How do you measure your "success"? How do you remain faithful?

Choir
The same question asked of the cantor can be asked of you: what is your mission, and how do you measure your "success"? How does participating in the choir lead you to greater faith and deeper response to the call of God in your life?

Music Directors
Look over your parish repertoire of Gospel acclamations and divide it into three categories: (1) the most festive and elaborate; (2) the less elaborate, yet energetic; (3) the ones whose tempo or style are not really acclamatory. Reserve the first group for festal seasons, use the second group for Ordinary Time, and throw out the third group. In deciding which ones from group two to use during Ordinary Time, narrow your choices. The success of an acclamation is not dependent upon how many variations of it you use, but on how well the assembly knows it and sings. All service music can do its job better if it is repetitive and has had time to become automatic for the assembly.

Liturgy Committee
The temptation is to cancel meetings during the summer months and put liturgy on "automatic pilot." What does this convey to the parish about liturgy? What does this convey about your own attitude about liturgy? How do you keep your "liturgical energy" up throughout the year, giving the proper balance to festive seasons and Ordinary Time?

During these long, hot summer months there is a tendency in many parishes to "go on vacation," so that your liturgies give the impression that they aren't so very important. All too frequently the choir disbands for the summer, the music is decreased, sometimes even the homily is omitted. In these ritual decisions, however, are you not catering more to the cultural rhythm and season than the liturgical? It minimizes the centrality of Ordinary Time by communicating (as contemporary culture does) that only the festal seasons of Christmas and Easter are important. When you do so, you downplay discipleship—the faithful walking with Jesus that is the main thrust of Ordinary Time.

JULY 9, 2000

Fifteenth Sunday in Ordinary Time

FAITH-SHARING
- Do you trust the authority given you as disciples of Jesus?
- Are you aware of what has been given you by sharing in Jesus' mission?
- Has anyone shaken the dust off their feet because you haven't welcomed them or listened?

PRESIDERS
It is tempting to use gimmicks to promote the liturgy or the good news of Jesus. The danger is that people may be entertained or moved emotionally but not really *struck by the Gospel*. Reflect carefully about the differences between gimmicks and the authority that Jesus gives in preaching the kingdom—one that will be welcomed by some and rejected by others.

DEACONS
In what ways is the authority of Jesus manifested through your service in the parish? within your neighborhood and family?

HOSPITALITY MINISTERS
Liturgical hospitality is more than a friendly exchange; it is the beginning of God's summoning the people, as Jesus summoned the Twelve in the Gospel. How might you welcome people with the awareness of gathering them to continue Jesus' mission?

MUSIC MINISTERS
It is so easy to turn music in liturgy in the direction of entertainment or performance. How can you keep it (and yourselves) focused on the mission of Jesus and the kingdom?

ALTAR MINISTERS
Jesus' mission included preaching repentance, expelling demons, healing the sick. When have you attended to these elements outside the sanctuary?

LECTORS
The mission of Jesus is continued whenever you proclaim the Scriptures. However, in what ways do you *live* the Scriptures and, thereby, continue the mission of Jesus?

EUCHARISTIC MINISTERS
Jesus "summoned" the Twelve and "sen[t] them out." How did Jesus summon you to be a Eucharistic minister? What have you witnessed by being sent in the name of Jesus to the infirm?

Spirituality

Reflecting on the Gospel
Marketing is a huge industry in today's consumer-crazed society. The tools of marketing include hype, repetition, acceptance, cleverness, gimmicks, recognition, desirability of product, company name. Clarity and truth aren't exactly priorities. The measure of success for a marketing campaign is tallied by profits, not necessarily by quality of product nor even by customer satisfaction. What a contrast to this Sunday's Gospel!

Jesus would hardly be a good candidate to climb the corporate marketing ladder. Oh, he could have a terrific gimmick if he chose to use it in such a way—after all, he forgives sins and casts out demons and cures illnesses, certainly "products" that are popular and desirable. Jesus has all the tools at hand to make a really big splash. But what does he do?

First, Jesus doesn't keep the action of spreading the good news to himself, but summons the Twelve and shares with them his authority, sending them out "two by two." Two was the minimum number of witnesses required for valid testimony (see Deut 17:6), suggesting that the disciples did not preach and do mighty deeds for their own self-promotion, but only as witnesses to Jesus and his authority.

Second, Jesus doesn't outfit the Twelve in fancy clothes, doesn't give them pedigreed horses or camels or carriages to ride in comfort, doesn't send advance parties to arrange comfortable accommodations. Quite the contrary: the Twelve are instructed to "take nothing," suggesting that the most important matter is the urgency of the mission, the clarity and truth of the message, and that nothing is needed except the authority given.

Third, Jesus instructs the Twelve to accept the first accommodation offered, rather than look around for the most convenient or comfortable. If rejection is met, they are not to become angry or retaliate but are simply to walk away, shaking "the dust off [their] feet."

With such unostentatious traveling gear and instructions, "they went off." And what did the Twelve do? They did what Jesus did: preached, drove out demons, healed. Their only "marketing strategy" was fidelity and witness to the authority given them in and by Jesus Christ.

Two millennia later, if we judge the campaign successful, it is a success based not on profit margins but on clarity and truth of word and sincerity of deed. This is one of the longest continuous marketing campaigns in the history of humanity! This campaign is different from all others; it announces God's kingdom is at hand.

Living the Paschal Mystery
Everything that happened to Jesus is happening in us: we are given the authority to witness to the good news of the coming of God's kingdom and in our witness we meet both acceptance and rejection. Our success is not measured by our acceptance/rejection ratio, but by the integrity of our words and deeds. Our authority is most fruitful when it is borne out by living as Jesus lived. Disciples of Jesus strip themselves of everything except the one thing that counts most: witnessing to the good news of God's reign.

GOSPEL [Mark 6:7-13; L104B]

Jesus summoned the Twelve and began to send them out two by two and gave them authority over unclean spirits. He instructed them to take nothing for the journey but a walking stick—no food, no sack, no money in their belts. They were, however, to wear sandals but not a second tunic. He said to them, "Wherever you enter a house, stay there until you leave. Whatever place does not welcome you or listen to you, leave there and shake the dust off your feet in testimony against them." So they went off and preached repentance. The Twelve drove out many demons, and they anointed with oil many who were sick and cured them.

Working with the Word

Key words and phrases from the Gospel: gave them authority, take nothing, preached repentance, drove out many demons, cured

Connecting to the first reading: Amos was taken from shepherding his flock and sent by God to prophesy. He was rejected and expelled from Bethel. The Twelve were sent out from Jesus and also met some rejection. Both Amos and the Twelve were sent out on the authority of someone else.

Connecting to biblical culture: Itinerant preachers were a staple of ancient life. One has only to look to Paul and his broad-ranging missionary journeys for documentary evidence of the popularity of, and the openness of the culture to, traveling missionaries with a message—as well as news and gossip!—from far-off places.

Exegetical points: According to Mark, the mission of the Church to preach the Gospel has its roots in the ministry and charge of Jesus. The disciples are sent in twos first, because the law requires two witnesses to establish valid testimony (see Deut 17:6; also Matt 26:60-61); and, second, to stress the communitarian aspect of the mission of the Church—life in Christ's community is not a private or personal affair. Their simple traveling gear stresses both the urgency of their task and their sole reliance on God for its effectiveness. This last point is reinforced by the fact that Jesus gives them his authority. It is noteworthy that the disciples do all that Jesus has done so far in the Gospel, and in the same order that Mark has presented it: they preach repentance (cf. Mark 1:14-15), expel demons (Mark 1:23-28), heal the sick (Mark 1:29-31).

To the point: The mission of Jesus continues through the work of his disciples—then and now! Everything that has happened to Jesus is recapitulated in his disciples, including struggle with opposition.

Celebration

Model Penitential Rite

Presider: We gather here in God's house this Sunday to offer our praise and thanksgiving to a God who always welcomes us. Let us prepare ourselves to accept hospitably God's Word and sacrament . . . [pause]

> Lord Jesus, you have authority to heal: Lord . . .
> Christ Jesus, you give us authority to be your disciples: Christ . . .
> Lord Jesus, you send us out to preach repentance and cure the sick: Lord . . .

Responsorial Psalm

"Lord, let us see your kindness, and grant us your salvation."
Like Amos in the first reading, the disciples are ordinary people, not self-appointed prophets. And, like Amos, they are sent on a mission. Jesus sends them two by two and instructs them to take along nothing extra. They won't need it, for they carry the very authority of Jesus himself to cast out demons and to heal the sick. Amos, given authority by God; the disciples, given authority by Jesus—ordinary people endowed with the power of God to overcome evil. This Sunday's psalm is a hymn of confidence in the surety of our salvation.

Model General Intercessions

Presider: We ask God now to hear our prayers and answer them with the same authority that he bestowed on Jesus and on us, his disciples.

Response:

(musical notation: Lord, hear our prayer.)

Cantor:

(musical notation: we pray to the Lord,)

May the Church always use the authority conferred by Jesus to preach the good news, overcome evil, and heal . . . [pause]

May the leaders of the world's nations always exercise authority rather than authoritarianism . . . [pause]

May those who cannot listen to the good news be opened to Jesus' authority . . . [pause]

May we not put anything in our lives ahead of preaching and living the good news of God's reign . . . [pause]

Presider: Good and gracious God, your authority brings forth life and truth: hear these our prayers that we may further your reign. We pray through your Son Jesus Christ our Lord. **Amen.**

OPENING PRAYER
Let us pray

Pause for silent prayer

God our Father,
your light of truth
guides us on the way of Christ.
May all who follow him
reject what is contrary to the gospel.

We ask this through our Lord Jesus
    Christ, your Son,
who lives and reigns with you and the
    Holy Spirit,
one God, for ever and ever. **Amen.**

RESPONSORIAL PSALM
[Ps 85:9-10, 11-12, 13-14]

℟. (8) Lord, let us see your kindness, and grant us your salvation.

I will hear what God proclaims;
    the LORD—for he proclaims peace.
Near indeed is his salvation to those
    who fear him,
    glory dwelling in our land.

℟. Lord, let us see your kindness, and grant us your salvation.

Kindness and truth shall meet;
    justice and peace shall kiss.
Truth shall spring out of the earth,
    and justice shall look down from
        heaven.

℟. Lord, let us see your kindness, and grant us your salvation.

The LORD himself will give his benefits;
    our land shall yield its increase.
Justice shall walk before him,
    and prepare the way of his steps.

℟. Lord, let us see your kindness, and grant us your salvation.

FIRST READING [Amos 7:12-15]

Amaziah, priest of Bethel, said to Amos,
    "Off with you, visionary, flee to the
        land of Judah!
There earn your bread by prophesying,
    but never again prophesy in Bethel;
    for it is the king's sanctuary and a
        royal temple."
Amos answered Amaziah, "I was no
    prophet,
    nor have I belonged to a company of
        prophets;
    I was a shepherd and a dresser of
        sycamores.
The LORD took me from following the
    flock, and said to me,
    Go, prophesy to my people Israel."

SECOND READING
[Eph 1:3-14]

Blessed be the God and Father of our Lord Jesus Christ,
  who has blessed us in Christ with every spiritual blessing in the heavens,
  as he chose us in him, before the foundation of the world,
  to be holy and without blemish before him.
In love he destined us for adoption to himself through Jesus Christ,
  in accord with the favor of his will,
  for the praise of the glory of his grace that he granted us in the beloved.
In him we have redemption by his blood,
  the forgiveness of transgressions,
  in accord with the riches of his grace that he lavished upon us.
In all wisdom and insight, he has made known to us
  the mystery of his will in accord with his favor
  that he set forth in him as a plan for the fullness of times,
  to sum up all things in Christ, in heaven and on earth.

In him we were also chosen,
  destined in accord with the purpose of the One
  who accomplishes all things according to the intention of his will,
  so that we might exist for the praise of his glory,
  we who first hoped in Christ.
In him you also, who have heard the word of truth,
  the gospel of your salvation, and have believed in him,
  were sealed with the promised Holy Spirit,
  which is the first installment of our inheritance
  toward redemption as God's possession, to the praise of his glory.

Catechesis

Cantors
As you prepare this Sunday's psalm, ask yourself, "What is God proclaiming in my life? Do I hear it? What am I proclaiming with my life? Do others hear it?"

Choir
How do you as a choir participate in the mission of Jesus? One way is through the kindness and truth, justice and peace with which you treat one another. Your commitment to living these virtues will affect the quality of your singing.

Music Directors
The verses of Michael Perry's text "How Shall They Hear the Word of God" [W3] are set up in question and answer form. How shall people hear the Gospel? How shall people come to know God's saving action in their lives? Each question is answered with a petition that God bless those engaged in the mission of Christ. The final petition, "So send us, Lord," is the clincher, however, when the singing assembly asks to be the ones sent on the mission. Because each phrase of the text begins on a pick-up beat, the hymn possesses a forward movement which fits the sense of mission about which it speaks. It would work well as a reflection on the Liturgy of the Word during the presentation of the gifts.

Liturgy Committee
It is often tempting to substitute your own creativity and resourcefulness in liturgy preparation rather than trust in God's authority to bring about fruitfulness. Do you let the ritual speak for itself? Do you let the ritual unfold, trusting its authority? It would be good to read and study together the *General Instruction of the Roman Missal,* paying special attention to those paragraphs that uncover the deep theology of liturgy (see especially nos. 6-9).

The second reading for this Sunday has a longer and shorter form. Since the second reading on Sundays in Ordinary Time is a sequential reading not specifically chosen for its relation to the other texts in the Liturgy of the Word, it would be pastorally appropriate to use the shorter form.

JULY 16, 2000

Sixteenth Sunday in Ordinary Time

FAITH-SHARING
- How do you respond to the balance between the needs of others and taking quality time for prayer and rest?
- Do you take time to "report" your ministerial activities to a spiritual director or someone else who can help you discern its fruitfulness?
- What are the qualities of effective shepherding?
- Where do you turn in times of need? Where ought you turn?

PRESIDERS
With regard to *extending* Jesus' shepherding, do people recognize the voice of Jesus in your shepherding? With regard to *receiving* Jesus' shepherding, how can you better balance the "coming and going in great numbers" with the need to rest in a "deserted place"?

DEACONS
What are the parallels between your ministry of service to the Christian community and that of the Good Shepherd?

HOSPITALITY MINISTERS
How is your ministry ultimately one of the care of the good shepherd? What practical shape might this take week after week? At church? In your everyday life?

MUSIC MINISTERS
A great deal of your ministry is teaching—choir members, cantors, other musicians, the assembly. How can you do this with the care and compassion of Jesus?

ALTAR MINISTERS
How might attentive, unobtrusive carrying out of your ministry help other ministers find balance between doing and resting?

LECTORS
How might your heart reaching out to others in care this week help you to proclaim better God's Word?

EUCHARISTIC MINISTERS
The Eucharistic eating and drinking is about communion—with God, with one another. How do you foster "communion" as part of Jesus' shepherding throughout the week?

Spirituality

Reflecting on the Gospel

Last Sunday Jesus sent the Twelve out with the authority to say and do as he had done. In this Sunday's Gospel the disciples return and report what "they had done and taught."

Twice Jesus and the apostles try to go away to a deserted place. The enthusiasm stirred up in the people, however, would not allow these teachers and miracle workers to rest. Word spread and the crowd runs to gather at the deserted place even before the apostles can get there. All of this sets the scene for a further unfolding of the identity of Jesus.

On the one hand, the scene sets up what will come next in chapter 6 of Mark (but is omitted from the Lectionary): the feeding of the five thousand. Probably the apostles had brought food to the deserted place to nourish themselves during their desired rest. But the people, in their haste, had come empty-handed. The compassion Jesus shows for his apostles in suggesting they come away to a deserted place to rest is now transferred to the "vast crowd." He responds by teaching them and (as Mark reports next in his Gospel) by multiplying the loaves and fishes to feed them.

On the other hand, the scene serves as a further revelation of who Jesus is: the shepherd come to gather and guide those who are "like sheep without a shepherd." The first reading from Jeremiah suggests to us that the Gospel is less about the sheep than it is about the faithful shepherd. The unfaithful shepherd misleads and scatters the sheep and does not care for them. The faithful shepherd gathers the sheep until "none [are] missing," cares for them so that they "no longer fear and tremble," sees that they "increase and multiply," and does whatever is needed so that they can "dwell in security." In this Gospel Mark is telling us that these qualities of the faithful shepherd outlined by Jeremiah have come to fulfillment in Jesus.

Sheep are notoriously smelly and dumb. But they are also loyal. Once they are taught the sound of the shepherd's voice, they follow faithfully. We learn the sound of the voice of our Shepherd through the Scriptures. Do we follow equally faithfully?

Living the Paschal Mystery

The Paschal Mystery calls us to enter into the dying and rising rhythm of Jesus and live it out in our everyday circumstances. The only way we can translate this call from theory to actual practice is to learn the voice of the Shepherd, listen to the good news, and follow him faithfully. Like our Shepherd we, too, must be moved to pity for others whom we encounter who seem lost or in need. We, too, must care for others and ease their fear and trembling. We, too, must search for those missing and bring them back to security.

But like the apostles, at times we, too, need to depart to a deserted place to rest. Part of living the rhythm of the Paschal Mystery is to discern when to care for others and when to care for ourselves. This is not always such an easy balance to achieve. So we look to the Good Shepherd to learn when to teach and do good deeds, and when to rest.

Do we learn the voice of our Shepherd? Do we know his voice? Jesus is the one to whom we turn, who invites us to rest, who is moved to pity at our hungers. Do we follow faithfully?

JULY 23, 2000

GOSPEL Mark 6:30-34; L107B]

The apostles gathered together with Jesus and reported all they had done and taught. He said to them, "Come away by yourselves to a deserted place and rest a while." People were coming and going in great numbers, and they had no opportunity even to eat. So they went off in the boat by themselves to a deserted place. People saw them leaving and many came to know about it. They hastened there on foot from all the towns and arrived at the place before them.

When he disembarked and saw the vast crowd, his heart was moved with pity for them, for they were like sheep without a shepherd; and he began to teach them many things.

Working with the Word

Key words and phrases from the Gospel: rest a while, hastened there on foot, moved with pity, like sheep without a shepherd, teach them many things

Connecting to the first reading: When authority is misused the sheep are scattered, driven away, not cared for; the shepherd will be punished. The apostles have been given the authority and modeling of Jesus; their use of it bears the fruit of care.

Connecting to the biblical culture: Sheep and shepherding were part of life in Israel, beginning already when they were nomads in the desert. In Scripture the shepherd became the image for kingship, leadership.

Exegetical points: The Lectionary skips Mark's account of the death of John the Baptist (Mark 6:14-33) and instead picks up the conclusion of the mission of the Twelve which was the subject of last Sunday's Gospel. This is unfortunate because Mark typically inserts (intercalates or "sandwiches") one story into another in order to interpret both in light of each other. In this case, the death of John is framed by the mission of the Twelve, thus stressing two points: (1) the preaching of the Gospel is inexorable and will not be deterred by resistance, rejection, or even by the death of its heralds; and (2) the mission of the Gospel is costly, as John's death poignantly and tragically attests. This close link between the fate of John and the preaching of the word recalls the Third Sunday in Ordinary Time (Mark 1:14-20) where the notice of John's arrest introduces the preaching of Jesus.

The Lectionary's choice from Jeremiah as the first reading puts the focus on the image of the shepherd. Jesus is the Good Shepherd who pities the crowd because they are like sheep without a shepherd. Unlike the self-serving shepherds in Jeremiah's time, Jesus and those he commissions to continue his work are to put the needs of others ahead of even their own need to rest. In the immediate context, Jesus perceives that what the wandering sheep most need is direction, which he supplies by "teaching them many things."

To the point: Even when Jesus' own needs and the immediate needs of his disciples loom, he is still moved with pity for the people; he is still the good shepherd who meets their hunger: he teaches them.

Celebration

Model Penitential Rite

Presider: God is the shepherd who cares for us and brings us back when we stray. Let us reflect on how we have strayed and surrender ourselves to God's love and care . . . [pause]

> Good Shepherd, you invite us to a deserted place to rest a while: Lord . . .
> Compassionate Shepherd, your heart is moved with pity as you gaze upon us: Christ . . .
> Wise Shepherd, you teach us the good news so that we learn your voice: Lord . . .

Responsorial Psalm

"The Lord is my shepherd; there is nothing I shall want."

Psalm 23, perhaps the best known and most loved of all the psalms, uses two metaphors for God: shepherd and host. Both are images of caring, feeding, nurturing, and protecting. The significance of these metaphors is greatly enhanced when we remember that Psalm 23 follows Psalm 22: "My God, my God, why have you forsaken me?"

This Sunday's readings suggest that God never abandons the people. In Jeremiah when the leaders fail to care, God intervenes and calls forth new shepherds (first reading). In the Gospel Jesus *is* the new shepherd, his "heart . . . moved with pity" both for the exhausted apostles and for the crowd that pursues them. When we sing Psalm 23 this Sunday, we express not only our knowledge of who Jesus is but also our absolute confidence in his care for us.

Model General Intercessions

Presider: Our God is a shepherd who cares for us beyond our imagining. Confidently we place our needs in our shepherd's hands.

Response:

[musical notation: Lord, hear our prayer.]

Cantor:

[musical notation: we pray to the Lord,]

That all disciples of Jesus faithfully teach as Jesus did . . . [pause]

That the people of the world have good shepherds to lead and guide them to truth and justice . . . [pause]

That those who are troubled or weary find a refreshing place to rest awhile . . . [pause]

That we are always moved to pity by those who are lost or in need . . . [pause]

Presider: O God, you take care that not one of your flock be lost: hear our prayers that we may rest only in you. We pray through Jesus Christ our Lord. **Amen.**

OPENING PRAYER

Let us pray

Pause for silent prayer

Lord,
be merciful to your people.
Fill us with your gifts
and make us always eager to serve you
in faith, hope, and love.

Grant this through our Lord Jesus
  Christ, your Son,
who lives and reigns with you and the
  Holy Spirit,
one God, for ever and ever. **Amen.**

RESPONSORIAL PSALM

[Ps 23:1-3, 3-4, 5-6]

℟. (1) The Lord is my shepherd; there is nothing I shall want.

The LORD is my shepherd; I shall not
    want.
  In verdant pastures he gives me
    repose;
beside restful waters he leads me;
  he refreshes my soul.

℟. The Lord is my shepherd; there is nothing I shall want.

He guides me in right paths
  for his name's sake.
Even though I walk in the dark valley
  I fear no evil; for you are at my side
with your rod and your staff
  that give me courage.

℟. The Lord is my shepherd; there is nothing I shall want.

You spread the table before me
  in the sight of my foes;
you anoint my head with oil;
  my cup overflows.

℟. The Lord is my shepherd; there is nothing I shall want.

Only goodness and kindness follow me
  all the days of my life;
and I shall dwell in the house of the LORD
  for years to come.

℟. The Lord is my shepherd; there is nothing I shall want.

FIRST READING

[Jer 23:1-6]

Woe to the shepherds
  who mislead and scatter the flock of
    my pasture,
  says the LORD.
Therefore, thus says the LORD, the God
  of Israel,

against the shepherds who shepherd
    my people:
  You have scattered my sheep and
    driven them away.
You have not cared for them,
  but I will take care to punish your evil
    deeds.
I myself will gather the remnant of my
    flock
  from all the lands to which I have
    driven them
  and bring them back to their meadow;
    there they shall increase and multiply.
I will appoint shepherds for them who
    will shepherd them
  so that they need no longer fear and
    tremble;
  and none shall be missing, says the
    LORD.

Behold, the days are coming, says the
    LORD,
  when I will raise up a righteous shoot
    to David;
as king he shall reign and govern wisely,
  he shall do what is just and right in
    the land.
In his days Judah shall be saved,
  Israel shall dwell in security.
This is the name they give him:
  "The LORD our justice."

SECOND READING
[Eph 2:13-18]

Brothers and sisters:
In Christ Jesus you who once were far
    off
  have become near by the blood of
    Christ.

For he is our peace, he who made both
    one
  and broke down the dividing wall of
    enmity, through his flesh,
  abolishing the law with its
    commandments and legal claims,
  that he might create in himself one
    new person in place of the two,
  thus establishing peace,
  and might reconcile both with God,
    in one body, through the cross,
  putting that enmity to death by it.
He came and preached peace to you
    who were far off
  and peace to those who were near,
  for through him we both have access
    in one Spirit to the Father.

Catechesis

Cantors
God promises that there is nothing you shall want. This is a tall order! Do you believe that God will fill it? Do you turn to God with your needs? What is it you want?

Choir
Whenever you feel worn out by the demands which singing in the choir place upon you—weekly rehearsal, always having to come early for Mass, extra practices at Christmas and Easter—remember the compassion with which Jesus looked upon the exhausted apostles in this Sunday's Gospel. He is not unaware of what your fidelity to this ministry costs you. Take time this week to thank Jesus for his shepherding care.

Music Directors
The temptation this Sunday is to use hymns which speak of God as shepherd. Since this is not really "Good Shepherd Sunday" (the Fourth Sunday of Easter is), let the psalm stand alone as the Good Shepherd text, and use hymns which focus on the call to mission which this stretch of Sunday Gospels has been proclaiming.

Numerous settings of Psalm 23 are available. Choose one in which the text shines as the dominant element rather than the music. One of the finest is Gelineau's classic [RS, W3, WC] where the flute-like accompaniment moves in counterpoint with the melody of the psalm tone. Two other good examples are the settings of Angelo della Picca [PC] and Stephen Somerville [CH].

Liturgy Committee
Are the members of the liturgy committee always so caught up in the immediate tasks of liturgy preparation that they never have time for prayer as a group? For a day of recollection? How might such prayer and rest together help improve the functioning of the committee?

Jesus' sensitivity to the apostles' need for rest provides an opportunity for you to reflect on your parish's Sunday observance. Is Sunday a day of rest? What catechesis might you provide to encourage this?

The English translations of this Gospel passage have a problem with pronoun antecedents that leave open its interpretation (the Greek text is equally ambiguous). In v. 31b ("People were coming and going in great numbers, and they had no opportunity to eat") does the "they" refer to the subject of that sentence, "People," or does it parallel the "they" in v. 30b with antecedent "apostles"? If "they" refers to "people," then this sentence sets the Gospel up nicely to lead into the ostensible reason for the multiplication of the loaves. If it refers to the apostles, then it gives a clue for the next verse, which says that "they went off in the boat by themselves to a deserted place." This remains a problem for the Gospel proclaimer, but it is not a good practice to change the text and impose one's own interpretation.

JULY 23, 2000

Seventeenth Sunday in Ordinary Time

FAITH-SHARING
- What are the hungers in your lives (in your parishes? in your cities?) that need your response?
- How might you satisfy those hungers, even with "fragments left over"?
- How does your participation in Eucharist each Sunday call you to be mindful of your need for sustenance on your paschal journey?
- How might your being fed with Eucharist lead you to the kind of believing in Jesus that draws forth from you signs of his presence?

PRESIDERS
What signs does Jesus give you and how does he sustain you on your ministerial paschal journey?

DEACONS
How is your service to the community as a deacon intimately bound up with feeding the hungry?

HOSPITALITY MINISTERS
When faced with human hunger, you can respond either like Philip and Andrew or like Jesus. How might your reception of others be a way of feeding the hungry?

MUSIC MINISTERS
Does the music you use for liturgy truly nourish the life of Christ in your people?

ALTAR MINISTERS
Jesus' "sign" of feeding the five thousand led people to see him as the awaited Prophet who is to come into the world. In what way does your service around the altar "signify" to others that Jesus is the awaited prophet in whom you must believe?

LECTORS
What is the connection between proclaiming God's word and being sustained for the paschal journey? How might you live this journey more faithfully?

EUCHARISTIC MINISTERS
How might paying attention to feeding the hungry enable you to minister the Body of Christ with greater faith?

Spirituality

Reflecting on the Gospel
Over these past Sundays, the Lectionary readings from the Gospel of Mark have been developing certain motifs: the kingdom or reign of God, discipleship, Jesus' authority, growing controversy over who Jesus is. This Sunday we interrupt the in-course reading of Mark's Gospel and insert chapter 6 from John's Gospel, to be proclaimed over five Sundays. John's "Bread of Life Discourse" replaces Mark's account of the multiplication of the loaves and of Jesus' walking on the water.

It is tempting to jump right in and get to what we are most comfortable with regarding Eucharist. But to do so blinds us to all the rich and gradual insights unfolded in the sixth chapter of John's Gospel, which does eventually culminate in Jesus' flesh and blood being true food and drink (see Twentieth Sunday in Ordinary Time).

John begins chapter 6 by setting the scene: the time is Passover, spring of the year when the grass is green and everything is fresh and bursting with new life. A large crowd follows Jesus. Making explicit what Mark only implies, John tells us that the crowd followed because "they saw the signs he was performing." Jesus summons faith from those he forgives and heals, but the crowd exhibits imperfect faith; they believe because of Jesus' signs. Jesus initiates the sequence of events that are to follow by asking Philip about buying food. Philip, too, misses the faith question because he answers Jesus literally, "Two hundred days' wages worth of food would not be enough . . ." Andrew pipes in with a parallel reservation: a boy has five loaves and two fish, "but what are these for so many?" After the people recline, Jesus offers the Jewish *berakah* (blessing) over the food and then *he himself distributes* (in the Synoptic Gospels the disciples distribute) the loaves and fishes, intimating the identity made later in the discourse about *himself* as the bread of life.

Jesus, knowing the people's weak faith, reaches out to them with a sign that they can immediately grasp: he feeds them. Not just a little bit, but "more than they could eat," for at Jesus' direction the disciples gather up twelve baskets of leftovers. Jesus' effort fails, however. Rather than leading the people to deeper faith, this sign merely strengthens their expectation that Jesus be the messiah-king who will restore their earthly power and wealth. Jesus, spurning this kind of kingship, is forced to withdraw from them. The people are a paradigm of what humankind's history repeats over and over. We see signs and interpret them to fit our own expectations. They recognized Jesus as "truly the Prophet," but missed the point of who Jesus really is.

Living the Paschal Mystery
This interruption of Mark, during Ordinary Time, gives us a description of the food that sustains us on *our* paschal journey. This Sunday's Gospel informs us that Jesus is the one who feeds us on the journey—feeds us himself in word (teachings) and deed (sacramental self). No matter how much "dying" we encounter on our journey, Jesus always nourishes us and sustains us if we have eyes to see and believe in the sign he gives. People are hungry. Jesus feeds them. In this sign we know that we are never alone on our journey to eternal life.

JULY 30, 2000

GOSPEL [John 6:1-15; L110B]

Jesus went across the Sea of Galilee. A large crowd followed him, because they saw the signs he was performing on the sick. Jesus went up on the mountain, and there he sat down with his disciples. The Jewish feast of Passover was near. When Jesus raised his eyes and saw that a large crowd was coming to him, he said to Philip, "Where can we buy enough food for them to eat?" He said this to test him, because he himself knew what he was going to do. Philip answered him, "Two hundred days' wages worth of food would not be enough for each of them to have a little." One of his disciples, Andrew, the brother of Simon Peter, said to him, "There is a boy here who has five barley loaves and two fish; but what good are these for so many?" Jesus said, "Have the people recline." Now there was a great deal of grass in that place. So the men reclined, about five thousand in number. Then Jesus took the loaves, gave thanks, and distributed them to those who were reclining, and also as much of the fish as they wanted. When they had had their fill, he said to his disciples, "Gather the fragments left over, so that nothing will be wasted." So they collected them, and filled twelve wicker baskets with fragments from the five barley loaves that had been more than they could eat. When the people saw the sign he had done, they said, "This is truly the Prophet, the one who is to come into the world." Since Jesus knew that they were going to come and carry him off to make him king, he withdrew again to the mountain alone.

Working with the Word

Key words and phrases from the Gospel: signs, food, distributed, gather the fragments left over, nothing will be wasted, withdrew again

Connecting to last Sunday: In the Gospel account this Sunday Jesus himself distributes the food to the hungry; he *is* the shepherd who feeds his flock.

Connecting to our culture: We all experience profound human need in our families, work places, and communities and we respond either like Philip and Andrew or like Jesus. Hunger is *real* in the world today.

Exegetical points: The Lectionary at this point departs from the reading of Mark to take up an important Johannine discourse on the Eucharist that would otherwise not be found in the Sunday cycle of readings. The feeding of the five thousand from John is inserted into the same spot that it occupies in Mark's Gospel, though John develops it at greater length.

The actual recounting of the "sign," as opposed to the theological development of it that occurs in the rest of John 6 (and on Sundays 19, 20, and 21 in Ordinary Time) is at pains to make the connection to Moses and Passover: Jesus ascending the mountain, the explicit mention of "the Jewish feast of Passover," and the reference to grass which is found in the springtime when Passover is celebrated.

Throughout John's Gospel, the evangelist shows many ways in which Jesus either fulfills or supersedes the institutions and feasts of Judaism. Here, Jesus is the promised "prophet like Moses" (Deut 18:15-18; cf. John 6:14), but greater because the "manna" he gives is in fact "living bread" that leads to eternal life. While the Eucharistic elements of this passage are unmistakable (e.g., "he took the bread . . . gave thanks [Greek: *eucharistein*] . . . and distributed" it), the focus is on the miraculous sign that leads people to see in Jesus the fulfillment of the long awaited "Prophet who is to come into the world." For John, the promises and institutions of Judaism are coming to fulfillment in Christ.

To the point: Human hunger is real. The astonishment is that, with God, so little feeds so many—even with leftovers in abundance.

Celebration

Model Penitential Rite

Presider: This Sunday we begin a series of readings from the Bread of Life discourse in John's Gospel. In today's Gospel, Jesus feeds the five thousand with just a few loaves and fish. Let us prepare for hearing God's Word and feasting abundantly at God's Table by emptying ourselves so we can be filled with the abundant food that God offers . . . [pause]

> Lord Jesus, you feed the hungry: Lord . . .
> Christ Jesus, you care for the needy: Christ . . .
> Lord Jesus, you renew us in our communion with you: Lord . . .

Responsorial Psalm

"The hand of the Lord feeds us; he answers all our needs."
Elisha had no doubt that the Lord would feed the people with just a few loaves of bread (first reading). Jesus has no doubt that he will do the same for the hungry crowd facing him (Gospel). In both cases it is the disciples who are skeptical. This Sunday's responsorial psalm is part of Psalm 145, the whole of which is an acrostic, that is, each verse begins in sequence with the next letter of the Hebrew alphabet. The psalm is a hymn of praise for the continuity of God's goodness from the beginning of things to their end. In singing it we share the confidence of Elisha and Jesus that the God who sees hunger will always satisfy it.

Model General Intercessions

Presider: Our God takes little and produces much. We are confident that our simple prayers will be answered in abundance. And so we pray.

Response:

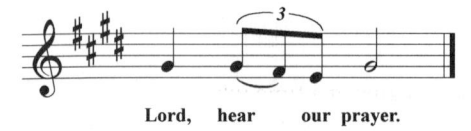

[Musical notation: "Lord, hear our prayer."]

Cantor:

[Musical notation: "we pray to the Lord,"]

That the people of God may believe in the signs of Jesus all around us . . . [pause]

That all people may recognize the Savior who is come into the world . . . [pause]

That the hungry may have their fill . . . [pause]

That our community, the Body of Christ, may be strengthened by the Eucharist on our paschal journey . . . [pause]

Presider: O God of abundance, you fill those who hunger: hear these our prayers that all may be filled and nothing will be wasted. We pray through Jesus Christ our Lord. **Amen.**

ALTERNATIVE OPENING PRAYER
Let us pray
> [for the faith to recognize God's presence in our world]

Pause for silent prayer

God our Father,
open our eyes to see your hand at work
in the splendor of creation,
in the beauty of human life.
Touched by your hand our world is holy.
Help us to cherish the gifts that surround us,
to share your blessings with our brothers and sisters,
and to experience the joy of life in your presence.
We ask this through Christ our Lord.
Amen.

RESPONSORIAL PSALM
[Ps 145:10-11, 15-16, 17-18]

℟. (cf. 16) The hand of the Lord feeds us; he answers all our needs.

Let all your works give you thanks, O Lord,
and let your faithful ones bless you.
Let them discourse of the glory of your kingdom
and speak of your might.

℟. The hand of the Lord feeds us; he answers all our needs.

The eyes of all look hopefully to you,
and you give them their food in due season;
you open your hand
and satisfy the desire of every living thing.

℟. The hand of the Lord feeds us; he answers all our needs.

The Lord is just in all his ways
and holy in all his works.
The Lord is near to all who call upon him,
to all who call upon him in truth.

℟. The hand of the Lord feeds us; he answers all our needs.

FIRST READING
[2 Kgs 4:42-44]

A man came from Baal-shalishah
　bringing to Elisha, the man of God,
　twenty barley loaves made from the
　　firstfruits,
　and fresh grain in the ear.
Elisha said, "Give it to the people to
　eat."
But his servant objected,
　"How can I set this before a hundred
　　people?"
Elisha insisted, "Give it to the people to
　eat.
For thus says the LORD,
　'They shall eat and there shall be
　　some left over.'"
And when they had eaten, there was
　some left over,
　as the LORD had said.

SECOND READING
[Eph 4:1-6]

Brothers and sisters:
I, a prisoner for the Lord,
　urge you to live in a manner worthy
　　of the call you have received,
　with all humility and gentleness, with
　　patience,
　bearing with one another through
　　love,
　striving to preserve the unity of the
　　spirit through the bond of peace:
　one body and one Spirit,
　as you were also called to the one
　　hope of your call;
　one Lord, one faith, one baptism;
　one God and Father of all,
　who is over all and through all and in
　　all.

Catechesis

Cantors

This Sunday's psalm invites you not only to remember that God feeds you, but also to reflect on what it is for which you hunger. What desires *does* God satisfy? What do you desire? So that you can sing this psalm with confidence, pray this week for greater integrity between what you seek and what God wishes.

Choir

Use the psalm refrain as a response to a litany of petitions to end choir rehearsal this week. Invite the choir to offer spontaneous petitions for those who hunger: for food, for justice, for acceptance, for freedom, for equality, etc. Pray for the world, for your parish, for your families.

Music Directors

A perfect hymn for Communion this Sunday is Kreutz/Westendorf's "Gift of Finest Wheat" ["You Satisfy the Hungry Heart"], found in all major hymnbooks. Kreutz' SATB arrangement is available as an octavo from OCP [#8005CC]. OCP also includes it in *Choral Praise* [9093GC] in both 4- and 2-part versions. GIA publishes a concertato by John Ferguson [G-3089]. Verses 1, 3, and 5 are SATB. Verses 2 and 4 are unison with organ doubling the melody in the pedal and manuals playing open chords in counterpoint on flute or string stops. It can be used without pedal, keeping strings on both manuals, with a flutist doubling the melody.

Liturgy Committee

This may be a good time to assess your personal and communal understanding of Eucharist and grow in its meaning for your Sunday celebrations as well as for your daily living. What is the connection between the action you do each Sunday and your identity as Body of Christ? How can you help your assembly to understand that on Sunday they are fed for their daily paschal journey?

　This important sequence of Gospels begins at a time when many people are not present (end of July, August: last vacation efforts). You must be careful not to slacken in your Sunday preparations. These Sundays afford you an excellent opportunity to insert some catechetical material into the homilies, but since these readings from John 6 cover a number of weeks be careful about moving too quickly to Eucharistic theology (even though this Sunday's Gospel does make explicit three of the four-fold traditional Eucharistic actions: take, bless [give thanks], break, and give [distribute]). This is a wonderful time to stress the reality of the paschal journey (walking with Jesus toward Jerusalem), and that no one is ever alone on this journey. Jesus gives signs along the way to intensify belief in him and the most sublime Food to sustain those on the journey.

　There may be a temptation during these Sundays when John's Bread of Life discourse is read to "decorate" the sacred space with a Eucharistic motif. Remember, it is Ordinary Time; the thrust of these Gospels is that you are on a paschal journey toward Jerusalem and learning the cost (and fruits) of that journey.

JULY 30, 2000

The Transfiguration of the Lord

FAITH-SHARING
- When do you have glimpses of Jesus' sovereign majesty? glory?
- How do these glimpses sustain you in the scandal of the cross?
- What does it mean to say that Jesus is transfigured? What does this mean for you?
- How well do you listen to God's voice?

PRESIDERS
When natural demands and frustrations make ministry discouraging, it might be well to recall this Gospel. How might you set time aside to glimpse Jesus' (and your) glorification so that you are encouraged?

DEACONS
How do your glimpses of glory empower you to serve? How do they bring balance to the cost of discipleship?

HOSPITALITY MINISTERS
Part of the experience of Jesus' glory is in Peter's words: "Rabbi, it is good that we are here!" How does your hospitality move you toward the glory of being gathered with God's chosen people?

MUSIC MINISTERS
Music more than any other act can transform the human heart. How does the music you choose for liturgy transform the assembly into showing the glory of Christ?

ALTAR MINISTERS
The Eucharistic liturgy mirrors, reflects, enables all to participate in the glorious kingship of Christ where "myriads upon myriads attend him." How does your liturgical service embody this transcendent glory in which you already participate?

LECTORS
How does your listening to Jesus, the beloved Son, in the Word help you to proclaim the Word with more conviction?

EUCHARISTIC MINISTERS
The Gospel reminds you that a wonderful posture before Jesus is one of listening. How well and frequently do you listen to the same Lord whom you give to your brothers and sisters in Communion?

Spirituality

Reflecting on the Gospel

Twice during the liturgical year (excluding the daily Lectionary), we hear proclaimed the transfiguration event, on the Second Sunday of Lent and on this Sunday's feast of the transfiguration. During Lent this Gospel stands in contrast to the First Sunday of Lent on which we proclaim Jesus' temptation in the wilderness. The contrast is between temptation and human weakness, on the one hand, and victory and glory, on the other hand. On August 6 this Gospel stands in contrast to our journey during Ordinary Time. The contrast is between our awakening to discipleship and its costs, on the one hand, and victory and glory, on the other hand. This feast is a splendid embodiment of the rhythm of the Paschal Mystery, a rhythm of dying and rising, of abasement and glory. Other contrasts between the cost of discipleship and glory mark the account.

Jesus takes Peter, James, and John and they ascend "a high mountain" (a place for theophanies, for God to be manifested and encountered), in contrast to their descent at the conclusion of the account (down the mountain, to the ordinary places of living and being where the cost of discipleship always shows its face). Present at Jesus' glorification are Elijah and Moses (from the old dispensation with its messianic expectation and the reminder that Law and prophets guide us in our journey toward God) and Jesus' three apostles (from the new dispensation with its messianic fulfillment and its glimpses of glory).

In this Sunday's Gospel we get a glimpse of what glory awaits us when we "listen to" Jesus. Even as we struggle to listen, to overcome our own human weakness and sinfulness as we plod along on our paschal journey, we already see the glory that awaits us. We are encouraged to embrace the cross of discipleship because we already know the promise of resurrection. The three apostles questioned "what rising from the dead meant." We already know. It means life.

Living the Paschal Mystery

Normally we do everything we can to avoid hardships. The road to glory, however, is not an easy one. The Paschal Mystery, paradoxically, tells us that the only way to have life is to surrender to dying.

Jesus' transfigured glory foreshadows his glorious resurrection, a new life that was his because he faithfully did the will of his Father, even to the point of suffering and ignominious dying. If we wish to share in this same transfigured glory, we must be equally faithful in surrendering our wills to God's will, to living the Gospel. The transfiguration of Jesus tells us that the kingdom of God is already here. We help establish that kingdom when we die to self and rise with Christ in glory.

The cost of discipleship is not something we would naturally embrace. This Gospel motivates us to be disciples because we already see what becomes of the faithful disciple: he or she is transfigured into glory. The challenge to our everyday living is that our life be transfigured (transformed) so that when people see us, they see Jesus.

AUGUST 6, 2000

GOSPEL [Mark 9:2-10; L614B]

Jesus took Peter, James, and John and led them up a high mountain apart by themselves. And he was transfigured before them, and his clothes became dazzling white, such as no fuller on earth could bleach them. Then Elijah appeared to them along with Moses, and they were conversing with Jesus. Then Peter said to Jesus in reply, "Rabbi, it is good that we are here! Let us make three tents: one for you, one for Moses, and one for Elijah." He hardly knew what to say, they were so terrified. Then a cloud came, casting a shadow over them; from the cloud came a voice, "This is my beloved Son. Listen to him." Suddenly, looking around, they no longer saw anyone but Jesus alone with them.

As they were coming down from the mountain, he charged them not to relate what they had seen to anyone, except when the Son of Man had risen from the dead. So they kept the matter to themselves, questioning what rising from the dead meant.

Working with the Word

Key words and phrases from the Gospel: This is my beloved Son, listen to him, saw [no one] but Jesus alone with them

Connecting to baptism: At Jesus' baptism in Mark's Gospel, only he hears God's voice; now, Jesus' relationship to God (beloved Son) is revealed to his disciples and we are to "listen to him."

Connecting to our culture: Movie buffs are familiar with a special effects technique known as "morphing," an effect usually achieved by computer manipulation of a figure in which one character is changed into another. The Greek word for "transfiguration" is actually "metamorphosis," i.e., to change form.

Exegetical points: Just as Moses and Elijah had encountered the living God on the mountain top (Sinai/Horeb) and there heard God's voice, Jesus, too, comes to the mountain top where God is revealed in vision and voice. The difference is that the glory which is God's at Sinai is here revealed as the glory of Jesus.

The presence of Elijah and Moses is variously interpreted. One option is that together they represent the fullness of divine revelation in the Law (Moses) and the prophets (Elijah). Alternately, Jesus is shown to be the fulfillment of prophecies: Jesus is the Messiah whose way is prepared by Elijah (Mal 4:1-6) and he is the one whom God raises up to be a prophet like Moses (Deut 18:15). The opening prayer for this feast tends toward this latter option in which the transfiguration "confirm[s] the witness of your prophets."

In the transfiguration, the voice from the cloud announces to the apostles that Jesus is God's beloved Son. This recalls the same announcement God made to Jesus at his baptism (Mark 1:9-11) and it anticipates the announcement by the Roman centurion at the foot of the cross which is the final, climactic, and complete statement of Jesus' true identity as revealed by his suffering and death (Mark 15:39).

To the point: As we listen to Jesus, the beloved Son of God, we will receive glimpses of his glory to sustain us on our journey of discipleship and remind us of our own awaited glory.

Celebration

Model Penitential Rite

Presider: Our Lord was revealed in all his glory to Peter, James, and John on the mountain. Let us open ourselves to God's revelation to each of us this day . . . [pause]

> Lord Jesus, you have received dominion, glory, and kingship: Lord . . .
> Christ Jesus, you are the fulfillment of the Law and Prophets: Christ . . .
> Lord Jesus, you are the beloved Son of God to whom we listen: Lord . . .

Responsorial Psalm

"The Lord is king, the Most High over all the earth."
Psalm 97 was an enthronement psalm sung by the Hebrew community to celebrate God's kingship. In the first reading Daniel describes the coming of the One who is to be king. In the Gospel Jesus shines with the same brightness and glory. He is, moreover, not only king but God's beloved Son. This psalm is an expression of our belief in the identity of Jesus.

Model General Intercessions

Presider: God desires that we all share in the Son's glory and so we are confident that God lifts up all those in need. Let us pray.

Response:

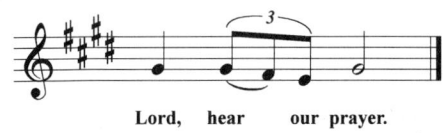

[Musical notation: "Lord, hear our prayer."]

Cantor:

[Musical notation: "we pray to the Lord,"]

Listening to the beloved Son, may the Church prepare for the glory that awaits all God's faithful . . . [pause]

Listening to the beloved Son, may the people of God proclaim the glory of what they have seen to all peoples . . . [pause]

Listening to the beloved Son, may the lowly and downtrodden be lifted up . . . [pause]

Listening to the beloved Son, may we be unafraid to speak the good news of Jesus' dying and rising and accept the cost of discipleship . . . [pause]

Presider: O glorious God, you hear the voices of all those who call to you: hear these our prayers and answer them so that all may be glorified in you. We pray through Jesus Christ our Lord. **Amen.**

OPENING PRAYER

Let us pray
  [that we may hear the Lord Jesus and share his everlasting life]

Pause for silent prayer

God our Father,
in the transfigured glory of Christ your Son,
you strengthen our faith
by confirming the witness of your prophets,
and show us the splendor of your beloved sons and daughters.
As we listen to the voice of your Son,
help us to become heirs to eternal life with him
who lives and reigns with you and the Holy Spirit,
one God, for ever and ever. **Amen.**

RESPONSORIAL PSALM
[Ps 97:1-2, 5-6, 9]

℟. (1a, 9a) The Lord is king, the Most High over all the earth.

The LORD is king; let the earth rejoice;
  let the many islands be glad.
Clouds and darkness are round about him;
  justice and judgment are the foundation of his throne.

℟. The Lord is king, the Most High over all the earth.

The mountains melt like wax before the LORD,
  before the LORD of all the earth.
The heavens proclaim his justice;
  all peoples see his glory.

℟. The Lord is king, the Most High over all the earth.

Because you, O LORD, are the Most High over all the earth,
  exalted far above all gods.

℟. The Lord is king, the Most High over all the earth.

FIRST READING [Dan 7:9-10, 13-14]

As I watched:
　Thrones were set up
　　and the Ancient One took his throne.
　His clothing was snow bright,
　　and the hair on his head as white as
　　　wool;
　his throne was flames of fire,
　　with wheels of burning fire.
　A surging stream of fire
　　flowed out from where he sat;
　thousands upon thousands were
　　ministering to him,
　and myriads upon myriads
　　attended him.
The court was convened and the books
　were opened.

As the visions during the night
　continued, I saw
　one like a Son of man coming,
　　on the clouds of heaven;
　when he reached the Ancient One
　　and was presented before him,
　the one like a Son of man received
　　dominion, glory, and kingship;
　all peoples, nations, and languages
　　serve him.
　His dominion is an everlasting
　　dominion
　　that shall not be taken away,
　　his kingship shall not be destroyed.

SECOND READING [2 Pet 1:16-19]

Beloved:
We did not follow cleverly devised
　myths
　when we made known to you
　the power and coming of our Lord
　　Jesus Christ,
　but we had been eyewitnesses of his
　　majesty.
For he received honor and glory from
　God the Father
　when that unique declaration came to
　　him from the majestic glory,
　"This is my Son, my beloved, with
　　whom I am well pleased."
We ourselves heard this voice come
　from heaven
　while we were with him on the holy
　　mountain.
Moreover, we possess the prophetic
　message that is altogether reliable.
You will do well to be attentive to it,
　as to a lamp shining in a dark place,
　until day dawns and the morning star
　rises in your hearts.

*C*atechesis

Cantors
When you sing this psalm you proclaim the absolute rule of God. You stand, as it were, on the mountaintop and see God's victory of justice in every corner of the world. Sing with conviction and joy!

Choir
Through your baptism you are one with Christ. You, too, are beloved sons and daughters of God. This week look with transfigured eyes at the faces of one another, and say, "It is good to be here!"

Music Directors
Since this is a feast of the Lord, sing the festive service music you use for Easter season. Do a long Gospel procession with extended verses.

Most hymnbooks include songs specific to the Transfiguration; for example, "O Light of Light, Love Given Birth" [CBW3], "Tis Good, Lord, to Be Here" [CH, RS, W3], "Transform Us" [RS], "O Wondrous Type! O Vision Faith" [CH]. Hymns for Christ the King, such as "Jesus Shall Reign" and "Rejoice the Lord Is King" would also fit this dominical feast.

Liturgy Committee
How does your committee's preparations and planning balance the transcendence of God's glory with the immanence of Jesus' ministry and presence through his disciples?

Solemnities and feasts of the Lord replace Sundays in Ordinary Time. The origins of this feast date to about the fifth century in the Eastern Church and the tenth century in the West. It was added to the calendar of the universal Church in the sixteenth century to mark the victory of St. John Capistrano and John Hunyadi over the Turks.

As with all solemnities and feasts, the second reading, in this case from 2 Peter, is chosen to fit with the first reading and Gospel. Often it clarifies the richness and depth of the solemnity or feast.

The placement of this account in Mark's Gospel immediately after the first prediction of the passion (8:27-35) is well explained in the preface for this feast: "He revealed his glory to the disciples to strengthen them for the scandal of the cross."

This feast calls for the color white and a more festive environment. It would be appropriate to visually tie the sacred space to Easter.

AUGUST 6, 2000

Nineteenth Sunday in Ordinary Time

FAITH-SHARING
- What causes you to murmur? Even more, do you ever (when?) find yourself saying, "Enough!"?
- During these times, how does Jesus' teaching become the food that sustains you?
- What might you do to increase your faith in the Word as the bread of life?
- How do you live out your belief that there is no knowledge of God apart from Jesus?

PRESIDERS
Sometimes, like Elijah, you might say to God, "This is enough, O Lord!" What is the Word from heaven that feeds you through the difficult times? How might your reflection assist you in preaching the good news of Jesus as the bread of life?

DEACONS
In the book of Kings the Lord orders Elijah, "Get up and eat, else the journey will be too long for you!" What food from the Lord do you need, lest the journey be "too long for you"?

HOSPITALITY MINISTERS
How is treating others as the body of Christ really at the heart of your ministry? How might your speaking hospitable words bring others to belief?

MUSIC MINISTERS
How is your preparing and leading music in worship a source of sustenance for you in your journey of discipleship? Is it ever a drudgery? When?

ALTAR MINISTERS
How does your prayer over God's word have an impact on your service in daily life? in the sanctuary?

LECTORS
How has your ministry as lector had an impact on your appreciation for and belief in the word of Jesus? How does this help draw you closer to eternal life?

EUCHARISTIC MINISTERS
How might your ministering the Eucharistic Bread draw others to a more belief-filled *Amen!* ? When you *show* the Eucharistic bread to a communicant, do you look through the bread to the person and really *believe* that both bread and person are Body of Christ? Is this the same belief that you have in the word?

Spirituality

Reflecting on the Gospel
This Sunday's Gospel opens with some Jews murmuring because Jesus claimed to be the "bread that came down from heaven." In next Sunday's Gospel, this bread from heaven will clearly refer to the Eucharistic bread. But let's not hurry too quickly to this kind of sacramental interpretation of the Gospel. This Sunday Jesus relates the bread of heaven to what is taught and believed.

The peoples' murmuring and their practical objection to Jesus' claim to be from heaven (they "know his father and mother") shows they have completely misunderstood the purpose of the multiplication of loaves. They move the discussion from what God offers from heaven to what they know to be true on earth. Jesus answers their misunderstanding and unbelief with a monologue in which he teaches that when we seek the "desert manna," we die. The true bread that comes down from heaven gives life, but does so only when we surrender ourselves in belief.

The "bread of life" (v. 48), then, also refers to what is taught and is to be believed: that there is no knowledge of the Father apart from Jesus; that Jesus is the revealer of the Father; that belief brings eternal life. The *word* is bread/food that sustains us on our journey and "whoever *believes* has eternal life." There is no easy road to eternal life. The multiplication of the loaves wasn't simply to *feed* the multitude; it was a sign meant to call forth *belief* in what they have been taught.

The plight of Elijah in the first reading sheds further light on the relationship of belief and bread. Elijah is the last of the prophets in his day; all others have been killed. The burden of being the last to announce God's message is overpowering. Elijah begs to die: "This is enough, O Lord!" It is God who gives Elijah bread for the journey to Horeb where the prophet encounters God. We, in turn, encounter God in Jesus. One kind of bread that sustains us on our journey is the good news taught by Jesus. When we believe—"eat" this "bread"—we also encounter God.

The way to the Father and to eternal life is through Jesus. This is why he is the bread of life. In this Gospel, belief, bread, and life all converge in the person Jesus.

Living the Paschal Mystery
Sometimes our dying to self can lead us, like Elijah, to say "Enough; take my life!" We need a bread that revives us and keeps us from despair. Jesus' words of life bring us such hope and strength.

Living the Paschal Mystery doesn't mean that our life unfolds on a simple, straight path to eternal life. Spiritual growth includes vicissitudes of ups and downs, risings and dyings, "not yets" and "alreadys," that are natural to the very rhythm of the Mystery itself. Our challenge is not to get discouraged, but to hand ourselves over to the nourishment of word and sacrament that God offers, a nourishment that carries us on our life's journey toward eternal life.

GOSPEL [John 6:41-51; L116B]

The Jews murmured about Jesus because he said, "I am the bread that came down from heaven," and they said, "Is this not Jesus, the son of Joseph? Do we not know his father and mother? Then how can he say, 'I have come down from heaven'?" Jesus answered and said to them, "Stop murmuring among yourselves. No one can come to me unless the Father who sent me draw him, and I will raise him on the last day. It is written in the prophets: *They shall all be taught by God.* Everyone who listens to my Father and learns from him comes to me. Not that anyone has seen the Father except the one who is from God; he has seen the Father. Amen, amen, I say to you, whoever believes has eternal life. I am the bread of life. Your ancestors ate the manna in the desert, but they died; this is the bread that comes down from heaven so that one may eat it and not die. I am the living bread that came down from heaven; whoever eats this bread will live forever; and the bread that I will give is my flesh for the life of the world."

Working with the Word

Key words and phrases from the Gospel: murmured, bread that came down from heaven, whoever believes has eternal life, bread of life

Connecting to the first reading: The miraculous provision of bread in the wilderness sustains Elijah's physical life for the journey to Horeb, the mountain of God. "Horeb" is another name for Sinai, the place where Moses encountered the living God in the burning bush and where he received the Decalogue. The bread Jesus' teaching provides sustains believers on the journey unto eternal life, the "new" Mt. Horeb.

Connecting to today's culture: Many people today experience plenty of weariness on the journey: family life, jobs, commitments, etc. There is much evidence that people have had enough: prozac, road rage, violence. Jesus as word and sacrament offers us an alternative.

Exegetical points: The feast of the transfiguration last Sunday preempted St. John's discourse on the Bread of Life in which Jesus compares the bread he provides to the manna God provided for the Hebrews in their wilderness journey. He further identifies himself as the living bread come down from heaven. This Sunday's Gospel picks up at that point, with the Jews wondering how this is possible. John's comment, "the Jews murmured about him," deliberately recalls the "murmuring" of the Hebrews in the wilderness with the lack of food and then their discontent with having nothing but manna (Exod 16:2-7; Num 11:4-6, 14:2). "Murmuring" in those traditions is tantamount to rebelling against Moses and God. The murmuring in John both recalls the Old Testament Traditions and anticipates the later rejection of Jesus by some of his followers; refusal to believe leads to darkness and death. By contrast, "those who believe have eternal life" and "those who eat this bread . . . will live forever."

To the point: Jesus offers the food of his teaching as well as his own flesh for the journey of life and unto life.

Celebration

Model Penitential Rite

Presider: Our God nourishes us with Word and Sacrament. Let us place ourselves in the divine presence and ask God to strengthen us in our belief . . . [pause]

> Lord Jesus, you are the word that comes down from heaven: Lord . . .
> Christ Jesus, you lead us to the Father when we listen to you: Christ . . .
> Lord Jesus, you are the bread that sustains us on our journey: Lord . . .

Responsorial Psalm

"Taste and see the goodness of the Lord."

For the next three Sundays while the Bread of Life discourse from John continues, we will sing parts of Psalm 34 as the responsorial psalm. The obvious reason for the choice of this psalm is the verse which is used as the refrain, "Taste and see the goodness of the Lord."

When Elijah in the desert has despaired of life, an angel comes with food to revitalize him (first reading). In the Gospel Jesus tells us that this food from heaven, his "bread of life," is none other than himself. Like Elijah, we can continue the difficult journey of discipleship because we are being fed by the very goodness of Christ himself.

Model General Intercessions

Presider: Just as God sent down bread from heaven for the Hebrews in the wilderness, so God will respond to us in all our needs. And so we pray.

Response:

(musical notation: "Lord, hear our prayer.")

Cantor:

(musical notation: "we pray to the Lord,")

That the Church may live out its belief that Jesus reveals the Father through the Body of Christ . . . [pause]

That the world may share its abundant bread with the hungry . . . [pause]

That those who murmur may believe in Jesus as the One sent down from heaven so that all might have eternal life . . . [pause]

That we may believe more fully that the Father draws us into divine life through Christ . . . [pause]

Presider: O God, you sent manna in the desert and you sent your Son to dwell among us so that all might live forever: hear these our prayers, that we might be drawn more closely to you. We pray through your Son Jesus Christ our Lord. Amen.

ALTERNATIVE OPENING PRAYER

Let us pray
  [that through us others may find the way to life in Christ]

Pause for silent prayer

Father,
we come, reborn in the Spirit,
to celebrate our sonship in the Lord Jesus Christ.
Touch our hearts,
help them grow toward the life you have promised.
Touch our lives,
make them signs of your love for all men.
Grant this through Christ our Lord.
Amen.

RESPONSORIAL PSALM

[Ps 34:2-3, 4-5, 6-7, 8-9]

℟. (9a) Taste and see the goodness of the Lord.

I will bless the LORD at all times;
  his praise shall be ever in my mouth.
Let my soul glory in the LORD;
  the lowly will hear me and be glad.

℟. Taste and see the goodness of the Lord.

Glorify the LORD with me,
  let us together extol his name.
I sought the LORD, and he answered me
  and delivered me from all my fears.

℟. Taste and see the goodness of the Lord.

Look to him that you may be radiant with joy,
  and your faces may not blush with shame.
When the afflicted man called out, the LORD heard,
  and from all his distress he saved him.

℟. Taste and see the goodness of the Lord.

The angel of the LORD encamps around those who fear him and delivers them.
Taste and see how good the LORD is;
  blessed the man who takes refuge in him.

℟. Taste and see the goodness of the Lord.

FIRST READING
[1Kgs 19:4-8]

Elijah went a day's journey into the desert,
　until he came to a broom tree and sat beneath it.
He prayed for death, saying:
　"This is enough, O LORD!
Take my life, for I am no better than my fathers."
He lay down and fell asleep under the broom tree,
　but then an angel touched him and ordered him to get up and eat.
Elijah looked and there at his head was a hearth cake
　and a jug of water.
After he ate and drank, he lay down again,
　but the angel of the LORD came back a second time,
　touched him, and ordered,
　"Get up and eat, else the journey will be too long for you!"
He got up, ate, and drank;
　then strengthened by that food,
　he walked forty days and forty nights to the mountain of God, Horeb.

SECOND READING
[Eph 4:30–5:2]

Brothers and sisters:
Do not grieve the Holy Spirit of God,
　with which you were sealed for the day of redemption.
All bitterness, fury, anger, shouting, and reviling
　must be removed from you, along with all malice.
And be kind to one another, compassionate,
　forgiving one another as God has forgiven you in Christ.

So be imitators of God, as beloved children, and live in love,
　as Christ loved us and handed himself over for us
　as a sacrificial offering to God for a fragrant aroma.

Catechesis

Cantors
The journey of discipleship is long and difficult. But God constantly surprises you with new nourishment right at the moment when you are most depleted and discouraged. You can sing with confidence in the goodness of this God who always feeds you. Take time this week to recognize the many ways God nourishes you.

Choir
Even persons who faithfully participate in Sunday Eucharist sometimes struggle with their faith in Jesus. You help them not so much by what you sing as by the fidelity of your prayerful presence at liturgy. How can you sustain your prayerful presence?

Music Directors
The bread of life Jesus speaks about in this Sunday's Gospel is his word, his teaching, which sustains those on the way to eternal life. One hymn text which expresses this idea is "Shepherd of Souls, [Refresh and Bless]" [BB, CH, W3, WC], especially in v. 2, "We would not live by bread alone, But by your word of grace, In strength of which we travel on . . ." This hymn could be used for either the entrance procession or at the presentation of the gifts. If used for the entrance, play it with a slightly detached rhythm that emphasizes the downbeats. If used for the presentation of the gifts, broaden the tempo and play in a smoother, more contemplative style. "I Received the Living God" [RS, W3, WC] would be a fitting Communion hymn because it speaks about receiving Jesus not only as bread, but also as way, truth, life.

Liturgy Committee
If the Word is truly "bread from heaven," then you ought not hurry the Liturgy of the Word. How might you enhance listening by moments of silence at the proclamation of the word?

　The *General Instruction of the Roman Missal* (no. 8) makes quite clear that the Liturgy of the Word is not simply a preamble to the Liturgy of the Eucharist, but they are "two parts so closely connected that they form but one single act of worship." It is good occasionally to evaluate the relationship of the Liturgy of the Word and the Liturgy of the Eucharist so that both are celebrated as equally important. Sufficient time and care must be taken in preparing the Liturgy of the Word and its ritual celebration.

AUGUST 13, 2000

Assumption of the Blessed Virgin Mary

Spirituality

Reflecting on the Gospel

From a fifth-century lectionary we have readings listed for an August 15 celebration of Mary the Mother of God. It soon came to be regarded as a festival honoring her "birth"; that is, her death and entry into eternal life. The Gospel selected for this solemnity was that of the visitation of Mary to her cousin Elizabeth—as we have now for this solemnity of the Assumption of the Blessed Virgin Mary. This Gospel underscores Elizabeth's and Mary's participation in God's plan to save us, John's relationship to Jesus, and—especially important for this festival of the assumption—it suggests to us that Mary's song of praise begun here on earth is continued in heaven.

Two women giving birth to sons because of miraculous events are at the heart of Luke's account of the dawning of salvation. This Gospel points out some interesting things about these women. Mary "set out" for the hill country "in haste." Her journey somewhat parallels our own journey through Ordinary Time; we both are seeking a sign of the marvelous things God is accomplishing. Mary stays for "about three months." We might conjecture that Luke has her leaving *before* John was born for a reason, or surely she would have stayed longer and helped her aged cousin with the newborn. Thus, Luke is saying that the purpose of Mary's visit was not primarily charitable and pragmatic—helping the pregnant Elizabeth. Instead these women received an insight into God's plan. Elizabeth is "filled with the Holy Spirit." The infant in her womb "leaped for joy" at hearing Mary's greeting. Elizabeth identifies the new life in Mary's womb as "my Lord," and she recognizes Mary as a believer—"blessed are you who believed that what was spoken to you by the Lord would be fulfilled." Through this visitation, Mary receives the sign confirming what Gabriel announced to her.

Mary's response to Elizabeth is that splendid hymn of praise which Christians from earliest times have sung each evening as a fitting doxology in the Church's Evening Prayer. In the first half of the *Magnificat* (as it is called), Mary exalts God because of the wonders that have happened to her, one of the poor servants of Israel. In the second half we get a glimpse of the new order of the Messianic Age in which things are turned upside down: the proud are scattered, the mighty are cast down, and the rich are empty while the lowly are lifted up and the hungry are filled. Such is God's "promise of mercy"!

Living the Paschal Mystery

From her own privileged conception to her miraculous conception of Jesus to her standing at the foot of the cross to her presence at Pentecost, Mary was always the servant of God. This is why she enjoys a privileged place in heaven where she continually sings her *magnificat*. Mary knew the cost of dying; she now enjoys the glory of everlasting life.

FAITH-SHARING
- What is God accomplishing in *you*? through *you*?
- How might you make your whole life a song of praise unto God?
- Recall some of the great things God has done for you.
- All generations remember Mary as blessed because she surrendered herself to God's plan. Where is God asking you to surrender yourself to the divine plan?

PRESIDERS
When is your ministry a song of praise? What are the things God is accomplishing in you?

DEACONS
Mary was always the servant of God—she faithfully surrendered to God's plan. Where does your life and service need to become more Mary-like?

HOSPITALITY MINISTERS
Elizabeth said, "How does this happen to me, that the mother of my Lord should come to me?" How does it happen to you that members of the body of Christ come to you?

MUSIC MINISTERS
Mary focused her song of praise, the *Magnificat*, on God and God's goodness. How do you keep your song focused on praise of God?

ALTAR MINISTERS
"God's temple in heaven [is] opened" to the faithful in a privileged way through the liturgy. How might your service witness the heavenly amidst the familiar?

LECTORS
Mary sings God's praise because "the Almighty has done great things for me." When you witness God's "great things," how does that affect your daily living? your Sunday proclamation?

EUCHARISTIC MINISTERS
Mary's *Magnificat* gives a glimpse of the messianic age: the proud scattered, the mighty cast down, and the rich are empty while the lowly are lifted up and the hungry are filled. How are you participating in the inauguration of this new order by your ministry to the body of Christ?

AUGUST 15, 2000

GOSPEL [Luke 1:39-56; L622]

Mary set out and traveled to the hill country in haste to a town of Judah, where she entered the house of Zechariah and greeted Elizabeth. When Elizabeth heard Mary's greeting, the infant leaped in her womb, and Elizabeth, filled with the Holy Spirit, cried out in a loud voice and said, "Blessed are you among women, and blessed is the fruit of your womb. And how does this happen to me, that the mother of my Lord should come to me? For at the moment the sound of your greeting reached my ears, the infant in my womb leaped for joy. Blessed are you who believed that what was spoken to you by the Lord would be fulfilled."

And Mary said: "My soul proclaims the greatness of the Lord; my spirit rejoices in God my Savior for he has looked upon his lowly servant. From this day all generations will call me blessed: the Almighty has done great things for me, and holy is his name. He has mercy on those who fear him in every generation. He has shown the strength of his arm, and has scattered the proud in their conceit. He has cast down the mighty from their thrones, and has lifted up the lowly. He has filled the hungry with good things, and the rich he has sent away empty. He has come to the help of his servant Israel for he has remembered his promise of mercy, the promise he made to our fathers, to Abraham and his children forever."

Mary remained with her about three months and then returned to her home.

Working with the Word

Key words and phrases from the Gospel: set out, leaped for joy, believed, all generations will call me blessed, the Almighty has done great things for me

Connecting to the second reading: The second reading from the First Letter to the Corinthians captures well the underlying intent of this festival. The key line is "in Christ all be brought to life." This Solemnity of the Assumption of the Blessed Virgin Mary celebrates Mary's fidelity to God's will and her sharing with her divine Son eternal life.

Connecting to our culture: There is no Gospel incident that gives rise to this feast; we know nothing about Mary's death. It is another of our "idea feasts," meaning that the commemoration arises more out of our doctrinal reflection than an actual biblical event. Vatican I closed before the Council Fathers got around to defining the assumption of Mary into Heaven as a dogma. That didn't come until Pope Pius XII declared it so on November 1 in the Marian year 1950.

Exegetical points: The choice of the *Magnificat* for the Gospel is appropriate for this solemnity. More problematic is the reading from Revelation. For whom does this woman clothed with the sun stand? The symbols of the twelve stars, sun, and moon almost certainly come from Genesis 37, where Joseph dreams of his father and mother and twelve brothers (i.e., all Israel) represented as the sun, moon, and stars bowing down to him. So first and foremost, the woman in Revelation represents ideal Israel who gives birth to the Messiah. But the meaning of the symbol is fluid, as symbols often are in apocalyptic literature. Just shortly after this passage, the same woman clearly stands for the Church whose children are pursued and persecuted by the dragon. In the Gospel of John the mother of Jesus, standing at the foot of the cross, can be a symbol of the Church. So, reading backwards: because the woman of Revelation is the Church, and Mary also stands for the Church, the woman of Revelation can also stand for Mary, which is precisely how this feast intends us to understand this reading.

To the point: The readings for this solemnity emphasize what *God* did in Mary. Her greatness comes from her participation in God's plan and from her surrender and fidelity to it. This is a posture of anyone genuinely committed to living the Paschal Mystery.

Celebration

Model Penitential Rite

Presider: Today we commemorate God's glorification of Mary for her fidelity to God's plan. Let us pause and reflect on what God does in and through us . . . [pause]

> Savior Lord, you were conceived in Mary's womb: Lord . . .
>
> Christ our Lord, you caused John to leap for joy in his mother's womb: Christ . . .
>
> Almighty Lord, you lift up the lowly and fill the hungry with good things: Lord . . .

Responsorial Psalm

"The queen stands at your right hand, arrayed in gold."

The responsorial psalm given for this solemnity is part of a royal wedding song. The queen is the new bride who has left her own family and homeland to stand at the right hand of Israel's king. Those "borne" into the palace "with gladness and joy" are her retinue of maidens. The psalm is used here to celebrate the kind of relationship Mary bears to Christ. Not only is she his mother (Gospel), she is also his queen. The two images, one actual and the other figurative, express the depth of her intimacy with Christ, and it is this intimacy which is the source of her identity for the Church. She is the queen whom "all generations" will call "blessed" (Gospel). In singing this psalm, we join those generations.

Model General Intercessions

Presider: God does marvelous deeds on behalf of humanity. Let us bring our prayers to the heavenly throne with confidence.

Response:

Lord, hear our prayer.

Cantor:

we pray to the Lord,

That members of the Church leap for joy at the many manifestations of God's presences . . . [pause]

That people of the world believe what is spoken to them by the Lord . . . [pause]

That the scattered, cast down, proud, and mighty surrender themselves to God's promise of mercy . . . [pause]

That we proclaim the greatness of the Lord faithfully in our prayer and daily living . . . [pause]

Presider: God of mercy, you have remained faithful to your promises throughout all generations: hear these our prayers that we might one day enjoy everlasting life with you and Mary our mother. We ask this through your divine Son, Jesus Christ our Lord. **Amen.**

ALTERNATIVE OPENING PRAYER

Let us pray

Pause for silent prayer

Father in heaven,
all creation rightly gives you praise,
for all life and all holiness come from you.
In the plan of your wisdom
she who bore the Christ in her womb
was raised body and soul in glory to be with him in heaven.
May we follow her example in reflecting your holiness
and join in her hymn of endless life and praise.
We ask this through Christ our Lord.
Amen.

RESPONSORIAL PSALM
[Ps 45:10, 11, 12, 16]

℞. (10bc) The queen stands at your right hand, arrayed in gold.

The queen takes her place at your right hand in gold of Ophir.

℞. The queen stands at your right hand, arrayed in gold.

Hear, O daughter, and see; turn your ear, forget your people and your father's house.

℞. The queen stands at your right hand, arrayed in gold.

So shall the king desire your beauty; for he is your lord.

℞. The queen stands at your right hand, arrayed in gold.

They are borne in with gladness and joy; they enter the palace of the king.

℞. The queen stands at your right hand, arrayed in gold.

FIRST READING
[Rev 11:19a; 12:1-6a, 10ab]

God's temple in heaven was opened, and the ark of his covenant could be seen in the temple.

A great sign appeared in the sky, a woman clothed with the sun,
with the moon beneath her feet,
and on her head a crown of twelve stars.
She was with child and wailed aloud in pain as she labored to give birth.
Then another sign appeared in the sky; it was a huge red dragon, with seven heads and ten horns,
and on its heads were seven diadems.

Its tail swept away a third of the stars in
   the sky
   and hurled them down to the earth.
Then the dragon stood before the
   woman about to give birth,
   to devour her child when she gave
      birth.
She gave birth to a son, a male child,
   destined to rule all the nations with
      an iron rod.
Her child was caught up to God and his
   throne.
The woman herself fled into the desert
   where she had a place prepared by
      God.
Then I heard a loud voice in heaven say:
   "Now have salvation and power
      come,
      and the kingdom of our God
      and the authority of his Anointed
         One."

SECOND READING
[1 Cor 15:20-27]

Brothers and sisters:
Christ has been raised from the dead,
   the firstfruits of those who have fallen
      asleep.
For since death came through man,
   the resurrection of the dead came also
      through man.
For just as in Adam all die,
   so too in Christ shall all be brought to
      life,
   but each one in proper order:
   Christ the firstfruits;
   then, at his coming, those who belong
      to Christ;
   then comes the end,
   when he hands over the kingdom to
      his God and Father,
   when he has destroyed every
      sovereignty
   and every authority and power.
For he must reign until he has put all his
   enemies under his feet.
The last enemy to be destroyed is death,
   for "he subjected everything under
      his feet."

Catechesis

Cantors
The responsorial psalm for this solemnity is awkward to sing unless you understand the verses in context of the whole of Psalm 45, which was a song composed for the wedding celebration of one of Israel's kings. It would be well to take time to read and pray over the entire psalm and reflect on the joy which the king and his new bride brought Israel because they symbolized God's saving love for all the people.

Choir
One aspect of this solemnity is the relationship of intimacy which Mary shares with Christ. Through your baptism you participate in this same intimacy. How does your singing as a choir express and deepen your intimacy with Christ? with the Church? with others?

Music Directors
"Mary the Dawn" [CH] expresses Mary's essential but subordinate relationship with Christ through paired imagery (e.g., dawn-day, root-vine, grape-wine) sung in responsorial fashion between choir and assembly. The setting itself—rich metaphors sung to a simple chant—mirrors the paired relationship. The hymn could be sung as a reflective litany of praise after Communion. It could also be sung as a prelude with the women's voices leading and the men responding.

This would also be an appropriate day to sing a setting of the *Magnificat* as a hymn of praise after Communion.

Liturgy Committee
How can you help your parishioners appreciate the meaning of this festival and choose to celebrate it because it invites them deeper into the Mystery of salvation rather than celebrate it because they are obliged to? What aspect of the Mystery of salvation is being revealed on this solemnity?

The Gospel's *Magnificat* text and the two lines used in the Hail Mary are not the translations from the revised New Testament of the New American Bible. Rather, the Lectionary inserted the translations familiar to people in the liturgical and devotional praying of these texts.

It is summertime in the northern hemisphere, so there should be abundant flowers to create a festive atmosphere in the sacred space.

AUGUST 15, 2000

Twentieth Sunday in Ordinary Time

FAITH-SHARING
- Do you ever find yourselves "murmuring" and "quarreling" about these mysteries? How can you overcome these tendencies?
- How can the times the Church provides for Eucharistic devotions (e.g., praying before the Blessed Sacrament, especially on Holy Thursday evening) help you to see Eucharist as an action nourishing the community and unifying it as the body of Christ?
- Does your Eucharistic devotion ever take you beyond Christ to the Father in the Spirit?

PRESIDERS
In what ways does your sharing in the Eucharistic banquet deepen your relationship to God? to those to whom you minister? How do you keep presiding at Eucharist from becoming just routine, a job?

DEACONS
"Whoever eats my flesh and drinks my blood remains in me and I in him." How does your diaconal service help you to "remain" in Jesus? How does your service help others to "remain" in Jesus?

HOSPITALITY MINISTERS
How does your devotion to the Eucharist shape your hospitality?

MUSIC MINISTERS
How does the music you use in the liturgy feed the faith of the people?

ALTAR MINISTERS
How might your belief in the Eucharist and your Eucharistic devotion be reflected in your ministry? in your daily life?

LECTORS
St. Jerome wrote, "Ignorance of the Scriptures is ignorance of Christ." How does your prayer with the readings deepen your devotion to the Eucharist? How does it help you to get to know Christ better? What is the relationship between Eucharist and Scripture?

EUCHARISTIC MINISTERS
How might you approach your ministry in such a way as to promote great awe, love, and respect for the mystery of the Eucharist? How do you relate to each other if Eucharist is central in your lives? What are the signs of belief in Eucharist?

Spirituality

Reflecting on the Gospel

Finally, with this Sunday, Jesus' revelation of the lofty Mystery which has been at the heart of our Catholic tradition for two millennia comes to full light. The Gospel opens with a repetition of the verse that concluded last Sunday's Gospel. Again, we find some Jews quarreling among themselves; this, because they continue to take Jesus' words about his being "the living bread that came down from heaven" on a literal level. Literally, Jesus cannot give us his human flesh to eat. Having said this, however, we cannot conclude that Jesus does not give us, truly, his flesh and blood as food and drink. This is the Mystery. This is the stumbling block.

Jesus' monologue about himself as the living bread begins with a negative warning: if we don't eat and drink Jesus' flesh and blood, we cannot have life. This is a startling and bold statement. We have no choice but to partake. Jesus is present to us in our taking, blessing, breaking, and giving his body and blood as true food and drink.

The monologue continues with what seems like repetition which serves to alert us to two aspects of this great Mystery. The phrase "Whoever eats my flesh and drinks my blood" introduces two different fruits of partaking in this food from heaven. First, we *have* eternal life and Jesus *will raise* us up on the last day. In this promise we see both the "already" of the life we now share and the "not yet" of the life that is yet to come. Eucharist has something to do with both present reality and our future life that has yet to come. Second, by eating the flesh and drinking the blood we remain in Jesus and Jesus in us, this Son who has life because of the Father. Our eating and drinking, then, has a relational aspect; the believer shares in the same life as the Father and Son and the only way to share in that life is to share in the heavenly food.

The word "eat" is repeated seven times in these few verses from John's Gospel. It is pretty difficult to miss the point: we truly are to *eat* "the flesh of the Son of Man and drink his blood" if we wish to have life. The concluding verse of the Gospel returns to an earlier theme: our ancestors ate the bread in the desert and they died. Jesus is revealing a startling, new bread from heaven, one that nourishes us to live forever.

Living the Paschal Mystery

It is easy to get caught up in definitions and interpretations of the Eucharistic Mystery. The sublime beauty of this Gospel text reminds us that no human words can exhaust the meaning of the Mystery. The first reading from Proverbs reminds us that the "simple" and those who "lack understanding" are invited to the banquet. We cannot take this literally, any more than we can take "flesh" and "blood" literally. Yet, the food from heaven upon which we feast is no less than Jesus himself.

Jesus is the source of our life. We share "already," but "not yet." We share in the Eucharistic banquet which foreshadows the Messianic banquet. We have life, but will still be raised up on the last day. This is the mystery. This is our food. This is the nourishment for our journey.

GOSPEL [John 6:51-58; L119B]

Jesus said to the crowds: "I am the living bread that came down from heaven; whoever eats this bread will live forever; and the bread that I will give is my flesh for the life of the world."

The Jews quarreled among themselves, saying, "How can this man give us his flesh to eat?" Jesus said to them, "Amen, amen, I say to you, unless you eat the flesh of the Son of Man and drink his blood, you do not have life within you. Whoever eats my flesh and drinks my blood has eternal life, and I will raise him on the last day. For my flesh is true food, and my blood is true drink. Whoever eats my flesh and drinks my blood remains in me and I in him. Just as the living Father sent me and I have life because of the Father, so also the one who feeds on me will have life because of me. This is the bread that came down from heaven. Unlike your ancestors who ate and still died, whoever eats this bread will live forever."

Working with the Word

Key words and phrases from the Gospel: eat, drink, flesh, blood, eternal life, remains in me

Connecting to the first reading: The selection from Proverbs reminds us that food is about wise/insightful living and that eating and drinking advances us in the way of understanding. This parallels Jesus' revelation of himself as both word that is food and flesh that is food.

Connecting to the biblical and our culture: To the first-century Jew, blood is equated with life. To spill blood is to take life. Modern culture also values blood as life. Medicine makes it possible—literally—to give blood so that others may live. With blood as the very gift of life, it is ironic that the sacrament of unity should be a means of disunity ecumenically.

Exegetical points: This passage begins by repeating the last line of last Sunday's Gospel in which the bread of life is identified for the first time with "my flesh." Jesus, in his flesh and blood, is the source of life for believers. These heavenly gifts evoke other Johannine images for Jesus as the source of life: in 8:12, Jesus is the "light of life" for the world (cf. also John 1:4); in his discourse with the woman at the well, Jesus reveals himself as the source of "living water" (John 4:10); his word is life (John 5:24); he is the bread of life (John 6:35, 48); his Spirit gives life (John 6:63, 68). In many and varied ways, John presents Jesus as the source of life. Moreover, the life of which he speaks is neither limited to this life, nor deferred to the next; rather, Jesus is the source of life now and in the age to come: "Whoever eats my flesh and drinks my blood has eternal life, and I will raise him on the last day" (John 6:54). The full significance of Jesus as Eucharist has already been disclosed: Jesus is the bread of life. In this way, the deepest meaning of the story of the multiplication of the loaves comes to expression in the Eucharist, recalling Jesus' own admonition, "Do not work for food that perishes but for the food that endures for eternal life" (John 6:27).

To the point: Our food is the personal Jesus: *com-union*, we are called to remain in him. Jesus is inviting us to participate in him and his promise of eternal life.

Celebration

Model Penitential Rite

Presider: Our God nourishes us with bread from heaven. Let us prepare ourselves for this great gift by surrendering ourselves to God so we can give fitting praise and thanksgiving . . . [pause]

> Lord Jesus, you are the bread that came down from heaven: Lord . . .
>
> Christ Jesus, you give us your flesh and blood as nourishment for our journey: Christ . . .
>
> Lord Jesus, you invite us to remain in you and share in your life: Lord . . .

Responsorial Psalm

"Taste and see the goodness of the Lord."

In this Sunday's responsorial psalm use of Psalm 34, the word "goodness" appears only in the refrain. But in the psalm as a whole the word "good" appears four times, creating a deliberate sequence of thought in vv. 9-15:

> "Taste and see how *good* the Lord is."
>
> ". . . those who seek the Lord want for no *good* thing."
>
> "Which of you desires life and [. . . many days to enjoy *good*?"; NRSV]
>
> "Turn from evil, and do *good*."

The source of all goodness is God. Those who have experienced (tasted) this goodness want more. And the way to find more good is to do good.

What is the food which wisdom provides for the simple (first reading) and which Jesus offers those who hear and understand him (Gospel), if not the goodness of God? In singing this psalm we proclaim with simplicity that we have tasted this goodness and that we desire more.

Model General Intercessions

Presider: The God who nourishes us with bread from heaven will hear our prayers of need. And so we confidently voice those prayers.

Response: Lord, hear our prayer.

Cantor: we pray to the Lord,

That all members of the Church may remain in Jesus and enjoy life with him and the Father . . . [pause]

That the divisions within Christianity may be healed so that all can share together in the sacrament of unity . . . [pause]

That the simple and those who lack understanding may be invited to our banquets and have their fill . . . [pause]

That our community may be strengthened in our love and care for one another by the sacrament of eternal life . . . [pause]

Presider: Bounteous God, you nourish us with food and drink from your own table and invite us to share in your life: hear these our prayers that we might be strengthened for our journey home to you. We pray through Jesus Christ our Lord. **Amen.**

OPENING PRAYER

Let us pray

Pause for silent prayer

God our Father,
may we love you in all things
and above all things and reach the joy
    you have prepared for us
beyond all our imagining.
We ask this through our Lord Jesus
    Christ, your Son,
who lives and reigns with you and the
    Holy Spirit,
one God, for ever and ever. **Amen.**

RESPONSORIAL PSALM

[Ps 34:2-3, 4-5, 6-7]

℞. (9a) Taste and see the goodness of the Lord.

I will bless the LORD at all times;
    his praise shall be ever in my mouth.
Let my soul glory in the LORD;
    the lowly will hear me and be glad.

℞. Taste and see the goodness of the Lord.

Glorify the LORD with me,
    let us together extol his name.
I sought the LORD, and he answered me
    and delivered me from all my fears.

℞. Taste and see the goodness of the Lord.

Look to him that you may be radiant
    with joy,
    and your faces may not blush with
        shame.
When the poor one called out, the LORD
    heard,
    and from all his distress he saved him.

℞. Taste and see the goodness of the Lord.

FIRST READING
[Prov 9:1-6]

Wisdom has built her house,
   she has set up her seven columns;
she has dressed her meat, mixed her
   wine,
   yes, she has spread her table.
She has sent out her maidens; she calls
   from the heights out over the city:
"Let whoever is simple turn in here;
   To the one who lacks understanding,
      she says,
Come, eat of my food,
   and drink of the wine I have mixed!
Forsake foolishness that you may live;
   advance in the way of
      understanding."

SECOND READING
[Eph 5:15-20]

Brothers and sisters:
Watch carefully how you live,
   not as foolish persons but as wise,
   making the most of the opportunity,
   because the days are evil.
Therefore, do not continue in ignorance,
   but try to understand what is the will
      of the Lord.
And do not get drunk on wine, in which
   lies debauchery,
   but be filled with the Spirit,
   addressing one another in psalms and
      hymns and spiritual songs,
   singing and playing to the Lord in
      your hearts,
   giving thanks always and for
      everything
in the name of our Lord Jesus Christ
   to God the Father.

Catechesis

Cantors
Where in your life do you taste the goodness of God? Pray this week for the wisdom to see the person of Jesus acting in your life to nourish you.

Choir
End rehearsal this week with a prayer of thanksgiving for the Eucharist. Pray for one another that you grow in your faith in this Bread of Life and that you let its nourishment truly change the way you live.

Music Directors
This Sunday Jesus reveals that the food of everlasting life is his own flesh and blood. You might use Kreutz' "Our Daily Bread" (BB, CBW3) for the Communion hymn, with cantor or choir singing the verses. The choir arrangement is included in OCP's *Choral Praise* collection, and is also available as an octavo [OCP #8717]. A second possibility for the Communion hymn is Herbert Brokering and Carl Schalk's simple but lovely "Take the Bread, Children" [RS; choir octavo GIA G-3368]. The first four verses of this text are based on the four actions of the Liturgy of the Eucharist : take, bless, break, give.

Liturgy Committee
How does receiving Communion under both species comprise a more complete sign of what Jesus is offering you? What can you do in your parish to promote this?

This Gospel suggests a compelling incentive for offering Communion under both species. In this Gospel, clearly eating *and* drinking are tied together into a single action that brings life (see GIRM, no. 240). Yet, no matter how many medical studies are undertaken and how many reports affirm that there is no more danger—when the ministers wipe both the inside and outside of the cup's lip and rotate it with each communicant—of getting sick by drinking from the cup than from many other of our daily activities (like drinking from a public water fountain), many people still refuse to take from the cup. It is better not to force the issue. At the same time, don't get discouraged (especially if the practice of offering the cup has recently been introduced) if few people avail themselves. With patient explanations and faithful modeling, receiving from the cup can once again be a life-giving Eucharistic experience.

There are four ways to receive the Precious Blood: drinking from the cup, through a tube, on a spoon, or by intinction (GIRM, no. 200). The usual way to receive the Precious Blood in North America is to receive from the cup. Intinction (dipping the Host in the consecrated wine and then placing it on the communicant's tongue) is permitted but not promoted because it takes away the option of receiving Communion in the hand.

One practical pastoral problem that frequently comes up is that communicants don't consume right away the host placed in their hand, but go to the cup minister and dip the host themselves into the Precious Blood. This is not permitted because it compromises the action of *taking* and *receiving* between minister and communicant.

AUGUST 20, 2000

Twenty-First Sunday in Ordinary Time

FAITH-SHARING
- Have there been times when you have found Jesus' teaching "hard" and left?
- The people responded to Joshua about why they would serve the LORD God with examples of what God has done for them. Why do you stay with Jesus? What has Jesus done for you?
- What words of Jesus are "Spirit and life" for you?

PRESIDERS
What does it mean in your ordained ministry to accept Jesus as the source of life? How do you see yourself as a source of life for others? When was the last time you had to choose whether you would leave or stay with Jesus as the source of life? What has been the consequence of "staying with Jesus"—in your personal life? in your priestly ministry?

DEACONS
As you walk with people on their faith journeys, it is not uncommon to hear people say at some point, about some teaching, "This saying is hard; who can accept it?" How might you witness that Jesus has the "words of eternal life"?

HOSPITALITY MINISTERS
Some accept Jesus and some don't. Some leave and some stay. How might your hospitality encourage people to accept Jesus and stay with him?

MUSIC MINISTERS
How have you experienced the goodness of God? What makes you keep singing?

ALTAR MINISTERS
How might your service around the altar witness to the assembly your belief that Jesus is the Holy One of God? How might your devotion assist others to stay with Jesus, even when some of his sayings are hard?

LECTORS
Joshua summoned all of Israel for a serious choice. How might your proclamation "summon" the assembly interiorly? How might your reading inform the people of the seriousness of responding to Jesus' words?

EUCHARISTIC MINISTERS
"Taste and see the goodness of the Lord." Walk and watch carefully this week and see how the psalmist is right!

Spirituality

Reflecting on the Gospel
With this Sunday we conclude John's Bread of Life discourse. Interestingly enough, it is the last line of both the Gospel and the first reading that give us a clue as to where John's Bread of Life discourse has been taking us these past few Sundays. The first reading concludes with, "Therefore we will also serve the LORD, for he is our God"; the Gospel concludes with, "We have come to believe and are convinced that you are the Holy One of God." In both cases a choice is being made in response to God's initiative. What God will we serve?

Joshua challenges the Israelites, "decide today whom you will serve." The Israelites choose to serve the LORD their God because of all the deeds God had done on their behalf: brought them from slavery to freedom, performed great miracles, protected, and nourished them.

Disciples of Jesus have heard Jesus call himself the bread of life. They have heard him say he will give them his flesh to eat. This Sunday, Jesus reminds the disciples that "the words I have spoken to you are Spirit and life." Their response? Some accept Jesus and some don't. Some leave and some stay. Those who leave cannot get past the demands of belief: "This saying is hard; who can accept it?" Those who stay have come to see Jesus as the *source of life*. Simon Peter answers that he and the other eleven will remain with Jesus because he has "the words of eternal life."

God's words and deeds not only reveal who God is; they also invite a response—either to leave or stay. John's Bread of Life discourse leads us to make a choice. What God will we serve? Will we stay with Jesus as the source of life?

Living the Paschal Mystery
It seems as though the stumbling block for some Jews was Jesus' flesh as food; for some of Jesus' disciples it was his word as life-giving. Which is easier: to believe that flesh is food or that word brings life? Does our choice to stay with Jesus or leave depend on ease of belief? Does it depend on the cost?

From experience we know that choosing to stay with Jesus—in spite of the nourishment and life it brings—costs us. Just as Jesus risked losing his disciples and standing alone because he spoke radical words of life so, too, we risk standing alone when we choose to follow Jesus, also speaking radical words of life. Choosing to stay with Jesus, then, moves us into the rhythm of death/life; when we choose to stay we die (to "old" or "foreign" gods); but at the same time we gain life. To follow Jesus, the source of life, promises us eternal life.

At times we are like the disciples who had trouble accepting those hard sayings of Jesus and even Jesus himself. We want to leave. At other times we are like Simon Peter and know that we have nowhere else to go but to follow Jesus who is life. We stay. Our staying is one other manifestation of the rhythm of dying and rising that is the Paschal Mystery.

AUGUST 27, 2000

GOSPEL [John 6:60-69; L122B]

Many of Jesus' disciples who were listening said, "This saying is hard; who can accept it?" Since Jesus knew that his disciples were murmuring about this, he said to them, "Does this shock you? What if you were to see the Son of Man ascending to where he was before? It is the spirit that gives life, while the flesh is of no avail. The words I have spoken to you are Spirit and life. But there are some of you who do not believe." Jesus knew from the beginning the ones who would not believe and the one who would betray him. And he said, "For this reason I have told you that no one can come to me unless it is granted him by my Father."

As a result of this, many of his disciples returned to their former way of life and no longer accompanied him. Jesus then said to the Twelve, "Do you also want to leave?" Simon Peter answered him, "Master, to whom shall we go? You have the words of eternal life. We have come to believe and are convinced that you are the Holy One of God."

Working with the Word

Key words and phrases from the Gospel: his saying is hard, who can accept it?, some . . . who do not believe, do you also want to leave?, word of eternal life

Connecting to the first reading: Both the first reading and the Gospel call upon us to decide whom we will serve. The opening line of this Sunday's Gospel presumes the controversy that closed last Sunday's Gospel: Jesus is the source of life. This opens up the question of leaving or staying with Jesus.

Connecting to our culture: We have to make many choices today, in spite of the standard attitudes in TV sitcoms, pop psychology, etc. that people are unable to make a commitment. With Jesus there is no neutral ground; not to choose Jesus is to reject him.

Exegetical points: The dismayed response of some of the disciples, "this saying is hard," refers not just to the previous words of Jesus ("this is the bread that came down from heaven . . . whoever eats this bread will live forever"), but to the entire discourse in which Jesus claims his origin in heaven ("Son of Man ascending to where he was before"), his identity as the bread of life, his unique intimacy with the Father, the necessity of consuming his flesh and blood. All of this is just too hard to accept.

Jesus' claim that his words are "spirit and life" is affirmed by Peter in his closing comments, "you have the words of eternal life." While some of Jesus' disciples can no longer walk with him, Peter is the one who fulfills the "work of God" that Jesus had spoken of earlier, namely to "believe in the One whom He sent." Thus it is that Peter declares, "we have come to believe and are convinced that you are the Holy One of God." While it is true that faith is required to understand the Eucharist, it is also true that Eucharist leads to faith.

To the point: Jesus is the source of life, and encounter with Jesus always requires a response.

Celebration

Model Penitential Rite

Presider: We come to Mass today to celebrate Jesus as the source of life and to learn how to follow him. Let us open ourselves to the Holy One of God . . . [pause]

Lord Jesus, you are the Holy One of God: Lord . . .
Christ Jesus, you speak words of Spirit and life: Christ . . .
Lord Jesus, you have the words of eternal life: Lord . . .

Responsorial Psalm

"Taste and see the goodness of the Lord."

The verses from Psalm 34 used this Sunday are different from those used the previous weeks. This time we sing of God's protection in times of trouble, of distress, of brokenheartedness.

Psalm 34 begins with a call to praise. The reason for this praise is the psalmist's experience of God's deliverance. For the past two Sundays we have sung with the psalmist, "I sought the Lord, and he answered me and delivered me from all my fears." This Sunday we sing, "When the just cry out, the Lord hears them, and from all their distress he rescues them." The first statement was in singular voice and used past tense; the second statement is plural and uses ongoing verbs. One who has known the goodness of God has no doubt that this goodness lasts for all time and is given to all who cry out for it.

Thus, the Israelites could pledge fidelity to God because they had come to know God's saving deeds (first reading). Peter could promise to stay with Jesus because he had come to know his saving words (Gospel). We can sing this psalm because we, too, have come to know the One whose goodness is the source of eternal life.

Model General Intercessions

Presider: Jesus is the source of life who nourishes us and cares for us. We can be confident when we bring to God our needs and prayers.

Response:

Lord, hear our prayer.

Cantor:

we pray to the Lord,

For the Church who accepts the hard sayings of Jesus . . . [pause]

For people of the world who do not believe in God . . . [pause]

For unbelievers who cannot hear words of life . . . [pause]

For ourselves who have come to believe in Jesus the source of life . . . [pause]

Presider: O God, your words are the source of life: hear these our prayers that we might choose only to follow you. We pray through Jesus Christ our Lord. **Amen.**

ALTERNATIVE OPENING PRAYER
Let us pray

Pause for silent prayer

Lord our God,
all truth is from you,
and you alone bring oneness of heart.
Give your people the joy
of hearing your word in every sound
and of longing for your presence more
 than for life itself.
May all the attractions of a changing
 world
serve only to bring us
the peace of your kingdom which this
 world does not give.
Grant this through Christ our Lord.
Amen.

RESPONSORIAL PSALM
[Ps 34:2-3, 16-17, 18-19, 20-21]

℟. (9a) Taste and see the goodness of the Lord.

I will bless the LORD at all times;
 his praise shall be ever in my mouth.
Let my soul glory in the LORD;
 the lowly will hear me and be glad.

℟. Taste and see the goodness of the Lord.

The LORD has eyes for the just,
 and ears for their cry.
The LORD confronts the evildoers,
 to destroy remembrance of them from
 the earth.

℟. Taste and see the goodness of the Lord.

When the just cry out, the LORD hears
 them,
 and from all their distress he rescues
 them.
The LORD is close to the brokenhearted;
 and those who are crushed in spirit he
 saves.

℟. Taste and see the goodness of the Lord.

Many are the troubles of the just one,
 but out of them all the LORD delivers
 him;
he watches over all his bones;
 not one of them shall be broken.

℟. Taste and see the goodness of the Lord.

FIRST READING [Josh 24:1-2a, 15-17, 18b]

Joshua gathered together all the tribes of
 Israel at Shechem,
 summoning their elders, their leaders,
 their judges, and their officers.
When they stood in ranks before God,
 Joshua addressed all the people:
 "If it does not please you to serve the
 LORD,

decide today whom you will serve,
   the gods your fathers served beyond
      the River
   or the gods of the Amorites in whose
      country you are now dwelling.
As for me and my household, we will
   serve the LORD."

But the people answered,
   "Far be it from us to forsake the LORD
      for the service of other gods.
For it was the LORD, our God,
   who brought us and our fathers up
      out of the land of Egypt,
      out of a state of slavery.
He performed those great miracles
   before our very eyes
   and protected us along our entire
      journey
   and among the peoples through
      whom we passed.
Therefore we also will serve the LORD,
   for he is our God."

SECOND READING [Eph 5:21-32]

Brothers and sisters:
Be subordinate to one another out of
   reverence for Christ.
Wives should be subordinate to their
   husbands as to the Lord.
For the husband is head of his wife
   just as Christ is head of the church,
   he himself the savior of the body.
As the church is subordinate to Christ,
   so wives should be subordinate to
      their husbands in everything.
Husbands, love your wives,
   even as Christ loved the church
   and handed himself over for her to
      sanctify her,
   cleansing her by the bath of water
      with the word,
   that he might present to himself the
      church in splendor,
   without spot or wrinkle or any such
      thing,
   that she might be holy and without
      blemish.
So also husbands should love their
   wives as their own bodies.
He who loves his wife loves himself.
For no one hates his own flesh
   but rather nourishes and cherishes it,
   even as Christ does the church,
   because we are members of his body.
*For this reason a man shall leave his father
   and his mother and be joined to his wife,
   and the two shall become one flesh.*
This is a great mystery,
   but I speak in reference to Christ and
      the church.

Catechesis

Cantors

For the third week you sing "Taste and see the goodness of the Lord," almost as if the Lectionary is giving you the opportunity to truly mean what you say by asking you again and again if you really believe it. Some in this Sunday's Gospel don't. What is the basis of *your* belief? What has been *your* experience of God's goodness?

Choir

When Jesus asks the apostles in this Sunday's Gospel if they wish to leave him, Peter answers, "Master, to whom shall we go?" Why do you stay with Jesus? Why do you come each week to Eucharist? Why do you remain faithful to the discipline of being in the choir?

Music Directors

This Sunday the Gospel confronts you with the choice to stay with Jesus the Bread of Life or to leave. An excellent hymn is "The Summons" [G2, RS] with its relentless challenge, "Will you come and follow me?" This text would be appropriate during the presentation of the gifts. A good choice for Communion would be Eugene Englert's "I Am the Bread of Life" [WC]. By combining Jesus' words, "I am the bread of life" (refrain) with the words of Psalm 63, "O God, for you I long" (verses), Englert connects Jesus' revelation about himself with a desire to follow him. The verses are set for cantor, the refrain is SAB.

Liturgy Committee

Joshua summoned the tribes of Israel for a serious task: to make a real choice about which God they would serve. Jesus asks the Twelve: "Do you also want to leave?" How does your work with liturgy enable the assembly to make a full, conscious, and active choice to serve the Lord? How does your planning communicate the seriousness of this choice?

The second reading this Sunday has both a short and longer form. Since the second reading is not connected to the first reading and Gospel during Ordinary Time, it is pastorally appropriate to choose the shorter form.

AUGUST 27, 2000

TWENTY-SECOND SUNDAY IN ORDINARY TIME

FAITH-SHARING
- What is truly worth following?
- How might you better interiorize God's law?
- How can you balance human traditions with God's law?

PRESIDERS
Ministerial ordination has thrust you into an extremely public life. When have you been tempted to hide? When have you assumed a mask or "persona" rather than continue the difficult task of interior transformation?

DEACONS
Isaiah prophesied: "This people honors me with their lips, but their hearts are far from me." How might your service to the community be guarded against being mere "lip service"?

HOSPITALITY MINISTERS
How might you greet those you meet this week and at Sunday liturgy so that they are helped to have just hearts turned toward God?

MUSIC MINISTERS
To live with integrity is to live in the presence of God. How does your ministry of music call you to integrity?

ALTAR MINISTERS
How might your paying attention to the "cups and jugs and kettles" of your ministry be interiorized so that it truly offers God honor?

LECTORS
How might you *interiorize* God's word this week so that you do not proclaim it as mere "lip service"?

EUCHARISTIC MINISTERS
"The Pharisees . . . carefully washed their hands, keeping the tradition of the elders." How might you interiorize your washing of your hands in preparation for ministering the Body or Blood of Christ?

Spirituality

Reflecting on the Gospel

Soon the stores will be filled with Halloween decorations and costumes. Many of us can remember when we were children and the anticipation we felt for "beggars' night." We thought long and hard about who we wanted to be. Often, our costume turned us into our current hero/heroine or allowed us to be a villain for a night. The masks we wore hid (so we thought) our identity. If we went trick or treating in a neighborhood where we were known, it was great fun to see if we could fool the adults about who we were. But the identity hypocrisy was only for a night and then was over. The next day was school and we were back to being ourselves. This Sunday's Gospel is about hypocrisy of a far more serious nature, one that pertains to putting on a false identity that is not so easily taken off.

The first reading presents a very clear perspective on the commandments: they come from God and humans are neither to add to nor subtract from them. The Hebraic tradition after Moses, however, had proposed all kinds of specifications about how to interpret and live out these commandments. Many of these norms had become their own law; the "tradition of the elders" had become as important as God's commandments. External conformity to "human tradition" had replaced the interior attitude of righteousness that comes from keeping God's commands.

The Greek term for hypocrite refers to a stage actor who plays a part and whose face is hidden behind a mask. For the duration of the play actors become someone other than who they really are. In this Gospel Jesus calls these Pharisees and scribes "hypocrites" because they are merely playing a role in their relationship with God. Paying more attention to a "persona," an assumed identity, than to the depth of who they have been called to be by God, their fidelity to the covenant has become nothing more than hiding behind a mask of traditions of their own making. Jesus abrogates this hypocrisy, this hiding behind an external conformity while neglecting the real work: turning to God interiorly, realizing that "nothing . . . from the outside . . . defile[s] . . . but the things that come from within are what defile."

God is not a distant God keeping track of our conformity to myriad external laws and regulations, but a God "close . . . to us whenever we call upon him" (first reading). What counts is that interior transformation which strips off our masks and allows us to "live in the presence of the Lord" (psalm response).

Living the Paschal Mystery

In baptism we are plunged into the waters that destroy our old selves so we might rise in the new identity of Body of Christ. This is who we are as Christians. Living the Paschal Mystery precludes our being hypocrites, for it calls us to enter into the everyday rhythm of dying and rising with Christ. We must surrender to God's action deep within us and allow that interiorization of our identity and relationship with God to be expressed in our observable actions. The dying and rising of the Paschal Mystery urge that our interior and exterior selves be the same. We wear no masks.

SEPTEMBER 3, 2000

GOSPEL [Mark 7:1-8, 14-15, 21-23; L125B]

When the Pharisees with some scribes who had come from Jerusalem gathered around Jesus, they observed that some of his disciples ate their meals with unclean, that is, unwashed, hands.—For the Pharisees and, in fact, all Jews, do not eat without carefully washing their hands, keeping the tradition of the elders. And on coming from the marketplace they do not eat without purifying themselves. And there are many other things that they have traditionally observed, the purification of cups and jugs and kettles and beds.—So the Pharisees and scribes questioned him, "Why do your disciples not follow the tradition of the elders but instead eat a meal with unclean hands?" He responded, "Well did Isaiah prophesy about you hypocrites, as it is written: *This people honors me with their lips, but their hearts are far from me; in vain do they worship me, teaching as doctrines human precepts.* You disregard God's commandment but cling to human tradition."

He summoned the crowd again and said to them, "Hear me, all of you, and understand. Nothing that enters one from outside can defile that person; but the things that come out from within are what defile.

"From within people, from their hearts, come evil thoughts, unchastity, theft, murder, adultery, greed, malice, deceit, licentiousness, envy, blasphemy, arrogance, folly. All these evils come from within and they defile."

Working with the Word

Key words and phrases from the Gospel: tradition of the elders, hypocrites, hearts, God's commandments

Connecting to the first reading: Moses enjoins the people to observe God's commandments carefully and not to add to or subtract from them. Jesus is saying that the Pharisees and scribes in the Gospel have become more concerned with *human* institutions than with God's Law. Observance of God's laws leads to a purity that is interior as well as exterior.

Connecting to the culture: Purity then was a cultic term that had to do with whether one could offer worship to God. Today we almost exclusively think of purity in sexual terms.

Exegetical points: After an extended reflection on John's Bread of Life discourse, we resume reading from Mark's Gospel. The Lectionary picks up after feeding the five thousand, having omitted the story of Jesus walking on the water and a brief report of Jesus' healing ministry (Mark 6:45-56).

The opening verse of this Sunday's Gospel tells us that those who oppose Jesus "come from Jerusalem," anticipating again Jesus' final struggle against his opposition in that city. There are two issues in this Sunday's controversy story, namely the question of defilement and the authority of tradition (vv. 3, 4, 5, 8). The two different English words used, "unclean" (vv. 2, 5) and "defiled" (vv. 15, 23) are the same word in Greek (*koinóō*=to make common, to defile, profane).

The issue of defilement is an instance of the larger concern about tradition. In their concern to fulfill the law as perfectly as humanly possible, observant Jews developed a body of practices that would help individuals keep from inadvertently breaking the law. Over time, these practices ("human traditions" or "traditions from the elders") took on the force of Law. Jesus' response does two things: it restores priority to God's Law over various interpretations of the law, and it moves the discussion from outward observances to inward intention. In this way, "defilement" as a ritual term is reinterpreted by Jesus as a moral term that refers to deliberate acts.

To the point: What is real observance of God's commandments? What is worth following? What are our priorities? Jesus calls us back to what is most fundamental about law and tradition: that which originates from God and dwells within.

Celebration

Model Penitential Rite

Presider: God has given us commandments to guide us. Let us reflect on how well those commandments have drawn us closer to God . . . [pause]

>Lord Jesus, you ask us to worship you with pure hearts: Lord . . .
>Christ Jesus, you take away the evil that comes from within: Christ . . .
>Lord Jesus, you call us to live by your word of truth: Lord . . .

Responsorial Psalm

"The one who does justice will live in the presence of the Lord."
Psalm 15 is a liturgical psalm used when Israel renewed its covenant with God. The psalm begins with the question, "LORD, who may abide in your tent?" and goes on to answer the question by describing a person who treats others with justice. The mark of fidelity to the covenant, then, was acting justly toward one's neighbor.

In the first reading Moses commands the people to be faithful to all the statutes and decrees given them by God because the law was a sign of God's closeness to them, and was a guide to justice. When the Pharisees confront Jesus about the failure of his disciples to keep the ritual laws of washing before eating, they are not concerned with either closeness to God or justice, but with their desire to undermine the integrity of Jesus' authority. Jesus responds by going to the core of fidelity to the law: living from a deep interiorization of its precepts. The responsorial psalm invites us to interiorize the law of God by just living. In singing this psalm we recommit ourselves to living out our covenant relationship with God.

Model General Intercessions

Presider: With pure hearts turned toward God, we make our needs and prayers known.

Response:

[musical notation: Lord, hear our prayer.]

Cantor:

[musical notation: we pray to the Lord,]

That the Church may honor God with a right heart . . . [pause]

That leaders of the world may be guided by God's law when formulating human laws that promote justice . . . [pause]

That those who are defiled by evil actions may put these aside and turn toward a loving and merciful God . . . [pause]

That our community may understand human tradition in light of what God asks of us . . . [pause]

Presider: O God, giver of Law and guarantor of justice, you guide us toward just hearts: hear our prayers that we may always honor you. We pray through Jesus Christ our Lord. **Amen.**

ALTERNATIVE OPENING PRAYER
Let us pray
Pause for silent prayer
Lord God of power and might,
nothing is good which is against your will,
and all is of value which comes from your hand.
Place in our hearts a desire to please you
and fill our minds with insight into love,
so that every thought may grow in wisdom
and all our efforts may be filled with your peace.
We ask this through Christ our Lord.
Amen.

RESPONSORIAL PSALM
[Ps 15:2-3, 3-4, 4-5]

℟. (1a) The one who does justice will live in the presence of the Lord.

Whoever walks blamelessly and does justice;
  who thinks the truth in his heart
  and slanders not with his tongue.

℟. The one who does justice will live in the presence of the Lord.

Who harms not his fellow man,
  nor takes up a reproach against his neighbor;
by whom the reprobate is despised,
  while he honors those who fear the LORD.

℟. The one who does justice will live in the presence of the Lord.

Who lends not his money at usury
  and accepts no bribe against the innocent.
Whoever does these things
  shall never be disturbed.

℟. The one who does justice will live in the presence of the Lord.

FIRST READING
[Deut 4:1-2, 6-8]

Moses said to the people:
"Now, Israel, hear the statutes and decrees
which I am teaching you to observe,
that you may live, and may enter in and take possession of the land
which the LORD, the God of your fathers, is giving you.
In your observance of the commandments of the LORD, your God,
which I enjoin upon you,
you shall not add to what I command you nor subtract from it.
Observe them carefully,
for thus will you give evidence
of your wisdom and intelligence to the nations,
who will hear of all these statutes and say,
'This great nation is truly a wise and intelligent people.'
For what great nation is there
that has gods so close to it as the LORD, our God, is to us
whenever we call upon him?
Or what great nation has statutes and decrees
that are as just as this whole law
which I am setting before you today?"

SECOND READING
[Jas 1:17-18, 21b-22, 27]

Dearest brothers and sisters:
All good giving and every perfect gift is from above,
coming down from the Father of lights,
with whom there is no alteration or shadow caused by change.
He willed to give us birth by the word of truth
that we may be a kind of firstfruits of his creatures.

Humbly welcome the word that has been planted in you
and is able to save your souls.

Be doers of the word and not hearers only, deluding yourselves.

Religion that is pure and undefiled before God and the Father is this:
to care for orphans and widows in their affliction
and to keep oneself unstained by the world.

Catechesis

Cantors

All of you desire to live in the presence of the Lord. This Sunday's psalm teaches you that you live in God's presence when you act justly. This psalm challenges you to examine patterns in your relationships with others. Do you act with the truth, justice, and love that motivated Jesus? Such acting only arises from an integrity deep within the heart. As you prepare to sing this psalm, ask God for the gift of such integrity.

Choir

Music-making requires attention to many details—entrances, cut-offs, rhythms, rests, pitch, diction, etc.—at the same time that it requires seeing a bigger picture—music in the service of liturgical prayer. How do you stay faithful to both the "laws" of music and to its deeper purpose? How do you bring both of these values together with integrity?

Music Directors

Two songs, one a hymn and the other a refrain-verse setting, which would be appropriate responses to this Sunday's Liturgy of the Word during the presentation of the gifts are Thomas Troeger and Carol Doran's "As a Chalice Cast of Gold" [CH] and David Haas' "Deep Within" [G, G2, RS]. "As a Chalice Cast of Gold" was composed to coincide with the Gospel reading for this Sunday. In it one prays to be saved "from the soothing sin of the empty cultic deed" and from the "tangled words that mask" the deeper questings of the soul. In the text of "Deep Within" God calls, begging that you understand the law as something planted "not on stone but in your heart." God pleads with you to renew your covenant relationship with God in all its intimacy and depth.

Liturgy Committee

It is always challenging and difficult to draw the fine line between doing liturgy "right" and getting caught up merely in rubrics and forgetting what you are really about: making present the Paschal Mystery. How might you find the balance between what is "correct" liturgy and what is "good" liturgy? between doing liturgy "right" and really praying?

Monday is Labor Day but it is not liturgically appropriate to introduce homily material, hymns, and other ritual elements that are not proper to the Lord's Day celebration. On Monday a proper Mass (For the Blessing of Human Labor, no. 25 in Masses and Prayers for Various Needs and Occasions in the Sacramentary) may be used.

September is a time of change: school has begun, vacations are generally over, a touch of fall may be in the air. There is a subtle change beginning to happen in the liturgical year, as well. Ordinary Time has unfolded over a number of months now; the Sunday Gospels are moving the assembly with Jesus on the journey toward Jerusalem and the cross. As you come nearer to Jerusalem, begin to feel more keenly the tension of the controversies. Already this early in the fall one is beginning to sense those events that lead to the end of the liturgical year with its predictions of the end of the world and Christ's second coming.

SEPTEMBER 3, 2000

Twenty-third Sunday in Ordinary Time

FAITH-SHARING
- When have you been closed to Jesus? What is it that moves you to be closed with him?
- When have you been open to Jesus? What has that been like for you?
- How hard are you willing to work to help open others to Jesus?

PRESIDERS
How open are you with being Jesus' instrument for others? Are there times when you prefer being closed? How has Jesus' healing opened you to be a better minister?

DEACONS
In what ways is your ministry a comfort to others ("Be strong, fear not!") because it points to Jesus ("Here is your God")?

HOSPITALITY MINISTERS
How might your greeting and hospitality help people to be open to life, to liturgy?

MUSIC MINISTERS
How does the very discipline of music immerse you in the dying and rising of the Paschal Mystery?

ALTAR MINISTERS
Service, by nature, moves you to be open to the other, to their needs over your own. How might you practice this openness by serving the needs of those with whom you live?

LECTORS
How has proclaiming the readings helped you to open your eyes to see anew? Are there times when you are closed to the word? How do you practice having an open heart to the word you proclaim?

EUCHARISTIC MINISTERS
You are open to being a Eucharistic minister at liturgy. How open are you to be the body of Christ in daily life—family, neighbors, colleagues? In contrast, with whom are you closed? How does that affect your Eucharistic ministry?

Spirituality

Reflecting on the Gospel

We all know what it is like to live "closed up." For example, with so much violence around us, we try to protect our families and ourselves; we close in on ourselves. There are occasions like these when being closed is prudent, yet, to live "closed up" all the time is not healthy, either. This Sunday's Gospel addresses the opposite energy in life; it is about being open!

The first "opening" is hinted at in the first sentence of the Gospel that goes to great lengths to give us a "biblical triptik"—Jesus went "into the district of Decapolis," an area that is largely Gentile. Jesus' ministry is not "closed in" and only for the Jews; it is *open* to *all* who seek salvation.

The second opening concerns a healing episode that occupies most of our attention in this Gospel selection. There are some surprises. The Gospel reports that *people* brought the man to Jesus and begged for healing; it says nothing of the desires or openness of the man himself. Jesus takes the man "off by himself, away from the crowd." Jesus uses many very intimate human gestures for this healing, seemingly working harder than for others: he puts his finger "into the man's ears," touches the man's tongue with his spittle, assumes a prayer posture ("looked up to heaven"), groans, and commands "be opened." Jesus' ministry of opening the man's ears and loosening his tongue seems not to have come easy but to have required effort. "Be opened" can have its demands.

The third opening is that—in spite of Jesus' command "not to tell anyone"—the people proclaimed the good news openly and often. Unlike those in previous Sunday Gospels who opposed the words and works of Jesus, this crowd is not only open to Jesus but can't contain their astonishment. They widely broadcast Jesus' ministry of healing.

These common folks don't enter into the controversies over commandments and traditions (as we saw with the Pharisees last Sunday) but accept things for what they are: "He has done all things well. He makes the deaf hear and the mute speak." There is a problem, however, with their response, for they are able to see only what is immediately at hand, the healing. They are closed to its deeper meaning, namely, that the vision of peace and restoration proclaimed by Isaiah is coming to fulfillment before their eyes in Jesus! Jesus, therefore, commands silence in order that the healing can be kept in perspective. The final opening proclaimed by this Gospel is only intimated: how hard it is for Jesus to open us to the deeper reality that salvation does not come quickly or easily but has a cost. Ultimately, Jesus will have to undergo suffering and death to achieve it.

Living the Paschal Mystery

It's easy to be open to living the Paschal Mystery when we are in the life-giving part of the rhythm. This Sunday's Gospel reminds us that we must be open to the *whole* of the mystery and that means we must be ready and willing to embrace the cross. If we try to ignore or get around embracing the suffering that is an inevitable part of surrendering our lives to doing God's will, then we are only living half the mystery (half the truth). The Paschal Mystery is both *dying* and *rising*. When we proclaim the good news, we must proclaim *all* of it.

SEPTEMBER 10, 2000

GOSPEL [Mark 7:31-37; L128B]

Again Jesus left the district of Tyre and went by way of Sidon to the Sea of Galilee, into the district of the Decapolis. And people brought to him a deaf man who had a speech impediment and begged him to lay his hand on him. He took him off by himself away from the crowd. He put his finger into the man's ears and, spitting, touched his tongue; then he looked up to heaven and groaned, and said to him, *"Ephphatha!"*—that is, "Be opened!"—And immediately the man's ears were opened, his speech impediment was removed, and he spoke plainly. He ordered them not to tell anyone. But the more he ordered them not to, the more they proclaimed it. They were exceedingly astonished and they said, "He has done all things well. He makes the deaf hear and the mute speak."

Working with the Word

Key words and phrases from the Gospel: lay his hand, off by himself, be opened, ordered them not to tell anyone

Connecting to the first reading: The reading from Isaiah and the Gospel are linked not only by the general theme of healing the deaf but by specific vocabulary. The particular word for deaf *(mogilalos)* occurs just twice in the Greek Bible: in the first reading from Isaiah (Isa 35:6) and in this Sunday's Gospel (Mark 7:32).

Connecting to the culture: Modern conveniences help us forget that sometimes the things we need the most are those for which we must work the hardest. Instant credit and other such things give us instant gratification. Jesus promises suffering and death.

Exegetical points: This Sunday's healing of the man from the district of Decapolis (together with the preceding story of the healing of the Syrophoenician woman in Mark 7:24-30, which the Lectionary omits) extends the healing ministry of Jesus to those outside the community of Israel: the kingdom of God as announced and inaugurated by Jesus is no national kingdom. Further, the allusion to the passage from Isaiah suggests that the eschatological vision of peace and restoration proclaimed by Isaiah is coming to fulfillment in Jesus of Nazareth. The wonderful deeds of Jesus—his healings, exorcisms, teachings, and miracles—are definitive signs that confirm his initial proclamation that "the kingdom of God is at hand" (Mark 1:15) and that God's kingdom is universal.

To the point: How hard Jesus must "work" to get us to hear beyond what we want to hear (what doesn't cost us) or are able to hear! The healings aren't all there is to Jesus; to be truly "exceedingly astonished" is also to open ourselves to his suffering and death.

Celebration

Model Penitential Rite

Presider: God desires for us to be healed of all that keeps us closed. Let us open ourselves to the divine presence and ask for healing and forgiveness . . . [pause]

> Lord Jesus, you lay your hand on us and heal us: Lord . . .
> Christ Jesus, you do all things well: Christ . . .
> Lord Jesus, you invite us to share in your ministry: Lord . . .

Responsorial Psalm

"Praise the Lord, my soul!"

Psalm 146 is the first of five psalms which together form the conclusion to the whole book of Psalms. These five are a shout of praise to the God who—throughout all of human history—continually saves the people, transforming impairment to wholeness, injustice to right, and suffering to joy. The reading from Isaiah proclaims the promise of God to do these very things. In the Gospel these promises become fully incarnate—touching and touchable—in Jesus. In the responsorial psalm we praise God for this healing and salvation realized in the ministry of Jesus and continued in our own lives today as we disciples take up Jesus' ministry.

Model General Intercessions

Presider: Our God is a compassionate God who greatly desires that we be healed of all that ails us. Let us pray for our needs.

Response:

[musical notation: Lord, hear our prayer.]

Cantor:

[musical notation: we pray to the Lord,]

That all in the Church be open to seeing suffering as a means of salvation . . . [pause]

That all in the world be open to God's offer of salvation . . . [pause]

That all who need healing be open to God's compassionate touch . . . [pause]

That we be open to Jesus' good news of healing and salvation . . . [pause]

Presider: Compassionate God, you desire to open us to the wonders of your salvific presence: hear these our prayers that we may always recognize you in those who suffer. We pray through Jesus Christ our Lord. **Amen.**

ALTERNATIVE OPENING PRAYER

Let us pray

Pause for silent prayer

Lord our God,
in you justice and mercy meet.
With unparalleled love you have saved
 us from death
and drawn us into the circle of your life.
Open our eyes to the wonders this life
 sets before us,
that we may serve you free from fear
and address you as God our Father.
We ask this in the name of Jesus the
 Lord. **Amen.**

RESPONSORIAL PSALM
[Ps 146:7, 8-9, 9-10]

℟. (1b) Praise the Lord, my soul!
 or:
℟. Alleluia.

The God of Jacob keeps faith forever,
 secures justice for the oppressed,
 gives food to the hungry.
The LORD sets captives free.

℟. Praise the Lord, my soul!
 or:
℟. Alleluia.

The LORD gives sight to the blind;
 the LORD raises up those who were
 bowed down.
The LORD loves the just;
 the LORD protects strangers.

℟. Praise the Lord, my soul!
 or:
℟. Alleluia.

The fatherless and the widow the LORD
 sustains,
 but the way of the wicked he thwarts.
The LORD shall reign forever;
 your God, O Zion, through all
 generations.
Alleluia.

℟. Praise the Lord, my soul!
 or:
℟. Alleluia.

FIRST READING
[Isa 35:4-7a]

Thus says the LORD:
   Say to those whose hearts are
      frightened:
      Be strong, fear not!
   Here is your God,
      he comes with vindication;
   with divine recompense
      he comes to save you.
   Then will the eyes of the blind be
      opened,
      the ears of the deaf be cleared;
   then will the lame leap like a stag,
      then the tongue of the mute will
        sing.
   Streams will burst forth in the desert,
      and rivers in the steppe.
   The burning sands will become pools,
      and the thirsty ground, springs of
        water.

SECOND READING
[Jas 2:1-5]

My brothers and sisters, show no
   partiality
      as you adhere to the faith in our
        glorious Lord Jesus Christ.
For if a man with gold rings and fine
   clothes
      comes into your assembly,
   and a poor person in shabby clothes
      also comes in,
   and you pay attention to the one
      wearing the fine clothes
   and say, "Sit here, please,"
   while you say to the poor one, "Stand
      there," or "Sit at my feet,"
   have you not made distinctions
      among yourselves
   and become judges with evil designs?

Listen, my beloved brothers and sisters.
Did not God choose those who are poor
   in the world
      to be rich in faith and heirs of the
        kingdom
   that he promised to those who love
      him?

Catechesis

Cantors

This psalm text is perhaps one of the easiest in the psalter to sing. You praise God for all the concrete ways salvation is granted to the suffering and the downtrodden. Perhaps not so evident is that you pray also in this psalm for all those in the midst of suffering so great that no salvation seems present or possible. As you prepare this psalm, keep all of these people in mind so that you will sing not only praise for what God has done but also instill in others confidence in what God will do.

Choir

In this Sunday's Gospel Jesus cures a deaf-mute person, opening his ears and loosening his tongue. Although you use tongue and voice each week to praise God in song, each of you—because you are human—remains deaf in some ways to the voice of Jesus. How can you open your ears more fully to Jesus so that what you sing is truly his good news?

Music Directors

Anna Hoppe's hymn "O Son of God, in Galilee" [CH, W3] relates directly to this Sunday's Gospel. The text speaks not only of the physical healing of the deaf and the mute but also of the need to hear on the level of faith. CH omits the final verse, and both CH and W3 eliminate the original fourth verse which on this Sunday would accord well with the Gospel's intimated struggle with the cost of salvation: "But if it be the Father's will That they should suffer loss, O lend them grace with patience still To bear a painful cross" [reprinted from the *American Lutheran Hymnal,* © 1930 Lutheran Intersynodical Hymnal Committee, used by permission of Augsburg Fortress]. This verse sheds light on the import of the fifth and final verse: "Then in your promised happy land Each loss will prove a gain; All myst'ries we shall understand, For you shall make them plain." You might use this hymn during the presentation of the gifts, with the choir alone singing the omitted verse before everyone sings the last verse. You may reprint the fourth verse for your choir; include the credit line given above.

Liturgy Committee

How might your concern for preparation of good liturgy help open the assembly more deeply to the totality of the Paschal Mystery—its dying and rising?

Often, as in this Sunday's Gospel, Jesus heals or forgives by laying on hands, a personal and intimate means of communication. It is a liturgical gesture found in all of our sacraments and is especially expressive in the Eucharistic liturgy.

In our present Eucharistic rite, the presider extends ("lays") his hands over the gifts of bread and wine during the Eucharistic Prayer in a gesture known as the *epiclesis,* a liturgical term for extending the hands and calling down the Holy Spirit. In many of the Eastern rites there is a "double" *epiclesis:* extending the hands over the gifts *and* over the people. The liturgical sign is that, as the Spirit comes "upon these gifts to make them holy, so that they may become for us the body and blood of our Lord, Jesus Christ" (Eucharist Prayer II) so, too, does the Spirit come upon the assembly and make them holy.

SEPTEMBER 10, 2000

Twenty-Fourth Sunday in Ordinary Time

FAITH-SHARING
- Where does following Jesus lead you?
- What gives you hope and consolation when you face suffering?
- What in your way of thinking needs to be changed? How do you go about changing it?
- Are you willing to look at the dark side of yourself and do the hard work to change?

PRESIDERS
What are the consequences for your own ordained ministry when you think like God does rather than as human beings do?

DEACONS
How does your taking up your cross of service for the community bring life to others? In what ways must you still "lose" your life?

HOSPITALITY MINISTERS
How might your reaching out and comforting those who suffer (e.g., in a nursing home) better enable you to greet others coming for Sunday liturgy as the Body of Christ?

MUSIC MINISTERS
The ministry of music demands a sacrifice of time, energy, and attention. How are these part of your participation in the cross of discipleship?

ALTAR MINISTERS
How is your ministry of simple service in the little things a perfect example of losing self in order to save your life? What ways do you still need to deny yourself so that you can serve better?

LECTORS
How might your coming to know Jesus better as the suffering servant affect your proclamation of the word? Affect how you live?

EUCHARISTIC MINISTERS
How do you participate in Jesus' suffering? How might this make you a better minister of the Eucharist?

Spirituality

Reflecting on the Gospel
By this time in September many of us are beginning to see changes that remind us fall is near. The leaves change to glorious colors, but this bit of pleasure is merely a harbinger of the dying that is happening in all of nature, a reminder of the bleakness and seeming deadness of winter. Nature moves relentlessly in a rhythm in which the lushness of life gives way to the starkness of death. This Sunday's Gospel is a pivotal one, not only in Mark's account but also in the liturgical year. It marks a clear change in the unfolding story of Jesus.

Right away the opening line clues us to a shift. Jesus sets out with his disciples to Caesarea Philippi. This is south of the district of Decapolis, where we journeyed with them last Sunday. *South.* Toward Jerusalem. *We* know what happens in Jerusalem. The disciples are still clueless. From now on Jesus openly begins to teach his disciples what is in store for him ("He spoke this openly"), but also what is in store for those who follow him.

Jesus turns the conversation on the journey with a pivotal question that opens the space for him to begin to nudge the disciples toward the real demands of discipleship. He asks about his identity. Peter responds "You are the Christ," an answer that shows both Peter's insight and his lack of it. Insight: he recognized Jesus as more than the prophets; Jesus was the long-awaited Messiah. Lack of insight: Peter's rebuke of Jesus shows that Peter limited his understanding of Messiah to the contemporary Jewish expectation. "Messiah" meant "anointed," and although the term could be used in a wide context (for example, prophets were anointed), by Jesus' time it was used especially in reference to kings. Peter's understanding of Messiah, more than likely, was that of a king in the line of David who would restore Israel as a great nation.

Jesus' meaning of Messiah, however, was quite different. He "warned them not to tell anyone about him" since he did not want the disciples to raise false expectations of what was to come. Jesus' reign as Messiah would be about something quite different from power and wealth. And so "he began to teach them" about his real identity: the Messiah would suffer, be rejected, killed, and rise after three days. Hardly like the great king David!

Jesus' own identity as the "suffering servant" (the first reading is from one of Isaiah's suffering servant songs) has implications for us as his disciples. We, too, must deny ourselves, take up our cross, and follow Jesus. It is telling that the first use of "cross" in Mark's Gospel is not in relation to Jesus' cross, but to our cross in following him as the Messiah.

Living the Paschal Mystery
Our denying ourselves, taking up our cross, and following Jesus is not about a dramatic martyrdom like in the early Church, nor about any great, showy response. Rather it is about how we live every single day: dying and rising in our simple, ordinary circumstances. For example, we must die to *our* way of thinking (taking the easy way of self-seeking, self-gratification, self-interest) and embrace how God thinks (carrying the cross of goodness, righteousness, justice, integrity, wholeness, fullness of life).

SEPTEMBER 17, 2000

GOSPEL [Mark 8:27-35; L131B]

Jesus and his disciples set out for the villages of Caesarea Philippi. Along the way he asked his disciples, "Who do people say that I am?" They said in reply, "John the Baptist, others Elijah, still others one of the prophets." And he asked them, "But who do you say that I am?" Peter said to him in reply, "You are the Christ." Then he warned them not to tell anyone about him.

He began to teach them that the Son of Man must suffer greatly and be rejected by the elders, the chief priests, and the scribes, and be killed, and rise after three days. He spoke this openly. Then Peter took him aside and began to rebuke him. At this he turned around and, looking at his disciples, rebuked Peter and said, "Get behind me, Satan. You are thinking not as God does, but as human beings do."

He summoned the crowd with his disciples and said to them, "Whoever wishes to come after me must deny himself, take up his cross, and follow me. For whoever wishes to save his life will lose it, but whoever loses his life for my sake and that of the gospel will save it."

Working with the Word

Key words and phrases from the Gospel: Whoever wishes to come after me, deny self, take up his [or her] cross, follow me

Connecting to the Lectionary: The passage from Isaiah 50:4-9, the so-called Third Song of the Servant of the Lord, is otherwise found only on Palm Sunday of the Lord's Passion (all three years) and on Wednesday of Holy Week. The tradition of associating this reading with the passion of the Lord makes it an appropriate complement to this Sunday's Gospel prediction of the Lord's forthcoming death.

Connecting to our culture: So much of today's culture is about "me." Many self-help books and much advertising announce whatever the cost, "I'm worth it." The Gospel is counter-cultural, announcing that the most important thing in life is "losing" self in order to find something greater: eternal life.

Exegetical points: This Gospel stands at the very middle of Mark's Gospel and signals both a climax and a change in focus. The persistent question about the identity of Jesus which has shaped the Gospel to this point finds an answer in Peter's response to Jesus: "You are the Messiah." But, like the blind man who is healed in stages (Mark 8:22-26, unfortunately omitted from the Lectionary), Peter's profession is at first imperfect: he fails to see that this Messiah must suffer and die.

The meaning of Christ's Messiahship becomes the focus of Jesus' teaching for the remainder of the Gospel. In fact, his prediction (that the Son of Man "must suffer . . . be rejected . . . be killed . . . and rise") is the outline of the plot from this point on. Along with Jesus' teaching about the Messiah goes a pronounced emphasis on what it means to be a disciple of this kind of Messiah: the disciple is likewise to deny self, take up the cross, and lose one's life. It is, therefore, ironic that Peter immediately attempts to become the Master and Teacher by "rebuking" Jesus! Jesus sharply reminds him that the proper place for a disciple is "behind" (v. 33) or "after" (v. 34) the Master. Disciples of Jesus can understand their proper role—their true "selves"—only when they understand that Jesus is a Messiah who suffers and dies.

To the point: The key here is not the revelation of the identity of Jesus as the Christ, but Jesus' proclamation of himself as suffering servant.

Celebration

Model Penitential Rite

Presider: Jesus asks us to deny ourselves, take up our cross, and follow him. Let us consider how well we have surrendered to God's will this week, and open ourselves to God's grace and healing in this celebration . . . [pause]

> Lord Jesus, you are the Servant of God who suffered for our sake: Lord . . .
> Christ Jesus, you are the Messiah who brings salvation: Christ . . .
> Lord Jesus, you offer us eternal life: Lord . . .

Responsorial Psalm

"I will walk before the Lord, in the land of the living."

Psalm 116 was a song of thanksgiving prayed by an individual while he or she offered a sacrifice in gratitude for God's deliverance from grave danger. On this Sunday when both the first reading and the Gospel place the reality of death before us, this psalm is a statement of profound confidence in God's presence and protection. The suffering servant of Isaiah faces persecution without "turn[ing] back" (first reading). Jesus begins to teach that the cost of discipleship is the cross (Gospel). If we remain faithful to discipleship we are, indeed, in grave danger. But we can grapple with death because we know, like the psalmist, that no suffering is greater than God's desire for our life. How wise of the Lectionary to have us sing such a psalm of confidence on this day!

Model General Intercessions

Presider: God calls us to life through death. Let us die to ourselves as we pray for the needs of the world.

Response:

[musical notation: Lord, hear our prayer.]

Cantor:

[musical notation: we pray to the Lord,]

That the disciples of Jesus may deny themselves, take up their cross, and follow him even to suffering and death . . . [pause]

That those who exercise power and authority may think more as God does and less as humans do . . . [pause]

That all those suffering for the sake of the Gospel may find comfort in Christ . . . [pause]

That our community may be faithful to our journey with Christ toward the cross . . . [pause]

Presider: O God, hear our prayers that our lives and the lives of those for whom we pray may be full in you. We ask this through Christ our Lord. **Amen.**

OPENING PRAYER

Let us pray
 [that God will keep us faithful in his service]

Pause for silent prayer

Almighty God,
our creator and guide,
may we serve you with all our heart
and know your forgiveness in our lives.
We ask this through our Lord Jesus
 Christ, your Son
who lives and reigns with you and the
 Holy Spirit,
one God, for ever and ever. **Amen.**

RESPONSORIAL PSALM

[Ps 116:1-2, 3-4, 5-6, 8-9]

℟. (9) I will walk before the Lord, in the land of the living.
 or:
℟. Alleluia.

I love the Lord because he has heard
 my voice in supplication,
because he has inclined his ear to me
 the day I called.

℟. I will walk before the Lord, in the land of the living.
 or:
℟. Alleluia.

The cords of death encompassed me;
 the snares of the netherworld seized
  upon me;
 I fell into distress and sorrow,
and I called upon the name of the Lord,
 "O Lord, save my life!"

℟. I will walk before the Lord, in the land of the living.
 or:
℟. Alleluia.

Gracious is the Lord and just;
 yes, our God is merciful.
The Lord keeps the little ones;
 I was brought low, and he saved me.

℟. I will walk before the Lord, in the land of the living.
 or:
℟. Alleluia.

For he has freed my soul from death,
 my eyes from tears, my feet from
  stumbling.
I shall walk before the Lord
 in the land of the living.

℟. I will walk before the Lord, in the land of the living.
 or:
℟. Alleluia.

FIRST READING
[Isa 50:4c-9a]

The Lord GOD opens my ear that I may hear;
and I have not rebelled,
have not turned back.
I gave my back to those who beat me,
my cheeks to those who plucked my beard;
my face I did not shield
from buffets and spitting.

The Lord GOD is my help,
therefore I am not disgraced;
I have set my face like flint,
knowing that I shall not be put to shame.
He is near who upholds my right;
if anyone wishes to oppose me,
let us appear together.
Who disputes my right?
Let that man confront me.
See, the Lord GOD is my help;
who will prove me wrong?

SECOND READING
[Jas 2:14-18]

What good is it, my brothers and sisters,
if someone says he has faith but does not have works?
Can that faith save him?
If a brother or sister has nothing to wear
and has no food for the day,
and one of you says to them,
"Go in peace, keep warm, and eat well,"
but you do not give them the necessities of the body,
what good is it?
So also faith of itself,
if it does not have works, is dead.

Indeed someone might say,
"You have faith and I have works."
Demonstrate your faith to me without works,
and I will demonstrate my faith to you from my works.

Catechesis

Cantors

To sing this Sunday's psalm well, you must combine a confidence in God's protection with a willingness to take up the cross. How, in your life, does the one feed the other?

Choir

You might end rehearsal this week by praying for yourselves and your parish for the grace of a ready response to the call of this Sunday's Gospel to take up the cross. You may wish to sing "Take Up Your Cross" or "Only This I Want" as part of your prayer.

Music Directors

One way to mark the change which characterizes the tenor of the Gospel readings from this Sunday until the end of the liturgical year is to change the service music you have been singing. You might begin using one of the other Ordinary Time settings which the parish has in its repertoire and a different Gospel acclamation. In line with this change, we have included a different musical setting for the general intercessions. All of this—far more than simply adding variety to what has become familiar—is to help us experience the shift in mood connected with the journey of Jesus and his disciples toward Jerusalem and the cross.

Hymns which invite you to take up the cross would be appropriate for this Sunday. "Take Up Your Cross" (in most hymnals, with varying tunes) would function well for the entrance procession. For the presentation of the gifts, or as a choir-only prelude, you might use "Only This I Want" [BB, CBW3, G2]. Especially strong because of its poetic imagery is "Before the Fruit Is Ripened by the Sun" [CH, W3], the mood and tempo of which would make it appropriate either as a choir prelude or for the presentation of the gifts.

Because the readings also speak of God's promise to bring life out of death, this would be a good Sunday to have the assembly sing a post-Communion hymn which celebrates resurrection. You might use "Sing with All the Saints in Glory" [CBW3, W3, WC]. Even more strongly connected to the readings is Edward McKenna's "The Paschal Hymn" [CH] which relates Christian service to cross and resurrection ("Facing death in our service to life, We rise freed from sin, redeemed from strife").

Liturgy Committee

It is surely not too early in the year to begin looking ahead to Advent. The Scriptures from now until the final Sunday of the liturgical year, the Solemnity of Our Lord Jesus Christ the King, all keep the assembly marching toward Jerusalem. What image of Christ will be portrayed in the Gospels these next Sundays that culminates in the Christ-who-comes of Advent?

This Sunday's Gospel marks a turning point in Mark's account of Jesus and it marks a turning point in these Sundays in Ordinary Time (to help bring home this turning point to the assembly, the music of the general intercessions has been changed). We hear today hints of what is in store for Jesus and his disciples as they journey closer to Jerusalem and the cross. For us, we are moving closer to the end of the liturgical year, closer to Advent, and closer to ending our in-course reading of the Gospel which ends just before the Passion account.

SEPTEMBER 17, 2000

Twenty-Fifth Sunday in Ordinary Time

FAITH-SHARING
- How is service a death to self? What does dying mean?
- How might you better bring home to yourselves that when you serve others *in Jesus' name* you serve him?
- Are you truly the servant of *all*?
- How does a life of service help you live the Paschal Mystery every day?

PRESIDERS
In your ministry do you tend to give more time and energy to those whom you know and enjoy and less to those whom you don't know or who annoy you? In what ways do you still need to die to self?

DEACONS
What does dying mean in the practical terms of your life of service to the community?

HOSPITALITY MINISTERS
Do you show favoritism and preferences when you greet others? Do you greet those you don't know with the same care and enthusiasm as you greet your friends?

MUSIC MINISTERS
In the ministry of music in your parish, who are the "least of all"?

ALTAR MINISTERS
How might your service ministry help others realize that God's ways are different from your ways?

LECTORS
How might you prepare your ministry so that the proclamation of God's word is a dying to self?

EUCHARISTIC MINISTERS
How is recognition of *all* others as the body of Christ a dying to self?

Spirituality

Reflecting on the Gospel

Jesus' journey toward Jerusalem now takes him through Galilee. This is the region where most of his public activity has taken place, but this phase of Jesus' ministry seems to be over ("he did not wish anyone to know" that he was traveling through Galilee). Jesus takes the opportunity the journey offers to continue to instruct his disciples about his true identity and mission. The Gospel unfolds in two seemingly opposing layers.

One layer is Jesus' continuous teaching about who he really is and what he is really all about. This Sunday's Gospel relates the second passion prediction: "The Son of Man is to be handed over to men and they will kill him and three days after his death the Son of Man will rise." However, in spite of Jesus' growing emphasis on what is really about to happen, the disciples "did not understand the saying." Further, "they were afraid to question him." How often in our own lives don't we avoid the unpleasant by ignoring it, putting it out of our minds, not pursuing any more information? How often are we afraid of the truth? Who wants to ask questions about something we would really rather not know about anyway?

The second layer to the Gospel shows how far the disciples are from truly following Jesus in the footsteps of his passion. As if to heighten the disciples' refusal to hear what Jesus is really saying, they carry on their own conversation quite apart from Jesus' message. Instead of paying close attention to where their journey will lead them, they argue about who among them is the greatest. This is about as far from Jesus' talk about personal suffering as they can get! How often in our own lives do we put the unpleasant out of our minds by focusing on what is much more to our liking and within our vision of how things ought to be?

Can't we just imagine how tried Jesus' patience was? Parents and teachers and others can readily identify with what must have been Jesus' great exasperation! Enough talk! Jesus *demonstrates* for them where their vision must be. He takes a child and hugs it ("putting his arms around it"). In a familiar, everyday gesture Jesus teaches us what discipleship actually is. He took a child—someone innocent, without legal status, totally dependent upon his or her parents or guardians, the negligible person of society—and tells the disciples to be servant *of all,* even of this least creature. And to do so is to serve Jesus himself as well as the "One who sent" him.

Living the Paschal Mystery

An incredible irony lies at the basis of Jesus' teaching: only the one who becomes least by serving the least of all can be first. This lays out for us a very practical, concrete way to live the Paschal Mystery. By dying to self and serving the least we rise. Dying to self doesn't simply mean we write a check for the United Way or bring non-perishable food gifts to Mass every Sunday to present with the bread and wine (as good as those gestures may be). It means surrendering our very selves for others—*all* others, not just those of our own picking and choosing.

GOSPEL [Mark 9:30-37; L134B]

Jesus and his disciples left from there and began a journey through Galilee, but he did not wish anyone to know about it. He was teaching his disciples and telling them, "The Son of Man is to be handed over to men and they will kill him, and three days after his death the Son of Man will rise." But they did not understand the saying, and they were afraid to question him.

They came to Capernaum and, once inside the house, he began to ask them, "What were you arguing about on the way?" But they remained silent. They had been discussing among themselves on the way who was the greatest. Then he sat down, called the Twelve, and said to them, "If anyone wishes to be first, he shall be the last of all and the servant of all." Taking a child, he placed it in their midst, and putting his arms around it, he said to them, "Whoever receives one child such as this in my name, receives me; and whoever receives me, receives not me but the One who sent me."

Working with the Word

Key words and phrases from the Gospel: journey, death, rise, they did not understand, arguing, servant of all

Connecting to the first reading: The selection from Wisdom helps us to focus on the forthcoming suffering of Christ. It also gives us a sense of *how* we also journey on the road of suffering, how we embrace death in the hope of having life—with "God [who] will take care of" us.

Connecting to our culture: We don't live in a society in which servants are a common commodity. Yet, we have cultural, economic, and social classes of people whom we definitely treat as the least. The Gospel calls us to serve these lowliest. Why is serving the least so central to Christian living? Because this is the way the Teacher lived!

Exegetical points: Jesus sets out on a journey. The geographical destination is Jerusalem, but the end point is really the cross. What lies ahead must be weighing heavily on his mind, for Jesus announces the second of three passion predictions (the first was last Sunday and the third is omitted from the Lectionary). Once again, the cross casts its shadow over this Sunday's reading.

In the same way that last Sunday's teaching was set against the misunderstanding of Peter, in this week's Gospel the disciples as a group "did not understand" Jesus' teaching: they, who are called to discipleship, are caught jockeying for position. In both Gospels, the suffering-death-resurrection of Jesus is the context in which he teaches the meaning of discipleship. Being a disciple in the sense Jesus describes is the way in which followers of Jesus enter into and share his Paschal Mystery.

The force of the saying, "the one who wishes to be first shall be the last of all" comes into clear focus in the final phrase, "and the servant of all." Just who that "all" includes is made clear in the child around whom Jesus places his arms. It is helpful to pay attention to this child, for "children" and "little ones" appear in the Gospels for the next three weeks as well. Children are the gospel symbol of the "least of all."

To the point: To be a disciple means to do as the Teacher did: Jesus died for the sake of all. For us, in the midst of everyday living, to die means to give our life in service. Service is a kind of dying (of self for others).

Celebration

Model Penitential Rite

Presider: God reaches out to *all*, without any prejudice or favoritism. Let us consider how God has touched each of us this week through others and open ourselves to having God touch us through this liturgy . . . [pause]

Son of Man, you suffered and died for us and rose for our salvation: Lord . . .
Son of God, you became the servant of all: Christ . . .
Lord Jesus, you receive the helpless and the lowly: Lord . . .

Responsorial Psalm

"The Lord upholds my life."

This Sunday's responsorial psalm is a cry of confidence in face of certain death. In the first reading the "wicked" plot "a shameful death" for one whose righteous manner of living was an affront to their unrighteous ways. In the Gospel Jesus warns the disciples that this same end is in store for him. But he promises also that on the third day he will rise. Like the psalmist, Jesus knows that God will be upholding his life. We, too, can face the cost of discipleship because we believe that even in death God will uphold us. Such confidence does not come from mere intellectual conviction, but from interpersonal relationship: we call on God's very name ("by your name save me") which we have come to know is "goodness" itself. In singing this psalm we profess our willingness to continue on the journey to the cross because we *know by name* the goodness of the One who calls us forward.

Model General Intercessions

Presider: God takes care of the least among us. By this we are encouraged to make our needs known.

Response:

[musical notation: Lord, hear our prayer.]

Cantor:

[musical notation: we pray to the Lord,]

May all members of the Church be willing to serve the least among us . . . [pause]

May all people of the world come to understand the power of being servant to others . . . [pause]

May the least among us be granted dignity and honor . . . [pause]

May our community be known for our unselfish service toward others . . . [pause]

Presider: O God, when we receive others we receive you: embrace us in your strength that we may serve you in others. We ask this through Christ our Lord. **Amen.**

OPENING PRAYER

Let us pray
 [that we may grow in the love of God and of one another]

Pause for silent prayer

Father,
guide us, as you guide creation
according to your law of love.
May we love one another
and come to perfection
in the eternal life prepared for us.
Grant this through our Lord Jesus
 Christ, your Son,
who lives and reigns with you and the
 Holy Spirit,
one God, for ever and ever. **Amen.**

RESPONSORIAL PSALM

[Ps 54:3-4, 5, 6-8]

℟. (6b) The Lord upholds my life.

O God, by your name save me,
 and by your might defend my cause.
O God, hear my prayer;
 hearken to the words of my mouth.

℟. The Lord upholds my life.

For the haughty men have risen up
 against me,
 the ruthless seek my life;
 they set not God before their eyes.

℟. The Lord upholds my life.

Behold, God is my helper;
 the Lord sustains my life.
Freely will I offer you sacrifice;
 I will praise your name, O LORD, for
 its goodness.

℟. The Lord upholds my life.

Catechesis

FIRST READING
[Wis 2:12, 17-20]

The wicked say:
>Let us beset the just one, because he is obnoxious to us;
>he sets himself against our doings, reproaches us for transgressions of the law
>and charges us with violations of our training.
>Let us see whether his words be true;
>let us find out what will happen to him.
>For if the just one be the son of God, God will defend him
>and deliver him from the hand of his foes.
>With revilement and torture let us put the just one to the test
>that we may have proof of his gentleness
>and try his patience.
>Let us condemn him to a shameful death;
>for according to his own words, God will take care of him.

SECOND READING
[Jas 3:16–4:3]

Beloved:
Where jealousy and selfish ambition exist,
>there is disorder and every foul practice.
>But the wisdom from above is first of all pure,
>then peaceable, gentle, compliant, full of mercy and good fruits,
>without inconstancy or insincerity.
>And the fruit of righteousness is sown in peace
>for those who cultivate peace.

Where do the wars
>and where do the conflicts among you come from?
>Is it not from your passions
>that make war within your members?
>You covet but do not possess.
>You kill and envy but you cannot obtain;
>you fight and wage war.
>You do not possess because you do not ask.
>You ask but do not receive,
>because you ask wrongly, to spend it on your passions.

Cantors
You would probably rather avoid the death which fidelity to discipleship makes inevitable. This Sunday's responsorial psalm sings about how God upholds you even in death. As you prepare to lead the assembly in singing this psalm, pray for this confidence which is the source of a disciple's courage.

Choir
In this Sunday's Gospel Jesus teaches you that rather than vying to be greatest, you should strive to serve one another. What opportunities does your collaboration as a choir offer you to live out this value?

Music Directors
A hymn which speaks of Christ as the model of service and which calls you to compassionate service with him is "Lord, Whose Love in Humble Service" [BB, CBW3, CH, RS, W3, WC]. All three of the tunes to which it is sung (HOLY MANNA, IN BABILONE, BEACH SPRING) would function well for the entrance procession.

A different twist on the call to service is given in Richard Guillard's "The Servant Song" [G, G2, RS]. In this hymn you ask one another for permission to be the servant, indicating that the receiving of service is itself gift and grace. You might sing this hymn during the presentation of the gifts with a broad, meditative tempo.

Liturgy Committee
Assess your service to the community in terms of the Paschal Mystery. How does your dying to self help your community rise in newness of life?

The gifts of bread and wine you bring to the altar-table in the presentation of the gifts represent yourselves and all your service to the least among you. You offer yourselves for each other just as Jesus offered himself for you. The only other appropriate gifts to present during Mass are food items for the poor and gifts for the needs of the Church (see GIRM, no. 101). Other kinds of gifts (for example, a trophy) might be wonderful symbols of your lives, but there is something far deeper going on here. The gifts that you present are taken by God, transformed, and returned to you as *food:* the Body of Christ for you or food to satisfy the physical hunger of members of the Body.

It is good pastoral practice to have baskets at the entrance to the sacred space and to encourage people regularly to make sacrifices for the poor rather than just at Thanksgiving time. It would be appropriate to make a brief comment about this in the context of the homily.

SEPTEMBER 24, 2000

Twenty-Sixth Sunday in Ordinary Time

FAITH-SHARING
- Is bringing about the kingdom of God a clear priority in your life? Could others read this in your actions?
- What do you do that brings life to God's kingdom?
- What does it mean to be *for* Jesus?
- What do you need to "cut off" in order for God's kingdom to be more present in your life?

PRESIDERS
Building the kingdom is your central concern. However, it is easy to let other things take over your life. If you were to examine where you put your time and energy, what would this identify as your ministerial priorities? Is it the kingdom? Does anything need to be "cut off" in order to keep the kingdom first?

DEACONS
Who needs from you a "cup of water to drink because [he or she] belong[s] to Christ"?

HOSPITALITY MINISTERS
Who are the "little ones" (at work, in the neighborhood) to whom you need to reach out? How does this shape your greeting people as the body of Christ on Sunday?

MUSIC MINISTERS
Music ministry can easily be a forum for subtle rivalries and petty jealousies. How might you be assured that what you do is in Jesus' name, not in the name of your own ego?

ALTAR MINISTERS
Jesus' continual usage of the phrase "cut it off" impresses upon all that nothing is more important than the kingdom. How might you serve to communicate the centrality of God's kingdom?

LECTORS
The root of the word "passion" means "to suffer with." Both Moses' and Jesus' response in the readings are passionate. In what way does the Word cause you to live passionately about the kingdom?

EUCHARISTIC MINISTERS
Where can you practice greater inclusivity in your daily life? How would this affect your ministerial contact with the members of the body of Christ?

Spirituality

Reflecting on the Gospel

Many organized team sports for younger children have league rules that require everyone on the team be given a chance to play regardless of talent. It is a good choice in favor of inclusivity and the inherent worth of each individual. These kinds of rules keep organized sports from doing what the "sandlot" sports tended to do. We adults can remember as kids "choosing up sides" for a game. Usually, the two best players were automatically assumed to be the "captains." They chose their respective teams by taking turns, inevitably choosing the best players first. This certainly fed the ego and strengthened the self-esteem of those chosen quickly, but had the opposite effect on those who got chosen last. Actually, these last players were more tolerated than chosen. Sometimes these last ones might have felt jealous of the better players; but more often they just felt the sting of not being wanted or of not really belonging. Jesus deals with a similar situation in this Sunday's Gospel and with unexpected candor.

Someone not chosen ("he does not follow us") was "driving out demons." Someone who doesn't "belong" was doing what Jesus did. Those who do belong—the disciples—do what is natural for most of us: they tried to prevent the "non-belonger" from acting as though he belonged. Jesus lays down a simple, clear rule: "Whoever is not against us is for us." Anyone who is doing good in Jesus' name—no matter how great ("driving out demons") or how small ("gives you a cup of water to drink")—cannot also speak ill of Jesus. To be a disciple of Jesus means letting go of the need to be the greatest (from last Sunday's Gospel) or letting go of our ideas of who belongs or who doesn't. This raises the question about what are our priorities with respect to the kingdom of God?

Four times does Jesus say "it would be better for you." Here is where Jesus speaks with utter candor: for his followers, there is nothing more important—not even our own human life or body parts!—than our entering the kingdom of God and our not being a cause for others to lose entering the kingdom. If anything whatsoever gets in the way of bringing us or others the life of the kingdom, get rid of it! Jesus can't get any clearer than that!

Living the Paschal Mystery

Each day we are faced with choices: to be *for* or *against* Christ. This is both as easy as it sounds and as profound. The entire second part of Mark's Gospel is about who Jesus is and what it costs to be his disciple. To be Jesus' disciple necessitates losing something, cutting some things out. But when we do, *life* comes. In other words, cutting off is a kind of dying; it is a way to be "against" something (that is attractive to us) so as to be "for" Jesus. The kingdom of God is so important that we must want to do everything and anything we can—great and small—to bring it about.

OCTOBER 1, 2000

GOSPEL [Mark 9:38-43, 45, 47-48; L137B]

At that time, John said to Jesus, "Teacher, we saw someone driving out demons in your name, and we tried to prevent him because he does not follow us." Jesus replied, "Do not prevent him. There is no one who performs a mighty deed in my name who can at the same time speak ill of me. For whoever is not against us is for us. Anyone who gives you a cup of water to drink because you belong to Christ, amen, I say to you, will surely not lose his reward.

"Whoever causes one of these little ones who believe in me to sin, it would be better for him if a great millstone were put around his neck and he were thrown into the sea. If your hand causes you to sin, cut it off. It is better for you to enter into life maimed than with two hands to go into Gehenna, into the unquenchable fire. And if your foot causes you to sin, cut if off. It is better for you to enter into life crippled than with two feet to be thrown into Gehenna. And if your eye causes you to sin, pluck it out. Better for you to enter into the kingdom of God with one eye than with two eyes to be thrown into Gehenna, where 'their worm does not die, and the fire is not quenched.'"

Working with the Word

Key words and phrases from the Gospel: Do not prevent, in my name, not against us, for us, kingdom of God

Connecting to last Sunday's Gospel: Last Sunday the Gospel included the disciples' argument about who is the greatest and least in the kingdom. This Sunday's Gospel offers another comment on service in the kingdom: it is not a question of *what* we do but for *whom:* the "little ones."

Connecting to the culture: Both Moses' and Jesus' response in the readings this Sunday are passionate ones: Moses is passionate about who may prophesy ("Would that all the people of the LORD were prophets!") and Jesus is passionate about advancing the kingdom (". . . better for you to enter into the kingdom of God with one eye . . ."). What are we passionate about with respect to the Gospel? What is our culture saying our passion should be about?

Exegetical points: The disciples tip their hand when they describe the man driving out demons as one who "does not follow *us.*" On one level, the problem is one of belonging: does the one performing service belong to "us" or to Jesus? The danger of forming the Church as an exclusive group of insiders "like us" is rejected by Jesus in a remarkably generous assessment: "whoever is not against us is for us." On another level, the nature of service is not determined by what is done: it can be as great an act as expelling demons, or as insignificant an act as giving a cup of water. Instead, what qualifies service as "Christian" is "in whose name" the service is done.

The child of last week's Gospel appears in this Sunday's Gospel as "these little ones" to whom the community has a responsibility to give sound teaching and good example. There are two points to these difficult and hyperbolic sayings. First, they recognize sin as something personal, as much a part of us as hand, foot, and eye. Second, these sayings highlight the surpassing value of life in the kingdom. Mere "life" or the "quality of life" is not the goal of Christian existence. Life is not valued by the number of hands or feet, or by physical ability or impairment, but by the willingness to live for Christ.

To the point: What does it mean to be *for* Jesus? (1) Advance the kingdom of God: nothing is more important than this, and (2) doing deeds in Christ's name, whether the deeds are as dramatic as casting out demons or as ordinary as giving a drink of water.

Celebration

Model Penitential Rite

Presider: Whoever is not against Jesus is for Jesus. Let us look at the past week and examine when we have made decisions for or against Jesus . . . [pause]

> Lord Jesus, your teaching makes present the kingdom: Lord . . .
> Teacher, your precepts give joy to our hearts: Christ . . .
> Lord Jesus, cleanse us from our unknown faults: Lord . . .

Responsorial Psalm

"The precepts of the Lord give joy to the heart."

Both this Sunday's first reading and Gospel raise the question of who is *for* God. Moses answered, anyone who prophesies through the power of God's spirit. Jesus responded, anyone who performs good deeds in his name. The responsorial psalm answers by speaking of the law of the Lord. For the Israelites the Law *(torah)* was the guide to a life directed wholeheartedly toward God. The Law sustained one's fidelity to God by leading the heart to what was "perfect," "trustworthy," "pure," and "true." The Law was the path to life. When we sing this psalm, we are thanking God for the gift of this guide and for the joy which following it brings.

Model General Intercessions

Presider: Nothing is more important than bringing about God's kingdom. We help to make God's kingdom present by praying for our brothers and sisters in need.

Response:

Lord, hear our prayer.

Cantor:

we pray to the Lord,

That nothing be more important in the lives of the people of God than bringing about God's kingdom . . . [pause]

That nothing be more important in the lives of the leaders of the world than caring for children, providing for the needy, and protecting the weak . . . [pause]

That nothing be more important in the lives of those who cause others to sin than repenting and cutting themselves off from their evil ways . . . [pause]

That nothing be more important in our lives than acting in Jesus' name . . . [pause]

Presider: O God, you call us to bear the name of your Son and reward us for being faithful: hear our prayers that we might serve you in others. We ask this through Christ our Lord. **Amen.**

ALTERNATIVE OPENING PRAYER

Let us pray

Pause for silent prayer

Father of our Lord Jesus Christ,
in your unbounded mercy
you have revealed the beauty of your power
through your constant forgiveness of our sins.
May the power of this love be in our hearts
to bring your pardon and your kingdom to all we meet.
We ask this through Christ our Lord.
Amen.

RESPONSORIAL PSALM
[Ps 19:8, 10, 12-13, 14]

℟. (9a) The precepts of the Lord give joy to the heart.

The law of the Lord is perfect,
  refreshing the soul;
the decree of the Lord is trustworthy,
  giving wisdom to the simple.

℟. The precepts of the Lord give joy to the heart.

The fear of the Lord is pure,
  enduring forever;
the ordinances of the Lord are true,
  all of them just.

℟. The precepts of the Lord give joy to the heart.

Though your servant is careful of them,
  very diligent in keeping them,
yet who can detect failings?
  Cleanse me from my unknown faults!

℟. The precepts of the Lord give joy to the heart.

From wanton sin especially, restrain your servant;
  let it not rule over me.
Then shall I be blameless and innocent of serious sin.

℟. The precepts of the Lord give joy to the heart.

FIRST READING
[Num 11:25-29]

The Lord came down in the cloud and spoke to Moses.
Taking some of the spirit that was on Moses,
    the Lord bestowed it on the seventy elders;
    and as the spirit came to rest on them, they prophesied.

Now two men, one named Eldad and the other Medad,
    were not in the gathering but had been left in the camp.
They too had been on the list, but had not gone out to the tent;
    yet the spirit came to rest on them also,
    and they prophesied in the camp.
So, when a young man quickly told Moses,
    "Eldad and Medad are prophesying in the camp,"
Joshua, son of Nun, who from his youth had been Moses' aide, said,
    "Moses, my lord, stop them."
But Moses answered him,
    "Are you jealous for my sake?
Would that all the people of the Lord were prophets!
Would that the Lord might bestow his spirit on them all!"

SECOND READING
[Jas 5:1-6]

Come now, you rich, weep and wail over your impending miseries.
Your wealth has rotted away, your clothes have become moth-eaten,
    your gold and silver have corroded,
    and that corrosion will be a testimony against you;
    it will devour your flesh like a fire.
You have stored up treasure for the last days.
Behold, the wages you withheld from the workers
    who harvested your fields are crying aloud;
    and the cries of the harvesters have reached the ears of the Lord of hosts.
You have lived on earth in luxury and pleasure;
    you have fattened your hearts for the day of slaughter.
You have condemned;
    you have murdered the righteous one;
    he offers you no resistance.

Catechesis

Cantors

As you prepare to sing this Sunday's psalm, pray for the grace to experience the joy which comes from remaining faithful to the law of God even when this fidelity entails removing from your life those things which stand in the way of this fidelity.

Choir

Living for Jesus means doing deeds—great or small—in his name. It also means removing from your lives those behaviors which get in the way of the kingdom. This week you might examine what motivates your singing in the choir and what behaviors you bring to the choir. Do your motives and behavior model for others that you are "for" Jesus and live in his name, or do they scandalize others by advertising that you are "against" Jesus?

Music Directors

Using an entrance hymn that connects directly to the text of the Gospel adds to the integrity of the celebration, but it is not always possible to find an entrance hymn that clearly connects. Nor is this always necessary. Any hymn which speaks of the gathering of the Church or of praise is also a good choice for a Sunday in Ordinary Time.

An example of such a hymn is Delores Dufner's "Sing a New Church" [BB]. She has set the text to the familiar American folk tune NETTLETON, using the last two phrases for an inviting refrain, "Let us bring the gifts that differ, and, in splendid, varied ways, Sing a new Church into being, One in faith and love and praise."

Liturgy Committee

At times with certain tasks of a liturgy committee (e.g., enhancing the environment), some individuals can create a "dynasty" in which they make the decisions and accept few suggestions or no advice. This can cause tension and even jealousy on the part of other committee members. Ultimately, the liturgy itself might suffer because the liturgy is not working together for the common good. Are there factions on your liturgy committee, or does anyone dominate? How inclusive are you as a committee? What affect does your inclusivity have on your parish's worship? If there are problems in this area, what is the most pastorally sensitive way to handle them?

Examine the ways in which your liturgies are inclusive of everyone, especially the "little ones." Is your sacred space accessible to the physically challenged? Do you include the physically and mentally challenged among your ministers?

OCTOBER 1, 2000

TWENTY-SEVENTH SUNDAY IN ORDINARY TIME

FAITH-SHARING
- Isn't it ironic that with the great overriding urgency of building the kingdom of God, children take precedence and show everyone what the kingdom is really all about?
- When and with whom do you tend to have a "hard heart"?
- What could be some concrete steps you can take to ensure fidelity to your commitments?
- In what areas of life are you most apt to act out of human weakness rather than according to God's plan?

PRESIDERS
Your openness is Christ's embrace, especially for the "little ones" most in need of his blessing. Where do you need to be more open?

DEACONS
Who are the (metaphoric) "children" you need to receive, embrace, and bless—in daily life? in ministry?

HOSPITALITY MINISTERS
How might your greeting "embrace" another with a loving touch so that they feel drawn to God's love, compassion, and peace?

MUSIC MINISTERS
In the Gospel Jesus blesses the children who seek his presence and his touch. Do you seek, in your music ministry, to be touched by Jesus? Do you ask for his blessing?

ALTAR MINISTERS
How faithful are you to service—at home? with your ministry? What are some concrete ways that your service can be deepened?

LECTORS
When do you find yourself testing or rebuking others by your speech? How does this adversely affect your proclamation of God's Word?

EUCHARISTIC MINISTERS
"May the Lord bless us all the days of our lives." How might you see distribution of Communion as a participation in God's blessing of people?

Spirituality

Reflecting on the Gospel
This Sunday's Gospel, at first reading, seems to tackle one of the thorniest problems facing our society: the question of divorce. The shorter form of the Gospel selection with a quick read of the first reading from Genesis would lead us to believe that legality of divorce is the whole point of this Gospel. However, a closer examination of the structure of the Lectionary directs our reflection in a broader way than merely sermonizing on divorce and the indissolubility of marriage. These readings bring to mind a number of other questions and challenges: communion and relationship, God's ways and our ways, human hardness of heart, and—most importantly—who belongs to the kingdom of God.

If divorce were the central issue, then we might expect the first reading to be Deuteronomy 24:1-4 where Moses takes divorce for granted and lays out the specifics of how to handle it. Instead, we have the second creation account from Genesis. The Deuteronomy reading would underscore human fickleness and loss of relationship; the Genesis account underscores communion and fidelity to relationship. Deuteronomy would illustrate human ways; Genesis underscores God's ways. The four Gospel verses on children added to the divorce material put the question of divorce into a larger perspective and also help us keep in mind the larger Marcan context of the gradual revelation of Jesus' identity, the true meaning of discipleship, and the inauguration of God's kingdom.

People were bringing children to Jesus so that "he might touch them," language used for blessing. The hard-hearted disciples rebuke the people; Jesus is indignant at the disciples but gentle and welcoming with the children ("he embraced them"), telling the disciples "not to prevent them" (a phrase we heard in last Sunday's Gospel) from coming to him. Why does Jesus welcome the children? Because "the kingdom of God belongs to such as these."

The arrangement of the readings in the Lectionary directs our reflection toward the profound difference between God's ways and human ways. These readings depict conflicts with God's ways: "testing" (Pharisees with Jesus), "divorce" (between husband and wife), and "rebuking" (the disciples with the children) are the ways of hearts grown hard. God's plan "in the beginning" and fulfilled in the establishment of the kingdom by Christ, on the other hand, is about *communion*—symbolized in the receiving, embracing, and blessing of children. These readings should not help us ignore society's serious problem with divorce. They don't dissolve the questions. But they do offer us a larger perspective. Would the problem and the questions be different if we were able to place our relationships in the larger context of God's ways and relationship with us?

Living the Paschal Mystery
The Paschal Mystery tension of dying and rising is played out many ways. This Sunday's Gospel suggests a number of them: God's ways vs. human ways; peace vs. "testing"; fidelity vs. fickleness; communion vs. separation; those without power (children) vs. those in power (Pharisees); come vs. rebuke; accept vs. does not enter. Which do we choose?

GOSPEL [Mark 10:2-16; L140B]

The Pharisees approached Jesus and asked, "Is it lawful for a husband to divorce his wife?" They were testing him. He said to them in reply, "What did Moses command you?" They replied, "Moses permitted a husband to write a bill of divorce and dismiss her." But Jesus told them, "Because of the hardness of your hearts he wrote you this commandment. But from the beginning of creation, *God made them male and female. For this reason a man shall leave his father and mother and be joined to his wife, and the two shall become one flesh.* So they are no longer two but one flesh. Therefore what God has joined together, no human being must separate." In the house the disciples again questioned Jesus about this. He said to them, "Whoever divorces his wife and marries another commits adultery against her; and if she divorces her husband and marries another, she commits adultery."

And people were bringing children to him that he might touch them, but the disciples rebuked them. When Jesus saw this he became indignant and said to them, "Let the children come to me; do not prevent them, for the kingdom of God belongs to such as these. Amen, I say to you, whoever does not accept the kingdom of God like a child will not enter it." Then he embraced them and blessed them, placing his hands on them.

Working with the Word

Key words and phrases from the Gospel: testing him, one flesh, do not prevent them, accept the kingdom of God, embraced them

Connecting to the Lectionary: The tendency this Sunday is to "sermonize" on the indissolubility of marriage. But this Gospel's Lectionary context tells us its point is otherwise: the kingdom of God takes priority over all things, even human law.

Connecting to culture: Historically, marriage and divorce have always been a problem. The Pharisees *tested* Jesus, which is to say they used a thorny issue to *nail* him. Notice how Jesus moves from a specific theological debate to the larger perspective of the ways of the kingdom. When are we as Church tempted to get caught up in theoretical arguments and lose sight of what's really important? How might we forestall this?

Exegetical points: In the matter of marriage and divorce, the Pharisees emerge as those concerned about divorce whereas Jesus is the champion of marriage; the Pharisees want to know what the Law permits, whereas Jesus tells them what God intended from creation. Thus, the controversy is really about the divine plan and human legalism. In such a contest, there is no doubt that God's creative design takes priority over all legalism. The Pharisees, in their concern for what is "lawful" and what is "permitted," lose focus on both the divine commandment and the human consequences that the sadness of divorce and remarriage causes. Remarriage is not merely a violation of law, as the term "adultery" implies. Jesus says that the man who divorces his wife and marries another "commits adultery against her." Human acts affect human persons. Hiding behind legalism is no excuse for ignoring either God's plans or the affects our actions have on others.

Moreover, in the context of this discussion about marriage, Mark has placed a story of Jesus blessing children. Children are especially dependent on others and thus reveal a crucial aspect of discipleship: our reliance on the Master for what we need. Awareness of dependence ideally fosters the ability to receive what others have to give.

To the point: Given human ways and God's plan, where do our loyalties lie? Using the thorny example of marriage and divorce, the Pharisees (and disciples) become spokesmen for human ways while Jesus is spokesman for God's intentions in creation and in furthering the kingdom.

Celebration

Model Penitential Rite

Presider: Each Sunday we gather in God's loving embrace and ask for God's blessing. Let us open ourselves to the divine presence . . . [pause]

>Lord Jesus, your love and mercy restore the goodness of creation: Lord . . .
>Christ Jesus, you desire that we follow God's ways, not our ways: Christ . . .
>Lord Jesus, you gather us, your children, into your kingdom: Lord . . .

Responsorial Psalm

"May the Lord bless us all the days of our lives."

This Sunday's responsorial psalm is a song of ascents, one of a sequential set (Pss 120–134) some scholars believe were sung as the Israelites "went up" to Jerusalem to celebrate the major feasts every year. Psalm 128 was perhaps a song of blessing over the people as they began the journey back home. The psalm is about the blessings which fidelity to "walking in [God's] ways" brings. The image of the happy family projected by the psalm was the symbol *par excellence* of Israel's covenant relationship with God. The blessings described—fruitfulness, fulfillment, prosperity, and peace—are extended to all of Jerusalem. Thus Psalm 128 is not so much about the blessings of marriage as it is about the blessings of a way of life faithful to the "ways" of God. When we sing it we pray for the "fear" of the Lord which is awe and gratitude for God's gift of covenant relationship with us.

Model General Intercessions

Presider: When Jesus embraces the children, he shows us that he pays attention to the "little ones." So we are encouraged to place our needs before God.

Response:

[musical notation: Lord, hear our prayer.]

Cantor:

[musical notation: we pray to the Lord,]

For the Church, that she may place God's plan above human ways . . . [pause]

For all married couples, that they may be faithful to their vocation to be united in one flesh . . . [pause]

For the divorced and separated, that they may overcome their pain and live in God's peace . . . [pause]

For our community, that we may appreciate the gift of God's kingdom offered to us . . . [pause]

Presider: O creating God, you will that all people be held in your loving embrace: hear these our prayers that pain may be healed and all may be united in you. We ask this through Christ our Lord. **Amen.**

OPENING PRAYER

Let us pray

Pause for silent prayer

Father,
your love for us
surpasses all our hopes and desires.
Forgive our failings,
keep us in your peace
and lead us in the way of salvation.
We ask this through our Lord Jesus Christ, your Son,
who lives and reigns with you and the Holy Spirit,
one God, for ever and ever. **Amen.**

RESPONSORIAL PSALM

[Ps 128:1-2, 3, 4-5, 6]

℟. (cf. 5) May the Lord bless us all the days of our lives.

Blessed are you who fear the LORD,
    who walk in his ways!
For you shall eat the fruit of your
    handiwork;
    blessed shall you be, and favored.

℟. May the Lord bless us all the days of our lives.

Your wife shall be like a fruitful vine
    in the recesses of your home;
your children like olive plants
    around your table.

℟. May the Lord bless us all the days of our lives.

Behold, thus is the man blessed
    who fears the LORD.
The LORD bless you from Zion:
    may you see the prosperity of
        Jerusalem
    all the days of your life.

℟. May the Lord bless us all the days of our lives.

May you see your children's children.
    Peace be upon Israel!

℟. May the Lord bless us all the days of our lives.

FIRST READING
[Gen 2:18-24]

The Lord God said: "It is not good for
   the man to be alone.
I will make a suitable partner for him."
So the Lord God formed out of the
      ground
   various wild animals and various
      birds of the air,
   and he brought them to the man to
      see what he would call them;
   whatever the man called each of them
      would be its name.
The man gave names to all the cattle,
   all the birds of the air, and all wild
      animals;
   but none proved to be the suitable
      partner for the man.

So the Lord God cast a deep sleep on
      the man,
   and while he was asleep,
   he took out one of his ribs and closed
      up its place with flesh.
The Lord God then built up into a
      woman the rib
   that he had taken from the man.
When he brought her to the man, the
      man said:
   "This one, at last, is bone of my bones
      and flesh of my flesh;
   this one shall be called 'woman,' for
      out of 'her man' this one has been
      taken."
That is why a man leaves his father and
      mother
   and clings to his wife,
   and the two of them become one
      flesh.

SECOND READING
[Heb 2:9-11]

Brothers and sisters:
He "for a little while" was made "lower
      than the angels,"
   that by the grace of God he might
      taste death for everyone.

For it was fitting that he,
   for whom and through whom all
      things exist,
   in bringing many children to glory,
   should make the leader to their
      salvation perfect through
      suffering.
He who consecrates and those who are
      being consecrated
   all have one origin.
Therefore, he is not ashamed to call
   them "brothers."

Catechesis

Cantors

The refrain for this Sunday's psalm is a prayer of blessing over the people. As you prepare to sing it, spend time praying for members of your parish and for the whole Church. Pray for the blessings of fruitfulness, fulfillment, and peace which come from walking in the ways of God. As you travel to church this Sunday, you might consider using the psalm as your own song of ascent.

Choir

You might begin rehearsal this week with a prayer that the fruit of your labor as a choir be the blessing of a closer relationship with God. Pray that through your singing God bless you, and the assembly, with greater fidelity to the covenant. Use the refrain of the responsorial psalm to frame your prayer.

Music Directors

This Sunday's readings call you to remain open to a relationship with Jesus lived out by being faithful to the ways of the kingdom. A fitting hymn would be George Herbert's "Come, My Way, My Truth, My Life" [BB, CH, RS, W3, WC]. Written in seventh-century England, its poetry may at first seem archaic. But a second read reveals its perennial power (and the reason why it is still included in so many contemporary hymnals). In the hymn you call Jesus to come to you. All of the words you sing, with one exception, are of a single syllable. Those who want to receive Jesus come, not with the duplicity of a Pharisee, but with the simplicity and directness of a child. The mood and tempo fit the presentation of the gifts. Or you might have the choir sing the text as a prelude. One lovely choral setting, for example, is Don Muro's SATB arrangement from GIA [G-3277].

Liturgy Committee

How might you prepare the Sunday liturgies so that there is a strong element of spirituality for the adults that encourages fidelity to living God's plan?

It is important this Sunday to use the long form of the Gospel for it puts the debate about divorce into the larger perspective of the kingdom of God (a central point in Mark's Gospel). Here the Lectionary—by taking into consideration all the readings—clearly aids an interpretation of the Gospel selection. This "Lectionary hermeneutic" has been a guiding principle in the preparation of these Sunday reflections.

OCTOBER 8, 2000

Twenty-Eighth Sunday in Ordinary Time

FAITH-SHARING

- As you consider your salvation, are you more comfortable with "inheriting" it as a gift or with "entering" it through your own doing of good works? How might you bring better balance to these two in your life?
- What do you hang on to or hold out on that keeps you from following Jesus' invitation and challenge?
- What is the hundredfold in your life that you already possess?

PRESIDERS

Of what do you need to dispossess yourself in order to do God's work better? How have you already experienced the promised hundredfold in your life?

DEACONS

How might you better recognize Jesus' invitation and challenge to follow him in your service to the community? in your proclamation of the Gospel?

HOSPITALITY MINISTERS

In what ways is your greeting of people part of God's hundredfold? How might you make this more apparent in your ministry?

MUSIC MINISTERS

How might praying for wisdom during this week help you to see your ministry not just as choosing hymns and leading singing, but on the deeper level of helping the assembly surrender to discipleship?

ALTAR MINISTERS

Those are saved who dispossess themselves of anything that stands in the way of doing *God's* work. How does your service witness to the utter centrality of following Jesus and doing God's work?

LECTORS

What is the hundredfold in your life that utterly convinces you of God's blessings? How might this help you proclaim God's word with more conviction?

EUCHARISTIC MINISTERS

Eucharist as the Messianic banquet is part of your hundredfold blessing in following Jesus. How is this true for you? In what ways do you share this hundredfold with those you meet outside liturgical celebrations?

Spirituality

Reflecting on the Gospel

This Sunday's Gospel concerns wealth and the kingdom and unfolds in three progressive vignettes. Each one has its own challenge and draws us deeper into understanding what inaugurating the kingdom of God means.

1. *Invitation and challenge.* The first vignette involves a man who humbly ("knelt down before him") asks a most important and profound question: "What must I do to inherit eternal life?" Jesus answers with the expected reply: keep the commandments, which the man claims he has done. Clearly this is not a false claim and the man understands true humility, for Jesus does not contradict his claim but looks at him lovingly in return. How touching for the man that gaze must have been! Then Jesus issues the invitation and challenge: to be disciple means to go beyond keeping the Law; it means to divest oneself of everything— empty oneself—and "come, follow" Jesus. The depth of the man's longing for eternal life is evident in that, hearing Jesus' invitation, "his face fell, and he went away sad." He couldn't surrender! He couldn't let go! He couldn't relinquish his possessions and satisfy his deepest longing!

2. *Reversal of meaning of God's blessings.* The second vignette is Jesus' brief, private instruction to his disciples concerning how difficult it is for the wealthy "to enter the kingdom of God." In Jewish society wealth was a sign of God's blessing. Here Jesus is qualifying this thinking; it is not possessions which assure one of entrance into the kingdom, but dispossession. The disciples "were amazed" at this change in the understanding of divine election. No wonder they began to question "who can be saved?" In response, Jesus answers that what seems impossible for human beings is, indeed, possible for God. Those are saved who dispossess themselves of anything that stands in the way of *God's* work.

3. *Rewards of discipleship.* The third vignette is a reassuring one for those who have sacrificed all to follow Jesus as disciples. Jesus assures his disciples of a hundredfold abundance both "in this present age" *and* "in the age to come." It may cost to be a disciple of Jesus, but the rewards of discipleship far exceed the sacrifices.

There we have it: to inherit eternal life we must dispossess ourselves of anything that gets in the way of responding to the invitation (the first vignette), look to God rather than to ourselves and our possessions for salvation (the second vignette), and if we do so we receive far more than we relinquish in this life as well as the next (third vignette). Indeed, "all things are possible for God"!

Living the Paschal Mystery

In this Gospel account the dying and rising of the Paschal Mystery might be captured in terms of enter and inherit, give up and hundredfold, seek and given. These tensions remind us that salvation is a gift of God *and* our own doing of good works. "Eternal life" appears at the beginning of the Gospel in the man's question and at the end of the Gospel in Jesus' promise of hundredfold reward for his disciples. In between the two comes the renunciation of anything that keeps us from surrendering to God's action to bring about the kingdom. Therein is the dying . . . and the rising to eternal life!

GOSPEL [Mark 10:17-30; L143B]

As Jesus was setting out on a journey, a man ran up, knelt down before him, and asked him, "Good teacher, what must I do to inherit eternal life?" Jesus answered him, "Why do you call me good? No one is good but God alone. You know the commandments: *You shall not kill; you shall not commit adultery; you shall not steal; you shall not bear false witness; you shall not defraud; honor your father and your mother.*" He replied and said to him, "Teacher, all of these I have observed from my youth." Jesus, looking at him, loved him and said to him, "You are lacking in one thing. Go, sell what you have, and give to the poor and you will have treasure in heaven; then come, follow me." At that statement his face fell, and he went away sad, for he had many possessions.

Jesus looked around and said to his disciples, "How hard it is for those who have wealth to enter the kingdom of God!" The disciples were amazed at his words. So Jesus again said to them in reply, "Children, how hard it is to enter the kingdom of God! It is easier for a camel to pass through the eye of a needle than for one who is rich to enter the kingdom of God." They were exceedingly astonished and said among themselves, "Then who can be saved?" Jesus looked at them and said, "For human beings it is impossible, but not for God. All things are possible for God." Peter began to say to him, "We have given up everything and followed you." Jesus said, "Amen, I say to you, there is no one who has given up house or brothers or sisters or mother or father or children or lands for my sake and for the sake of the gospel who will not receive a hundred times more now in this present age: houses and brothers and sisters and mothers and children and lands, with persecutions, and eternal life in the age to come."

Working with the Word

Key words and phrases from the Gospel: inherit eternal life; come, follow me; enter the kingdom of God; all things are possible with God; receive a hundred times more

Connecting to the Lectionary: Often, this passage (especially about receiving a hundredfold) is applied to those who answer the call to ordained priesthood or religious life but, in reality, this Gospel passage refers to *all* who accept the invitation to be disciples of Jesus. This man is asked to give his riches to the poor to follow Christ.

Connecting to the Jewish culture: For Jews, wealth was a sign of blessings from God (e.g., Prov 10:22; Eccl 5:18). In this Gospel the question becomes, if a person who is blessed can't be saved, who can be? Jesus answers, the one who makes the kingdom first in life, above all else, is the one who can be saved.

Exegetical points: This demanding teaching on wealth and discipleship is offered by Jesus as he is on his "journey" to the cross. Though the rich man is called to "follow me," instead he "went away sad"—the only person in Mark's Gospel to walk away from a call to discipleship.

The rich man's flattery, "Good teacher" (otherwise attested in the entire Bible only in Luke's parallel version of this story), is rebuffed by Jesus somewhat testily. As difficult as Jesus' demands to the rich man are—go, sell, give, come, follow—his generalized teaching to the disciples is even more difficult: "how hard it is for those who have wealth to enter the kingdom of God." The force of Peter's question is: "If those blessed by God cannot be saved, then who can?" (In preaching, avoid the hypothesis that "Needle's Eye" refers to a small gate in Jerusalem; no such gate is known to have existed until the ninth century C.E.) A clue is found in Jesus' addressing his disciples as "children," that is, those who must depend on God to accomplish what neither human wealth nor achievements can. Would-be disciples who cannot give up their wealth will certainly be unable to give up their lives, for this is where the journey of discipleship will end—at the cross.

To the point: Our journey of discipleship leads to eternal life. We both *inherit* it (eternal life is a gift of God, a grace) and *enter* it (we do good works; e.g., keep the commandments, dispossess ourselves and give to the poor).

Celebration

Model Penitential Rite

Presider: God promises a hundredfold abundance to those who surrender to being disciples. Let us reflect on our opportunities for discipleship during this past week and how well we have responded . . . [pause]

> Good Teacher, you love us and call us to follow you: Lord . . .
> Christ Jesus, you show us the way to salvation: Christ . . .
> Lord Jesus, you promise a hundredfold to your disciples: Lord . . .

Responsorial Psalm

"Fill us with your love, O Lord, and we will sing for joy!"

In order to fully understand this Sunday's responsorial psalm, we must read the entirety of Psalm 90. This psalm meditates on the fragility and brevity of human life by poignantly contrasting all that is human with the power and eternity of God. Typical of Hebrew thought, the psalm construes of death and suffering as punishment for sin, and prays for respite ("Make us glad, for the day when you afflicted us, for the years when we saw evil"). Ultimately—again, typical of Hebrew thought—it is a psalm of hope, a sure statement that God will give prosperity to that which is radically tenuous: human life and endeavor.

This Sunday's responsorial psalm, then, prays for the wisdom described in the first reading while it identifies with the struggle with possession/dispossession presented in the Gospel. In singing it we acknowledge our human fragility and proclaim the omnipotence of God for whom "all things are possible."

Model General Intercessions

Presider: All things are possible for God, and so we are encouraged to pray for what we need.

Response:

[musical notation: Lord, hear our prayer.]

Cantor:

[musical notation: we pray to the Lord,]

That all the baptized may value life in Christ more than any earthly possessions . . . [pause]

That the peoples of the world may know peace and justice by keeping God's commandments . . . [pause]

That those who struggle to follow Jesus may hear his call to dispossess themselves and follow him . . . [pause]

That we recognize with grateful hearts the hundredfold God has already given each of us . . . [pause]

Presider: Good and gracious God, all things are possible with you: hear these our prayers that we may inherit eternal life. We pray through Jesus Christ our Lord. **Amen.**

OPENING PRAYER

Let us pray

Pause for silent prayer

Lord,
our help and guide,
make your love the foundation of our lives.
May our love for you express itself
in our eagerness to do good for others.
Grant this through our Lord Jesus Christ, your Son,
who lives and reigns with you and the Holy Spirit,
one God, for ever and ever. **Amen.**

RESPONSORIAL PSALM
[Ps 90:12-13, 14-15, 16-17]

℟. (14) Fill us with your love, O Lord, and we will sing for joy!

Teach us to number our days aright,
    that we may gain wisdom of heart.
Return, O LORD! How long?
    Have pity on your servants!

℟. Fill us with your love, O Lord, and we will sing for joy!

Fill us at daybreak with your kindness,
    that we may shout for joy and gladness all our days.
Make us glad, for the days when you afflicted us,
    for the years when we saw evil.

℟. Fill us with your love, O Lord, and we will sing for joy!

Let your work be seen by your servants
    and your glory by their children;
and may the gracious care of the Lord our God be ours;
    prosper the work of our hands for us!
    Prosper the work of our hands!

℟. Fill us with your love, O Lord, and we will sing for joy!

Catechesis

FIRST READING
[Wis 7:7-11]

I prayed, and prudence was given me;
 I pleaded, and the spirit of wisdom came to me.
I preferred her to scepter and throne,
and deemed riches nothing in comparison with her,
 nor did I liken any priceless gem to her;
because all gold, in view of her, is a little sand,
 and before her, silver is to be accounted mire.
Beyond health and comeliness I loved her,
and I chose to have her rather than the light,
 because the splendor of her never yields to sleep.
Yet all good things together came to me in her company,
 and countless riches at her hands.

SECOND READING
[Heb 4:12-13]

Brothers and sisters:
Indeed the word of God is living and effective,
 sharper than any two-edged sword,
 penetrating even between soul and spirit, joints and marrow,
 and able to discern reflections and thoughts of the heart.
No creature is concealed from him,
 but everything is naked and exposed to the eyes of him
 to whom we must render an account.

Cantors
If surrendering to discipleship means dispossessing yourselves of much that you hold dear, who can do it? The psalm refrain gives a clue: you pray to be filled with God's love, that which will ultimately satisfy. Use this refrain for daily prayer this week so that your longing for God can be heard in your singing.

Choir
In this Sunday's psalm you pray that God will "prosper the work of [your] hands." What kind of "prosperity" marks your ministry as a choir? Do you experience yourselves growing in discipleship because of your participation in the choir, and do you see this as a kind of prosperity? Do you see the assembly growing in discipleship because of your ministry as a choir?

Music Directors
Michael Joncas' "The Love of the Lord" [G, G2, RS] connects with both this Sunday's readings and the responsorial psalm refrain ("Fill us with your love, O Lord, and we will sing for joy!"). The verses speak of riches, wealth, honors, all that one cherishes as worthless "in the light of the love of the Lord." The refrain ties this abandonment of all things to the satisfaction which comes from a "share in [Christ's] suffering and death." Because of its meditative mood, this hymn would work well either at the presentation of the gifts, or as a second Communion song. You might have cantor or choir only sing the verses with the assembly joining in the refrain.

Liturgy Committee
Especially with the environment of the sacred space, it can look like there needs to be some examination about "dispossessing." Is your liturgical environment cluttered? What are the principles you use to judge the appropriateness of the environment? Is more better? What is the difference between "lush" that draws each member of the assembly into liturgical prayer and season and "overdone" that, ultimately, distracts? Are they the same principles that you might use if you were "decorating" a space for another public event? Of what do you need to dispossess yourselves in order to serve your community better in the preparation of liturgies? What is blocking this dispossession?

It is essential to use the long form of the Gospel this Sunday because it leads to the ultimate goal of discipleship: eternal life.

OCTOBER 15, 2000

Twenty-Ninth Sunday in Ordinary Time

FAITH-SHARING
- Where do you exercise "lording it over"? What step could you take to move toward humility and self-emptying?
- What does Jesus give/offer you instead of places of honor?
- Consider what it means to say, "baptism is an *ongoing yes* to daily dying and rising in Christ."

PRESIDERS
How is your own baptism related to your ordained ministry? At this point in your life, what does your baptismal *yes* look like? What kind of daily shape does your servanthood take?

DEACONS
How does this Sunday's Gospel further the discussion that discipleship = service? What does this mean for you, one ordained to service?

HOSPITALITY MINISTERS
It was *not* Jesus' place to give the honor of sitting at his right or left to James and John. In your ministry are you tempted to honor your friends more than others? How might you practice this week treating everyone with dignity and honor?

MUSIC MINISTERS
The very nature of leading music for the assembly to some extent puts you at "center stage" during liturgy. How do you remain humble servants?

ALTAR MINISTERS
How might you perform your ministry in simple service, *not* drawing attention to yourself?

LECTORS
Proclamation of God's word is *not* something you do merely at the ambo. Living your baptism is a daily proclamation. How might you live this week Jesus' proclamation that disciples are "servants" and not glory-seekers?

EUCHARISTIC MINISTERS
Discipleship is *not* about seeking glory. Sometimes special ministers of the Eucharist are considered to be "better" than others. The very title "special" ministers of the Eucharist may support this in some peoples' minds. How might you serve in your ministry so that you convey true discipleship—"servant," "slave of all."

Spirituality

Reflecting on the Gospel

Manipulation is one of those things we all get caught up in once in a while. It is an act whereby we shrewdly exercise an "authority" over another, getting them to say or do something that benefits us. It is taking advantage of another person. James and John were two of the "favored" Twelve. In this Sunday's Gospel we see them trying to manipulate Jesus into giving them places of honor and power. These verses immediately follow Jesus' third prediction of his Passion (vv. 32-34) in Mark's Gospel (these verses come between last Sunday's Gospel and this Sunday's, but they are omitted in the Lectionary). The disciples still don't get it, do they?

The longer form of the Gospel selection may be divided into four segments. Each of these four sections has the word "not" in it, underscoring the misconception about discipleship not only by James and John but by all the Twelve.

In the first segment James and John ask for places of honor at Jesus' right and left in heaven. Jesus replies, "You do *not* know what you are asking." He redirects their seeking places of honor to what is at the core of discipleship: drink the cup of suffering and be baptized into his death. James and John reply that they can do these things, although their later desertion of Jesus during his Passion and death (in Mark's Gospel) suggest that their resolve was not very deep. In the second segment Jesus tells James and John that they will share in his cup and baptism, but the places of honor are "*not* mine to give." Their manipulation to get privileged places leaves them nowhere near what they really want and closer to what they don't want: suffering and death. This is a direct statement about the disciples' participation in the Paschal Mystery and describes what a disciple can expect.

In the third segment Jesus points to the manipulative authority of the rulers (who already have their position of privilege and honor and abuse it at the expense of others; cf. first segment) and says "it shall *not* be so among you." In the fourth segment Jesus describes the disciple who is great: one who does "*not* come to be served but to serve," one who gives up his or her life (cf. second segment) for all.

This Gospel is perhaps the clearest statement so far that the *disciples will participate* in Jesus' death and resurrection ("drink the cup," "be baptized"). James and John ask for places of honor in the time of fulfillment; the other ten apostles are "indignant"—they, too, want a share in Christ's glory. The Twelve thought they understood Jesus' mission and were ready to follow. Are we?

Living the Paschal Mystery

This Gospel reminds us that discipleship plunges us into the dying and rising Mystery of Christ. The disciples kept misunderstanding this. We must recall that our baptism, as our entrance into discipleship, is an *ongoing yes* to the daily dying and rising in Christ. Discipleship means emptying ourselves to be servant (practical, every day putting others ahead of ourselves) over and over again and constantly learning what the cost of our baptismal *yes* is. Our *yes*, in turn, brings us honor and glory in the age to come.

GOSPEL [Mark 10:35-45; L146B]

James and John, the sons of Zebedee, came to Jesus and said to him, "Teacher, we want you to do for us whatever we ask of you." He replied, "What do you wish me to do for you?" They answered him, "Grant that in your glory we may sit one at your right and the other at your left." Jesus said to them, "You do not know what you are asking. Can you drink the cup that I drink or be baptized with the baptism with which I am baptized?" They said to him, "We can." Jesus said to them, "The cup that I drink, you will drink, and with the baptism with which I am baptized, you will be baptized; but to sit at my right or at my left is not mine to give but is for those for whom it has been prepared." When the ten heard this, they became indignant at James and John. Jesus summoned them and said to them, "You know that those who are recognized as rulers over the Gentiles lord it over them, and their great ones make their authority over them felt. But it shall not be so among you. Rather, whoever wishes to be great among you will be your servant; whoever wishes to be first among you will be the slave of all. For the Son of Man did not come to be served but to serve and to give his life as a ransom for many."

Working with the Word

Key words and phrases from the Gospel: drink the cup, be baptized, to serve, to give his life

Connecting to the Twenty-fifth Sunday in Ordinary Time: A month ago the Gospel already made the point that discipleship means giving our life in service. The disciples still don't grasp this difficult point, so Jesus attempts to explain again by saying what discipleship is *not*.

Connecting to culture: The human tendency to grandiosity is prevalent; it is evident in this Sunday's Gospel and it is evident today. Discipleship is not about seeking places of honor, but about serving. Jesus tells us service is the lot of *all of us* who want to follow him to real glory.

Exegetical points: The Lectionary omits Mark 10:31-34 (the third passion prediction) which is the necessary background for understanding this Sunday's Gospel: after Jesus describes his coming suffering and death, we find the disciples squabbling over placement in the kingdom! Even after such explicit and repeated instructions, the disciples still do not understand what it means to follow Jesus. James and John still imagine that somehow this journey will end in glory and they want to sit at the right and left of Jesus. As that journey in fact ends, those to the right and left of Jesus are those who are crucified with him! Truly, "you do not know what you are asking"!

But James and John aren't alone in their misunderstanding; the rest of the Twelve become indignant, fearing that all the good seats have been taken. Jesus must repeat, almost verbatim, the teaching he had given earlier (9:35; see comments for the twenty-fifth Sunday). But here, Jesus goes further in summarizing his entire ministry: "to give his life as a ransom for many." The concept of "ransom" refers to a sum of money paid to free slaves, prisoners of war, and criminals. Thus, sinful humanity is held in captivity, and Jesus' life and death is like a ransom fee paid for their deliverance. The phrase "for many" contrasts "the multitude as opposed to the individual." Jesus is not so much "my personal savior" as he is "our community savior."

To the point: If even the Son of Man serves humanity to the point of death, those who follow in his way must also "be the slave of all." The greatness of discipleship is measured, not in terms of glory or position in the community or the kingdom, but to the extent that the disciple resembles the Master who serves and gives his life.

Celebration

Rite of Blessing and Sprinkling Holy Water

Presider: Dear friends, this water will be used to remind us of our baptism. By baptism we enter into Christ's dying and rising. Let us ask God to bless this water, and to keep us faithful to our commitment to serve as disciples of Jesus Christ. . . . [pause]

[*Continue with form A of the blessing of water*]

Responsorial Psalm

"Lord, let your mercy be upon us, as we place our trust in you."

Over and over again in the refrain of this Sunday's responsorial psalm we sing of God's mercy. And in the verses we hear the word "kindness" three times. Both words are translations of the Hebrew *chesed*, a word which belongs to terminology about covenant and refers to the loyalty established between covenanting parties. What Israel understood was that the fundamental and enduring faithfulness upon which their covenant with God stood began with God, who could be counted upon to be faithful at all times, in every situation, to the ends of the earth.

The call of discipleship is to serve as Christ served by laying down our lives for the sake of others (Gospel). How can we have the courage to accept a call which means death? Only by "plac[ing] our trust" in the One who will "deliver [us] from death" (psalm), the God of everlasting *chesed*. This is our prayer as we sing this Sunday's psalm.

Model General Intercessions

Presider: God sent Jesus to show us what it means to serve others. One of our services to the Church and world and an expression of our baptismal priesthood is to pray for those in need.

Response:

♪ Lord, hear our prayer.

Cantor:

♪ . . . we pray to the Lord,

That all the baptized have the courage to embrace the suffering and death that leads to new life . . . [pause]

That world leaders exercise the authority that brings justice, peace, and life to all . . . [pause]

That those suffering and dying, uniting their agony to that of Jesus, come to experience his life more deeply . . . [pause]

That all of us here serve and give our life for the salvation of all . . . [pause]

Presider: O God, you draw near to you those who are disciples of your Son: hear our prayers that we may be strengthened in our service. We ask this through Christ our Lord. **Amen.**

OPENING PRAYER

Let us pray
　[for the gift of simplicity and joy in
　　our service of God and man]

Pause for silent prayer

Almighty and ever-living God,
our source of power and inspiration,
give us strength and joy
in serving you as followers of Christ,
who lives and reigns with you and the
　Holy Spirit,
one God, for ever and ever. **Amen.**

RESPONSORIAL PSALM

[Ps 33:4-5, 18-19, 20, 22]

℟. (22) Lord, let your mercy be on us, as we place our trust in you.

Upright is the word of the Lord,
　and all his works are trustworthy.
He loves justice and right;
　of the kindness of the Lord the earth
　　is full.

℟. Lord, let your mercy be on us, as we place our trust in you.

See, the eyes of the Lord are upon those
　who fear him,
　upon those who hope for his
　　kindness,
to deliver them from death
　and preserve them in spite of famine.

℟. Lord, let your mercy be on us, as we place our trust in you.

Our soul waits for the Lord,
　who is our help and our shield.
May your kindness, O Lord, be upon us
　who have put our hope in you.

℟. Lord, let your mercy be on us, as we place our trust in you.

FIRST READING
[Isa 53:10-11]

The LORD was pleased
  to crush him in infirmity.

If he gives his life as an offering for sin,
  he shall see his descendants in a long
    life,
  and the will of the LORD shall be
    accomplished through him.

Because of his affliction
  he shall see the light in fullness of
    days;
through his suffering, my servant shall
  justify many,
  and their guilt he shall bear.

SECOND READING
[Heb 4:14-16]

Brothers and sisters:
Since we have a great high priest who
  has passed through the heavens,
  Jesus, the Son of God,
  let us hold fast to our confession.
For we do not have a high priest
  who is unable to sympathize with our
    weaknesses,
  but one who has similarly been tested
    in every way,
  yet without sin.
So let us confidently approach the
  throne of grace
  to receive mercy and to find grace for
    timely help.

Catechesis

Cantors
The call of this Sunday's psalm is to sing confidently of the steadfast love (*chesed:* mercy, kindness) of God who supports you in your journey into the Paschal Mystery. God will deliver you from death by transforming that death into life. Let your prayer this week be for trust.

Choir
Discipleship is a participation in the passion and death of Jesus, as well as his resurrection. How does singing in the choir call you to die to yourself? Is it being faithful to rehearsal? Cooperating with others, some of whom may not be so easy to get along with? Stepping aside to let another's voice shine? Ever-present efforts to blend with other voices and talents? How, through this dying, do you experience fuller life in Christ?

Music Directors
Hymns which speak of discipleship as service would be appropriate this Sunday, but texts which speak of your participation in Jesus' death and resurrection would also be fitting. David Haas' "Now We Remain" [BB, G, G2, RS, WC] would work well as a Communion song with its refrain "We hold the death of the Lord deep in our hearts . . . ," and its fourth verse, ". . . for to live with the Lord, we must die with the Lord." An excellent hymn for the entrance procession would be Thomas Herbranson's "This Is the Spirit's Entry Now" [CH, W3], particularly if the Rite of Sprinkling is used. Verse 3 connects baptism with the daily dying of discipleship: "Let water be the sacred sign That we must die each day To rise again by his design As fol-l'wers of his way." Note that this verse contains no commas; its text, like the discipleship of which it speaks, is continually ongoing.

Liturgy Committee
This would be a good Sunday to schedule baptisms at one of the parish Masses. Some parishes celebrate baptisms at Sunday Mass more often than others. It is good to strive for a balance (not always so easy to achieve in actual practice) in the frequency of celebrating baptisms at Sunday Mass, keeping in mind these points: (1) baptism is an entry into the Christian community and the body of Christ and so it is fitting to celebrate this initiation sacrament in the presence of the whole community, not just the family; (2) when there is a large number of baptisms, the celebration can take so long that it might create a pastorally undesirable imbalance between the Liturgy of the Word (with baptisms) and the Liturgy of the Eucharist; and (3) when baptism is celebrated at every Sunday Mass, initiating members may seem to be the main purpose of the assembly's gathering.

It would be fitting to use the Rite of Blessing and Sprinkling Holy Water this Sunday because the Gospel speaks so pronouncedly about baptism. It would be helpful to connect discipleship with baptism as an ongoing reality in your lives.

It is best to use the long form of the Gospel this Sunday so that all the statements about what discipleship is *not* can be evident.

OCTOBER 22, 2000

Thirtieth Sunday in Ordinary Time

Spirituality

Reflecting on the Gospel

Over the past few Sundays we have seen how the disciples have impaired vision—they are unable to *see* the meaning of Jesus' death and resurrection, and they don't understand the nature of discipleship as imitation of Jesus' servanthood (recall last Sunday). Their lack of sight hinders their ability to follow Jesus. In this Sunday's Gospel, on the other hand, we have Mark's capsule of the true meaning of discipleship: the blind man recognizes who Jesus is ("Son of David"), encounters Jesus ("I want to see"), and follows ("and followed him on the way"). (Compare this with the "come," "see," and "stay" on the Second Sunday in Ordinary Time from John's Gospel).

Jesus asks Bartimaeus, "What do you want me to do for you," the same question put to James and John in last Sunday's Gospel. We can almost *feel* the intensity with which Jesus wants his disciples to understand who he is and what he is about. Bartimaeus answers rightly, "I want to see," which is a metaphor with meaning beyond the healing of his blindness. If Jesus can bring the blind beggar to see, certainly he can bring the disciples to "see." The beggar shows the disciples how to ask ("cry out . . . Jesus, son of David, have pity on me"), for what to ask ("Master, I want to see"), and how to respond ("followed him on the way").

Several other hints in the Gospel alert us to "follow" Jesus all the way to the cross and resurrection. First hint: Jesus was leaving *Jericho*. A few Sundays ago Jesus was at Caesarea Philippi, way up north and a good distance from Jerusalem. This Sunday Jesus leaves Jericho, a town only about fifteen miles to the northeast of Jerusalem. He is getting closer to his destination. A second hint: a "sizable crowd" was with him, probably foreshadowing the gathering of the crowd that meets Jesus at his entry into Jerusalem. A third hint: the beggar addresses Jesus as the "son of David," the first time this title is used in the Gospel. This is a regal title pointing to Jesus' kingship, a theme at his trial (and also the upcoming solemnity of Christ the King on the Thirty-fourth Sunday in Ordinary Time). A fourth hint: after Bartimaeus is given his sight, he begins "following him *on the way*"; since Jesus' journey was heading to Jerusalem, we may surmise that Bartimaeus followed him there.

Isn't it interesting that the disciples are with Jesus all along—witness his healings, casting out demons, forgiving sin—and still don't get it? Bartimaeus the beggar has this one encounter and he "sees" right away!

Living the Paschal Mystery

The blind beggar Bartimaeus can teach the disciples the truth about "seeing" because he knows who he is (a beggar) and his need (to see). Seeing can be a metaphor for knowing the truth, and this is seldom very easy. Part of the dying that is required for us to be true disciples means that we see ourselves for who we are: already redeemed, but "not yet." Living the Paschal Mystery means that we take a deep look at ourselves and root out whatever it is that keeps us from seeing who Jesus is, whether that is self-centeredness, preoccupation with getting ahead, amassing more money and material goods, seeking comfort above all else. All this demands a dying to self, and only by dying can we rise to "see" the glory of new life.

FAITH-SHARING
- What do you want Jesus to do for you? What does Jesus want you to do for him?
- Bartimaeus recognized Jesus, encountered him personally, and followed him. Can you identify times when you have "recognized" Jesus? when you have "encountered" him personally? when you have followed him? Can you identify this as a pattern of discipleship in your life?

PRESIDERS
What part of discipleship—recognizing, encountering, or following Jesus—do you need to learn from Bartimaeus?

DEACONS
If you prayed faithfully like Bartimaeus—"Jesus, Son of David, have pity on me"—how might that shape you and your diaconal service?

HOSPITALITY MINISTERS
The psalmist sings: "The Lord has done great things for us; we are filled with joy." What great things has the Lord done for you? As you recall them, are you able to let your joy enliven your hospitality?

MUSIC MINISTERS
When you become discouraged about your ministry because you cannot see where it is leading or what good it is doing, ask Jesus for his vision.

ALTAR MINISTERS
Generally, you are one of the "silent busy-bodies" behind the scenes or in the background. You are always "doing" for the Lord. What is it like for you to hear Jesus ask, "What do you want me to do for you?"

LECTORS
Bartimaeus was told, "Take courage; get up, Jesus is calling you." How might you proclaim God's Word so that people "take courage" and recognize Jesus' call to them?

EUCHARISTIC MINISTERS
Bartimaeus can be seen as an icon of human frailty—blind, begging, crying out. How do you respond to the Bartimaeuses in your life ("many rebuked him, telling him to remain silent" *or* "saying to him, 'Take courage; get up, Jesus is calling you'")? How do your daily responses affect your liturgical ministry?

OCTOBER 29, 2000

GOSPEL [Mark 10:46-52; L149B]

As Jesus was leaving Jericho with his disciples and a sizable crowd, Bartimaeus, a blind man, the son of Timaeus, sat by the roadside begging. On hearing that it was Jesus of Nazareth, he began to cry out and say, "Jesus, son of David, have pity on me." And many rebuked him, telling him to be silent. But he kept calling out all the more, "Son of David, have pity on me." Jesus stopped and said, "Call him." So they called the blind man, saying to him, "Take courage; get up, Jesus is calling you." He threw aside his cloak, sprang up, and came to Jesus. Jesus said to him in reply, "What do you want me to do for you?" The blind man replied to him, "Master, I want to see." Jesus told him, "Go your way; your faith has saved you." Immediately he received his sight and followed him on the way.

Working with the Word

Key words and phrases from the Gospel: blind, call him, I want to see, followed him

Connecting to Mark's Gospel: This Sunday completes our reading of a unit in Mark's Gospel on the identity of Jesus and discipleship. Mark frames his teaching on discipleship with two pericopes about blind men (the first, 8:22-26, is omitted in the Lectionary cycle) and by so doing implies that coming to sight is a metaphor for discipleship.

Connecting to the culture: The disciples rebuked the blind man who called out to Jesus and tried to silence him. We all too often tend to overlook the marginalized. Here, the blind man Bartimaeus ends up doing what the disciples haven't done to this point, "seeing" and "following."

Exegetical points: The section of Mark's Gospel that deals with discipleship (8:22–10:52) began with the healing of a blind man (omitted from the Lectionary) and concludes with this Sunday's story of blind Bartimaeus. The focus of this story on the call to discipleship is clear both in v. 49 where the verb "call" occurs three times, and in the dramatic final notice that Bartimaeus "followed him [Jesus] on the way." That way leads to Jerusalem, a fact already hinted at in Bartimaeus' address to Jesus as "Son of David."

Year B of the Lectionary began Ordinary Time with a passage in which Jesus invited would-be disciples to "come and see": seeing was an image for experiencing and knowing Jesus. In this Sunday's Gospel blindness is a metaphor for the disciples' inability to understand Jesus' mission and his teaching on discipleship. The link between seeing and understanding is evident in Jesus' question to the blind man: "What do you want me to do for you?" This is the same question Jesus asked James and John in last Sunday's Gospel (10:36). They asked for glory, Bartimaeus asks for sight; the disciples follow Jesus in confusion, Bartimaeus follows him "immediately." "Seeing" leads to discipleship. This "outsider" has clearer vision than the disciples!

To the point: In this Sunday's Gospel we finally "see" how we come to be disciples: call (from Jesus), see (who Jesus is), and follow him (to the cross).

Celebration

Model Penitential Rite

Presider: God always hears us when we call out for mercy. Let us ask God to have mercy on us in our need . . . [pause]

> Jesus, son of David, you encourage us by calling us to yourself: Lord . . .
> Christ, Messiah King, you never lose sight of our needs: Christ . . .
> Jesus, son of David, you invite us to join in your passion and resurrection: Lord . . .

Responsorial Psalm

"The Lord has done great things for us; we are filled with joy."

Psalm 126 is a song of ascents (see the remarks on the responsorial psalm for the Twenty-seventh Sunday in Ordinary Time), probably composed at the time when the Israelites were freed from their captivity in Babylon. Because of this experience, Israel is certain of God's intervention on their behalf in the future. The psalm's connection to the first reading is, therefore, easy to detect. The God who "has delivered his people . . . will gather them from the ends of the earth." Its connection to the Gospel, however, is not so obvious. From what are we delivered in the Gospel? What hope are we promised?

The answer lies in seeing the blind man's cure as a metaphor for our own spiritual condition. We are delivered from the "blindness" which keeps us from seeing Jesus and his mission clearly, and from choosing wholehearted discipleship. The hope that the Gospel promises is that we can be healed of this "blindness" if we call to Jesus for help. This is an ironic healing, however, for its outcome means that we will be walking with open eyes toward the cross. The deeper hope expresses itself in the connection that what begins with "weeping" will end with "rejoicing."

Model General Intercessions

Presider: Just as Jesus took pity on Bartimaeus and gave him his sight, so will God have pity on us and grant us our prayers.

Response:

Lord, hear our prayer.

Cantor:

we pray to the Lord,

For the Church to walk faithfully in the footsteps of Jesus . . . [pause]

For the world leaders to see the urgent need for justice, peace, and equality for all peoples . . . [pause]

For those without faith to have the courage to call out "Son of David, have pity on me!" . . . [pause]

For us not to waver as we follow Jesus to the cross . . . [pause]

Presider: Merciful God, you hear the prayers of those who cry out to you: be with us as we follow Jesus on the way. We pray through that same Jesus Christ our Lord. **Amen.**

ALTERNATIVE OPENING PRAYER

Let us pray
 [in humble hope for salvation]

Pause for silent prayer

Praised be you, God and Father of our
 Lord Jesus Christ.
There is no power for good
which does not come from your
 covenant,
and no promise to hope in,
that your love has not offered.
Strengthen our faith to accept your
 covenant
and give us the love to carry out your
 command.
We ask this through Christ our Lord.
Amen.

RESPONSORIAL PSALM
[Ps 126:1-2, 2-3, 4-5, 6]

℟. (3) The Lord has done great things for us; we are filled with joy.

When the Lord brought back the
 captives of Zion,
 we were like men dreaming.
Then our mouth was filled with
 laughter,
 and our tongue with rejoicing.

℟. The Lord has done great things for us; we are filled with joy.

Then they said among the nations,
 "The Lord has done great things for
 them."
The Lord has done great things for us;
 we are glad indeed.

℟. The Lord has done great things for us; we are filled with joy.

Restore our fortunes, O Lord,
 like the torrents in the southern
 desert.
Those that sow in tears
 shall reap rejoicing.

℟. The Lord has done great things for us; we are filled with joy.

Although they go forth weeping,
 carrying the seed to be sown,
they shall come back rejoicing,
 carrying their sheaves.

℟. The Lord has done great things for us; we are filled with joy.

FIRST READING
[Jer 31:7-9]

Thus says the LORD:
Shout with joy for Jacob,
    exult at the head of the nations;
    proclaim your praise and say:
The LORD has delivered his people,
    the remnant of Israel.
Behold, I will bring them back
    from the land of the north;
I will gather them from the ends of the world,
    with the blind and the lame in their midst,
the mothers and those with child;
    they shall return as an immense throng.
They departed in tears,
    but I will console them and guide them;
I will lead them to brooks of water,
    on a level road, so that none shall stumble.
For I am a father to Israel,
    Ephraim is my first-born.

SECOND READING
[Heb 5:1-6]

Brothers and sisters:
Every high priest is taken from among men
    and made their representative before God,
    to offer gifts and sacrifices for sins.
He is able to deal patiently with the ignorant and erring,
    for he himself is beset by weakness
    and so, for this reason, must make sin offerings for himself
    as well as for the people.
No one takes this honor upon himself
    but only when called by God,
    just as Aaron was.
In the same way,
    it was not Christ who glorified himself in becoming high priest,
    but rather the one who said to him:
        You are my son: this day I have begotten you;
    just as he says in another place:
        You are a priest forever according to the order of Melchizedek.

Catechesis

Cantors
Past deliverance = future hope. Can you see in your life where God has already kept his promise? For what things in your life now do you need to pray for present deliverance?

Choir
As part of your rehearsal prayer this week, sing the first verse of "Amazing Grace" (try it in three- or four-part canon). Sing it softly, almost at whisper level, while you pray for members of your parish, your families, the Church, and yourselves to have the grace to see Jesus clearly and follow him willingly.

Music Directors
This Sunday's Gospel is about healing, but the cure is more spiritual than physical. The blind man's affliction is a metaphor for your inability to see the real nature of Jesus' mission and willingly to follow. Choose hymns which refer to healing this deeper inability to see.

One good choice would be "Amazing Grace," best used at the presentation of the gifts or as a prelude. One way to give this hymn a lift out of the over familiarity which often plagues it would be to sing a verse or two in canon, beginning the second voice at the end of the second full measure. Another way to give this hymn a lift would be singing it in 4/4 rather than the usual 3/4. To do so you need to fill in the extra beat with some keyboard embellishment; you also need either to warn the assembly or to have only the choir sing it.

A second effective hymn would be Kathleen Thomerson's "I Want to Walk as a Child of the Light" [G, G2, RS, W3, WC]. The text speaks strongly of the desire to follow Jesus whom you have come to see as the light. This hymn would work well at the presentation of the gifts, as a hymn of thanksgiving after Communion, or as a choir prelude (GIA publishes a SATB arrangement [G-2786]).

Liturgy Committee
Bartimaeus was blind and begging, yet he knew how to pray. Perfect liturgies are not our goal; prayerful liturgies are. What are some ways you can worry less about "good performance" and, instead, enhance genuine prayerfulness?

These two pericopes of blind men that frame Mark's account of who Jesus is and what it means to be his disciples shed light on the demands of our own baptismal commitment. Parallel this Sunday's Gospel with that of the Second Sunday of Lent, year A (John 9:1-41). The Johannine account is also about a blind man to whom Jesus gives sight. We see there the same pattern of what it means to be baptized, to be a disciple: persistence (asking, praying, recognizing), faith (encountering), following Jesus. These various miracles in which Jesus gives sight are important reflections for the catechumens and candidates participating in the RCIA process. You may want to spend a few minutes pointing this out during your weekly session with them. Perhaps you might use this Gospel as your prayer and take some time for faith-sharing.

OCTOBER 29, 2000

All Saints

FAITH-SHARING

- Which beatitude is most comforting to you? most challenging to you?
- Who are the saintly people in your life? What has each of them taught you about Christian living? Who looks to you for guidance in sanctity?
- "See what love the Father has bestowed on us." What is it like for you to realize that you are God's child *now*? In what ways do you live out this dignity?

PRESIDERS

Identify the ways in which the beatitudes are the blueprint for your ministry. How do they contribute to your holiness? How do they challenge you?

DEACONS

How is your ministry making you into a saint? How are you helping others to become saints? How are you part of people's blessedness when they are insulted and persecuted?

HOSPITALITY MINISTERS

How you perceive others shapes how you greet them. As you meet people, what do you see—people "longing to see [God's] face" (psalm)? people who are "God's children now" (second reading)? How might you begin to perceive others as God sees them?

MUSIC MINISTERS

Liturgical singing is one of the ways the assembly enters into God's presence. How can you stand at the doorway with them, seeking God's face?

ALTAR MINISTERS

You prepare, set up, clean, etc. the sacred space for worship. How is Christ preparing you as one of the saints through your ministry?

LECTORS

When you remember that earthly worship is united to the heavenly worship, what difference does that make to you? to your proclamation?

EUCHARISTIC MINISTERS

"Blessed are they who hunger and thirst for righteousness." How might you "feed" people in their work for what is just and right?

Spirituality

Reflecting on the Gospel

It is unfortunate that Halloween gets far better press and response than the feast for which it prepares, All Saints! This festival has its origins in the Eastern Church, dating all the way back to the fourth century when there was celebrated a memorial of all martyrs (on various dates, depending on the local church). The Emperor Constantine in effect ended martyrdom in 313 C.E. when he issued the Edict of Milan making Christianity a free religion. It was natural that the Church would want to honor those men and women who had died for their faith. Further, martyrs commanded special esteem because they so totally—even to the point of death—likened themselves to Christ. With the end of the age of martyrdom others were soon singled out as being special examples of those who had conformed their life to Christ. By the ninth century a festival was held on November 1 commemorating all the saints, martyrs and otherwise.

The first reading from Revelation draws us to honor those saints (from the Latin word *sanctus* meaning "holy") who have died and won their eternal reward. The throng who was sealed (the anointing that we now know as the sacrament of confirmation was called a *sphragis* in the Eastern Church, which means "seal") were those "who have survived the time of distress" and have been redeemed by Christ. There is a baptismal allusion at the conclusion of the Revelation reading: "they have washed their robes and made them white in the blood of the Lamb."

The second reading from the first letter of St. John reminds us that we ought not consider "saints" only those few ascetics and extraordinarily holy people who seem beyond us. *We* are already God's saints because we are children of God (through baptism). Heaven will reveal how "we shall be like him," but we are already conformed to Christ in his dying and rising. In a very real way, then, this solemnity is also a celebration of how God has already graced us with divine life. It is our own feastday.

The beatitudes describe profoundly the "blueprint" for Christian living, reminding us of all the right relationships between God and neighbor. Whenever these relationships are enfleshed, God's heavenly kingdom is inaugurated in the here and now. In this way, the Gospel (indeed, the whole liturgy) envisions the communion between the saints in heaven and us faithful disciples here on earth. All of us—living and deceased, named and unnamed—in our living of the beatitudes make up the one "great multitude which no one can count." Let us rejoice and be glad, "for [our] reward will be great in heaven"!

Living the Paschal Mystery

The beatitudes characterize our paschal dying and rising. Whenever we hear the blessedness of being poor in spirit, meek, clean of heart, insulted, persecuted, etc., we know vividly how counter-cultural living the Paschal Mystery is. We must die to many ways of the world so that Gospel values may come alive in us. In so doing, we live as God's children now; and, we bring about a new kingdom of justice and righteousness.

NOVEMBER 1, 2000

GOSPEL [Matt 5:1-12a; L667]

When Jesus saw the crowds, he went up the mountain, and after he had sat down, his disciples came to him. He began to teach them, saying: "Blessed are the poor in spirit, for theirs is the kingdom of heaven. Blessed are they who mourn, for they will be comforted. Blessed are the meek, for they will inherit the land. Blessed are they who hunger and thirst for righteousness, for they will be satisfied. Blessed are the merciful, for they will be shown mercy. Blessed are the clean of heart, for they will see God. Blessed are the peacemakers, for they will be called children of God. Blessed are they who are persecuted for the sake of righteousness, for theirs is the kingdom of heaven. Blessed are you when they insult you and persecute you and utter every kind of evil against you falsely because of me. Rejoice and be glad, for your reward will be great in heaven."

Working with the Word

Key words and phrases from the Gospel: Blessed, rejoice and be glad, reward will be great

Connecting to the communion of saints: Sometimes we forget that worship is always an act of the *whole* Church, that is, the whole communion of saints—we who are still living and those who have died in Christ (both the poor souls and saints in heaven.) The privilege of our earthly worship is that it is united with the heavenly throng worshiping eternally before the throne of God.

Connecting to our culture: We must be careful not to treat this solemnity as the Church's "hall of fame." Our culture's way of honoring people focuses on individual accomplishments. This festival does otherwise. We focus on what *Christ* accomplishes in us.

Exegetical points: The Beatitudes stand as one of the defining texts of Christianity. Yet its meaning must be understood in light of the Hebrew Scriptures. The principles of retribution set forth in the classic theology of Deuteronomy—that good is rewarded and evil punished in this life—over time proved inadequate because it just wasn't borne out in everyday experience. Particularly problematic was working backwards from evidence to conclusions: seeing success, prosperity, children, and long life, one could reasonably conclude that a person was blessed for righteousness and goodness. Conversely, seeing infirmity, poverty, childlessness, and hardship, one could conclude that such a person must have done something wrong to be so punished. Against all this background, the Beatitudes are radical, indeed. The Beatitudes are part of Jesus' penchant for reversals, the "blessed" are the poor, the meek, the hungry—just as the first shall be last, the proud will be humbled but the humble will be exalted, the greatest must become the least, the master must be the servant, and so on. Life in the Kingdom does not measure success in the same way the world does. As a reading for the solemnity of All Saints, the Gospel challenges notions of spiritual "success" or religious "prosperity" and redefines Christian life as a life of discipleship lived in imitation of the Master. In this way, the Beatitudes are not only descriptive of life in the Kingdom, they are also prescriptive, setting forth the way disciples are actually to live their lives.

To the point: The solemnity of All Saints is about the culmination of the Paschal Mystery. Real people (both named and unnamed) become like Christ *now* through their faithful living of the Paschal Mystery.

Celebration

Rite of Blessing and Sprinkling Holy Water:

Presider: Dear friends, saints of God each one of us, this water will be used to remind us of our baptism. By baptism we were plunged into Christ's dying and rising and were made to be like him. Let us ask God to bless this water and to keep us faithful to our baptismal commitment so that one day we might join the heavenly choir before the throne of God . . . [pause]

[Continue with form B of the blessing of water]

Responsorial Psalm

"Lord, this is the people that longs to see your face."

The verses of Psalm 24 used for the solemnity of All Saints were originally part of a ritual entrance into the temple. As the worshipers approached the entryway, a designated person would ask, "Who can ascend the mountain of the LORD? or who may stand in his holy place?" A temple representative responded with, "One whose hands are sinless, whose heart is clean, who desires not what is vain." Having thus examined those at the doorway he declared, "This is the people that seeks the face . . . of the God of Jacob," and allowed the worshipers to enter.

On this solemnity we celebrate those who have entered into the presence of God because they have been faithful to the demands of the covenant, both old (psalm) and new (Gospel). Seeing at last the face for which they have longed, they have discovered their own identity: "children of God . . . we shall be like him" (second reading). When we sing this psalm we stand at the threshold which they have crossed.

Model General Intercessions

Presider: God calls each one into the divine presence to offer praise and thanksgiving alongside the throng before the heavenly throne. We voice our prayers, confident that God hears them.

Response:

Lord, hear our prayer.

Cantor:

we pray to the Lord,

That members of the Church lead lives of holiness befitting the saints of God . . . [pause]

That peoples of the world be meek, just, merciful, pure of heart, and peaceful in their relations with others . . . [pause]

That the poor, sorrowful, and persecuted may find hope in God . . . [pause]

That we witness by the saintliness of our lives to the dawn of salvation . . . [pause]

Presider: God most holy, you gather us among your elect: hear these our prayers that one day we might worship in heaven before your throne. We ask this through Christ our Lord. **Amen.**

ALTERNATIVE OPENING PRAYER

Let us pray

Pause for silent prayer

God our Father,
source of all holiness,
the work of your hands is manifest in your saints,
the beauty of your truth is reflected in their faith.
May we who aspire to have part in their joy
be filled with the Spirit that blessed their lives,
so that having shared their faith on earth
we may also know their peace in your kingdom.
Grant this through Christ our Lord.
Amen.

RESPONSORIAL PSALM
[Ps 24:1-2, 3-4, 5-6]

℟. (cf. 6) Lord, this is the people that longs to see your face.

The LORD's are the earth and its fullness;
    the world and those who dwell in it.
For he founded it upon the seas
    and established it upon the rivers.

℟. Lord, this is the people that longs to see your face.

Who can ascend the mountain of the LORD?
    or who may stand in his holy place?
One whose hands are sinless, whose heart is clean,
    who desires not what is vain.

℟. Lord, this is the people that longs to see your face.

He shall receive a blessing from the LORD,
    a reward from God his savior.
Such is the race that seeks for him,
    that seeks the face of the God of Jacob.

℟. Lord, this is the people that longs to see your face.

FIRST READING [Rev 7:2-4, 9-14]

I, John, saw another angel come up from the East,
    holding the seal of the living God.
He cried out in a loud voice to the four angels
    who were given power to damage the land and the sea,
"Do not damage the land or the sea or the trees
    until we put the seal on the foreheads
    of the servants of our God."

I heard the number of those who had
	been marked with the seal,
	one hundred and forty-four thousand
		marked
	from every tribe of the Israelites.
After this I had a vision of a great
	multitude,
	which no one could count,
	from every nation, race, people, and
		tongue.
They stood before the throne and before
	the Lamb,
	wearing white robes and holding
		palm branches in their hands.
They cried out in a loud voice:
	"Salvation comes from our God,
		who is seated on the throne,
		and from the Lamb."
All the angels stood around the throne
	and around the elders and the four
		living creatures.
They prostrated themselves before the
	throne,
	worshiped God, and exclaimed:
	"Amen. Blessing and glory, wisdom
		and thanksgiving,
		honor, power, and might
		be to our God forever and ever.
			Amen."
Then one of the elders spoke up and
	said to me,
	"Who are these wearing white robes,
		and where did they come from?"
I said to him, "My lord, you are the one
	who knows."
He said to me,
	"These are the ones who have
		survived the time of great distress;
		they have washed their robes
		and made them white in the blood of
			the Lamb."

SECOND READING [1 John 3:1-3]

Beloved:
See what love the Father has bestowed
	on us
	that we may be called the children of
		God.
Yet so we are.
The reason the world does not know us
	is that it did not know him.
Beloved, we are God's children now;
	what we shall be has not yet been
		revealed.
We do know that when it is revealed we
	shall be like him,
	for we shall see him as he is.
Everyone who has this hope based on
	him makes himself pure,
	as he is pure.

Catechesis

Cantors
Your role in singing the psalm for this solemnity is like that of the official who granted worshipers entrance into the temple. You call the people to fidelity to the covenant, and you identify them to God. This is a humbling position for it challenges your own fidelity and your own relationship with God.

Choir
It is not enough just to sing about the beatitudes, you must live them. How can you bring these values and attitudes into choir rehearsal? into Sunday worship?

Music Directors
The sprinkling rite on this solemnity is not penitential in nature but celebratory of the re-creation God has wrought in you, the saints. Texts using variations of "Springs of water, bless the Lord" or of "You will draw water joyfully from the springs of salvation" would be the most appropriate. Refrain-style settings of the Beatitudes are excellent for the Communion procession. In addition to David Haas' well-known "Blest Are They," there is a lovely arrangement by Stephen Dean [OCP #7200] in which the choir continues to hum the SATB parts of the refrain while the cantor sings each verse. The setting is satisfying in its very simplicity.

Douglas E. Wagner's "Canticle: For All the Saints" is a combination prelude-entrance hymn. The choir sings first about the famous who are remembered because of the mark they have made on history, then about those for whom there is "no memorial." The concluding verse "but their names liveth forevermore" blossoms dramatically into the full congregational singing of "For All the Saints."

Liturgy Committee
Since this All Saints is a solemnity and a holy day of obligation, you need to work toward celebrating it with a festive atmosphere at *all* the liturgies. How might you begin moving your parish in this direction?

The Rite of Blessing and Sprinkling Holy Water is suggested for this solemnity because by our baptism we are welcomed into the communion of saints.

The liturgical calendar has separate days for All Saints and the Commemoration of All the Faithful Departed. All Souls day (a commemoration) following immediately upon All Saints day (a solemnity) is one way the Church is alerting us that *all* those who die in the Lord are already saints.

NOVEMBER 1, 2000

Thirty-First Sunday in Ordinary Time

Spirituality

Reflecting on the Gospel

We have skipped two chapters in our journey through Mark's Gospel. At the point where we pick up the story in this Sunday's Gospel, Jesus and his disciples have arrived in Jerusalem. We are into the first part of passion week (in the Gospel's time frame). Jesus has been in the temple area and a number of controversies have arisen in conversations with leading Jews (Mark mentions the chief priests, scribes, elders, Pharisees, Herodians, and Sadducees). A scribe approaches Jesus with yet another question, but this scribe is different. Both his question and response to Jesus are not marked with any antagonism; it seems to be simply a learning exercise. The question about which of the 613 precepts is greatest was a common one put to teachers, and their answers marked clearly those teachers who were orthodox.

"Orthodoxy" is a hot topic these days. Literally, the term means "right opinion" or "right thinking." On the very brink of his passion, with not much time left, Jesus gets to the heart of things. Drawing on Scripture familiar to Jews, he creatively juxtaposes two passages and then places them in proper relationship to what takes place in the temple. Jesus does more than answer the scribe's question; he brings to explicit statement the whole underlying meaning of his ministry and what discipleship and inaugurating the kingdom of God are really all about.

The greatest of the commandments concerns the singularity of God and the command to love God with our whole person (Deut 6:4-5). This passage is actually a prayer the observant Jew prays three times a day and is a short-hand statement of the Jewish "creed." Jesus, however, goes one step further and in addition to the commandment to love God above all else, Jesus tells his listeners to "love your neighbor as yourself" (Lev 19:18). What links our relationship to God, neighbor, and self is love. Law is not kept for its own sake; ideally, law sustains and protects relationships in a loving way.

This particular scribe demonstrates how well he grasps who Jesus is and his message. He affirms Jesus' answer ("Well said, teacher") by repeating what Jesus had said, then adds a line that takes the discussion beyond all expectations: this love of God and neighbor "is worth more than all burnt offerings and sacrifices." Right in the Temple area, the scribe unequivocally states what is really important: not only the legality of keeping laws and not even the religious obligation of Temple sacrifice (so utterly dear to the Jews), but *love! Doing* right must precede sacrifice (see Hos 6:6; Mic 6:6-8; Ps 51:18-21). No wonder Jesus tells the scribe "You are not far from the kingdom of God."

Living the Paschal Mystery

The Paschal Mystery's dying that leads to rising does not refer to physical death, but to the whole-hearted giving of self in unselfish love. Loving is a dying (of selfishness) and rising (to life in profound communion). The link between keeping the commandments and the nearness of God's kingdom is *love* of God, neighbor, self. Only then can we offer fitting sacrifice to God.

FAITH-SHARING
- Jesus suggests that keeping the Law is more than what takes place in the temple. Identify this "more."
- Calvary is the perfect manifestation of love of God and love of neighbor. How far are you willing to travel toward Calvary?
- How can you be catalysts transforming the shallow kind of love rampant today to the lasting love of the Paschal Mystery?

PRESIDERS
What is the relationship between orthopraxis and orthodoxy in your own ordained ministry? Is there something you need to put "right"?

DEACONS
"Take to heart these words I enjoin on you today." As you try to step aside from all of your busy-ness, what word needs to be taken to heart?

HOSPITALITY MINISTERS
To what extent is the spirit of your ministerial greeting that of *duty* rather than *love*? How might your greeting, when extended in love and with care, help the assembly to love God better?

MUSIC MINISTERS
How does your ministry measure up in terms of this commandment of love, i.e., how you direct the choir, how you lead the assembly, how you interact with other members of the parish staff?

ALTAR MINISTERS
"You are not far from the kingdom." How does your ministry around the altar-table of the Lord help you to *live* in a manner that is "not far from the kingdom"?

LECTORS
"Hear, O Israel!" Real proclamation begins not with clarity of voice, but with genuine hearing of the Word. How well do you listen to the Word you proclaim?

EUCHARISTIC MINISTERS
"Love . . . is worth more than all burnt offerings and sacrifices." The greatest part of your ministry is not being "near" the altar-table nor having the privilege of "touching" the host or cup. You genuinely reverence and love the Lord by loving neighbor and self. Where do you need to work on "loving neighbor as yourself"?

NOVEMBER 5, 2000

GOSPEL [Mark 12:28b-34; L152B]

One of the scribes came to Jesus and asked him, "Which is the first of all the commandments?" Jesus replied, "The first is this: *Hear, O Israel! The Lord our God is Lord alone! You shall love the Lord your God with all your heart, with all your soul, with all your mind, and with all your strength.* The second is this: *You shall love your neighbor as yourself.* There is no other commandment greater than these." The scribe said to him, "Well said, teacher. You are right in saying, 'He is One and there is no other than he.' And 'to love him with all your heart, with all your understanding, with all your strength, and to love your neighbor as yourself' is worth more than all burnt offerings and sacrifices." And when Jesus saw that he answered with understanding, he said to him, "You are not far from the kingdom of God." And no one dared to ask him any more questions.

Working with the Word

Key words and phrases from the Gospel: first of all the commandments, love God, love neighbor as yourself, answered with understanding, not far from the kingdom of God

Connecting to Mark's Gospel: (1) The last reference to where Jesus is geographically located is Mark 11:27 which has Jesus in the Temple area fielding a whole series of disputes with some of the Jewish leaders. (2) Last Sunday we had Mark's summary of discipleship and Jesus' ministry; this Sunday we get Jesus' own summary. (3) This Sunday's Gospel is a summation of Jesus' previous teaching on discipleship and God's kingdom and is the foundation for what is coming, the bridge from good news to cross.

Connecting to our culture: The movie *Love Story* has been out for a long time and has been largely forgotten in spite of its sequel's attempt to keep it going. Yet the line "Love is never having to say 'I'm sorry'" seems to endure! Jesus' teaching about love in this Sunday's Gospel takes us so much deeper into the mystery of love! Love isn't never-ending romance, but self-sacrifice for the sake of others.

Exegetical points: Mark has two distinctive features. (1) Jesus begins his quotation of the Law with the *Shema*, "Hear, O Israel . . ." The inclusion of the *Shema* roots the observance of these great commandments in the prayer life of Israel and links it to the primary affirmation of Israel's confession of faith: God is God alone. Thus, both prayer and faith find their fulfillment in the love of God, neighbor, and self. (2) The scribe affirms the surpassing value of these commandments to the offering of sacrifice. Love and sacrifice come together on the cross where the love of Jesus attains its most perfect expression. For disciples, then and now, the greatest commandment not only sums up the life and teaching of Jesus, it identifies the path of discipleship as the way of love.

To the point: Our "Ordinary Time journey" with Mark has directed us to understand discipleship as love of God, neighbor, and self. Being a disciple and building the kingdom is not an intellectual exercise of knowing the law, but an *experience* of relationship founded on love.

Celebration

Model Penitential Rite

Presider: We gather here today to offer our sacrifice of praise and thanksgiving to God. Let us examine ourselves on how our actions this week have prepared us to enter into the divine presence. How well have we loved God, neighbor, self? . . . [pause]

> Lord Jesus, you teach us to love with our whole heart, soul, mind, and strength: Lord . . .
>
> Teacher, you show us the way to truth and understanding: Christ . . .
>
> Lord Jesus, you reveal to us your kingdom of love: Lord . . .

Responsorial Psalm

"I love you, Lord, my strength."

Perhaps the best way to understand the relationship between this Sunday's responsorial psalm and the readings is to consider re-writing the syntax of its refrain. The particular Hebrew verb for "love" used in this refrain is *raham*, the root of which means the compassion of a mother for the child in her womb. The Scripture scholar Irene Nowell points out that this verb is never used with God as its object (*Sing a New Song: the Psalms in the Sunday Lectionary* [Collegeville: The Liturgical Press, 1993] 72). God is the source of such tender mother-love, never its recipient. So this refrain, which is taken directly from the psalm, is a puzzlement. Nowell suggests that it might originally have been a dialogue: God said, "I love you" and David, the psalmist, responded, "Lord, my strength." In other words, the very source of the strength by which we are commanded to love God (first reading and Gospel) is a love which God has first given us even before we were born. What an encouragement this psalm offers us, then, that we *can* love as we have been commanded!

Model General Intercessions

Presider: Because God loves us first, we are confident that our prayers are always answered, and so we pray.

Response:

Lord, hear our prayer.

Cantor:

we pray to the Lord,

That all members of the Church may surrender their heart, soul, mind, and strength to God in love . . . [pause]

That world leaders may remember that love is the foundation and motivation for making and keeping laws that sustain life . . . [pause]

That those who rigidly keep laws but without love may have the understanding to know what really leads to fullness of life . . . [pause]

That we may sacrifice self to serve our God in each other . . . [pause]

Presider: God, you alone are Lord and you love us above all things: hear these our prayers and help us to offer you fitting sacrifices of praise and thanksgiving. We ask this through Jesus Christ our Lord. **Amen.**

ALTERNATIVE OPENING PRAYER

Let us pray

Pause for silent prayer

Father in heaven, God of power and
    Lord of mercy,
from whose fullness we have received,
direct our steps in our everyday efforts.
May the changing moods of the human
    heart
and the limits which our failings impose
    on hope
never blind us to you, source of every
    good.
Faith gives us the promise of peace
and makes known the demands of love.
Remove the selfishness that blurs the
    vision of faith.
Grant this through Christ our Lord.
Amen.

RESPONSORIAL PSALM

[Ps 18:2-3, 3-4, 47, 51]

℟. (2) I love you, Lord, my strength.

I love you, O Lord, my strength,
    O Lord, my rock, my fortress, my
    deliverer.

℟. I love you, Lord, my strength.

My God, my rock of refuge,
    my shield, the horn of my salvation,
    my stronghold!
Praised be the Lord, I exclaim,
    and I am safe from my enemies.

℟. I love you, Lord, my strength.

The Lord lives! And blessed be my rock!
    Extolled be God my savior,
you who gave great victories to your
    king
    and showed kindness to your
    anointed.

℟. I love you, Lord, my strength.

FIRST READING
[Deut 6:2-6]

Moses spoke to the people, saying:
"Fear the LORD, your God,
    and keep, throughout the days of
        your lives,
    all his statutes and commandments
        which I enjoin on you,
    and thus have long life.
Hear then, Israel, and be careful to
    observe them,
    that you may grow and prosper the
        more,
    in keeping with the promise of the
        LORD, the God of your fathers,
    to give you a land flowing with milk
        and honey.

"Hear, O Israel! The LORD is our God,
    the LORD alone!
Therefore, you shall love the LORD, your
    God,
    with all your heart,
    and with all your soul,
    and with all your strength.
Take to heart these words which I enjoin
    on you today."

SECOND READING
[Heb 7:23-28]

Brothers and sisters:
The levitical priests were many
    because they were prevented by death
        from remaining in office,
    but Jesus, because he remains forever,
        has a priesthood that does not pass
        away.
Therefore, he is always able to save
    those who approach God through
        him,
    since he lives forever to make
        intercession for them.

It was fitting that we should have such a
    high priest:
    holy, innocent, undefiled, separated
        from sinners,
    higher than the heavens.
He has no need, as did the high priests,
    to offer sacrifice day after day,
    first for his own sins and then for
        those of the people;
    he did that once for all when he
        offered himself.
For the law appoints men subject to
    weakness to be high priests,
    but the word of the oath, which was
        taken after the law,
    appoints a son,
    who has been made perfect forever.

Catechesis

Cantors
Listen this week for the ways that God is saying to you, "I love you."

Choir
To love God with your whole being and your neighbor as yourself is a tall order. How can the awareness of God's love for you help you reach out to those in need of your love—in your family, your parish, in the choir itself?

Music Directors
Three settings of "Ubi Caritas" are readily available: Richard Proulx' translation and arrangement of the original chant [CBW3, RS, W3], Westendorf/Benoit's "Where Charity and Love Prevail" (BB, CH, G, G2, RS, WC], the Taizé setting [CB, G, G2, RS, W3, WC]. WC has an additional setting by Joyce Glover. All would be appropriate for Communion, or as a prelude.

More directly related to the readings are "What Shall I Bring" [CH] and Eugene Englert's "You Shall Love the Lord Your God" [WLP octavo #7940]. The first would work well at the presentation of the gifts. Have the assembly sing the first verse as a refrain, since it is in first person addressed to God, and choir or cantor sing the other verses which are the voice of God directed to the people. The refrain of Englert's choral piece is the *Shema Israel*. The verses are the rest of the text from this Sunday's first reading from Deuteronomy. The setting would be suitable for either the presentation of the gifts or as a prelude.

Liturgy Committee
The balance between prayerful celebration and rubrics is very well demonstrated in the *General Instruction of the Roman Missal* in both a general way (e.g., the introduction and chapter I forming an important backdrop for the rest of the document) and specific ways (e.g., GIRM, nos. 9, 19, 31, 48, 56, and 62). Sometimes this document is used only for the "how to" laid out in chapters II to VIII. It would be good to review and discuss the theology of Eucharist proposed there. How well have you as a committee worked out of this theology?

One of the greatest challenges in celebrating good liturgy is finding the right balance between being careful about rubrics (orthodoxy) and good pastoral practice that truly promotes full, conscious, and active participation leading to heartfelt worship (orthopraxis). In a nutshell, your goal must be genuine prayer and celebration, not simply "getting it right" (a point also made in last Sunday's catechesis for the liturgy committee).

NOVEMBER 5, 2000

Thirty-Second Sunday in Ordinary Time

FAITH-SHARING GROUPS
- What is the real measure of your generosity?
- Who are the unexpected people who may serve as models of discipleship for you?

PRESIDERS
In your ministry, does your behavior line you up with the scribes or the widow? Are you caught up in prestige and honors and getting as much as you can while giving as little as possible, or is your practiced inclination to give all, as did the widow?

DEACONS
All tend to serve well when they have a "surplus" of time, talent, energy, etc. What is it like for you to serve out of your "poverty" of time, talent, energy, etc.?

HOSPITALITY MINISTERS
How does this Sunday's Gospel help you not to overlook those who seem the least, to have the least?

MUSIC MINISTERS
When you are leading music for more than one liturgy every weekend, you may often feel that you have nothing left to give by the last Mass. How can you be like the widow in this Sunday's Gospel who gives even from her poverty?

ALTAR MINISTERS
The widow demonstrates how to give extravagantly while being of simple means. How might your unassuming preparations for the liturgy be the expression of giving yourself extravagantly to God?

LECTORS
If you rely on yourselves and amass your own treasures, you will lose everything. If you surrender yourselves in loving self-sacrifice, you gain everything. How might you *live* and *proclaim* so that people are aware of the seriousness of this choice?

EUCHARISTIC MINISTERS
Many people-in-the-pews perceive your ministry as the "highest." How does that perception tempt you (as the scribes) from the real call to give of yourself as the widow?

Spirituality

Reflecting on the Gospel

In any other context than our almost complete reading of Mark's Gospel up to the passion account, this episode about the widow would be totally senseless if not downright irresponsible. She is described as a *poor* widow; she contributes "*all* she had." Most of us would hang on to our little, hoping to survive until maybe our luck would change. Not this widow; she contributes her "whole livelihood." We are supposed to trust in God, right? But this is ridiculous! Unless we contrast this episode with the first one given in this Sunday's Gospel. What seems to link these two incidents is each has a reference to widows, but deeper reflection takes us into the very heart of the Paschal Mystery.

The Gospel opens with Jesus teaching the crowds who have gathered around him in Jerusalem. He uses strong language: beware! The scribes were the ones learned in the law; since they studied God's precepts so diligently, we might expect that they would be the models for others. Some, no doubt, were. Yet Jesus goes after those scribes who dress and put on airs, puffing up their own importance. Two of their most important obligations according to the law were to take care of the widow (and orphan and sojourner) and to pray. What do some scribes do? They take advantage of the widows (often it was the scribes as the "lawyers" of their day who administered the estates of widows) and rattle through "lengthy prayers" instead of really praying. After describing this deplorable and unloving behavior, Jesus uses the strongest language possible: "They will receive a very severe condemnation."

Jesus points to the result of these scribes' behavior: condemnation. He makes no mention of the widow's reward, but the contrasting stories suggest that Jesus would have considered her "not far from the kingdom" (similar to the good scribe from last Sunday's Gospel). The abusive scribes have it all now—status, clothes, seats of honor, power, wealth—and end up losing everything. The poor widow has little and surrenders even that—and ends up gaining everything!

Living the Paschal Mystery

Placing ourselves at the center of worldly values—status, clothes, seats of honor, power, wealth—gains us condemnation. Surrendering ourselves as disciples at the service of the cross gains us salvation. But how easily we are fooled about where our hearts truly lay!

We might look at the widow's giving all she had as a foreshadowing of Jesus giving his all on the cross. The good news is that when we surrender our all there is a constant reversal in the order of things: oppressed → protected; beneficiary → benefactor; master → servant; least → greatest; last → first; condemnation → salvation; poverty → surplus; death → life. When we give our all, we never run out. God is the one who is always there to provide. The Paschal Mystery reminds us that if we rely on ourselves and amass our own treasures, we will lose everything. If we surrender ourselves in loving self-sacrifice, we gain everything. The choice is ours!

NOVEMBER 12, 2000

GOSPEL [Mark 12:38-44; L155B]

In the course of his teaching Jesus said to the crowds, "Beware of the scribes, who like to go around in long robes and accept greetings in the marketplaces, seats of honor in synagogues, and places of honor at banquets. They devour the houses of widows and, as a pretext recite lengthy prayers. They will receive a very severe condemnation."

He sat down opposite the treasury and observed how the crowd put money into the treasury. Many rich people put in large sums. A poor widow also came and put in two small coins worth a few cents. Calling his disciples to himself, he said to them, "Amen, I say to you, this poor widow put in more than all the other contributors to the treasury. For they have all contributed from their surplus wealth, but she, from her poverty, has contributed all she had, her whole livelihood."

Working with the Word

Key words and phrases from the Gospel: beware, severe condemnation, from her poverty, her whole livelihood

Connecting to the first reading: The Gospel widow gives her last monies; Elijah's widow gives her last meal; the Gospel widow's reward isn't explicit, but implied; Elijah's widow is rewarded with eating for a year.

Connecting to the culture: Often the poor tend to be incredibly generous; they understand what deprivation and need are. We are sometimes inclined to think of the poor as only on the receiving end; they often can teach us much about giving.

Exegetical points: Apart from the temple discourse in Mark 13, the episode in this Sunday's Gospel is the last public act of Jesus before his passion and death. With the sober reality of the cross looming large, the religious posturing of the scribes in the Temple precincts is especially onerous. Their clothing, seating, public acts of piety, and marks of respect are all designed to show them in a positive light. But their hypocrisy is clear for all to see as they "devour the houses of widows" (see Isa 3:14).

By contrast, the otherwise unnoticed widow acts with genuine piety. We may presume that the "large sums" of the rich were exactly calculated tithes, while the offering of the widow was complete and unstinting: she "contributed everything she had." On the one hand, she is a model of discipleship as she humbly gives what she can. On the other hand, her offering everything she has anticipates the offering Jesus will soon make when he, too, gives his entire life.

To the point: The kingdom of God many times catches us by surprises, by reversals. We expect the scribes to be the models and the surprise is that the lowly one, the widow, is the model.

Celebration

Model Penitential Rite

Presider: The selfless love of God is revealed to us in Jesus. As we begin our liturgy, let us open our hearts to receive and celebrate God's merciful love . . . [pause]

> Lord Jesus, you reveal to us God's selfless love : Lord . . .
> Christ Jesus, you model for us on the cross how to give our all: Christ . . .
> Lord Jesus, you teach us the generosity of self-sacrifice: Lord . . .

Responsorial Psalm

"Praise the Lord, my soul!"
We sang these verses from Psalm 146 on the Twenty-third Sunday in Ordinary Time. In the Gospel of that week Jesus cured a deaf-mute brought to him by the people. In this Sunday's readings we are given glimpses of two women who have lost what is dearest to them (husband, family) yet who willingly give to God what little they have left. God rewards the first with abundant sustenance; the second Jesus identifies as the model for all discipleship. True disciples give all that they have for the sake of the kingdom. In singing this psalm we express our faith that those who give all will be given all in return.

Model General Intercessions

Presider: Bountiful God, you take care of the lowly ones and those in need. We are confident that when we speak our prayers you answer them with abundance.

Response:

[Musical notation: "Lord, hear our prayer."]

Cantor:

[Musical notation: "we pray to the Lord,"]

That the Church beware of pretentiousness and eyes closed to the lowly . . . [pause]

That the leaders of the world beware of using their power for anything but the good of all . . . [pause]

That widows, orphans, and strangers be supported, protected, and received with generosity . . . [pause]

That we contribute generously from both our surplus and our poverty . . . [pause]

Presider: O God, you hear the cries of the poor and reach out to those in need: hear these our prayers and help us always to rely on you for what we need. We ask this through Christ our Lord. **Amen.**

ALTERNATIVE OPENING PRAYER
Let us pray

Pause for silent prayer

Almighty Father,
strong is your justice and great is your mercy.
Protect us in the burdens and challenges of life.
Shield our minds from the distortion of pride
and enfold our desire with the beauty of truth.
Help us to become more aware of your loving design
so that we may more willingly give our lives in service to all.
We ask this through Christ our Lord.
Amen.

RESPONSORIAL PSALM
[Ps 146:7, 8-9, 9-10]

℟. (1b) Praise the Lord, my soul!
or:
℟. Alleluia.

The LORD keeps faith forever,
　secures justice for the oppressed,
　gives food to the hungry.
The LORD sets captives free.

℟. Praise the Lord, my soul!
or:
℟. Alleluia.

The LORD gives sight to the blind;
　the LORD raises up those who were bowed down.
The LORD loves the just;
　the LORD protects strangers.

℟. Praise the Lord, my soul!
or:
℟. Alleluia.

The fatherless and the widow he sustains,
　but the way of the wicked he thwarts.
The LORD shall reign forever;
　your God, O Zion, through all generations. Alleluia.

℟. Praise the Lord, my soul!
or:
℟. Alleluia.

FIRST READING [1 Kgs 17:10-16]

In those days, Elijah the prophet went to Zarephath.
As he arrived at the entrance of the city,
　a widow was gathering sticks there;
　he called out to her,
　"Please bring me a small cupful of water to drink."

She left to get it, and he called out after her,
"Please bring along a bit of bread."
She answered, "As the LORD, your God, lives,
I have nothing baked; there is only a handful of flour in my jar
and a little oil in my jug.
Just now I was collecting a couple of sticks,
to go in and prepare something for myself and my son;
when we have eaten it, we shall die."
Elijah said to her, "Do not be afraid.
Go and do as you propose.
But first make me a little cake and bring it to me.
Then you can prepare something for yourself and your son.
For the LORD, the God of Israel, says,
'The jar of flour shall not go empty,
nor the jug of oil run dry,
until the day when the LORD sends rain upon the earth.'"
She left and did as Elijah had said.
She was able to eat for a year, and he and her son as well;
the jar of flour did not go empty,
nor the jug of oil run dry,
as the LORD had foretold through Elijah.

SECOND READING [Heb 9:24-28]

Christ did not enter into a sanctuary made by hands,
a copy of the true one, but heaven itself,
that he might now appear before God on our behalf.
Not that he might offer himself repeatedly,
as the high priest enters each year into the sanctuary
with blood that is not his own;
if that were so, he would have had to suffer repeatedly
from the foundation of the world.
But now once for all he has appeared at the end of the ages
to take away sin by his sacrifice.
Just as it is appointed that human beings die once,
and after this the judgment, so also Christ,
offered once to take away the sins of many,
will appear a second time, not to take away sin
but to bring salvation to those who eagerly await him.

Catechesis

Cantors
This psalm is meant to be sung with confidence in God's goodness, God's protection, God's providence. But unless you give all that you have—your whole hearts—you never discover what God is giving in return. What are you holding back?

Choir
Have you ever noticed how you derive the most out of singing in choir when you simply stop thinking about yourself and let the music take over? In this way singing in the choir is a paradigm of the message of this Sunday's readings. The more you give, the more you receive, but what makes the giving possible is forgetting about yourselves. How might you practice this forgetting of self more faithfully in your everyday living?

Music Directors
This would be another good Sunday to sing "The Love of the Lord" [G, G2, RS] because it speaks of faith in "the love of the Lord" and "the promise of Christ" as the ultimate wealth. The hymn could be sung either during Communion or as a song of thanksgiving after Communion. A second option for Communion or after Communion would be to sing the *Magnificat* which speaks of God's feeding the hungry and exalting the humble.

Liturgy Committee
Cultural preferences are often very similar to some of the scribes' in this Sunday's Gospel—nice clothes (long robes), places of honor, lengthy prayers. While fitting worship to God may and should include beauty and fine things (see EACW, nos. 19-23), the core of right worship is the interior, total self-sacrifice of the community. In what ways does your committee move people from exterior "fineries" to the extravagant surrendering of the widow?

Using the long form of the Gospel this Sunday completes the contrast between the two parts of the Gospel.

The end of Ordinary Time is quickly approaching and the readings are already pointing to next Sunday's prediction of Christ's Second Coming and the Thirty-fourth Sunday's Solemnity of Our Lord Jesus Christ the King. As this Sunday's Gospel hints, the final judgment brings either "severe condemnation" or fulfillment.

NOVEMBER 12, 2000

Thirty-Third Sunday in Ordinary Time

FAITH-SHARING
- Is the coming of Christ something you long for? fear? never consider?
- What do you need to do to be prepared for Christ's coming?
- What are happenings around you that let you "know that he is near"? How do these experiences assist your vigilance until Christ comes in glory?

PRESIDERS
The inevitable cares and worries within your ministry can make you feel "in the dark." What helps you to live in the light and hope that Christ's resurrection promises? What might you do to move from "darkness" to "light"?

DEACONS
Christian discipleship is more than good social work (a wonderful, necessary kind of service). In what way is your service an aid for people's preparation for Christ's Second Coming?

HOSPITALITY MINISTERS
Styles of reception can foster either suspicion and fear or promote acceptance and trust. How might your greeting people over the next weeks (both at liturgy and other times) encourage people to "abide in confidence" (psalm)?

MUSIC MINISTERS
How is the day in, day out pursuit of your ministry already a participation in the inheritance of eternal life?

ALTAR MINISTERS
If you really believed that the end were near, how might this affect how you perform your service?

LECTORS
St. Jerome wrote, "Ignorance of the Scriptures is ignorance of Christ." Can you sense how your prayerful preparation with God's word enables you to know Christ, to be prepared for his coming?

EUCHARISTIC MINISTERS
Viaticum (Holy Communion for the dying) is a most important sacrament for those passing from death to life. As you visit the elderly and infirm, how might you witness a preparation for Christ's coming that underscores joyful expectation rather than fear?

Spirituality

Reflecting on the Gospel

It's five weeks shy of a year since we celebrated that great feast of light, Christmas. Then we celebrated Jesus' first coming as a babe in Bethlehem. It was night. Winter solstice: the longest night of the year. Jesus, the light of the world enters and dispels darkness. As we approach the end of the liturgical year (next Sunday is the final Sunday of this year), we encounter these same images of darkness and light.

The Gospel opens with the great lights in the heavens "going out" after a time of tribulation. We have the image, once again, that darkness reigns. (These portents of Christ's Second Coming are a reverse of what happened at creation where from darkness and chaos God's creative word brought forth light and order.) Further, just as at the first coming, Christ at the Second Coming enters a dark world and brings light and life ("coming . . . with great power and glory"). The same contrast of darkness and light is implied in the first, apocalyptic reading from the prophet Daniel. "In those days" there will be "unsurpassed distress," surely a "dark" image. "But the wise shall shine brightly like the splendor of the firmament, and those who lead the many to justice shall be like the stars forever." In both Daniel and the Gospel there is a gathering of the elect. The first reading suggests to us that either we find ourselves among the elect or not (some shall escape and some shall not).

The dark portents of the first part of the Gospel give way to positive images of new growth in the second part of the Gospel (the fig tree's "branch becomes tender and sprouts leaves"). When we see these things happening, we will know that the Son of Man "is near." Since the spring and summer growth of the fig tree is recurring, this image reminds us that we need to be constantly ready for the Second Coming, and if we are there is nothing to fear. The last verse of the Gospel recommends that same kind of constant vigilance: "But of that day or hour, no one knows." Who are the elect? Those who are constantly vigilant and who pay attention to the Son of Man's words which "will not pass away."

For the disciple of Jesus, the Second Coming of Christ need not be something to fear. As long as we are vigilant, we can long with joyful expectation to see "the Son of Man coming in the clouds with great power and glory."

Living the Paschal Mystery

At the end of times—and we know not the day or hour—this world as we know it will pass and Christ will come to judge all people and the general resurrection will take place. For those of us immersed by baptism into the Paschal Mystery and who have surrendered ourselves in our everyday living of its rhythm, we can be assured that we are promised to be numbered among God's elect. And, just as the Paschal Mystery constantly teaches us that when we surrender to the dying there is *always* new life beyond that dying, so will there be resurrection for the elect beyond the final judgment. There is no need to fear Christ's Second Coming. All we need do is surrender ourselves to living the Paschal Mystery.

NOVEMBER 19, 2000

GOSPEL [Mark 13:24-32; L158B]

Jesus said to his disciples: "In those days after that tribulation the sun will be darkened, and the moon will not give its light, and the stars will be falling from the sky, and the powers in the heavens will be shaken.

"And then they will see 'the Son of Man coming in the clouds' with great power and glory, and then he will send out the angels and gather his elect from the four winds, from the end of the earth to the end of the sky.

"Learn a lesson from the fig tree. When its branch becomes tender and sprouts leaves, you know that summer is near. In the same way, when you see these things happening, know that he is near, at the gates. Amen, I say to you, this generation will not pass away until all these things have taken place. Heaven and earth will pass away, but my words will not pass away.

"But of that day or hour, no one knows, neither the angels in heaven, nor the Son, but only the Father."

Working with the Word

Key words and phrases from the Gospel: will be darkened, great power and glory, gather his elect, he is near, my words will not pass away, no one knows

Connecting to the liturgical year: This Gospel about the end times comes in the context of the end of the liturgical year. Our journey of discipleship (through Mark's eyes) is coming to an end; next Sunday we celebrate the victory!

Connecting to the culture: A year ago, for months on end we heard about the new millennium and this Sunday's Gospel is another candid reminder that we are living in it. We've heard many things about catastrophes; did we let this paralyze us? Or are we living the new millennium with courage and hope, because we have Jesus' promise that "my words will not pass away."

Exegetical points: This passage, which presents Jesus as sharing the apocalyptic expectations of his day, indicates that while the end is certainly coming, the exact time is unknown. Significantly, the end is here associated, not just with calamity, but with the coming of the Son of Man in glory and power. While many of the themes of this passage are taken directly from the Old Testament (e.g., the darkening of the sun and moon and the gathering of the elect), these themes are not associated with the coming of the Son of Man. In the Old Testament the collapse of nature is associated with God's day of judgment; the gathering of the elect is associated with God's day of restoration. That Mark associates them with the coming of the Son of Man indicates that the kingdom of God whose coming Jesus announced (1:15; 3rd Sunday) will come to its consummation with his return. The effective power of God in creating and redeeming is now realized in Jesus. It is crucial to the proper understanding of this passage that the reader or preacher not lose sight of the "good news" that the end is not calamity and "tribulation" but redemption.

To the point: We see here another Gospel of contrasts, between the Second Coming with all its impending catastrophes or the Second Coming as a joyful expectation of the elect being gathered. It is an invitation to place our hope and faith in what does not pass away.

Celebration

Model Penitential Rite

Presider: Our God comes with great power and glory to be near us. Let us open ourselves to that divine presence . . . [pause]

> Son of Man, you will come in the clouds to gather the elect to enjoy everlasting life with you: Lord . . .
> Christ Jesus, you are always near to bring us to new growth: Christ . . .
> Son of God, your words will not pass away: Lord . . .

Responsorial Psalm

"You are my inheritance, O Lord!"

This Sunday's responsorial psalm reaffirms the positive vision of the end times and the Second Coming of Christ presented in the readings. These tell us that it is not catastrophes which will dominate, but the light of Christ coming with "great power and glory" (Gospel). Nor is it the passing of heaven and earth which should be our focus, but the words of Christ which "will not pass away" (Gospel). Discipleship does not mean that we will be protected from tragedy, suffering, conflict, or death. It does mean that no matter what the future, God will not abandon to the "netherworld" (death) those who have led "many to justice" (first reading), but will show them the "path to life" (psalm). Our psalm this Sunday is a song of confidence in and thanksgiving for what our inheritance will be: the God of everlasting life.

Model General Intercessions

Presider: Our God is always near and always gathers us under the divine care. So we are encouraged to make our needs known.

Response:

[musical notation: Lord, hear our prayer.]

Cantor:

[musical notation: we pray to the Lord,]

That the Church always bring the light of Christ to darkened places in our world . . . [pause]

That the world be ready from the end of the earth to the end of the sky for the coming of our God . . . [pause]

That those paralyzed by fear may find hope in signs of new life around them . . . [pause]

That our community may live with quiet resolve to be witnesses of the endurance of the Son of Man's words . . . [pause]

Presider: Good and gracious God, you are near to us in our need: hear our prayers of petition and help us to realize our dependence on you. We ask this through Jesus Christ our Lord. **Amen.**

ALTERNATIVE OPENING PRAYER

Let us pray

Pause for silent prayer

Father in heaven,
ever-living source of all that is good,
from the beginning of time you promised man salvation
through the future coming of your Son, our Lord Jesus Christ.
Help us to drink of his truth
and expand our hearts with the joy of his promises,
so that we may serve you in faith and in love
and know for ever the joy of your presence.
We ask this through Christ our Lord.
Amen.

RESPONSORIAL PSALM
[Ps 16:5, 8, 9-10, 11]

℟. (1) You are my inheritance, O Lord!

O LORD, my allotted portion and my cup,
 you it is who hold fast my lot.
I set the LORD ever before me;
 with him at my right hand I shall not be disturbed.

℟. You are my inheritance, O Lord!

Therefore my heart is glad and my soul rejoices,
 my body, too, abides in confidence;
because you will not abandon my soul to the netherworld,
 nor will you suffer your faithful one to undergo corruption.

℟. You are my inheritance, O Lord!

You will show me the path to life,
 fullness of joys in your presence,
 the delights at your right hand forever.

℟. You are my inheritance, O Lord!

FIRST READING
[Dan 12:1-3]

In those days, I, Daniel,
   heard this word of the LORD:
"At that time there shall arise
   Michael, the great prince,
   guardian of your people;
it shall be a time unsurpassed in distress
   since nations began until that time.
At that time your people shall escape,
   everyone who is found written in the
   book.

Many of those who sleep in the dust of
   the earth shall awake;
   some shall live forever,
   others shall be an everlasting horror
   and disgrace.

But the wise shall shine brightly
   like the splendor of the firmament,
   and those who lead the many to justice
   shall be like the stars forever."

SECOND READING
[Heb 10:11-14, 18]

Brothers and sisters:
Every priest stands daily at his ministry,
   offering frequently those same
      sacrifices
   that can never take away sins.
But this one offered one sacrifice for
      sins,
   and took his seat forever at the right
      hand of God;
   now he waits until his enemies are
      made his footstool.
For by one offering
   he has made perfect forever those
      who are being consecrated.

Where there is forgiveness of these,
   there is no longer offering for sin.

Catechesis

Cantors
Your preparation of this Sunday's psalm may raise unsettling questions for you. Do you truly believe that God is your inheritance? On what do you base this belief? Are you willing to pay the price which gaining eternal life requires? How might these reflections help you in your music ministry?

Choir
No one can see the future. Your confidence that its outcome will be the kingdom rests on your personal relationship with Jesus whose "words will not pass away" (Gospel). You might end rehearsal this week with a litany praying for fidelity to discipleship. Using the refrain from Paul Inwood's "Center of My Life" as the response, pray for courage, for fidelity, for confidence, etc.

Music Directors
Two hymns especially relevant to this Sunday's Gospel are Bob Moore's "When the Lord in Glory Comes" [G2, RS] and Richard Proulx' "Now the Day of the Lord Is at Hand" [W3]. The first is meant to be sung in responsorial fashion with the assembly joining in on the repeat of the refrain. The text speaks of what will be most important at the Second Coming: the voice and face of Christ. This would make a good hymn after Communion. The Proulx hymn sings of the darkness and pain of the final day being transformed into joy for those with "true hearts." It would work well as an entrance song.

Another song which this Sunday's Liturgy of the Word brings to mind is Paul Inwood's "Center of My Life" [BB, G, G2], a setting of Psalm 16 (this week's responsorial psalm). Because it uses different verses from those given in the Lectionary, it would not be advisable to use it as the responsorial psalm; it would make a good Communion hymn, with cantor or choir doing the verses and the assembly joining in on the refrain.

Liturgy Committee
How might you use this Sunday's message of hope to draw the assembly more deeply into an experience of the Paschal Mystery during liturgy? Since this is almost the end of this liturgical year, you might review your committee work by identifying any ways your liturgy preparation might promote a joyful expectation of Christ's Second Coming.

This is the second last Sunday of the liturgical year and is an important one for understanding where your Gospel journey has brought your parish or liturgical community. This is a good time to assess your growth: are you liturgically more "advanced" than you were last year at this time? Where are your areas of growth? What are the areas you need to address?

You would be cheating your assemblies if you would focus this Sunday Mass on Thanksgiving, tempting as that might be. There is a proper Mass for Thursday, and it would be well to encourage your parishioners to come, for everyone has much for which to be grateful. But let this Sunday speak its own powerful message.

NOVEMBER 19, 2000

THE SOLEMNITY OF OUR LORD JESUS CHRIST

FAITH-SHARING
- Where does your heart lie? How do you live in the earthly kingdom and the heavenly kingdom at the same time?
- When/where have you been called upon to "testify to the truth"? Where did/do you find the courage to do this?
- In what ways have you grown closer to Jesus during the past liturgical year? In what ways has your own self-identity as a *disciple* grown?

PRESIDERS
To what truth do you testify in your ministry? To what voice(s) do you listen?

DEACONS
Before Christ bore a crown of glory, he carried a cross of wood. What does that tell you about your servant-ministry?

HOSPITALITY MINISTERS
No matter how you come or who you are, Jesus has made you into his kingdom with the price of his blood. What do you see and notice while the assembly gathers—idiosyncrasies? friends vs. strangers? *or* a kingdom gathered together? What would help you to recognize Christ's kingdom here on earth—with these people of your liturgical community?

MUSIC MINISTERS
During this past liturgical year, how has the kingdom of God become more evident because of your ministry? How has your parish grown in discipleship because of your ministry?

ALTAR MINISTERS
Jesus your king shows the way: from dying as a servant *to* being enthroned in glory. Over the past year, what growth have you noticed by attending carefully to your service?

LECTORS
Over the past liturgical year, you have read the great stories of your faith. How has that changed you? How has being a lector made this year different from if you weren't a lector?

EUCHARISTIC MINISTERS
Each Sunday you participate in the life-giving banquet of the heavenly King. How has this banquet been life-giving for you? How has this affected your daily living? your ministry?

Spirituality

Reflecting on the Gospel

If there were an international contest for double-talk, Jesus would surely win the grand master title and Pilate would come in a close second! This Sunday's Gospel is one long linguistic sparring incident; questions are asked (four by Pilate and one by Jesus) but none directly answered. On this, the solemnity of Our Lord Jesus Christ the King, very little seems to be accomplished between Pilate and Jesus. And yet everything is revealed and salvific events are inexorably set in motion. We have come to the end of the liturgical year. This day both reveals and celebrates what our journey all these long months has really been about: (1) now we know who Jesus really is: the one lifted up on the cross who is enthroned in glory; and (2) now we know the paschal journey of our own discipleship: dying to self to eternal glory.

This Gospel is, for one thing, about truth; it is also about admitting, facing, and accepting the consequences of truth. Pilate asks Jesus, "Are you the King of the Jews?" Jesus replies with a question of his own: "Do you say this on your own or have others told you about me?" The implication in Jesus' response is not only that Jesus truly is king, but also that Pilate has been told so. At least two other points become clear as the sparring continues.

First, Jesus makes quite clear that his kingdom is not of this world. The ostensible reason for Pilate's concern and the "legal" reason for Jesus' condemnation is really no concern at all. Jesus is no threat to Pilate's (or Caesar's) earthly power. Second, Jesus once again witnesses to the integrity of his word and deed. Pilate asks, "What have you done?" Jesus says that he testifies "to the truth" and those who belong "to the truth" listen "to my voice." Pilate knows in the depths of his heart the truth upon which he should act—release this man for he has done nothing wrong; he is an innocent man (see John 18:38; 19:4, 6, 8, 12). But Pilate's deed belies what he knows is true: "In the end, Pilate handed Jesus over to be crucified" (John 19:16). Jesus speaks the truth and by so doing seals his own condemnation but *his* deed witnesses to the truth of *his* word: he carries his cross and rises as the eternal king.

Living the Paschal Mystery

This solemnity makes a statement about Christ, but also about our own self-identity: he has made us into a kingdom. Jesus was born to be king and "to testify to the truth." The truth of his earthly existence led to the cross. The truth of our existence as subjects also leads to the cross. Only through the cross is Jesus brought to glory; only through the cross are we brought to glory.

The contrasting images from the Revelation reading sum up the Paschal Mystery character of this solemnity: first-born, ruler, glory, power forever vs. pierced, lament, by his blood. We all like the positive images invoked by this solemnity. In our own moments of truth we admit to our very human propensity for power and wealth. Much about society and our own daily lives carries us in this direction. We would like to avoid the reality of the challenge offered by the contrasting negative images that remind us to embrace the cross. One last time, on this last Sunday of the liturgical year, we say: the road to glory is through the cross.

THE KING

NOVEMBER 26, 2000

GOSPEL [John 18:33b-37; L161B]

Pilate said to Jesus, "Are you the King of the Jews?" Jesus answered, "Do you say this on your own or have others told you about me?" Pilate answered, "I am not a Jew, am I? Your own nation and the chief priests handed you over to me. What have you done?" Jesus answered, "My kingdom does not belong to this world. If my kingdom did belong to this world, my attendants would be fighting to keep me from being handed over to the Jews. But as it is, my kingdom is not here." So Pilate said to him, "Then you are a king?" Jesus answered, "You say I am a king. For this I was born and for this I came into the world, to testify to the truth. Everyone who belongs to the truth listens to my voice."

Working with the Word

Key words and phrases from the Gospel: king; what have you done?; My kingdom is not here; testify to the truth; listens to my voice

Connecting the three readings: On a solemnity celebrating the kingship of Christ, we read a Gospel from his passion. It is telling that this selection is not a post-resurrection account. The first reading focuses on the glory of the Son's kingship and the Gospel focuses on the passion. The second reading from Revelation holds the two together: the shedding of Jesus' blood out of his love "has freed us" and "made us into a kingdom." Beyond the passion is glory; and we cannot understand glory without the passion.

Connecting to our culture: Our notions of kingship tend toward being rather negative (exercise of unlimited power or simply an outdated, expensive institution) or romantic (e.g., King Arthur). What does "king" mean for us today as shown in the Gospel? What are we really celebrating on this solemnity? Christ's kingship is contextualized by the cross.

Exegetical points: The "Son of Man" who figured so prominently in last Sunday's Gospel appears in this Sunday's first reading as the effective agent of God who receives everlasting kingship. In the Old Testament, the king was the adoptive "son of God" (Pss 2:6-7; 110:1-3) who is to uphold God's reign of justice and righteousness (Pss 89:15; 97:2; Isa 9:6; 16:5).

The reading from Revelation alludes to Exodus 19:6 in which God makes Israel a "kingdom of priests," i.e., Israel's presence among the nations is to be like that of the priest in Israel—one set apart by holiness to serve God. Those redeemed by the blood of Jesus are a "kingdom," i.e., they are under the rule of God; they are also made priests, i.e., they are dedicated to the service of God. Priests are those who mediate between God and humanity: this is the vocation of the Christian.

It should not escape notice that the liturgical understanding of the kingship of Jesus points, not to his power and glory, but to his service in dying on the cross.

To the point: The Gospel reveals to us the unexpected—the ignominious one is claimed as king which has implications for us: Christ as king has a kingdom and *we* are his subjects, a kingdom of "priests for his God and Father."

Celebration

Model Penitential Rite

Presider: On this, the last Sunday of the liturgical year and the solemnity of our Lord Jesus Christ the King, we celebrate Christ's victory over earthly power and even the power of death itself. Let us pause and reflect on our own surrender to the mystery of Christ's dying and rising in our daily living . . . [pause]

> Faithful Witness, you testify to the truth: Lord . . .
> Christ the King, you inaugurate a kingdom not of this world: Christ . . .
> Savior of the world, you free us from sin by your blood: Lord . . .

Responsorial Psalm

"The Lord is king; he is robed in majesty."

Although Psalm 93 is short, the Lectionary unfortunately omits vv. 3-4: "The floods lift up, O Lord, the floods lift up their voice; the floods lift up their tumult. More powerful than the roaring of many waters, more powerful than the breakers of the sea—powerful on high is the Lord." The biblical concept of the world saw the earth as a platform balanced on the chaotic waters of the sea. The surging waters constantly threatened to overwhelm the earth, and would have done so were it not of the equally constant intervention of a more powerful stabilizing force: the hand of God. This is the meaning behind v. 1b, "And he has made the world firm, not to be moved." The omitted verses strengthen this psalm's theme of the power of God's kingship—expressed at the beginning and the end of the psalm—because they pit God's kingship against the forces of chaos which threaten the earth and its peoples. In the Bible, as in Canaan and Mesopotamia, creation is prelude to kingship: God establishes the credentials to rule by the power to create.

The very structure of this psalm, then, expresses the cosmic conflict between the power of God and the forces of evil and, by framing the images of chaos with assertions of God's power and trustworthiness, assures us of the outcome. Truly, the Lord is king.

Model General Intercessions

Presider: Jesus' testimony to the truth led him through the cross to resurrection where he sits in glory at the right hand of the Father. We pray through the intercession of Christ our King.

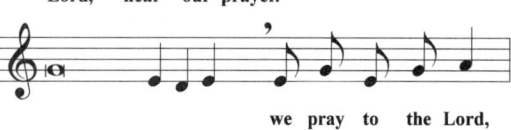

Response: Lord, hear our prayer.

Cantor: . . . we pray to the Lord,

That the Church witness to the eternal truth of God's kingdom . . . [pause]

That nations live the truth that life-giving power lies in the everlasting kingdom and is not of this world . . . [pause]

That those who abuse power and belie truth recognize the destructiveness of their deeds . . . [pause]

That our community celebrate this day with the joy of those already living in the eternal kingdom . . . [pause]

Presider: God our Father, you raised up Jesus Christ your Son and seated him at your right hand to have dominion, glory, and kingship: hear these our prayers that we might one day enjoy everlasting life. We pray through Christ our Lord. **Amen.**

ALTERNATIVE OPENING PRAYER

Let us pray

Pause for silent prayer

Father all-powerful, God of love,
you have raised our Lord Jesus Christ
    from death to life,
resplendent in glory as King of creation.
Open our hearts,
free all the world to rejoice in his peace,
to glory in his justice, to live in his love.
Bring all mankind together in Jesus
    Christ your Son,
whose kingdom is with you and the
    Holy Spirit,
one God, for ever and ever. **Amen.**

RESPONSORIAL PSALM

[Ps 93:1, 1-2, 5]

℟. (1a) The Lord is king; he is robed in majesty.

The Lord is king, in splendor robed;
    robed is the Lord and girt about with strength.

℟. The Lord is king; he is robed in majesty.

And he has made the world firm,
    not to be moved.
Your throne stands firm from of old;
    from everlasting you are, O Lord.

℟. The Lord is king; he is robed in majesty.

Your decrees are worthy of trust indeed;
    holiness befits your house,
    O Lord, for length of days.

℟. The Lord is king; he is robed in majesty.

FIRST READING
[Dan 7:13-14]

As the visions during the night
    continued, I saw
    one like a Son of man coming,
        on the clouds of heaven;
    when he reached the Ancient One
        and was presented before him,
    the one like a Son of man received
        dominion, glory, and kingship;
    all peoples, nations, and languages
        serve him.
His dominion is an everlasting
    dominion
    that shall not be taken away,
    his kingship shall not be destroyed.

SECOND READING
[Rev 1:5-8]

Jesus Christ is the faithful witness,
    the firstborn of the dead and ruler of
        the kings of the earth.
To him who loves us and has freed us
    from our sins by his blood,
    who has made us into a kingdom,
        priests for his God and Father,
    to him be glory and power forever
        and ever. Amen.
Behold, he is coming amid the clouds,
    and every eye will see him,
        even those who pierced him.
    All the peoples of the earth will
        lament him.
        Yes. Amen.

"I am the Alpha and the Omega," says
    the Lord God,
    "the one who is and who was and
        who is to come, the almighty."

Catechesis

Cantors
Even though the middle verses of Psalm 93 are missing from the Lectionary, keep them and their significance in mind as you prepare to sing the psalm. Remember that Christ's kingship is dynamic, acting continuously against the forces of evil, and that you must continuously choose to act with him.

Choir
On this solemnity of Our Lord Jesus Christ the King, you say a last *Amen* to your journey of this year through Ordinary Time. The reading from the Passion of John reminds you of what the Sundays in Ordinary Time have been teaching you all along: that the kingdom of Christ is a kingdom achieved through the cross. Look over this past liturgical year and see how, as a choir, you have grown in discipleship, how you have embraced the cross, and how you have experienced the kingdom.

Music Directors
This Sunday's solemnity calls for the most festive service music in your parish repertoire.

Because of the Gospel reading from the Passion of John, "Lift High the Cross" [CBW3, CH, RS, W3, WC] would be a fitting entrance hymn. Organ and brass fanfare are included in Carl Schalk's concertato on this hymn [Concordia #98-2468]. You will need to alert the choir to variations between this setting and revised texts given in most hymnals, e.g., "Captain" has become "Master," "soldiers" has been changed to "followers."

Liturgy Committee
As you know, generally people view Sunday Mass in the context of a single week; they are not as aware of Sundays being connected to each other in a year-long unfolding of the Paschal Mystery. Christ the King as a solemnity is the culmination of an entire liturgical year. How might you communicate this solemnity as a *culmination of a year* rather than an isolated, special day in a week?

Last January on the Second Sunday in Ordinary Time you read from John's Gospel. You were faced with the question of Jesus' identity and learned that he is the Lamb of God, the long-expected Messiah. In August you read from the sixth chapter in John's Gospel and, again, considered the identity of Jesus and learned he is the Bread of Life. This Sunday you once again read from John's Gospel and learn something anew about Jesus' identity: he is your eternal king. Over this past liturgical year you have gradually deepened your knowledge of who Christ is. This also draws you into a greater awareness of your own self-identity as followers of Christ. By recognizing the marvelous connections in the Lectionary, you are better able to see the connections from one Sunday to the next of your Eucharistic celebrations. Sunday Mass is not an isolated event in your week. It is the unfolding of Christ's identity and, consequently, of your identity, too.

The sacred space may be enhanced so that there is a joyful, festive environment. However, do not remove all vestiges of Ordinary Time since the weekdays to come are still in Ordinary Time.

NOVEMBER 26, 2000

APPENDIX A

Readings *(continued)*

The Nativity of the Lord, *December 25, 1999*

For the Vigil Mass

SECOND READING
[Acts 13:16-17, 22-25]

When Paul reached Antioch in Pisidia and entered the synagogue,
  he stood up, motioned with his hand, and said,
  "Fellow Israelites and you others who are God-fearing, listen.
The God of this people Israel chose our ancestors
  and exalted the people during their sojourn in the land of Egypt.
With uplifted arm he led them out of it.
Then he removed Saul and raised up David as king;
  of him he testified,
  'I have found David, son of Jesse, a man after my own heart;
    he will carry out my every wish.'
From this man's descendants God,
  according to his promise,
  has brought to Israel a savior, Jesus.
John heralded his coming by proclaiming a baptism of repentance
  to all the people of Israel;
  and as John was completing his course, he would say,
  'What do you suppose that I am? I am not he.
Behold, one is coming after me;
  I am not worthy to unfasten the sandals of his feet.'"

For the Mass at Midnight

SECOND READING [Titus 2:11-14]

Beloved:
The grace of God has appeared, saving all
  and training us to reject godless ways and worldly desires
  and to live temperately, justly, and devoutly in this age,
as we await the blessed hope,
  the appearance of the glory of our great God
  and savior Jesus Christ,
  who gave himself for us to deliver us from all lawlessness
  and to cleanse for himself a people as his own,
  eager to do what is good.

For the Mass at Dawn

SECOND READING [Titus 3:4-7]

Beloved:
When the kindness and generous love of God our savior appeared,
not because of any righteous deeds we had done
  but because of his mercy,
he saved us through the bath of rebirth and renewal by the Holy Spirit,
whom he richly poured out on us through Jesus Christ our savior,
so that we might be justified by his grace
  and become heirs in hope of eternal life.

For the Mass during the Day

SECOND READING
[Heb 1:1-6]

Brothers and sisters:
In times past, God spoke in partial and various ways
  to our ancestors through the prophets;
in these last days, he has spoken to us through the Son,
  whom he made heir of all things
  and through whom he created the universe,
who is the refulgence of his glory,
  the very imprint of his being,
  and who sustains all things by his mighty word.
When he had accomplished purification from sins,
  he took his seat at the right hand of the Majesty on high,
as far superior to the angels
  as the name he has inherited is more excellent than theirs.

For to which of the angels did God ever say:
  "You are my son; this day I have begotten you"?
Or again:
  "I will be a father to him, and he shall be a son to me"?
And again, when he leads the firstborn into the world, he says:
  "Let all the angels of God worship him."

Palm Sunday of the Lord's Passion, *April 16, 2000*

GOSPEL

[Mark 14:1–15:47; L38B]

The Passover and the Feast of Unleavened Bread were to take place in two days' time. So the chief priests and the scribes were seeking a way to arrest him by treachery and put him to death. They said, "Not during the festival, for fear that there may be a riot among the people."

When he was in Bethany reclining at table in the house of Simon the leper, a woman came with an alabaster jar of perfumed oil, costly genuine spikenard. She broke the alabaster jar and poured it on his head. There were some who were indignant. "Why has there been this waste of perfumed oil? It could have been sold for more than three hundred days' wages and the money given to the poor." They were infuriated with her. Jesus said, "Let her alone. Why do you make trouble for her? She has done a good thing for me. The poor you will always have with you, and whenever you wish you can do good to them, but you will not always have me. She has done what she could. She has anticipated anointing my body for burial. Amen, I say to you, wherever the gospel is proclaimed to the whole world, what she has done will be told in memory of her."

Then Judas Iscariot, one of the Twelve, went off to the chief priests to hand him over to them. When they heard him they were pleased and promised to pay him money. Then he looked for an opportunity to hand him over.

On the first day of the Feast of Unleavened Bread, when they sacrificed the Passover lamb, his disciples said to him, "Where do you want us to go and prepare for you to eat the Passover?" He sent two of his disciples and said to them, "Go into the city and a man will meet you, carrying a jar of water. Follow him. Wherever he enters, say to the master of the house, 'The Teacher says, "Where is my guest room where I may eat the Passover with my disciples?"'" Then he will show you a large upper room furnished and ready.

Make the preparations for us there." The disciples then went off, entered the city, and found it just as he had told them; and they prepared the Passover.

When it was evening, he came with the Twelve. And as they reclined at table and were eating, Jesus said, "Amen, I say to you, one of you will betray me, one who is eating with me." They began to be distressed and to say to him, one by one, "Surely it is not I?" He said to them, "One of the Twelve, the one who dips with me into the dish. For the Son of Man indeed goes, as it is written of him, but woe to that man by whom the Son of Man is betrayed. It would be better for that man if he had never been born."

While they were eating, he took bread, said the blessing, broke it, and gave it to them, and said, "Take it; this is my body." Then he took a cup, gave thanks, and gave it to them, and they all drank from it. He said to them, "This is my blood of the covenant, which will be shed for many. Amen, I say to you, I shall not drink again the fruit of the vine until the day when I drink it new in the kingdom of God." Then, after singing a hymn, they went out to the Mount of Olives.

Then Jesus said to them, "All of you will have your faith shaken, for it is written: *'I will strike the shepherd, and the sheep will be dispersed.'* But after I have been raised up, I shall go before you to Galilee." Peter said to him, "Even though all should have their faith shaken, mine will not be." Then Jesus said to him, "Amen, I say to you, this very night before the cock crows twice you will deny me three times." But he vehemently replied, "Even though I should have to die with you, I will not deny you." And they all spoke similarly. Then they came to a place named Gethsemane, and he said to his disciples, "Sit here while I pray." He took with him Peter, James, and John, and began to be troubled and distressed. Then he said to them, "My soul is sorrowful even to death. Remain here and keep watch." He advanced a little and fell to the ground and prayed that if it were possible the hour might pass by him; he said, "Abba, Father, all things are possible to you. Take this cup away from me, but not what I will but what you will." When he returned he found them asleep. He said to Peter, "Simon, are you asleep? Could you not keep watch for one hour? Watch and pray that you may not undergo the test. The spirit is willing but the flesh is weak." Withdrawing again, he prayed, saying the same thing. Then he returned once more and found them asleep, for they could not keep their eyes open and did not know what to answer him. He returned a third time and said to them, "Are you still sleeping and taking your rest? It is enough. The hour has come. Behold, the Son of Man is to be handed over to sinners. Get up, let us go. See, my betrayer is at hand."

Then, while he was still speaking, Judas, one of the Twelve, arrived, accompanied by a crowd with swords and clubs who had come from the chief priests, the scribes, and the elders. His betrayer had arranged a signal with them, saying, "The man I shall kiss is the one; arrest him and lead him away securely." He came and immediately went over to him and said, "Rabbi." And he kissed him. At this they laid hands on him and arrested him. One of the bystanders drew his sword, struck the high priest's servant, and cut off his ear. Jesus said to them in reply, "Have you come out as against a robber, with swords and clubs, to seize me? Day after day I was with you teaching in the temple area, yet you did not arrest me; but that the Scriptures may be fulfilled." And they all left him and fled. Now a young man followed him wearing nothing but a linen cloth about his body. They seized him, but he left the cloth behind and ran off naked.

They led Jesus away to the high priest, and all the chief priests and the elders and the scribes came together. Peter followed him at a distance into the high priest's courtyard and was seated with the guards, warming himself at the fire. The chief priests and the entire Sanhedrin kept trying to obtain testimony against Jesus in order to put him to death, but they found none. Many gave false witness against him, but their testimony did not agree. Some took the stand and testified falsely against him, alleging, "We heard him say, 'I will destroy this temple made with hands and within three days I will build another not made with hands.'" Even so their testimony did not agree. The high priest rose before the assembly and questioned Jesus, saying, "Have you no answer? What are these men testifying against you?" But he was silent and answered nothing. Again the high priest asked him and said to him, "Are you the Christ, the son of the Blessed One?" Then Jesus answered, "I am; and 'you will see the Son of Man seated at the right hand of the Power and coming with the clouds of heaven.'" At that the high priest tore his garments and said, "What further need have we of witnesses? You have heard the blasphemy. What do you think?" They all condemned him as deserving to die. Some began to spit on him. They blindfolded him and struck him and said to him, "Prophesy!" And the guards greeted him with blows. While Peter was below in the courtyard, one of the high priest's maids came along. Seeing Peter warming himself, she looked intently at him and said, "You too were with the Nazarene, Jesus." But he denied it saying, "I neither know nor understand what you are talking about." So he went out into the outer court. Then the cock crowed. The maid saw him and began again to say to the bystanders, "This man is one of them." Once again he denied it. A little later the bystanders said to Peter once more, "Surely you are one of them; for you too are a Galilean." He began to curse and to swear, "I do not know this man about whom you are talking." And immediately a cock crowed a second time. Then Peter remembered the word that Jesus had said to him, "Before the cock crows twice you will deny me three times." He broke down and wept.

As soon as morning came, the chief priests with the elders and the scribes, that is, the whole Sanhedrin, held a council. They bound Jesus, led him away, and handed him over to Pilate. Pilate questioned him, "Are you the king of the Jews?" He said to him in reply, "You say so." The chief priests accused him of many things. Again Pilate questioned him, "Have you no answer? See how many things they accuse you of." Jesus gave him no further answer, so that Pilate was amazed.

Now on the occasion of the feast he used to release to them one prisoner whom they requested. A man called Barabbas was then in prison along with the rebels who had committed murder in a rebellion. The crowd came forward and began to ask him to do for them as he was accustomed. Pilate answered, "Do you want me to release to you the king of the Jews?" For he knew that it was out of envy that the chief priests had handed him over. But the chief priests stirred up the crowd to have him release Barabbas for them instead. Pilate again said to them in reply, "Then what do you want me to do with the man you call the king of the Jews?" They shouted again, "Crucify him." Pilate said to them, "Why? What evil has he done?" They only shouted the louder, "Crucify him." So Pilate, wishing to satisfy the crowd, released Barabbas to them and, after he had Jesus scourged, handed him over to be crucified.

The soldiers led him away inside the palace, that is, the praetorium, and assembled the whole cohort. They clothed him in purple and, weaving a crown of thorns, placed it on him. They began to salute him with, "Hail, King of the Jews!" and kept striking his head with a reed and spitting upon him. They knelt before him in homage. And when they had mocked him, they stripped him of the purple cloak, dressed him in his own clothes, and led him out to crucify him.

They pressed into service a passer-by, Simon, a Cyrenian, who was coming in from the country, the father of Alexander and Rufus, to carry his cross.

They brought him to the place of Golgotha—which is translated Place of the Skull—. They gave him wine drugged with myrrh, but he did not take it. Then they crucified him and divided his garments by casting lots for them to see what each should take. It was nine o'clock in the morning when they crucified him. The inscription of the charge against him read, "The King of the Jews." With him they crucified two revolutionaries, one on his right and one on his left. Those passing by reviled him, shaking their heads and saying, "Aha! You who would destroy the temple and rebuild it in three days, save yourself by coming down from the cross." Likewise the chief priests, with the scribes, mocked him among themselves and said, "He saved others; he cannot save himself. Let the Christ, the King of Israel, come down now from the cross that we may see and believe." Those who were crucified with him also kept abusing him. At noon darkness came over the whole land until three in the afternoon. And at three o'clock Jesus cried out in a loud voice, *"Eloi, Eloi, lema sabachthani?"* which is translated, "My God, my God, why have you forsaken me?" Some of the bystanders who heard it said, "Look, he is calling Elijah." One of them ran, soaked a sponge with wine, put it on a reed and gave it to him to drink saying, "Wait, let us see if Elijah comes to take him down." Jesus gave a loud cry and breathed his last.

(Here all kneel and pause for a short time.)

The veil of the sanctuary was torn in two from top to bottom. When the centurion who stood facing him saw how he breathed his last he said, "Truly this man was the Son of God!" There were also women looking on from a distance. Among them were Mary Magdalene, Mary the mother of the younger James and of Joses, and Salome. These women had followed him when he was in Galilee and ministered to him. There were also many other women who had come up with him to Jerusalem.

When it was already evening, since it was the day of preparation, the day before the sabbath, Joseph of Arimathea, a distinguished member of the council, who was himself awaiting the kingdom of God, came and courageously went to Pilate and asked for the body of Jesus. Pilate was amazed that he was already dead. He summoned the centurion and asked him if Jesus had already died. And when he learned of it from the centurion, he gave the body to Joseph. Having bought a linen cloth, he took him down, wrapped him in the linen cloth, and laid him in a tomb that had been hewn out of the rock. Then he rolled a stone against the entrance to the tomb. Mary Magdalene and Mary the mother of Joses watched where he was laid.

Good Friday, April 21, 2000

GOSPEL (cont.)

[John 18:1–19:42; L40ABC]

When Pilate heard these words he brought Jesus out and seated him on the judge's bench in the place called Stone Pavement, in Hebrew, Gabbatha. It was preparation day for Passover, and it was about noon. And he said to the Jews, "Behold, your king!" They cried out, "Take him away, take him away! Crucify him!" Pilate said to them, "Shall I crucify your king?" The chief priests answered, "We have no king but Caesar." Then he handed him over to them to be crucified. So they took Jesus, and, carrying the cross himself, he went out to what is called the Place of the Skull, in Hebrew, Golgotha. There they crucified him, and with him two others, one on either side, with Jesus in the middle. Pilate also had an inscription written and put on the cross. It read, "Jesus the Nazarene, the King of the Jews." Now many of the Jews read this inscription, because the place where Jesus was crucified was near the city; and it was written in Hebrew, Latin, and Greek. So the chief priests of the Jews said to Pilate, "Do not write 'The King of the Jews,' but that he said, 'I am the King of the Jews'." Pilate answered, "What I have written, I have written."

When the soldiers had crucified Jesus, they took his clothes and divided them into four shares, a share for each soldier. They also took his tunic, but the tunic was seamless, woven in one piece from the top down. So they said to one another, "Let's not tear it, but cast lots for it to see whose it will be," in order that the passage of Scripture might be fulfilled that says: *They divided my garments among them, and for my vesture they cast lots.* This is what the soldiers did. Standing by the cross of Jesus were his mother and his mother's sister, Mary the wife of Clopas, and Mary of Magdala. When Jesus saw his mother and the disciple there whom he loved he said to his mother, "Woman, behold, your son." Then he said to the disciple, "Behold, your mother." And from that hour the disciple took her into his home.

After this, aware that everything was now finished, in order that the Scripture might be fulfilled, Jesus said, "I thirst." There was a vessel filled with common wine. So they put a sponge soaked in wine on a sprig of hyssop and put it up to his mouth. When Jesus had taken the wine, he said, "It is finished." And bowing his head, he handed over the spirit.

(Here all kneel and pause for a short time.)

Now since it was preparation day, in order that the bodies might not remain on the cross on the sabbath, for the sabbath day of that week was a solemn one, the Jews asked Pilate that their legs be broken and that they be taken down. So the soldiers came and broke the legs of the first and then of the other one who was crucified with Jesus. But when they came to Jesus and saw that he was already dead, they did not break his legs, but one soldier thrust his lance into his side, and immediately blood and water flowed out. An eyewitness has testified, and his testimony is true; he knows that he is speaking the truth, so that you also may come to believe. For this happened so that the Scripture passage might be fulfilled: *Not a bone of it will be broken.* And again another passage says: *They will look upon him whom they have pierced.*

After this, Joseph of Arimathea, secretly a disciple of Jesus for fear of the Jews, asked Pilate if he could remove the body of Jesus. And Pilate permitted it. So he came and took his body. Nicodemus, the one who had first come to him at night, also came bringing a mixture of myrrh and aloes weighing about one hundred pounds. They took the body of Jesus and bound it with burial cloths along with the spices, according to the Jewish burial custom. Now in the place where he had been crucified there was a garden, and in the garden a new tomb, in which no one had yet been buried. So they laid Jesus there because of the Jewish preparation day; for the tomb was close by.

Good Friday, April 21, 2000

RESPONSORIAL PSALM
[Ps 31:2, 6, 12-13, 15-16, 17, 25]

℟. (Luke 23:46) Father, into your hands I commend my spirit.

In you, O LORD, I take refuge;
    let me never be put to shame.
In your justice rescue me.
    Into your hands I commend my spirit;
you will redeem me, O LORD, O faithful God.

℟. Father, into your hands I commend my spirit.

For all my foes I am an object of reproach,
    a laughingstock to my neighbors, and a dread to my friends;
they who see me abroad flee from me.
I am forgotten like the unremembered dead;
    I am like a dish that is broken.

℟. Father, into your hands I commend my spirit.

But my trust is in you, O LORD;
    I say, "You are my God.
In your hands is my destiny; rescue me
    from the clutches of my enemies and my persecutors."

℟. Father, into your hands I commend my spirit.

Let your face shine upon your servant;
    save me in your kindness.
Take courage and be stouthearted,
    all you who hope in the LORD.

℟. Father, into your hands I commend my spirit.

FIRST READING
[Isa 52:13–53:12]

See, my servant shall prosper,
    he shall be raised high and greatly exalted.
Even as many were amazed at him—
    so marred was his look beyond human semblance
    and his appearance beyond that of the sons of man—
so shall he startle many nations,
    because of him kings shall stand speechless;
for those who have not been told shall see,
    those who have not heard shall ponder it.

Who would believe what we have heard?
    To whom has the arm of the LORD been revealed?
He grew up like a sapling before him,
    like a shoot from the parched earth;
there was in him no stately bearing to make us look at him,
    nor appearance that would attract us to him.
He was spurned and avoided by people,
    a man of suffering, accustomed to infirmity,
one of those from whom people hide their faces,
    spurned, and we held him in no esteem.

Yet it was our infirmities that he bore,
    our sufferings that he endured,
while we thought of him as stricken,
    as one smitten by God and afflicted.
But he was pierced for our offenses,
    crushed for our sins;
upon him was the chastisement that makes us whole,
    by his stripes we were healed.
We had all gone astray like sheep,
    each following his own way;
but the LORD laid upon him
    the guilt of us all.

Though he was harshly treated, he submitted
    and opened not his mouth;
like a lamb led to the slaughter
    or a sheep before the shearers,
    he was silent and opened not his mouth.
Oppressed and condemned, he was taken away,
    and who would have thought any more of his destiny?
When he was cut off from the land of the living,
    and smitten for the sin of his people,
a grave was assigned him among the wicked
    and a burial place with evildoers,
though he had done no wrong
    nor spoken any falsehood.
But the LORD was pleased
    to crush him in infirmity.

If he gives his life as an offering for sin,
    he shall see his descendants in a long life,
and the will of the LORD shall be accomplished through him.

Because of his affliction
    he shall see the light
    in fullness of days;
through his suffering, my servant shall justify many,
    and their guilt he shall bear.
Therefore I will give him his portion among the great,
    and he shall divide the spoils with the mighty,
because he surrendered himself to death
    and was counted among the wicked;
and he shall take away the sins of many,
    and win pardon for their offenses.

SECOND READING
[Heb 4:14-16; 5:7-9]

Brothers and sisters:
Since we have a great high priest who has passed through the heavens,
    Jesus, the Son of God,
    let us hold fast to our confession.
For we do not have a high priest
    who is unable to sympathize with our weaknesses,
    but one who has similarly been tested in every way,
    yet without sin.
So let us confidently approach the throne of grace
    to receive mercy and to find grace for timely help.

In the days when Christ was in the flesh,
    he offered prayers and supplications with loud cries and tears
    to the one who was able to save him from death,
    and he was heard because of his reverence.
Son though he was, he learned obedience from what he suffered;
    and when he was made perfect,
    he became the source of eternal salvation for all who obey him.

Easter Vigil, April 22, 2000

FIRST READING
[Gen 1:1–2:2] (cont.)

God set them in the dome of the sky,
  to shed light upon the earth,
  to govern the day and the night,
  and to separate the light from the darkness.
God saw how good it was.
Evening came, and morning followed—the fourth day.

Then God said,
  "Let the water teem with an abundance of living creatures,
  and on the earth let birds fly beneath the dome of the sky."
And so it happened:
  God created the great sea monsters
  and all kinds of swimming creatures with which the water teems,
  and all kinds of winged birds.
God saw how good it was, and God blessed them, saying,
  "Be fertile, multiply, and fill the water of the seas;
  and let the birds multiply on the earth."
Evening came, and morning followed—the fifth day.

Then God said,
  "Let the earth bring forth all kinds of living creatures:
  cattle, creeping things, and wild animals of all kinds."
And so it happened:
  God made all kinds of wild animals, all kinds of cattle,
  and all kinds of creeping things of the earth.
God saw how good it was.
Then God said:
  "Let us make man in our image, after our likeness.
  Let them have dominion over the fish of the sea,
  the birds of the air, and the cattle,
  and over all the wild animals
  and all the creatures that crawl on the ground."
God created man in his image;
  in the image of God he created him;
  male and female he created them.
God blessed them, saying:
  "Be fertile and multiply;
  fill the earth and subdue it.
  Have dominion over the fish of the sea, the birds of the air,
  and all the living things that move on the earth."
God also said:
  "See, I give you every seed-bearing plant all over the earth
  and every tree that has seed-bearing fruit on it to be your food;
  and to all the animals of the land, all the birds of the air,
  and all the living creatures that crawl on the ground,
  I give all the green plants for food."
And so it happened.
God looked at everything he had made, and he found it very good.
Evening came, and morning followed—the sixth day.

Thus the heavens and the earth and all their array were completed.
Since on the seventh day God was finished with the work he had been doing,
  he rested on the seventh day from all the work he had undertaken.

SECOND READING
[Gen 22:1-18]

God put Abraham to the test.
He called to him, "Abraham!"
"Here I am," he replied.
Then God said:
  "Take your son Isaac, your only one, whom you love,
  and go to the land of Moriah.
There you shall offer him up as a holocaust on a height that I will point out to you."
Early the next morning Abraham saddled his donkey,
  took with him his son Isaac and two of his servants as well,
  and with the wood that he had cut for the holocaust,
  set out for the place of which God had told him.
On the third day Abraham got sight of the place from afar.
Then he said to his servants:
  "Both of you stay here with the donkey,
  while the boy and I go on over yonder.
We will worship and then come back to you."
Thereupon Abraham took the wood for the holocaust
  and laid it on his son Isaac's shoulders,
  while he himself carried the fire and the knife.
As the two walked on together, Isaac spoke to his father Abraham:
  "Father!" Isaac said.
"Yes, son," he replied.
Isaac continued, "Here are the fire and the wood,
  but where is the sheep for the holocaust?"
"Son," Abraham answered,
  "God himself will provide the sheep for the holocaust."
Then the two continued going forward.
When they came to the place of which God had told him,
  Abraham built an altar there and arranged the wood on it.
Next he tied up his son Isaac,
  and put him on top of the wood on the altar.
Then he reached out and took the knife to slaughter his son.
But the LORD's messenger called to him from heaven,
  "Abraham, Abraham!"
"Here I am," he answered.
"Do not lay your hand on the boy," said the messenger.
"Do not do the least thing to him.
I know now how devoted you are to God,
  since you did not withhold from me your own beloved son."
As Abraham looked about,
  he spied a ram caught by its horns in the thicket.
So he went and took the ram
  and offered it up as a holocaust in place of his son.
Abraham named the site Yahweh-yireh;
  hence people now say, "On the mountain the LORD will see."

Again the LORD's messenger called to Abraham from heaven and said:
  "I swear by myself, declares the LORD,
  that because you acted as you did
  in not withholding from me your beloved son,
  I will bless you abundantly
  and make your descendants as countless
  as the stars of the sky and the sands of the seashore;
  your descendants shall take possession of the gates of their enemies,
  and in your descendants all the nations of the earth
  shall find blessing—
  all this because you obeyed my command."

RESPONSORIAL PSALM
[Ps 16:5, 8, 9-10, 11]

℟. (1) You are my inheritance, O Lord.

O LORD, my allotted portion and my cup,
  you it is who hold fast my lot.
I set the LORD ever before me;
  with him at my right hand I shall not be disturbed.

℟. You are my inheritance, O Lord.

Therefore my heart is glad and my soul rejoices,
  my body, too, abides in confidence;
because you will not abandon my soul to the netherworld,

Easter Vigil, April 22, 2000

nor will you suffer your faithful one to undergo corruption.

℟. You are my inheritance, O Lord.

You will show me the path to life,
fullness of joys in your presence,
the delights at your right hand forever.

℟. You are my inheritance, O Lord.

THIRD READING
[Exod 14:15–15:1]

The Lord said to Moses, "Why are you crying out to me?
Tell the Israelites to go forward.
And you, lift up your staff and, with hand outstretched over the sea,
split the sea in two,
that the Israelites may pass through it on dry land.
But I will make the Egyptians so obstinate that they will go in after them.
Then I will receive glory through Pharaoh and all his army,
his chariots and charioteers.
The Egyptians shall know that I am the Lord,
when I receive glory through Pharaoh and his chariots and charioteers."

The angel of God, who had been leading Israel's camp,
now moved and went around behind them.
The column of cloud also, leaving the front, took up its place behind them,
so that it came between the camp of the Egyptians
and that of Israel.
But the cloud now became dark, and thus the night passed
without the rival camps coming any closer together
all night long.
Then Moses stretched out his hand over the sea,
and the Lord swept the sea
with a strong east wind throughout the night
and so turned it into dry land.
When the water was thus divided,
the Israelites marched into the midst of the sea on dry land,
with the water like a wall to their right and to their left.

The Egyptians followed in pursuit;
all Pharaoh's horses and chariots and charioteers went after them
right into the midst of the sea.
In the night watch just before dawn
the Lord cast through the column of the fiery cloud
upon the Egyptian force a glance that threw it into a panic;
and he so clogged their chariot wheels that they could hardly drive.
With that the Egyptians sounded the retreat before Israel,
because the Lord was fighting for them against the Egyptians.
Then the Lord told Moses, "Stretch out your hand over the sea,
that the water may flow back upon the Egyptians,
upon their chariots and their charioteers."
So Moses stretched out his hand over the sea,
and at dawn the sea flowed back to its normal depth.
The Egyptians were fleeing head on toward the sea,
when the Lord hurled them into its midst.
As the water flowed back,
it covered the chariots and the charioteers of Pharaoh's whole army
which had followed the Israelites into the sea.
Not a single one of them escaped.
But the Israelites had marched on dry land through the midst of the sea,
with the water like a wall to their right and to their left.
Thus the Lord saved Israel on that day from the power of the Egyptians.
When Israel saw the Egyptians lying dead on the seashore
and beheld the great power that the Lord had shown against the Egyptians,
they feared the Lord and believed in him and in his servant Moses.

Then Moses and the Israelites sang this song to the Lord:
I will sing to the Lord, for he is gloriously triumphant;
horse and chariot he has cast into the sea.

RESPONSORIAL PSALM
[Exod 15:1-2, 3-4, 5-6, 17-18]

℟. (1b) Let us sing to the Lord; he has covered himself in glory.

I will sing to the Lord, for he is gloriously triumphant;
horse and chariot he has cast into the sea.
My strength and my courage is the Lord,
and he has been my savior.
He is my God, I praise him;
the God of my father, I extol him.

℟. Let us sing to the Lord; he has covered himself in glory.

The Lord is a warrior,
Lord is his name!
Pharaoh's chariots and army he hurled into the sea;
the elite of his officers were submerged in the Red Sea.

℟. Let us sing to the Lord; he has covered himself in glory.

The flood waters covered them,
they sank into the depths like a stone.
Your right hand, O Lord, magnificent in power,
your right hand, O Lord, has shattered the enemy.

℟. Let us sing to the Lord; he has covered himself in glory.

You brought in the people you redeemed
and planted them on the mountain of your inheritance—
the place where you made your seat, O Lord,
the sanctuary, Lord, which your hands established.
The Lord shall reign forever and ever.

℟. Let us sing to the Lord; he has covered himself in glory.

FOURTH READING
[Isa 54:5-14]

The One who has become your husband is your Maker;
his name is the Lord of hosts;
your redeemer is the Holy One of Israel,
called God of all the earth.
The Lord calls you back,
like a wife forsaken and grieved in spirit,
a wife married in youth and then cast off,
says your God.
For a brief moment I abandoned you,
but with great tenderness I will take you back.
In an outburst of wrath, for a moment I hid my face from you;
but with enduring love I take pity on you,
says the Lord, your redeemer.
This is for me like the days of Noah,
when I swore that the waters of Noah should never again deluge the earth;
so I have sworn not to be angry with you,
or to rebuke you.
Though the mountains leave their place and the hills be shaken,
my love shall never leave you
nor my covenant of peace be shaken,
says the Lord, who has mercy on you.
O afflicted one, storm-battered and unconsoled,
I lay your pavements in carnelians,
and your foundations in sapphires;

Easter Vigil, April 22, 2000

I will make your battlements of rubies,
  your gates of carbuncles,
  and all your walls of precious stones.
All your children shall be taught by the Lord,
  and great shall be the peace of your
    children.
In justice shall you be established,
  far from the fear of oppression,
  where destruction cannot come near you.

RESPONSORIAL PSALM
[Ps 30:2, 4, 5-6, 11-12, 13]

℟. (2a) I will praise you, Lord, for you have rescued me.

I will extol you, O Lord, for you drew me clear
  and did not let my enemies rejoice over me.
O Lord, you brought me up from the netherworld;
  you preserved me from among those going down into the pit.

℟. I will praise you, Lord, for you have rescued me.

Sing praise to the Lord, you his faithful ones,
  and give thanks to his holy name.
For his anger lasts but a moment;
  a lifetime, his good will.
At nightfall, weeping enters in,
  but with the dawn, rejoicing.

℟. I will praise you, Lord, for you have rescued me.

Hear, O Lord, and have pity on me;
  O Lord, be my helper.
You changed my mourning into dancing;
  O Lord, my God, forever will I give you thanks.

℟. I will praise you, Lord, for you have rescued me.

FIFTH READING
[Isa 55:1-11]

Thus says the Lord:
All you who are thirsty,
  come to the water!
You who have no money,
  come, receive grain and eat;
come, without paying and without cost,
  drink wine and milk!
Why spend your money for what is not bread,
  your wages for what fails to satisfy?
Heed me, and you shall eat well,
  you shall delight in rich fare.
Come to me heedfully,
  listen, that you may have life.

I will renew with you the everlasting covenant,
  the benefits assured to David.
As I made him a witness to the peoples,
  a leader and commander of nations,
so shall you summon a nation you knew not,
  and nations that knew you not shall run to you,
because of the Lord, your God,
  the Holy One of Israel, who has glorified you.

Seek the Lord while he may be found,
  call him while he is near.
Let the scoundrel forsake his way,
  and the wicked man his thoughts;
let him turn to the Lord for mercy;
  to our God, who is generous in forgiving.
For my thoughts are not your thoughts,
  nor are your ways my ways, says the Lord.
As high as the heavens are above the earth,
  so high are my ways above your ways
  and my thoughts above your thoughts.

For just as from the heavens
  the rain and snow come down
and do not return there
  till they have watered the earth,
  making it fertile and fruitful,
giving seed to the one who sows
  and bread to the one who eats,
so shall my word be
  that goes forth from my mouth;
my word shall not return to me void,
  but shall do my will,
  achieving the end for which I sent it.

RESPONSORIAL PSALM
[Isa 12:2-3, 4, 5-6]

℟. (3) You will draw water joyfully from the springs of salvation.

God indeed is my savior;
  I am confident and unafraid.
My strength and my courage is the Lord,
  and he has been my savior.
With joy you will draw water
  at the fountain of salvation.

℟. You will draw water joyfully from the springs of salvation.

Give thanks to the Lord, acclaim his name;
  among the nations make known his deeds,
  proclaim how exalted is his name.

℟. You will draw water joyfully from the springs of salvation.

Sing praise to the Lord for his glorious achievement;
  let this be known throughout all the earth.
Shout with exultation, O city of Zion,
  for great in your midst
  is the Holy One of Israel!

℟. You will draw water joyfully from the springs of salvation.

SIXTH READING
[Bar 3:9-15, 32–4:4]

Hear, O Israel, the commandments of life:
  listen, and know prudence!
How is it, Israel,
  that you are in the land of your foes,
  grown old in a foreign land,
defiled with the dead,
  accounted with those destined for the netherworld?
You have forsaken the fountain of wisdom!
  Had you walked in the way of God,
  you would have dwelt in enduring peace.
Learn where prudence is,
  where strength, where understanding;
that you may know also
  where are length of days, and life,
  where light of the eyes, and peace.
Who has found the place of wisdom,
  who has entered into her treasuries?

The One who knows all things knows her;
  he has probed her by his knowledge—
the One who established the earth for all time,
  and filled it with four-footed beasts;
he who dismisses the light, and it departs,
  calls it, and it obeys him trembling;
before whom the stars at their posts
  shine and rejoice;
when he calls them, they answer, "Here we are!"
  shining with joy for their Maker.
Such is our God;
  no other is to be compared to him:
he has traced out the whole way of understanding,
  and has given her to Jacob, his servant,
  to Israel, his beloved son.

Since then she has appeared on earth,
  and moved among people.
She is the book of the precepts of God,
  the law that endures forever;
all who cling to her will live,
  but those will die who forsake her.
Turn, O Jacob, and receive her:
  walk by her light toward splendor.
Give not your glory to another,
  your privileges to an alien race.
Blessed are we, O Israel;
  for what pleases God is known to us!

Easter Vigil, April 22, 2000

RESPONSORIAL PSALM
[Ps 19:8, 9, 10, 11]

℟. (John 6:68c) Lord, you have the words of everlasting life.

The law of the Lord is perfect,
  refreshing the soul;
the decree of the Lord is trustworthy,
  giving wisdom to the simple.

℟. Lord, you have the words of everlasting life.

The precepts of the Lord are right,
  rejoicing the heart;
the command of the Lord is clear,
  enlightening the eye.

℟. Lord, you have the words of everlasting life.

The fear of the Lord is pure,
  enduring forever;
the ordinances of the Lord are true,
  all of them just.

℟. Lord, you have the words of everlasting life.

They are more precious than gold,
  than a heap of purest gold;
sweeter also than syrup
  or honey from the comb.

℟. Lord, you have the words of everlasting life.

SEVENTH READING
[Ezek 36:16-17a, 18-28]

The word of the Lord came to me, saying:
  Son of man, when the house of Israel
    lived in their land,
    they defiled it by their conduct and deeds.
Therefore I poured out my fury upon them
  because of the blood that they poured out
    on the ground,
  and because they defiled it with idols.
I scattered them among the nations,
  dispersing them over foreign lands;
  according to their conduct and deeds I
    judged them.
But when they came among the nations
  wherever they came,
  they served to profane my holy name,
  because it was said of them: "These are
    the people of the Lord,
  yet they had to leave their land."
So I have relented because of my holy name
  which the house of Israel profaned
    among the nations where they came.
Therefore say to the house of Israel: Thus
  says the Lord God:
  Not for your sakes do I act, house of
    Israel,
  but for the sake of my holy name,
    which you profaned among the nations
      to which you came.
I will prove the holiness of my great name,
  profaned among the nations,
  in whose midst you have profaned it.
Thus the nations shall know that I am the
  Lord, says the Lord God,
  when in their sight I prove my holiness
    through you.
For I will take you away from among the
  nations,
  gather you from all the foreign lands,
  and bring you back to your own land.
I will sprinkle clean water upon you
  to cleanse you from all your impurities,
  and from all your idols I will cleanse you.
I will give you a new heart and place a new
  spirit within you,
  taking from your bodies your stony hearts
    and giving you natural hearts.
I will put my spirit within you and make
  you live by my statutes,
  careful to observe my decrees.
You shall live in the land I gave your
  fathers;
  you shall be my people, and I will be
    your God.

RESPONSORIAL PSALM
[Ps 42:3, 5; 43:3, 4]

℟. (42:2) Like a deer that longs for running streams, my soul longs for you, my God.

Athirst is my soul for God, the living God.
  When shall I go and behold the face of
    God?

℟. Like a deer that longs for running streams, my soul longs for you, my God.

I went with the throng
  and led them in procession to the house
    of God,
  amid loud cries of joy and thanksgiving,
    with the multitude keeping festival.

℟. Like a deer that longs for running streams, my soul longs for you, my God.

Send forth your light and your fidelity;
  they shall lead me on
and bring me to your holy mountain,
  to your dwelling-place.

℟. Like a deer that longs for running streams, my soul longs for you, my God.

Then will I go in to the altar of God,
  the God of my gladness and joy;
then will I give you thanks upon the harp,
  O God, my God!

℟. Like a deer that longs for running streams, my soul longs for you, my God.

EPISTLE
[Rom 6:3-11]

Brothers and sisters:
Are you unaware that we who were
  baptized into Christ Jesus
  were baptized into his death?
We were indeed buried with him through
  baptism into death,
  so that, just as Christ was raised from the
    dead
  by the glory of the Father,
  we too might live in newness of life.
For if we have grown into union with him
  through a death like his,
  we shall also be united with him in the
    resurrection.
We know that our old self was crucified
  with him,
  so that our sinful body might be done
    away with,
  that we might no longer be in slavery to
    sin.
For a dead person has been absolved from
  sin.
If, then, we have died with Christ,
  we believe that we shall also live with
    him.
We know that Christ, raised from the dead,
  dies no more;
  death no longer has power over him.
As to his death, he died to sin once and for
  all;
  as to his life, he lives for God.
Consequently, you too must think of
  yourselves as being dead to sin
  and living for God in Christ Jesus.

RESPONSORIAL PSALM
[Ps 118:1-2, 16-17, 22-23]

℟. Alleluia, alleluia, alleluia.

Give thanks to the Lord, for he is good,
  for his mercy endures forever.
Let the house of Israel say,
  "His mercy endures forever."

℟. Alleluia, alleluia, alleluia.

The right hand of the Lord has struck with
  power;
  the right hand of the Lord is exalted.
I shall not die, but live,
  and declare the works of the Lord.

℟. Alleluia, alleluia, alleluia.

The stone which the builders rejected
  has become the cornerstone.
By the Lord has this been done;
  it is wonderful in our eyes.

℟. Alleluia, alleluia, alleluia.

Easter Sunday, April 23, 2000

SEQUENCE

Victimae paschali laudes

Christians, to the Paschal Victim
   Offer your thankful praises!
A Lamb the sheep redeems;
   Christ, who only is sinless,
   Reconciles sinners to the Father.
Death and life have contended in that
   combat stupendous:
   The Prince of life, who died, reigns
   immortal.
Speak, Mary, declaring
   What you saw, wayfaring.
"The tomb of Christ, who is living,
   The glory of Jesus' resurrection;
Bright angels attesting,
   The shroud and napkin resting.
Yes, Christ my hope is arisen;
   To Galilee he goes before you."
Christ indeed from death is risen, our new
   life obtaining.
   Have mercy, victor King, ever reigning!
Amen. Alleluia.

The Ascension of the Lord, June 1, 2000

SECOND READING
[Eph 4:1-13]

Brothers and sisters,
I, a prisoner for the Lord,
   urge you to live in a manner worthy of
      the call you have received,
   with all humility and gentleness, with
      patience,
   bearing with one another through love,
   striving to preserve the unity of the spirit
      through the bond of peace:
   one body and one Spirit,
   as you were also called to the one hope of
      your call;
one Lord, one faith, one baptism;
one God and Father of all,
   who is over all and through all and in all.

But grace was given to each of us
   according to the measure of Christ's gift.
Therefore, it says:
   *He ascended on high and took prisoners
   captive;*
   he gave gifts to men.
What does "he ascended" mean except that
   he also descended
      into the lower regions of the earth?
The one who descended is also the one who
   ascended
far above all the heavens,
   that he might fill all things.

And he gave some as apostles, others as
   prophets,
   others as evangelists, others as pastors
      and teachers,
   to equip the holy ones for the work of
      ministry,
   for building up the body of Christ,
   until we all attain the unity of faith
   and knowledge of the Son of God, to
      mature manhood,
   to the extent of the full stature of
      Christ.

Pentecost, June 11, 2000

SEQUENCE

Veni, Sancte Spiritus

Come, Holy Spirit, come!
And from your celestial home
   Shed a ray of light divine!
Come, Father of the poor!
Come, source of all our store!
   Come, within our bosoms shine.
You, of comforters the best;
You, the soul's most welcome guest;
   Sweet refreshment here below;
In our labor, rest most sweet;
Grateful coolness in the heat;
   Solace in the midst of woe.
O most blessed Light divine,
Shine within these hearts of yours,
   And our inmost being fill!
Where you are not, we have naught,
Nothing good in deed or thought,
   Nothing free from taint of ill.
Heal our wounds, our strength renew;
On our dryness pour your dew;
Wash the stains of guilt away:
Bend the stubborn heart and will;
Melt the frozen, warm the chill;
   Guide the steps that go astray.
On the faithful, who adore
And confess you, evermore
   In your sevenfold gift descend;
Give them virtue's sure reward;
Give them your salvation, Lord;
   Give them joys that never end. Amen.
Alleluia.

The Solemnity of the Most Holy Body and Blood of Christ, June 25, 2000

SEQUENCE

Lauda Sion

Laud, O Zion, your salvation,
Laud with hymns of exultation,
    Christ, your king and shepherd true:

Bring him all the praise you know,
He is more than you bestow.
    Never can you reach his due.

Special theme for glad thanksgiving
Is the quick'ning and the living
    Bread today before you set:

From his hands of old partaken,
As we know, by faith unshaken,
    Where the Twelve at supper met.

Full and clear ring out your chanting,
Joy nor sweetest grace be wanting,
    From your heart let praises burst:

For today the feast is holden,
When the institution olden
    Of that supper was rehearsed.

Here the new law's new oblation,
By the new king's revelation,
    Ends the form of ancient rite:

Now the new the old effaces,
Truth away the shadow chases,
    Light dispels the gloom of night.

What he did at supper seated,
Christ ordained to be repeated,
    His memorial ne'er to cease:

And his rule for guidance taking,
Bread and wine we hallow, making
    Thus our sacrifice of peace.

This the truth each Christian learns,
Bread into his flesh he turns,
    To his precious blood the wine:

Sight has fail'd, nor thought conceives,
But a dauntless faith believes,
    Resting on a pow'r divine.

Here beneath these signs are hidden
Priceless things to sense forbidden;
    Signs, not things are all we see:

Blood is poured and flesh is broken,
Yet in either wondrous token
    Christ entire we know to be.

Whoso of this food partakes,
Does not rend the Lord nor breaks;
    Christ is whole to all that taste:

Thousands are, as one, receivers,
One, as thousands of believers,
    Eats of him who cannot waste.

Bad and good the feast are sharing,
Of what divers dooms preparing,
    Endless death, or endless life.

Life to these, to those damnation,
See how like participation
    Is with unlike issues rife.

When the sacrament is broken,
Doubt not, but believe 'tis spoken,
    That each sever'd outward token
        Doth the very whole contain.

Nought the precious gift divides,
Breaking but the sign betides
    Jesus still the same abides,
        Still unbroken does remain.

The shorter form of the sequence begins here.

Lo! the angel's food is given
To the pilgrim who has striven;
    See the children's bread from heaven,
        Which on dogs may not be spent.

Truth the ancient types fulfilling,
Isaac bound, a victim willing,
    Paschal lamb, its lifeblood spilling,
        Manna to the fathers sent.

Very bread, good shepherd, tend us,
Jesu, of your love befriend us,
    You refresh us, you defend us,
    Your eternal goodness send us
In the land of life to see.

You who all things can and know,
Who on earth such food bestow,
    Grant us with your saints, though lowest,
    Where the heav'nly feast you show,
Fellow heirs and guests to be. Amen.
    Alleluia.

APPENDIX B

Choral Settings for the General Intercessions

Purchasers of this volume may reproduce these choral arrangements for use in their parish or community. The music must be reproduced as given below, with composer's name and copyright line.

ADVENT

Cantor: we pray to the Lord,

SATB Response (Descant): Lord, hear our prayer.
Lord, hear our prayer.
Lord, hear our prayer.

Music: Kathleen Harmon, SNDdeN, ©1999, Institute for Liturgical Ministry, 4960 Salem Avenue, Dayton OH 45416. All rights reserved.

CHRISTMAS and EASTER

Cantor: we pray to the Lord,

SATB Response (Descant): Lord, hear our prayer.
Lord, hear our prayer.

Music: Kathleen Harmon, SNDdeN, ©1999, Institute for Liturgical Ministry, 4960 Salem Avenue, Dayton OH 45416. All rights reserved.

LENT

Cantor: we pray to the Lord,

SATB Response: Lord, hear our prayer.

Music: Kathleen Harmon, SNDdeN, ©1999, Institute for Liturgical Ministry, 4960 Salem Avenue, Dayton OH 45416. All rights reserved.

SOLEMNITIES

Cantor: we pray to the Lord,

SATB Response (Descant): Lord, hear our prayer.
Lord, hear our prayer.

Music: Kathleen Harmon, SNDdeN, ©1999, Institute for Liturgical Ministry, 4960 Salem Avenue, Dayton OH 45416. All rights reserved.

ORDINARY TIME, WEEKS 2-9

Cantor: ... we pray to the Lord,

SATB Response (Descant): Lord, hear our prayer.

Lord, hear our prayer.

Music: Kathleen Harmon, SNDdeN, ©1999, Institute for Liturgical Ministry, 4960 Salem Avenue, Dayton OH 45416. All rights reserved.

ORDINARY TIME, WEEKS 13-23

Cantor: ... we pray to the Lord,

SATB Response: Lord, hear our prayer.

Music: Kathleen Harmon, SNDdeN, ©1999, Institute for Liturgical Ministry, 4960 Salem Avenue, Dayton OH 45416. All rights reserved.

ORDINARY TIME, WEEKS 24-33

Cantor: ... we pray to the Lord,

SATB Response: Lord, hear our prayer.

Music: Kathleen Harmon, SNDdeN, ©1999, Institute for Liturgical Ministry, 4960 Salem Avenue, Dayton OH 45416. All rights reserved.